Chevrolet/GMC S-10 & S-15 Automotive Repair Manual

by David Hayden and John H Haynes

Member of the Guild of Motoring Writers

Models covered:
Chevrolet S-10 pick-up and Blazer
GMC S-15 pick-up and Jimmy
1982 thru 1990

ISBN 1 85010 704 1

Printed in the USA

AEC

(1T5 – 831)

MEMBER

Haynes Publishing Group
Sparkford Nr Yeovil
Somerset BA22 7JJ England

Haynes North America, Inc.
861 Lawrence Drive
Newbury Park
California 91320 USA

Acknowledgments

Special thanks are due General Motors Corporation for supplying technical information and certain illustrations for this manual, and to the Champion Spark Plug Company, who supplied the illustrations of various spark plug conditions.

About this manual

Its purpose

The purpose of this manual is to help you get the best value from your vehicle. It can do so in several ways. It can help you decide what work must be done, even if you choose to have it done by a dealer service department or a repair shop; it provides information and procedures for routine maintenance and servicing; and it offers diagnostic and repair procedures to follow when trouble occurs.

It is hoped that you will use the manual to tackle the work yourself. For many simpler jobs, doing it yourself may be quicker than arranging an appointment to get the vehicle into a shop and making the trips to leave it and pick it up. More importantly, a lot of money can be saved by avoiding the expense the shop must pass on to you to cover its labor and overhead costs. An added benefit is the sense of satisfaction and accomplishment that you feel after having done the job yourself.

Using the manual

The manual is divided into Chapters. Each Chapter is divided into numbered Sections, which are headed in bold type between horizontal lines. Each Section consists of consecutively numbered paragraphs.

The two types of illustrations used (figures and photographs), are referenced by a number preceding their caption. Figure reference numbers denote Chapter and numerical sequence within the Chapter; (i.e. Fig. 3.4 means Chapter 3, figure number 4). Figure captions are followed by a Section number which ties the figure to a specific portion of the text. All photographs apply to the Chapter in which they appear and the reference number pinpoints the pertinent Section and paragraph; i.e., 3.2 means Section 3, paragraph 2.

Procedures, once described in the text, are not normally repeated. When it is necessary to refer to another Chapter, the reference will be given as Chapter and Section number i.e. Chapter 1/16). Cross references given without use of the word 'Chapter' apply to Sections and/or paragraphs in the same Chapter. For example, 'see Section 8' means in the same Chapter.

Reference to the left or right side of the vehicle is based on the assumption that one is sitting in the driver's seat, facing forward.

Even though extreme care has been taken during the preparation of this manual, neither the publisher nor the author can accept responsibility for any errors in, or omissions from, the information given.

Introduction to the S-10 and S-15

The Chevrolet S-10 and GMC S-15 are available in a Jeep-style passenger vehicle or pick-up truck configuration.

Power from the engine is transmitted through the transmission to the rear axle via a driveshaft on two-wheel drive vehicles, and from the transmission to a transfer case, then to the front and rear axles by driveshafts on four-wheel drive models. Both manual and automatic transmissions are available on these vehicles.

Power assisted brakes are available as an option or as standard equipment, depending on the model. Power steering is available as an option on all models.

Independent front suspension with torsion bars on four-wheel drive and coil springs on two-wheel drive is utilized, with semi-elliptic springs comprising the rear suspension. Conventional tubular shock absorbers are used front and rear.

Contents

The Chevrolet S-10 and GMC S-15 truck, club cab truck and Blazer

General dimensions

Overall length
Short wheelbase truck and Blazer/Jimmy . . . . 178.2 in
Long wheelbase truck . . . . 194.2 in
Truck with club cab . . . . 192.8 in

Width . . . . 64.8 in

Wheelbase
Short wheelbase truck and Blazer/Jimmy . . . . 108.3 in
Long wheelbase truck . . . . 117.9 in
Truck with club cab . . . . 122.9 in

Vehicle identification numbers

Modifications are a continuing and unpublicized process in vehicle manufacturing. Since spare parts manuals and lists are compiled on a numerical basis, the individual vehicle numbers are essential to correctly identify the component required.

Vehicle identification number (VIN)

This very important identification number is located on a plate attached to the top left corner of the dashboard and can easily be seen while looking through the windshield from the outside of the vehicle. The VIN also appears on the Vehicle Certificate of Title and Registra-

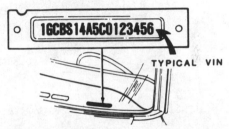

Location of the Vehicle Identification Number plate

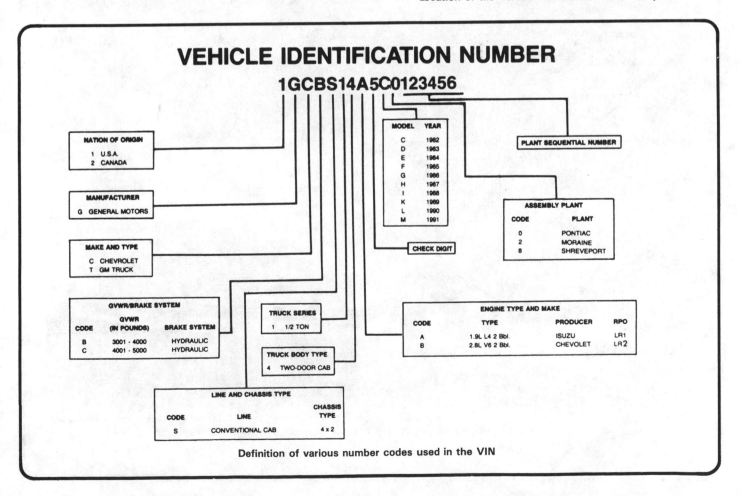

Definition of various number codes used in the VIN

tion. It contains valuable information such as where and when the vehicle was manufactured, the model year and the body style.

Engine identification numbers

The ID number on the four-cylinder engine is found at the left rear side of the engine, on the casting to the rear of the exhaust manifold.

The ID number on the V6 engine is found either below the left cylinder head or below the right cylinder head, to the rear of the timing cover.

Automatic transmission numbers

Automatic transmission ID numbers may be stamped in a variety of locations on pads on either side of the transmission (refer to the accompanying illustration).

Manual transmission numbers

Manual transmission ID numbers are located on a tag attached to an extension housing bolt on the driver's side.

Rear axle numbers

The rear axle ID number is located on the right axle tube, adjacent to the carrier.

Alternator numbers

The alternator ID number is located on top of the drive end frame.

Starter numbers

The starter ID number is stamped on the outer case, toward the rear.

Battery numbers

The battery ID number is located on the cell cover segment on top of the battery.

Emissions Control Information label

The Emissions Control Information label is attached to the radiator fan shroud (photo).

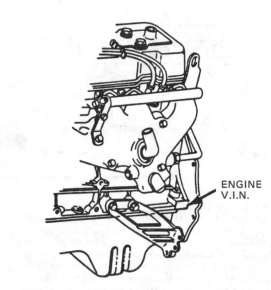

Location of the engine ID number on 1.9 liter four-cylinder engines

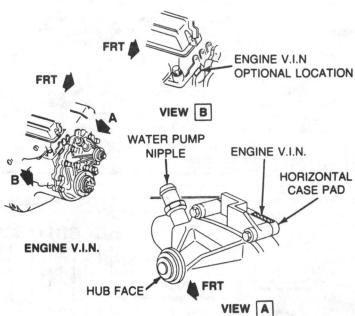

Location of the engine ID number on V6 engines

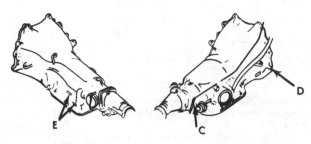

Locations of the ID numbers on automatic transmissions

C   THM 200 and 200-4R ID tag location
D   THM 200 and 200-4R VIN location
E   THM 200 and 200-4R optional VIN location

The Emissions Control Information label is located on the fan shroud

Buying parts

Replacement parts are available from many sources, which generally fall into one of two categories — authorized dealer parts departments and independent retail auto parts stores. Our advice concerning these parts is as follows:

Authorized dealer parts department: This is the best source for parts which are unique to your vehicle and not generally available elsewhere (i.e. major engine parts, transmission parts, trim pieces, etc.). It is also the only place you should buy parts if your vehicle is still under warranty, as non-factory parts may invalidate the warranty. To be sure of obtaining the correct parts, have your vehicle's engine and chassis numbers available and, if possible, take the old parts along for positive identification.

Retail auto parts stores: Good auto parts stores will stock frequently needed components which wear out relatively fast (i.e. clutch components, exhaust systems, brake parts, tune-up parts, etc.). These stores often supply new or reconditioned parts on an exchange basis, which can save a considerable amount of money. Discount auto parts stores are often very good places to buy materials and parts needed for general vehicle maintenance (i.e. oil, grease, filters, spark plugs, belts, touch-up paint, bulbs, etc.). They also usually sell tools and general accessories, have convenient hours, charge lower prices, and can often be found not far from your home.

Maintenance techniques, tools and working facilities

Maintenance techniques

There are a number of techniques involved in maintenance and repair that will be referred to throughout this manual. Application of these techniques will enable the home mechanic to be more efficient, better organized and capable of performing the various tasks properly, which will ensure that the repair job is thorough and complete.

Fasteners

Fasteners are nuts, bolts, studs and screws used to hold two or more parts together. There are a few things to keep in mind when working with fasteners. Almost all of them use a locking device of some type, either a lock washer, locknut, locking tab or thread adhesive. All threaded fasteners should be clean and straight, with undamaged threads and undamaged corners on the hex head where the wrench fits. Develop the habit of replacing all damaged nuts and bolts with new ones. Special locknuts with nylon or fiber inserts can only be used once. If they are removed, they lose their locking ability and must be replaced with new ones.

Rusted nuts and bolts should be treated with a penetrating fluid to ease removal and prevent breakage. Some mechanics use turpentine in a spout-type oil can, which works quite well. After applying the rust penetrant, let it "work" for a few minutes before trying to loosen the nut or bolt. Badly rusted fasteners may have to be chiseled or sawed off or removed with a special nut breaker, available at tool stores.

If a bolt or stud breaks off in an assembly, it can be drilled and removed with a special tool commonly available for this purpose. Most automotive machine shops can perform this task, as well as other repair procedures (such as repair of threaded holes that have been stripped out).

Flat washers and lock washers, when removed from an assembly, should always be replaced exactly as removed. Replace any damaged washers with new ones. Always use a flat washer between a lock washer and any soft metal surface (such as aluminum), thin sheet metal or plastic.

Fastener sizes

For a number of reasons, automobile manufacturers are making wider and wider use of metric fasteners. Therefore, it is important to be able to tell the difference between standard (sometimes called U.S., English or SAE) and metric hardware, since they cannot be interchanged.

All bolts, whether standard or metric, are sized according to diameter, thread pitch and length. For example, a standard 1/2 — 13 x 1 bolt is 1/2 inch in diameter, has 13 threads per inch and is 1 inch long. An M12 — 1.75 x 25 metric bolt is 12 mm in diameter, has a thread pitch of 1.75 mm (the distance between threads) and is 25 mm long. The two bolts are nearly identical, and easily confused, but they are not interchangeable.

In addition to the differences in diameter, thread pitch and length, metric and standard bolts can also be distinguished by examining the bolt heads. To begin with, the distance across the flats on a standard bolt head is measured in inches, while the same dimension on a metric bolt is measured in millimeters (the same is true for nuts). As a result, a standard wrench should not be used on a metric bolt and a metric wrench should not be used on a standard bolt. Also, standard bolts have slashes radiating out from the center of the head to denote the grade or strength of the bolt (which is an indication of the amount of torque that can be applied to it). The greater the number of slashes, the greater the strength of the bolt (grades 0 through 5 are commonly used on automobiles). Metric bolts have a property class (grade) number, rather than a slash, molded into their heads to indicate bolt strength. In this case, the higher the number, the stronger the bolt (property class numbers 8.8, 9.8 and 10.9 are commonly used on automobiles).

Strength markings can also be used to distinguish standard hex nuts from metric hex nuts. Standard nuts have dots stamped into one side,

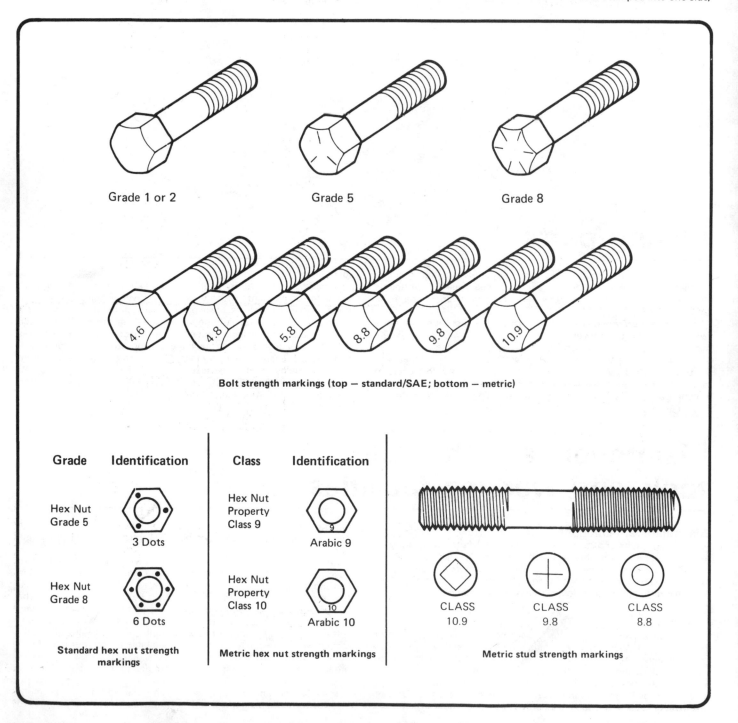

Bolt strength markings (top — standard/SAE; bottom — metric)

Standard hex nut strength markings

Metric hex nut strength markings

Metric stud strength markings

while metric nuts are marked with a number. The greater the number of dots, or the higher the number, the greater the strength of the nut.

Metric studs are also marked on their ends according to property class (grade). Larger studs are numbered (the same as metric bolts), while smaller studs carry a geometric code to denote grade.

It should be noted that many fasteners, especially Grades 0 through 2, have no distinguishing marks on them. When such is the case, the only way to determine whether it is standard or metric is to measure the thread pitch or compare it to a known fastener of the same size.

Since fasteners of the same size (both standard and metric) may have different strength ratings, be sure to reinstall any bolts, studs or nuts removed from your vehicle in their original locations. Also, when replacing a fastener with a new one, make sure that the new one has a strength rating equal to or greater than the original.

Tightening sequences and procedures

Most threaded fasteners should be tightened to a specific torque value (torque is basically a twisting force). Over-tightening the fastener can weaken it and cause it to break, while under-tightening can cause it to eventually come loose. Bolts, screws and studs, depending on the material they are made of and their thread diameters, have specific torque values (many of which are noted in the Specifications at the beginning of each Chapter). Be sure to follow the torque recommendations closely. For fasteners not assigned a specific torque, a general torque value chart is presented here as a guide. As was previously mentioned, the size and grade of a fastener determine the amount of torque that can safely be applied to it. The figures listed here are approximate for Grade 2 and Grade 3 fasteners (higher grades can tolerate higher torque values).

Metric thread sizes	Ft-lb	Nm
M-6	6 to 9	9 to 12
M-8	14 to 21	19 to 28
M-10	28 to 40	38 to 54
M-12	50 to 71	68 to 96
M-14	80 to 140	109 to 154
Pipe thread sizes		
1/8	5 to 8	7 to 10
1/4	12 to 18	17 to 24
3/8	22 to 33	30 to 44
1/2	25 to 35	34 to 47
U.S. thread sizes		
1/4 — 20	6 to 9	9 to 12
5/16 — 18	12 to 18	17 to 24
5/16 — 24	14 to 20	19 to 27
3/8 — 16	22 to 32	30 to 43
3/8 — 24	27 to 38	37 to 51
7/16 — 14	40 to 55	55 to 74
7/16 — 20	40 to 60	55 to 81
1/2 — 13	55 to 80	75 to 108

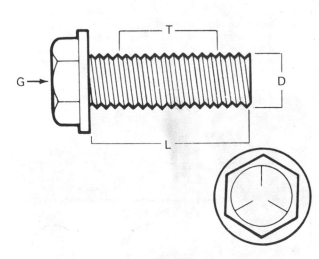

Standard (SAE) bolt dimensions/grade marks

G — Grade marks (bolt strength)
L — Length (in inches)
T — Thread pitch (number of threads per inch)
D — Nominal diameter (in inches)

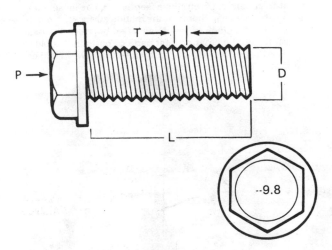

Metric bolt dimensions/grade marks

P — Property class (bolt strength)
L — Length (in millimeters)
T — Thread pitch (distance between threads; in millimeters)

Fasteners laid out in a pattern (i.e. cylinder head bolts, oil pan bolts, differential cover bolts, etc.) must be loosened or tightened in a sequence to avoid warping the component. This sequence will normally be shown in the appropriate Chapter. If a specific pattern is not given, the following procedures can be used to prevent warping. Initially, the bolts or nuts should be assembled finger-tight only. Next, they should be tightened one full turn each, in a crisscross or diagonal pattern. After each one has been tightened one full turn, return to the first one and tighten them all one-half turn, following the same pattern. Finally, tighten each of them one-quarter turn at a time until each fastener has been tightened to the proper torque. To loosen and remove the fasteners, the procedure would be reversed.

Component disassembly

Component disassembly should be done with care and purpose to help ensure that the parts go back together properly. Always keep track of the sequence in which parts are removed. Make note of special characteristics or marks on parts that can be installed more than one way (such as a grooved thrust washer on a shaft). It is a good idea to lay the disassembled parts out on a clean surface in the order that they were removed. It may also be helpful to make sketches or take instant photos of components before removal.

When removing fasteners from a component, keep track of their locations. Sometimes threading a bolt back in a part, or putting the washers and nut back on a stud, can prevent mix-ups later. If nuts and bolts cannot be returned to their original locations, they should be kept in a compartmented box or a series of small boxes. A cupcake or muffin tin is ideal for this purpose, since each cavity can hold the bolts and nuts from a particular area (i.e. oil pan bolts, valve cover bolts, engine mount bolts, etc.). A pan of this type is especially helpful when working on assemblies with very small parts, such as the carburetor, alternator, valve train or interior dash and trim pieces. The cavities can be marked with paint or tape to identify the contents.

Whenever wiring looms, harnesses or connectors are separated, it's a good idea to identify the two halves with numbered pieces of masking tape so they can be easily reconnected.

Gasket sealing surfaces

Throughout any vehicle, gaskets are used to seal the mating surfaces between two parts and keep lubricants, fluids, vacuum or pressure contained in an assembly.

Many times these gaskets are coated with a liquid or paste-type gasket sealing compound before assembly. Age, heat and pressure can sometimes cause the two parts to stick together so tightly that they are very difficult to separate. Often, the assembly can be loosened by striking it with a soft-faced hammer near the mating surfaces. A regular hammer can be used if a block of wood is placed between the hammer and the part. Do not hammer on cast parts or parts that could be easily damaged. With any particularly stubborn part, always recheck to make sure that every fastener has been removed.

Avoid using a screwdriver or bar to pry apart an assembly, as they can easily mar the gasket sealing surfaces of the parts (which must remain smooth). If prying is absolutely necessary, use an old broom handle, but keep in mind that extra clean-up will be necessary if the wood splinters.

After the parts are separated, the old gasket must be carefully scraped off and the gasket surfaces cleaned. Stubborn gasket material can be soaked with rust penetrant or treated with a special chemical to soften it so it can be easily scraped off. A scraper can be fashioned from a piece of copper tubing by flattening and sharpening one end. Copper is recommended because it is usually softer than the surfaces to be scraped, which reduces the chance of gouging the part. Some gaskets can be removed with a wire brush, but regardless of the method used, the mating surfaces must be left clean and smooth. If for some reason the gasket surface is gouged, then a gasket sealer thick enough to fill scratches will have to be used during reassembly of the components. For most applications, a non-drying (or semi-drying) gasket sealer should be used.

Hose removal tips

Caution: *If the vehicle is equipped with air conditioning, do not disconnect any of the A/C hoses without first having the system depressurized by a dealer service department or an air conditioning specialist.*

Hose removal precautions closely parallel gasket removal precautions. Avoid scratching or gouging the surface that the hose mates against or the connection may leak. This is especially true for radiator hoses. Because of various chemical reactions, the rubber in hoses can bond itself to the metal spigot that the hose fits over. To remove a hose, first loosen the hose clamps that secure it to the spigot. Then, with slip-joint pliers, grab the hose at the clamp and rotate it around the spigot. Work it back and forth until it is completely free, then pull it off. Silicone or other lubricants will ease removal if they can be applied between the hose and the outside of the spigot. Apply the same lubricant to the inside of the hose and the outside of the spigot to simplify installation.

As a last resort (and if the hose is to be replaced with a new one anyway), the rubber can be slit with a knife and the hose peeled from the spigot. If this must be done, be careful that the metal connection is not damaged.

If a hose clamp is broken or damaged, do not reuse it. Wire-type clamps usually weaken with age, so it is a good idea to replace them with screw-type clamps whenever a hose is removed.

Tools

A selection of good tools is a basic requirement for anyone who plans to maintain and repair his or her own vehicle. For the owner who has few tools, if any, the initial investment might seem high, but when compared to the spiraling costs of professional auto maintenance and repair, it is a wise one.

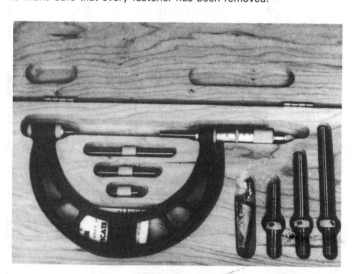

Micrometer set

Dial indicator set

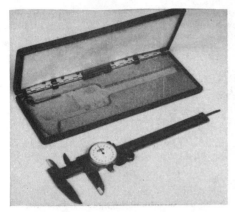

Dial caliper

Hydraulic lifter removal tool

Universal-type puller

Hand-operated vacuum pump

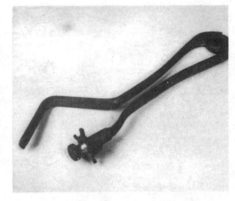

Piston ring groove cleaning tool

Piston ring compressor

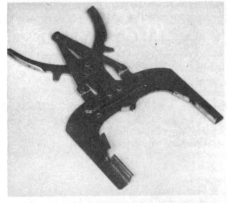

Piston ring removal/installation tool

Cylinder ridge reamer

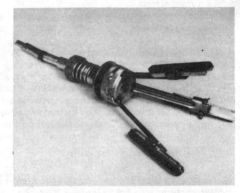

Cylinder surfacing hone

Cylinder bore gauge

Brake shoe spring tool

Valve spring compressor

To help the owner decide which tools are needed to perform the tasks detailed in this manual, the following tool lists are offered: *Maintenance and minor repair, Repair and overhaul* and *Special.* The newcomer to practical mechanics should start off with the *Maintenance and minor repair tool kit,* which is adequate for the simpler jobs performed on a vehicle. Then, as confidence and experience grow, the owner can tackle more difficult tasks, buying additional tools as they are needed. Eventually the basic kit will be expanded into the *Repair and overhaul tool set.* Over a period of time, the experienced do-it-yourselfer will assemble a tool set complete enough for most repair and overhaul procedures and will add tools from the *Special* category when it is felt that the expense is justified by the frequency of use.

Maintenance and minor repair tool kit

The tools in this list should be considered the minimum required for performance of routine maintenance, servicing and minor repair work. We recommend the purchase of combination wrenches (box-end and open-end combined in one wrench); while more expensive than open-ended ones, they offer the advantages of both types of wrench.

> Combination wrench set (1/4 in to 1 in or 6 mm to 19 mm)
> Adjustable wrench — 8 in
> Spark plug wrench (with rubber insert)
> Spark plug gap adjusting tool
> Feeler gauge set
> Brake bleeder wrench
> Standard screwdriver (5/16 in x 6 in)
> Phillips screwdriver (No. 2 x 6 in)
> Combination pliers — 6 in
> Hacksaw and assortment of blades
> Tire pressure gauge
> Grease gun
> Oil can
> Fine emery cloth
> Wire brush
> Battery post and cable cleaning tool
> Oil filter wrench
> Funnel (medium size)
> Safety goggles
> Jackstands (2)
> Drain pan

Note: *If basic tune-ups are going to be part of routine maintenance, it will be necessary to purchase a good quality stroboscopic timing light and combination tachometer/dwell meter. Although they are included in the list of Special tools, it is mentioned here because they are absolutely necessary for tuning most vehicles properly.*

Repair and overhaul tool set

These tools are essential for anyone who plans to perform major repairs and are in addition to those in the *Maintenance and minor repair tool kit.* Included is a comprehensive set of sockets which, though expensive, are invaluable because of their versatility (especially when various extensions and drives are available). We recommend the 1/2-inch drive over the 3/8-inch drive. Although the larger drive is bulky and more expensive, it has the capacity of accepting a very wide range of large sockets (ideally, the mechanic would have a 3/8-inch drive set and a 1/2-inch drive set).

> Socket set(s)
> Reversible ratchet
> Extension — 10 in
> Universal joint
> Torque wrench (same size drive as sockets)
> Ball peen hammer — 8 oz
> Soft-faced hammer (plastic/rubber)
> Standard screwdriver (1/4 in x 6 in)
> Standard screwdriver (stubby — 5/16 in)
> Phillips screwdriver (No. 3 x 8 in)
> Phillips screwdriver (stubby — No. 2)
> Pliers — vise grip
> Pliers — lineman's
> Pliers — needle nose
> Pliers — snap-ring (internal and external)

> Cold chisel — 1/2 in
> Scriber
> Scraper (made from flattened copper tubing)
> Center punch
> Pin punches (1/16, 1/8, 3/16 in)
> Steel rule/straightedge — 12 in
> Allen wrench set (1/8 to 3/8 in or 4 mm to 10 mm)
> A selection of files
> Wire brush (large)
> Jackstands (second set)
> Jack (scissor or hydraulic type)

Note: *Another tool which is often useful is an electric drill motor (with a chuck capacity of 3/8-inch) and a set of good-quality drill bits.*

Special tools

The tools in this list include those which are not used regularly, are expensive to buy, or which need to be used in accordance with their manufacturer's instructions. Unless these tools will be used frequently, it is not very economical to purchase many of them. A consideration would be to split the cost and use between yourself and a friend or friends. In addition, most of these tools can be obtained from a tool rental shop on a temporary basis.

This list primarily contains only those tools and instruments widely available to the public, and not those special tools produced by the vehicle manufacturer for distribution to dealer service departments. Occasionally, references to the manufacturer's special tools are included in the text of this manual. Generally, an alternative method of doing the job without the special tool is offered. However, sometimes there is no alternative to their use. Where this is the case, and the tool cannot be purchased or borrowed, the work should be turned over to the dealer service department or an automotive repair shop.

> Valve spring compressor
> Piston ring groove cleaning tool
> Piston ring compressor
> Piston ring installation tool
> Cylinder compression gauge
> Cylinder ridge reamer
> Cylinder surfacing hone
> Cylinder bore gauge
> Micrometer(s) and/or dial calipers
> Hydraulic lifter removal tool
> Balljoint separator
> Universal-type puller
> Impact screwdriver
> Dial indicator set
> Stroboscopic timing light (inductive pick-up)
> Hand-operated vacuum/pressure pump
> Tachometer/dwell meter
> Universal electrical multimeter
> Cable hoist
> Brake spring removal and installation tools
> Floor jack

Buying tools

For the do-it-yourselfer who is just starting to get involved in vehicle maintenance and repair, there are a number of options available when purchasing tools. If maintenance and minor repair is the extent of the work to be done, the purchase of individual tools is satisfactory. If, on the other hand, extensive work is planned, it would be a good idea to purchase a modest tool set from one of the large retail chain stores. A set can usually be bought at a substantial savings over the individual tool prices (and they often come with a tool box). As additional tools are needed, add-on sets, individual tools and a larger tool box can be purchased to expand the tool selection. Building a tool set gradually allows the cost of the tools to be spread over a longer period of time and gives the mechanic the freedom to choose only those tools that will actually be used.

Tool stores will often be the only source of some of the special tools that are needed, but regardless of where tools are bought, try to avoid cheap ones (especially when buying screwdrivers and sockets) because they won't last very long. The expense involved in replacing cheap tools will eventually be greater than the initial cost of quality tools.

Care and maintenance of tools

Good tools are expensive, so it makes sense to treat them with respect. Keep them clean and in usable condition and store them properly when not in use. Always wipe off any dirt, grease or metal chips before putting them away. Never leave tools lying around in the work area. Upon completion of a job, always check closely under the hood for tools that may have been left there (so they don't get lost during a test drive).

Some tools, such as screwdrivers, pliers, wrenches and sockets, can be hung on a panel mounted on the garage or workshop wall, while others should be kept in a tool box or tray. Measuring instruments, gauges, meters, etc. must be carefully stored where they cannot be damaged by weather or impact from other tools.

When tools are used with care and stored properly, they will last a very long time. Even with the best of care, tools will wear out if used frequently. When a tool is damaged or worn out, replace it; subsequent jobs will be safer and more enjoyable if you do.

Working facilities

Not to be overlooked when discussing tools is the workshop. If anything more than routine maintenance is to be carried out, some sort of suitable work area is essential.

It is understood, and appreciated, that many home mechanics do not have a good workshop or garage available and end up removing an engine or doing major repairs outside. It is recommended, however, that the overhaul or repair be completed under the cover of a roof.

A clean, flat workbench or table of comfortable working height is an absolute necessity. The workbench should be equipped with a vise that has a jaw opening of at least four inches.

As mentioned previously, some clean, dry storage space is also required for tools, as well as the lubricants, fluids, cleaning solvents, etc. which soon become necessary.

Sometimes waste oil and fluids, drained from the engine or cooling system during normal maintenance or repairs, present a disposal problem. To avoid pouring them on the ground or into a sewage system, simply pour the used fluids into large containers, seal them with caps and take them to an authorized disposal site or recycling center. Plastic jugs (such as old antifreeze containers) are ideal for this purpose.

Always keep a supply of old newspapers and clean rags available. Old towels are excellent for mopping up spills. Many mechanics use rolls of paper towels for most work because they are readily available and disposable. To help keep the area under the vehicle clean, a large cardboard box can be cut open and flattened to protect the garage or shop floor.

Whenever working over a painted surface (such as when leaning over a fender to service something under the hood), always cover it with an old blanket or bedspread to protect the finish. Vinyl covered pads, made especially for this purpose, are available at auto parts stores.

Booster battery (jump) starting

Certain precautions must be observed when using a booster battery to 'jump start' a vehicle.

a) Before connecting the booster battery, make sure that the ignition switch is in the Off position.
b) Turn off the lights, heater and other electrical loads.
c) The eyes should be shielded; safety goggles are a good idea.
d) Make sure the booster battery is the same voltage as the dead one in the vehicle.
e) The two vehicles must not touch each other.
f) Make sure the transmission is in Neutral (manual transmission) or Park (automatic transmission).

Connect the red jumper cable to the *positive* (+) terminals of each battery.

Connect one end of the black jumper cable to the *negative* (–) terminal of the booster battery. The other end of this cable should be connected to a good ground on the vehicle to be started, such as a bolt or bracket on the engine block.

Start the engine using the booster battery, then, with the engine running at idle speed, disconnect the jumper cables in the reverse order of connection.

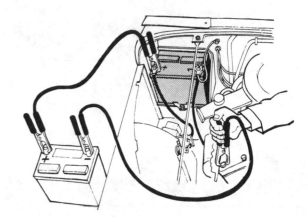

Booster battery cable connections (note that the negative cable is *not* attached to the negative terminal of the dead battery)

Jacking and towing

Jacking

The jack supplied with the vehicle should only be used for raising the vehicle when changing a tire or placing jackstands under the frame. **Caution:** *Never work under the vehicle or start the engine while this jack is being used as the only means of support.*

The vehicle should be on level ground with the wheels blocked and the transmission in Park (automatic) or Reverse (manual). Pry off the hub cap (if equipped) using the tapered end of the lug wrench. Loosen the wheel nuts one-half turn and leave them in place until the wheel is raised off the ground.

Place the jack under the side of the vehicle in the indicated position and place the jack lever in the 'up' position. Raise the jack until the jack head groove fits into the rocker flange notch. Operate the jack with a slow, smooth motion, using your hand or foot to pump the handle until the wheel is raised off the ground. Remove the wheel nuts, pull off the wheel and replace it with the spare. (If you have a stowaway spare, refer to the instructions accompanying the supplied inflator.)

With the beveled side in, replace the wheel nuts and tighten them until snug. Place the jack lever in the 'down' position and lower the vehicle. Remove the jack and tighten the nuts in a crisscross sequence by turning the wrench clockwise. Replace the hub cap (if equipped) by placing it into position and using the heel of your hand or a rubber mallet to seat it.

Towing

The vehicle can be towed with all four wheels on the ground, provided that speeds do not exceed 35 mph and the distance is not over 50 miles, otherwise transmission damage can result.

Towing equipment specifically designed for this purpose should be used and should be attached to the main structural members of the vehicle and not the bumper or brackets.

Safety is a major consideration when towing and all applicable state and local laws must be obeyed. A safety chain system must be used for all towing.

While towing, the parking brake should be released and the transmission should be in Neutral. The steering must be unlocked (ignition switch in the Off position). Remember that power steering and power brakes will not work with the engine off.

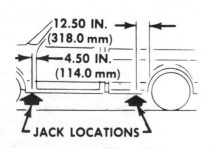

Front and rear jack locations for raising the vehicle

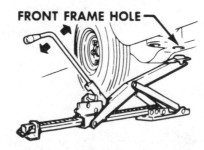

A special frame hole is provided behind the front wheel to accept the jack pad

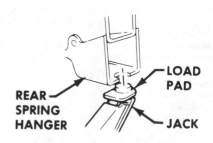

When raising the rear of the vehicle, the jack should be placed under the spring hanger

Automotive chemicals and lubricants

A number of automotive chemicals and lubricants are available for use during vehicle maintenance and repair. They include a wide variety of products ranging from cleaning solvents and degreasers to lubricants and protective sprays for rubber, plastic and vinyl.

Contact point/spark plug cleaner is a solvent used to clean oily film and dirt from points, grime from electrical connectors and oil deposits from spark plugs. It is oil free and leaves no residue. It can also be used to remove gum and varnish from carburetor jets and other orifices.

Carburetor cleaner is similar to contact point/spark plug cleaner but it is a stronger solvent and may leave a slight oily residue. It is not recommended for cleaning electrical components or connections.

Brake system cleaner is used to remove grease or brake fluid from brake system components where clean surfaces are absolutely necessary and petroleum-based solvents cannot be used. It also leaves no residue.

Silicone-based lubricants are used to protect rubber parts such as hoses, weatherstripping and grommets, and are used as lubricants for hinges and locks.

Multi-purpose grease is an all-purpose lubricant used wherever grease is more practical than a liquid lubricant such as oil. Some multi-purpose grease is white and specially formulated to be more resistant to water than ordinary grease.

Bearing grease/wheel bearing grease is a heavy grease used where increased loads and friction are encountered (i.e. wheel bearings, universal joints, etc.).

High-temperature wheel bearing grease is designed to withstand the extreme temperatures encountered by wheel bearings in disc-brake equipped vehicles. It usually contains molybdenum disulfide, which is a 'dry' type lubricant.

Gear oil (sometimes called gear lube) is a specially designed oil used in differentials, manual transmissions and transfer cases, as well as other areas where high-friction, high-temperature lubrication is required. It is available in a number of viscosities (weights) for various applications.

Motor oil, of course, is the lubricant specially formulated for use in engines. It normally contains a wide variety of additives to prevent corrosion and reduce foaming and wear. Motor oil comes in various weights (viscosity ratings) of from 5 to 80. The recommended weight of the oil depends on the seasonal temperature and the demands on the engine. Light oil is used in cold climates and under light load conditions; heavy oil is used in hot climates and where high loads are encountered. Multi-viscosity oils are designed to have characteristics of both light and heavy oils and are available in a number of weights from 5W-20 to 20W-50.

Oil additives range from viscosity index improvers to slick chemical treatments that purportedly reduce friction. It should be noted that most oil manufacturers caution against using additives with their oils.

Gas additives perform several functions, depending on their chemical makeup. They usually contain solvents that help dissolve gum and varnish that build up on carburetor and intake parts. They also serve to break down carbon deposits that form on the inside surfaces of the combustion chambers. Some additives contain upper cylinder lubricants for valves and piston rings.

Brake fluid is a specially formulated hydraulic fluid that can withstand the heat and pressure encountered in brake systems. Care must be taken that this fluid does not come in contact with painted surfaces or plastics. An opened container should always be resealed to prevent contamination by water or dirt.

Undercoating is a petroleum-based, tar-like substance that is designed to protect metal surfaces on the underside of a vehicle from corrosion. It also acts as a sound-deadening agent by insulating the bottom of the vehicle.

Weatherstrip cement is used to bond weatherstripping around doors, windows and trunk lids. It is sometimes used to attach trim pieces as well.

Degreasers are heavy-duty solvents used to remove grease and grime that may accumulate on engine and chassis components. They can be sprayed or brushed on and, depending on the type, are rinsed off with either water or solvent.

Solvents are used alone or in combination with degreasers to clean parts and assemblies during repair and overhaul. The home mechanic should use only solvents that are non-flammable and that do not produce irritating fumes.

Gasket sealing compounds may be used in conjunction with gaskets, to improve their sealing capabilities, or alone, to seal metal-to-metal joints. Many gasket sealers can withstand extreme heat, some are impervious to gasoline and lubricants, while others are capable of filling and sealing large cavities. Depending on the intended use, gasket sealers either dry hard or stay relatively soft and pliable. They are usually applied by hand, with a brush, or are sprayed on the gasket sealing surfaces.

Thread cement is an adhesive locking compound that prevents threaded fasteners from loosening because of vibration. It is available in a variety of types for different applications.

Moisture dispersants are usually sprays that can be used to dry out electrical components such as the distributor, fuse block and wiring connectors. Some types can also be used as treatment for rubber and as a lubricant for hinges, cables and locks.

Waxes and polishes are used to help protect painted and plated surfaces from the weather. Different types of paint may require the use of different types of wax polish. Some polishes utilize a chemical or abrasive cleaner to help remove the top layer of oxidized (dull) paint on older vehicles. In recent years many non-wax polishes that contain a wide variety of chemicals such as polymers and silicones have been introduced. These non-wax polishes are usually easier to apply and last longer than conventional waxes and polishes.

Safety first!

Regardless of how enthusiastic you may be about getting on with the job at hand, take the time to ensure that your safety is not jeopardized. A moment's lack of attention can result in an accident, as can failure to observe certain simple safety precautions. The possibility of an accident will always exist, and the following points should not be considered a comprehensive list of all dangers. Rather, they are intended to make you aware of the risks and to encourage a safety conscious approach to all work you carry out on your vehicle.

Essential DOs and DON'Ts

DON'T rely on a jack when working under the vehicle. Always use approved jackstands to support the weight of the vehicle and place them under the recommended lift or support points.

DON'T attempt to loosen extremely tight fasteners (i.e. wheel lug nuts) while the vehicle is on a jack — it may fall.

DON'T start the engine without first making sure that the transmission is in Neutral (or Park where applicable) and the parking brake is set.

DON'T remove the radiator cap from a hot cooling system — let it cool or cover it with a cloth and release the pressure gradually.

DON'T attempt to drain the engine oil until you are sure it has cooled to the point that it will not burn you.

DON'T touch any part of the engine or exhaust system until it has cooled sufficiently to avoid burns.

DON'T siphon toxic liquids such as gasoline, antifreeze and brake fluid by mouth, or allow them to remain on your skin.

DON'T inhale brake lining dust — it is potentially hazardous (see *Asbestos* below)

DON'T allow spilled oil or grease to remain on the floor — wipe it up before someone slips on it.

DON'T use loose fitting wrenches or other tools which may slip and cause injury.

DON'T push on wrenches when loosening or tightening nuts or bolts. Always try to pull the wrench toward you. If the situation calls for pushing the wrench away, push with an open hand to avoid scraped knuckles if the wrench should slip.

DON'T attempt to lift a heavy component alone — get someone to help you.

DON'T rush or take unsafe shortcuts to finish a job.

DON'T allow children or animals in or around the vehicle while you are working on it.

DO wear eye protection when using power tools such as a drill, sander, bench grinder, etc. and when working under a vehicle.

DO keep loose clothing and long hair well out of the way of moving parts.

DO make sure that any hoist used has a safe working load rating adequate for the job.

DO get someone to check on you periodically when working alone on a vehicle.

DO carry out work in a logical sequence and make sure that everything is correctly assembled and tightened.

DO keep chemicals and fluids tightly capped and out of the reach of children and pets.

DO remember that your vehicle's safety affects that of yourself and others. If in doubt on any point, get professional advice.

Asbestos

Certain friction, insulating, sealing, and other products — such as brake linings, brake bands, clutch linings, torque converters, gaskets, etc. — contain asbestos. *Extreme care must be taken to avoid inhalation of dust from such products since it is hazardous to health.* If in doubt, assume that they *do* contain asbestos.

Fire

Remember at all times that gasoline is highly flammable. Never smoke or have any kind of open flame around when working on a vehicle. But the risk does not end there. A spark caused by an electrical short circuit, by two metal surfaces contacting each other, or even by static electricity built up in your body under certain conditions, can ignite gasoline vapors, which in a confined space are highly explosive. Do not, under any circumstances, use gasoline for cleaning parts. Use an approved safety solvent.

Always disconnect the battery ground (–) cable *at the battery* before working on any part of the fuel system or electrical system. Never risk spilling fuel on a hot engine or exhaust component.

It is strongly recommended that a fire extinguisher suitable for use on fuel and electrical fires be kept handy in the garage or workshop at all times. Never try to extinguish a fuel or electrical fire with water.

Fumes

Certain fumes are highly toxic and can quickly cause unconsciousness and even death if inhaled to any extent. Gasoline vapor falls into this category, as do the vapors from some cleaning solvents. Any draining or pouring of such volatile fluids should be done in a well ventilated area.

When using cleaning fluids and solvents, read the instructions on the container carefully. Never use materials from unmarked containers.

Never run the engine in an enclosed space, such as a garage. Exhaust fumes contain carbon monoxide, which is extremely poisonous. If you need to run the engine, always do so in the open air, or at least have the rear of the vehicle outside the work area.

If you are fortunate enough to have the use of an inspection pit, never drain or pour gasoline and never run the engine while the vehicle is over the pit. The fumes, being heavier than air, will concentrate in the pit with possibly lethal results.

The battery

Never create a spark or allow a bare light bulb near a battery. They normally give off a certain amount of hydrogen gas, which is highly explosive.

Always disconnect the battery ground (–) cable *at the battery* before working on the fuel or electrical systems.

If possible, loosen the filler caps or cover when charging the battery from an external source (this does not apply to sealed or maintenance-free batteries). Do not charge at an excessive rate or the battery may burst.

Take care when adding water to a non maintenance-free battery and when carrying a battery. The electrolyte, even when diluted, is very corrosive and should not be allowed to contact clothing or skin.

Always wear eye protection when cleaning the battery to prevent the caustic deposits from entering your eyes.

Household current

When using an electric power tool, inspection light, etc., which operates on household current, always make sure that the tool is correctly connected to its plug and that, where necessary, it is properly grounded. Do not use such items in damp conditions and, again, do not create a spark or apply excessive heat in the vicinity of fuel or fuel vapor.

Secondary ignition system voltage

A severe electric shock can result from touching certain parts of the ignition system (such as the spark plug wires) when the engine is running or being cranked, particularly if components are damp or the insulation is defective In the case of an electronic ignition system, the secondary system voltage is much higher and could prove fatal.

Troubleshooting

Contents

This section provides an easy-reference guide to the more common problems which may occur during the operation of your vehicle. These problems and possible causes are grouped under various components or systems i.e. Engine, Cooling system, etc., and also refer to the Chapter and/or Section which deals with the problem.

Remember that successful troubleshooting is not a mysterious 'black art' practiced only by professional mechanics; it's simply the result of a bit of knowledge combined with an intelligent, systematic approach to the problem. Always work by a process of elimination, starting with the simplest solution and working through to the most complex — and never overlook the obvious. Anyone can forget to fill the gas tank or leave the lights on overnight, so don't assume that you are above such oversights.

Finally, always get clear in your mind why a problem has occurred and take steps to ensure that it doesn't happen again. If the electrical system fails because of a poor connection, check all other connections in the system to make sure that they don't fail as well; if a particular fuse continues to blow, find out why — don't just go on replacing fuses. Remember, failure of a small component can often be indicative of potential failure or incorrect functioning of a more important component or system.

Engine

1   Engine will not rotate when attempting to start

1   Battery terminal connections loose or corroded. Check the cable terminals at the battery; tighten the cable or remove corrosion as necessary.
2   Battery discharged or faulty. If the cable connections are clean and tight on the battery posts, turn the key to the On position and switch on the headlights and/or windshield wipers. If they fail to function, the battery is discharged.
3   Automatic transmission not completely engaged in Park or clutch not completely depressed.
4   Broken, loose or disconnected wiring in the starting circuit. Inspect all wiring and connectors at the battery, starter solenoid and ignition switch.
5   Starter motor pinion jammed in flywheel ring gear. If manual transmission, place transmission in gear and rock the vehicle to manually turn the engine. Remove starter and inspect pinion and flywheel at earliest convenience.
6   Starter solenoid faulty (Chapter 5).
7   Starter motor faulty (Chapter 5).
8   Ignition switch faulty (Chapter 10).

2   Engine rotates but will not start

1   Fuel tank empty.
2   Battery discharged (engine rotates slowly). Check the operation of electrical components as described in previous Section.
3   Battery terminal connections loose or corroded. See previous Section.
4   Carburetor flooded and/or fuel level in carburetor incorrect. This will usually be accompanied by a strong fuel odor from under the hood. Wait a few minutes, depress the accelerator pedal all the way to the floor and attempt to start the engine.
5   Choke control inoperative (Chapter 1).
6   Fuel not reaching carburetor. With ignition switch in Off position, open hood, remove the top plate of air cleaner assembly and observe the top of the carburetor (manually move choke plate back if necessary). Have an assistant depress accelerator pedal and check that fuel spurts into carburetor. If not, check fuel filter (Chapter 1), fuel lines and fuel pump (Chapter 4).
7   Fuel pump faulty (Chapter 4).
8   Excessive moisture on, or damage to, ignition components (Chapter 5).
9   Worn, faulty or incorrectly gapped spark plugs (Chapter 1).
10 Spark plug fouling (on V6 engines only) after repeated short trips, leading to a no-start condition. A General Motors dealer technical service bulletin concerning this problem has been issued. Take the vehicle to your dealer and inform him of the problem.
11 Broken, loose or disconnected wiring in the starting circuit (see previous Section).
12 Distributor loose, causing ignition timing to change. Turn the distributor as necessary to start the engine, then set ignition timing as soon as possible (Chapter 1).
13 Broken, loose or disconnected wires at the ignition coil or faulty coil (Chapter 5).

3   Starter motor operates without rotating engine

1   Starter pinion sticking. Remove the starter (Chapter 5) and inspect.
2   Starter pinion or flywheel teeth worn or broken. Remove the cover at the rear of the engine and inspect.

4   Engine hard to start when cold

1   Battery discharged or low. Check as described in Section 1.
2   Choke control inoperative or out of adjustment (Chapter 4).
3   Carburetor flooded (see Section 2).

4   Fuel supply not reaching the carburetor (see Section 2).
5   Carburetor in need of overhaul (Chapter 4).
6   Distributor rotor carbon tracked and/or mechanical advance mechanism rusted (Chapter 5).

5   Engine hard to start when hot

1   Choke sticking in the closed position (Chapter 1).
2   Carburetor flooded (see Section 2).
3   Air filter clogged (Chapter 1).
4   Fuel not reaching the carburetor (see Section 2).

6   Starter motor noisy or excessively rough in engagement

1   Pinion or flywheel gear teeth worn or broken. Remove the cover at the rear of the engine (if so equipped) and inspect.
2   Starter motor mounting bolts loose or missing.

7   Engine starts but stops immediately

1   Loose or faulty electrical connections at distributor, coil or alternator.
2   Insufficient fuel reaching the carburetor. Disconnect the fuel line at the carburetor and remove the filter (Chapter 1). Place a container under the disconnected fuel line. Observe the flow of fuel from the line. If little or none at all, check for blockage in the lines and/or replace the fuel pump (Chapter 4).
3   Vacuum leak at the gasket surfaces of the intake manifold and/or carburetor. Make sure that all mounting bolts (nuts) are tightened securely and that all vacuum hoses connected to the carburetor and manifold are positioned properly and in good condition.

8   Engine lopes while idling or idles erratically

1   Vacuum leakage. Check mounting bolts (nuts) at the carburetor and intake manifold for tightness. Make sure that all vacuum hoses are connected and in good condition. Use a stethoscope or a length of fuel hose held against your ear to listen for vacuum leaks while the engine is running. A hissing sound will be heard. A soapy water solution will also detect leaks. Check the carburetor and intake manifold gasket surfaces.
2   Leaking EGR valve or plugged PCV valve (see Chapters 1 and 6).
3   Air filter clogged (Chapter 1).
4   Fuel pump not delivering sufficient fuel to the carburetor (see Section 7).
5   Carburetor out of adjustment (Chapter 4).
6   Leaking head gasket. If this is suspected, take the vehicle to a repair shop or dealer where the engine can be pressure checked.
7   Timing chain and/or gears worn (Chapter 2).
8   Camshaft lobes worn (Chapter 2).
9   Spark plug fouling (on V6 engines only) after repeated short trips. A General Motors dealer technical service bulletin concerning this problem has been issued. Take the vehicle to your dealer annd inform him of the problem.

9   Engine misses at idle speed

1   Spark plugs worn or not gapped properly (Chapter 1).
2   Spark plug fouling (on V6 engines only) after repeated short trips (see Section 8).
3   Faulty spark plug wires (Chapter 1).
4   Choke not operating properly (Chapter 1).

10   Engine misses throughout driving speed range

1   Fuel filter clogged and/or impurities in the fuel system (Chap-

ter 1). Also check fuel output at the carburetor (see Section 7).
2   Faulty or incorrectly gapped spark plugs (Chapter 1).
3   Incorrect ignition timing (Chapter 1).
4   Check for cracked distributor cap, disconnected distributor wires and damaged distributor components (Chapter 1).
5   Leaking spark plug wires (Chapter 1).
6   Faulty emissions system components (Chapter 6).
7   Low or uneven cylinder compression pressures. Remove spark plugs and test compression with gauge (Chapter 1).
8   Weak or faulty ignition system (Chapter 5).
9   Vacuum leaks at carburetor, intake manifold or vacuum hoses (see Section 8).

11   Engine stalls

1   Idle speed incorrect (Chapter 1).
2   Fuel filter clogged and/or water and impurities in the fuel system (Chapter 1).
3   Choke improperly adjusted or sticking (Chapter 1).
4   Distributor components damp or damaged (Chapter 5).
5   Faulty emissions system components (Chapter 6).
6   Faulty or incorrectly gapped spark plugs (Chapter 1). Also check spark plug wires (Chapter 1).
7   Vacuum leak at the carburetor, intake manifold or vacuum hoses. Check as described in Section 8.
8   Valve clearances incorrectly set (Chapter 1).

12   Engine lacks power

1   Incorrect ignition timing (Chapter 1).
2   Excessive play in distributor shaft. At the same time, check for worn rotor, faulty distributor cap, wires, etc. (Chapters 1 and 5).
3   Faulty or incorrectly gapped spark plugs (Chapter 1).
4   Spark plug fouling (on V6 engines only) after repeated short trips (see Section 8).
5   Carburetor not adjusted properly or excessively worn (Chapter 4).
6   Faulty coil (Chapter 5).
7   Brakes binding (Chapter 1).
8   Automatic transmission fluid level incorrect (Chapter 1).
9   Clutch slipping (Chapter 8).
10 Fuel filter clogged and/or impurities in the fuel system (Chapter 1).
11 Emissions control system not functioning properly (Chapter 6).
12 Use of sub-standard fuel. Fill tank with proper octane fuel.
13 Low or uneven cylinder compression pressures. Test with compression tester, which will detect leaking valves and/or blown head gasket (Chapter 1).

13   Engine backfires

1   Emissions system not functioning properly (Chapter 6).
2   Ignition timing incorrect (Chapter 1).
3   Faulty secondary ignition system (cracked spark plug insulator, faulty plug wires, distributor cap and/or rotor) (Chapters 1 and 5).
4   Carburetor in need of adjustment or worn excessively (Chapter 4).
5   Vacuum leak at carburetor, intake manifold or vacuum hoses. Check as described in Section 8.
6   Valve clearances incorrectly set, and/or valves sticking (Chapter 1).

14   Pinging or knocking engine sounds during acceleration or uphill

1   Incorrect grade of fuel. Fill tank with fuel of the proper octane rating.
2   Ignition timing incorrect (Chapter 1).
3   Carburetor in need of adjustment (Chapter 4).
4   Improper spark plugs. Check plug type against Emissions Control Information label located in engine compartment. Also check plugs and wires for damage (Chapter 1).
5   Worn or damaged distributor components (Chapter 5).
6   Faulty emissions system (Chapter 6).
7   Vacuum leak. Check as described in Section 8.

15   Engine 'diesels' (continues to run) after switching off

1   Idle speed too high (Chapter 1).
2   Electrical solenoid at side of carburetor not functioning properly (not all models, see Chapter 4).
3   Ignition timing incorrectly adjusted (Chapter 1).
4   Thermo-controlled air cleaner heat valve not operating properly (Chapter 1).
5   Excessive engine operating temperature. Probable causes of this are malfunctioning thermostat, clogged radiator, faulty water pump (Chapter 3).

Engine electrical system

16   Battery will not hold a charge

1   Alternator drivebelt defective or not adjusted properly (Chapter 1).
2   Electrolyte level low or battery discharged (Chapter 1).
3   Battery terminals loose or corroded (Chapter 1).
4   Alternator not charging properly (Chapter 5).
5   Loose, broken or faulty wiring in the charging circuit (Chapter 5).
6   Short in vehicle wiring causing a continual drain on battery.
7   Battery defective internally.

17   Ignition light fails to go out

1   Fault in alternator or charging circuit (Chapter 5).
2   Alternator drivebelt defective or not properly adjusted (Chapter 1).

18   Ignition light fails to come on when key is turned on

1   Warning light bulb defective (Chapter 10).
2   Alternator faulty (Chapter 5).
3   Fault in the printed circuit, dash wiring or bulb holder (Chapter 10).

19   'Check engine' light comes on

See Chapter 6.

Fuel system

20   Excessive fuel consumption

1   Dirty or clogged air filter element (Chapter 1).
2   Incorrectly set ignition timing (Chapter 1).
3   Choke sticking or improperly adjusted (Chapter 1).
4   Emissions system not functioning properly (not all vehicles, see Chapter 6).
5   Carburetor idle speed and/or mixture not adjusted properly (Chapter 1).
6   Carburetor internal parts excessively worn or damaged (Chapter 4).
7   Low tire pressure or incorrect tire size (Chapter 1).

21   Fuel leakage and/or fuel odor

1   Leak in a fuel feed or vent line (Chapter 4).
2   Tank overfilled. Fill only to automatic shut-off.
3   Emissions system filter clogged (Chapter 1).
4   Vapor leaks from system lines (Chapter 4).
5   Carburetor internal parts excessively worn or out of adjustment (Chapter 4).

Engine cooling system

22   Overheating

1   Insufficient coolant in system (Chapter 1).

2   Water pump drivebelt defective or not adjusted properly (Chapter 1).
3   Radiator core blocked or radiator grille dirty and restricted (Chapter 3).
4   Thermostat faulty (Chapter 3).
5   Fan blades broken or cracked (Chapter 3).
6   Radiator cap not maintaining proper pressure. Have cap pressure tested by gas station or repair shop.
7   Ignition timing incorrect (Chapter 1).

23   Overcooling

1   Thermostat faulty (Chapter 3).
2   Inaccurate temperature gauge (Chapter 10)

24   External coolant leakage

1   Deteriorated or damaged hoses. Tighten clamps at hose connections (Chapter 1).
2   Water pump seals defective. If this is the case, water will drip from the 'weep' hole in the water pump body (Chapter 1).
3   Leakage from radiator core or header tank. This will require the radiator to be professionally repaired (see Chapter 3 for removal procedures).
4   Engine drain plugs or water jacket core plugs leaking (see Chapter 2).

25   Internal coolant leakage

Note: *Internal coolant leaks can usually be detected by examining the oil. Check the dipstick and inside of the rocker arm cover(s) for water deposits and an oil consistency like that of a milkshake.*

1   Leaking cylinder head gasket. Have the cooling system pressure-tested.
2   Cracked cylinder bore or cylinder head. Dismantle engine and inspect (Chapter 2).

26   Coolant loss

1   Too much coolant in system (Chapter 1).
2   Coolant boiling away due to overheating (see Section 15).
3   Internal or external leakage (see Sections 24 and 25).
4   Faulty radiator cap. Have the cap pressure-tested.

27   Poor coolant circulation

1   Inoperative water pump. A quick test is to pinch the top radiator hose closed with your hand while the engine is idling, then let it loose. You should feel the surge of coolant if the pump is working properly (Chapter 1).
2   Restriction in cooling system. Drain, flush and refill the system (Chapter 1). If necessary, remove the radiator (Chapter 3) and have it reverse-flushed.
3   Water pump drivebelt defective or not adjusted properly (Chapter 1).
4   Thermostat sticking (Chapter 3).

Clutch

28   Fails to release (pedal pressed to the floor — shift lever does not move freely in and out of Reverse)

1   Improper linkage free play adjustment (Chapter 1).
2   Clutch fork off ball stud. Look under the vehicle, on the left side of transmission.
3   Clutch plate warped or damaged (Chapter 8).

29   Clutch slips (engine speed increases with no increase in vehicle speed)

1   Linkage out of adjustment (Chapter 8).
2   Clutch plate oil soaked or lining worn. Remove clutch (Chapter 8) and inspect.
3   Clutch plate not seated. It may take 30 or 40 normal starts for a new one to seat.

30   Grabbing (chattering) as clutch is engaged

1   Oil on clutch plate lining. Remove (Chapter 8) and inspect. Correct any leakage source.
2   Worn or loose engine or transmission mounts. These units move slightly when clutch is released. Inspect mounts and bolts.
3   Worn splines on clutch plate hub. Remove clutch components (Chapter 8) and inspect.
4   Warped pressure plate or flywheel. Remove clutch components and inspect.

31   Squeal or rumble with clutch fully engaged (pedal released)

1   Improper adjustment; no free play (Chapter 1).
2   Release bearing binding on transmission bearing retainer. Remove clutch components (Chapter 8) and check bearing. Remove any burrs or nicks, clean and relubricate before reinstallation.
3   Weak linkage return spring. Replace the spring.

32   Squeal or rumble with clutch fully disengaged (pedal depressed)

1   Worn, defective or broken release bearing (Chapter 8).
2   Worn or broken pressure plate springs (or diaphragm fingers) (Chapter 8).

33   Clutch pedal stays on floor when disengaged

1   Bind in linkage or release bearing. Inspect linkage or remove clutch components as necessary.
2   Linkage springs being over-extended. Adjust linkage for proper free play. Make sure proper pedal stop (bumper) is installed.

Manual transmission

34   Noisy in Neutral with engine running

1   Input shaft bearing worn.
2   Damaged main drive gear bearing.
3   Worn countershaft bearings.
4   Worn or damaged countershaft end play shims.

35   Noisy in all gears

1   Any of the above causes, and/or:
2   Insufficient lubricant (see checking procedures in Chapter 1).

36   Noisy in one particular gear

1   Worn, damaged or chipped gear teeth for that particular gear.
2   Worn or damaged synchronizer for that particular gear.

37   Slips out of high gear

1   Transmission loose on clutch housing (Chapter 7).
2   Damaged mainshaft pilot bearing.
3   Dirt between transmission case and engine or misalignment of transmission (Chapter 7).
4   Worn or improperly adjusted linkage (Chapter 7).

38   Difficulty in engaging gears

1   Clutch not releasing completely (see clutch adjustment in Chapter 1).
2   Loose, damaged or out-of-adjustment shift linkage. Make a thorough inspection, replacing parts as necessary (Chapter 7).

39   Oil leakage

1   Excessive amount of lubricant in transmission (see Chapter 1 for correct checking procedures). Drain lubricant as required.
2   Side cover loose or gasket damaged.
3   Rear oil seal or speedometer oil seal in need of replacement (Chapter 7).

Automatic transmission

Note: *Due to the complexity of the automatic transmission, it is difficult for the home mechanic to properly diagnose and service this component. For problems other than the following, the vehicle should be taken to a dealer or reputable mechanic.*

40   General shift mechanism problems

1   Chapter 7 deals with checking and adjusting the shift linkage on automatic transmissions. Common problems which may be attributed to poorly adjusted linkage are:

Engine starting in gears other than Park or Neutral.
Indicator on shifter pointing to a gear other than the one actually being used.
Vehicle moves when in Park.

2   Refer to Chapter 7 to adjust the linkage.

41   Transmission will not downshift with accelerator pedal pressed to the floor

Chapter 7 deals with adjusting the throttle valve (TV) cable to enable the transmission to downshift properly.

42   Engine will start in gears other than Park or Neutral

Chapter 7 deals with adjusting the Neutral start switch used with automatic transmissions.

43   Transmission slips, shifts rough, is noisy or has no drive in forward or reverse gears

1   There are many probable causes for the above problems, but the home mechanic should be concerned with only one possibility — fluid level.
2   Before taking the vehicle to a repair shop, check the level and condition of the fluid as described in Chapter 1. Correct fluid level as necessary or change the fluid and filter if needed. If the problem persists, have a professional diagnose the probable cause.

44   Fluid leakage

1   Automatic transmission fluid is a deep red color. Fluid leaks should not be confused with engine oil, which can easily be blown by air flow to the transmission.
2   To pinpoint a leak, first remove all built-up dirt and grime from around the transmission. Degreasing agents and/or steam cleaning will achieve this. With the underside clean, drive the vehicle at low speeds so air flow will not blow the leak far from its source. Raise the vehicle and determine where the leak is coming from. Common areas of leakage are:

  a) Pan: Tighten mounting bolts and/or replace pan gasket as necessary (see Chapters 1 and 7).
  b) Rear extension: Tighten bolts and/or replace oil seal as necessary (Chapter 7).
  c) Filler pipe: Replace the rubber seal where pipe enters transmission case.
  d) Transmission oil lines: Tighten connectors where lines enter transmission case and/or replace lines.
  e) Vent pipe: Transmission over-filled and/or water in fluid (see checking procedures, Chapter 1).
  f) Speedometer connector: Replace the O-ring where speedometer cable enters transmission case (Chapter 7).

Transfer case

45   Transfer case difficult to shift into the desired range

1   Speed may be too great to permit engagement. Stop the vehicle and shift into the desired range.
2   Shift linkage loose, bent or binding. Check the linkage for damage or wear and replace or lubricate as necessary (Chapter 7).
3   If the vehicle has been driven on a paved surface for some time, the driveline torque can make shifting difficult. Stop and shift into 2-wheel drive on paved or hard surfaces.
4   Insufficient or incorrect grade of lubricant. Drain and refill the transfer case with the specified lubricant (Chapter 1).
5   Worn or damaged internal components. Disassembly and overhaul of the transfer case may be necessary (Chapter 7).

46   Transfer case noisy in all gears

Insufficient or incorrect grade of lubricant. Drain and refill (Chapter 1).

47   Noisy or jumps out of 4-wheel drive Low range

1   Transfer case not fully engaged. Stop the vehicle, shift into Neutral and then engage 4L.
2   Shift linkage loose, worn or binding. Tighten, repair or lubricate linkage as necessary.
3   Shift fork cracked, inserts worn or fork binding on the rail. Disassemble and repair as necessary (Chapter 7).

48   Lubricant leaks from the vent or output shaft seals

1   Transfer case is overfilled. Drain to the proper level (Chapter 1).
2   Vent is clogged or jammed closed. Clear or replace the vent.
3   Output shaft seal incorrectly installed or damaged. Replace the seal and check the seal contact surfaces for nicks and scoring.

Driveshaft

49   Oil leak at front of driveshaft

Defective transmission rear oil seal. See Chapter 7 for replacement procedures. While this is done, check the splined yoke for burrs or a rough condition which may be damaging the seal. They can be removed with crocus cloth or a fine whetstone.

50 Knock or clunk when the transmission is under initial load (just after transmission is put into gear)

1   Loose or disconnected rear suspension components. Check all mounting bolts and bushings (Chapter 11).
2   Loose driveshaft bolts. Inspect all bolts and nuts and tighten them to the specified torque (Chapter 8).
3   Worn or damaged universal joint bearings. Check for wear (Chapter 8).

51 Metallic grating sound consistent with vehicle speed

Pronounced wear in the universal joint bearings. Check as described in Chapter 8.

52 Vibration

Note: *Before assuming that the driveshaft is at fault, make sure the tires are perfectly balanced and perform the following test.*

1   Install a tachometer inside the vehicle to monitor engine speed as the vehicle is driven. Drive the vehicle and note the engine speed at which the vibration (roughness) is most pronounced. Now shift the transmission to a different gear and bring the engine speed to the same point.
2   If the vibration occurs at the same engine speed (rpm) regardless of which gear the transmission is in, the driveshaft is NOT at fault since the driveshaft speed varies.
3   If the vibration decreases or is eliminated when the transmission is in a different gear at the same engine speed, refer to the following probable causes.
4   Bent or dented driveshaft. Inspect and replace as necessary (Chapter 8).
5   Undercoating or build-up dirt, etc. on the driveshaft. Clean the shaft thoroughly and recheck.
6   Worn universal joint bearings. Remove and inspect (Chapter 8).
7   Driveshaft and/or companion flange out of balance. Check for missing weights on the shaft. Remove driveshaft (Chapter 8) and reinstall 180° from original position, then retest. Have driveshaft professionally balanced if problem persists.

Axles

53 Noise (same when in drive as when vehicle is coasting)

1   Road noise. No corrective procedures available.
2   Tire noise. Inspect tires and check tire pressures (Chapter 1).
3   Front wheel bearings loose, worn or damaged (Chapter 1).

54 Vibration

See probable causes under *Driveshaft*. Proceed under the guidelines listed for the driveshaft. If the problem persists, check the rear axleshaft bearings by raising the rear of the vehicle and spinning the wheels by hand. Listen for evidence of rough (noisy) bearings. Remove and inspect (Chapter 8).

55 Oil leakage

1   Pinion seal damaged (Chapter 8).
2   Axleshaft oil seals damaged (Chapter 8).
3   Differential cover leaking. Tighten mounting bolts or replace the gasket as required (Chapter 8).

Brakes

Note: *Before assuming that a brake problem exists, make sure that the tires are in good condition and inflated properly (see Chapter 1), that*

the front end alignment is correct and that the vehicle is not loaded with weight in an unequal manner.

56 Vehicle pulls to one side during braking

1   Defective, damaged or oil contaminated disc brake pads on one side. Inspect as described in Chapter 9.
2   Excessive wear of brake pad material or disc on one side. Inspect and correct as necessary.
3   Loose or disconnected front suspension components. Inspect and tighten all bolts to the specified torque (Chapter 11).
4   Defective caliper assembly. Remove caliper and inspect for stuck piston or other damage (Chapter 9).

57 Noise (high-pitched squeal without the brakes applied)

Disc brake pads worn out. The noise comes from the wear sensor rubbing against the disc (does not apply to all vehicles). Replace pads with new ones immediately (Chapter 9).

58 Excessive brake pedal travel

1   Partial brake system failure. Inspect entire system (Chapter 9) and correct as required. .
2   Insufficient fluid in master cylinder. Check (Chapter 1), add fluid and bleed system if necessary (Chapter 9).
3   Rear brakes not adjusting properly. Make a series of starts and stops while the vehicle is in Reverse. If this does not correct the situation, remove drums and inspect self-adjusters (Chapter 9).

59 Brake pedal feels spongy when depressed

1   Air in hydraulic lines. Bleed the brake system (Chapter 9).
2   Faulty flexible hoses. Inspect all system hoses and lines. Replace parts as necessary.
3   Master cylinder mounting bolts/nuts loose.
4   Master cylinder defective (Chapter 9).

60 Excessive effort required to stop vehicle

1   Power brake booster not operating properly (Chapter 9).
2   Excessively worn linings or pads. Inspect and replace if necessary (Chapter 9).
3   One or more caliper pistons or wheel cylinders seized or sticking. Inspect and rebuild as required (Chapter 9).
4   Brake linings or pads contaminated with oil or grease. Inspect and replace as required (Chapter 9).
5   New pads or shoes installed and not yet seated. It will take a while for the new material to seat against the drum (or rotor).

61 Pedal travels to the floor with little resistance

Little or no fluid in the master cylinder reservoir caused by leaking wheel cylinder(s), leaking caliper piston(s), loose, damaged or disconnected brake lines. Inspect entire system and correct as necessary.

62 Brake pedal pulsates during brake application

1   Wheel bearings not adjusted properly or in need of replacement (Chapter 1).
2   Caliper not sliding properly due to improper installation or obstructions. Remove and inspect (Chapter 9).
3   Rotor defective. Remove the rotor (Chapter 9) and check for excessive lateral runout and parallelism. Have the rotor resurfaced or replace it with a new one.

63 Rattle in front brake pads (1982 models only)

A General Motors dealer technical service bulletin concerning this problem has been issued. Take the vehicle to your dealer and inform him of the problem.

Suspension and steering systems

64 Vehicle pulls to one side

1 Tire pressures uneven (Chapter 1).
2 Defective tire (Chapter 1).
3 Excessive wear in suspension or steering components (Chapter 11).
4 Front end in need of alignment.
5 Front brakes dragging. Inspect brakes as described in Chapter 9.

65 Shimmy, shake or vibration

1 Tire or wheel out-of-balance or out-of-round. Have professionally balanced.
2 Loose, worn or out-of-adjustment wheel bearings (Chapters 1 and 8).
3 Shock absorbers and/or suspension components worn or damaged (Chapter 11).

66 Excessive pitching and/or rolling around corners or during braking

1 Defective shock absorbers. Replace as a set (Chapter 11).
2 Broken or weak springs and/or suspension components. Inspect as described in Chapter 11.

67 Excessively stiff steering

1 Lack of fluid in power steering fluid reservoir (Chapter 1).
2 Incorrect tire pressures (Chapter 1).
3 Lack of lubrication at steering joints (Chapter 1).
4 Front end out of alignment.
5 See also section titled *Lack of power assistance*.

68 Excessive play in steering

1 Loose front wheel bearings (Chapter 1).
2 Excessive wear in suspension or steering components (Chapter 11).
3 Steering gearbox out of adjustment (Chapter 11).

69 Lack of power assistance

1 Steering pump drivebelt faulty or not adjusted properly (Chapter 1).
2 Fluid level low (Chapter 1).
3 Hoses or lines restricted. Inspect and replace parts as necessary.
4 Air in power steering system. Bleed system (Chapter 11).

70 Excessive tire wear (not specific to one area)

1 Incorrect tire pressures (Chapter 1).
2 Tires out of balance. Have professionally balanced.
3 Wheels damaged. Inspect and replace as necessary.
4 Suspension or steering components excessively worn (Chapter 11).

71 Excessive tire wear on outside edge

1 Inflation pressures incorrect (Chapter 1).
2 Excessive speed in turns.
3 Front end alignment incorrect (excessive toe-in). Have professionally aligned.
4 Suspension arm bent or twisted (Chapter 11).

72 Excessive tire wear on inside edge

1 Inflation pressures incorrect (Chapter 1).
2 Front end alignment incorrect (toe-out). Have professionally aligned.
3 Loose or damaged steering components (Chapter 11).

73 Tire tread worn in one place

1 Tires out of balance.
2 Damaged or buckled wheel. Inspect and replace if necessary.
3 Defective tire (Chapter 1).

Chapter 1 Tune-up and routine maintenance

Refer to Chapter 13 for specifications and information related to 1985 and later models

Contents

Specifications

Recommended lubricants, fluids and capacities

Engine oil type	Grade SF, SF/CC or SF/CD
Engine oil viscosity	
40° to 100° + F (4° to 38° + C)	SAE 30
20° to 100° + F (–7° to 38° + C)	SAE 20W-20, 20W-40, 20W-50
10° to 100° + F (–14° to 38° + C)	SAE 15W-40
0° to 100° + F (–18° to 38° + C)	SAE 10W-30, 10W-40
0° to 60° F (–18° to 17° C)	SAE 10W
Below –20° to 60° F (below –30° to 17° C)	SAE 5W-30
Engine oil capacity (without filter)	
1.9 liter four-cylinder engine	3 qts
2.0 liter four-cylinder engine	4 qts
2.8 liter V6 engine	4 qts
Coolant type	Ethylene glycol
Cooling system capacity	
Four-cylinder engine (all)	9.5 qts
2.8 liter V6 engine	12 qts
Brake fluid type	DOT-3
Manual transmission oil type	
4-speed without overdrive	GL-5 gear lubricant, SAE 80W or 80W-90
S-10 truck or 4-speed with overdrive	Dexron II or equivalent ATF
Manual transmission oil capacity	
4-speed	2.4 qts
5-speed	3.5 qts
Transfer case oil type	Dexron II ATF
Automatic transmission	
Fluid type	Dexron II or equivalent
Fluid capacity*	
200-C	3.5 qts
700-R4	4.7 qts
Power steering fluid type	GM no. 1050017 or equivalent
Front wheel bearing grease	GM no. 1051344 or equivalent
Windshield washer solvent	GM Optikleen or equivalent

Note: Capacities are approximate for refill after draining for routine maintenance; actual capacity should be measured on the transmission dipstick as discussed in Section 26.

Radiator cap opening pressure .... 15 psi

Engine idle speed .... See *Emission Control Information label* in engine compartment

Valve clearances (1.9 liter four-cylinder engine)
Intake . . . .   0.006 in
Exhaust . . . .   0.010 in

Ignition system
Distributor direction of rotation . . . .   Clockwise (all)
Firing order
    Four-cylinder engines   1-3-4-2
    2.8 liter V6 engine   1-2-3-4-5-6
Spark plug type and gap . . . .   See *Emission Control Information label* in engine compartment
Ignition timing . . . .   *See Emission Control Information label* in engine compartment

Clutch pedal free play (non-hydraulic clutch) . . . .   Approx. 2 in

Torque specifications
	Ft-lbs
Oil pan drain plug	
2.0 liter four-cylinder	20
1.9 liter four-cylinder	N/A
V6	N/A
Spark plugs	
2.0 liter four-cylinder	7 to 19
1.9 liter four-cylinder	N/A
V6	7 to 15
Carburetor mounting nuts/bolts	
V6 and 2.0 liter engine	9
Distributor hold-down bolt	20
Manual transmission fill plug	
4-speed	30
5-speed	20
Automatic transmission pan bolts	
700-R4	18
200C	10 to 13
Brake caliper mounting bolts	35
Rocker arm shaft bracket nuts (1.9 liter engine)	16
Wheel lug nuts	90

---

1   Introduction and routine maintenance schedule

This Chapter was designed to help the home mechanic maintain his (or her) vehicle for peak performance, economy, safety and long life.

On the following pages you will find a maintenance schedule along with Sections which deal specifically with each item on the schedule. Included are visual checks, adjustments and item replacements.

Servicing your vehicle using the time/mileage maintenance schedule and the sequenced Sections will give you a planned program of maintenance. Keep in mind that it is a full plan, and maintaining only a few items at the specified intervals will not give you the same results.

You will find as you service your vehicle that many of the procedures can, and should, be grouped together, due to the nature of the job at hand. Examples of this are as follows:

If the vehicle is fully raised for a chassis lubrication, for example, this is the ideal time for the following checks: manual transmission oil, rear axle oil, exhaust system, suspension, steering and the fuel system.

If the tires and wheels are removed, as during a routine tire rotation, go ahead and check the brakes and wheel bearings at the same time.

If you must borrow or rent a torque wrench, it is a good idea to service the spark plugs, repack (or replace) the wheel bearings and check the carburetor mounting bolt torque all in the same day to save time and money.

The first step of this or any maintenance plan is to prepare yourself before the actual work begins. Read through the appropriate Sections for all work that is to be performed before you begin. Gather together all necessary parts and tools. If it appears that you could have a problem during a particular job, don't hesitate to seek advice from your local parts man or dealer service department.

Routine maintenance intervals

The following recommendations are given with the assumption that the vehicle owner will be doing the maintenance or service work (as opposed to having a dealer service department do the work). The following are factory maintenance recommendations; however, subject to the preference of the individual owner, in the interest of keeping his or her vehicle in peak condition at all times and with the vehicle's ultimate

resale in mind, many of these operations may be performed more often. We encourage such owner initiative.

When the vehicle is new, it should be serviced initially by a factory authorized dealer service department to protect the factory warranty. In most cases the initial maintenance check is done at no cost to the owner.

Every 250 miles or weekly, whichever comes first

Check the engine oil level (Sec 4)
Check the engine coolant level (Sec 4)
Check the windshield washer fluid level (Sec 4)
Check the tires and tire pressures (Sec 3)

Every 6000 miles or 6 months, whichever comes first

Check the automatic transmission fluid level (Sec 4)
Check the power steering fluid level (Sec 4)
Change the engine oil and oil filter (Sec 16)
Lubricate the chassis components (Sec 10)
Check the cooling system (Sec 7)
Check and replace (if necessary) the underhood hoses (Sec 8)
Check the exhaust system (Sec 11)
Check the steering and suspension components (Sec 12)
Check and adjust (if necessary) the engine drivebelts (Sec 12)
Check the brake master cylinder fluid level (Sec 4)
Check the manual transmission oil level (Sec 4)
Check the rear axle oil level (Sec 4)
Check the operation of the choke (at this interval, then every 12000 miles or 12 months, whichever comes first) (Sec 14)
Check and adjust (if necessary) the engine idle speed (at this interval, then every 12000 miles or 12 months, whichever comes first) (Sec 15)
Check the disc brake pads (Sec 13)
Check the brake system (Sec 13)

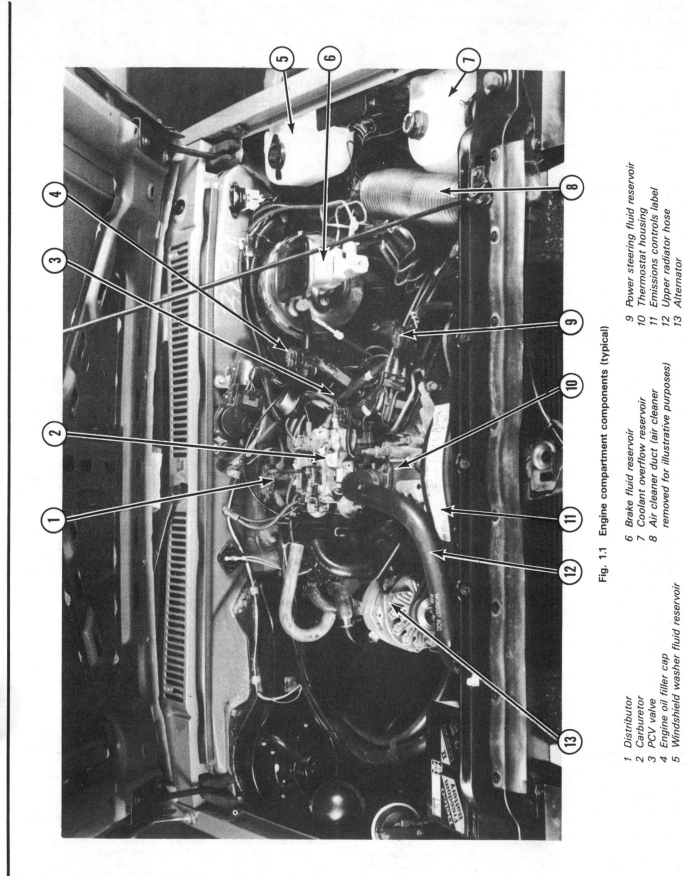

Fig. 1.1 Engine compartment components (typical)

1 Distributor
2 Carburetor
3 PCV valve
4 Engine oil filler cap
5 Windshield washer fluid reservoir
6 Brake fluid reservoir
7 Coolant overflow reservoir
8 Air cleaner duct (air cleaner removed for illustrative purposes)
9 Power steering fluid reservoir
10 Thermostat housing
11 Emissions controls label
12 Upper radiator hose
13 Alternator

Check and service the battery (Sec 5)
Check and replace (if necessary) the windshield wiper blades (Sec 9)
Check the clutch pedal free play (Sec 24)
Rotate the tires (Sec 23)
Change the differential oil (if the vehicle is used to pull a trailer) (Sec 25)

Every 12000 miles or 12 months, whichever comes first

Check the drum brake linings (Sec 13)
Check the parking brake (Sec 13)
Check the Thermo-controlled Air Cleaner (TAC) for proper operation (Sec 20)
Check the EFE system (Sec 22)
Check the fuel system components (Sec 17)
Replace the fuel filter (Sec 18)
Check the operation of the EGR valve (Sec 33)
Check the throttle linkage (Sec 19)
Check and adjust (if necessary) the valve clearance (1.9 liter engine only) (Sec 39)
Change the oil in the differentials (4 x 4 — severe operating conditions) (Sec 25)

Every 18000 miles or 18 months, whichever comes first

Check and repack the front wheel bearings (perform this procedure whenever brake pads are replaced, regardless of maintenance interval) (Sec 30)
Change the automatic transmission fluid and filter (if driven mainly in heavy city traffic in hot-climate regions, in hilly or mountainous areas, or for frequent trailer pulling) (Sec 26)
Check the torque of the carburetor mounting bolts (Sec 21)
Drain, flush and refill the cooling system (Sec 29)

Every 24000 miles or 24 months, whichever comes first

Check the EGR system (Sec 33)
Replace the PCV valve (Sec 32)
Replace the air filter and PCV filter (Sec 31)
Replace the spark plugs (Sec 36)
Check the spark plug wires, distributor cap and rotor (Sec 37)
Check and adjust (if necessary) the ignition timing (Sec 35)
Check the EEC emissions system and replace the canister filter (Sec 34)
Change the automatic transmission fluid (if driven under severe conditions, see 18000 mile interval) (Sec 26)
Change the rear differential oil (if driven under severe conditions, see 12000 or 18000 mile interval) (Sec 25)
Lubricate the clutch cross-shaft (Sec 10)
Check the engine compression (Sec 38)

2 Tune-up sequence

The term 'tune-up' is loosely used for any general operation that puts the engine back in its proper running condition. A tune-up is not a specific operation, but rather a combination of individual operations, such as replacing the spark plugs, adjusting the idle speed, setting the ignition timing, etc.

If, from the time the vehicle is new, the routine maintenance schedule (Section 1) is followed closely and frequent checks are made of fluid levels and high wear items, as suggested throughout this manual, the engine will be kept in relatively good running condition and the need for additional tune-ups will be minimized.

More likely than not, however, there will be times when the engine is running poorly due to lack of regular maintenance. This is even more likely if a used vehicle (which has not received regular and frequent maintenance checks) is purchased. In such cases, an engine tune-up will be needed outside of the regular routine maintenance intervals.

The following series of operations are those most often needed to bring a generally poor running engine back into a proper state of tune.

Minor tune-up

Clean, inspect and test battery (Sec 5)
Check all engine-related fluids (Sec 4)
Check engine compression (Sec 38)
Check and adjust drivebelts (Sec 6)
Replace spark plugs (Sec 36)
Inspect distributor cap and rotor (Sec 37)
Inspect spark plug and coil wires (Sec 37)
Check and adjust idle speed (Sec 15)
Check and adjust timing (Sec 35)
Check and adjust fuel/air mixture (see underhood VECI label)
Replace fuel filter (Sec 18)
Check PCV valve (Sec 32)
Check cooling system (Sec 7)

Major tune-up

(the above operations and those listed below)
Check EGR system (Chapter 6)
Check ignition system (Chapter 5)
Check charging system (Chapter 5)
Check fuel system (Sec 17)

3 Tire and tire pressure checks

1   Periodically inspecting the tires may not only prevent you from being stranded with a flat tire, but can also give you clues as to possible problems with the steering and suspension systems before major damage occurs.
2   Proper tire inflation adds miles to the lifespan of the tires, allows the vehicle to achieve maximum miles per gallon figures and contributes to the overall quality of the ride.
3   When inspecting the tires, first check the wear of the tread. Irregularities in the tread pattern (cupping, flat spots, more wear on one side than the other) are indications of front end alignment and/or balance problems. If any of these conditions are noted, take the vehicle to a reputable repair shop to correct the problem.
4   Also check the tread area for cuts and punctures. Many times a nail or tack will embed itself into the tire tread and yet the tire will hold its air pressure for a short time. In most cases, a repair shop or gas

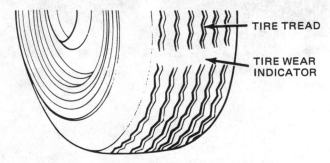

TIRE TREAD
TIRE WEAR INDICATOR

Fig. 1.2   If the tire wear indicators look like this, it is time for replacement (Sec 3)

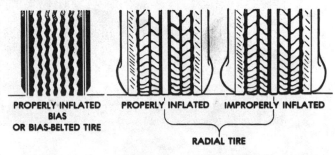

PROPERLY INFLATED BIAS OR BIAS-BELTED TIRE
PROPERLY INFLATED
IMPROPERLY INFLATED
RADIAL TIRE

Fig. 1.3   An accurate tire gauge should always be used when checking tire pressures, but a quick visual inspection might alert you to a slow leak (Sec 3)

station can repair the punctured tire.

5   It is also important to check the sidewalls of the tires, both inside and outside. Check for deteriorated rubber, cuts, and punctures. Also inspect the inboard side of the tire for signs of brake fluid leakage, indicating that a thorough brake inspection is needed immediately.

6   Incorrect tire pressure cannot be determined merely by looking at the tire. This is especially true for radial tires. A tire pressure gauge must be used . If you do not already have a reliable gauge, it is a good idea to purchase one and keep it in the glovebox. Built-in pressure gauges at gas stations are often unreliable.

7   Always check tire inflation when the tires are cold. Cold, in this case, means the vehicle has not been driven more than one mile after sitting for three hours or more. It is normal for the pressure to increase four to eight pounds or more when the tires are hot.

8   Unscrew the valve cap protruding from the wheel or hubcap and press the gauge firmly onto the valve stem. Observe the reading on the gauge and compare the figure to the recommended tire pressure listed on the tire placard. The tire placard is usually attached to the driver's door.

9   Check all tires and add air as necessary to bring them up to the recommended pressure levels. Do not forget the spare tire. Be sure to reinstall the valve caps (which will keep dirt and moisture out of the valve stem mechanism).

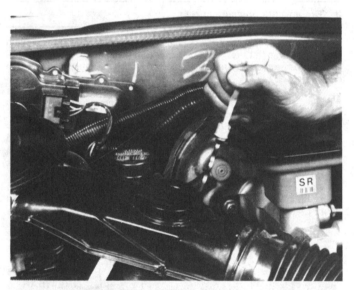

4.4a   After wiping off the engine oil dipstick, make sure it is reinserted all the way before withdrawing it for the oil level check

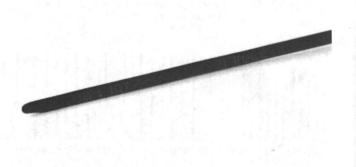

4.4b   The oil level should appear between the Add and Full marks; do not overfill the crankcase

4 Fluid level checks

1   There are a number of components on a vehicle which rely on the use of fluids to perform their job. During normal operation of the vehicle, these fluids are used up and must be replenished before damage occurs. See *Recommended lubricants and fluids* at the front of this Chapter for the specific fluid to be used when addition is required. When checking fluid levels, it is important to have the vehicle on a level surface.

Engine oil

2   The engine oil level is checked with a dipstick which is located at the side of the engine block. The dipstick travels through a tube and into the oil pan to the bottom of the engine.

3   The oil level should be checked preferably before the vehicle has been driven, or about 15 minutes after the engine has been shut off. If the oil is checked immediately after driving the vehicle, some of the oil will remain in the upper engine components, producing an inaccurate reading on the dipstick.

4   Pull the dipstick from the tube (photo) and wipe all the oil from the end with a clean rag. Insert the clean dipstick all the way back into the oil pan and pull it out again. Observe the oil at the end of the dipstick (photo). At its highest point, the level should be between the Add and Full marks.

5   It takes approximately one quart of oil to raise the level from the Add mark to the Full mark on the dipstick. Do not allow the level to drop below the Add mark as engine damage due to oil starvation may occur. On the other hand, do not overfill the engine by adding oil above the Full mark since it may result in oil-fouled spark plugs, oil leaks or oil seal failures.

6   Oil is added to the engine after removing a twist-off cap located on the rocker arm cover or through a raised tube near the front of the engine (photo). The cap should be marked 'Engine oil' or 'Oil.' An oil can spout or funnel will reduce spills as the oil is poured in.

7   Checking the oil level can also be an important preventative maintenance step. If you find the oil level dropping abnormally, it is an indication of oil leakage or internal engine wear which should be corrected. If there are water droplets in the oil, or if it is milky looking, component failure is indicated and the engine should be checked immediately. The condition of the oil can also be checked along with the level. With the dipstick removed from the engine, take your thumb and index finger and wipe the oil up the dipstick, looking for small dirt or metal particles which will cling to the dipstick. This is an indication that the oil should be drained and fresh oil added (Section 16).

Engine coolant

8   All vehicles covered by this manual are equipped with a pressurized coolant recovery system which makes coolant level checks very

4.6   The engine oil filler cap is located on the left rocker arm cover on V6 engines

easy. A clear or white coolant reservoir attached to the inner fender panel is connected by a hose to the radiator cap. As the engine heats up during operation, coolant is forced from the radiator, through the connecting tube and into the reservoir. As the engine cools, the coolant is automatically drawn back into the radiator to keep the level correct.

9   The coolant level should be checked when the engine is hot. Merely observe the level of fluid in the reservoir, which should be at or near the Full Hot mark on the side of the reservoir (photo). If the system is completely cool, also check the level in the radiator by removing the cap (photo).

10 **Caution:** *Under no circumstances should either the radiator cap or the coolant recovery reservoir cap be removed when the system is hot, because escaping steam and scalding liquid could cause serious personal injury. In the case of the radiator cap, wait until the system has cooled completely, then wrap a thick cloth around the cap and turn it to the first stop. If any steam escapes, wait until the system has cooled further, then remove the cap. The coolant recovery cap may be removed carefully after it is apparent that no further 'boiling' is occurring in the recovery tank.*

11 If only a small amount of coolant is required to bring the system up to the proper level, regular water can be used. However, to maintain the proper antifreeze/water mixture in the system, both should be mixed together to replenish a low level. High-quality antifreeze offering protection to −20°F should be mixed with water in the proportion specified on the container. Do not allow antifreeze to come in contact with your skin or painted surfaces of the vehicle. Flush contacted areas immediately with plenty of water.

12 Coolant should be added to the reservoir until it reaches the Full Cold mark.

13 As the coolant level is checked, note the condition of the coolant. It should be relatively clear. If it is brown or a rust color, the system should be drained, flushed and refilled (Section 29).

14 If the cooling system requires repeated additions to maintain the proper level, have the radiator cap checked for proper sealing ability. Also check for leaks in the system (cracked hoses, loose hose connections, leaking gaskets, etc.).

Windshield washer fluid

15 Fluid for the windshield washer system is located in a plastic reservoir (photo). The level in the reservoir should be maintained at the Full mark, except during periods when freezing temperatures are expected, at which times the fluid level should be maintained no higher than 3/4 full to allow for expansion should the fluid freeze. The use of an additive such as Optikleen will help lower the freezing point of the fluid and will result in better cleaning of the windshield surface. *Do not use antifreeze because it will cause damage to the vehicle's paint.*

16 Also, to help prevent icing in cold weather, warm the windshield with the defroster before using the washer.

Battery electrolyte

17 All vehicles with which this manual is concerned are equipped with a 'freedom' battery which is permanently sealed (except for vent holes) and has no filler caps (photo). Water does not have to be added to these batteries at any time.

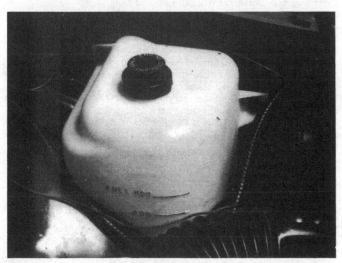

4.9a   The engine coolant level should appear near the Full Hot mark with the engine at normal operating temperature

4.9b   If the engine is completely cool, this is a good time to check the coolant level in the radiator

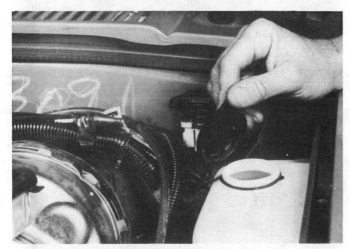

4.15   Special windshield cleaning fluid should be used in the windshield washer reservoir, since water solutions can freeze up and clog the lines (do not use antifreeze)

4.17   This type of battery never requires adding water, but normal maintenance should be performed

Brake fluid

18 The master cylinder is mounted directly on the firewall (manual brake models) or on the front of the power booster unit (power brake models) in the engine compartment.

19 The master cylinder reservoir incorporates two windows, which allow checking the brake fluid level without removal of the reservoir cover. The level should be maintained at 1/4-inch below the lowest edge of each reservoir opening (photo).

20 If a low level is indicated, be sure to wipe the top of the reservoir cover with a clean rag, to prevent contamination of the brake system, before lifting the cover.

21 When adding fluid, pour it carefully into the reservoir, taking care not to spill any onto surrounding painted surfaces. Be sure the specified fluid is used, since mixing different types of brake fluid can cause damage to the system. See *Recommended lubricants and fluids* or your owner's manual.

22 At this time the fluid and master cylinder can be inspected for contamination. Normally, the brake system will not need periodic draining and refilling, but if rust deposits, dirt particles or water droplets are seen in the fluid, the system should be dismantled, drained and refilled with fresh fluid.

23 After filling the reservoir to the proper level, make sure the lid is properly seated to prevent fluid leakage and/or system pressure loss.

24 The brake fluid in the master cylinder will drop slightly as the brake shoes or pads at each wheel wear down during normal operation. If the master cylinder requires repeated replenishing to keep it at the proper level, this is an indication of leakage in the brake system, which should be corrected immediately. Check all brake lines and connections, along with the wheel cylinders and booster (see Section 13 for more information).

25 If upon checking the master cylinder fluid level you discover one or both reservoirs empty or nearly empty, the brake system should be bled (Chapter 9).

Manual transmission oil

26 Manual shift transmissions do not have a dipstick. The fluid level is checked with the engine cold by removing a plug from the side of the transmission case. Locate the plug and use a rag to clean the plug and the area around it, then remove it with a wrench (photo).

27 If oil immediately starts leaking out, thread the plug back into the transmission because the level is all right. If there is no leakage, completely remove the plug and place your little finger inside the hole. The oil level should be just at the bottom of the plug hole.

28 If the transmission needs more oil, use a syringe to squeeze the appropriate lubricant into the plug hole until the level is correct.

29 Thread the plug back into the transmission and tighten it securely.

30 Drive the vehicle a short distance, then check to make sure the plug is not leaking.

Automatic transmission fluid

31 The level of the automatic transmission fluid should be carefully maintained. Low fluid level can lead to slipping or loss of drive, while overfilling can cause foaming and loss of fluid.

32 With the parking brake set, start the engine, then move the shift lever through all the gear ranges, ending in Park. The fluid level must be checked with the vehicle level and the engine running at idle. **Note:** *Incorrect fluid level readings will result if the vehicle has just been driven at high speeds for an extended period, in hot weather in city traffic, or if it's been pulling a trailer.* If any of these conditions apply, wait until the fluid has cooled (about 30 minutes).

33 Locate the dipstick at the rear of the engine compartment on the passenger's side and pull it out of the filler tube.

34 Carefully touch the end of the dipstick to determine if the fluid is cool (about room temperature), or warm or hot (uncomfortable to the touch).

35 Wipe the fluid from the dipstick and push it back into the filler tube until the cap seats.

36 Pull the dipstick out again and note the fluid level.

37 If the fluid felt cool, the level should be 1/8 to 3/8-inch below the Add mark (photo). The two dimples below the Add mark indicate this range.

38 If the fluid felt warm, the level should be close to the Add mark (just above or below it).

39 If the fluid felt hot, the level should be at the Full mark.

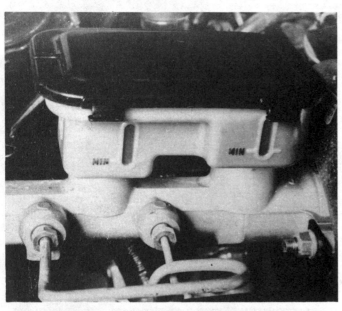

4.19   It is essential that dirt and grease be wiped off the master cylinder cover before it is removed

4.26   The oil fill/inspection plug is located on the right side on all 'S' series manual transmissions

4.37   Follow the directions stamped on the dipstick to get an accurate reading (use high quality transmission fluid, as a few cents saved on 'bargain brands' could lead to a high repair bill)

40 Add just enough of the recommended fluid to fill the transmission to the proper level. It takes about one pint to raise the level from the Add mark to the Full mark with a hot transmission, so add the fluid a little at a time and keep checking the level until it is correct.

41 The condition of the fluid should also be checked along with the level. If the fluid at the end of the dipstick is a dark reddish-brown color, or if the fluid has a burnt smell, the transmission fluid should be changed. If you are in doubt about the condition of the fluid, purchase some new fluid and compare the two for color and smell.

Transfer case lubricant

42 The transfer case lubricant level should be checked at the same time as the manual transmission and differentials.

43 Remove the filler plug and determine whether or not the lubricant level is even with the bottom of the filler hole (photo).

44 Fill the transfer case and, if so equipped, the reduction unit to the proper level with the specified lubricant. Replace the filler plugs, drive the vehicle and check for leaks.

Differential lubricant

45 Like the manual transmission and transfer case, the front and rear differentials have an inspection and fill plug which must be removed to check the level.

46 Remove the plug, which is located on the side of the differential carrier (photos). Use your little finger to reach inside the housing to feel the level of the oil. It should be at the bottom of the plug hole.

47 If such is not the case, add the proper lubricant to the carrier through the plug hole. A syringe or a small funnel can be used for this.

48 Make certain the correct lubricant is used, as regular and locking rear axles require different lubricants. A locking axle with the wrong lubricant will make a chattering noise and must be drained and refilled with the proper lubricant.

49 Tighten the plug securely and check for leaks after the first few miles of driving.

Power steering fluid

50 Unlike manual steering, the power steering system relies on fluid which may, over a period of time, require replenishing.

51 The reservoir for the power steering pump will be located near the front of the engine and can be mounted on either the left or right side.

52 For the check, the front wheels should be pointed straight ahead and the engine should be off.

53 Use a clean rag to wipe off the reservoir cap and the area around the cap. This will help prevent any foreign matter from entering the reservoir during the check.

54 Make sure the engine is at normal operating temperature.

55 Remove the dipstick (photo), wipe it off with a clean rag, reinsert it, then withdraw it and read the fluid level. The level should be between the Add and Full Hot marks.

56 If additional fluid is required, pour the specified type directly into the reservoir using a funnel to prevent spills.

57 If the reservoir requires frequent fluid additions, all power steering hoses, hose connections, the power steering pump and the steering box should be carefully checked for leaks.

4.43   Location of the transfer case drain and filler plugs

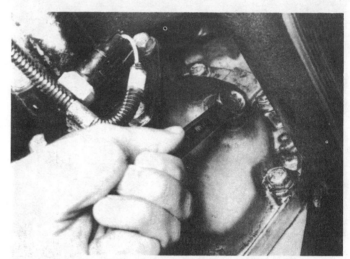

4.46a   The front differential oil fill/inspection plug can be found on the right side of the housing (4x4 vehicles only)

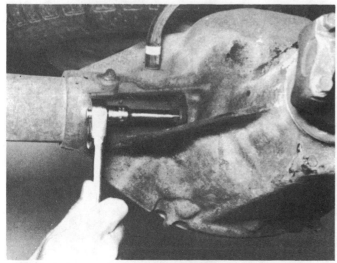

4.46b   A one-half inch socket extension works fine for removing the rear filler plug on this differential housing

4.55   Make certain that no foreign matter gets into the power steering fluid reservoir when the check is made

5   Battery check and maintenance

1   A sealed 'freedom' battery is standard equipment on all vehicles with which this manual is concerned. Although this type of battery has many advantages over the older, capped cell type and never requires the addition of water, it should nevertheless be routinely maintained according to the procedures which follow. **Warning:** *Hydrogen gas in small quantities is present in the area of the two small side vents on sealed batteries, so keep lighted tobacco and open flames or sparks away from them.*

2   The external condition of the battery should be monitored periodically for damage such as a cracked case or cover.

3   Check the tightness of the battery cable clamps to ensure good electrical connections and check the entire length of each cable for cracks and frayed conductors.

4   If corrosion (visible as white, fluffy deposits) is evident, remove the cables from the terminals, clean them with a battery brush and reinstall the cables. Corrosion can be kept to a minimum by applying a layer of petroleum jelly or grease to the terminals and cable clamps after they are assembled.

5   Make sure that the rubber protector (if so equipped) over the positive terminal is not torn or missing. It should completely cover the terminal.

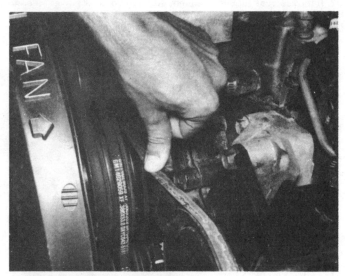

6.4   Checking the drivebelt tension

6   Make sure that the battery carrier is in good condition and that the hold-down clamp bolts are tight. If the battery is removed from the carrier, make sure that no parts remain in the bottom of the carrier when the battery is reinstalled. When reinstalling the hold-down clamp bolts, do not overtighten them.

7   Corrosion on the hold-down components, battery case and surrounding areas may be removed with a solution of water and baking soda, but take care to prevent any solution from coming in contact with your eyes, skin or clothes, as it contains acid. Protective gloves should be worn. Thoroughly wash all cleaned areas with plain water.

8   Any metal parts of the vehicle damaged by corrosion should be covered with a zinc-based primer, then painted after the affected areas have been cleaned and dried.

9   Further information on the battery, charging and jump-starting can be found in Chapter 5.

6   Drivebelt check and adjustment

1   The drivebelts, or V-belts as they are sometimes called, are located at the front of the engine and play an important role in the overall operation of the vehicle and its components. Due to their function and material make-up, the belts are prone to failure after a period of time and should be inspected and adjusted periodically to prevent major engine damage.

2   The number of belts used on a particular vehicle depends on the accessories installed. Drivebelts are used to turn the generator/alternator, air injection smog pump, power steering pump, water pump, fan and air-conditioning compressor. Depending on the pulley arrangement, a single belt may be used to drive more than one of these components.

3   With the engine off, open the hood and locate the various belts at the front of the engine. Using your fingers (and a flashlight, if necessary), move along the belts checking for cracks and separation of the belt plies. Also check for fraying and glazing, which gives the belt a shiny appearance. Both sides of the belt should be inspected, which means you will have to twist the belt to check the underside.

4   The tension of each belt is checked by pushing on the belt at a distance halfway between the pulleys. Push firmly with your thumb and see how much the belt moves down (deflects) (photo). A rule of thumb is that if the distance from pulley center-to-pulley center is between 7 and 11 inches, the belt should deflect 1/4-inch. If the belt is longer and travels between pulleys spaced 12 to 16 inches apart, the belt should deflect 1/2-inch.

5   If it is necessary to adjust the belt tension, either to make the belt tighter or looser, it is done by moving the belt-driven accessory on the bracket.

6   For each component there will be an adjustment or strap bolt and a pivot bolt (photos). Both bolts must be loosened slightly to enable you to move the component.

6.6a   To adjust drivebelt tension, first loosen the component pivot bolt

6.6b   After loosening the pivot bolt, loosen the adjustment bolt just enough to move the component

7   After the two bolts have been loosened, move the component away from the engine (to tighten the belt) or toward the engine (to loosen the belt). Hold the accessory in position and check the belt tension. If it is correct, tighten the two bolts until just snug, then recheck the tension. If it is all right, tighten the bolts.

8   It will often be necessary to use some sort of pry bar to move the accessory while the belt is adjusted. If this must be done to gain the proper leverage, be very careful not to damage the component being moved or the part being pried against.

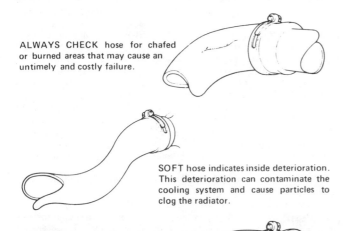

ALWAYS CHECK hose for chafed or burned areas that may cause an untimely and costly failure.

SOFT hose indicates inside deterioration. This deterioration can contaminate the cooling system and cause particles to clog the radiator.

HARDENED hose can fail at any time. Tightening hose clamps will not seal the connection or stop leaks.

SWOLLEN hose or oil soaked ends indicate danger and possible failure from oil or grease contamination. Squeeze the hose to locate cracks and breaks that cause leaks.

Fig. 1.4 Simple checks can detect radiator hose defects (Sec 8)

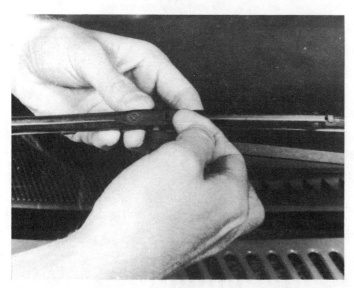

9.4   The wiper blade assembly can be removed by simply releasing the lever and sliding the wiper blade off the arm

7 Cooling system check

1   Many major engine failures can be attributed to a faulty cooling system. If the vehicle is equipped with an automatic transmission, the cooling system also plays an important role in prolonging its life.

2   The cooling system should be checked with the engine cold. Do this before the vehicle is driven for the day or after it has been shut off for at least three hours.

3   Remove the radiator cap and thoroughly clean the cap (inside and out) with clean water. Also clean the filler neck on the radiator. All traces of corrosion should be removed.

4   Carefully check the upper and lower radiator hoses along with the smaller diameter heater hoses. Inspect each hose along its entire length, replacing any hose which is cracked, swollen or shows signs of deterioration. Cracks may become more apparent if the hose is squeezed.

5   Also make sure that all hose connections are tight. A leak in the cooling system will usually show up as white or rust colored deposits on the areas adjoining the leak.

6   Use compressed air or a soft brush to remove bugs, leaves, etc. from the front of the radiator or air-conditioning condenser. Be careful not to damage the delicate cooling fins or cut yourself on them.

7   Finally, have the cap and system pressure tested. If you do not have a pressure tester, most gas stations and repair shops will do this for a minimal change.

8 Underhood hose check and replacement

Caution: *Replacement of air-conditioner hoses must be left to a dealer or air-conditioning specialist who can depressurize the system and perform the work safely.*

1   The high temperatures present under the hood can cause deterioration of the numerous rubber and plastic hoses.

2   Periodic inspection should be made for cracks, loose clamps and leaks because some of the hoses are part of the emissions control systems and can affect the engine's performance.

3   Remove the air cleaner if necessary and trace the entire length of each hose. Squeeze each hose to check for cracks and look for swelling, discoloration and leaks.

4   If the vehicle has considerable mileage or if one or more of the hoses is suspect, it is a good idea to replace all of the hoses at one time.

5   Measure the length and inside diameter of each hose and obtain and cut the replacement to size. Since original equipment hose clamps are often good for only one or two uses, it is a good idea to replace them with screw-type clamps.

6   Replace each hose one at a time to eliminate the possibility of confusion. Hoses attached to the heater and radiator contain coolant, so newspapers or rags should be kept handy to catch the spills when they are disconnected.

7   After installation, run the engine until it reaches operating temperature, shut it off and check for leaks. After the engine has cooled, retighten all of the screw-type clamps.

9 Windshield wiper blade inspection and replacement

1   The windshield wiper and blade assembly should be inspected periodically for damage, loose components and cracked or worn blade elements.

2   Road film can build up on the wiper blades and affect their efficiency so they should be washed regularly with a mild detergent solution.

3   The action of the wiping mechanism can loosen the bolts, nuts and fasteners so they should be checked and tightened, as necessary, at the same time the wiper blades are checked.

4   If the wiper blade elements are cracked, worn or warped, they should be replaced with new ones. The wiper blade assemblies are equipped with release levers. Pull the lever up and slide the old wiper blade assembly off the wiper arm pin (photo). Install the new blade by positioning it over the wiper arm pin and pressing on it until it snaps into place.

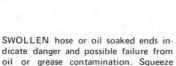

1

5   The wiper blade element is locked in place at either end of the wiper blade assembly by a spring-loaded retainer and metal tabs. To remove the element, use a screwdriver to slide the blade under the element near the tabs and rotate the screwdriver, then slide the element up, out of the tabs.

6   To install, slide the element into the retaining tabs, lining up the slot in the element with the tabs, and snap the element into place.

7   Snap the blade assembly into place on the wiper arm pin.

10   Chassis lubrication

1   A grease gun and a cartridge filled with the proper grease (see *Recommended lubricants and fluids*) are usually the only equipment necessary to lubricate the chassis components. In some chassis locations, plugs may be installed rather than grease fittings, in which case grease fittings will have to be purchased and installed.

2   Refer to the accompanying photos, which show where the various grease fittings are located. Look under the vehicle to find these components and determine if grease fittings or solid plugs are installed. If there are plugs, remove them with a wrench and buy grease fittings which will thread into the component. A GM dealer or auto parts store will be able to supply replacement fittings. Straight, as well as angled, fittings are available.

3   For easier access under the vehicle, raise it with a jack and place jackstands under the frame. Make sure the vehicle is securely supported by the stands.

4   Before proceeding, force a little of the grease out of the nozzle to remove any dirt from the end of the gun. Wipe the nozzle clean with a rag.

5   With the grease gun, plenty of clean rags and the diagram, crawl under the vehicle and begin lubricating the components

6   Wipe the grease fitting nipple clean and push the nozzle firmly over the fitting nipple. Squeeze the trigger on the grease gun to force grease into the component. **Note:** *The lower control arm balljoints (one for each front wheel) should be lubricated until the rubber reservoir is firm to the touch. Do not pump too much grease into these fittings as it could rupture the reservoir.* For all other suspension and steering fittings, continue pumping grease into the nipple until grease seeps out of the joint between the two components. If the grease seeps out around the grease gun nozzle, the nipple is clogged or the nozzle is not seated on the fitting nipple. Resecure the gun nozzle to the fitting and try again. If necessary, replace the fitting.

7   Wipe the excess grease from the components and the grease fitting. Follow the procedures for the remaining fittings.

8   While you are under the vehicle, clean and lubricate the parking brake cable, along with the cable guides and levers. This can be done by smearing some of the chassis grease onto the cable and its related parts with your fingers.

9   Lower the vehicle to the ground for the remaining body lubrication process.

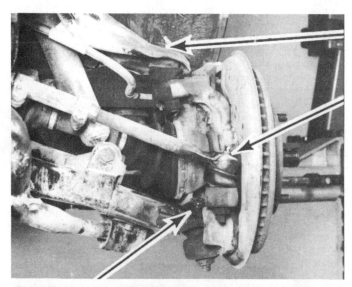

10.2a   Upper and lower balljoint and steering arm lubrication fittings

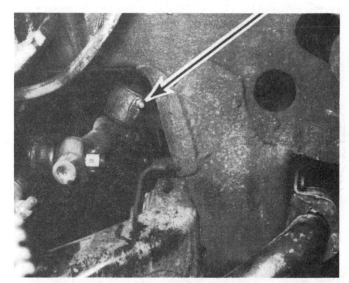

10.2b   Location of the idler arm lubrication fitting

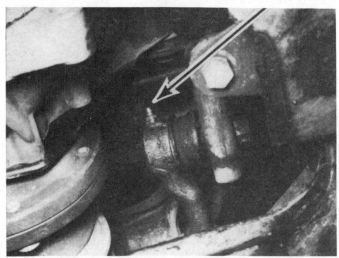

10.2c   Relay rod-to-tie rod lubrication fitting

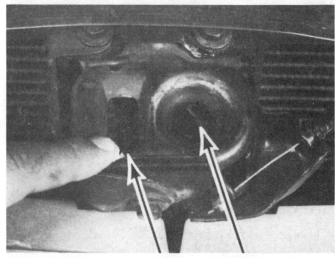

10.10   Multi-purpose grease is used to lubricate the hood latch mechanism

10 Open the hood and smear a little chassis grease on the hood latch mechanism (photo). If the hood has an inside release, have an assistant pull the release knob from inside the vehicle as you lubricate the cable at the latch.

11 Lubricate all the hinges (door, hood, hatch) with a few drops of light engine oil to keep them in proper working order.

12 Finally, the key lock cylinders can be lubricated with spray-on graphite which is available at auto parts stores.

11 Exhaust system check

1 With the engine cold (at least three hours after the vehicle has been driven), check the complete exhaust system from its starting point at the engine to the end of the tailpipe. This should be done on a hoist where unrestricted access is available.

2 Check the pipes and connections for signs of leakage and/or corrosion indicating a potential failure. Make sure that all brackets and hangers are in good condition and tight (photo).

3 At the same time, inspect the underside of the body for holes, corrosion, open seams, etc. which may allow exhaust gases to enter the passenger compartment. Seal all body openings with silicone or body putty.

4 Rattles and other noises can often be traced to the exhaust system, especially the mounts and hangers. Try to move the pipes, muffler and

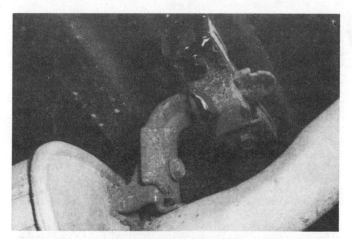

11.2 A broken hanger bracket here will cause noise and lead to further exhaust system damage

13.6 The disc brake pad wear inspection hole is visible at the center of the caliper

catalytic converter (if so equipped). If the components can come in contact with the body or driveline parts, secure the exhaust system with new mounts.

5 This is also an ideal time to check the running condition of the engine by inspecting inside the very end of the tailpipe. The exhaust deposits here are an indication of engine state-of-tune. If the pipe is black and sooty or coated with white deposits, the engine is in need of a tune-up (including a thorough carburetor inspection and adjustment).

12 Suspension and steering check

1 Whenever the front of the vehicle is raised for service, it is a good idea to visually check the suspension and steering components for wear.

2 Indications of a fault in these systems are excessive play in the steering wheel before the front wheels react, excessive sway around corners, body movement over rough roads or binding at some point as the steering wheel is turned.

3 Before the vehicle is raised for inspection, test the shock absorbers by pushing down to rock the vehicle at each corner. If you push down and the vehicle does not come back to a level position within one or two bounces, the shocks/struts are worn and must be replaced. As this is done, check for squeaks and strange noises coming from the suspension components. Information on suspension components can be found in Chapter 11.

4 Now raise the front end of the vehicle and support it firmly on jackstands placed under the frame rails. Because of the work to be done, make sure the vehicle cannot fall from the stands.

5 Grab the top and bottom of the front tire with your hands and rock the tire/wheel on the spindle. If there is movement of more than 0.005 inch, the wheel bearings should be serviced (see Section 30).

6 Crawl under the vehicle and check for loose bolts, broken or disconnected parts and deteriorated rubber bushings on all suspension and steering components. Look for grease or fluid leaking from around the steering box. Check the power steering hoses and connections for leaks. Check the balljoints for wear.

7 Have an assistant turn the steering wheel from side-to-side and check the steering components for free movement, chafing and binding. If the steering does not react with the movement of the steering wheel, try to determine where the slack is located.

13 Brake check

Note: *For detailed photographs of the brake system, refer to Chapter 9.*

1 The brakes should be inspected every time the wheels are removed or whenever a defect is suspected. Indications of a potential brake system defect are: the vehicle pulls to one side when the brake pedal is depressed; noises coming from the brakes when they are applied; excessive brake pedal travel; pulsating pedal; and leakage of fluid, usually seen on the inside of the tire or wheel.

Disc brakes

2 The front disc brakes can be visually checked without removing any parts except the wheels.

3 Raise the vehicle and place it securely on jackstands. Remove the wheels (see *Jacking and towing* at the front of the manual, if necessary).

4 The disc brake calipers, which contain the pads, are now visible. There is an outer pad and an inner pad in each caliper. All pads should be inspected.

5 The inner pads on the front wheels are equipped with a wear sensor. This is a small, bent piece of metal which is visible from the inboard side of the brake caliper. When the pads wear to the danger limit, the metal sensor rubs against the rotor and makes a screeching sound.

6 Check the pad thickness by looking at each end of the caliper and through the inspection hole in the caliper body (photo). If the wear sensor clip is very close to the rotor, or if the lining material is 1/16-inch or less in thickness, the pads should be replaced. Keep in mind that the lining material is riveted or bonded to a metal backing shoe and the metal portion is not included in this measurement.

7 Since it will be difficult, if not impossible, to measure the exact thickness of the remaining lining material, remove the pads for further inspection or replacement if you are in doubt as to the quality of the pad.

8   Before installing the wheels, check for leakage around the brake hose connections leading to the caliper and damage (cracking, splitting, etc.) to the brake hose. Replace the hose or fittings as necessary, referring to Chapter 9.

9   Also check the condition of the rotor. Look for scoring, gouging and burnt spots. If these conditions exist, the hub/rotor assembly should be removed for servicing (Chapter 9).

Drum brakes — rear

10 Using a scribe or chalk, mark the drum, hub and backing plate so they can be reinstalled in the same positions.

11 Pull the brake drum off the axle and brake assembly. If this proves difficult, make sure the parking brake is released, then squirt some penetrating oil around the center hub area. Allow the oil to soak in and again try to pull the drum off. Then, if the drum cannot be pulled off, the brake shoes will have to be adjusted in. This is done by first removing the lanced knock-out in the backing plate with a hammer and chisel. With the lanced area punched in, pull the lever off the sprocket and then use a small screwdriver to turn the adjuster wheel, which will move the shoes away from the drum.

12 With the drum removed, carefully brush away any accumulations of dirt and dust. **Warning:** *Do not blow the dust out with compressed air. Make an effort not to inhale the dust because it contains asbestos and is harmful to your health.*

13 Note the thickness of the lining material on both the front and rear brake shoes (photo). If the material has worn away to within 1/16-inch of the recessed rivets or metal backing, the shoes should be replaced. If the linings look worn, but you are unable to determine their exact thickness, compare them with a new set at an auto parts store. The shoes should also be replaced if they are cracked, glazed (shiny surface) or contaminated with brake fluid.

14 Check to see that all the brake assembly springs are connected and in good condition.

15 Check the brake components for signs of fluid leakage. With your finger, carefully pry back the rubber cups on the wheel cylinder located at the top of the brake shoes. Any leakage is an indication that the wheel cylinders should be overhauled immediately (Chapter 9). Also check the hoses and connections for signs of leakage.

16 Wipe the inside of the drum with a clean rag and denatured alcohol. Again, be careful not to breathe the dangerous asbestos dust.

17 Check the inside of the drum for cracks, scores, deep scratches and hard spots which will appear as small discolored areas. If imperfections cannot be removed with fine emery cloth, the drum must be taken to a machine shop for resurfacing.

18 After the inspection process, if all parts are found to be in good condition, reinstall the brake drum (using a metal plug if the lanced knock-out was removed). Install the wheel and lower the vehicle to the ground.

Parking brake

19 The easiest way to check the operation of the parking brake is to park the vehicle on a steep hill with the parking brake set and the transmission in Neutral. If the parking brake cannot prevent the vehicle from rolling, it is in need of adjustment (see Chapter 9).

14 Carburetor choke check

1   The choke only operates when the engine is cold, so this check should be performed before the vehicle has been started for the day.

2   Open the hood and remove the top plate of the air cleaner assembly. It is usually held in place by a wing nut. If any vacuum hoses must be disconnected, make sure you tag them to ensure reinstallation in their original positions. Place the top plate and wing nut aside, out of the way of moving engine components.

3   Look at the top of the carburetor at the center of the air cleaner housing. You will notice a flat plate at the carburetor opening (photo).

4   Have an assistant press the accelerator pedal to the floor. The plate should close completely. Start the engine while you observe the plate at the carburetor. **Caution:** *Do not position your face directly over the carburetor, because the engine could backfire and cause serious burns.* When the engine starts, the choke plate should open slightly.

5   Allow the engine to continue running at an idle speed. As the engine warms up to operating temperature, the plate should slowly open, allowing more air to enter through the top of the carburetor.

6   After a few minutes, the choke plate should be all the way open to the vertical position.

7   You will notice that the engine speed corresponds with the plate opening. With the plate completely closed, the engine should run at a fast idle. As the plate opens, the engine speed will decrease.

8   If a malfunction is detected during the above checks, refer to Chapter 4 for specific information related to adjusting and servicing the choke components.

15 Engine idle speed check and adjustment

1   Engine idle speed is the speed at which the engine operates when no accelerator pedal pressure is applied. This speed is critical to the performance of the engine itself, as well as many engine sub-systems.

2   A hand-held tachometer must be used when adjusting the idle speed to get an accurate reading. The exact hook-up for these meters varies with the manufacturer, so follow the particular directions included.

3   Since these models were equipped with many different carburetors in the time period covered by this manual, and each has its own peculiarities when setting idle speed, it would be impractical to cover all types in this Section. Chapter 4 contains information on each individual carburetor used. The carburetor used on your particular engine can be found in the Specifications Section of Chapter 4. However, all vehicles covered in this manual have an Emission Control Information

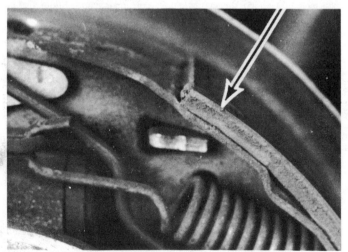

13.13   If the shoe lining material has worn to within 1/16-inch of the recessed rivets or metal backing to which the lining is bonded, new brake shoes are needed.

14.3   With the air cleaner top plate removed, the choke plate is easily checked

label in the engine compartment, usually placed near the top of the radiator. The printed instructions for setting idle speed can be found on the label, and should be followed since it is for your particular engine.

4   Basically, for most applications, the idle speed is set by turning an adjustment screw located at the side of the carburetor (photo). Turning the screw changes the position of the throttle valve in the carburetor. This screw may be on the linkage itself or may be part of the idle stop solenoid. Refer to the Emission Control Information label or Chapter 4.

5   Once you have located the idle speed screw, experiment with different length screwdrivers until the adjustments can easily be made without coming into contact with hot or moving engine components.

6   Follow the instructions on the Emission Control Information label, which may include disconnecting certain vacuum or electrical connections. To plug a vacuum hose after disconnecting it, insert a properly sized metal rod into the opening or thoroughly wrap the open end with tape to prevent any vacuum loss through the hose.

7   If the air cleaner is removed, the vacuum hose to the snorkel should be plugged.

8   Make sure the parking brake is firmly set and the wheels blocked to prevent the vehicle from rolling. This is especially true if the transmission is to be in Drive. An assistant inside the vehicle pushing on the brake pedal is the safest method.

9   For all applications, the engine must be completely warmed-up to operating temperature, which will automatically render the choke fast idle inoperative.

10   Turn the idle speed screw in or out, as required, until the idle speed listed in the Specifications is obtained.

16   Engine oil and filter change

1   Frequent oil changes may be the best form of preventative maintenance available for the home mechanic. When engine oil ages, it gets diluted and contaminated, which ultimately leads to premature engine wear.

2   Although some sources recommend oil filter changes every other oil change, we feel that the minimal cost of an oil filter and the relative ease with which it is installed dictate that a new filter be used whenever the oil is changed.

3   The tools necessary for a normal oil and filter change are a wrench to fit the drain plug at the bottom of the oil pan, an oil filter wrench to remove the old filter, a container with at least a six-quart capacity to drain the old oil into and a funnel or oil can spout to help pour fresh oil into the engine.

4   In addition, you should have plenty of clean rags and newspapers handy to mop up any spills. Access to the underside of the vehicle is greatly improved if the vehicle can be lifted on a hoist, driven onto ramps or supported by jackstands. *Do not work under a vehicle which is supported only a bumper, hydraulic or scissors-type jack.*

5   If this is your first oil change on the vehicle, it is a good idea to crawl underneath and familiarize yourself with the locations of the oil drain plug and the oil filter. The engine and exhaust components will be warm during the actual work, so it is a good idea to figure out any potential problems before the engine and its accessories are hot.

6   Allow the engine to warm up to normal operating temperature. If the new oil or any tools are needed, use this warm-up time to gather everything necessary for the job. The correct type of oil to buy for your application can be found in *Recommended lubricants and fluids* near the front of this manual.

7   With the engine oil warm (warm engine oil will drain better and more built-up sludge will be removed with the oil), raise and support the vehicle. Make sure it is firmly supported. If jackstands are used, they should be placed toward the front of the frame rails which run the length of the vehicle.

8   Move all necessary tools, rags and newspapers under the vehicle. Position the drain pan under the drain plug. Keep in mind that the oil will initially flow from the pan with some force, so place the pan accordingly.

9   Being careful not to touch any of the hot exhaust pipe components, use the wrench to remove the drain plug near the bottom of the oil pan (photo). Depending on how hot the oil has become, you may want to wear gloves while unscrewing the plug the final few turns.

10   Allow the old oil to drain into the pan. It may be necessary to move the pan farther under the engine as the oil flow slows to a trickle.

11   After all the oil has drained, wipe off the drain plug with a clean rag. Small metal particles may cling to the plug and would immediately contaminate the new oil.

12   Clean the area around the drain plug opening and reinstall the plug. Tighten the plug securely with the wrench. If a torque wrench is available, use it to tighten the plug.

13   Move the drain pan into position under the oil filter. Lower the vehicle.

14   Now go to the engine compartment and use the filter wrench to loosen the oil filter (photo). Chain or metal band-type filter wrenches may distort the filter canister, but this is of no concern as the filter will be discarded anyway. A heavy glove should also be used, due to the close proximity to hot engine components.

15   Sometimes the oil filter is on so tight it cannot be loosened, or it is positioned in an area which is inaccessible with a filter wrench. As a last resort, you can punch a metal bar or long screwdriver directly through the side of the canister and use it as a T-bar to turn the filter. If so, be prepared for oil to spurt out of the canister as it is punctured.

16   Completely unscrew the old filter. Be careful, it is full of oil. Empty the oil inside the filter into the drain pan.

17   Compare the old filter with the new one to make sure they are the same type.

18   Use a clean rag to remove all oil, dirt and sludge from the area where the oil filter mounts to the engine. Check the old filter to make sure the rubber gasket is not stuck to the engine mounting surface. If the gasket is stuck to the engine (use a flashlight if necessary), remove it.

15.4   Typical location for the engine idle speed adjustment on Rochester 2SE carburetors (2.0 liter four-cylinder and V6 engines)

16.9   The engine oil drain plug is located on the rear of the oil pan

19 Open one of the cans of new oil and fill the new filter about half-full of fresh oil. Also, apply a light coat of oil to the rubber gasket of the new oil filter.

20 Attach the new filter to the engine following the tightening directions printed on the filter canister or packing box. Most filter manufacturers recommend against using a filter wrench due to the possibility of overtightening and damage to the seal.

21 Remove all tools, rags, etc. from under the vehicle, being careful not to spill the oil in the drain pan.

22 Move to the engine compartment and locate the oil filler cap on the engine. In most cases there will be a screw-off cap on the rocker arm cover (at the side of the engine) or a cap at the end of a fill tube at the front of the engine. In any case, the cap will most likely be labeled 'Engine Oil' or 'Oil.'

23 If an oil can spout is used, push the spout into the top of the oil can and pour the fresh oil through the filler opening. A funnel may also be used.

24 Pour about three (3) quarts of fresh oil into the engine. Wait a few minutes to allow the oil to drain into the pan, then check the level on the oil dipstick (see Section 4 if necessary). If the oil level is at or near the lower Add mark, start the engine and allow the new oil to circulate.

25 Run the engine for only about a minute and then shut it off. Immediately look under the vehicle and check for leaks at the oil pan drain plug and around the oil filter. If either is leaking, tighten with a bit more force.

26 With the new oil circulated and the filter now completely full, recheck the level on the dipstick and add enough oil to bring the level to the Full mark on the dipstick.

27 During the first few trips after an oil change, make it a point to check frequently for leaks and proper oil level.

28 The old oil drained from the engine cannot be reused in its present state and should be disposed of. Oil reclamation centers, auto repair shops and gas stations will normally accept the oil, which can be refined and used again. After the oil has cooled, it can be drained into a suitable container (capped plastic jugs, topped bottles, milk cartons, etc.) for transport to one of these disposal sites.

17 Fuel system check

Caution: *There are certain precautions to take when inspecting or servicing the fuel system components. Work in a well-ventilated area and do not allow open flames (cigarettes, appliance pilot lights, etc.) to get near the work area. Mop up spills immediately and do not store fuel-soaked rags where they could ignite.*

1 The fuel system is under a small amount of pressure, so if any fuel lines are disconnected for servicing, be prepared to catch the fuel as it spurts out. Plug all disconnected fuel lines immediately after disconnection to prevent the tank from emptying itself.

2 The fuel system is most easily checked with the vehicle raised on a hoist so the components underneath the vehicle are readily visible and accessible.

3 If the smell of gasoline is noticed while driving or after the vehicle has been in the sun, the system should be thoroughly inspected immediately.

4 Remove the gas filler cap and check for damage, corrosion and an unbroken sealing imprint on the gasket (photo). Replace the cap with a new one, if necessary.

5 With the vehicle raised, inspect the gas tank and filler neck for punctures, cracks and other damage. The connection between the filler neck and the tank is especially critical. Sometimes a rubber filler neck will leak due to loose clamps or deteriorated rubber, problems a home mechanic can usually rectify. **WARNING:** *Do not, under any circumstances, try to repair a fuel tank yourself (except rubber components) unless you have had considerable experience. A welding torch or any open flame can easily cause the fuel vapors to explode if the proper precautions are not taken.*

6 Carefully check all rubber hoses and metal lines leading away from the fuel tank. Check for loose connections, deteriorated hoses, crimped lines and other damage. Follow the lines up to the front of the vehicle, carefully inspecting them all the way. Repair or replace damaged sections as necessary.

7 If a fuel odor is still evident after the inspection, refer to Section 34.

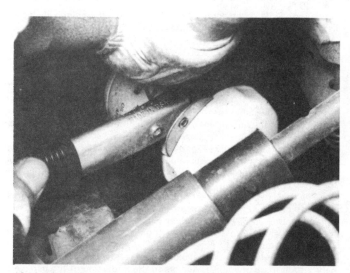

16.14   An oil filter wrench is used to break the seal on the filter before removal

17.4   With today's sophisticated emissions systems, it is essential that seals in the gas tank cap be checked regularly

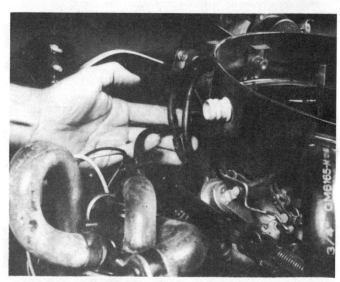

18.3   Tag all hoses as they are removed from the air cleaner assembly; this will make installation much easier

18 Fuel filter replacement

1   The fuel filter is located inside the fuel inlet at the carburetor on 2.0 liter and V-6 models. It is made of pleated paper and cannot be cleaned or reused.

2   This job should be done with the engine cold (after sitting at least three hours). The necessary tools include open-end wrenches to fit the fuel line nuts. Flare nut wrenches (which wrap around the nut) should be used, if available. In addition, you will have to obtain the replacement filter (make sure it is for your specific vehicle and engine) and some clean rags.

3   Remove the air cleaner assembly. If vacuum hoses must be disconnected, be sure to note their positions and/or tag them to ensure that they are reinstalled correctly (photo).

4   On 2.0 liter and V6 models, locate the fuel filter housing at the left rear of the carburetor body (photo). On 1.9 liter engines, locate the fuel pump (upper right side of engine towards the front) and follow the metal line to the fuel filter.

5   Place some rags under the fuel inlet fittings to catch spilled fuel as the fittings are disconnected.

6   With the proper size wrench, hold the nut immediately next to the carburetor body. Now loosen the nut fitting and the end of the metal fuel line. A flare nut wrench on this fitting will help prevent slipping and possible damage. However, an open-end wrench should do

18.4   The fuel filter is located at the rear of the carburetor on all models equipped with a 2.0 liter four-cylinder or V6 engine

19.5   The pivot points on the accelerator cable mechanism should be lubricated with clean engine oil (2SE carburetor shown)

the job. Make sure the larger nut next to the carburetor is held securely while the fuel line is disconnected.

7   After the fuel line is disconnected, move it aside for better access to the inlet filter nut. Do not crimp the fuel line.

8   Now unscrew the fuel inlet filter nut which was previously held steady. As this fitting is drawn away from the carburetor body, be careful not to lose the thin washer-type gasket or the spring located behind the fuel filter. Also, pay close attention to how the filter is installed.

9   Compare the old filter with the new one to make sure they are the same length and design.

10   Reinstall the spring in the carburetor body.

11   Place the new filter in position behind the spring. It will have a rubber gasket and check valve at one end, which should point *away* from the carburetor.

12   Install a new washer-type gasket on the fuel inlet filter nut (a gasket is usually supplied with the new filter) and tighten the nut in the carburetor. Make sure it is not cross-threaded. Tighten it securely (if a torque wrench is available, tighten the nut to 18 ft-lbs). Do not over-tighten it, as the hole can strip easily, causing fuel leaks.

13   Hold the fuel inlet nut securely with a wrench while the fuel line is connected. Again, be careful not to cross-thread the connector. Tighten the fitting securely.

14   Plug the vacuum hose which leads to the air cleaner snorkel motor so the engine can be run.

15   Start the engine and check carefully for leaks. If the fuel line connector leaks, disconnect it using the above procedures and check for stripped or damaged threads. If the fuel line connector has stripped threads, remove the entire line and have a repair shop install a new fitting. If the threads look all right, purchase some thread sealing tape and wrap the connector threads with it. Now reinstall and tighten it securely. Inlet repair kits are available at most auto parts stores to overcome leaking at the fuel inlet filter nut.

16   Reinstall the air cleaner assembly, connecting the hoses in their original positions.

19 Throttle linkage check

1   The throttle linkage is a cable type and, although there are no adjustments for the linkage itself, periodic maintenance is necessary to assure its proper function.

2   Remove the air cleaner so the entire linkage is visible.

3   Check the entire length of the cable to make sure that it is not binding.

4   Check all nylon bushings for wear, replacing them with new ones as necessary.

5   Lubricate the cable mechanisms with engine oil at the pivot points (photo).

20 Thermo-controlled Air Cleaner (TAC) check

1   All engines are equipped with a thermostatically controlled air cleaner which draws air to the carburetor from different locations, depending upon engine temperature.

2   This is a simple visual check; however, if access is limited, a small mirror may have to be used.

3   Open the hood and locate the damper door inside the air cleaner assembly. It will be located inside the long snorkel of the metal air cleaner housing. Make sure that the flexible air hose(s) are securely attached and undamaged (photo).

4   If there is a flexible air duct attached to the end of the snorkel, leading to an area behind the grille, disconnect it at the snorkel. This will enable you to look through the end of the snorkel and see the damper door inside.

5   The check should be done when the engine and outside air are cold. Start the engine and look through the snorkel at the damper door, which should move to a closed position. With the damper door closed, air cannot enter through the end of the snorkel, but instead enters the air cleaner through the flexible duct attached to the exhaust manifold.

6   As the engine warms up to operating temperature, the damper door should open to allow air through the snorkel end. Depending on ambient temperature, this may take 10 to 15 minutes. To speed this up you can reconnect the snorkel air duct, drive the vehicle and then check

1

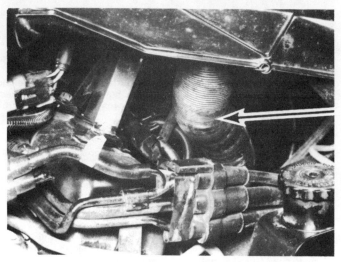

20.3   A loose fitting or torn air hose here will greatly affect cold engine driveability and exhaust emissions

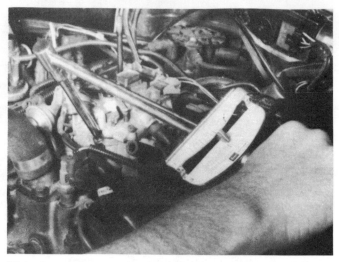

21.4   A socket extention and universal joint will be needed to torque the carburetor mounting bolts

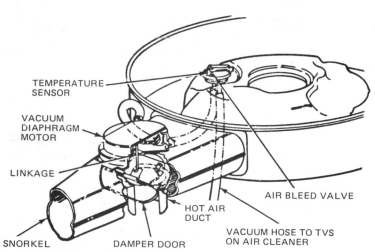

TEMPERATURE SENSOR

VACUUM DIAPHRAGM MOTOR

LINKAGE

SNORKEL

DAMPER DOOR

HOT AIR DUCT

AIR BLEED VALVE

VACUUM HOSE TO TVS ON AIR CLEANER

Fig. 1.5   The thermo-controlled air cleaner improves the vehicle's warmup characteristics and emission levels (V6 shown) (Sec 20)

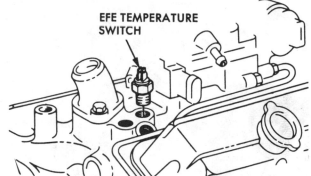

EFE TEMPERATURE SWITCH

Fig. 1.6   Typical location of the EFE heater switch (V6 shown) (Sec 22)

to see if the damper door is completely open.
7   If the thermo-controlled air cleaner is not operating properly, see Chapter 6 for more information.

21   Carburetor mounting torque check

1   The carburetor is attached to the top of the intake manifold by four nuts or bolts. These fasteners can sometimes work loose from vibration and temperature changes during normal engine operation and cause a vacuum leak.
2   To properly tighten the mounting nuts/bolts, a torque wrench is necessary. If you do not own one, they can usually be rented on a daily basis.
3   Remove the air cleaner assembly, tagging each hose to be disconnected with a piece of numbered tape to make reassembly easier.
4   Locate the mounting nuts/bolts at the base of the carburetor. Decide what special tools or adapters will be necessary, if any, to tighten the fasteners with a socket and the torque wrench (photo).
5   Tighten the nuts/bolts to the specified torque. Do not overtighten

them, as the threads could strip.
6   If you suspect that a vacuum leak exists at the bottom of the carburetor, obtain a length of hose about the diameter of fuel hose. Start the engine and place one end of the hose next to your ear as you probe around the base with the other end. You will hear a hissing sound if a leak exists.
7   If, after the nuts/bolts are properly tightened, a vacuum leak still exists, the carburetor must be removed and a new gasket installed. See Chapter 4 for more information.
8   After tightening the fasteners, reinstall the air cleaner and return all hoses to their original positions.

22   Early Fuel Evaporation (EFE) system check

1   The EFE system improves cold engine driveability and, by reducing the time that the choke is closed, exhaust emissions levels. The system utilizes a ceramic heater grid located between the carburetor base and intake manifold. This electrically heated unit improves vaporization of the air/fuel mixture during engine warmup.
2   To check the EFE, disconnect the electrical leads at the EFE temperature switch (refer to the accompanying illustration).
3   Connect a 12-volt test light across the connector terminals of the wire leads. If the test light glows when the ignition switch is turned on (engine off), the EFE system is working properly.
4   If the test light does not glow, refer to Chapter 6 for further tests and information concerning the EFE system.

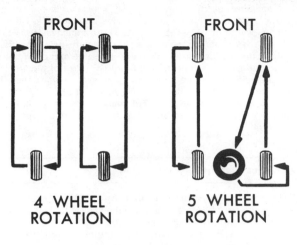

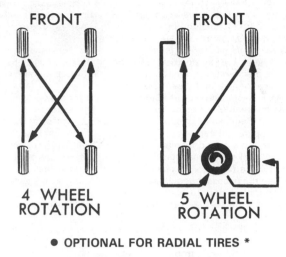

* The optional 'X' rotation pattern for radials is acceptable when required for more uniform tire wear.

Fig. 1.7 Tire rotation diagram (Sec 23)

23 Tire rotation

1   The tires should be rotated at the specified intervals and whenever uneven wear is noticed. Since the vehicle will be raised and the tires removed anyway, this is a good time to check the brakes (Section 13) and/or repack the wheel bearings (Section 30). Read over these Sections if this is to be done at the same time.
2   Refer to the accompanying illustration of the 'preferred' and 'optional' tire rotation patterns. Do not include 'Temporary Use Only' spare tires in the rotation sequence. The 'optional' X-rotation procedure is acceptable when required for more uniform tire wear.
3   Refer to the information in *Jacking and towing* at the front of this manual for the proper procedures to follow when raising the vehicle and changing a tire; however, if the brakes are to be checked, do not apply the parking brake as stated. Make sure the tires are blocked to prevent the vehicle from rolling.
4   Preferably, the entire vehicle should be raised at the same time. This can be done on a hoist or by jacking up each corner and then lowering the vehicle onto jackstands placed under the frame rails. Always use four jackstands and make sure the vehicle is firmly supported.
5   After rotation, check and adjust the the tire pressures as necessary and be sure to check the lug nut tightness.

24 Clutch pedal free play check and adjustment

Note: *The information which follows applies to 1982 and 1983 vehicles only (non-hydraulic assisted clutch assemblies). A hydraulic clutch operating mechanism is used on all 1984 vehicles. This system locates the clutch pedal and provides automatic clutch adjustment, so no adjustment of the clutch linkage or pedal position is required.*

1   If your vehicle is equipped with a manual transmission, it is important to have the clutch free play properly adjusted. Basically, free play is the distance the clutch pedal moves before all play in the linkage is removed and the clutch begins to disengage. It is measured at the pedal pad. Slowly depress the pedal and determine how far it moves before resistance is felt.
2   There is only one linkage adjustment to compensate for all normal clutch wear.
3   Lift the clutch pedal all the way up to the stop. Now depress the pedal slowly several times (to make sure the pawl engages completely with the detent teeth on the self-adjusting ratchet).
4   Refer to Chapter 8 for further clutch service information.

25 Differential oil change

1   Some differentials can be drained by removing a drain plug, while on others it is necessary to remove the cover plate on the differential housing. Because of this, be sure to buy a new gasket at the same time the gear lubricant is purchased.
2   Move a drain pan (at least five-pint capacity), rags, newspapers and wrenches under the vehicle.
3   On four-wheel drive models, a suction pump will be needed to remove the oil from the front differential. Remove the filler plug and insert the flexible suction hose. Work the hose down to the bottom of the differential housing and pump the oil out.
4   Fill the front differential with the specified lubricant to the base of the fill plug hole. Install the fill plug and tighten it securely.
5   On rear differentials, remove the bolts on the lower half of the differential cover plate. Use the upper bolts to keep the cover loosely attached to the differential. Allow the lubricant to drain into the drain pan, then completely remove the cover.
6   Using a lint-free rag, clean the inside of the cover and accessible areas of the differential housing. As this is done, check for chipped gears and metal particles in the lubricant, indicating the differential should be more thoroughly inspected or repaired.
7   Thoroughly clean the gasket mating surface on the cover and the differential housing. Use a gasket scraper or putty knife to remove all traces of the old gasket.
8   Apply a thin film of RTV-type gasket sealant to the cover flange and then press a new gasket into position on the cover. Make sure the bolt holes align properly.
9   Place the cover on the differential housing and install the bolts. Tighten the bolts a little at a time, working across the cover in a diagonal fashion until all bolts are tight.
10   Remove the fill plug on the side of the differential housing and fill the housing with the proper lubricant until the level is at the bottom of the plug hole.
11   Securely install the plug.

26 Automatic transmission fluid change

1   At the specified time intervals, the transmission fluid should be changed and the filter replaced with a new one. Since there is no drain plug, the transmission oil pan must be removed from the bottom of the transmission to drain the fluid.

2   Before draining, purchase the specified transmission fluid (see *Recommended lubricants and fluids*) and a new filter. The necessary gaskets should be included with the filter; if not, purchase an oil pan gasket and a strainer-to-valve body gasket.

3   Other tools necessary for this job include jackstands to support the vehicle in a raised position, a wrench to remove the oil pan bolts, a standard screwdriver, a drain pan capable of holding at least eight pints, newspapers and clean rags.

4   The fluid should be drained immediately after the vehicle has been driven. This will remove any built-up sediment better than if the fluid were cold. Because of this, it may be wise to wear protective gloves (fluid temperature can exceed 350°F in a hot transmission).

5   After it has been driven to warm up the fluid, raise the vehicle and place it on jackstands for access underneath. Make sure it is firmly supported by the four stands placed under the frame rails.

6   Move the necessary equipment under the vehicle, being careful not to touch any of the hot exhaust components.

7   Remove the keeper at the rear of the transmission selector cable assembly.

8   Remove the clip that retains the transmission selector cable to the transmission selector lever.

9   Remove the cable from the selector lever.

10   Remove the cable housing from the transmission selector cable bracket.

11   Remove the selector cable bracket. To avoid confusion when re-installing the transmission pan, note that the bolts retaining the cable bracket are a different size than those retaining the pan.

12   Place the drain pan under the transmission oil pan and remove the oil pan bolts along the rear and sides of the pan. Loosen, but do not remove, the bolts at the front of the pan.

13   Carefully pry the pan down at the rear, allowing the hot fluid to drain into the container. If necessary, use a screwdriver to break the gasket seal at the rear of the pan; however, do not damage the pan or transmission in the process.

14   Support the pan and remove the remaining bolts at the front. Lower the pan and drain the remaining fluid into the container. As this is done, check the fluid for metal particles, which may be an indication of internal failure.

15   Now visible on the bottom of the transmission is the filter/strainer held in place by two screws.

16   Remove the two screws, the filter and the gasket.

17   Thoroughly clean the transmission oil pan with solvent. Inspect it for metal particles and foreign matter. Dry it with compressed air if available. It is important that all remaining gasket material be removed from the oil pan mounting flange. Use a gasket scraper or putty knife for this.

18   Clean the filter mounting surface on the valve body. Again, this surface should be smooth and free of any leftover gasket material.

19   Clean the screen assembly with solvent, then dry it thoroughly (use compressed air, if available). Paper or felt-type filters should be replaced with new ones.

20   Place the new filter into position, with a new gasket between it and the transmission valve body. Install the two mounting screws and tighten them securely.

21   Apply a light bead of gasket sealant around the oil pan mounting surface, with the sealant to the inside of the bolt holes. Press the new gasket into place on the pan, making sure all bolt holes line up.

22   Lift the pan up to the bottom of the transmission and install the mounting bolts. Tighten the bolts in a diagonal fashion, working around the pan. Using a torque wrench, tighten the bolts to the specified torque.

23   Lower the vehicle off the jackstands.

24   Open the hood and remove the transmission fluid dipstick from the guide tube.

25   Since fluid capacities vary between the various transmission types, it is best to add a little fluid at a time, continually checking the level with the dipstick. Allow the fluid time to drain into the pan. Add fluid until the level just registers on the end of the dipstick. In most cases, a good starting point will be four to five pints added to the transmission through the filler tube (use a funnel to prevent spills).

26   With the selector lever in Park, apply the parking brake and start the engine without depressing the accelerator pedal (if possible). Do not race the engine at a high speed; run it at slow idle only.

27   Depress the brake pedal and shift the transmission through each gear. Place the selector back into Park and check the level on the dipstick (with the engine still idling). Look under the vehicle for leaks around

the transmission oil pan mating surface.

28   Add more fluid through the dipstick tube until the level on the dipstick is 1/4-inch below the Add mark on the dipstick. Do not allow the fluid level to go above this point, as the transmission would then be overfull, necessitating the removal of the pan to drain the excess fluid.

29   Push the dipstick firmly back into the tube and drive the vehicle to reach normal operating temperature (15 miles of highway driving or its equivalent in the city). Park on a level surface and check the fluid level on the dipstick with the engine idling and the transmission in Park. The level should now be at the Full mark on the dipstick. If not, add more fluid as necessary to bring the level up to this point. Again, do not overfill.

27 Manual transmission oil change

1   The manual transmission lubricant should be drained and replaced at the specified intervals. Drive the vehicle to bring the transmission lubricant to operating temperature.

2   Raise the vehicle and support it securely. Before beginning this job, you will need:

> A wrench to remove the transmission plug
> A drain pan of at least six-quart capacity
> An adequate supply of the specified lubricant
> Jackstands to support the vehicle in a raised position
> Newspapers and clean rags

3   Place the drain pan under the drain plug and remove the fill plug.

4   Remove the drain plug (photo) and allow the transmission lubricant to drain into the pan. Inspect the lubricant for signs of contamination and metal particles, which could indicate a malfunction in the transmission.

5   Install the fill plug and fill the transmission with the specified lubricant (see *Recommended lubricants and fluids*) to the bottom of the fill plug hole. Install the fill plug and tighten it securely.

6   Lower the vehicle, drive it and check for leaks.

28 Transfer case oil change

1   The transfer case oil should be drained and replaced at the same time as the manual transmission (Sec 27).

2   Follow the procedures in Steps 2 and 3 of Section 27.

3   Remove the drain plug and allow the lubricant to run into the pan.

4   Inspect the lubricant for clues as to the condition of the transfer case, such as metal particles, water and other contamination.

5   Install the drain plug.

6   Fill the transfer case to just below the filler hole with the specified lubricant and install the plug. Tighten it securely.

7   Lower the vehicle, test drive it and check for leaks.

27.4   Locations of the drain and fill plugs on all 'S' series manual transmissions

29 Cooling system servicing (draining, flushing and refilling)

1 Periodically, the cooling system should be drained, flushed and refilled to replenish the antifreeze mixture and prevent formation of rust and corrosion, which can impair the performance of the cooling system and ultimately cause engine damage.

2 At the same time the cooling system is serviced, all hoses and the radiator cap should be inspected and replaced if defective (see Section 8).

3 Since antifreeze is a corrosive and poisonous solution, be careful not to spill any of the coolant mixture on the vehicle's paint or your skin. If this happens, rinse immediately with plenty of clean water. Also, consult your local authorities about the dumping of antifreeze before draining the cooling system. In many areas, reclamation centers have been set up to collect automobile oil and drained antifreeze/water mixtures rather than allowing them to be added to the sewage system.

4 With the engine cold, remove the radiator cap.

5 Move a large container under the radiator to catch the coolant as it is drained.

6 Drain the radiator. Most models are equipped with a drain plug at the bottom (photo). If this drain has excessive corrosion and cannot be turned easily, or if the radiator is not equipped with a drain, disconnect the lower radiator hose to allow the coolant to drain. Be careful that none of the solution is splashed on your skin or into your eyes.

7 If accessible, remove the two engine drain plugs. There is one plug on each side of the engine about halfway back, on the lower edge near the oil pan rail. These will allow the coolant to drain from the engine itself.

8 Disconnect the hose from the coolant reservoir and remove the reservoir. Flush it out with clean water.

9 Place a garden hose in the radiator filler neck at the top of the radiator and flush the system until the water runs clear at all drain points.

10 In severe cases of contamination or clogging of the radiator, remove it (see Chapter 3) and reverse flush it. This involves simply inserting the hose in the bottom radiator outlet to allow the clear water to run against the normal flow, draining through the top. A radiator repair shop should be consulted if further cleaning or repair is necessary.

11 When the coolant is regularly drained and the system refilled with the correct antifreeze/water mixture, there should be no need to use chemical cleaners or descalers.

12 To refill the system, reconnect the radiator hoses and install the drain plugs securely in the engine. Special thread-sealing tape (available at auto parts stores) should be used on the drain plugs. Install the reservoir and the overflow hose where applicable.

13 Fill the radiator to the base of the filler neck and then add more coolant to the reservoir until it reaches the mark.

14 Run the engine until normal operating temperature is reached and,

with the engine idling, add coolant up to the Full Hot level. Install the radiator cap so that the arrows are in alignment with the overflow hose. Install the reservoir cap.

15 Always refill the system with a mixture of high quality antifreeze and water in the proportion called for on the antifreeze container or in your owner's manual. Chapter 3 also contains information on antifreeze mixtures.

16 Keep a close watch on the coolant level and the various cooling system hoses during the first few miles of driving. Tighten the hose clamps and/or add more coolant as necessary.

30 Wheel bearing check and repack

Note: *The four-wheel drive vehicles covered by this manual incorporate sealed front wheel bearings which do not require adjustment or lubrication maintenance.*

1 In most cases, the front wheel bearings will not need servicing until the brake pads are changed. However, these bearings should be checked whenever the front wheels are raised for any reason.

2 With the vehicle securely supported on jackstands, spin the wheel and check for noise, rolling resistance and free play. Now grab the top of the tire with one hand and the bottom of the tire with the other. Move the tire in-and-out on the spindle. If it moves more than 0.005-inch, the bearings should be checked and then repacked with grease or replaced if necessary.

3 To remove the bearings for replacement or repacking, begin by removing the hub cap and wheel.

4 Using an Allen wrench of the proper size, remove the two bolts which secure the disc brake caliper to the support (see Chapter 9).

5 Fabricate a wood block (1-1/16-inch by 1-1/16-inch by 2 inches in length) which will be slid between the brake pads to keep them separated. Carefully slide the caliper off the disc and insert the wood block between the pads. Use wire to hang the caliper assembly out of the way. Be careful not to kink or damage the brake hose.

6 Pry the dust cap out of the hub using a screwdriver or hammer and chisel (photo). The cap is located at the center of the hub.

7 Use needle-nose pliers or a screwdriver to straighten the bent ends of the cotter pin and then pull the cotter pin out of the locking nut (photos). Discard the cotter pin and use a new one during reassembly.

8 Remove the spindle nut and washer from the end of the spindle (photos).

9 Pull the hub assembly out slightly and then push it back into its original position. This should force the outer bearing off the spindle enough so that it can be removed with your fingers (photo). Remove the outer bearing, noting how it is installed on the end of the spindle (photo).

29.6 Location of the radiator drain plug

30.6 Removing the wheel bearing dust cap

30.7a   Straightening the ends of the cotter pin

30.7b   Removing the cotter pin

30.8a   Removing the spindle nut

30.8b   Removing the spindle washer

30.9   Removing the outer wheel bearing

30.10   Removing the hub assembly from the spindle

30.11   Removing the inner bearing lip seal

10   Now the hub assembly can be pulled off the spindle (photo).
11   On the rear side of the hub, use a screwdriver to pry out the inner bearing lip seal (photo). As this is done, note the direction in which the seal is installed.
12   The inner bearing can now be removed from the hub, again noting how it is installed.
13   Use solvent to remove all traces of the old grease from the bearings, hub and spindle. A small brush may prove useful; however, make sure no bristles from the brush embed themselves inside the bearing rollers. Allow the parts to air dry.
14   Carefully inspect the bearings for cracks, heat discoloration, bent rollers, etc. Check the bearing races inside the hub for cracks, scoring and uneven surfaces. If the bearing races are defective, the hubs should be taken to a machine shop with the facilities to remove the old races and press new ones in.
15   Use an approved high-temperature front wheel bearing grease to pack the bearings. Work the grease completely into the bearings, forcing it between the rollers, cone and cage (photo).
16   Apply a thin coat of grease to the spindle at the outer bearing seat, inner bearing seat, shoulder and seal seat (photo).
17   Put a small quantity of grease inboard of each bearing race inside the hub. Using your finger, form a dam at these points to provide extra grease availability and to keep thinned grease from flowing out of the bearing.

30.15   Packing a bearing with special high-temperature wheel bearing grease (work it well into the rollers)

30.16   Applying a thin coat of grease to the spindle surfaces

30.19   Installing a new seal over the inner bearing using a soft-faced hammer (tap around the entire circumference)

30.20   Installing the outer bearing

18 Place the grease-packed inner bearing into the rear of the hub and put a little more grease outboard of the bearing.
19 Place a new seal over the inner bearing and tap the seal with a hammer until it is flush with the hub (photo).
20 Carefully place the hub assembly onto the spindle and push the grease-packed outer bearing into position (photo).
21 Install the washer and spindle nut. Tighten the nut only slightly (12 ft-lbs of torque) (photos).
22 Spin the hub in a forward direction to seat the bearings and remove any grease or burrs which could cause excessive bearing play later.
23 Put a little grease outboard of the outer bearing to provide extra grease availability.
24 Now check to see that the tightness of the spindle nut is still 12 ft-lbs.
25 Loosen the spindle nut until it is just loose, no more.
26 Using your hand (not a wrench of any kind), tighten the nut until it is snug. Install a new cotter pin through the hole in the spindle and spindle nut (photo). If the nut slits do not line up, loosen the nut slightly until they do. From the hand-tight position, the nut should not be loosened more than one-half flat to install the cotter pin.
27 Bend the ends of the new cotter pin until they are flat against the nut (photo). Cut off any extra length which could interfere with the dust cap.
28 Install the dust cap, tapping it into place with a rubber mallet.
29 Place the brake caliper near the rotor and carefully remove the wood

spacer. Slide the caliper over the rotor. Tighten the caliper mounting bolts to 35 ft-lbs. Chapter 9 contains details on the disc brake caliper assembly.
30 Install the tire/wheel assembly on the hub and tighten the lug nuts.
31 Grab the top and bottom of the tire and check the bearings in the same manner as described at the beginning of this Section.
32 Lower the vehicle to the ground and tighten the lug nuts completely. Install the hub cap, using a rubber mallet to seat it.

31 Air filter and PCV filter replacement

1   At the specified intervals, the air filter and PCV filter should be replaced with new ones. A thorough program of preventative maintenance would call for the two filters to be inspected between changes.
2   The air filter is located inside the air cleaner housing on the top of the engine. The filter is generally replaced by removing the wing nut at the top of the air cleaner assembly and lifting off the top plate (photo). If vacuum hoses are connected to the plate, note their positions and disconnect them.
3   While the top plate is off, be careful not to drop anything down into the carburetor.
4   Lift the air filter element out of the housing.

30.21a   Installing the spindle washer (make sure that the tab lines up with the groove)

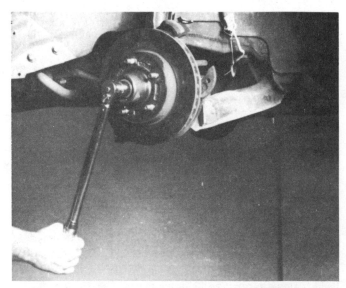

30.21b   Tighten the spindle nut only slightly (no more than 12 ft-lbs)

30.26   Installing the cotter pin after lining up the hole in the spindle with a groove in the spindle nut

30.27   Bending the ends of the cotter pin to secure it

5 To check the filter, hold it up to strong sunlight or place a flashlight or droplight on the inside of the filter. If you can see light coming through the paper element, the filter is all right. Check all the way around the filter.

6 Wipe out the inside of the air cleaner housing with a clean rag.

7 Place the old filter (if in good condition) or the new filter (if the specified interval has elapsed) back into the air cleaner housing. Make sure it seats properly in the bottom of the housing.

8 Connect any disconnected vacuum hoses to the top plate and reinstall the plate.

9 The PCV filter is also located inside the air cleaner housing. Remove the top plate and air filter as described previously, then locate the PCV filter on the side of the housing.

10 Remove the retaining clip from the outside of the housing, then remove the PCV filter (photo).

11 Install a new PCV filter, then reinstall the retaining clip, air filter, top plate and any hoses that were disconnected.

32 Positive Crankcase Ventilation (PCV) valve replacement

1 The PCV valve is located in the rocker arm cover or intake manifold (photo). A hose connected to the valve runs to either the carburetor or intake manifold.

31.2 The air cleaner top plate and wing nut must be removed in order to gain access to the air filter and PCV filter

32.1 The PCV valve is located in the left rocker arm cover on V6 engines

2 When purchasing a replacement PCV valve, make sure it is for your particular vehicle, model year and engine size.

3 Pull the valve (with hose attached) from the rubber grommet in the rocker arm cover or manifold.

4 Loosen the retaining clamp and pull the PCV valve from the end of the hose, noting its installed position and direction.

5 Compare the old valve with the new one to make sure they are the same.

6 Push the new valve into the end of the hose until it is seated and reinstall the clamp.

7 Inspect the rubber grommet for damage and replace it with a new one, if faulty.

8 Push the PCV valve and hose securely into position.

9 More information on the PCV system can be found in Chapter 6.

33 Exhaust Gas Recirculation (EGR) valve check

1 On GM vehicles, the EGR valve is located on the intake manifold, adjacent to the carburetor. Most of the time when a problem develops in this emissions system, it is due to a stuck or corroded EGR valve.

2 With the engine cold to prevent burns, reach under the EGR valve and manually push on the diaphragm. Using moderate pressure, you should be able to press the diaphragm up and down within the housing.

3 If the diaphragm does not move or moves only with much effort, replace the EGR valve with a new one. If in doubt about the quality of the valve, compare the free movement of your EGR valve with a new valve.

4 Refer to Chapter 6 for more information on the EGR system.

34 Evaporative Emissions Control System (EEC) filter replacement

1 The function of the Evaporative Emissions Control System is to draw fuel vapors from the tank and carburetor, store them in a charcoal canister and then burn them during normal engine operation.

2 The filter at the bottom of the charcoal canister should be replaced at the specified intervals. If, however, a fuel odor is detected, the canister, filter and system hoses should immediately be inspected.

3 To replace the filter, locate the canister at the front of the engine compartment. It will have between three and six hoses running out of the top (photo).

4 Mark the hoses with tape to simplify reinstallation, then disconnect them from the canister.

5 Remove the two bolts which secure the bottom of the canister to the body.

6 Turn the canister upside-down and pull the old filter from the bottom of the canister.

34.3 The EEC canister is located in the front of the engine compartment, just behind the headlight assembly

1

7   Push the new filter into the bottom of the canister, making sure it is seated all the way around.

8   Place the canister back into position and tighten the two mounting bolts. Connect the various hoses if disconnected.

9   The EEC is explained in more detail in Chapter 6.

35   Ignition timing check and adjustment

Note: *It is imperative that the procedures included on the Vehicle Emissions Control Information label be followed when adjusting the ignition timing. The label will include all information concerning preliminary steps to be performed before adjusting the timing, as well as the timing specifications.*

1   Locate the VECI label under the hood and read through and perform all preliminary instructions concerning ignition timing.

2   Locate the timing mark pointer plate located beside the crankshaft pulley. The O mark represents top dead center (TCD). The pointer plate will be marked in either one or two-degree increments and should have the proper timing mark for your particular engine noted. If not, count back from the 0 mark the correct number of degrees BTDC, as noted on the VECI label, and mark the plate.

3   Locate the notch on the crankshaft balancer of pulley and mark

35.4   Typical wiring hookup for an inductive-type timing light

35.5   The timing light must be held fairly close to the timing marks (arrow) for good visibility, so be careful of the fan!

it with chalk or a dab or paint so it will be visible under the timing light.

4   With the ignition off, connect the pick-up lead of the timing light to the number one spark plug. Use either a jumper lead between the wire and plug or an inductive-type pick-up (photo). *Do not pierce the wire or attempt to insert a wire between the boot and the wire.* Connect the timing light power leads according to the manufacturer's instructions. **Note:** *Some engines incorporate a magnetic timing probe hole for use with special electronic timing equipment. Consult the manufacturer's instructions for proper use of this equipment.*

5   Start the engine, aim the timing light at the timing mark by the crankshaft pulley and note which timing mark the notch on the pulley is lining up with (photo).

6   If the notch is not lining up with the correct mark, loosen the distributor hold-down bolt and rotate the distributor until the notch is lined up with the correct timing mark.

7   Retighten the hold-down bolt and recheck the timing.

8   Turn off the engine and disconnect the timing light. Reconnect the number one spark plug wire, if removed.

36   Spark plug replacement

1   The spark plugs are located on each side of V6 engines and on the left side of four-cylinder engines. They may or may not be easily accessible for removal. If the vehicle is equipped with air-conditioning or power steering, some of the plugs may be tricky to remove. Special extension or swivel tools may be necessary. Make a survey under the hood to determine if special tools will be needed.

2   In most cases, the tools necessary for a spark plug replacement job include a plug wrench or spark plug socket which fits onto a ratchet wrench (this special socket will be padded inside to protect the plug) and a feeler gauge to check and adjust the spark plug gaps. Also, a special spark plug wire removal tool is available for separating the wires from the spark plugs. To ease installation, obtain a piece of 3/16-inch inside diameter rubber hose, 8 to 12 inches in length.

3   The best procedure to follow when replacing the spark plugs is to purchase the new spark plugs beforehand, adjust them to the proper gap and then replace each plug one at a time. When buying the new spark plugs, it is important to obtain the correct plugs for your specific engine. This information can be found in the Specifications at the front of this Chapter, but should be checked against the information found on the Emissions Control Information label located under the hood or in the owner's manual. If differences exist between these sources, purchase the spark plug type specified on the Emissions Control label because the information was printed for your specific engine.

4   With the new spark plugs at hand, allow the engine to cool completely before attempting plug removal. During this time, each of the new spark plugs can be inspected for defects and the gaps can be checked.

5   The gap is checked by inserting the proper thickness gauge between the electrodes at the tip of the plug. The gap between the electrodes should be the same as that given in the Specifications or on the Emissions Control label. The wire should just touch each of the electrodes. If the gap is incorrect, use the notched adjuster on the feeler gauge body to bend the curved side electrode slightly until the proper gap is achieved. If the side electrode is not exactly over the center electrode, use the notched adjuster to align the two. Also at this time check for cracks in the porcelain insulator, indicating the spark plug should not be used.

6   Cover the fenders of the vehicle to prevent damage to the paint.

7   With the engine cool, remove the spark plug wire from one spark plug. Do this by grabbing the boot at the end of the wire, not the wire itself. Sometimes it is necessary to use a twisting motion while the boot and plug wire are pulled free. Using a plug wire removal tool is the easiest and safest method.

8   If compressed air is available, use it to blow any dirt or foreign material away from the spark plug area. A common bicycle pump will also work. The idea here is to eliminate the possibility of material falling into the cylinder as the spark plug is removed.

9   Now place the spark plug wrench or socket over the plug and remove it from the engine by turning in a counterclockwise direction.

10   Compare the spark plug with those shown in the accompanying color photos to get an indication of the overall running condition of the engine.

CARBON DEPOSITS
Symptoms: Dry sooty deposits indicate a rich mixture or weak ignition. Causes misfiring, hard starting and hesitation.

Recommendation: Check for a clogged air cleaner, high float level, sticky choke and worn ignition points. Use a spark plug with a longer core nose for greater anti-fouling protection.

OIL DEPOSITS
Symptoms: Oily coating caused by poor oil control. Oil is leaking past worn valve guides or piston rings into the combustion chamber. Causes hard starting, misfiring and hesition.

Recommendation: Correct the mechanical condition with necessary repairs and install new plugs.

TOO HOT
Symptoms: Blistered, white insulator, eroded electrode and absence of deposits. Results in shortened plug life.

Recommendation: Check for the correct plug heat range, over-advanced ignition timing, lean fuel mixture, intake manifold vacuum leaks and sticking valves. Check the coolant level and make sure the radiator is not clogged.

PREIGNITION
Symptoms: Melted electrodes. Insulators are white, but may be dirty due to misfiring or flying debris in the combustion chamber. Can lead to engine damage.

Recommendation: Check for the correct plug heat range, over-advanced ignition timing, lean fuel mixture, clogged cooling system and lack of lubrication.

HIGH SPEED GLAZING
Symptoms: Insulator has yellowish, glazed appearance. Indicates that combustion chamber temperatures have risen suddenly during hard acceleration. Normal deposits melt to form a conductive coating. Causes misfiring at high speeds.

Recommendation: Install new plugs. Consider using a colder plug if driving habits warrant.

GAP BRIDGING
Symptoms: Combustion deposits lodge between the electrodes. Heavy deposits accumulate and bridge the electrode gap. The plug ceases to fire, resulting in a dead cylinder.

Recommendation: Locate the faulty plug and remove the deposits from between the electrodes.

NORMAL
Symptoms: Brown to grayish-tan color and slight electrode wear. Correct heat range for engine and operating conditions.

Recommendation: When new spark plugs are installed, replace with plugs of the same heat range.

ASH DEPOSITS
Symptoms: Light brown deposits encrusted on the side or center electrodes or both. Derived from oil and/or fuel additives. Excessive amounts may mask the spark, causing misfiring and hesitation during acceleration.

Recommendation: If excessive deposits accumulate over a short time or low mileage, install new valve guide seals to prevent seepage of oil into the combustion chambers. Also try changing gasoline brands.

WORN
Symptoms: Rounded electrodes with a small amount of deposits on the firing end. Normal color. Causes hard starting in damp or cold weather and poor fuel economy.

Recommendation: Replace with new plugs of the same heat range.

1

DETONATION
Symptoms: Insulators may be cracked or chipped. Improper gap setting techniques can also result in a fractured insulator tip. Can lead to piston damage.

Recommendation: Make sure the fuel anti-knock values meet engine requirements. Use care when setting the gaps on new plugs. Avoid lugging the engine.

SPLASHED DEPOSITS
Symptoms: After long periods of misfiring, deposits can loosen when normal combustion temperature is restored by an overdue tune-up. At high speeds, deposits flake off the piston and are thrown against the hot insulator, causing misfiring.

Recommendation: Replace the plugs with new ones or clean and reinstall the originals.

MECHANICAL DAMAGE
Symptoms: May be caused by a foreign object in the combustion chamber or the piston striking an incorrect reach (too long) plug. Causes a dead cylinder and could result in piston damage.

Recommendation: Remove the foreign object from the engine and/or install the correct reach plug.

11   Due to the angle at which the spark plugs must be installed on most engines, installation will be simplified by inserting the plug wire terminal of the new spark plug into the 3/16-inch rubber hose, mentioned previously, before it is installed in the cylinder head (photo). This procedure serves two purposes: the rubber hose gives you flexibility for establishing the proper angle of plug insertion in the head and, should the threads be improperly lined up, the rubber hose will merely slip on the spark plug terminal when it meets resistance, preventing damage to the cylinder head threads.

12   After installing the plug to the limit of the hose grip, tighten it with the socket. It is a good idea to use a torque wrench for this to ensure that the plug is seated correctly. The correct torque figure is included in the Specifications.

13   Before pushing the spark plug wire onto the end of the plug, inspect it following the procedures outlined in Section 37.

14   Attach the plug wire to the new spark plug, again using a twisting motion on the boot until it is firmly seated on the spark plug. Make sure the wire is routed away from the exhaust manifold.

15   Follow the above procedure for the remaining spark plugs, replacing them one at a time to prevent mixing up the spark plug wires.

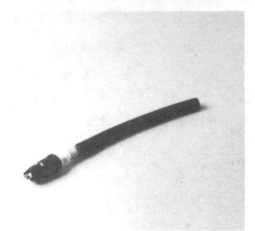

36.11   A length of 3/16-inch ID rubber hose will save time and prevent damaged threads when installing spark plugs

37   Spark plug wires, distributor cap and rotor check and replacement

1   Begin this procedure by making a visual check of the spark plug wires while the engine is running. In a darkened garage (make sure there is ventilation) start the engine and observe each plug wire. Be careful not to come into contact with any moving engine parts. If there is a break in the wire, you will see arcing or a small spark at the damaged area. If arcing is noticed, make a note to obtain new wires, then allow the engine to cool and check the distributor cap and rotor.

2   Disconnect the negative cable from the battery. At the distributor, disconnect the ECM connector and coil wire.

3   Remove the distributor cap by placing a screwdriver on the slotted head of each latch. Press down on the latch and turn it 180° to release the hooked end at the bottom (photo). On some engines, due to restricted working room, a stubby screwdriver will work best. With all latches disengaged, separate the cap from the distributor with the spark plug wires still attached.

4   Inspect the cap for cracks and other damage. Closely examine the contacts on the inside of the cap for excessive corrosion (photo). Slight scoring is normal. Deposits on the contacts may be removed with a small file.

5   If the inspection reveals damage to the cap, make a note to obtain a replacement for your particular engine, then examine the rotor.

6   The rotor is visible, with the cap removed, at the top of the

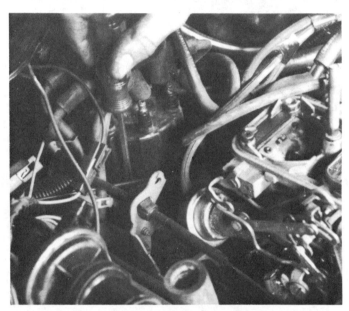

37.3   Releasing the distributor cap hold-down latches (the spark plug wire ring has previously been removed for visibility)

37.4   Close-up shows deposit build-up on cap terminals

37.7   Close-up of the metal contact on this rotor reveals a normal wear pattern

distributor shaft. It is held in place by two screws. Remove the screws and the rotor.

7   Inspect the rotor for cracks and other damage. Carefully check the condition of the metal contact at the top of the rotor for excessive burning and pitting (photo).

8   If it is determined that a new rotor is required, make a note to that effect. If the rotor and cap are in good condition, reinstall them at this time. Note that the rotor has two raised pegs on the bottom and that it has a wide slot and a narrow slot. Make sure that the slots are correctly aligned and that the pegs are firmly seated when the rotor is installed.

9   If the cap must be replaced, do not reinstall it. Leave it off the distributor with the wires still connected.

10 If the spark plug wires are being replaced, now is the time to obtain a new set, along with a new cap and rotor as determined in the checks above. Purchase a wire set for your particular engine, pre-cut to the proper size, with the rubber boots already installed.

11 If the spark plug wires passed the check in Step 1, they should be checked further as follows.

12 Examine the wires one at a time to avoid mixing them up.

13 Disconnect the plug wire from the spark plug. A removal tool can be used for this, or you can grab the rubber boot, twist slightly and then pull the wire free. Do not pull on the wire itself, only on the rubber boot.

14 Inspect inside the boot for corrosion, which will look like a white crusty powder. Some models use a conductive white silicone lubricant which should not be mistaken for corrosion.

15 Now push the wire and boot back onto the end of the spark plug. It should be a tight fit on the plug end. If not, remove the wire and use pliers to carefully crimp the metal connector inside the wire boot until the fit is snug.

16 Now, using a clean rag, clean the entire length of the wire. Remove all built-up dirt and grease. As this is done, check for burns, cracks and any other form of damage. Bend the wires in several places to ensure that the conductive wire inside has not hardened.

17 Next, the wires should be checked at the distributor cap in the same manner. On four-cylinder engines, remove the wire from the cap by pulling on the boot, again examining the wires one at a time, and reinstalling each one after examination. Apply new silicone lubricant before reinstallation. On V6 engines, the distributor boots are connected to a circular retaining ring attached to the distributor cap. Release the locking tabs, turn the ring upside down and check all wire boots at the same time.

18 If the wires appear to be in good condition, reinstall the retaining ring (V6 engines) and make sure that all wires are secure at both ends. If the cap and rotor are also in good condition, the check is finished. Reconnect the wires at the distributor and at the battery.

19 If it was determined in Steps 12 through 17 that new wires are

required, obtain them at this time, along with a new cap and rotor if so determined in the checks above.

20 Attach the rotor to the distributor. Make sure that the carbon brush is properly installed in the cap, as a wide gap between the carbon brush and the rotor will cause rotor burn-through and/or damage to the distributor cap.

21 If new wires are being installed, replace them one at a time. **Note:** *It is important to replace the wires one at a time, noting the routing as each wire is removed and installed, to maintain the correct firing order and to prevent short-circuiting.*

22 Attach the cap to the distributor, reconnecting all wires disconnected in Step 2, then reconnect the battery cable.

38 Compression check

1   A compression check will tell you what mechanical condition the engine is in. Specifically, it can tell you if the compression is down due to leakage caused by worn piston rings, defective valves and seats or a blown head gasket.

2   Begin by cleaning the area around the spark plugs before you remove them. This will keep dirt from falling into the cylinders while you are performing the compression test.

3   Remove the coil high-tension lead from the distributor and ground it on the engine block. Block the throttle and choke valves wide open.

4   With the compression gauge in the number one cylinder's spark plug hole, crank the engine over at least four compression strokes and observe the gauge (the compression should build up quickly in a healthy engine) (photo). Low compression on the first stroke, followed by gradually increasing pressure on successive strokes, indicates worn piston rings. A low compression reading on the first stroke, which does not build up during successive strokes, indicates leaking valves or a blown head gasket (a cracked head could also be the cause). Record the highest gauge reading obtained.

5   Repeat the procedure for the remaining cylinders and compare the results to the Specifications. Compression readings approximately 10 percent above or below the specified amount can be considered normal.

6   Pour a couple of teaspoons of engine oil (a squirt can works great for this) into each cylinder, through the spark plug hole, and repeat the test.

7   If the compression increases after the oil is added, the piston rings are definitely worn. If the compression does not increase significantly, the leakage is occurring at the valves or head gasket. Leakage past the valves may be caused by burned valve seats or faces, warped, cracked or bent valves or valves that require adjustment.

8   If two adjacent cylinders have equally low compression, there is a strong possibility that the head gasket between them is blown. The appearance of coolant in the combustion chambers or the crankcase would verify this condition.

9   If the compression is higher than normal, the combustion chambers are probably coated with carbon deposits. If that is the case, the cylinder head(s) should be removed and decarbonized.

10 If compression is way down or varies greatly between cylinders, it would be a good idea to have a leak-down test performed by a reputable automotive repair shop. This test will pinpoint exactly where the leakage is occurring and how severe it is.

39 Valve clearance adjustment (1.9 liter engine only)

1   Tag and remove the emissions hoses from the rocker arm cover. Remove the rocker arm cover.

2   Before adjusting the valves, check the tightness of the rocker shaft bracket nuts with a torque wrench. Tighten them to the specified torque if necessary.

3   Position the number 1 piston at top dead center (TDC) on the compression stroke. To do this, first number each spark plug wire, then remove all of the spark plugs from the engine.

4   Locate the number 1 cylinder spark plug wire and trace it back to the distributor. Write a number 1 on the distributor body directly below the terminal where the number 1 spark plug wire attaches to the distributor cap. Do this for the number 4 cylinder as well, then remove the cap and wires from the distributor.

5   Slip a wrench or socket over the large bolt at the front of the

38.4   Using a special gauge to check cylinder compression

crankshaft and slowly turn it in a *clockwise* direction until the groove in the crankshaft pulley is aligned with the 0 (zero) on the timing mark tag. The rotor should be pointing directly at the number 1 you made on the distributor body. If it is not, turn the crankshaft one more complete revolution (360°) in a *clockwise* direction. If the rotor is now pointing at the number 1 on the distributor body, then the number 1 piston is at TDC on the compression stroke and the clearances for some of the valves can be checked and adjusted (refer to the accompanying illustration).

6   Insert an appropriate size feeler gauge between the valve stem and the adjusting screw. If the feeler gauge fits with a slight drag, then the clearance is correct and no adjustment is required. Be sure to use the correct feeler gauge, as the intake and exhaust valves require different clearances for proper engine operation.

7   If the feeler gauge will not fit between the valve stem and adjusting screw or if it is loose, loosen the adjusting screw locknut and carefully tighten or loosen the adjusting screw until you can feel a slight drag on the feeler gauge as it is withdrawn.

8   Hold the adjusting screw with a wrench to keep it from turning and tighten the locknut securely.

9   Turn the crankshaft 360° and align the rotor with the number 4 on the distributor. Adjust the clearance for the remaining valves.

10   Install the rocker arm cover (use a new gasket) and tighten the mounting bolts evenly and securely.

11   Install the distributor cap and spark plugs, then hook up the spark plug wires and the various hoses and vacuum lines.

12   Start the engine and check for oil leakage between the rocker arm cover and the cylinder head.

---

40   Underbody flushing

1   At least every spring, the underbody should be flushed with plain water to remove corrosive materials picked up from road surfaces. Materials used for ice and snow removal and dust control will cause premature rusting of the underbody sheet metal.

2   Be sure to thoroughly clean areas where mud and other debris can collect. Areas with large deposits of sediment should be pre-soaked before being flushed.

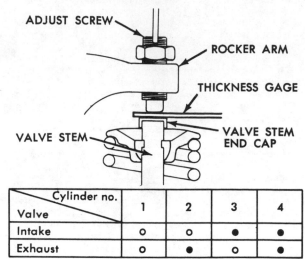

Valve / Cylinder no.	1	2	3	4
Intake	o	o	●	●
Exhaust	o	●	o	●

Note: o When piston in No. 1 cylinder is at TDC on compression stroke.
   ● When piston in No. 4 cylinder is at TDC on compression stroke.

Fig. 1.8   The intake and exhaust valves can be adjusted with the two crankshaft positions indicated (Sec 39)

Chapter 2 Part A   1.9L four-cylinder engine

Contents

2A

Specifications

General

Rocker shaft runout limit	0.0079 in (0.2 mm)
Rocker shaft diameter	
Standard	0.8071 in (20.5 mm)
Service limit	0.8012 in (20.35 mm)
Rocker shaft-to-rocker arm clearance limit	0.0078 in (0.2 mm)
Timing chain wear measurement (forty links)	
Standard	15 in (381 mm)
Service limit	15.16 in (385 mm)
Intake manifold-to-cylinder head surface warpage limit	0.0157 in (0.4 mm)
Exhaust manifold-to-cylinder head surface warpage limit	0.0156 in (0.4 mm)

Torque specifications

	Ft-lb	Nm
Rocker shaft bracket nuts	16	22
Timing sprocket bolt	58	78
Cylinder head bolts..................................	72	98
Crankshaft pulley bolt	87	118
Flywheel bolts	76	103
Oil pan mounting bolts	4	5
Camshaft cover nuts	4	5
Timing cover mounting bolts	18	19
Exhaust manifold mounting nuts	16	22

1   General information

The Isuzu engine used in some S-10/S-15 pick-ups is equipped with a forged crankshaft supported by four main bearings, with the number three bearing used as the thrust bearing. An overhead camshaft directly operates the rocker arms, and periodic valve lash adjustment is required. An automatic adjuster tensions the timing chain.

The Sections in this Part of Chapter 2 are devoted to 'in vehicle' repair procedures for the Isuzu 1.9 liter engine. All information concerning engine block and cylinder head servicing can be found in Part D of this Chapter.

The repair procedures included in this Part are based on the assumption that the engine is still installed in the vehicle. Therefore, if this information is being used during a complete engine overhaul — with the engine already out of the vehicle and on a stand — many of the steps included here will not apply.

The Specifications included in this Part of Chapter 2 apply only to the engine and procedures found here. For Specifications regarding engines other than the Isuzu, see Part B or C, whichever applies. Part D of Chapter 2 contains the Specifications necessary for engine block and cylinder head rebuilding.

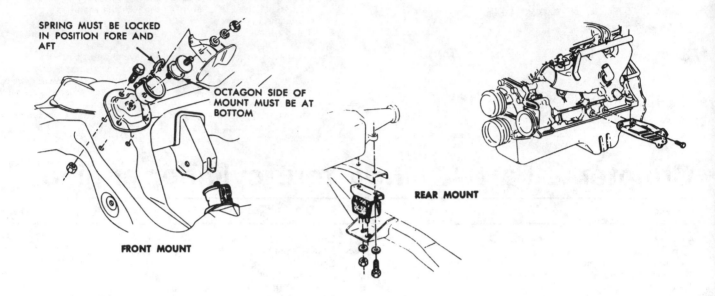

Fig. 2.A.1   Typical front and rear motor mounts used on the 1.9 liter engine (Sec 2)

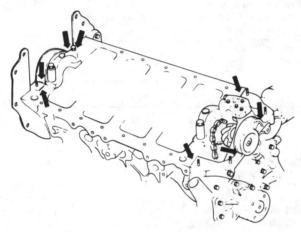

Fig. 2A.2   A thin coat of sealer must be applied to these locations before installing the oil pan gasket (Sec 3)

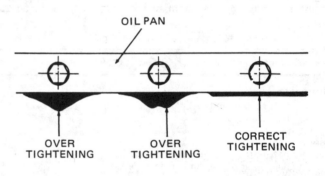

Fig. 2A.3   Overtightening of the oil pan bolts can cause gasket distortion and oil leakage (Sec 3)

2   Engine mounts — replacement with engine in vehicle

Front mounts

1   Disconnect the negative battery cable.
2   Remove the air filter assembly.
3   Remove the upper fan shroud.
4   Remove the safety wire from the engine mount bolt and remove the engine mount retaining nut from the connecting stud.
5   Raise the engine with a jack (position a block of wood underneath the oil pan). Make sure that the engine mounts do not bind as the engine is raised off the insulator assembly.
6   Remove the mount-to-engine bracket.
7   Remove the engine mount using GM factory tool No. J-25510.
8   Installation is the reverse of removal.

Rear mount

9   Disconnect the negative battery cable.
10   Remove the retaining nut and bolt from the engine mount.
11   Place a jack under the transmission extension housing and raise the transmission until the mount can be removed from the frame crossmember.
12   Installation is the reverse of removal.

3   Oil pan — removal and installation

Note: *The engine must be removed from the vehicle before the oil pan can be removed.*

1   Remove the engine as described in Part D of this Chapter.
2   Remove the oil pan retaining bolts and nuts and separate the oil pan from the engine block. Do not damage the gasket sealing surfaces.
3   Remove the dipstick guide tube from the intake manifold and oil pan.
4   Clean the oil pan and block sealing surfaces. Inspect the gasket sealing surfaces for distortion due to overtightening of the bolts. Repair with a wood block and hammer as necessary.
5   Before installing the oil pan, apply a thin coat of Permatex No. 2 gasket sealant or equivalent to the locations shown in the accompanying illustration.
6   Attach the new oil pan gasket to the oil pan. Make sure that all the holes are properly aligned.
7   Attach the dipstick guide tube and oil pan to the engine block.
8   Starting at the center of the pan and working out to the corners, tighten the retaining bolts and nuts to the specified torque.
9   Install the engine (Chapter 2D).

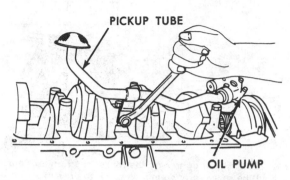

PICKUP TUBE

OIL PUMP

Fig. 2A.4   The oil pump (a non-serviceable assembly) is mounted at the front of the engine (Sec 4)

4   Oil pump — removal and installation

1   Remove the oil pan as described in Section 3.
2   Remove the mounting bolts from the oil pump and oil pump pickup tube.
3   Remove the oil pump. The oil pump is not rebuildable and must be replaced as a unit.
4   Installation is the reverse of removal.

5   Intake manifold — removal and installation

Removal

1   Drain the coolant from the radiator and engine block. The cooling system must be completely drained before removing the intake manifold or coolant will flow into the cylinders when the manifold is removed.
2   Remove the air cleaner assembly.
3   Disconnect the upper radiator hose from the front of the intake manifold.
4   Disconnect the vacuum hose from the intake manifold.
5   Disconnect the heater hoses from the rear of the intake manifold and from the connector under the dashboard.
6   Disconnect the accelerator cable from the carburetor.
7   Disconnect the vacuum hose from the distributor and disconnect the thermo-unit wiring at the connector.
8   Disconnect the carburetor automatic choke and solenoid wiring at the connectors.
9   Disconnect the PCV hose from the camshaft cover.
10 Remove the bolt that attaches the oil dipstick guide tube to the intake manifold.
11 Disconnect the EGR pipe from the EGR valve adapter.
12 Disconnect the AIR vacuum hose from the three-way joint.
13 Remove the eight retaining nuts and separate the intake manifold from the cylinder head.
14 Check the manifold for cracks and damage. Replace it if necessary.
15 Scrape away all traces of gasket material from the manifold-to-cylinder head surfaces.
16 Using a straightedge and a feeler gauge, check the cylinder head mating surface of the manifold for distortion and compare it to the Specifications. If the manifold is distorted beyond the specified limit, a machine shop should be able to correct the condition with a surface grinder.

Installation

17 Installation is the reverse of removal. Be sure to use a new gasket. Tighten the mounting bolts in four or five increments, working from the center of the manifold out in a criss-cross pattern.

6   Exhaust manifold — removal and installation

Note: *Before beginning, see the warning below.*
1   Disconnect the negative battery cable.

2   Raise the vehicle and support it securely on jackstands.
3   Disconnect the exhaust pipe from the exhaust manifold.
4   Disconnect the EGR pipe from the exhaust manifold.
5   Lower the vehicle.
6   Remove the air cleaner mounting bolts. Loosen the air cleaner clamp bolts.
7   Lift the air cleaner slightly and remove the hot air hose.
8   Remove the air-conditioning compressor adjustment brackets and remove the compressor, if equipped. **Warning:** *Do not disconnect or in any way damage the pressurized refrigerant lines. If necessary, have the system depressurized by a professional.*
9   Remove the power steering pump adjustment bracket and remove the pump, if equipped.
10 Remove the four mounting bolts from the manifold cover and remove the manifold cover.
11 Remove the seven mounting nuts from the exhaust manifold and remove the exhaust manifold.
12 Scrape away all traces of gasket material from the cylinder head-to-exhaust manifold surfaces.
13 Check the exhaust manifold for cracks and damage. Replace it if necessary.
14 Using a straightedge and a feeler gauge, measure the cylinder head mating surface of the exhaust manifold for distortion and compare it to the Specifications. If the manifold is warped beyond the specified limit, a machine shop should be able to correct the condition with a surface grinder.
15 Installation is the reverse of removal. Be sure to use a new gasket.
16 Tighten the exhaust manifold nuts a little at a time, in sequence, starting with the inner nuts and working out. Finally, tighten the exhaust manifold nuts to the specified torque.

7 Camshaft cover and valve train components — removal, inspection and installation

2A

Removal

1   Disconnect the negative battery cable.
2   Remove the air cleaner assembly.
3   Disconnect the spark plug wires from the routing bracket on the cam cover and secure them out of the way.
4   Disconnect the evaporator pipe at the air injection manifold and at the engine lift bracket.
5   Remove the cam cover retaining nuts and washers and remove the cam cover.
6   Loosen the rocker shaft bracket nuts a little at a time in sequence, beginning with the outer brackets and working toward the center.
7   Remove the retaining nuts from the rocker shaft brackets.
8   The valve train components can be disassembled by removing the spring from the rocker arm shaft and then removing the rocker arm brackets and rocker arms.

Inspection

9   Inspect the rocker shafts for runout. Support the shaft on V blocks at the ends and position a dial indicator at the center of the shaft. Turn the shaft slowly and then note the amount of runout shown on the dial indicator. Replace the rocker shaft if it is not within the specified limits.
10 Use a micrometer to measure the shaft diameter at the four rocker arm locations. Replace the shaft if it is less than the specified diameter.
11 Using a telescoping gauge, measure the inside diameter of the rocker arms. Compare this measurement to the rocker shaft diameter at the corresponding rocker arm location. If the clearance exceeds the specified limits, replace the rocker shaft or rocker arms as necessary.
12 Check the valve contact area of the rocker arms for step wear and scoring. Replace the rocker arm(s) if there is considerable step wear or scoring.

Installation

13 Apply liberal amounts of engine oil to the rocker shaft, rocker arms and valve stems.
14 Install the longer shaft on the exhaust valve side and the short rocker shaft on the intake side. The alignment marks on the shafts should face up and towards the front of the engine (refer to the accompanying illustration).

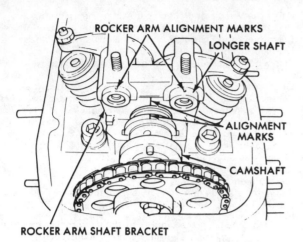

Fig. 2A.5 The non-interchangeable rocker shafts have alignment marks for correct installation (Sec 7)

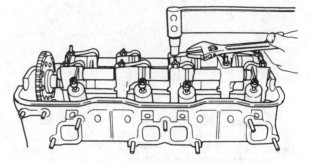

Fig. 2A.6 When tightening the rocker shaft bracket nuts, hold the rocker arm springs in place to prevent spring damage (Sec 7)

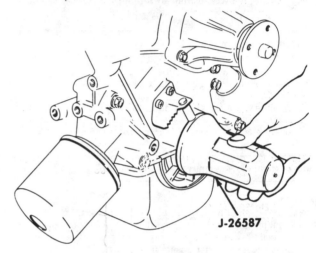

Fig. 2A.7 A special tool (as shown) or a large piece of pipe is needed to install a new timing cover seal without removing the cover (Sec 8)

15 Install the rocker shaft brackets and rocker arms. Make sure that the cylinder number on the upper face of the brackets points to the front of the engine.
16 Align the mark on the number one rocker shaft bracket with the marks on the intake and exhaust side rocker shafts. The rocker shaft on the exhaust side should extend past the outer face of the number one rocker shaft bracket farther than on the intake side.
17 Place the rocker shaft springs in position between the rocker shaft brackets and rocker arms.
18 Make sure that the punch marks are still aligned properly and then install the rocker shaft bracket assembly on the cylinder head studs. Align the mark on the camshaft with the mark on the number one rocker shaft bracket.
19 While holding the rocker arm springs with an adjustable wrench to prevent damage to the springs, tighten the rocker shaft bracket nuts to the specified torque.
20 Adjust the valves as described in Chapter 1.
21 The rest of installation is the reverse of removal.

8 Timing cover seal — replacement

1 Disconnect the negative battery cable.
2 Drain the cooling system.
3 Remove the engine fan.
4 Disconnect the upper and lower radiator hoses.
5 Remove the radiator mounting bolts and carefully remove the radiator.
6 Remove the engine drivebelts.
7 Remove the crankshaft pulley bolt and remove the pulley assembly.
8 Pry out the timing cover seal with a large screwdriver.
9 Use a large piece of pipe (or GM tool No. J26587) to install the new seal.
10 Align the groove in the crankshaft pulley with the crankshaft key and install the pulley assembly. Install the washer and crankshaft pulley bolt and tighten the bolt to the specified torque.
11 The rest of installation is the reverse of removal.

9 Timing cover and chain — removal and installation

Note: Before beginning, see warning below.
1 Remove the engine as described in Part D of this Chapter.
2 Remove the cam cover as described in Section 7.
3 Remove the bolt from the EGR pipe clamp at the rear of the cylinder head.
4 Raise the vehicle and support it securely on jackstands.
5 Disconnect the exhaust pipe at the exhaust manifold.
6 Lower the vehicle.
7 Drain the cooling system, including the engine block.
8 Disconnect the heater hoses at the intake manifold and at the front

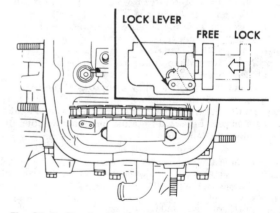

Fig. 2A.8 Tension is released on the timing chain by pivoting the lock lever (Sec 9)

of the cylinder head.
9 Remove the engine drivebelts.
10 Remove the air conditioning compressor and power steering pump and brackets, if equipped. Warning: Do not disconnect or in any way damage the refrigerant lines. If necessary have the system depressurized by a professional.
11 Disconnect the accelerator linkage and fuel line at the carburetor.
12 Disconnect all electrical wires, spark plug wires and vacuum lines from the cylinder head.
13 Remove the distributor (refer to Chapter 5).
14 Lock the automatic adjuster shoe in the fully retracted position by depressing the adjuster lock lever with a screwdriver as shown in Fig. 2A.8 and Fig. 2A.9.

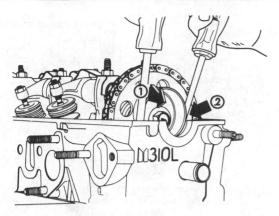

Fig. 2A.9 Two screwdrivers work well when unlocking the timing chain tensioner (Sec 9)

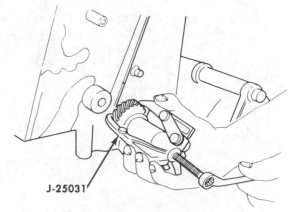

Fig. 2A.10 If the crankshaft timing sprocket must be replaced, a puller will be needed (Sec 9)

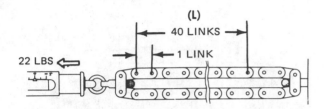

Fig. 2A.11 A section of the timing chain can be measured to check for chain wear (Sec 9)

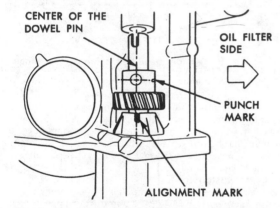

Fig. 2A.13 When installing the timing cover, the marks on the oil pump pinion gear must be as shown (Sec 9)

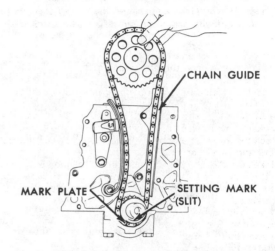

Fig. 2A.12 With the camshaft timing sprocket mark at top dead center, the crankshaft sprocket and chain timing marks should be positioned as shown (Sec 9)

25 Check the timing chain for wear by stretching it with an approximate pull of 22 pounds as shown in the accompanying illustration. Measure the length of 40 links on one side of the chain and compare the measurement to the Specifications. Replace the chain if the links exceed the specified length or if the chain shows signs of excessive wear.

26 Remove the mounting bolt from the timing chain tensioner and remove the tensioner. Make sure that the shoe becomes locked when the show is pushed in with the lock lever released.

27 Make sure that the lock releases when the shoe is pushed in. Replace the tensioner assembly if it does not operate properly or if the rack teeth show excessive wear.

28 Inspect the tensioner pin in the engine block for wear and damage. If replacement is necessary, the pin can be removed with locking pliers.

29 If a new tensioner pin is being installed, lubricate it with clean engine oil before installation. Start the pin into the block and place the chain tensioner over the pin. Place the e-clip on the pin and carefully tap the pin into the block until the clip just clears the tensioner.

30 Inspect the tensioner guide for wear and damage. Make sure that the lower oil jet is not clogged. If necessary, remove the mounting bolts and clean or replace the guides as needed.

31 If the crankshaft timing sprocket is being replaced, install the sprocket and pinion gear (groove side toward the front) on the crankshaft and align the key grooves with the crankshaft key. Drive the sprocket into position using a large section of pipe.

32 Turn the crankshaft so that the key is toward the cylinder head.

33 Reinstall the head (Section 11).

34 Install the timing chain by aligning the chain mark plate with the crankshaft sprocket as shown in the accompanying illustration. Next, install the camshaft sprocket with the timing mark at the top as shown.

15 Remove the timing sprocket to camshaft bolt and remove the sprocket and the fuel pump drive cam. Keep the sprocket on the chain damper and tensioner. Do not remove the sprocket from the chain at this time.

16 Remove the oil pan (Section 3).

17 Remove the retaining bolt from the oil pickup tube and unthread the pickup tube from the oil pump.

18 Remove the crankshaft pulley (Section 8).

19 Remove the timing cover mounting bolts and separate the timing cover from the engine.

20 Remove the cylinder head mounting bolts in a criss-cross sequence, starting with the outer bolts.

21 Remove the cylinder head, intake manifold and exhaust manifold as an assembly.

22 Scrape away all traces of gasket material from the timing cover and engine block sealing surfaces.

23 Inspect the timing cover for cracks, leakage and deterioration. If necessary, the seal can be pried out and a new seal installed.

24 Check the timing sprockets for wear and damage. If the crankshaft sprocket must be replaced, a puller such as GM tool No. J-25031 will be needed.

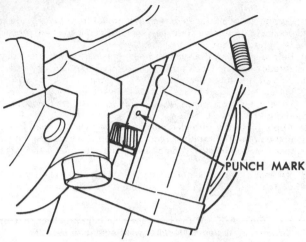

Fig. 2A.14   By sighting between the rear of the timing cover and the engine block, correct alignment of the oil pump pinion gear can be checked (Sec 9)

35   Install the timing chain tensioner. Release the lock by depressing the tensioner shoe by hand and then make sure that the chain is properly tensioned.
36   Use a new gasket when installing the timing cover.
37   Align the punch mark on the oil pump drive gear with the oil filter side of the cover. Next, align the center of the dowel pin with the alignment mark on the oil pump case as shown in the accompanying illustration.
38   Install the timing cover by engaging the pinion gear with the oil pump drive gear in the crankshaft.
39   Make sure that the punch mark on the oil pump drive gear can be viewed through the clearance area between the front cover and the engine block as shown in the accompanying illustration.
40   Check to be sure that the slot at the end of the oil pump shaft is parallel to the face of the engine block and offset forward as shown in the accompanying illustration.
41   Install the timing cover bolts and tighten them to the specified torque.
42   The rest of the installation procedure is the reverse of removal. Check the ignition timing after the installation is complete.

10   Camshaft — removal and installation

Note: *The engine must be removed from vehicle before the camshaft can be removed.*

1   Remove the camshaft cover as described in Section 7.
2   Remove the number 4 spark plug.
3   Place your finger over the spark plug hole while turning the crankshaft wrench on the pulley bolt at the front of the engine.
4   When you feel compression, continue turning the crankshaft slowly until the timing mark on the crankshaft pulley is aligned with the 0 of the engine timing indicator on the front cover.
5   Remove the distributor as described in Chapter 5. Do not rotate the crankshaft again until the distributor has been reinstalled.
6   Remove the fuel pump mounting bolts and remove the fuel pump.
7   Remove the timing cover and chain as described in Section 9.
8   Remove the rocker arm, shaft and bracket assembly as described in Section 7.
9   Remove the camshaft.
10   Refer to Part D of this Chapter for camshaft inspection procedures.
11   Apply liberal amounts of clean engine oil to the camshaft and cylinder head journals before installation.
12   Install the camshaft.
13   Install the rocker arm, shaft and bracket assembly as described in Section 7.
14   Make sure that the mark on the number one rocker shaft bracket aligns with the mark on the camshaft and that the timing mark on the crankshaft pulley aligns with the top dead center mark on the front cover.

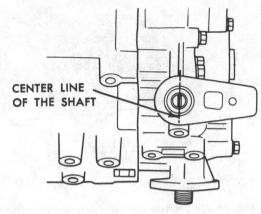

Fig. 2A.15   The centerline of the oil pump shaft should be parallel to the front face of the engine block (Sec 9)

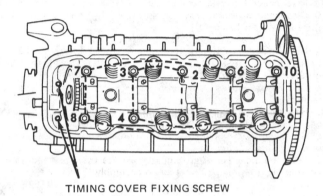

Fig. 2A.16   Cylinder head bolt tightening sequence (1.9 liter engine) (Sec 11)

15   While keeping the chain and sprocket together, attach the timing sprocket to the camshaft by aligning it with the pin on the camshaft.
16   Install the fuel pump drive cam, washer and sprocket bolt.
17   Remove the half-moon seal at the front of the cylinder head and tighten the sprocket bolt to the specified torque. Replace the half-moon seal in the cylinder head.
18   Install the distributor.
19   Release the lock on the timing chain tensioner by depressing the shoe with a screwdriver. Make sure that the timing chain is at the proper tension.
20   Check to be sure that the rotor and mark on the distributor housing line up when the number four cylinder is in the firing position.
21   Install the distributor cap. Install the camshaft cover, referring to Section 7 if necessary.

11   Cylinder head — removal and installation

Note: *The engine must be removed from vehicle before the cylinder head can be removed. Before beginning, see warning below.*

1   Remove the camshaft cover, referring to Section 7 if necessary.
2   Remove the bolt from the EGR pipe clamp at the rear of the cylinder head.
3   Raise the vehicle and support it securely on jackstands.
4   Disconnect the exhaust pipe at the exhaust manifold.
5   Lower the vehicle.
6   Drain the cooling system, including the engine block.
7   Disconnect the heater hoses at the intake manifold and at the front of the cylinder head.
8   Remove the air-conditioning compressor and power steering pump and brackets, if equipped. **Warning:** *Do not disconnect or in any way damage the refrigerant lines. If necessary, have the system depres-*

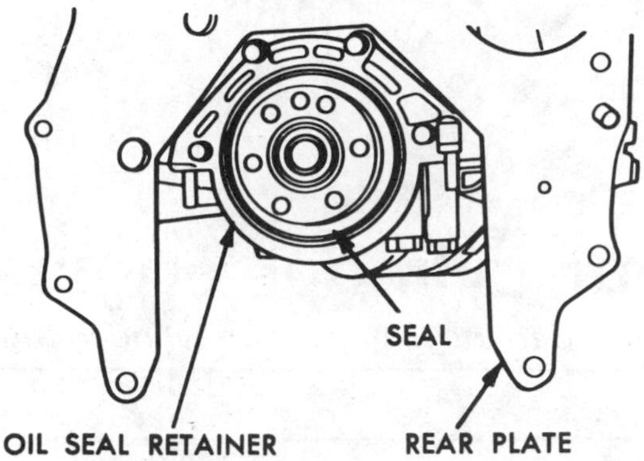

OIL SEAL RETAINER   **SEAL**   **REAR PLATE**

Fig. 2A.17 The rear main seal can be pried out and replaced without removing the seal retainer (Sec 12)

surized by a professional.

9   Disconnect the accelerator linkage and fuel line at the carburetor.

10 Disconnect all electrical wirers, spark plug wires and vacuum lines from the cylinder head.

11 Remove the distributor (refer to Chapter 5).

12 Remove the fuel pump mounting bolts and remove the fuel pump.

13 Remove the timing chain and cam sprocket as described in Section 9.

14 Disconnect the AIR hose and check valve at the air injection manifold.

15 Remove the upper timing cover bolts which thread into the cylinder head.

16 Remove the cylinder head mounting bolts in a criss-cross sequence, starting with the outer bolts.

17 With the aid of an assistant, remove the cylinder head, intake manifold and exhaust manifold as an assembly.

18 Scrape away all traces of gasket material from the cylinder head and engine block mating surfaces. Cylinder head inspection procedures can be found in Part D of this Chapter.

19 Before installing the cylinder head, make sure that the mounting bolt threads, engine block threads and both gasket surfaces are clean and free of any foreign matter.

20 Install a new gasket over the dowel pin ('top' side up).

21 With the aid of an assistant, carefully install the cylinder head assembly.

22 Apply oil to the threaded portion of the cylinder head bolts and install the bolts. Tighten the cylinder head bolts a little at a time in the sequence shown in the accompanying illustration until the specified torque is reached.

23 The rest of the installation procedure is the reverse of removal. Refer to Section 9 for timing chain installation procedures.

12   Rear main oil seal — replacement (engine in vehicle)

1   Remove the starter motor mounting bolts and separate the starter motor from the engine. Lay the starter motor to one side or wire the motor to a frame member.

2   Remove the transmission as described in Chapter 7.

3   On models with a manual transmission, remove the clutch cover and pressure plate assembly (Chapter 8).

4   Remove the flywheel and flywheel cover on models with an automatic transmission.

5   Carefully pry the old seal out of the retainer.

6   Before installing the replacement seal, fill the groove between the seal lips with grease. Also, lubricate the seal lips with clean engine oil.

7   Position the seal in the retainer and drive it into place using a section of large pipe.

8   The rest of the installation procedure is the reverse of removal. Tighten the flywheel or clutch cover bolts to the specified torque.

2A

Chapter 2 Part B   2.0L four-cylinder engine

Refer to Chapter 13 for specifications and information related to the 2.5 liter four-cylinder engine

Contents

Specifications

Torque specifications

	Ft-lbs	M-kg
Oil pan bolts	6	0.8
Oil pan drain plug	25	3.4
Oil screen support bolt	37	5.1
Oil pump-to-block bolts	22	3.0
Oil pump cover bolts	10	1.4
Crank pulley hub bolts	160	21.2
Flywheel/driveplate-to-crankshaft bolts	44	6.0
Intake manifold-to-cylinder head bolts	29	4.0
Exhaust manifold-to-cylinder head bolts	44	6.0
Fuel pump-to-block bolts	18	2.5
Distributor hold-down bolt	22	3.0
EGR valve-to-manifold bolts	10	1.4
Water outlet housing bolts	20	2.7
Thermostat housing bolts	20	2.7
Water pump bracket-to-block bolts	25	3.4
Timing cover-to-block bolts	see Fig. 2B.8	
Fan and pulley-to-water pump bolts	18	2.4
Cylinder head bolts	85	11.5
Rocker arm nuts	10	1.3
Rocker arm cover bolts	3	0.4
Camshaft thrust plate-to-block bolts	7	1.0
Engine mount nuts/bolts upper	41	5.6

1   General information

The L4 engine utilizes a cast iron crankshaft supported by five main bearings, with the number four bearing used as the thrust bearing. Hydraulic lifters and hollow push rods activate rocker arms which operate on stud-mounted pivots.

The Sections in this Part of Chapter 2 are devoted to 'in vehicle' repair procedures for the 2.0 liter four-cylinder engine. All information concerning engine block and cylinder head servicing can be found in Part D of this Chapter.

The repair procedures included in this Part are based on the assumption that the engine is still installed in the vehicle. Therefore, if this information is being used during a complete overhaul — with the engine already out of the vehicle and on a stand — many of the steps included here will not apply.

The Specifications included in this Part of Chapter 2 apply only to the engine and procedures found here. For Specifications regarding engines other than the 2.0 liter four cylinder, see Part A or C, whichever applies. Part D of Chapter 2 contains the Specifications necessary for engine block and cylinder head rebuilding.

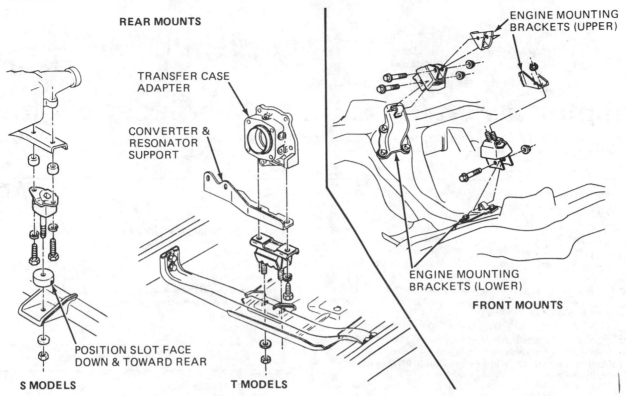

REAR MOUNTS

TRANSFER CASE
ADAPTER

CONVERTER &
RESONATOR
SUPPORT

POSITION SLOT FACE
DOWN & TOWARD REAR

S MODELS   T MODELS

ENGINE MOUNTING
BRACKETS (UPPER)

ENGINE MOUNTING
BRACKETS (LOWER)

FRONT MOUNTS

Fig. 2B.1   The front and rear engine mounts used on the 2.0 liter four-cylinder engine (Sec 2)

2B

2   Engine mounts — replacement with engine in vehicle

Front mounts

1   Disconnect the battery cables (negative first, then positive).
2   Remove the upper fan shroud.
3   Raise the vehicle.
4   On the left side engine mount, remove the nuts attaching the mount to the upper engine bracket. On the right side, remove the mount through bolt.
5   Position a jack and a block of wood beneath the oil pan and raise the front of the engine just enough to remove the mount-to-engine bolt.
Note: *Distributor or EGR component damage can result from raising the engine higher than necessary. Check for interference between the rear of the engine and the cowl panel while raising the engine.*
6   Remove the old engine mount and install the replacement.
7   Lower the engine into place and install the retaining bolt.
8   The rest of installation is the reverse of removal. Tighten all nuts/bolts to the specified torque.

Rear mount

9   Remove the crossmember-to-mount bolts, then raise the transmission slightly with a jack.
10   Remove the mount-to-transmission bolts, followed by the mount.
11   Install the new mount, lower the transmission and align the crossmember-to mount bolts.
12   Tighten all bolts to the specified torque.

3   Oil pan — removal and installation

Two-wheel drive truck

1   Disconnect the negative battery cable.
2   Remove the engine as described in Chapter 2D.
3   Remove the oil pan mounting bolts and separate the oil pan from the engine.
4   Clean the oil pan and sealing surfaces. Inspect the gasket sealing surfaces for distortion. Repair with a wood block and hammer if necessary.

5   Before installing the oil pan apply a thin coat of RTV-type sealant to both ends of the new rear oil pan seal. Do not let the sealant extend beyond the tabs of the seal. Install the seal firmly into the rear main bearing cap.
6   Apply a uniform bead of RTV-type sealant (about 1/8-inch diameter) to the oil pan side rails. The bead should run between the bolt holes and to the the inside edge of each bolt hole. *Do not apply sealant to the rear oil pan seal mating surface.*
7   Apply a thin bead of RTV-type sealant to the timing cover mating surface on the oil pan. Make sure that the sealant meets the beads on the oil pan side rails.
8   Immediately attach the oil pan to the engine block, taking care not to smear the sealant.
9   Tighten the mounting bolts, working from the center of the pan out, to the specified torque.

4x4 truck

10   Disconnect the negative battery cable.
11   Remove the starter front brace bolt.
12   Remove the motor mount through bolts
13   Raise the vehicle, support it on jackstands, and remove the front splash shield.
14   Remove the brake and fuel line clip retaining bolts.
15   Remove the crossmember bolts, and rotating the crossmember around the lines drop it from beneath the truck.
16   Drain the oil pan
17   Remove the starter bolts.
18   Disconnect the steering damper at the frame.
19   Scribe the idler arm location, then disconnect the idler arm and steering gear from the frame.
20   Disconnect the front axle at the frame.
21   Disconnect the front driveshaft at the front differential.
22   Slide the differential forward.
23   Remove the oil pan bolts and raise the engine just enough to remove the pan.
24   Before installation clean the oil pan sealing surfaces.
25   Apply a thin coat of RTV-type sealant to both ends of the new rear oil pan seal. Do not let the sealant extend beyond the tabs of the seal. Install the seal firmly into the rear main bearing cap.
26   Apply a uniform bead of RTV-type sealant (about 1/8 inch diameter)

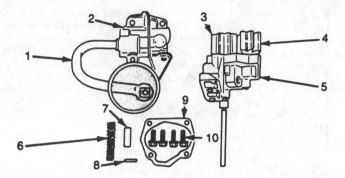

Fig. 2B.2   Exploded view of the oil pump (Sec 4)

1 Pick up tube and screen	6 Pressure regulator spring
2 Pump cover	7 Pressure regulator valve
3 Drive gear and shaft	8 Retaining pin
4 Idler gear	9 Gasket
5 Pump body	10 Attaching bolts

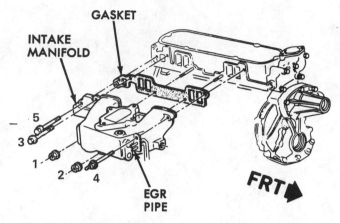

Fig. 2B.3   Intake manifold for the 2.0 liter four-cylinder engine (Sec 5)

to the oil pan side rails. The bead should run between the bolt holes and to the inside edge of each bolt hole. *Do not apply sealant to the rear oil pan seal mating surface.*

27 Apply a thin bead of RTV-type sealant to the timing cover mating surface on the oil pan. Make sure that the sealant meets the beads on the oil pan side rails.

28 Immediately attach the oil pan to the engine block, taking care not to smear the sealant.

29 Tighten the mounting bolts working from the center of the pan out, to the specified torque.

30 Reverse the removal procedures for the remainder of the installation.

4   Oil pump — removal, inspection and installation

1   Remove the oil pan (refer to Section 3).

2   Remove the oil pump mounting bolt.

3   Remove the pump and extension shaft.

4   To disassemble the pump for inspection, first remove the cover attaching bolts and the cover. Mark the gear teeth so that the gears can be reassembled with the same teeth indexing.

5   Remove the idler gear, drive gear and shaft from the pump body.

6   Remove the pressure regulator valve retaining pin.

7   Remove the pressure regulator spring and valve.

8   If the pickup screen and pipe assembly need replacing, it is possible to remove the pipe and press the replacement in (with sealant). However, it is recommended that anyone without experience in this operation consult a GM dealer before proceeding.

9   Clean all parts with solvent. Allow to air dry or, if available, use compressed air.

10 Inspect the pump body and cover for cracks and signs of excessive wear.

11 Inspect the pump gears for damage or excessive wear.

12 If the pump gears or body are damaged and worn, the entire oil pump assembly will have to be replaced. The pump gears and body are not available separately.

13 Inspect the drive gear shaft and the pressure regulator valve for any looseness where they fit into the oil pump body.

14 Finally, before reassembling the oil pump, check to make sure that the oil pump shaft retainer is not split. Replace it if necessary.

15 Install the pressure regulator valve, spring and retaining pin.

16 Install the drive gear and shaft in the oil pump body.

17 Install the idler gear in the pump body. Use the alignment marks to position the gears as they were before disassembly.

18 Install a new cover gasket.

19 Install the pump cover and tube brace and tighten the bolts to the specified torque.

20 Turn the pump drive shaft by hand to make sure the components are meshing smoothly.

21 Attach the pump and extension shaft with retainer to the rear main bearing cap. While aligning the pump with the two dowel pins at the bottom of the main bearing cap, align the top end of the hexagon ex-

tension shaft with the hexagon lower end of the distributor drive gear.

22 Install the pump mounting bolt and tighten it to the specified torque.

23 Install the oil pan (refer to Section 3).

5   Intake manifold — removal and installation

1   Disconnect the negative battery cable.

2   Remove the air cleaner assembly, tagging each hose to be disconnected with a piece of numbered tape to simplify reinstallation.

3   Remove the distributor cap.

4   Raise the vehicle and support it securely on jackstands.

5   Remove the middle right hand bellhousing bolt from the engine block. Move the wiring harness out of the way.

6   Remove the distributor hold down nut and clamp.

7   Disconnect the vacuum hose and primary wires at the coil.

8   Remove the fuel pump mounting bolts. It is not necessary to disconnect the fuel line: the fuel pump can hang in place.

9   Lower the vehicle.

10 Disconnect the fuel delivery line, accelerator cable and necessary wires and vacuum hoses.

11 Remove the carburetor.

12 Drain the cooling system.

13 Disconnect the fuel vapor harness pipes from the cylinder head.

14 Remove the vacuum pipe bolt from the rear of the cylinder head and disconnect the adjacent vacuum hoses.

15 Disconnect the heater hose and bypass hose from the intake manifold.

16 Disconnect the remaining hoses and wires from the intake manifold.

17 Remove the retaining nuts and bolts from the intake manifold.

18 Remove the intake manifold and gasket. Scrape away all traces of gasket material from the intake manifold mating surfaces.

19 Installation is the reverse of removal. Be sure to use a new gasket. Tighten the retaining nuts/bolts to the specified torque, working in a criss-cross fashion from the center out.

6   Exhaust manifold — removal and installation

1   Disconnect the negative battery cable.

2   Remove the air cleaner assembly.

3   Raise the vehicle and support it securely on jackstands.

4   Remove the exhaust pipe mounting bolts from the manifold and disconnect the exhaust pipe from the manifold.

5   Remove the AIR hose, AIR pipe bracket bolt and dipstick tube bracket.

6   Remove the fuel vapor harness pipes from the left and right side of the engine.

7   Remove the exhaust manifold mounting bolts and remove the exhaust manifold.

8   If a replacement exhaust manifold is going to be installed, remove

NOTE: AT TIME OF INSTALLATION, FLANGES MUST BE FREE OF OIL. A 2.0-3.0 BEAD OF SEALANT MUST BE APPLIED TO FLANGES AND SEALANT MUST BE WET TO TOUCH WHEN BOLTS ARE TORQUED.

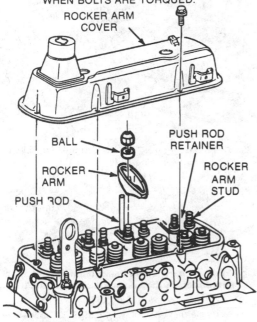

ROCKER ARM COVER

BALL

PUSH ROD RETAINER

ROCKER ARM

ROCKER ARM STUD

PUSH ROD

Fig. 2B.4   Exploded view of the rocker arm cover and rocker arm components (Sec 7)

the AIR injection manifold and exhaust manifold seal.

9   Scrape away all traces of gasket material from the exhaust manifold mating surfaces.

10 Clean all manifold-related threads before installation. A wire brush can be used on the manifold mounting bolts while a tap works well when cleaning the cylinder head bolt holes.

11 Installation is the reverse of removal. Tighten all bolts to the specified torque.

7   Rocker arm cover — removal and installation

1   Remove the air cleaner assembly, tagging each hose to be disconnected with a piece of numbered tape to simplify installation.

2   Disconnect the throttle cable from the carburetor, making careful note of the exact locations of the cable components and hardware to ensure correct reinstallation.

3   Disconnect the fuel vapor hoses from the harness pipes on both sides of the engine. Remove the retaining bolts from the harness pipes and remove the harness pipes.

4   Remove the rocker arm cover bolts.

5   Remove the rocker arm cover. **Note:** *If the cover sticks to the cylinder head, use a block of wood and a hammer to dislodge it. If the cover still will not come loose, pry on it carefully, but do not distort the sealing flange surface.*

6   Prior to installation of the cover, clean all dirt, oil and old gasket material from the sealing surfaces of the cover and cylinder head with a scraper and degreaser.

7   Apply a continuous 1/8-inch (5 mm) diameter bead of RTV-type sealant to the sealing flange of the cover. Be sure to apply the sealant *inboard* of the bolt holes.

8   Place the rocker arm cover on the cylinder head while the sealant is still wet and install the mounting bolts. Tighten the bolts a little at a time to the specified torque.

9   Complete the installation by reversing the removal procedure.

8   Valve train components — replacement (cylinder head installed)

1   Remove the rocker arm cover as described in Section 7.

2   If only the pushrod is to be replaced, loosen the rocker nut enough to allow the rocker arm to be rotated away from the pushrod. Pull the pushrod out of the hole in the cylinder head. If the rocker arm is to be removed, remove the rocker nut and pivot and lift off the rocker arm.

3   If the valve spring is to be removed, remove the spark plug from the affected cylinder.

4   There are two methods that will allow the valve to remain in place while the valve spring is removed. If you have access to compressed air, install an air hose adapter (GM part number J-23590) in the spark plug hole. When air pressure is applied to the adapter, the valves will be held in place by the pressure.

5   If you do not have access to compressed air, bring the piston of the affected cylinder to just before top dead center (TDC) on the compression stroke. Feed a long piece of 1/4-inch nylon cord in through the spark plug hole until it fills the combustion chamber. Be sure to leave the end of the cord hanging out of the spark plug hole so it can be removed easily. Rotate the crankshaft with a wrench (in the normal direction of rotation) until slight resistance is felt.

6   Install the rocker arm nut (without the rocker arm).

7   Insert the slotted end of a valve spring compressing tool under the bolt head and compress the spring just enough to remove the spring keepers, then release the pressure on the tool.

8   Remove the retainer, cup shield, O-ring seal, spring, spring damper (if so equipped) and valve stem oil seal (if so equipped).

9   Inspection procedures for valve train components are covered in Section 10 and in Chapter 2, Part D.

10 Installation of the valve train components is the reverse of the removal procedure. *Always use new valve stem oil seals whenever the spring keepers have been disturbed.* Prior to installing the rocker arms, coat the bearing surfaces of the arms and rocker arm pivots with moly-based grease or engine assembly lube. Be sure to adjust the valve lash as detailed in Section 9.

2B

9   Valve lash — adjustment

1   Disconnect the cable from the negative battery terminal.

2   If the rocker arm cover is still on the engine, refer to Section 7 and remove it.

3   If the valve train components have been serviced just prior to this procedure, make sure that the components are completely reassembled.

4   Rotate the crankshaft until the number one piston is at top dead center (TDC) on the compression stroke. To make sure that you do not mix up the TDC positions of the number one and four pistons, check the position of the rotor in the distributor to see which terminal it is pointing at. Another method is to place your fingers on the number one rocker arms as the timing marks line up at the crankshaft pulley. If the rocker arms are not moving, the number one piston is at TDC. If they move as the timing marks line up, the number four piston is at TDC.

5   Back off the rocker arm nut until play is felt at the pushrod, then turn it back in just until all play is removed. This can be determined by rotating the pushrod while tightening the nut. Just when drag is felt at the pushrod, all lash has been removed. Now turn the nut in an additional 1-1/2 turns.

6   Adjust the number one and two cylinder intake valves and the number one and three cylinder exhaust valves with the crankshaft in this position, using the method just described.

7   Rotate the crankshaft until the number four piston is at TDC on the compression stroke and adjust the number three and four cylinder intake valves and the number two and four cylinder exhaust valves.

8   Refer to Section 7 and install the rocker arm covers.

10   Cylinder head — removal and installation

Removal

1   Remove the intake manifold as described in Section 5.

2   Remove the exhaust manifold as described in Section 6.

3   Remove the bolts that secure the alternator bracket to the cylinder head.

4   If so equipped, unbolt the air-conditioner compressor and swing it out of the way for clearance. **Caution:** *Do not disconnect any of the air-conditioning lines unless the system has been depressurized by a dealer or repair shop, because personal injury may occur.* Disconnection of the lines should not be necessary in this case.

5   Disconnect all electrical and vacuum lines from the cylinder head. Be sure to label the lines to simplify reinstallation.

6   Remove the upper radiator hose.

7   Remove the heater hoses.

8   Disconnect the spark plug wires and remove the spark plugs. Be sure to label the plug wires to simplify reinstallation.

9   Remove the distributor as described in Chapter 5.

10   Remove the rocker arm cover. To break the gasket seal it may be necessary to strike the cover with your hand or a rubber hammer. Do not pry between the sealing surfaces. Refer to Section 7 if necessary.

11   When disassembling the valve mechanisms, keep all of the components separate so they can be reinstalled in their original positions. A cardboard box or rack, numbered to correspond to the engine cylinders, can be used for this purpose.

12   Remove each of the rocker arm nuts and separate the rocker arms and pivots from the cylinder head.

13   Remove the pushrods.

14   Remove the upper fan shroud.

15   Remove the four mounting bolts from the fan and remove the fan.

16   Remove the air diverter valve from its mounting bracket.

17   Remove the air pump mounting bolts and remove the pump. Remove the upper air pump bracket.

18   Disconnect and plug the fuel line at the fuel pump.

19   Loosen each of the cylinder head mounting bolts one turn at a time until they can be removed. Note the length and position of each bolt to ensure correct reinstallation.

20   Lift the head off of the engine. If it is stuck to the engine block, do not attempt to pry it free, as you could damage the sealing surfaces. Instead, use a hammer and block of wood to tap the head and break the gasket seal. Place the head on a block of wood to prevent damage to the gasket surface.

21   Remove the cylinder head gasket.

22   Refer to Chapter 2D for cylinder head disassembly and valve service procedures.

Installation

23   If a new cylinder head is being installed, transfer all external parts from the old cylinder head to the new one.

24   If not already done, thoroughly clean the gasket surfaces on the cylinder head and the engine block. Do not gouge or otherwise damage the gasket surfaces.

25   To get the proper torque readings, the threads of the head bolts must be clean. This also applies to the threaded holes in the engine block. Run a tap through the holes to ensure that they are clean.

26   Place the gasket in position over the engine block dowel pins.

27   Carefully lower the cylinder head onto the engine, over the dowel pins and the gasket.

28   Coat the threads of each cylinder head bolt and the point at which the head and the bolt meet with a sealing compound and install the bolts finger tight. Do not tighten any of the bolts at this time.

29   Tighten each of the bolts a little at a time in the sequence shown in the accompanying illustration. Continue tightening in this sequence until the proper torque reading is obtained. As a final check, work around the head in a front-to-rear sequence to make sure none of the bolts have been left out of the sequence.

30   The remaining installation steps are the reverse of removal.

---

11   Hydraulic lifters — removal, inspection and installation

1   A noisy valve lifter can be isolated when the engine is idling. Place a length of hose or tubing near the position of each valve while listening at the other end of the tube. Another method is to remove the rocker arm cover and, with the engine idling, place a finger on each of the valve spring retainers, one at a time. If a valve lifter is defective, it will be evident from the shock felt at the retainer as the valve seats.

2   The most likely cause of a noisy valve lifter is a piece of dirt trapped between the plunger and the lifter body.

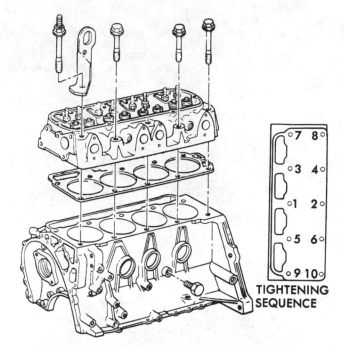

Fig. 2B.5   The cylinder head mounting bolts must be *tightened* **in the sequence shown (Sec 10)**

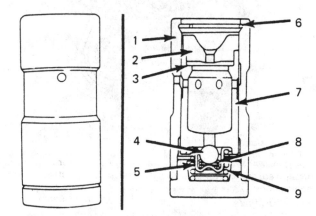

Fig. 2B.6   Cut-away view of hydraulic lifter (Sec 11)

1 *Lifter body*	6 *Push rod seat retainer*
2 *Push rod seat*	7 *Plunger*
3 *Metering valve*	8 *Check ball spring*
4 *Check ball*	9 *Plunger spring*
5 *Check ball retainer*	

3   Remove the rocker arm cover as described in Section 7.

4   Loosen the rocker arm nut and rotate the rocker arm away from the pushrod.

5   Remove the pushrod.

6   To remove the lifter, a special hydraulic lifter removal tool must be used.

7   The lifters should be kept separate for reinstallation in their original positions.

8   To dismantle a valve lifter, hold the plunger down with a pushrod and then extract the retainer spring with a small screwdriver.

9   Remove the pushrod seat and the metering valve.

10   Remove the plunger, ball check valve and plunger spring. Remove the ball check valve and spring by prying them out with a small screwdriver.

11   Clean the lifter components with solvent and dry them with compressed air. Examine the internal components for wear and check the ball carefully for flat spots. **Note:** *Refer to Chapter 2, Part D, for additional lifter (and camshaft) inspection procedures.*

12   If the lifters are worn, they must be replaced with new ones and

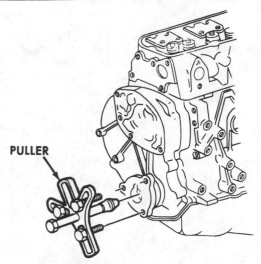

Fig. 2B.7 A special puller is needed to remove the crankshaft pulley hub (Sec 12)

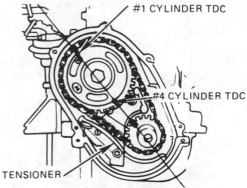

Fig. 2B.9 The timing marks on the crankshaft and camshaft sprockets must line up as shown before removing the timing chain and sprockets (Sec 14)

the camshaft must be replaced as well (see Chapter 2, Part D). If the lifters were contaminated with dirt, they can be reinstalled — they *may* operate normally.

13 Reassembly should be done in the following manner:

 a) Place the ball check valve on the small hole in the bottom of the plunger.

 b) Insert the ball check spring into the seat in the valve retainer and place the retainer over the ball so that the spring rests on the ball. Using a small screwdriver, carefully press the retainer into position in the plunger.

 c) Place the plunger spring over the ball retainer, invert the lifter body and slide it over the spring and plunger. Make sure the oil holes in the body and plunger line up.

 d) Fill the assembly with 10-weight oil. Place the metering valve and pushrod seat in position, press down on the seat and install the retainer spring.

14 When installing the lifters, make sure they are replaced in their original bores and coat them with moly-based grease or engine assembly lube.

15 The remaining installation steps are the reverse of removal.

---

12 Crankshaft pulley, hub and front oil seal — removal and installation

1 Remove the cable from the negative battery terminal.

2 Loosen the accessory drivebelt tension adjusting bolts, as necessary, and remove the drivebelts. Tag each belt as it is removed to simplify reinstallation.

3 With the parking brake applied and the shifter in Park (automatic) or in gear (manual) to prevent the engine from turning over, remove the crank pulley bolts. A breaker bar will probably be necessary, since

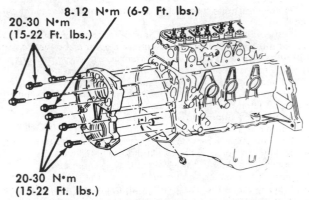

Fig. 2B.8 Location of the timing cover mounting bolts — note the bolts which must be removed from the bottom flange (Sec 13)

the bolts are very tight.

4 Mark the position of the pulley in relation to the hub. Remove the bolts and separate the pulley from the hub.

5 Remove the hub center bolt, then, using a puller, remove the hub from the crankshaft.

6 Carefully pry the oil seal out of the front cover with a large screwdriver. Be careful not to distort the cover.

7 Install the new seal with the helical lip toward the *rear* of the engine. Drive the seal into place using a seal installation tool or a large socket. If there is enough room, a block of wood and hammer can also be used.

8 Apply a thin layer of clean multi-purpose grease to the seal contact surface of the hub.

9 Position the pulley hub on the crankshaft and slide it through the seal until it bottoms against the crankshaft gear. Note that the slot in the hub must be aligned with the Woodruff key in the end of the crankshaft. The hub-to-crankshaft bolt can be used to press the hub into position.

10 Install the crank pulley on the hub, noting the alignment marks made during removal. The pulley-to-hub bolts should be coated with Drylock 299, or equivalent, whenever they are removed and installed.

11 Tighten the hub-to-crankshaft and pulley-to-hub bolts to the specified torque.

12 The remaining installation steps are the reverse of removal. Tighten the drivebelts to the proper tension (refer to Chapter 1).

---

13 Timing gear cover — removal and installation

1 Remove the crankshaft pulley and hub as described in Section 12.

2 Remove the water pump.

3 Remove the oil pan-to-timing gear cover bolts.

4 Using a scraper and degreaser, remove all dirt and old gasket material from the sealing surfaces of the timing gear cover, engine block and oil pan.

5 Replace the front oil seal by carefully prying it out of the timing gear cover with a large screwdriver. Do not distort the cover.

6 Install the new seal with the helical lip towards the *inside* of the cover. Drive the seal into place using a seal installation tool or a large socket and hammer. A block of wood will also work (photo).

7 Apply a thin (2 mm) bead of RTV sealant to the timing gear cover-to-engine block mating surface.

8 Apply a slightly thicker (3 mm) bead of RTV sealant to the oil pan mating surface of the timing gear cover.

9 Insert the crankshaft hub through the cover seal and place the cover in position on the block, sliding the hub onto the nose of the crankshaft.

10 Install the oil pan-to-cover bolts and partially tighten them.

11 Install the bolts that secure the cover to the block, then tighten all of the mounting bolts, including the pan bolts, to the specified torque.

12 Complete the installation by reversing the removal procedure.

---

14 Timing chain and sprockets — inspection, removal and installation

1 Remove the timing chain cover (refer to Section 13).

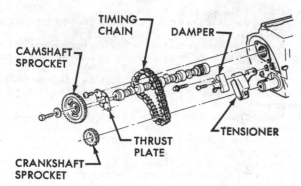

Fig. 2B.10   Timing chain components (exploded view)
(Sec 14)

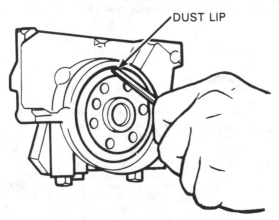

Fig. 2B.12   The rear main oil seal can be carefully pried out
of the block (models equipped with thick seals only)
(Sec 16)

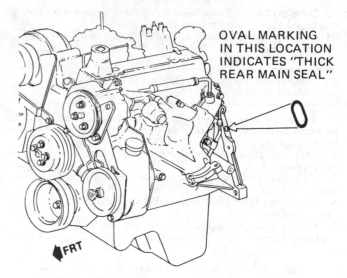

Fig. 2B.11   This mark indicates a rear main seal which can
be serviced without dropping the oil pan (Sec 16)

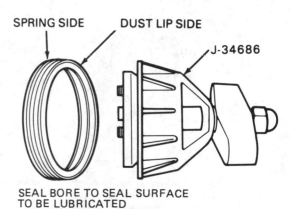

SEAL BORE TO SEAL SURFACE
TO BE LUBRICATED
WITH ENGINE OIL BEFORE
ASSEMBLY

Fig. 2B.12   A special tool is needed to install the rear main
seal (Sec 16)

2   Align the marks on the camshaft and crankshaft sprockets. Do not attempt to remove any of the timing chain components until these marks are properly aligned.

3   Remove the chain tensioner and damper.

4   Remove the camshaft sprocket center bolt and lift off the cam sprocket and chain.

5   Inspect the camshaft and crankshaft sprockets, timing chain and chain tensioner for excessive or unusual wear. Failure to replace worn components can result in erratic engine performance, loss of power and decreased gas mileage. If any one component requires replacement all related components, including both sprockets and the chain, must be replaced.

6   A special puller is required to remove the crankshaft sprocket from the crankshaft should replacement of the timing chain assembly be required.

7   Replacement of the camshaft and crankshaft sprockets and timing chain is the reverse of removal. Make sure the timing marks on the camshaft and crankshaft sprockets line up and coat the thrust face of the camshaft sprocket with moly-base lubricant or assembly lube.

8   Before reinstalling the chain tensioner the spring loading unit must be 'cocked'. This is best accomplished with special tool J-33875. After compressing the spring a cotterkey or nail is inserted through the small hole in the tensioner provided for the purpose, holding the spring compressed until the tensioner unit is installed. After bolting the tensioner in place remove the pin, releasing the spring.

9   Lubricate the chain with engine oil and reinstall the timing chain cover as previously outlined.

15   Camshaft — removal and installation

1   Remove the cable from the negative battery terminal.
2   Drain the coolant from the radiator (refer to Chapter 1).
3   Remove the radiator (refer to Chapter 3).

4   If equipped with air conditioning, remove the condenser (refer to Chapter 3). **Caution:** *The air conditioning system must be evacuated by an air-conditioning system technician before the condenser can be removed. Under no circumstances should this be attempted by the home mechanic, as personal injury may result.*

5   Remove the water pump.
6   Mark the distributor for proper alignment.
7   Remove the fuel pump.
8   Remove the distributor holddown nut and clamp.
9   Remove the distributor.
10   Remove the rocker arms and pushrods (refer to Section 7).
11   Remove the rocker arm studs and pushrod guide plates.
12   Remove the lifters (refer to Section 11).
13   Remove the timing cover and timing chain (refer to Sections 13 and 14).
14   Remove the camshaft thrust plate.
15   Carefully support the camshaft and slide it out of the block, being careful that none of the lobes nick or scratch the camshaft bearings.
16   Refer to Chapter 2, Part D for camshaft inspection procedures. Whenever a new camshaft is installed it is recommended that a complete new set of valve lifters be installed at the same time, along with new oil and a new oil filter.
17   Prior to reinstalling the camshaft coat each of the lobes and journals with engine assembly lube or moly-based grease.
18   Slide the camshaft into the engine block, again being extra careful not to damage the bearings.
19   Install the camshaft thrust plate and tighten the mounting bolts to the specified torque.

20 Complete the installation by reversing the removal procedure, referring to the appropriate Sections or Chapters.
21 Have the air conditioning system recharged (if so equipped).

16 Flywheel/driveplate and rear main bearing oil seal — removal and installation

1 If your engine is equiped with a 'thick' rear main seal (identified by a mark on the engine — see the accompanying illustration), the seal can be replaced without removing the oil pan or crankshaft.
2 Refer to Chapter 7. Follow all precautionary notes and remove the transmission.
3 If equipped with a manual transmission, remove the clutch pressure plate and disc.
4 Remove the flywheel/driveplate mounting bolts and separate it from the crankshaft.
5 Using a screwdriver or pry bar, carefully remove the oil seal from the block. It is very important here not to damage the crankshaft O.D.

surface while prying with the tool.
6 Check the I.D. of the seal bore for nicks or scratches and carefully file if necessary.
7 A special tool will be needed to install the replacement oil seal (GM no. J-34686). Slide the seal on the mandril until the dust lip bottoms squarely against the the collar of the tool.
8 Align the dowel pin of the tool with the dowel pin hole in the crankshaft and attach the tool to the crankshaft by hand-tightening the attaching bolts.
9 Turn the handle of the tool until the collar bottoms against the case, seating the seal.
10 Loosen the tool handle and remove the attaching bolts. Remove the special tool.
11 Check the seal and make sure that it is seated squarely in the bore.
12 Install the flywheel/driveplate and tighten the bolts to the specified torque.
13 If equipped with a manual transmission, install the clutch disc and pressure plate and tighten the pressure plate bolts to the specified torque.
14 Install the transmission as described in Chapter 7.

Chapter 2 Part C 2.8 liter V6 engine

Refer to Chapter 13 for specifications and information related to the 4.3 liter V6 engine

Contents

Specifications

Torque specifications

	Ft-lbs	M-kg
Camshaft sprocket bolts	18	2.5
Clutch cover-to-flywheel bolts	15	2.0
Rear camshaft cover bolts	7	1.0
Cylinder head bolts	68	9.4
Connecting rod cap nuts	37	5.1
Crankshaft pulley bolts	25	3.4
Crankshaft pulley hub bolt	75	10.3
Distributor hold-down bolt	25	3.4
Driveplate-to-torque converter bolts	27	3.7
EGR valve mounting bolts	15	2.0
Engine mounting bracket bolts	80	11.0
Engine strut bracket	35	4.8
Exhaust manifold mounting bolts	25	3.4
Flywheel mounting bolts	50	7.0
Front cover mounting bolts (small)	15	2.0
Front cover mounting bolts (large)	25	3.4
Fuel pump mounting bolts	15	2.0
Intake manifold mounting bolts/nuts	23	3.2
Main bearing cap bolts	70	9.6
Oil filter bolt	15	2.0
Oil filter connector bolt	29	3.9
Oil pan mounting bolts (small)	7	1.0
Oil pan mounting bolts (large)	18	2.5
Oil pump mounting bolt	30	4.1
Oil pump cover bolts	8	1.1
Oil pressure switch	5	0.7
Oil drain plug	18	2.5
Rear lifting bracket bolt	25	3.4
Rocker arm cover bolts	8	1.1
Rocker arm studs	45	6.2
Spark plugs	12	1.6
Starter motor mounting bolts	32	4.4
Strut bracket assembly nut and bolt	35	4.8
Timing chain tensioner bolts	15	2.0
Water outlet housing bolts	25	3.4
Water pump mounting bolts (small)	7	1.0
Water pump mounting bolts (medium)	15	2.0
Water pump mounting bolts (large)	25	3.4
Water pump pulley bolt	15	2.0

Note: *Refer to Chapter 2, Part D for additional specifications.*

1   General information

The 2.8 liter V6 engine uses a cast iron crankshaft supported by four main bearings (the number three bearing is the thrust bearing). Hydraulic lifters and hollow pushrods actuate rocker arms which operate on studmounted ball pivots.

The forward Sections in this Part of Chapter 2 are devoted to "in-vehicle" repair procedures for the 2.8 liter V6 engine. The latter Sections in this Part of Chapter 2 involve the removal and installation procedures for the 2.8 liter V6 engine. All information concerning engine block and cylinder head servicing can be found in Part D of this Chapter.

The repair procedures included in this Part are based on the assumption that the engine is still installed in the vehicle. Therefore, if this information is being used during a complete engine overhaul – with the engine already out of the vehicle and on a stand – many of the steps included here will not apply.

The Specifications included in this Part of Chapter 2 apply only to the engine and procedures found here. For Specifications regarding engines other than the 2.8 liter V6, see Part A or B, whichever applies. Part D of Chapter 2 contains the Specifications necessary for engine block and cylinder head rebuilding procedures.

2   Rocker arm covers — removal and installation

Right side

1   Disconnect the cable from the negative battery terminal.
2   Remove the air cleaner assembly, tagging each hose to be disconnected with a piece of numbered tape to simplify reinstallation.
3   Remove the bolts retaining the air management valve/coil bracket.
4   Disconnect the wires and hoses that would interfere with the removal of the rocker arm covers, tagging them as they are disconnected.
5   Disconnect the carburetor controls at the carburetor, then remove them from the support bracket.
6   Remove the rocker arm cover bolts.
7   Remove the rocker arm cover. **Note:** *If the cover sticks to the cylinder head, use a block of wood and a rubber hammer to dislodge it. If the cover still will not come loose, pry on it carefully, but do not distort the sealing flange surface.*
8   Before installing the cover, clean all dirt, oil and old gasket material from the sealing surfaces of the cover and cylinder head with a scraper and degreaser.
9   Apply a continuous 3/16-inch (5 mm) diameter bead of RTV-type sealant to the flange of the cover. Be sure to apply the sealant inboard of the bolt holes.
10   Place the rocker arm cover on the cylinder head while the sealant is still wet and install the mounting bolts. Tighten the bolts a little at a time to the specified torque.
11   Complete the installation by reversing the removal procedure.

Left side

12   Disconnect the cable from the negative battery terminal.
13   Disconnect the hoses at the PCV valve and label them.
14   Remove the air cleaner assembly, tagging each hose to be disconnected with a piece of numbered tape to simplify reinstallation.
15   Disconnect all other wires and hoses that would interfere with the removal of the rocker arm cover, tagging them as they are disconnected.
16   Remove the three way hose bracket from the front of the cover and set the assembly aside.
17   Remove the rocker arm cover bolts.
18   Disconnect the fuel line at the carburetor, plugging the fitting at the carburetor and the disconnected fuel line to prevent leakage and contamination.
19   Refer to Paragraphs 7 through 11 in this Section.

3   Valve train components — replacement (cylinder head installed)

1   Remove the rocker arm cover(s) as described in Section 2.
2   If only the pushrod is to be replaced, loosen the rocker nut enough to allow the rocker arm to be rotated away from the pushrod (photos).

Pull the pushrod out of the hole in the cylinder head.
3   If the rocker arm is to be removed, remove the rocker arm nut and pivot and lift off the rocker arm.
4   If the valve spring is to be removed, remove the spark plug from the affected cylinder.
5   There are two methods that will allow the valve to remain in place while the valve spring is removed. If you have access to compressed air, install an air hose adapter (GM part number J-23590) in the spark plug hole. When air pressure is applied to the adapter, the valves will be held in place by the pressure.
6   If you do not have access to compressed air, bring the piston of the affected cylinder almost to top dead center (TDC) on the compression stroke. Feed a long piece of 1/4-inch nylon cord in through the spark plug hole until it fills the combustion chamber. Be sure to leave the end of the cord hanging out of the spark plug hole so it can be removed easily. Rotate the crankshaft with a wrench (in the normal direction of rotation) until slight resistance is felt.
7   Reinstall the rocker arm nut (without the rocker arm).
8   Insert the slotted end of a valve spring compression tool under the nut and compress the spring just enough to remove the spring keepers, then release the pressure on the tool.
9   Remove the retainer, cup shield, O-ring seal, spring, spring damper (if so equipped) and valve stem oil seal (if so equipped).
10   The threaded rocker arm studs may be replaced by simply removing the damaged one and replacing it with a new one. Be sure to reinstall the pushrod guide (if so equipped) under the stud nut and tighten the nut to the specified torque.
11   Inspection procedures for the hydraulic lifters are detailed in Section 5. Procedures regarding other valve train components are detailed in Chapter 2, Part D.
12   Installation of the valve train components is the reverse of the removal procedure. Always use new valve stem oil seals whenever the spring keepers have been disturbed. Before installing the rocker arms, coat the bearing surfaces of the arms and pivots with moly-based grease or engine assembly lube. Be sure to adjust the valve lash as detailed in Section 6.

2C

4   Intake manifold — removal and installation

1   If the vehicle is equipped with air-conditioning, carefully examine the routing of the hoses and the mounting of the compressor. You may be able to remove the intake manifold without disconnecting the system. If you are in doubt, take the vehicle to a dealer or refrigeration

3.2   To remove the pushrod, simply loosen the rocker arm nuts

Fig. 2C.1   2.8 liter V6 engine front view

A   Vacuum break diaphagm
B   Thermal vacuum switch
C   Intake manifold
D   Coolant temperature sending unit
E   Fuel pump

Fig. 2C.2   2.8 liter V6 engine left side view

A   Water pump
B   Timing chain cover
C   PCV valve
D   Oil pressure sending unit
E   Vibration damper
F   Engine drivebelt pulley

Fig. 2C.3   2.8 liter V6 engine rear view

A   Deceleration valve
B   EGR valve
C   AIR pump output pipe

2C

Fig. 2C.4   2.8 liter V6 engine right side view

A   Ignition coil
B   AIR management valve
C   Soft plug

specialist to have the system depressurized. *Do not, under any circumstances, disconnect the hoses while the system is under pressure.*

2   Disconnect the cable from the negative battery terminal.

3   Drain the coolant from the radiator (Chapter 1).

4   Remove the air cleaner assembly, tagging each hose to be disconnected with a piece of numbered tape to simplify reinstallation.

5   Label and disconnect all electrical wires and vacuum hoses at the carburetor.

6   Disconnect the fuel line at the carburetor. Be prepared to catch some fuel, then plug the fuel line to prevent contamination.

7   Disconnect the throttle cable, making careful note of how it was installed.

8   Disconnect the spark plug wires at the spark plugs, referring to the removal technique described in Chapter 1.

9   Disconnect the wires at the coil, again using numbered pieces of tape to label them.

10 Remove the distributor cap and the attached spark plug wires (refer to Chapter 5).

11 Remove the distributor (refer to Chapter 5).

12 Remove the power brake fitting from the rear of the manifold (photo).

13 Remove the power brake tube mounting bracket from the manifold boss (photo).

14 Move the power brake tube/hose aside so it will not interfere with the removal of the manifold.

15 Remove the three way hose bracket from the front of the left rocker arm cover.

16 Remove the mounting bolts from the left rocker arm cover, then remove the cover.

17 Remove the AIR management valve/coil mounting bracket assembly bolts from the right cylinder head, disconnect the AIR management hose and remove the assembly.

18 Remove the bolts from the right rocker arm cover, then remove the cover.

19 Remove the upper radiator hose from the manifold.

20 Disconnect the heater hose at the manifold (photo).

4.12   The power brake tube fitting is located at the rear of the intake manifold

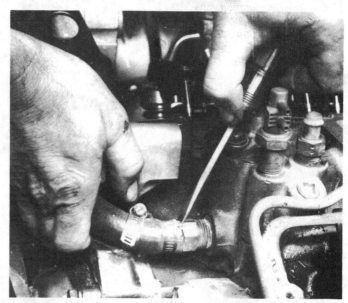

4.20   A screwdriver can be used to remove a stubborn heater hose from the intake manifold fitting

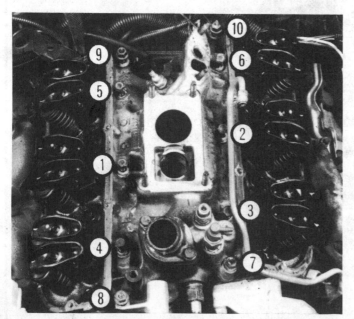

4.27   Recommended **tightening** sequence for the intake manifold bolts (V6)

5.7   A scribe can be used to remove the lifters

21 Disconnect the vacuum lines from the TVS switch at the front of the manifold.

22 Label and remove the remaining vacuum hoses from the rear of the manifold.

23 Loosen the air conditioning compressor pivot bolt and remove the adjusting bolt, if equipped. Remove the compressor drivebelt and rotate the compressor out of the way. **Caution:** *Do not, under any circumstances, disconnect the hoses while the system is under pressure.*

24 Remove the electrical connector from the coolant switch at the front of the manifold.

25 Make sure that all wires, vacuum hoses and coolant hoses that would interfere with manifold removal have been disconnected.

26 If the manifold is to be replaced with a new one, the external components remaining on the manifold must be removed for transfer to the new manifold. These components may be removed either before or after the manifold has been separated from the engine. These components include:

> The carburetor studs or bolts
> The coolant switch
> The EGR valve (use a new gasket when installing)
> The emissions system TVS valve

27 Loosen the manifold bolts in a sequence **opposite** to the one used for tightening them (photo). Remove the manifold bolts.

28 Separate the manifold from the engine. Do not pry between the mating surfaces because it could damage them. Tap the manifold with a hammer and wooden block to loosen it if necessary.

29 If a new manifold is being installed, transfer the external components from the old manifold to the new one.

30 Before installing the manifold, place clean, lint-free rags in the engine cavity and clean the engine block, cylinder head and manifold gasket surfaces. All gasket material and sealant must be removed prior to installation. Remove all dirt and gasket remnants from the engine cavity.

31 Clean the gasket sealing surfaces with degreaser, then apply a 3/16-inch (5 mm) diameter bead of RTV-type sealant to the engine block gasket surfaces only.

32 Install the new intake gaskets on the cylinder heads. Notice that the gaskets are marked *Right* and *Left.* Be sure to use the correct gasket on each cylinder head.

33 Hold the gaskets in place by extending the bead of RTV up about 1/4-inch onto the gasket ends. The new gaskets will have to be cut so they can be installed behind the pushrods.

34 Carefully lower the intake manifold into position, making sure that you do not disturb the gaskets.

35 Install the intake manifold mounting bolts/nuts and tighten them following the sequence illustrated. Tighten the bolts a little at a time until they are all at the specified torque.

36 Install the remaining components in the reverse order of removal.

37 Fill the radiator with coolant, start the engine and check for leaks. Adjust the ignition timing and idle speed as necessary (refer to Chapter 1).

5   Hydraulic lifters — removal, inspection and installation

1 A noisy hydraulic lifter can be isolated when the engine is idling. Place a length of hose or tubing near the position of each valve while listening at the other end of the tube. Another method is to remove the rocker arm cover and, with the engine idling, place a finger on each of the valve spring retainers, one at a time. If a valve lifter is defective, it will be evident from the shock felt at the retainer as the valve seats.

2 Assuming that adjustment is correct, the most likely cause of a noisy valve lifter is a piece of dirt trapped between the plunger and the lifter body.

3 Remove the rocker arm covers as described in Section 2.

4 Remove the intake manifold as described in Section 4.

5 Loosen the rocker arm nut and rotate the rocker arm away from the pushrod.

6 Remove the pushrod.

7 To remove the lifter, a special hydraulic lifter removal tool should be used, or a scribe can be positioned at the top of the lifter and used to force the lifter up (photo). *Do not use pliers or other tools on the outside of the lifter body, as they will damage the finished surface and*

render the lifter useless.

8 The lifters should be kept separate for reinstallation in their original positions.

9 To dismantle a valve lifter, hold the plunger down with a pushrod and then extract the retainer spring with a small screwdriver.

10 Remove the pushrod seat and the metering valve.

11 Remove the plunger, ball check valve and plunger spring. Remove the ball check valve and spring by prying them out with a small screwdriver.

12 Clean the lifter components with solvent and dry them with compressed air. Examine the internal components for wear and check the ball carefully for flat spots. Refer to Chapter 2, Part D, for additional lifter (and camshaft) inspection procedures.

13 If the lifters are worn, they must be replaced with new ones and the camshaft must be replaced as well (see Chapter 2, Part D). If the lifters were contaminated with dirt, they can be reinstalled — they *may* operate normally.

14 Reassembly should be done in the following manner:

a) Place the ball check valve on the small hole in the bottom of the plunger.

b) Insert the ball check valve spring into the seat in the retainer and place the retainer over the ball so that the spring rests on the ball. Using a small screwdriver, carefully press the retainer into position in the plunger.

c) Place the plunger spring over the ball retainer, invert the lifter body and slide it over the spring and plunger. Make sure the oil holes in the body and plunger line up.

d) Fill the assembly with 10-weight oil. Place the metering valve and pushrod seat in position, press down on the seat and install the retainer spring.

15 When installing the lifters, make sure they are replaced in their original bores and coat them with moly-based grease or engine assembly lube.

16 The remaining installation steps are the reverse of removal.

6   Valve lash — adjustment

1 Disconnect the cable from the negative battery terminal.

2 If the rocker arm covers are still on the engine, refer to Section 2 and remove them.

3 If the valve train components have been serviced just prior to this procedure, make sure that the components are completely reassembled.

4 Rotate the crankshaft until the number one piston is at top dead center (TDC) on the compression stroke. To make sure that you do not mix up the TDC positions of the number one and four pistons, check the position of the rotor in the distributor to see which terminal it is

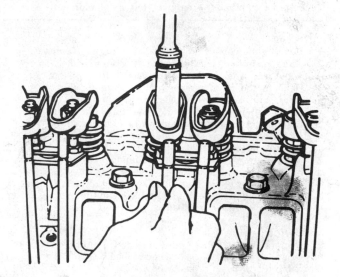

Fig. 2C.5   The valve lash must be adjusted whenever new rocker arms or pivots are installed (Sec 6)

2C

7.7   Locations of the top three exhaust manifold bolts (right side shown)

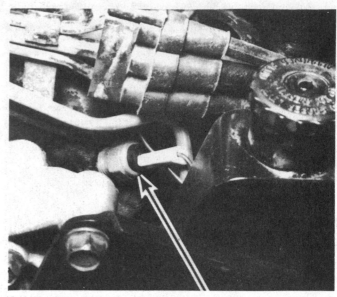

8.11   Location of the coolant temperature sending unit (V6)

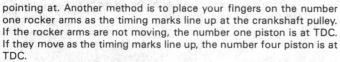

pointing at. Another method is to place your fingers on the number one rocker arms as the timing marks line up at the crankshaft pulley. If the rocker arms are not moving, the number one piston is at TDC. If they move as the timing marks line up, the number four piston is at TDC.

5   Back off the rocker arm nut until play is felt at the pushrod, then turn it back in until all play is just removed. This can be determined by rotating the pushrod while tightening the nut. Just when drag is felt at the pushrod, all lash has been removed. Now turn the nut in an additional 1-1/2 turns.

6   Adjust the number one, five and six cylinder intake valves and the number one, two and three cylinder exhaust valves, with the crankshaft in this position, using the method just described.

7   Rotate the crankshaft until the number four piston is at TDC on the compression stroke and adjust the number two, three and four cylinder intake valves and the number four, five and six cylinder exhaust valves.

8   Refer to Section 2 and install the rocker arm covers.

---

7   Exhaust manifolds — removal and installation

Right side

1   Remove the cable from the negative battery terminal.

2   Raise the front of the vehicle and support it securely on jackstands. Block the rear wheels to keep the vehicle from rolling.

3   Remove the bolts attaching the exhaust pipe to the exhaust manifold, then separate the pipe from the manifold.

4   Remove the jackstands and lower the vehicle.

5   Disconnect the air management hose at the check valve.

6   Disconnect the spark plug wires from the spark plugs, labeling them as they are disconnected to simplify installation.

7   Remove the exhaust manifold mounting bolts (photo) and separate the manifold from the engine.

8   Installation is the reverse of the removal procedure. Before installing the manifold, be sure to thoroughly clean the mating surfaces on the manifold and cylinder head.

Left side

9   Disconnect the cable from the negative battery terminal.

10   Raise the front of the vehicle and place it securely on jackstands. Block the rear wheels to keep the vehicle from rolling.

11   Remove the bolts retaining the exhaust pipe to the manifold, then disconnect the pipe from the manifold.

12   Remove the four bolts and one nut accessible at the rear of the manifold.

13   Remove the jackstands and lower the vehicle.

14   Remove the air cleaner assembly, labeling all hoses.

15   Disconnect the hoses leading to the air management valve.

16   Disconnect and label any wires that will interfere with the removal of the manifold.

17   Remove the power steering pump bracket from the cylinder head. Loosen the pump adjusting bracket bolt and remove the pump drivebelt from the pulley first. After removing the bracket from the cylinder head, place the steering pump assembly aside, out of the way.

18   Remove the remaining manifold bolts and separate the manifold and heat shield from the engine.

19   Installation is the reverse of the removal procedure. Be sure to thoroughly clean the cylinder head and manifold surfaces before installing the manifold.

---

8   Cylinder heads — removal and installation

Left side

1   Remove the intake manifold (refer to Section 4).

2   Raise the vehicle and place it securely on jackstands.

3   Locate the engine block drain plugs to the rear of the motor mounts (the plug on the left side is just above the oil filter). Remove the plugs and drain the block.

4   Disconnect the exhaust pipe from the exhaust manifold.

5   Remove the oil dipstick tube assembly from the side of the engine.

6   Remove the jackstands and lower the vehicle.

7   **Note:** *Steps 8 through 11 are to be followed if the head is to be replaced with a new one. These Steps may be performed either before or after the head has been removed. In the accompanying illustrations, the procedures were performed before the head was removed.*

8   Remove the exhaust manifold (refer to Section 7).

9   Remove the power steering pump bracket from the side of the cylinder head.

10   Remove the air-conditioner compressor bracket from the front of the cylinder head, if equipped.

11   Remove the coolant temperature sending unit from the front of the cylinder head (photo).

12   Loosen the rocker arm nuts enough to allow removal of the pushrods, then remove the pushrods (photo).

13   Loosen the head bolts in a sequence *opposite* to the one used for tightening them (photo).

14   Remove the cylinder head. To break the gasket seal, use a long screwdriver or pry bar under the cast ''ears'' of the cylinder head. Be sure not to damage the cylinder head sealing surface.

15   If a new cylinder head is being installed, attach the components

8.12 When removing the pushrods, be sure to store them separately to ensure reinstallation in their original positions

8.14 Be careful not to damage the cylinder head sealing surface when breaking the gasket loose with a screwdriver or pry bar

previously removed from the old head. Before installing the cylinder head, the gasket surfaces of both the head and the engine block must be clean and free of nicks and scratches. Also, the threads in the block and on the head bolts must be completely clean, as any dirt remaining in the threads will affect bolt torque.

16 Place the gasket in position over the locating dowels, with the note 'This Side Up' visible.

17 Position the cylinder head over the gasket.

18 Coat the cylinder head bolts with an appropriate sealer (GM part number 1052080, or equivalent) and install the bolts.

19 Tighten the bolts in the proper sequence (see the accompanying illustration) to the specified torque. Work up to the final torque in three steps.

20 Install the pushrods, making sure the lower ends are in the lifter seats, place the rocker arm ends over the pushrods and loosely install the rocker arm nuts.

21 The remaining installation steps are the reverse of those for removal. Before installing the rocker arm covers, adjust the valve lash (refer to Section 6).

Right side

22 Remove the intake manifold (refer to Section 4).

23 Raise the vehicle and place it securely on jackstands.

24 Locate the engine block drain plugs to the rear of the motor mounts (the plug on the left side is just above the oil filter), remove the plugs and drain the block.

25 Disconnect the exhaust pipe from the exhaust manifold.

26 Remove the jackstands and lower the vehicle.

27 Remove the alternator from the alternator bracket, then remove the bracket from the head.

28 Remove the lifting 'eye' from the rear of the head (necessary only if the head is to be replaced with a new one).

29 Remove the exhaust manifold (if the head is to be replaced with a new one).

30 Loosen the rocker arm nuts sufficiently to allow removal of the pushrods, then remove the pushrods.

31 Loosen the head bolts in a sequence **opposite** to the one used for tightening them (see accompanying illustration).

32 Remove the cylinder head. To break the gasket seal, insert a bar into one of the exhaust ports, then carefully lift on the tool.

33 To install the head, refer to Steps 15 through 21.

9 Oil pan — removal and installation

Note: *On rear wheel drive vehicles, due to the close proximity of the*

frame crossmember to the oil pan, the engine must be removed to remove the oil pan. Refer to Chapter 2D and then follow Steps 23 through 27.

1 On four-wheel drive vehicles, disconnect the negative battery cable.

2 Remove the oil dipstick.

3 Raise the vehicle and support it securely on jackstands.

4 Remove the drivebelt splash shield.

5 Remove the front axle shield.

6 Remove the transfer case shield.

7 Disconnect the brake lines from the clips on the crossmember.

8 Remove the number two crossmember.

9 If equipped with an automatic transmission, remove the converter hanger bolts and disconnect the exhaust pipe clamp at the converter. Disconnect the exhaust pipes at the manifolds and slide the pipes to the rear.

10 Disconnect the front driveshaft at the drive pinion.

11 Disconnect the engine braces at the flywheel cover and loosen the braces attached to the engine block.

12 Remove the starter motor wires and mounting bolts. Remove the starter motor.

13 Disconnect the steering shock absorber at the frame bracket.

14 Remove the steering gear mounting bolts.

15 Scribe a line indicating the position of the idler arm bracket and remove the idler arm mounting bolts

2C

16 Pull the steering gear and linkage forward.
17 On the right side, remove the differential housing mounting bolts from the mounting bracket. On the left side, remove the mounting bolts from the frame.
18 Move the differential housing forward.
19 Remove the through bolts from the engine mounts.
20 Drain the oil pan.
21 Remove the oil pan mounting bolts.
22 Raise the engine with a floor jack.
23 Remove the oil pan.
24 Before installing the pan, make sure that the sealing surfaces on the pan, block and timing cover are clean and free of oil. If the old pan is being reinstalled, make sure that all sealant has been removed from the pan sealing flange and from the blind attaching holes.
25 With all the sealing surfaces clean, place a 1/8-inch bead of RTV-type sealant on the oil pan sealing flange.
26 Install all bolts finger tight before tightening any bolts. Tighten the pan bolts to the specified torque (after lowering the engine on four-wheel drive models).
27 The rest of installation is the reverse of removal.

10   Oil pump — removal and installation

1   Remove the oil pan (refer to Section 9).
2   Remove the pump-to-rear main bearing cap bolt and separate the

pump and extension shaft from the engine.
3   To install the pump, move it into position and align the top end of the hexagonal extension shaft with the hexagonal socket in the lower end of the distributor drive gear. The distributor drives the oil pump, so it is essential that this alignment is correct.
4   Install the oil pump-to-rear main bearing cap bolt and tighten it to the specified torque.
5   Reinstall the oil pan.

11   Rear main bearing oil seal — replacement (engine in vehicle)

1982 and 1983 engines

Note: *Special tools, as noted in the Steps which follow, are required for this procedure. They are available from your dealer or may in some cases be rented from an auto parts store or tool rental shop.*

1   Although the crankshaft must be removed to install a new seal, the upper portion of the seal can be repaired with the crankshaft in place.
2   Remove the oil pan and oil pump (Sections 9 and 10).
3   Using GM tool J-29114-2, drive the old seal gently back into the groove, packing it tight. It will pack in to a depth of 1/4-to-3/4-inch.
4   Repeat the procedure on the other end of the seal.
5   Measure the amount that the seal was driven up into the groove on one side and add 1/16-inch. Remove the old seal from the main bearing cap. Use the main bearing cap as a fixture and cut off a piece of

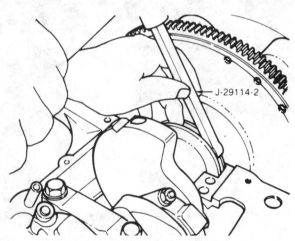

Fig. 2C.6   Using a packing tool to pack the old rear main bearing oil seal into the groove — 1982 and 1983 V6 engines (Sec 11)

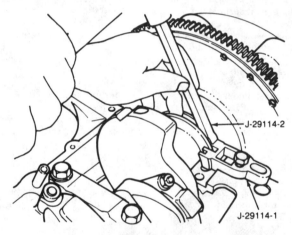

Fig. 2C.7   Using guide tools to install short pieces of seal cut from the old main bearing seal in the upper seal groove — 1982 and 1983 V6 engines (Sec 11)

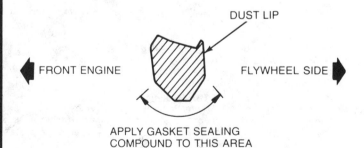

Fig. 2C.8   A very thin coat of RTV-type gasket sealant should be applied to the area shown on 1984 rear main bearing seals (avoid getting sealant on the seal lips) (Sec 11)

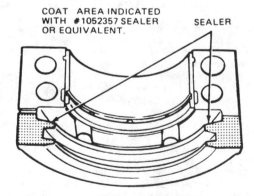

Fig. 2C.9   Apply anaerobic sealant to the areas shown on the rear main bearing cap of 1984 engines prior to installation (do not get sealant in the grooves or on the seal) (Sec 11)

the old seal to the predetermined length. Repeat this process for the other side.

6   Install the guide tool J-29114-1 on the block.

7   Using the packing tool J-29114-2, work the short pieces of the previously cut seal into the guide tool J-29114-1 and pack them into the block groove on each side. The guide and packing tools have been machined to provide a built-in stop. Use of oil on the seal pieces will ease installation.

8   Remove the guide tool.

9   Install a new seal in the main bearing cap.

10 Apply a thin, even coat of anaerobic-type gasket sealant to the areas of the rear main bearing cap indicated in the illustration. **Caution:** *Do not get any sealant on the bearing or seal faces.*

11 Tighten the rear main bearing cap bolts to the specified torque.

12 Install the oil pump and oil pan.

1984 engines

13 Always service both halves of the rear main oil seal. While replacement of this seal is much easier with the engine removed from the vehicle, the job can be done with the engine in place.

14 Remove the oil pan and oil pump as described previously in this Chapter.

15 Remove the rear main bearing cap from the engine.

16 Using a screwdriver, pry the lower half of the oil seal from the bearing cap.

17 To remove the upper half of the seal, use a small hammer and a brass pin punch to roll the seal around the crankshaft journal. Tap one end of the seal with the hammer and punch (be careful not to strike the crankshaft) until the other end of the seal protrudes enough to pull the seal out with pliers.

18 Remove all sealant and foreign material from the main bearing cap. Do not use an abrasive cleaner for this.

19 Inspect the components for nicks, scratches and burrs at all sealing surfaces. Remove any defects with a fine file or deburring tool.

20 Apply a very thin coat of RTV-type gasket sealant to the outer surface of the upper seal as shown in the accompanying illustration. Do not get any sealant on the seal lips.

21 Included in the purchase of the rear main oil seal should be a small plastic installation tool.

22 With the upper half of the seal positioned so that the seal lip faces toward the *front* of the engine and the small dust lip faces toward the flywheel, install the seal by rolling it around the crankshaft using the installation tool as a 'shoehorn' for protection.

23 Apply sealing compound as described in Step 20 to the other half of the seal and install it in the bearing cap.

24 Apply a 1/32-inch bead of anaerobic sealant to the cap between the rear main oil seal end and oil pan rear seal groove. Be sure to keep the sealant off the rear main oil seal and bearing and out of the drain slot.

25 Just before installing the cap, apply a light coat of moly-based grease or engine assembly lube to the crankshaft surface that will contact the seal.

26 Install the rear main bearing cap and tighten the bolts to the specified torque.

27 Install the oil pump and oil pan.

---

12   Vibration damper — removal and installation

---

1   Remove the hose from the retaining strap atop the radiator shroud by releasing the end of the strap from the underside of the shroud with pliers. Move the hose to the side, out of the way.

2   Remove the bolts and separate the upper radiator shroud from the radiator.

3   Remove the cooling fan from the fan pulley.

4   Loosen the accessory drivebelt adjusting bolts as necessary, then remove the drivebelts, tagging each one as it is removed to simplify reinstallation.

5   Remove the bolts from the crankshaft pulley (a screwdriver can be used to lock the starter ring gear on the flywheel), then remove the pulley. Remove the damper center bolt.

6   Attach a puller to the damper. Draw the damper off the crankshaft, being careful not to drop it as it breaks free. A common gear puller should not be used to draw the damper off, as it may separate the outer portion of the damper from the hub. Use only a puller which bolts to the hub.

12.6   A puller is needed to remove the crankshaft vibration damper

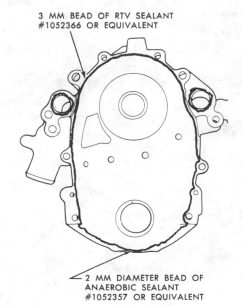

3 MM BEAD OF RTV SEALANT
#1052366 OR EQUIVALENT

2 MM DIAMETER BEAD OF
ANAEROBIC SEALANT
#1052357 OR EQUIVALENT

Fig. 2.10   Apply sealant to the front cover as shown prior to installation (Sec 13)

7   Before installing the damper, coat the front cover seal area (on the damper) with moly-based grease.

8   Place the damper in position over the key on the crankshaft. Make sure the damper keyway lines up with the key.

9   Using a damper installation tool (GM no. J-23523 or equivalent), push the damper onto the crankshaft. The special tool distributes the pressure evenly around the hub.

10 Remove the installation tool and install the damper retaining bolt. Tighten the bolt to the specified torque.

11 Follow the removal procedure in the reverse order for the remaining components.

12 Adjust the drivebelts (refer to Chapter 1).

---

13   Crankcase front cover — removal and installation

---

1   Remove the water pump as described in Chapter 3.

2   If equipped with air-conditioning, remove the compressor from the mounting bracket and secure it out of the way. *Do not disconnect any of the air-conditioning system hoses without having the system*

13.6a   Locations of the remaining front cover mounting bolts (the bottom two bolts and top bolt are not visible)

13.6b   Some of the timing cover bolts pass through to the oil pan

14.7   Driving the seal out of the front cover

14.9   Installing the front cover oil seal with a wood block and a hammer

15.8   The camshaft and crankshaft timing marks should be aligned before removing the timing gear sprockets and chain

15.9   A screwdriver will hold the camshaft sprocket in place while loosening the mounting bolts

15.10 A puller will be needed to remove the crankshaft sprocket,

15.12 Lubricating the thrust surface of the camshaft sprocket

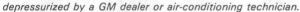

depressurized by a GM dealer or air-conditioning technician.
3   Remove the compressor mounting bracket.
4   Remove the vibration damper as described in Section 12.
5   Disconnect the lower radiator hose at the front cover.
6   Remove the front cover mounting bolts and separate the cover from the engine (photos).
7   Clean all oil, dirt and old gasket material from the sealing surfaces of the front cover and engine block. Replace the front cover oil seal as described in Section 14.
8   Apply a continuous 3/32-inch (2 mm) bead of anaerobic sealant to both mating surfaces of the front cover (except the cover-to-block mating surface where the cover engages the oil pan lip). Apply RTV-type sealant to the cover-to-oil pan area. Also apply anaerobic sealant to the areas surrounding the coolant passages.
9   Place the front cover in position on the engine block and install the mounting bolts. Tighten the bolts to the specified torque.
10   The remaining installation procedures are the reverse of removal.

14   Front cover oil seal — replacement

With front cover installed on engine
1   With the vibration damper removed (Section 12), pry the old seal out of the crankcase front cover with a large screwdriver. Be very careful not to damage the surface of the crankshaft.
2   Place the new seal in position with the open end of the seal (seal lip) toward the *inside* of the cover.
3   Drive the seal into the cover until it is seated. GM tool J-23042 is available for this purpose. These tools are designed to exert even pressure around the entire circumference of the seal as it is hammered into place. A section of large-diameter pipe or a large socket could also be used.
4   Be careful not to distort the front cover.

With front cover removed from engine
5   This method is preferred, as the cover can be supported while the old seal is removed and the new one is installed.
6   Remove the crankcase front cover (refer to Section 13).
7   Using a large screwdriver, pry the old seal out of the bore from the front of the cover. Alternatively, support the cover and drive the seal out from the rear (photo). Be careful not to damage the cover.
8   With the front of the cover facing up, place the new seal in position with the open end of the seal toward the *inside* of the cover.
9   Using a wooden block and hammer, drive the new seal into the cover until it is completely seated (photo).
10   If the cover was removed, install it by reversing the removal procedure.

15   Timing chain and sprockets — inspection, removal and installation

1   Disconnect the cable from the negative battery terminal.
2   Remove the vibration damper (refer to Section 12).
3   Remove the crankcase front cover (refer to Section 13).
4   Before removing the chain and sprockets, visually inspect the teeth on the sprockets for signs of wear and the chain for looseness.
5   If either or both sprockets show any signs of wear (edges on the teeth of the camshaft sprocket not 'square,' bright or blue areas on the teeth of either sprocket, chipping, pitting, etc.), they should be replaced with new ones. Wear in these areas is very common. Failure to replace a worn timing chain may result in erratic engine performance, loss of power and lowered gas mileage.
6   If any one component requires replacement, all related components should be replaced as well.
7   If it is determined that the timing components require replacement, proceed as follows.
8   Turn the engine over until the marks on the camshaft and crankshaft are in exact alignment (photo). At this point the number one and four pistons will be at top dead center with the number four piston in the firing position (verify by checking the position of the rotor in the distributor). *Do not attempt to remove either sprocket or the timing chain until this is done and do not turn the crankshaft or camshaft after the sprockets/chain are removed.*
9   Remove the three camshaft sprocket retaining bolts (photo) and lift the camshaft sprocket and timing chain off the front of the engine. It may be necessary to tap the sprocket with a soft-faced hammer to dislodge it.
10   If it is necessary to remove the crankshaft sprocket, it can be withdrawn from the crankshaft with a special puller (photo).
11   Attach the crankshaft sprocket to the crankshaft using a bolt and washer from the puller set.
12   Lubricate the thrust (rear) surface of the camshaft sprocket with moly-based grease or engine assembly lube (photo). Install the timing chain over the camshaft sprocket with slack in the chain hanging down over the crankshaft sprocket.
13   With the timing marks aligned, slip the chain over the crankshaft sprocket and then draw the camshaft sprocket into place with the three retaining bolts. Do not hammer or attempt to drive the camshaft sprocket into place, as it could dislodge the welch plug at the rear of the engine.
14   With the chain and both sprockets in place, check again to ensure that the timing marks on the two sprockets are properly aligned. If not, remove the camshaft sprocket and move it until the marks align.
15   Lubricate the chain with engine oil and install the remaining components in the reverse order of removal.

2C

16.11 A hooked wire comes in handy when removing the camshaft

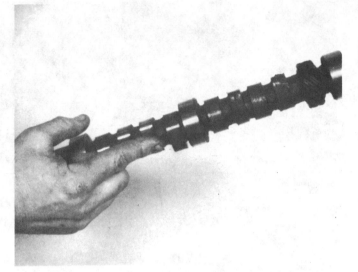

16.13 Be sure to apply engine assembly lube or moly-based grease to the cam lobes and bearing journals before installing the camshaft

16 Camshaft — removal and installation

Note: *Before removing the camshaft, refer to Chapter 2, Part D (Section 16), and measure the lobe lift.*
1 Remove the cable from the negative battery terminal.
2 Drain the oil from the crankcase (refer to Chapter 1).
3 Drain the coolant from the radiator (refer to Chapter 1).
4 Remove the radiator (refer to Chapter 3).
5 If equipped with air-conditioning, remove the condenser (refer to Chapter 3). **Caution:** *The air-conditioning system must be evacuated by an air-conditioning technician before the condenser can be removed. Under no circumstances should this be attempted by the home mechanic, as personal injury may result.*
6 Remove the valve lifters (refer to Section 5).
7 Remove the crankcase front cover (refer to Section 13).
8 Remove the fuel pump and pushrod (refer to Chapter 4).
9 Remove the timing chain and sprocket (refer to Section 15).
10 Install a long bolt in one of the camshaft bolt holes to be used as a handle to pull on and support the camshaft.
11 Carefully draw the camshaft out of the engine block (photo). Do this very slowly to avoid damage to the camshaft bearings as the lobes pass over the bearing surfaces. Always support the camshaft with one hand near the engine block.
12 Refer to Chapter 2, Part D, for the camshaft inspection procedures.
13 Prior to installing the camshaft, coat each of the lobes and journals with engine assembly lube or moly-based grease (photo).
14 Slide the camshaft into the engine block, again taking extra care not to damage the bearings.
15 Install the camshaft sprocket and timing chain as described in Section 15.
16 Install the remaining components in the reverse order of removal by referring to the appropriate Chapter or Section.
17 Adjust the valve lash (refer to Section 6).
18 Have the air-conditioning system (if so equipped) recharged.

17 Engine mounts — replacement with engine in vehicle

1 If the mounts have become hard, split or separated from the metal backing, they must be replaced. This operation may be carried out with the engine/transmission still in the vehicle. See Section 9 for the proper way to raise the engine while it is still in place.

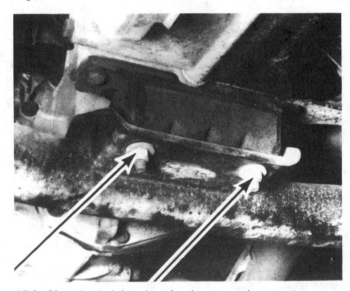

17.6 Mounting bolt locations for the rear engine mount

Front mount

2 Remove the through-bolt and nut.
3 Remove the upper fan shroud.
4 Raise the engine slightly using a hoist or jack with a wood block under the oil pan, then remove the mount and frame bracket assembly from the crossmember.
5 Position the new mount, install the through-bolt and nut, then tighten all the bolts to the specified torque.

Rear mount

6 Remove the crossmember-to-mount bolts (photo), then raise the transmission slightly with a jack.
7 Remove the mount-to-transmission bolts, followed by the mount.
8 Install the new mount, lower the transmission and align the crossmember-to-mount bolts.
9 Tighten all the bolts to the specified torque.

Chapter 2 Part D
General engine overhaul procedures

Refer to Chapter 13 for specifications and information related to 1985 and later models

Contents

Specifications

Isuzu 1.9 liter four-cylinder engine
Valves

Valve stem diameter (service limit)	
Intake	0.3102 in (7.88 mm)
Exhaust	0.3091 in (7.85 mm)
Stem-to-guide clearance (standard)	
Intake	0.0009 to 0.0022 in (0.023 to 0.056 mm)
Exhaust	0.0015 to 0.0031 in (0.038 to 0.078 mm)
Stem-to-guide clearance (service limit)	
Intake	0.01298 in (0.33 mm)
Exhaust	0.0097 in (0.25 mm)
Valve head thickness (service limit)	
Intake	0.0315 in (0.8 mm)
Exhaust	0.0394 in (1.0 mm)

Crankshaft and connecting rods

Crankshaft end play (feeler gauge)	0.0117 in (0.3 mm)
Connecting rod end play (side clearance)	0.0137 in (0.35 mm)
Main bearing journal diameter	
Standard	2.2016 to 2.2022 in (55.920 to 55.935 mm)
Service limit	2.1555 in (54.75 mm)
Main bearing oil clearance	
Standard	0.0008 to 0.0025 in (0.021 to 0.064 mm)
Service limit	0.0046 in (0.12 mm)
Connecting rod bearing journal diameter	
Standard	0.0007 to 0.0030 in (0.018 to 0.064 mm)
Service limit	0.0046 in (0.12 mm)
Crankshaft journal taper/out-of-round limit	0.00028 in (0.007 mm)

Engine block

Cylinder bore diameter	3.43 in (4.87cm)
Taper limit	0.0026 in (0.065 mm)

Torque specifications	**Ft-lbs**
Main bearing cap bolts	72
Connecting rod cap nuts	43

2.0 liter four-cylinder engine

Valves and related components

Valve face angle	45°
Valve seat angle	46°
Stem-to-guide clearance	
Intake	0.0011 to 0.0026 in (0.028 to 0.066 mm)
Exhaust	0.0014 to 0.003 in (0.035 to 0.078 mm)
Valve seat width	
Intake	0.049 to 0.059 (1.25 to 1.50 mm)
Exhaust	0.063 to 0.075 (1.60 to 1.90 mm)
Valve spring installed height	No less than 1.60 in (40.6 mm)
Valve spring pressure and length (intake and exhaust)	
Valve closed	1.6 in at 73 to 81 lbs.
Valve open	1.33 in at 176 to 188 lbs.

Crankshaft and connecting rods

Crankshaft end play	0.002 to 0.008 in (0.05 to 0.21 mm)
Connecting rod end play (side clearance)	0.004 to 0.015 in (0.10 to 0.38 mm)
Main bearing journal diameter	
Nos. 1 through 4	2.4945 to 2.4954 in (63.360 to 63.384 mm)
No. 5	2.4937 to 2.4946 in (63.340 to 63.364 mm)
Main bearing oil clearance	
1983	
Nos. 1 through 4	0.001 to 0.023 in (0.026 to 0.058 mm)
No. 5	0.0018 to 0.0031 in (0.046 to 0.078 mm)
1984	
No. 1 through 4	0.0006 to 0.0019 in (0.015 to 0.047 mm)
No. 5	0.014 to 0.0027 in (0.036 to 0.068 mm)
Connecting rod bearing journal diameter	1.9983 to 1.9994 in (50.758 to 50.784 mm)
Connecting rod bearing oil clearance	0.0001 to 0.0031 in (0.025 to 0.079 mm)
Crankshaft journal taper/out-of-round limit	0.0002 in (0.005 mm)

Engine block

Cylinder bore diameter	3.50 in (89 mm)
Out-of-round limit	0.001 in (0.02mm)
Taper limit	0.001 in (0.02mm)

Pistons and rings

Compression ring side clearance	0.001 to 0.003 in (0.03 to 0.07 mm)
Oil ring side clearance	0.008 in (0.20 mm)
Compression ring end gap	0.01 to 0.02 in (0.25 to 0.50 mm)
Oil ring end gap	0.02 to 0.06 in (0.5 to 1.5 mm)

Camshaft

Lobe lift (intake and exhaust)	0.26 in (6.67 mm)
Bearing journal diameter	1.867 to 1.869 in (47.44 to 47.49 mm)
Bearing oil clearance	0.001 to 0.004 in (0.026 to 0.101 mm)

Cylinders

Cylinder numbers	1—2—3—4 (front-to-rear)
Firing order	1—3—2—4

Torque specifications   Ft-lbs

Main bearing cap bolts	70
Connecting rod cap nuts	32

2.8 liter V6 engine

Valves and related components

Valve face angle	45°
Valve seat angle	46°
Valve seat runout	0.002 in (0.05 mm) maximum
Stem-to-guide clearance	0.001 to 0.0028 in (0.026 to 0.068 mm)
Valve seat width	
Intake	0.049 to 0.059 in (1.25 to 1.50 mm)
Exhaust	0.063 to 0.075 in (1.60 to 1.90 mm)
Valve spring installed height	1.57 in (40.0 mm)
Valve spring free length	1.91 in (48.5 mm)
Valve spring pressure and length (intake and exhaust)	
Valve closed	1.57 in at 87.9 lbs.
Valve open	1.18 in at 194.9 lbs.

Crankshaft and connecting rods

Crankshaft end play	0.002 to 0.007 in (0.05 to 0.17 mm)
Connecting rod end play (side clearance)	0.006 to 0.017 in (0.16 to 0.44 mm)

Main bearing journal diameter
    1982 (all) .... 2.4937 to 2.4946 in (63.340 to 63.364 mm)
    1983 and 1984 (1, 2 and 4) .... 2.4937 to 2.4946 in (63,340 to 63.364 mm)
    1983 and 1984 (3 only) .... 2.4932 to 2.4941 in (63.327 to 63.351 mm)
Main bearing oil clearance
    1982 (all) .... 0.0017 to 0.0030 in (0.044 to 0.076 mm)
    1983 and 1984 (all) .... 0.0016 to 0.0032 in (0.041 to 0.081 mm)
Connecting rod bearing journal diameter .... 1.9983 to 1.9994 in (50.758 to 50.784 mm)
Connecting rod bearing oil clearance .... 0.0012 to 0.0037 in (0.035 to 0.095 mm)
Crankshaft journal taper/out-of-round limit .... 0.0002 in (0.05 mm)

Engine block
Cylinder bore diameter .... 3.504 to 3.507 in (88.992 to 89.070 mm)
Out-of-round limit .... 0.0008 in (0.02 mm)
Taper limit .... 0.0008 in (0.02 mm)

Pistons and rings
Compression ring side clearance
    Top ring .... 0.0019 to 0.0028 in (0.030 to 0.070 mm)
    Second ring .... 0.0016 to 0.0037 in (0.040 to 0.095 mm)
Oil ring side clearance .... 0.0078 in (0.199 mm)
Piston-to-bore clearance .... 0.0017 to 0.0027 in (0.043 to 0.069 mm)
Piston pin diameter .... 0.90526 to 0.90557 in (22.994 to 23.002 mm)
Pin-to-piston clearance .... 0.00026 to 0.00036 in (0.0065 to 0.0091 mm)
Pin-to-rod clearance (press fit) .... 0.00074 to 0.00203 in (0.0187 to 0.0515 mm) (press)
Piston ring end gap
    Top ring .... 0.0098 to 0.0196 in (0.25 to 0.50 mm)
    Second ring .... 0.0098 to 0.0196 in (0.25 to 0.50 mm)
    Oil ring .... 0.020 to 0.055 in (0.51 to 1.40 mm)

Camshaft
Lobe lift
    Intake .... 0.231 in (5.87 mm)
    Exhaust .... 0.262 in (6.67 mm)
Bearing journal diameter .... 1.868 to 1.870 in (47.44 to 47.49 mm)
Bearing oil clearance .... 0.001 to 0.004 in (0.026 to 0.101 mm)

Cylinders
Right bank (passenger's side) .... 1–3–5 (front-to-rear)
Left bank (driver's side) .... 2–4–6 (front-to-rear)
Firing order 1-2-3-4-5-6

Torque specifications   Ft-lbs
Main bearing cap bolts 70
Connecting rod cap nuts 37

2D

1 General information

Included in this portion of Chapter 2 are the general overhaul procedures for the cylinder head(s) and internal engine components. The information ranges from advice concerning preparation for an overhaul and the purchase of replacement parts to detailed, step-by-step procedures covering removal and installation of internal engine components and the inspection of parts.

The following Sections have been written based on the assumption that the engine has been removed from the vehicle. For information concerning in-vehicle engine repair, as well as removal and installation of the external components necessary for the overhaul, see Part A, B or C of Chapter 2 (depending on engine type) and Section 2 of this Part.

The Specifications included here in Part D are only those necessary for the inspection and overhaul procedures which follow. Refer to Part A, B or C for additional Specifications related to the various engines covered in this manual.

2 Repair operations possible with the engine in the vehicle

Some repair operations can be accomplished without removing the engine from the vehicle.

It is a very good idea to clean the engine compartment and the exterior of the engine with some type of pressure washer before any work is begun. A clean engine will make the job easier and will prevent the possibility of getting dirt into the internal areas of the engine.

Remove the hood (Chapter 12) and cover the fenders to provide as much working room as possible and to prevent damage to the painted surfaces.

3 Engine overhaul — general information

It is not always easy to determine when, or if, an engine should be completely overhauled, as a number of factors must be considered.

High mileage is not necessarily an indication that an overhaul is needed while low mileage, on the other hand, does not preclude the need for an overhaul. Frequency of servicing is probably the single most important consideration. An engine that has regular (and frequent) oil and filter changes, as well as other required maintenance, will most likely give many thousands of miles of reliable service. Conversely, a neglected engine may require an overhaul very early in its life.

Excessive oil consumption is an indication that piston rings and/or valve guides are in need of attention (make sure that oil leaks are not responsible before deciding that the rings and guides are bad). Have a cylinder compression or leak-down test performed by an experienced tune-up mechanic to determine for certain the extent of the work required.

If the engine is making obvious knocking or rumbling noises, the connecting rod and/or main bearings are probably at fault. Check the oil pressure with a gauge (installed in place of the oil pressure sending unit). Your GM dealer should be able to supply you with oil pressure specifications. If it is extremely low, the bearings and/or oil pump are probably worn out.

Loss of power, rough running, excessive valve train noise and high fuel consumption rates may also point to the need for an overhaul (especially if they are all present at the same time). If a complete tune-up does not remedy the situation, major mechanical work is the only solution.

An engine overhaul generally involves restoring the internal parts to the specifications of a new engine. During an overhaul, the piston rings are replaced and the cylinder walls are reconditioned (rebored and/or honed). If a rebore is done, then new pistons are also required. The main and connecting rod bearings are replaced with new ones and, if necessary, the crankshaft may be reground to restore the journals. Generally, the valves are serviced as well since they are usually in less-than-perfect condition at this point. While the engine is being overhauled, other components such as the carburetor, the distributor, the starter and the alternator can be rebuilt also. The end result should be a like-new engine that will give as many trouble-free miles as the original.

Before beginning the engine overhaul, read through the entire procedure to familiarize yourself with the scope and requirements of the job. Overhauling an engine is not that difficult, but it is time consuming. Plan on the vehicle being tied up for a minimum of two weeks, especially if parts must be taken to an automotive machine shop for repair or reconditioning. Check on availability of parts and make sure that any necessary special tools and equipment are obtained in advance. Most work can be done with typical shop hand tools, although a number of precision measuring tools are required for inspecting parts to determine if they must be replaced. Often a reputable automotive machine shop will handle the inspection of parts and offer advice concerning reconditioning and replacement. **Note:** *Always wait until the engine has been completely disassembled and all components, especially the engine block, have been inspected before deciding what service and repair operations must be performed by an automotive machine shop.* Since the block's condition will be the major factor to consider when determining whether to overhaul the original engine or buy a rebuilt one, never purchase parts or have machine work done on other components until the block has been thoroughly inspected. As a general rule, time is the primary cost of an overhaul, so it does not pay to install worn or sub-standard parts.

As a final note, to ensure maximum life and minimum trouble from a rebuilt engine, everything must be assembled with care in a spotlessly clean environment.

4　Engine rebuilding alternatives

The do-it-yourselfer is faced with a several options when performing an engine overhaul. The decision to replace the block, piston/connecting rod assemblies and crankshaft depends on a number of factors, with the number one consideration being the condition of the block. Other factors are cost, access to machine shop facilities, parts availability, time required to complete the project and experience.

Some of the rebuilding alternatives include:

Individual parts — *If the inspection procedures reveal that the engine block and most engine components are in reusable condition, purchasing individual parts may be the most economical alternative. The block, crankshaft and piston/connecting rod assemblies should all be inspected carefully. Even if the block shows little wear, the cylinder bores should receive a finish hone; a job for an automotive machine shop.*

Master kit *(crankshaft kit) — This rebuild package usually consists of a reground crankshaft and a matched set of pistons and connecting rods. The pistons will already be installed on the connecting rods. Piston rings and the necessary bearings may or may not be included in the kit. These kits are commonly available for standard cylinder bores, as well as for engine blocks which have been bored to a regular oversize.*

Short block — *A short block consists of an engine block with a crankshaft and piston/connecting rod assemblies already installed. All new bearings are incorporated and all clearances will be correct. Depending on where the short block is purchased, a guarantee may be included. The existing camshaft, valve train components, cylinder head(s) and external parts can be bolted to the short block with little or no machine shop work necessary.*

Long block — *A long block consists of a short block plus an oil pump, oil pan, cylinder head(s), rocker arm cover(s), camshaft and valve train components, timing gears or sprockets and chain and timing gear/chain*

cover. All components are installed with new bearings, seals and gaskets incorporated throughout. The installation of manifolds and external parts is all that is necessary. Some form of guarantee is usually included with the purchase.

Give careful thought to which alternative is best for you and discuss the situation with local automotive machine shops, auto parts dealers or dealership partsmen before ordering or purchasing replacement parts.

5　Engine removal — methods and precautions

If it has been decided that an engine must be removed for overhaul or major repair work, certain preliminary steps should be taken.

Locating a suitable work area is extremely important. A shop is, of course, the most desirable place to work. Adequate work space along with storage space for the vehicle is very important. If a shop or garage is not available, at the very least a flat, level, clean work surface made of concrete or asphalt is required.

Cleaning the engine compartment and engine prior to removal will help keep tools clean and organized.

An engine hoist or A-frame will also be necessary. Make sure that the equipment is rated in excess of the combined weight of the engine and its accessories. Safety is of primary importance, considering the potential hazards involved in lifting the engine out of the vehicle.

If the engine is being removed by a novice, a helper should be available. Advice and aid from someone more experienced would also be helpful. There are many instances when one person cannot simultaneously perform all of the operations required when lifting the engine out of the vehicle.

Plan the operation ahead of time. Arrange for or obtain all of the tools and equipment you will need prior to beginning the job. Some of the equipment necessary to perform engine removal and installation safely and with relative ease are (in addition to an engine hoist) a heavy-duty floor jack, complete sets of wrenches and sockets as described in the front of this manual, wooden blocks and plenty of rags and cleaning solvent for mopping up the inevitable spills. If the hoist is to be rented, make sure that you arrange for it in advance and perform beforehand all of the operations possible without it. This will save you money and time.

Plan for the vehicle to be out of use for a considerable amount of time. A machine shop will be required to perform some of the work which the do-it-yourselfer cannot accomplish due to a lack of special equipment. These shops often have a busy schedule so it would be wise to consult them before removing the engine in order to accurate-

7.3　Before removing the hood, mark the hinge position by lightly scribing a line around the hinge edges

ly estimate the amount of time required to rebuild or repair components that may need work.

Always use extreme caution when removing and installing the engine; serious injury can result from careless actions. Plan ahead. Take your time and a job of this nature, although major, can be accomplished successfully.

6 Engine overhaul disassembly sequence

1   It is much easier to disassemble and work on the engine if it is mounted on a portable engine stand. These stands can often be rented for a reasonable fee from an equipment rental yard. Before the engine is mounted on a stand, the flywheel/driveplate should be removed from the engine (refer to Chapter 8).

2   If a stand is not available, it is possible to disassemble the engine with it blocked up on a sturdy workbench or on the floor. Be extra careful not to tip or drop the engine when working without a stand.

3   If you are going to obtain a rebuilt engine, all external components must come off first in order to be transferred to the replacement engine (just as they will if you are doing a complete engine overhaul yourself). These include:

Alternator and brackets
Emissions control components
Distributor, spark plug wires and spark plugs
Thermostat and housing cover
Water pump
Carburetor
Intake/exhaust manifolds
Oil filter
Fuel pump
Engine mounts
Flywheel/driveplate

Note: *When removing the external components from the engine, pay close attention to details that may be helpful or important during installation. Note the installed position of gaskets, seals, spacers, pins, washers, bolts and other small items.*

4   If you are obtaining a short block (which consists of the engine block, crankshaft, pistons and connecting rods all assembled), then the cylinder heads, oil pan and oil pump will have to be removed also. See *Engine rebuilding alternatives* for additional information regarding the different possibilities to be considered.

5   If you are planning a complete overhaul, the engine must be

disassembled and the internal components removed in the following order:

Rocker arm cover(s)
Cylinder head(s) and pushrods/valve gear
Valve lifters
Timing chain/gear cover
Timing chain/sprockets or gears
Camshaft
Oil pan
Oil pump
Piston/connecting rod assemblies
Crankshaft

6   Before beginning the disassembly and overhaul procedures, make sure the following items are available:

Common hand tools
Small cardboard boxes or plastic bags for storing parts
Gasket scraper
Ridge reamer
Vibration damper puller
Micrometers
Small hole gauges
Telescoping gauges
Dial indicator set
Valve spring compressor
Cylinder surfacing hone
Piston ring groove cleaning tool
Electric drill motor
Tap and die set
Wire brushes
Cleaning solvent

7 Engine — removal and installation

Note: *The following sequence of operations does not necessarily need to be performed in the order given. It is, rather, a checklist of everything that must be disconnected or removed before the engine can be lifted out of the vehicle. If a component mentioned does not apply to your particular vehicle, simply move on to the next step. It is very important that all linkages, electrical wiring, hoses and cables are removed or disconnected before attempting to lift the engine out of the vehicle. It should also be noted that the 'S' series vehicles are fitted with both metric and standard size fasteners. Therefore, both types of tools will be needed for this operation.*

1   Disconnect the negative battery cable.

2   Disconnect the underhood light.

3   Scribe very light lines on the underside of the hood, around the hood mounting bracket, so the hood can be installed in the same position (photo).

4   Unbolt the hood and, with the aid of an asistant, remove the hood from the vehicle.

5   Remove the air cleaner assembly.

6   Drain the cooling system.

7   Drain the engine oil.

8   Remove the upper radiator hose.

9   Remove the upper fan shroud (photo).

10   Disconnect the automatic transmission oil cooler lines, if equipped.

11   Remove the lower radiator hose.

12   Unbolt the radiator mounting bolts and carefully remove the radiator.

13   Remove the four mounting bolts from the fan. Remove the fan, and if equipped, remove the fan clutch.

14   Unbolt the air-conditioning compressor, if equipped, and lay it to the side out of the way. **Caution:** *Do not disconnect any of the air-conditioning lines unless the system has been depressurized by a dealer service department or air-conditioning technician, as personal injury may occur.*

15   Due to the inaccessability of the top bellhousing bolts on the 'S' series vehicles, it is necessary to raise the body off the chassis to gain adequate working clearance.

16   Remove the two front body mount bolts located behind the front bumper (photo).

17   Remove the two middle body mount bolts located behind the door

7.9   Location of the upper fan shroud mounting bolts

2D

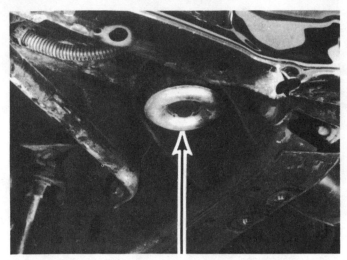

7.16   To gain working clearance, the front body mounts must be removed (most models) to allow the body to be raised off the chassis

7.17   Location of the right side middle body mount bolt

7.20   Spacer blocks are used to hold the body off the chassis

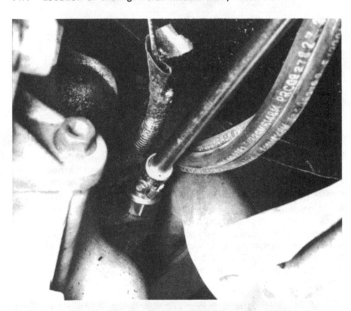

7.22   A socket extension and universal joint will probably be needed to remove the upper bellhousing bolts

pillars (photo).

18 Loosen the two rear body mount bolts.

19 Remove the front bumper mounting bolts and remove the front bumper.

20 Position a jack and a wood block under the front crossbrace. Raise the body off of the chassis just enough to insert a 2x4 wood block between the crossbrace and the frame rail on each side (photo).

21 Lower the jack.

22 Remove the two upper bellhousing-to-engine bolts (photo).

23 Disconnect the AIR pump hoses at the pump fittings and at the AIR injection manifold. Remove the hoses.

24 Remove the exhaust pipe mounting bolts from the exhaust manifold(s).

25 On *V6-equipped models*, remove the upper mounting bolts from the right side exhaust manifold.

26 Remove the lower mounting bolts from the right side exhaust manifold *(V6 engines)*. It may be necessary to raise the vehicle (be sure to support it securely on jackstands) to gain access to the lower manifold bolts.

27 Remove the electrical connectors from the starter motor and remove the starter lead clamp located at the right front corner of the oil pan. Position the wiring out of the way.

28 Remove the starter motor mounting bolts and remove the starter

motor (Chapter 5).

29 Disconnect the clutch cable at the clutch actuating lever (if equipped).

30 Remove the alternator electrical connectors.

31 Disconnect the alternator wiring harness from the two harness clamps and position the harness out of the way.

32 Remove the electrical connector from the diverter valve.

33 Remove the diverter valve from the mounting bracket on the rocker arm cover.

34 Disconnect all electrical connections from the carburetor.

35 Disconnect the vacuum hose from the intake manifold fitting located just below the secondary choke pulloff. Disconnect the vacuum brake hose from the filter, and any other manifold vacuum hoses which would later interfere with engine removal.

36 Disconnect the throttle cable from the the carburetor throttle lever and from the cable routing bracket on the rocker arm cover.

37 Remove the spark plug wires from the spark plugs.

38 Remove the distributor cap along with the spark plug wires. Disconnect the distributor electrical connector (photo).

39 Disconnect the fuel vapor hose three-way connector at the front of the engine. Remove the vapor hose harness clip from the power steering bracket and position the hoses out of the way.

40 Remove the electrical connector from the coolant temperature

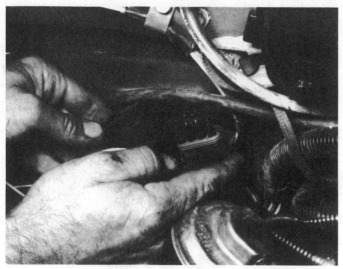

7.38 Disconnecting the distributor electrical leads

7.40 Location of the electrical connector for the coolant temperature sending unit

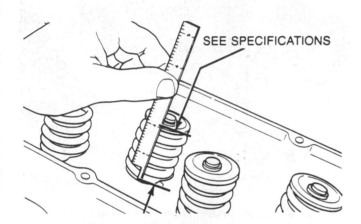

Fig. 2D.1 Measuring the installed valve spring height with a steel rule (V6 engine *intake* valves only) (Sec 8)

SEE SPECIFICATIONS

8.3 Use a valve spring compressor to compress the springs, then remove the keepers from the valve stem

2D

sending unit at the front of the engine (photo).
41 Remove the four remaining bellhousing-to-engine bolts.
42 Position a moveable jack (floor jack or transmission jack) under the transmission oil pan using a block of wood as an insulator. Support the transmission securely.
43 Attach the hoist lifting chains to the lifting brackets on the engine. There is one bracket at the front of the engine and one at the rear, diagonally opposite the front one. Make sure the chain is looped properly through the engine brackets and secured with bolts and nuts through the chain links. The hook on the lifting hoist should be at the center of the engine.
44 Raise the engine slightly and then pull it forward to clear the input shaft (manual transmission). Where an automatic transmission is involved, keep the torque coverter pushed well to the rear to retain engagement of the converter tangs with the oil pump inside the transmission.
45 Carefully lift the engine straight up and out of the engine compartment, continually checking clearances around it.
46 The transmission should remain supported by the floor jack or wood blocks while the engine is out.
47 Attach the engine to an engine stand.
48 Refer to other Sections in this Chapter for further disassembly and rebuilding procedures.

8 Cylinder head — disassembly

Note: *New and rebuilt cylinder heads are commonly available for most engines at dealerships and auto parts stores. Due to the fact that some specialized tools are necessary for the disassembly and inspection procedures, and replacement parts may not be readily available, it may be more practical and economical for the home mechanic to purchase a replacement head (or heads) rather than taking the time to disassemble, inspect and recondition the original head(s).*

1 Cylinder head disassembly involves removal and disassembly of the intake and exhaust valves and their related components. If they are still in place, remove the nuts or bolts and pivot balls, then separate the rocker arms from the cylinder head. Label the parts or store them separately so they can be reinstalled in their original locations.
2 Before the valves are removed, arrange to label and store them, along with their related components, so they can be kept separate and reinstalled in the same valve guides they are removed from. Also, measure the valve spring installed height (for each valve) and compare it to the Specifications. If it is greater than specified, the valve seats and valve faces need attention.
3 Compress the valve spring on the first valve with a spring compressor and remove the keepers (photo). Carefully release the valve spring compressor and remove the retainer (or rotator), the shield (if so equipped), the springs, the valve guide seal and/or O-ring seal, the spring seat and the valve from the head. If the valve binds in the guide (won't pull through), push it back into the head and deburr the area around the keeper groove with a fine file or whetstone.

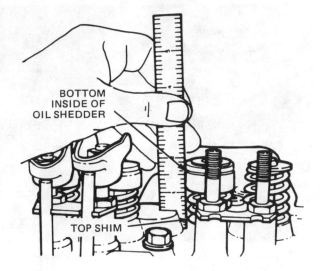

Fig. 2D.2   When checking the valve spring height on V6 engine exhaust valves and all four-cylinder engine valves, the measurement is made up to the bottom inside surface of the oil shedder (Sec 8)

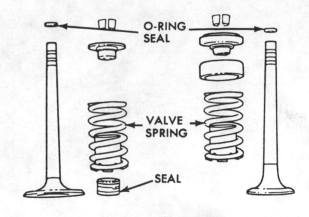

Fig. 2D.3   V6 engine valve components — note the valve stem seal locations (Sec 8)

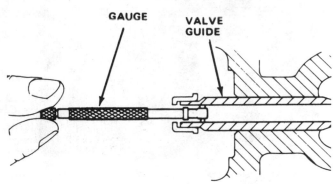

Fig. 2D.4   Use a small hole gauge to determine the inside diameter of the valve guides (the gauge is then measured with a micrometer) (Sec 9)

Fig. 2D.5   A dial indicator can also be used to determine the valve stem-to-guide clearance (Sec 9)

4   Repeat the procedure for the remaining valves. Remember to keep together all the parts for each valve so they can be reinstalled in the same locations.

5   Once the valves have been removed and safely stored, the head should be thoroughly cleaned and inspected. If a complete engine overhaul is being done, finish the engine disassembly procedures before beginning the cylinder head cleaning and inspection process.

9   Cylinder head — cleaning and inspection

1   Thorough cleaning of the cylinder head and related valve train components, followed by a detailed inspection, will enable you to decide how much valve service work must be done during the engine overhaul.

Cleaning

2   Scrape away all traces of old gasket material and sealing compound from the head gasket, intake manifold and exhaust manifold sealing surfaces.

3   Remove any built-up scale around the coolant passages.

4   Run a stiff wire brush through the oil holes to remove any deposits that may have formed in them.

5   It is a good idea to run an appropriate size tap into each of the threaded holes to remove any corrosion and thread sealant that may be present. If compressed air is available, use it to clear the holes of debris produced by this operation.

6   Clean the exhaust and intake manifold stud threads in a similar manner with an appropriate size die. Clean the rocker arm pivot bolt or stud threads with a wire brush.

7   Next, clean the cylinder head with solvent and dry it thoroughly. Compressed air will speed the drying process and ensure that all holes and recessed areas are clean. **Note:** *Decarbonizing chemicals are available and may prove very useful when cleaning cylinder heads and valve train components. They are very caustic and should be used with caution. Be sure to follow the instructions on the container.*

8   Clean the rocker arms, pivot balls and pushrods with solvent and dry them thoroughly. Compressed air will speed the drying process and can be used to clean out the oil passages.

9   Clean all the valve springs, keepers, retainers, rotators, shields and spring seats with solvent and dry them thoroughly. Do the components from one valve at a time to avoid mixing up the parts.

10   Scrape off any heavy deposits that may have formed on the valves, then use a motorized wire brush to remove deposits from the valve heads and stems. Again, make sure the valves do not get mixed up.

Inspection

Cylinder head

11   Inspect the head very carefully for cracks, evidence of coolant leakage and other damage. If cracks are found, a new cylinder head should be obtained.

12   Using a straightedge and feeler gauges, check the head gasket mating surface for warpage. If the head is warped beyond the limits given in the Specifications, it can be resurfaced at an automotive

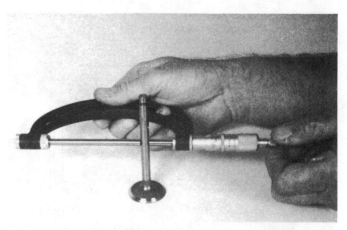

9.20 Measure the valve stem diameter at three points

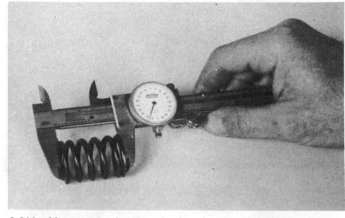

9.21A Measure the free length of each valve spring with a dial or vernier caliper

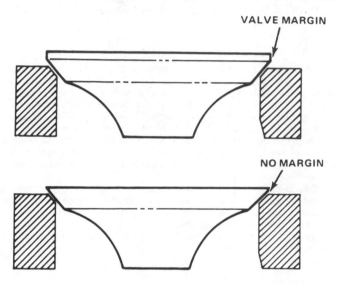

VALVE MARGIN

NO MARGIN

Fig. 2D.6 The margin width on each valve must be as specified (if no margin exists, the valve must be replaced) (Sec 9)

9.21B Check each valve spring for squareness

2D

machine shop.

13 Examine the valve seats in each of the combustion chambers. If they are pitted, cracked or burned, the head will require valve service that is beyond the scope of the home mechanic.

14 Measure the inside diameters of the valve guides (at both ends and the center of each guide) with a small hole gauge and a 0-to-1-inch micrometer. Record the measurements for future reference. These measurements, along with the valve stem diameter measurements, will enable you to compute the valve stem-to-guide clearances. These clearances, when compared to the Specifications, will be one factor that will determine the extent of valve service work required. The guides are measured at the ends and at the center to determine if they are worn in a bell-mouth pattern (more wear at the ends). If they are, guide reconditioning or replacement is necessary. As an alternative, use a dial indicator to measure the lateral movement of each valve stem with the valve in the guide and approximately 1/16-inch off the seat (see the accompanying illustration).

Rocker arm components

15 Check the rocker arm faces (that contact the pushrod ends and valve stems) for pits, wear and rough spots. Check the pivot contact areas as well.

16 Inspect the pushrod ends for scuffing and excessive wear. Roll the pushrod on a flat surface, such as a piece of glass, to determine if it is bent.

17 Any damaged or excessively worn parts must be replaced with new ones.

Valves

18 Carefully inspect each valve face for cracks, pits and burned spots. Check the valve stem and neck for cracks. Rotate the valve and check for any obvious indication that it is bent. Check the end of the stem for pits and excessive wear. The presence of any of these conditions indicates the need for valve service by a properly equipped professional.

19 Measure the width of the valve margin (on each valve) and compare it to the Specifications. Any valve with a margin narrower than specified will have to be replaced with a new one.

20 Measure the valve stem diameter (photo). By subtracting the stem diameter from the corresponding valve guide diameter, the valve stem-to-guide clearance is obtained. Compare the results to the Specifications. If the stem-to-guide clearance is greater than specified, the guides will have to be reconditioned and new valves may have to be installed, depending on the condition of the old ones.

Valve components

21 Check each valve spring for wear (on the ends) and pits. Measure the free length (photo) and compare it to the Specifications. Any springs that are shorter than specified have sagged and should not be reused. Stand the spring on a flat surface and check it for squareness (photo).

22 Check the spring retainers or rotators and keepers for obvious wear and cracks. Any questionable parts should be replaced with new ones, as extensive damage will occur in the event of failure during engine operation.

23 If the inspection process indicates that the valve components are in generally poor condition and worn beyond the limits specified, which

12.2 A special tool is required to remove the ridge from the top of each cylinder (do it *before* removing the piston)

12.6 Checking connecting rod end play with a feeler gauge

is usually the case in an engine that is being overhauled, reassemble the valves in the cylinder head and refer to Section 10 for valve servicing recommendations.
24 If the inspection turns up no excessively worn parts, and if the valve faces and seats are in good condition, the valve train components can be reinstalled in the cylinder head without major servicing. Refer to the appropriate Section for cylinder head reassembly procedures.

10 Valves — servicing

1 Because of the complex nature of the job and the special tools and equipment needed, servicing of the valves, the valve seats and the valve guides (commonly known as a 'valve job') is best left to a professional.
2 The home mechanic can remove and disassemble the head, do the initial cleaning and inspection, then reassemble and deliver the head to a dealer service department or a reputable automotive machine shop for the actual valve servicing.
3   The dealer service department, or automotive machine shop, will remove the valves and springs, recondition or replace the valves and valve seats, recondition the valve guides, check and replace the valve springs, spring retainers or rotators and keepers (as necessary), replace the valve seals with new ones, reassemble the valve components and make sure the installed spring height is correct. The cylinder head gasket surface will also be resurfaced if it is warped.
4 After the valve job has been performed by a professional, the head will be in like-new condition. When the head is returned, be sure to clean it again, very thoroughly (before installation on the engine), to remove any metal particles and abrasive grit that may still be present from the valve service or head resurfacing operations. Use compressed air, if available, to blow out all the oil holes and passages.

11 Cylinder head — reassembly

1   Regardless of whether or not the head was sent to an automotive machine shop for valve servicing, make sure it is clean before beginning reassembly.
2   If the head was sent out for valve servicing, the valves and related components will already be in place. Begin the reassembly procedure with Step 6.
3   Lay all the springs in position, then lubricate and install new seals (or deflectors) on each of the valve guides (V6 intake valves). Using a hammer and an appropriate size deep socket, gently tap each seal into place until it is properly seated on the guide. Do not twist or cock the seals during installation or they will not seal properly on the valve stems.

4   Next, install the valves (taking care not to damage the new valve guide seals), the springs, the shields (if so equipped), the retainers or rotators, the O-ring valve stem seals and the keepers. Coat the valve stems with clean moly-based grease or engine assembly lube before slipping them into the guides. Install the O-ring seals in the lower valve stem grooves (one in each groove). Make sure they are not twisted (a light coat of oil will prevent twisting). When compressing the springs with the valve spring compressor, do not let the retainers contact the valve guide seals. Make certain that the keepers are securely locked in their retaining grooves.
5   Double-check the installed valve spring height. If it was correct before disassembly, it should still be within the specified limits.
6   Check the valve stem O-ring seals with a vacuum pump and adapter. A properly installed seal should not leak.
7   Install the rocker arms and tighten the bolts/nuts to the specified torque. Be sure to lubricate the ball pivots with moly-based grease or engine assembly lube.

12 Piston/connecting rod assembly — removal

1   Prior to removal of the piston/connecting rod assemblies, the engine should be positioned upright.
2   Using a ridge reamer, completely remove the ridge at the top of each cylinder (follow the manufacturer's instructions provided with the ridge reaming tool) (photo). *Failure to remove the ridge before attempting to remove the piston/connecting rod assemblies will result in piston breakage.*
3   After all of the cylinder wear ridges have been removed, turn the engine upside-down.
4   Before the connecting rods are removed, check the end play as follows. Mount a dial indicator with its stem in line with the crankshaft and touching the side of the number one cylinder connecting rod cap.
5   Push the connecting rod forward, as far as possible, and zero the dial indicator. Next, push the connecting rod all the way to the rear and check the reading on the dial indicator. The distance that it moves is the end play. If the end play exceeds the service limit, a new connecting rod will be required. Repeat the procedure for the remaining connecting rods.
6   An alternative method is to slip feeler gauges between the connecting rod and the crankshaft throw until the play is removed (photo). The end play is then equal to the thickness of the feeler gauge(s).
7   Check the connecting rods and connecting rod caps for identification marks. If they are not plainly marked, identify each rod and cap using a small punch to make the appropriate number of indentations to indicate the cylinder they are associated with.
8   Loosen each of the connecting rod cap nuts approximately 1/2-turn each. Remove the number one connecting rod cap and bearing insert. Do not drop the bearing insert out of the cap. Slip a short length

12.8   To prevent damage to the crankshaft journals and cylinder walls, slip sections of hose over the rod bolts before removing the pistons

13.3   Checking crankshaft end play with a feeler gauge (V6 engine shown)

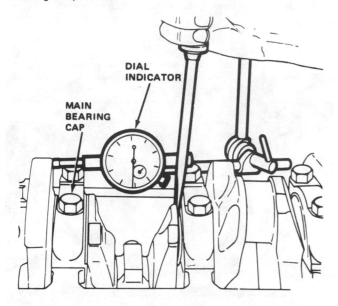

Fig. 2D.7   Checking crankshaft end play with a dial indicator (Sec 13)

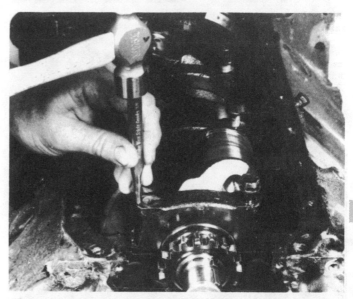

13.4   Mark the bearing caps with a center punch before removing them

of plastic or rubber hose over each connecting rod cap bolt (to protect the crankshaft journal and cylinder wall when the piston is removed) (photo) and push the connecting rod/piston assembly out through the *top* of the engine. Use a wooden tool to push on the upper bearing insert in the connecting rod. If resistance is felt, double-check to make sure that all of the ridge was removed from the cylinder.

9   Repeat the procedure for the remaining cylinders. After removal, reassemble the connecting rod caps and bearing inserts in their respective connecting rods and install the cap nuts finger tight. Leaving the old bearing inserts in place until reassembly will help prevent the connecting rod bearing surfaces from being accidentally nicked or gouged.

13   Crankshaft — removal

1   Before the crankshaft is removed, check the end play as follows. Mount a dial indicator with the stem in line with the crankshaft and just touching one of the crank throws (see accompanying illustration).

2   Push the crankshaft all the way to the rear and zero the dial indicator. Next, pry the crankshaft to the front as far as possible and check the reading on the dial indicator. The distance that it moves is

the end play. If it is greater than specified, check the crankshaft thrust surfaces for wear. If no wear is apparent, new main bearings should correct the end play.

3   If a dial indicator is not available, feeler gauges can be used. Gently pry or push the crankshaft all the way to the front of the engine. Slip feeler gauges between the crankshaft and the front face of the thrust main bearing (photo) to determine the clearance (which is equivalent to crankshaft end play).

4   Loosen each of the main bearing cap bolts 1/4 of a turn at a time, until they can be removed by hand. Check the main bearing caps to see if they are marked as to their locations. They are usually numbered consecutively (beginning with 1) from the front of the engine to the rear. If they are not, mark them with number stamping dies or a center punch (photo). Most main bearing caps have a cast-in arrow, which points to the front of the engine.

5   Gently tap the caps with a soft-faced hammer, then separate them from the engine block. If necessary, use the main bearing cap bolts as levers to remove the caps. Try not to drop the bearing insert if it comes out with the cap.

6   Carefully lift the crankshaft out of the engine. It is a good idea to have an assistant available, since the crankshaft is quite heavy. With the bearing inserts in place in the engine block and in the main bearing caps, return the caps to their respective locations on the engine block and tighten the bolts finger tight.

2D

14.1A   A hammer and large punch can be used to drive the soft plugs into the block

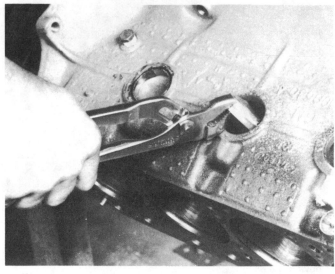

14.1B   Using pliers to remove a soft plug from the block

14.10   A large socket on an extension can be used to force the new soft plugs into their bores

15.4A   A telescoping gauge can be used to determine the cylinder bore diameter

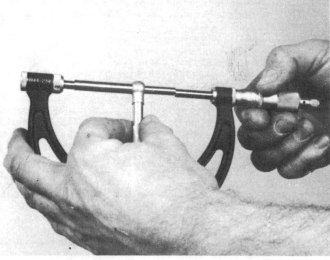

15.4B   The gauge is then measured with a micrometer to determine the bore size

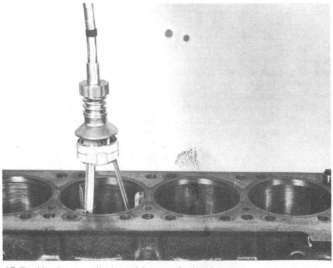

15.7   Honing a cylinder with a surfacing hone

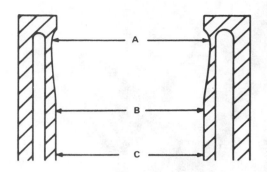

Fig. 2D.8 Measure the diameter of each cylinder just under the wear ridge (A), at the center (B) and at the bottom (C) (Sec 15)

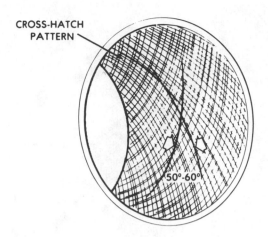

Fig. 2D.9 The cylinder hone should leave a cross-hatch pattern with the lines intersecting at approximately a 60° angle (Sec 15)

14 Engine block — cleaning

1   Remove the soft plugs from the engine block. To do this, knock the plugs into the block (using a hammer and punch), then grasp them with large pliers and pull them back through the holes (photo).
2   Using a gasket scraper, remove all traces of gasket material from the engine block. Be very careful not to nick or gouge the gasket sealing surfaces.
3   Remove the main bearing caps and separate the bearing inserts from the caps and the engine block. Tag the bearings according to which cylinder they removed from (and whether they were in the cap or the block) and set them aside.
4   Using a hex wrench of the appropriate size, remove the threaded oil gallery plugs from the front and back of the block.
5   If the engine is extremely dirty, it should be taken to an automotive machine shop to be steam cleaned or hot tanked. Any bearings left in the block (such as the camshaft bearings) will be damaged by the cleaning process, so plan on having new ones installed while the block is at the machine shop.
6   After the block is returned, clean all oil holes and oil galleries one more time (brushes for cleaning oil holes and galleries are available at most auto parts stores). Flush the passages with warm water until the water runs clear, dry the block thoroughly and wipe all machined surfaces with a light, rust-preventative oil. If you have access to compressed air, use it to speed the drying process and to blow out all the oil holes and galleries.
7   If the block is not extremely dirty or sludged up, you can do an adequate cleaning job with warm soapy water and a stiff brush. Take plenty of time and do a thorough job. Regardless of the cleaning method used, be very sure to thoroughly clean all oil holes and galleries, dry the block completely and coat all machined surfaces with light oil.
8   The threaded holes in the block must be clean to ensure accurate torque readings during reassembly. Run the proper size tap into each of the holes to remove any rust, corrosion, thread sealant or sludge and to restore any damaged threads. If possible, use compressed air to clear the holes of debris produced by this operation. Now is a good time to thoroughly clean the threads on the head bolts and the main bearing cap bolts as well.
9   Reinstall the main bearing caps and tighten the bolts finger tight.
10 After coating the sealing surfaces of the new soft plugs with a good quality gasket sealer, install them in the engine block (photo). Make sure they are driven in straight and seated properly or leakage could result. Special tools are available for this purpose, but equally good results can be obtained using a large socket (with an outside diameter that will just slip into the soft plug) and a large hammer.
11 If the engine is not going to be reassembled right away, cover it with a large plastic trash bag to keep it clean.

15 Engine block — inspection

1   Thoroughly clean the engine block as described in Section 14 and double-check to make sure that the ridge at the top of each cylinder

has been completely removed.
2   Visually check the block for cracks, rust and corrosion. Look for stripped threads in the threaded holes. It is also a good idea to have the block checked for hidden cracks by an automotive machine shop that has the special equipment to do this type of work. If defects are found, have the block repaired, if possible, or replaced.
3   Check the cylinder bores for scuffing and scoring.
4   Using the appropriate precision measuring tools, measure each cylinder's diameter at the top (just under the ridge), center and bottom of the cylinder bore, *parallel* to the crankshaft axis (photos). Next, measure each cylinder's diameter at the same three locations *across* the crankshaft axis. Compare the results to the Specifications. If the cylinder walls are badly scuffed or scored, or if they are out-of-round or tapered beyond the limits given in the Specifications, have the engine block rebored and honed at an automotive machine shop. If a rebore is done, oversize pistons and rings will be required as well.
5   If the cylinders are in reasonably good condition and not worn to the outside of the limits, and if the piston-to-cylinder clearances can be maintained properly, then they do not have to be rebored; honing is all that is necessary.
6   Before honing the cylinders, install the main bearing caps (without the bearings) and tighten the bolts to the specified torque.
7   To perform the honing operation, you will need the proper size flexible hone (with fine stones), plenty of light oil or honing oil, some rags and an electric drill motor. Mount the hone in the drill motor, compress the stones and slip the hone into the first cylinder (photo). Lubricate the cylinder thoroughly, turn on the drill and move the hone up and down in the cylinder at a pace which will produce a fine cross-hatch pattern on the cylinder walls (with the cross-hatch lines intersecting at approximately a 60° angle). Be sure to use plenty of lubricant and do not take off any more material than is absolutely necessary to produce the desired finish. Do not withdraw the hone from the cylinder while it is running. Instead, shut off the drill and continue moving the hone up and down in the cylinder until it comes to a complete stop, then compress the stones and withdraw the hone. Wipe the oil out of the cylinder and repeat the procedure on the remaining cylinders. Remember, do not remove too much material from the cylinder wall. If you do not have the tools or do not desire to perform the honing operation, most automotive machine shops will do it for a reasonable fee.
8   After the honing job is complete, chamfer the top edges of the cylinder bores with a small file so the rings will not catch when the pistons are installed.
9   Next, the entire engine block must be thoroughly washed again with warm, soapy water to remove all traces of the abrasive grit produced during the honing operation. Be sure to run a brush through all oil holes and galleries and flush them with running water. After rinsing, dry the block and apply a coat of light rust preventative oil to all machined surfaces. Wrap the block in a plastic trash bag to keep it clean and set it aside until reassembly.

2D

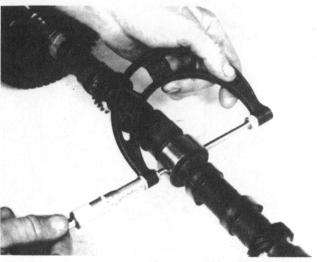

16.9   The camshaft bearing journal diameter is subtracted from the bearing inside diameter to obtain the oil clearance, which must be as specified

16.12   If the bottom of any of the lifters is worn concave, scratched or galled, they should all be replaced with new ones

16   Camshaft, lifters and bearings — inspection and bearing replacement

Camshaft

1   The most critical camshaft inspection procedure is lobe lift measurement, which must be done *before* the engine is disassembled.
2   Remove the rocker arm cover(s), then remove the nuts/bolts and separate the rocker arms and ball pivots from the cylinder head(s).
3   Beginning with the number one (1) cylinder, mount a dial indicator with the stem resting on the end of, and directly in line with, the exhaust valve pushrod.
4   Rotate the crankshaft very slowly in the direction of rotation until the lifter is on the heel of the cam lobe. At this point the pushrod will be at its lowest position.
5   Zero the dial indicator, then very slowly rotate the crankshaft in the direction of rotation until the pushrod is at its highest position. Note and record the reading on the dial indicator, then compare it to the lobe lift specifications.
6   Repeat the procedure for each of the remaining valves. Note that intake and exhaust valves may have different lobe lift specifications.
7   If the lobe lift measurements are not as specified, a new camshaft should be installed.
8   After the camshaft has been removed from the engine, cleaned with solvent and dried, inspect the bearing journals for uneven wear, pitting and evidence of seizure. If the journals are damaged, the bearing inserts in the block are probably damaged as well. Both the camshaft and bearings will have to be replaced with new ones. Measure the inside diameter of each camshaft bearing and record the results (take two measurements, 90° apart, at each bearing).
9   Measure the bearing journals with a micrometer (photo) to determine if they are excessively worn or out-of-round. If they are more than 0.001-inch out-of-round, the camshaft should be replaced with a new one. Subtract the bearing journal diameter(s) from the corresponding bearing inside diameter measurement to obtain the oil clearance. If it is excessive, new bearings must be installed.
10 Check the camshaft lobes for heat discoloration, score marks, chipped areas, pitting and uneven wear. If the lobes are in good condition and if the lobe lift measurements (Steps 1 through 7) were as specified, the camshaft can be reused.

Lifters

11 Clean the lifters with solvent and dry them thoroughly *without mixing them up.*
12 Check each lifter wall, pushrod seat and foot for scuffing, score marks and uneven wear. Each lifter foot (the surface that rides on the cam lobe) must be slightly convex — if they are concave (photo), the lifters and camshaft must be replaced with new ones. If the lifter walls

Fig. 2D.10   A dial indicator can be mounted as shown here to check the camshaft lobe lift (Sec 16)

are damaged or worn (which is not very likely), inspect the lifter bores in the engine block as well. If the pushrod seats are worn, check the pushrod ends.
13 If new lifters are being installed, a new camshaft must also be installed. If a new camshaft is installed, then use new lifters as well. *Never install used lifters unless the original camshaft is used and the lifters can be installed in their original locations.*

Bearing replacement

14 Camshaft bearing replacement requires special tools and expertise that place it outside the scope of the do-it-yourselfer. Take the block to an automotive machine shop to ensure that the job is done correctly.

17   Piston/connecting rod assembly — inspection

1   Before the inspection process can be carried out, the piston/connecting rod assemblies must be cleaned and the original piston rings removed from the pistons. **Note:** *Always use new piston rings when the engine is reassembled.*
2   Using a piston ring installation tool, carefully remove the rings from

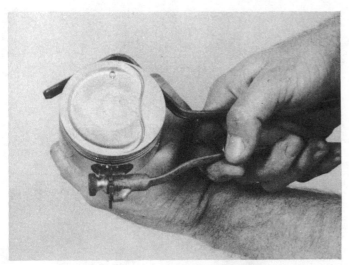

17.4   Cleaning the piston ring grooves with a piston ring groove cleaning tool

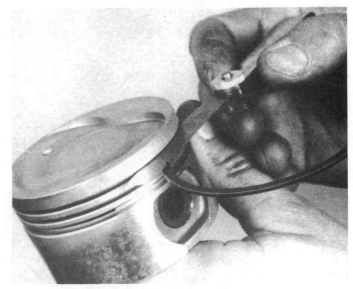

17.10   Checking the piston ring side clearance with a feeler gauge

17.11   Measure the piston diameter at 90° to piston pin hole

the pistons. Do not nick or gouge the pistons in the process.

3   Scrape all traces of carbon from the top (or crown) of the piston. A hand-held wire brush or a piece of fine emery cloth can be used once the majority of the deposits have been scraped away. Do not, under any circumstances, use a wire brush mounted in a drill motor to remove deposits from the pistons. The piston material is soft and will be eroded away by the wire brush.

4   Use a piston ring groove cleaning tool to remove any carbon deposits from the ring grooves. If a tool is not available, a piece broken off the old ring will do the job. Be very careful to remove only the carbon deposits. Do not remove any metal and do not nick or scratch the sides of the ring grooves (photo).

5   Once the deposits have been removed, clean the piston/rod assemblies with solvent and dry them thoroughly. Make sure that the oil hole in the big end of the connecting rod and the oil return holes in the back sides of the ring grooves are clear.

6   If the pistons are not damaged or worn excessively, and if the engine block is not rebored, new pistons will not be necessary. Normal piston wear appears as even vertical wear on the piston thrust surfaces and slight looseness of the top ring in its groove. New piston rings, on the other hand, should always be used when an engine is rebuilt.

7   Carefully inspect each piston for cracks around the skirt, at the pin bosses and at the ring lands.

8   Look for scoring and scuffing on the thrust faces of the skirt, holes in the piston crown and burned areas at the edge of the crown. If the skirt is scored or scuffed, the engine may have been suffering from overheating and/or abnormal combustion, which caused excessively high operating temperatures. The cooling and lubrication systems should be checked thoroughly. A hole in the piston crown, an extreme to be sure, is an indication that abnormal combustion (preignition) was occurring. Burned areas at the edge of the piston crown are usually evidence of spark knock (detonation). If any of the above problems exist, the causes must be corrected or the damage will occur again.

9   Corrosion of the piston (evidenced by pitting) indicates that coolant is leaking into the combustion chamber and/or the crankcase. Again, the cause must be corrected or the problem may persist in the rebuilt engine.

10   Measure the piston ring side clearance by laying a new piston ring in each ring groove and slipping a feeler gauge in beside it (photo). Check the clearance at three or four locations around each groove. Be sure to use the correct ring for each groove; they are different. If the side clearance is greater than specified, new pistons will have to be used.

11   Check the piston-to-bore clearance by measuring the bore (see Section 15) and the piston diameter (photo). Make sure that the pistons and bores are correctly matched. Measure the piston across the skirt, on the thrust faces (at a 90° angle to the piston pin), directly in line with the center of the pin hole. Subtract the piston diameter from the bore diameter to obtain the clearance. If it is greater than specified, the block will have to be rebored and new pistons and rings installed. Check the piston-to-rod clearance by twisting the piston and rod in opposite directions. Any noticeable play indicates that there is excessive wear, which must be corrected. The piston/connecting rod assemblies should be taken to an automotive machine shop to have new piston pins installed and the pistons and connecting rods rebored.

12   If the pistons must be removed from the connecting rods, such as when new pistons must be installed, or if the piston pins have too much play in them, they should be taken to an automotive machine shop. While they are there, it would be convenient to have the connecting rods checked for bend and twist, as automotive machine shops have special equipment for this purpose. *Unless new pistons or connecting rods must be installed, do not disassemble the pistons from the connecting rods.*

13   Check the connecting rods for cracks and other damage. Temporarily remove the rod caps, lift out the old bearing inserts, wipe the rod and cap bearing surfaces clean and inspect them for nicks, gouges and scratches. After checking the rods, replace the old bearings, slip the caps into place and tighten the nuts finger tight.

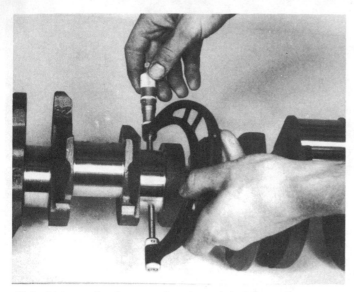

18.2   Measure the diameter of each crankshaft journal at several points to detect taper and out-of-round conditions

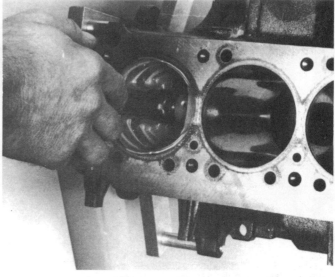

20.3A   Use the piston to square up the ring in the cylinder prior to checking the ring end gap

18   Crankshaft — inspection

1   Clean the crankshaft with solvent and dry it thoroughly. Be sure to clean the oil holes with a stiff brush and flush them with solvent. Check the main and connecting rod bearing journals for uneven wear, scoring, pitting and cracks. Check the remainder of the crankshaft for cracks and damage.

2   Using an appropriate size micrometer, measure the diameter of the main and connecting rod journals (photo) and compare the results to the Specifications. By measuring the diameter at a number of points around the journal's circumference, you will be able to determine whether or not the journal is worn out-of-round. Take the measurement at each end of the journal, near the crank throw, to determine whether the journal is tapered.

3   If the crankshaft journals are damaged, tapered, out-of-round or worn beyond the limits given in the Specificatioins, have the crankshaft reground by a reputable automotive machine shop. Be sure to use the correct undersize bearing inserts if the crankshaft is reconditioned.

4   Refer to Section 19 and examine the main and rod bearing inserts.

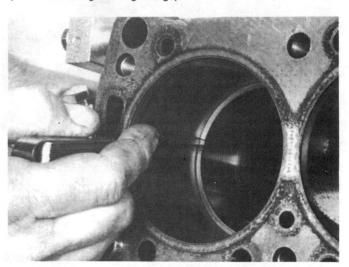

20.3B   Measure the ring end gap with a feeler gauge

19   Main and connecting rod bearings — inspection

1   Even though the main and connecting rod bearings should be replaced with new ones during the engine overhaul, the old bearings should be retained for close examination, as they may reveal valuable information about the condition of the engine.

2   Bearing failure occurs mainly because of lack of lubrication, the presence of dirt or other foreign particles, overloading the engine and corrosion. Regardless of the cause of bearing failure, it must be corrected before the engine is reassembled to prevent it from happening again.

3   When examining the bearings, remove them from the engine block, the main bearing caps, the connecting rods and the rod caps and lay them out on a clean surface in the same general position as their location in the engine. This will enable you to match any noted bearing problems with the corresponding crankshaft journal.

4   Dirt and other foreign particles get into the engine in a variety of ways. If may be left in the engine during assembly, or it may pass through filters or breathers. It may get into the oil, and from there into the bearings. Metal chips from machining operations and normal engine wear are often present. Abrasives are sometimes left in engine components after reconditioning, especially when parts are not thoroughly cleaned using the proper cleaning methods. Whatever the source, these foreign objects often end up embedded in the soft bearing material and are easily recognized. Large particles will not embed in the bearing and will score or gouge the bearing and shaft. The best prevention for this cause of bearing failure is to clean all parts thoroughly and keep everything spotlessly clean during engine assembly. Frequent and regular engine oil and filter changes are also recommended.

5   Lack of lubrication (or lubrication breakdown) has a number of interrelated causes. Excessive heat (which thins the oil), overloading (which squeezes the oil from the bearing face) and oil leakage or throw-off (from excessive bearing clearances, worn oil pump or high engine speeds) all contribute to lubrication breakdown. Blocked oil passages, which usually are the result of misaligned oil holes in a bearing shell, will also oil-starve a bearing and destroy it. When lack of lubrication is the cause of bearing failure, the bearing material is wiped or extruded from the steel backing of the bearing. Temperatures may increase to the point where the steel backing turns blue from overheating.

6   Driving habits can have a definite effect on bearing life. Full-throttle, low-speed operation (or 'lugging' the engine) puts very high loads on bearings, which tends to squeeze out the oil film. These loads cause the bearings to flex, which produces fine cracks in the bearing face (fatigue failure). Eventually the bearing material will loosen in pieces and tear away from the steel backing. Short-trip driving leads to corrosion of the bearing because insufficient engine heat is produced to drive off the condensed water and corrosive gases. These products collect in the engine oil, forming acid and sludge. As the oil is carried to the engine bearings, the acid attacks and corrodes the bearing material.

20.9A   Installing the spacer/expander in the oil control ring groove

20.12   Installing the compression rings with the special tool — the mark (arrow) must face *up*

7   Incorrect bearing installation during engine assembly will lead to bearing failure as well. Tight-fitting bearings leave insufficient bearing oil clearance and will result in oil starvation. Dirt or foreign particles trapped behind a bearing insert result in high spots on the bearing which lead to failure.

20   Piston rings — installation

1   Before installing the new piston rings, the ring end gaps must be checked. It is assumed that the piston ring side clearance has been checked and verified correct (Section 17).
2   Lay out the piston/connecting rod assemblies and the new ring sets so the ring sets will be matched with the same piston and cylinder during the end gap measurement and engine assembly.
3   Insert the top (number one) ring into the first cylinder and square it up with the cylinder walls by pushing it in with the top of the piston (photo). The ring should be near the bottom of the cylinder at the lower limit of ring travel. To measure the end gap, slip a feeler gauge between the ends of the ring (photo). Compare the measurement to the Specifications.
4   If the gap is larger or smaller than specified, double-check to make sure that you have the correct rings before proceeding.

20.9B   *Do not* use a piston ring tool when installing the oil ring side rails

5   If the gap is too small, it must be enlarged or the ring ends may come in contact with each other during engine operation, which can cause serious damage to the engine. The end gap can be increased by filing the ring ends very carefully with a fine file. Mount the *file* in a vise equipped with soft jaws, slip the ring over the file with the ends contacting the file face and slowly move the ring to remove material from the ends. *When performing this operation, file only from the outside in.*
6   Excess end gap is not critical unless it is greater than 0.040-inch (1 mm). Again, double-check to make sure you have the correct rings for your engine.
7   Repeat the procedure for each ring that will be installed in the first cylinder and for each ring in the remaining cylinders. Remember to keep rings, pistons and cylinders matched up.
8   Once the ring end gaps have been checked/corrected, the rings can be installed on the pistons.
9   The oil control ring (lowest one on the piston) is installed first. It is composed of three separate components. Slip the spacer expander into the groove (photo), then install the upper side rail. *Do not use a piston ring installation tool on the oil ring side rails, as they may be damaged.* Instead, place one end of the side rail into the groove between the spacer expander and the ring land, hold it firmly in place and slide a finger around the piston while pushing the rail into the groove (photo). Next, install the lower side rail in the same manner.
10   After the three oil ring components have been installed, check to make sure that both the upper and lower side rails can be turned smoothly in the ring groove.
11   The number two (middle) ring is installed next. It should be stamped with a mark so it can be readily distinguished from the top ring. **Note:** *Always follow the instructions printed on the package that the new rings are in — different manufacturers may require different approaches. Do not mix up the top and middle rings, as they have different cross sections.*
12   Use a piston ring installation tool and *make sure that the identification mark is facing the top of the piston,* then slip the ring into the middle groove on the piston (photo). Do not expand the ring any more than is necessary to slide it over the piston.
13   Finally, install the number one (top) ring in the same manner. Make sure the identifying mark is facing up.
14   Repeat the procedure for the remaining pistons and rings. Be careful not to confuse the number one and number two rings.

21   Rear main oil seal (2.8 liter V6 engine only) – installation

Rope-type seal

1   Lay one seal section on edge in the seal groove in the block and

2D

21.1   When correctly installed, the ends of the rope-type seal should extend out of the block

21.2   Seat the seal in the groove, but do not depress it below the bearing surface (the seal must contact the crankshaft journal)

21.3A   Trim the ends flush with the block, . . .

21.3B   . . . but leave the inner edge (arrow) protruding slightly

21.4   Lubricate the seal with assembly lube or moly-based grease

21.5   When applying the sealant, be sure it gets into the corner and onto the vertical cap-to-block mating surface or oil leaks will result

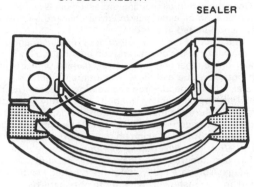

COAT AREA INDICATED
WITH #1052357 SEALER
OR EQUIVALENT.

SEALER

Fig. 2D.11 Apply anaerobic-type gasket sealant to the shaded
areas of the rear main bearing cap (V6 engine) (Sec 21)

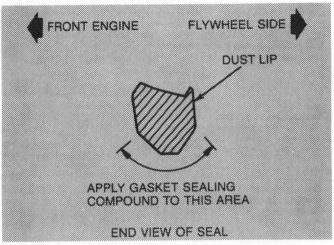

FRONT ENGINE   FLYWHEEL SIDE

DUST LIP

APPLY GASKET SEALING
COMPOUND TO THIS AREA

END VIEW OF SEAL

Fig. 2D.12 When installing the rear main oil seal on 1984 V6
engines, apply RTV-type sealant to the area indicated (Sec 21)

push it into place with your thumbs. Both ends of the seal should extend out of the block slightly (photo).

2   Seat it in the groove by rolling a large socket or piece of bar stock along the entire length of the seal (photo). As an alternative, push the seal very carefully into place with a wooden hammer handle.

3   Once you are satisfied that the seal is completely seated in the groove, trim off the excess on the ends with a single-edge razor blade or razor knife (the seal ends must be flush with the block-to-cap mating surfaces) (photos). Make sure that no seal fibers get caught between the block and cap.

4   Repeat the entire procedure to install the other half of the seal in the bearing cap. Apply a thin film of engine assembly lube to the edge of the seal (where it contacts the crankshaft) (photo).

5   During final installation of the crankshaft (after the main bearing oil clearances have been checked with Plastigage) as described in Section 22, apply a thin, even film of anaerobic-type gasket sealant to the areas of the rear main bearing cap indicated in the accompanying illustration and photo. **Caution:** *Do not get any sealant on the bearing or seal faces.*

Neoprene lip-type seal (two-piece)

6   Inspect the bearing cap and engine block mating surfaces and seal grooves for nicks, burrs and scratches. Remove any defects with a fine file or deburring tool.

7   Install one seal section in the block with the lip facing the *front* of the engine. Leave one end protruding from the block approximately 1/4 to 3/8-inch and make sure it is completely seated. **Note:** *On V6 models only, apply a very thin coat of RTV-type gasket sealant to the outer surface of the seal as shown in the accompanying illustration. Do not get any sealant on the seal lips.*

8   Repeat the procedure to install the remaining seal half in the rear main bearing cap. In this case, leave the opposite end of the seal protruding from the cap approximately the same distance the block seal is protruding from the block.

9   During final installation of the crankshaft (after the main bearing oil clearances have been checked with Plastigage) as described in Section 22, apply a thin, even film of anaerobic-type gasket sealant to the areas of the cap or block indicated in the accompanying illustration. **Caution:** *Do not get any sealant on the bearing face, crankshaft journal or seal lip.* Also, lubricate the seal lips with moly-based grease or engine assembly lube.

Neoprene lip-type seal (one-piece)

10 Apply a very thin coat (1.0 mm) of RTV-type gasket sealant to the outer surface of the seal as shown in the accompanying illustration. Do not get any sealant on the seal lips.

11 Place the seal tool (included with the replacement seal) and seal on the rear of the crankshaft so that the arrow on the tool points toward the crankshaft.

12 Carefully set the crankshaft into place.

13 Remove the tool and discard it.

14 Apply sealant as described in Step 9.

22 Crankshaft — installation and main bearing oil clearance check

1   Crankshaft installation is generally one of the first steps in engine reassembly; it is assumed at this point that the engine block and crankshaft have been cleaned, inspected and repaired or reconditioned. **Note:** *On V6 and 2.0 liter four-cylinder engines only, refer to Section 21 and install the rear main oil seal sections before proceeding.*

2   Position the engine with the bottom facing up.

3   Remove the main bearing cap bolts and lift out the caps. Lay them out in the proper order to help ensure that they are installed correctly.

4   If they are still in place, remove the old bearing inserts from the block and the main bearing caps. Wipe the main bearing surfaces of the block and caps with a clean, lint-free cloth (they must be kept spotlessly clean).

5   Clean the back sides of the new main bearing inserts and lay one bearing half in each main bearing saddle in the block. Lay the other bearing half from each bearing set in the corresponding main bearing cap. Make sure the tab on the bearing insert fits into the recess in the block or cap. Also, the oil holes in the block and cap must line up with the oil holes in the bearing insert. *Do not hammer the bearing into place and do not nick or gouge the bearing faces. No lubrication should be used at this time.*

6   The flanged thrust bearing must be installed in the number three (3) cap and saddle on V6 and 1.9 liter four-cylinder engines and the number four (4) cap and saddle on 2.0 liter four-cylinder engines.

7   Clean the faces of the bearings in the block and the crankshaft main bearing journals with a clean, lint-free cloth. Check or clean the oil holes in the crankshaft, as any dirt here can only go one way — straight through the new bearings.

8   Once you are certain that the crankshaft is clean, carefully lay it in position (an assistant would be very helpful here) in the main bearings with the counterweights lying sideways.

9   Before the crankshaft can be permanently installed, the main bearing oil clearance must be checked.

10 Trim several pieces of the appropriate type of Plastigage (so they are slightly shorter than the width of the main bearings) and place one piece on each crankshaft main bearing journal, parallel with the journal axis. Do not lay them across the oil holes.

11 Clean the faces of the bearings in the caps and install the caps in their respective positions (do not mix them up) with the arrows pointing toward the front of the engine. Do not disturb the Plastigage.

12 Starting with the center main and working out toward the ends, tighten the main bearing cap bolts, in three steps, to the specified torque. *Do not rotate the crankshaft at any time during this operation.*

13 Remove the bolts and carefully lift off the main bearing caps. Keep them in order. Do not disturb the Plastigage or rotate the crankshaft. If any of the main bearing caps are difficult to remove, tap them gently from side-to-side with a soft-faced hammer to loosen them.

14 Compare the width of the crushed Plastigage on each journal to the scale printed on the Plastigage container to obtain the main bearing oil clearance. Check the Specifications to make sure it is correct.

2D

15 If the clearance is not correct, double-check to make sure you have the right size bearing inserts. Also, make sure that no dirt or oil was between the bearing inserts and the main bearing caps or the block when the clearance was measured.

16 Carefully scrape all traces of the Plastigage material off the main bearing journals and/or the bearing faces. Do not nick or scratch the bearing faces.

17 Carefully lift the crankshaft out of the engine. Clean the bearing faces in the block, then apply a thin, uniform layer of clean, high-quality moly-based grease or engine assembly lube to each of the bearing faces. Be sure to coat the thrust flange faces as well as the journal face of the thrust bearing.

18 Lubricate the rear main oil seal (where it contacts the crankshaft) with moly-based grease or engine assembly lube. Note that on four-cylinder engines the oil seal is installed *after* the crankshaft is in place.

19 If you are working on a V6 or 2.0 four-cylinder engine, refer to Section 21 and apply anaerobic-type gasket sealant to the rear main bearing cap or block as described there. Make sure the crankshaft journals are clean, then lay it back in place in the block. Clean the faces of the bearings in the caps, then apply a thin, uniform layer of clean, moly-based grease to each of the bearing faces and install the caps in their respective positions with the arrows pointing toward the front of the engine. Install the bolts and tighten them to the specified torque, starting with the center main and working out toward the ends. Work up to the final torque in three steps.

20 Rotate the crankshaft a number of times by hand and check for any obvious binding.

21 The final step is to check the crankshaft end play. This can be done with a feeler gauge or a dial indicator set. Refer to Section 13 for the procedure.

23 Piston/connecting rod assembly — installation and bearing oil clearance check

1 Before installing the piston/connecting rod assemblies, the cylinder walls must be perfectly clean, the top edge of each cylinder must be chamfered, and the crankshaft must be in place.

2 Remove the connecting rod cap from the end of the number one connecting rod. Remove the old bearing inserts and wipe the bearing surfaces of the connecting rod and cap with a clean, lint-free cloth (they must be kept spotlessly clean).

3 Clean the back side of the new upper bearing half, then lay it in place in the connecting rod. Make sure that the tab on the bearing fits into the recess in the rod. Do not hammer the bearing insert into place and be very careful not to nick or gouge the bearing face. *Do not lubricate the bearing at this time.*

4 Clean the back side of the other bearing insert and install it in the rod cap. Again, make sure the tab on the bearing fits into the recess in the cap, and do not apply any lubricant. It is critically important that the mating surfaces of the bearing and connecting rod are perfectly clean and oil-free when they are assembled.

5 Position the piston ring gaps as shown in the accompanying illustrations, then slip a section of plastic or rubber hose over the connecting rod cap bolts.

6 Lubricate the piston and rings with clean engine oil and attach a piston ring compressor to the piston. Leave the skirt protruding about 1/4-inch to guide the piston into the cylinder. The rings must be compressed as far as possible.

7 Rotate the crankshaft until the number one connecting rod journal is as far from the number one cylinder as possible (bottom dead center), and apply a uniform coat of engine oil to the cylinder walls.

8 With the notch on top of the piston facing to the front of the engine, gently place the piston/connecting rod assembly into the number one cylinder bore and rest the bottom edge of the ring compressor on the engine block. Tap the top edge of the ring compressor to make sure it is contacting the block around its entire circumference.

9 Clean the number one connecting rod journal on the crankshaft and the bearing faces in the rod.

10 Carefully tap on the top of the piston with the end of a wooden hammer handle (photo) while guiding the end of the connecting rod into place on the crankshaft journal. The piston rings may try to pop out of the ring compressor just before entering the cylinder bore, so keep some downward pressure on the ring compressor. Work slowly, and if any resistance is felt as the piston enters the cylinder, stop im-

mediately. Find out what is hanging up and fix it before proceeding. *Do not, for any reason, force the piston into the cylinder, as you will break a ring and/or the piston.*

11 Once the piston/connecting rod assembly is installed, the connecting rod bearing oil clearance must be checked before the rod cap is permanently bolted in place.

12 Cut a piece of the the appropriate type Plastigage slightly shorter than the width of the connecting rod bearing and lay it in place on the number one connecting rod journal, parallel with the journal axis (it must not cross the oil hole in the journal) (photo).

13 Clean the connecting rod cap bearing face, remove the protective hoses from the connecting rod bolts and gently install the rod cap in place. Make sure the mating mark on the cap is on the same side as the mark on the connecting rod. Install the nuts and tighten them to the specified torque, working up to it in three steps. *Do not rotate the crankshaft at any time during this operation.*

14 Remove the rod cap, being very careful not to disturb the Plastigage. Compare the width of the crushed Plastigage to the scale printed on the Plastigage container to obtain the oil clearance (photo). Compare it to the Specifications to make sure the clearance is correct. If the clearance is not correct, double-check to make sure that you have the correct size bearing inserts. Also, recheck the crankshaft connecting rod journal diameter and make sure that no dirt or oil was between the bearing inserts and the connecting rod or cap when the clearance was measured.

15 Carefully scrape all traces of the Plastigage material off the rod journal and/or bearing face (be very careful not to scratch the bearing — use your fingernail or a piece of hardwood). Make sure the bearing faces are perfectly clean, then apply a uniform layer of clean, high-quality moly-based grease or engine assembly lube to both of them.

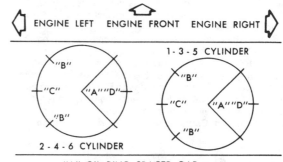

"A" OIL RING SPACER GAP
(Tang in Hole or Slot within Arc)
"B" OIL RING RAIL GAPS
"C" 2ND COMPRESSION RING GAP
"D" TOP COMPRESSION RING GAP

Fig. 2D.13 Before installing the pistons, position the ring end gaps as shown here (2.0 liter four-cylinder and V6 engines) (Sec 23)

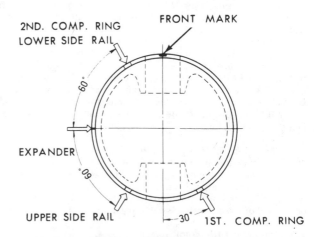

Fig. 2D.14 On 1.9 liter four-cylinder engines, the piston ring end gaps must be positioned as shown here (Sec 23)

You will have to push the piston into the cylinder to expose the face of the bearing insert in the connecting rod; be sure to slip the protective hoses over the rod bolts first.

16 Slide the connecting rod back into place on the journal, remove the protective hoses from the rod cap bolts, install the rod cap and tighten the nuts to the specified torque. Again, work up to the torque in three steps.

17 Repeat the entire procedure for the remaining piston/connecting rod assemblies. Keep the back sides of the bearing inserts and the inside of the connecting rod and cap perfectly clean when assembling them. Make sure you have the correct piston for the cylinder and that the notch, arrow or F on the piston faces to the front of the engine when the piston is installed. Remember, use plenty of oil to lubricate the piston before installing the ring compressor and cap. Also, when installing the rod caps for the final time, be sure to lubricate the bearing faces adequately.

18 After all the piston/connecting rod assemblies have been properly installed, rotate the crankshaft a number of times by hand and check for any obvious binding.

19 As a final step, the connecting rod end play must be checked. Refer to Section 12 for the procedure to follow. Compare the measured end play to the Specifications to make sure it is correct.

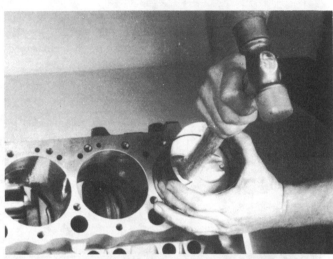

23.10 If resistance is encountered when tapping the piston/connecting rod assembly into the block, *stop immediately* and make sure the rings are fully compressed

23.12 Position the Plastigage strip on the bearing journal, parallel to the journal axis

24   Engine overhaul — reassembly sequence

1 Before beginning engine reassembly, make sure you have all the necessary new parts, gaskets and seals as well as the following items on hand:

Common hand tools
A 1/2-inch drive torque wrench
Piston ring installation tool
Piston ring compressor
Short lengths of rubber or plastic hose to fit over connecting rod bolts
Plastigage
Feeler gauges
A fine-tooth file
New, clean engine oil
Engine assembly lube or moly-based grease
RTV-type gasket sealant
Anaerobic-type gasket sealant
Thread locking compound

2 In order to save time and avoid problems, engine reassembly must be done in the following order.

Rear main oil seal (V6 and 2.0 liter four-cylinder engines only)
Crankshaft and main bearings
Piston rings
Piston/connecting rod assemblies
Oil pump
Oil pan
Camshaft
Timing chain/sprockets or gears
Timing chain/gear cover
Valve lifters
Cylinder head(s) and pushrods
Intake and exhaust manifolds
Oil filter
Pre-oil the engine (V6 engine only — Section 25)
Rocker arm cover(s)
Fuel pump
Water pump
Rear main oil seal
Flywheel/driveplate
Carburetor
Thermostat and housing cover
Distributor, spark plug wires and spark plugs
Emissions control components
Alternator

2D

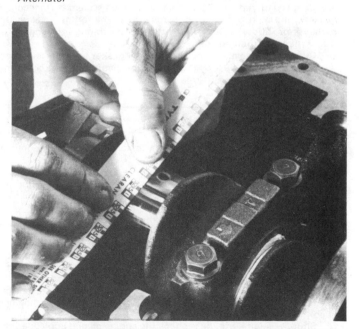

23.14 The crushed Plastigage is compared to the scale printed on the container to obtain the bearing oil clearance

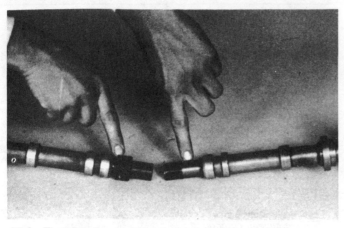

25.3   The pre-oiling tool (right) has the gear and advance weights ground off

25   Pre-oiling engine after overhaul (V6 engine only)

1   After an overhaul it is a good idea to pre-oil the engine before it is installed and initially started. This will reveal any problems with the lubrication system at a time when corrections can be made easily and without major engine damage. Pre-oiling the engine will also allow the parts to be lubricated thoroughly in a normal fashion, but without the heavy loads associated with the combustion process placed upon them.
2   The engine should be assembled completely with the exception of the distributor and the rocker arm covers.
3   A modified distributor will be needed for this procedure. This pre-oil tool is a distributor body with the bottom gear ground off and the advance weight assembly removed from the top of the shaft (photo).
4   Place the pre-oiler into the distributor shaft access hole at the rear of the intake manifold and make sure the bottom of the shaft mates with the oil pump. Clamp the modified distributor into place just as you would an ordinary distributor. Now attach an electric drill motor to the top of the shaft (photo).
5   With the oil filter installed, all oil ways plugged (oil-pressure sending unit at rear of block) and the crankcase full of oil as shown on the dipstick, rotate the pre-oiler with the drill. Make sure the rotation is in a *clockwise* direction. Soon, oil should start to flow from the rocker arms, signifying that the oil pump and lubrication system are functioning properly. It may take two or three minutes for oil to flow to all of the rocker arms (photo). Allow the oil to circulate through the engine for a few minutes, then shut off the drill motor.
6   Check for oil leaks at the filter and all gasket and seal locations.
7   Remove the pre-oil tool, then install the distributor and rocker arm covers.

26   Initial start-up and break-in after overhaul

1   Once the engine has been properly installed in the vehicle, double-check the engine oil and coolant levels.
2   With the spark plugs out of the engine and the coil high-tension lead grounded to the engine block, crank the engine over until oil pressure registers on the gauge (if so equipped) or until the oil light goes off.
3   Install the spark plugs, hook up the plug wires and the coil high-tension lead.
4   Make sure the carburetor choke plate is closed, then start the engine. It may take a few moments for the gasoline to reach the carburetor, but the engine should start without a great deal of effort.
5   As soon as the engine starts, it should be set at a fast idle (to ensure proper oil circulation) and allowed to warm up to normal operating temperature. While the engine is warming up, make a thorough check for oil and coolant leaks.
6   Shut the engine off and recheck the engine oil and coolant levels. Also, check the ignition timing and the engine idle speed (refer to

25.4   A drill motor connected to the modified distributor drives the oil pump

25.5   Oil and assembly lube or grease will spurt out of the holes in the rocker arms if the lubrication system is functioning properly

Chapter 1) and make any necessary adjustments.
7   Drive the vehicle to an area with minimum traffic, accelerate at full throttle from 30 to 50 mph, then allow the vehicle to slow to 30 mph with the throttle closed. Repeat the procedure 10 or 12 times. This will load the piston rings and cause them to seat properly against the cylinder walls. Check again for oil and coolant leaks.
8   Drive the vehicle gently for the first 500 miles (no sustained high speeds) and keep a constant check on the oil level. It is not unusual for an engine to use oil during the break-in period.
9   At approximately 500 to 600 miles, change the oil and filter, re-torque the cylinder head bolts and recheck the valve clearances (if applicable).
10   For the next few hundred miles, drive the vehicle normally. Do not pamper it or abuse it.
11   After 2000 miles, change the oil and filter again and consider the engine fully broken in.

Chapter 3
Cooling, heating and air conditioning systems

Refer to Chapter 13 for specifications related to 1985 and later models

Contents

Specifications

Cooling system
Operating pressure .... 14 to 17 psi
Coolant capacity .... See Chapter 1

Torque specifications   Ft-lbs
Fan-to-water pump bolts 20
Water pump bolts 15
Water outlet (thermostat housing) bolts 25
Coolant temperature sending unit....................... 20

1 General information

The cooling system is conventional in design, utilizing a cross-flow radiator, an engine driven water pump and a thermostat controlled coolant flow. Air conditioned models are equipped with a fan clutch, which allows the fan to draw air through the radiator at lower speeds. At higher speeds the fan is not needed for cooling, so the clutch automatically lowers the fan speed and reduces the engine power required for fan operation.

The water pump is mounted on the front of the engine and is driven by a belt from the pulley mounted on the front of the crankshaft. The belt is also used to drive other components.

The heater utilizes the heat produced by the engine and absorbed by the coolant to warm the interior of the vehicle. It is manually controlled from inside by the driver or passenger.

Air conditioning is optional equipment. All components of the system are mounted in the engine compartment and the system is driven by a belt from the pulley mounted on the front of the crankshaft. Output of the system is controlled from inside the vehicle.

2 Antifreeze — general information

Caution: *Do not allow antifreeze to come in contact with your skin or the painted surfaces of the vehicle. Flush contacted areas immediately with of water. Antifreeze can be fatal to children and pets, and they like because it is sweet. Wipe up garage floor and drip pan coolant spills immediately. Keep antifreeze containers covered and repair leaks in your cooling system immediately.*

The cooling system should be filled with a water/ethylene glycol based antifreeze solution, which will prevent freezing down to at least -20° F at all times. It also provides protection against corrosion and increases the coolant boiling point.

The cooling system should be drained, flushed and refilled at least every other year (see Chapter 1). The use of antifreeze solutions for periods of longer than two years is likely to cause damage and encourage the formation of rust and scale in the system.

Before adding antifreeze to the system, check all hose connections and retorque the cylinder head bolts. Antifreeze tends to search out and leak through very minute openings.

The exact mixture of antifreeze-to-water which you should use depends on the relative weather conditions. The mixture should contain at least 50 percent antifreeze, but should never contain more than 70 percent antifreeze.

3 Thermostat — replacement

Caution: *The engine must be completely cool before beginning this procedure. Also, when working in the vicinity of the electric fan, disconnect the negative battery cable from the battery to prevent the fan from starting accidentally.*

1.9L four-cylinder engine
1   Refer to the Caution in Section 2.
2   Disconnect the cable from the negative battery terminal (if not done previously).

3.27A If the old thermostat gasket is made of RTV-type sealant, it may be necessary to scrape away some of the excess sealant

3   Drain the cooling system until the level is below the thermostat by opening the petcock at the bottom of the radiator. Close the petcock when enough coolant has drained.

4   Label and disconnect the PCV hose, ECS hose, AIR hose and TCA hose (from the hot idle compensator to the intake manifold).

5   Remove the two air cleaner mounting bolts and loosen the clamp bolt.

6   Lift the air cleaner from the carburetor and disconnect the TCA hose from the thermosensor on the air cleaner snorkel. On California models there will be two additional emissions hoses to label and disconnect.

7   Remove the air cleaner.

8   Disconnect the upper radiator hose from the water outlet.

9   Remove the two water outlet mounting bolts and separate the outlet from the intake manifold.

10   Remove the thermostat from the thermostat housing.

11   Before installing the thermostat, clean the gasket sealing surfaces on the water outlet and the thermostat housing.

12   Install the replacement thermostat in the thermostat housing.

13   Apply a thin coat of gasket adhesive to both sides of the new gasket and install the gasket on the thermostat housing.

14   Install the water outlet and tighten the bolts to the specified torque.

15   Install the upper radiator hose.

16   Fill the cooling system with the proper antifreeze/water mixture

3.27B The thermostat can then be lifted from the housing

3.28 Make sure that the thermostat housing and water outlet sealing surfaces are completely free of old sealant and gasket material

3.29 A 1/8-inch bead of RTV-type sealant must be applied to the water outlet or thermostat housing sealing surface on V6 and 2.0L four-cylinder engines

3.30 A torque wrench should be used when tightening the thermostat housing bolts because of the soft threads in the aluminum intake manifold

(refer to Chapter 1).

17 Reconnect the battery cable and start the engine.

18 Run the engine with the radiator cap removed until the upper radiator hose is hot (thermostat open).

19 With the engine idling, add coolant to the radiator until the level reaches the bottom of the filler neck.

20 Install the radiator cap, making sure the arrows on the cap line up with the radiator overflow tube.

2.0L four-cylinder engine

21 Refer to the Caution in Section 2.

22 Disconnect the negative battery cable.

23 Drain the cooling system until the level is below the thermostat (refer to Step 3).

24 Remove the steel vacuum pipes from the intake manifold to gain adequate working clearance.

25 Disconnect the upper radiator hose from the water outlet.

26 Remove the two water outlet mounting bolts and separate the water outlet from the thermostat housing.

27 Remove the thermostat from the thermostat housing. It may be necessary to scrape away some excess sealant to break the bond (photo).

28 Before installation, use a gasket scraper or putty knife to carefully remove all traces of the old gasket from the thermostat housing and the engine sealing surface (photo). Do not allow the gasket pieces to drop down into the intake manifold.

29 Apply a 1/8-inch bead of RTV sealant to the water outlet-to-engine sealing surface (photo) and place the thermostat into the recess.

30 Immediately place the thermostat housing with sealant and a new gasket into positon and tighten the bolts to the specified torque (photo).

31 Where applicable, install the alternator brace and/or the TVS switch and vacuum hoses.

32 Connect the upper radiator hose and tighten the clamp securely.

33 Reinstall the air cleaner.

34 To complete the installation, refer to Steps 16 through 20.

V6 engines

35 Refer to the Caution in Section 2.

36 Disconnect the cable from the negative battery terminal.

37 Drain the cooling system until the level is below the thermostat (refer to Step 3).

38 Disconnect the upper radiator hose from the thermostat housing.

39 If the present gasket is made of RTV-type sealant, it may be necessary to scrape away some excess sealant to break the bond.

40 The thermostat can now be lifted out. Note how the thermostat is positioned in the recess, as it must be replaced in the same position.

41 Refer to Steps 28 through 30.

42 Connect the upper radiator hose and tighten the hose clamp securely.

43 To complete the installation, refer to Steps 16 through 20.

4 Thermostat — check

1 The best way to check the operation of the thermostat is with it removed from the engine. In most cases, if the thermostat is suspect, it is more economical to simply buy and install a replacement thermostat, as they are not very costly.

2 To check, first remove the thermostat as described in Section 3.

3 Inspect the thermostat for excessive corrosion or damage. Replace it with a new one if either of these conditions is noted.

4 Place the thermostat in hot water (25 degrees above the temperature stamped on the thermostat). When submerged the valve should open all the way.

5 Next, remove the thermostat using a piece of bent wire and place it in water which is 10 degrees below the temperature on the thermostat. At this temperature the thermostat valve should close completely.

6 Reinstall the thermostat if it operates properly. If it does not, purchase a new thermostat of the same temperature rating.

5 Radiator — removal, servicing and installation

Caution: *The engine must be completely cool before beginning this procedure. Also, when working in the vicinity of the electric fan, disconnect the negative battery cable to prevent the fan from starting accidentally.*

1 Refer to the Caution in Section 2.

2 Disconnect the cable from the negative battery terminal.

3 Drain the radiator (refer to Chapter 1 if necessary).

4 Disconnect the upper and lower radiator hoses from the radiator.

5 On vehicles equipped with an automatic transmission, disconnect the fluid cooler lines at the radiator and immediately plug the lines.

Caution: *Do not disconnect the air-conditioning refrigerant lines (if equipped) leading to the condenser unit in front of the radiator.*

6 If equipped with air-conditioning, remove the air-conditioning hose from the retaining clip.

7 Remove the clamp securing the coolant reservoir hose to the radiator outlet. On V6 models, remove the hose from the upper radiator shroud retainers. Disconnect the coolant reservoir hose from the radiator.

8 Remove the bolts securing the top of the upper radiator shroud to the metal support (photo).

9 Remove the bolts securing the upper radiator shroud to the lower shroud (photo).

10 Pull straight up on the radiator and shroud assembly and remove it from the vehicle.

11 Carefully examine the radiator for evidence of leaks or damage. It is recommended that any necessary repairs be performed by a radiator

3

5.8 Location of the upper radiator shroud mounting bolts

5.9 Location of the upper shroud-to-lower shroud attaching bolts

repair shop.

12 With the radiator removed, brush accumulations of insects and leaves from the fins and examine and replace, if necessary, any hoses or clamps which have deteriorated.

13 The radiator can be flushed as described in Chapter 1.

14 Check the pressure rating of the radiator cap and have it tested by a service station.

15 If you are installing a new radiator, transfer the fittings from the old unit to the new one.

16 Installation is the reverse of the removal procedure. When setting the radiator in the chassis, make sure the bottom of the radiator is seated correctly in the two bottom cradles secured to the radiator support.

17 After installing the radiator, refill it with the proper coolant mixture (refer to Chapter 1), then start the engine and check for leaks.

18 If equipped with a new automatic transmission, check the transmission fluid level (refer to Chapter 1).

6   Water pump — check

1   A failure in the water pump can cause overheating and serious engine damage (the pump will not circulate coolant through the engine).

2   There are three ways to check the operation of the water pump while it is installed on the engine. If the pump is defective, it should be replaced with a new or rebuilt unit.

3   With the engine at normal operating temperature, squeeze the upper radiator hose. If the water pump is working properly a pressure surge will be felt as the hose is released.

4   Water pumps are equipped with 'weep' or vent holes. If a pump seal failure occurs, small amounts of coolant will leak from the weep holes. In most cases it will be necessary to use a flashlight from under the vehicle to see evidence of leakage from this point on the pump body.

5   If the water pump shaft bearings fail there may be a squealing sound emitted from the front of the engine while it is running. Shaft wear can be felt if the water pump pulley is forced up and down. Do not mistake drivebelt slippage (which also causes a squealing sound) for water pump failure.

7   Water pump — removal and installation

Caution: *The engine must be completely cool before beginning this procedure. Also, when working in the vicinity of the electric fan, disconnect the negative battery cable from the battery to prevent the fan from starting accidentally.*

1   Refer to the Caution in Section 2.

2   Disconnect the cable from the negative battery terminal.

3   Drain the cooling system (refer to Chapter 1 if necessary).

4   Mark the accessory drivebelts with white paint to simplify installation (photo).

5   On V6 models, remove the upper fan shroud (refer to Section 5 if necessary).

6   Remove the accessory drivebelts (alternator, air-conditioning compressor, AIR system pump, power steering pump, as applicable) by loosening the pivot and adjusting bolts and pushing the accessory toward the engine.

7   On some engines it may be necessary to remove one or more accessories to gain access to the water pump. Refer to the appropriate Chapter(s) for removal details.

8   Remove the bolts retaining the fan to the fan pulley hub, then separate the fan and pulley hub from the water pump.

9   Disconnect the heater and lower radiator hoses from the water pump.

10 Remove the water pump mounting bolts (photo) and separate the water pump from the engine. **Caution:** *On V6 engines, the water pump bolts hold the timing cover to the block. Removal of the water pump may break the chemical seal and allow coolant into the oil. To prevent this secure the timing cover to the block with the clamping device shown in the accompanying illustrations before removing the water pump.*

11 Prior to installing the water pump remove all old gasket material and sealant from the gasket sealing surfaces. Clean the threaded holes in the block as well.

12 Installation is the reverse of the removal procedure.

13 If a new water pump is being installed transfer the heater hose fitting from the old pump to the new one.

14 On 2.0L four-cylinder engines use a new gasket or RTV-type sealant

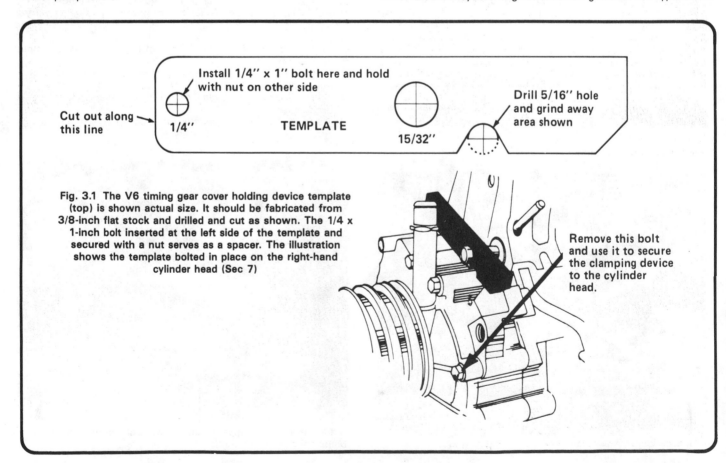

Fig. 3.1 The V6 timing gear cover holding device template (top) is shown actual size. It should be fabricated from 3/8-inch flat stock and drilled and cut as shown. The 1/4 x 1-inch bolt inserted at the left side of the template and secured with a nut serves as a spacer. The illustration shows the template bolted in place on the right-hand cylinder head (Sec 7)

Install 1/4" x 1" bolt here and hold with nut on other side

Cut out along this line

1/4"   TEMPLATE

15/32"

Drill 5/16" hole and grind away area shown

Remove this bolt and use it to secure the clamping device to the cylinder head.

when installing the pump.
15 On V6 engines use a new gasket when installing the pump.
16 Tighten the bolts to the specified torque after coating the threads with RTV-type sealant to prevent leaks. Follow a crisscross pattern and work up to the final torque in three steps.
17 Adjust all drivebelts (see Chapter 1).
18 Connect the negative battery cable and fill the radiator with a mixture of antifreeze and water. Start the engine and allow it to idle until the upper radiator hose gets hot. Check for leaks. With the engine hot, fill the radiator with more coolant mixture until the level is at the bottom of the filler neck. Install the radiator cap and check the coolant level periodically during the first few miles of driving.

8 Coolant temperature sending unit — check and replacement

1 The coolant temperature indicator system is composed of a light mounted in the instrument panel and a coolant temperature sending unit located at the left rear corner of the cylinder head on 2.0L engines and at the front of the left cylinder head on V6 engines. The sending unit on the 1.9L four-cylinder engine is located at the front of the intake manifold. If a temperature gauge is included in the instrument cluster the temperature sending unit is replaced by a transducer. **Caution:** *Since the ignition key will be in the On position for some of the*

diagnostic steps, be especially careful to stay clear of the electric fan blades.
2 If overheating occurs, check the coolant level in the system and then make sure that the wiring between the light or gauge and the sending unit is secure.
3 When the ignition switch is turned On and the starter motor is turning, the indicator light should be on (overheated engine indication). If the light is not on, the bulb may be burned out, the ignition switch may be faulty or the circuit may be open.
4 As soon as the engine starts the light should go out and remain out unless the engine overheats. Failure of the light to go out may be due to grounded wiring between the light and the sending unit, a defective sending unit or a faulty ignition switch.
5 If the sending unit is to be replaced it is unscrewed from the cylinder head using a six-point socket, and a replacement installed (photo). Make sure that the engine is cool before removing the defective sending unit. There will be some coolant loss, so check the level after the replacement has been installed.

9 Heater blower motor — removal and installation.

1 Disconnect the cable from the negative battery terminal.
2 Working in the engine compartment, disconnect the wires at the

7.4 Mark the drivebelts before removing them to ensure reinstallation on the correct pulleys

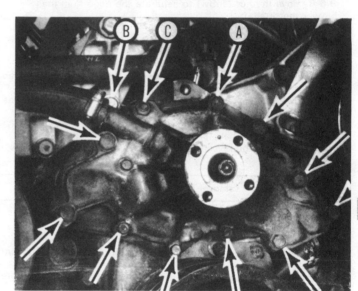

7.10 On V6 engines in which stud C goes through both the timing cover and the water pump, remove the water pump mounting bolts (arrows) *after* using bolt A to attach the tool mentioned in the text to the right cylinder head at location B

8.1 Location of the coolant temperature sending unit

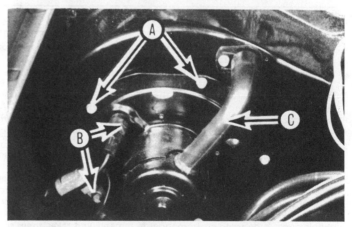

9.2 To remove the heater blower motor, remove the mounting bolts (A — 6 total), the motor and resistor wire (B) and the cooling tube (C)

3

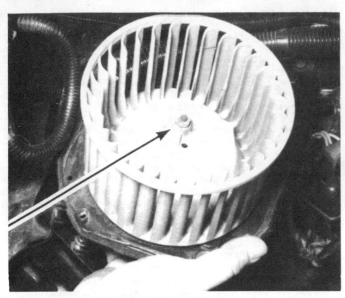

9.6 Remove the nut (arrow) to separate the cage from the blower motor shaft

lower blower motor and resistor (photo).
3   Disconnect the blower motor cooling tube.
4   On some models it may be necessary to disconnect the radio capacitor to allow removal of the blower motor.
5   Remove the blower motor mounting bolts and separate the motor/cage assembly from the case.
6   While holding the cage, remove the cage retaining nut and slide the cage off the motor shaft (photo).
7   Installation is the reverse of the removal procedure.

10   Heater core — removal and installation

1   Disconnect the negative battery cable.
2   Drain the coolant from the radiator (Chapter 1).
3   From inside the passenger compartment, remove the mounting bolts from the modular duct and remove the duct from the dashboard side of the firewall.
4   Disconnect the heater hoses at the heater core and plug the core tubes.
5   Remove the four mounting screws from the heater core and remove the core.
6   Installation is the reverse of removal.

11   Air conditioning system — servicing

1   Regularly inspect the condenser fins (located ahead of the radiator) and brush away leaves and bugs.
2   Clean the evaporator drain tubes.
3   Check the condition of the system hoses. If there is any sign of deterioration or hardening, have them replaced by your dealer. **Caution:** *Air conditioning system hoses cannot be disconnected until the presssurized refreigerant has been evacuated by an air conditioning technician. Serious injury can result from working on a system which is not properly evacuated.*
4   At the recommended intervals, check and adjust the compressor drivebelt as described in Chapter 1.
5   Because of the special tools, equipment and skills required to service air-conditioning systems major air-conditioner servicing procedures cannot be covered in this Manual. We will, however, cover component removal, as the home mechanic may realize a substantial savings in repair costs if he removes components himself and takes them to a professional for repair and/or replaces them with new ones.
6   As stated above, problems in the air-conditioning system should be diagnosed, and the system refrigerant evacuated by an air-

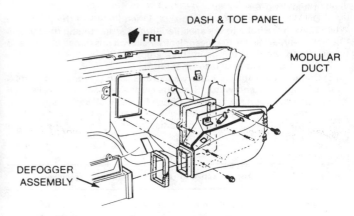

Fig. 3.2 The modular duct must be removed from beneath the dashboard to gain access to the heater core (Sec 10)

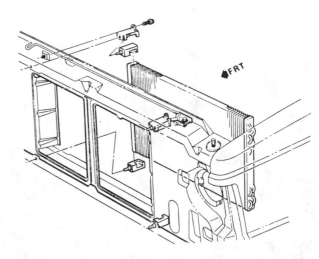

Fig. 3.3 Mounting details of the air-conditioning condenser (typical) (Sec 12)

conditioning technician before component removal/replacement is attempted.
7   Once the new or reconditioned component has been installed, the system should then be recharged and checked by an air-conditioning technician.
8   Before indiscriminately removing the air-conditioning system components, get more than one estimate of repair costs from reputable air-conditioning service centers. You may find it to be cheaper and less trouble to let the entire operation be performed by someone else.

12   Air-conditioning system condenser — removal and installation

Caution: *Before removing the condenser the system must be evacuated by an air-conditioning technician. Do not attempt to do this yourself — the refrigerant used in the system can cause serious injuries and respiratory irritation.*

1   After having the system evacuated, disconnect the coupled hose and liquid line fittings.
2   Remove the screws retaining the top radiator shroud.
3   Remove the radiator (Section 5).
4   Remove the shields from each side of the radiator support.
5   Remove the condenser mounting bolts.
6   Carefully tilt the radiator to the rear and lift the condenser out of the bottom cradle supports.
7   If the condenser is being replaced with a new one, transfer the

brackets and mounts from the old unit to the new one.

8   The installation procedures are the reverse of those for removal. When installing the hose and fittings, use new O-rings and lubricate them with 525 viscosity refrigerant oil.

9   After the condenser is installed, have the system recharged.

---

13   Air conditioning system compressor — removal and installation

Caution: *Before removing the compressor the system must be evacuated by an air-conditioning technician. Do not attempt to do this yourself — the refrigerant in the system can cause serious injuries and respiratory irritation.*

1   After having the system evacuated, remove the compressor pivot and adjusting bolts.

2   Disconnect the wire.

3   On four-cylinder models, remove the brace from the power steering bracket.

4   Remove the drivebelt, routing the lower loop behind the vibration damper to gain additional slack if necessary.

5   Remove the compressor from the mount.

6   Remove the fitting block (coupled hose assembly) bolt at the rear of the compressor.

7   If the compressor is being replaced with a new one, transfer the usable switches from the old unit to the new one.

8   Installation procedures are the reverse of those for removal. When installing the fitting block, use new O-rings and lubricate them with 525 viscosity refrigerant oil.

9   After the compressor is installed, have the system recharged.

3

Chapter 4 Fuel and exhaust systems

Refer to Chapter 13 for specifications and information related to 1985 and later models

Contents

Specifications

Rochester 2SE and E2SE carburetors

1982 models

Float adjustment, all	7/16-in (11.5 mm)
Fast idle cam (choke rod) adjustment, all	22 deg.
Primary vacuum break adjustment	
Carburetor numbers 17082348 and 17082350	26 deg.
All others	28 deg.
Air valve rod link adjustment, all	1 deg.
Secondary vacuum break adjustment	
Carburetor numbers 17082353 and 17082355	35 deg.
All others	32 deg.
Unloader adjustment	
Carburetor numbers 17082353 and 17082355	30 deg.
All others	35 deg.

1983 models

Float adjustment

Carburetor numbers:	13/32-in (10.3 mm)
17083356	
17083357	
17083358	
17083359	
Carburetor numbers:	1/8-in (3.2 mm)
17083368	
17083370	
17083450	
17083451	
17083452	
17083453	
17083454	
17083455	
17083456	
17083650	
Carburetor numbers:	1/4-in (6.5mm)
17083630	
17083631	
17083632	
17083633	
17083634	
17083635	
17083636	

Air valve spring adjustment
    Carburetor number 17083650 . . . .   1/2 turn
    All others . . . .   1 turn
Choke coil lever adjustment, all . . . .   0.085 in (2.18 mm)
Fast idle cam (choke rod) adjustment
    Carburetor numbers: . . . .   22 deg.
        17083356
        17083357
        17083358
        17083359
        17083368
        17083370
    All others . . . .   28 deg.

Primary vacuum break adjustment
    Carburetor numbers: . . . .   25 deg.
        17083356
        17083357
        17083358
        17083359
        17083368
        17083370
    All others . . . .   27 deg.
Air valve rod link adjustment, all . . . .   1 deg.
Secondary vacuum break adjustment, all . . . .   35 deg.
Unloader adjustment
    Carburetor numbers: . . . .   30 deg.
        17083356
        17083357
        17083358
        17083359
        17083368
        17083370
    All others . . . .   45 deg.

1984 models

Float adjustment
    Carburetor numbers: . . . .   9/32-in (7.0 mm)
        17084356
        17084357
        17084358
        17084359
        17084632
        17084633
        17084635
        17084636
    Carburetor numbers: . . . .   1/8-in (3.2 mm)
        17084368
        17084370
        17084542
    Carburetor numbers: . . . .   5/32-in (3.6 mm)
        17084360
        17084362
        17084364
        17084366
        17084534
        17084535
        17084537
        17084538
        17084540
    Carburetor numbers: . . . .   7/16-in (11.5 mm)
        17084390
        17084391
        17084392
        17084393
    All others . . . .   11/32-in (8.4 mm)
Air valve spring adjustment
    Carburetor numbers: . . . .   3/4 turn
        17084356
        17084357
        17084358
        17084359
        17084368
        17084370

4

Carburetor numbers: . . . .   1/2 turn
    17084534
    17084535
    17084537
    17084538
    17084540
    17084542
    17084632
    17084633
    17084635
    17084636
All others . . . .   1 turn
Coil choke lever adjustment . . . .   0.085 in (2.18 mm)
Fast idle cam (choke rod) adjustment
Carburetor numbers: . . . .   22 deg.
    17084348
    17084349
    17084350
    1708435l
    17084352
    17084353
    17084354
    17084355
    17084356
    17084357
    17084358
    17084359
    17084360
    17084362
    17084364
    17084366
    17084368
    17084370
Carburetor numbers: . . . .   15 deg.
    17084410
    17084412
    17084425
    17084427
    17084430
    17084431
    17084434
    17084435
    17084560
    17084562
    17084569
All others . . . .   28 deg.
Primary vacuum break adjustment
Carburetor numbers: . . . .   26 deg.
    17084425
    17084427
    17084430
    17084431
    17084434
    17084435
Carburetor numbers: . . . .   30 deg.
    17084348
    17084349
    17084350
    17084351
    17084352
    17084353
    17084354
    17084355
    17084360
    17084362
    17084364
    17084366
    17084390
    17084391
    17084392
17084393
All others . . . .   25 deg.
Air valve rod link adjustment, all . . . .   1 deg.

Secondary vacuum break adjustment
    Carburetor numbers: . . . . 30 deg.
        17084356
        17084357
        17084358
        17084359
        17084368
        17084370
    Carburetor numbers: . . . . 38 deg.
        17084390
        17084391
        17084392
        17084393
        17084410
        17084412
        17084430
        17084431
        17084434
        17084435
    All others . . . . 35 deg.
Unloader adjustment
    Carburetor numbers: . . . . 30 deg.
        17084356
        17084357
        17084358
        17084359
        17084368
        17084370
    Carburetor numbers: . . . . 38 deg.
        17084390
        17084391
        17084392
        17084393
        17084560
        17084562
        17084569
    Carburetor numbers: . . . . 40 deg.
        17084348
        17084349
        17084350
        17084351
        17084352
        17084353
        17084354
        17084355
        17084360
        17084362
        17084364
        17084366
        17084425
        17084427
    All others . . . . 45 deg.

Torque specifications   **Ft-lbs**
Carburetor mounting nuts (V6 and 2.0L 4-cyl) 13
Fuel inlet nut-to-carburetor 18
Carburetor fuel line-to-inlet nut 24
Fuel tank strap-to-frame rail bolts 25
Fuel tank strap-to-crossmember bolt 5
Fuel tank strap clamp bolt 5
Fuel pump mounting bolts 15

1 General information

The fuel system consists of a side mounted fuel tank, a mechanically operated fuel pump, a carburetor and an air cleaner. An electronically-controlled carburetor is used on California models.

The exhaust system includes a catalytic converter, muffler, related emissions equipment and associated pipes and hardware.

2 Fuel pump — check

Warning: *Gasoline is extremely flammable, so extra precautions must be taken when working on any part of the fuel system. Do not smoke or allow open flames or bare light bulbs near the work area. Also, do not work in a garage if a natural gas-type appliance with a pilot light is present.*

1   The fuel pump, located toward the front of the engine, is sealed and no repairs are possible. However, the pump can be inspected and tested as follows.
2   Make sure that there is fuel in the fuel tank.
3   With the engine running, check for leaks at all gasoline line connections between the fuel tank and the carburetor. Tighten any loose connections. Inspect all hoses for flat spots and kinks which would restrict the fuel flow. Air leaks or restrictions on the suction side of the fuel pump will greatly affect the pump's output.

4

4   Check for leaks at the fuel pump diaphragm flange.
5   Disconnect the high energy ignition (HEI) connector at the distributor, then disconnect the fuel inlet line from the carburetor and place it in a metal container.
6   Crank the engine a few revolutions and make sure that well-defined spurts of fuel are ejected from the open end of the line. If not, the fuel line is clogged or the fuel pump is defective.
7   Disconnect the fuel line at both ends and blow through it with compressed air. If the fuel line is not clogged, replace the fuel pump with a new one.

3   Fuel pump — removal and installation

Warning: *Gasoline is extremely flammable, so extra precautions must be taken when working on any part of the fuel system. Do not smoke or allow open flames or bare light bulbs near the work area. Also, do not work in a garage if a natural gas-type appliance with a pilot light is present.*

1   Disconnect the cable from the negative battery terminal.
2   Remove the fuel inlet and outlet lines. Use two wrenches to prevent damage to the pump and connections.
3   Remove the fuel pump mounting bolts, the pump and the gasket.
4   If the pushrod is to be removed, first remove the pipe plug or the pump adapter and gasket, as appropriate.
5   When installing the pump, first install the pushrod using gasket sealant on the pipe plug or gasket (where applicable). Hold the pushrod in position with heavy grease.
6   Install the pump using a new gasket. Use gasket sealant on the screw threads.
7   Connect the fuel lines, start the engine and check for leaks.

4   Fuel line — repair and replacement

Warning: *Gasoline is extremely flammable, so extra precautions must be taken when working on any part of the fuel system. Do not smoke or allow open flames or bare light bulbs near the work area. Also, do not work in a garage if a natural gas-type appliance with a pilot light is present.*

1   If a section of metal fuel line must be replaced, only brazed, seamless steel tubing should be used, since copper or aluminum does not have enough durability to withstand normal operating vibrations.
2   If only one section of a metal fuel line is damaged, it can be cut out and replaced with a piece of rubber hose. Be sure to use only reinforced fuel resistant hose, identified by the word 'Fluroelastomer' on the hose. The inside diameter of the hose should match the outside diameter of the metal line. The rubber hose should be cut four (4) in-

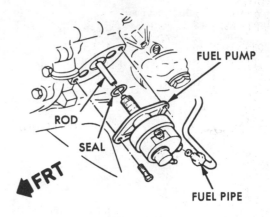

Fig. 4.1 V6 engine fuel pump installation — exploded view (Sec 3)

ches longer than the section it's replacing, so there are two (2) inches of overlap between the rubber and metal line at either end of the section. Hose clamps should be used to secure both ends of the repaired section.
3   If a section of metal line longer than six (6) inches is being removed, use a combination of metal tubing and rubber hose so the hose lengths will be no longer than 10 inches.
4   Never use rubber hose within four (4) inches of any part of the exhaust system or within 10 inches of the catalytic converter.
5   When replacing clamps, make sure the replacement clamp is identical to the one being replaced, as different clamps are used depending on location.

5   Fuel tank — removal and installation

Warning: *Gasoline is extremly flammable, so extra precautions must be taken when working on any part of the fuel system. Do not smoke or allow open flames or bare light bulbs near the work area. Also, do not work in a garage if natural gas-type appliance with a pilot light is present.*

1   Remove the cable from the negative battery terminal.
2   Remove the filler cap from the fuel tank.
3   Drain all fuel from the tank into a clean container. Since there are no drain plugs on the fuel tank and there is a restriction in the filler neck which prevents siphoning, the fuel will have to be drained through the line which feeds fuel from the tank to the fuel pump. Do not start

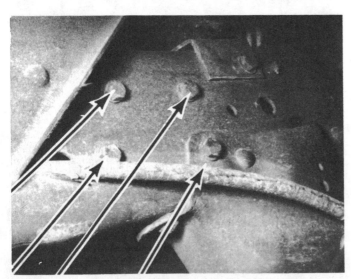

5.8   Location of the fuel tank mounting bolts which must be removed from the frame rail

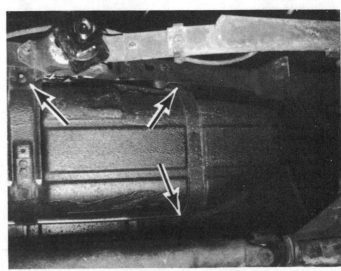

5.9   Location of the crossmember-to-fuel tank strap mounting bolts

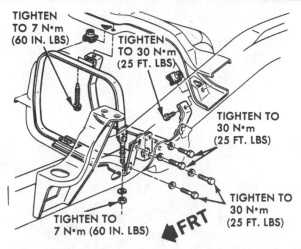

TIGHTEN TO 7 N·m (60 IN. LBS)

TIGHTEN TO 30 N·m (25 FT. LBS)

TIGHTEN TO 30 N·m (25 FT. LBS)

TIGHTEN TO 30 N·m (25 FT. LBS)

TIGHTEN TO 7 N·m (60 IN. LBS)

FRT

Fig. 4.2 Typical fuel tank installation details (Sec 5)

the siphoning process with your mouth — serious personal injury could result.

4   Raise the vehicle and support it securely on jackstands.

5   Disconnect the fuel gauge wire at the body wiring harness and the ground strap wire at the fuel tank reinforcement.

6   Disconnect the tank ventilator hose, fuel vapor hose and fuel feed and return hoses from the sender unit by loosening the hose clamps and pulling the hoses off the fittings.

7   Support the tank with a floor jack and wood block.

8   Remove the four fuel tank strap support bolts from the frame rail (photo).

9   Lower the jack to remove the tank.

10 Installation is the reverse of removal.

11 When the installation is complete, carefully check all lines, hoses and fittings for leaks.

6   Fuel tank — repair

1   Any repairs to the fuel tank or filler neck should be carried out by a professional who has experience in this critical and potentially dangerous work. Even after cleaning and flushing of the fuel system, explosive fumes can remain and ignite during repair of the tank.

2   If the fuel tank is removed from the vehicle, it should not be placed in an area where sparks or open flames could ignite the fumes coming out of the tank. Be especially careful inside garages where a natural gas-type appliance is located, because the pilot light could cause an explosion.

7   Carburetor — removal and installation

Warning: *Gasoline is extremly flammable, so extra precautions must be taken when working on any part of the fuel system. Do not smoke or allow open flames or bare light bulbs near the work area. Also, do not work in a garage if natural gas-type appliance with a pilot light is present.*

1   Remove the negative battery cable from the battery.

2   Label the air cleaner hoses and remove the air cleaner.

3   On V6 models, remove the mounting bolt from the three-way connector on the left rocker arm cover. Remove the fuel vapor hose from the carburetor (photo), and disconnect the coolant sensor lead wire. Place the hose and lead wire out of the way.

4   Label and remove all vacuum hoses from the carburetor.

5   Remove all electrical leads from the carburetor and position them out of the way (photo).

6   Disconnect the throttle return spring and accelerator linkage (photo).

7   Disconnect the downshift cable (automatic transmission only).

8   Remove the carburetor mounting nuts and/or bolts and separate the carburetor from the manifold.

9   Remove the gasket and/or EFE insulator.

10 Installation is the reverse of the removal procedure, but the following points should be noted:

   a) By filling the carburetor bowl with fuel, the initial start-up will

7.3   Removing the fuel vapor hose

7.5   All electrical leads and hoses should be placed out of the way before carburetor removal

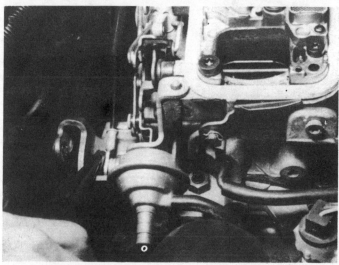

7.6   Needle nose pliers work well when removing the cable retaining circlip from the throttle linkage

4

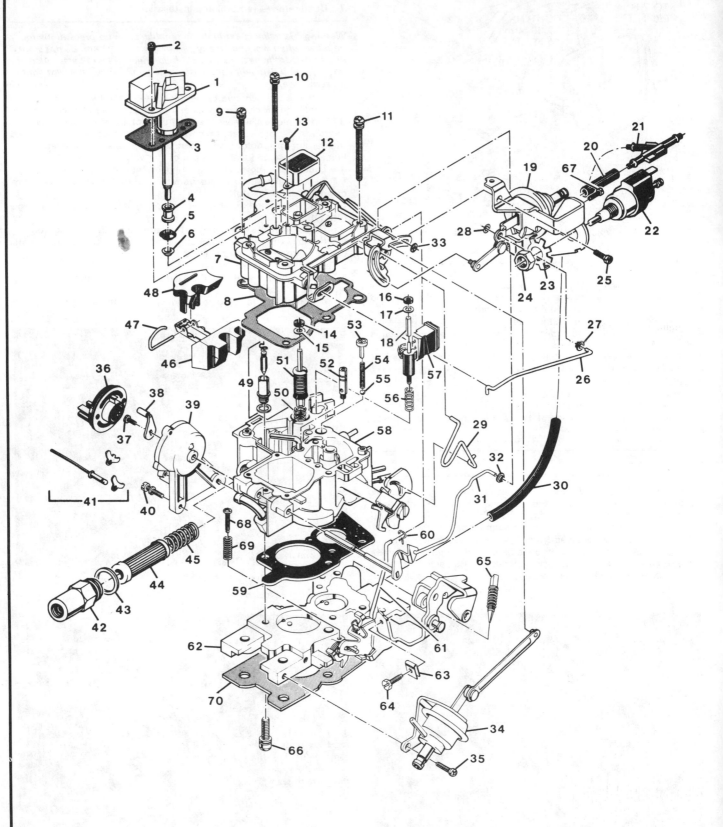

Fig. 4.3 E2SE carburetor — exploded view (Sec 8)

Air horn parts
1 Mixture control solenoid
2 Screw — M/C solenoid (3)
3 Gasket — M/C solenoid
4 Spacer — M/C solenoid
5 Seal — M/C solenoid
6 Retainer — M/C solenoid seal
7 Air horn assembly
8 Gasket — air horn
9 Screw — air horn, short (2)
10 Screw — air horn, long (3)
11 Screw — air horn, large
12 Vent stack
13 Screw — vent stack (2)
14 Seal — pump plunger
15 Retainer — pump plunger seal
16 Seal — TPS plunger
17 Retainer — TPS plunger seal
18 Plunger — TPS (throttle position sensor)
Choke parts
19 Vacuum break and bracket assembly — primary
20 Hose — vacuum break connecting
21 Tee — vacuum break connecting
22 Solenoid — idle speed
23 Retainer — idle speed solenoid
24 Nut — idle speed solenoid
25 Screw — vacuum break bracket attaching
26 Link — air valve
27 Bushing — air valve link
28 Retainer — air valve link
29 Link — fast idle cam
30 Hose — vacuum break
31 Intermediate choke shaft/lever/link assembly
32 Bushing — intermediate choke link
33 Retainer — intermediate choke link
34 Vacuum break and bracket assembly — secondary
35 Screw — vacuum break attaching (2)
36 Choke — cover and coil assembly
37 Screw — choke lever attaching
38 Choke lever and contact assembly
39 Choke housing
40 Screw — choke housing attaching (2)
41 Stat cover retainer kit
Float bowl parts
42 Nut — fuel inlet
43 Gasket — fuel inlet nut
44 Filter — fuel inlet
45 Spring — fuel filter
46 Float assembly
47 Hinge pin — float
48 Insert — float bowl
49 Needle and seat assembly
50 Spring — pump return
51 Pump assembly
52 Metering jet
53 Retainer — pump spring and check ball
54 Spring — pump check ball
55 Ball — pump check
56 Spring, TPS
57 Throttle position sensor (TPS)
58 Float bowl assembly
59 Gasket — float bowl
Throttle body parts
60 Clip — pump rod
61 Pump rod
62 Throttle body assembly
63 Clip — cam screw
64 Screw — fast idle cam
65 Idle needle and spring
66 Screw — throttle body attaching
67 Screw — vacuum break bracket attaching (new)
68 Screw — idle stop
69 Spring — idle stop screw
70 Gasket — intake manifold

be easier and less drain on the battery will occur.
b) New gaskets should be used.
c) Idle speed and mixture settings should be checked and, if necessary, adjusted.
d) Be sure to tighten the carburetor mounting nuts/bolts to the specified torque.

8 Carburetor (E2SE and 2SE) — overhaul and adjustment

Note: *Carburetor overhaul is an involved procedure that requires some experience. The home mechanic without much experience should have the overhaul done by a dealer service department or repair shop. Because of running production changes, some details of the unit overhauled here may not exactly match those of your carburetor, although the home mechanic with previous experience should be able to detect the differences and modify the procedure.*

Disassembly

1 Before disassembling the carburetor, purchase a carburetor rebuild kit for your particular model (the model number will be found on a metal tag at the side of the carburetor). This kit will have all the necessary replacement parts for the overhaul procedure.
2 It will be necessary to have a relatively large, clean workbench to lay out all of the parts as they are removed. Many of the parts are very small and can be lost easily if the work space is cluttered.
3 Carburetor disassembly is illustrated in the following step-by-step photo sequence to make the operation as easy as possible. Work slowly through the procedure and if at any point you feel the reassembly of a certain component may prove confusing, stop and make a rough sketch or apply identification marks. The time to think about reassembling the carburetor is when it is being taken apart. The disassembly photo sequence begins with photo 8.3/1.

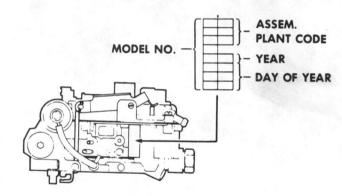

Fig. 4.4 Location of carburetor identification tag (Sec 8)

4

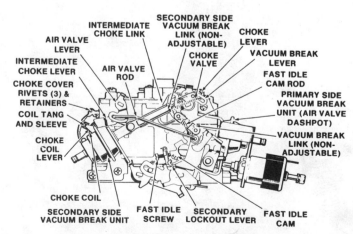

Fig. 4.5 E2SE carburetor choke system (Sec 8)

8.3/1   Remove the gasket from the top of the air horn

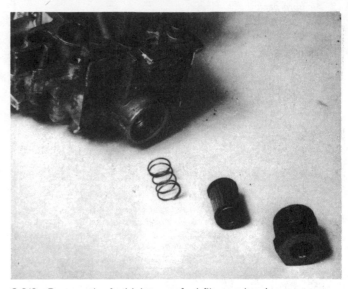

8.3/2   Remove the fuel inlet nut, fuel filter and spring

8.3/3   Remove the pump lever attaching screw

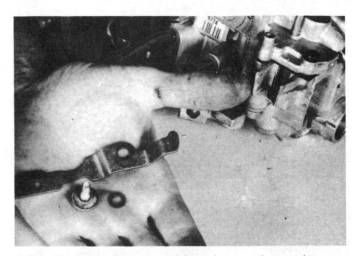

8.3/4   Disconnect the pump rod from the pump lever and remove the pump lever

8.3/5   Disconnect the primary vacuum break diaphragm hose from the throttle body

8.3/6   Remove the screws that retain the idle speed solenoid/vacuum break diaphragm bracket

8.3/7 Lift off the idle speed solenoid/vacuum break diaphragm assembly and disconnect the air valve link from the vacuum break plunger (repeat this step for the secondary vacuum break assembly, disconnecting the link from the slot in the choke lever

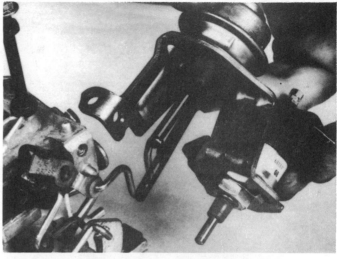

8.3/8 Disconnect the vacuum break and air valve links from the levers. Note: It is not necessary to disconnect the links from the vacuum break plungers unless either the rods or the vacuum break units are being replaced.

8.3/9 Pry off the clip that retains the intermediate choke link to the choke lever and separate the link from the lever

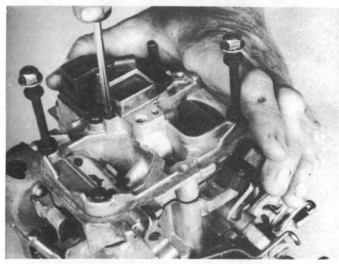

8.3/10 Remove the screws that retain the vent/screen assembly to the air horn and lift off the assembly

8.3/11 Remove the screws that retain the mixture control solenoid and, using a slight twisting motion, lift the solenoid out of the air horn

8.3/12 Remove the screws securing the air horn to the float bowl, noting their lengths and positions to simplify installation

4

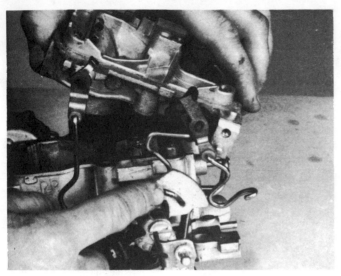

8.3/13   Rotate the fast idle cam up, lift off the air horn and disconnect the fast idle cam link from the fast idle cam

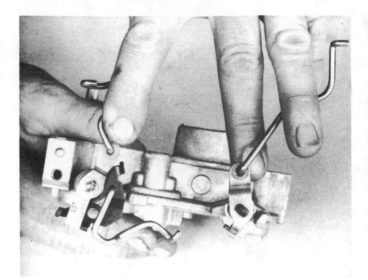

8.3/14   The links attached to the air horn need not be removed unless their reaplacement or removal is required to service other components

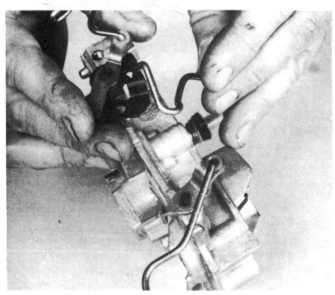

8.3/15   Disengage the fast idle cam link from the choke lever and save the bushing for reassembly

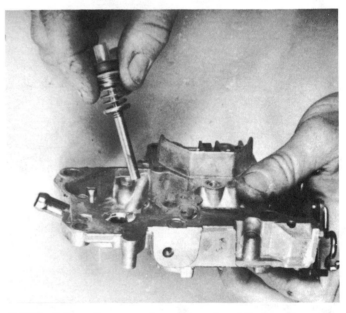

8.3/16   Remove the pump plunger from the air horn or the pump well in the float bowl. Note: For throttle position sensor (TPS) equipped carburetors, refer to the exploded-view drawing at this time and remove the TPS.

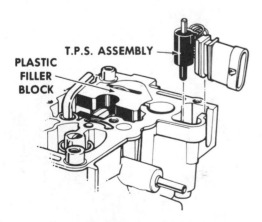

T.P.S. ASSEMBLY

PLASTIC FILLER BLOCK

Fig. 4.6 TPS removal on E2SE carburetors (push up from the bottom of the electrical connector and remove the TPS and connector assembly from the float bowl. Also remove the spring from the bottom of the float bowl) (Sec 8)

8.3/17   Compress the pump plunger spring and separate the spring retainer clip and spring from the piston

8.3/18   Remove the air horn gasket from the float bowl

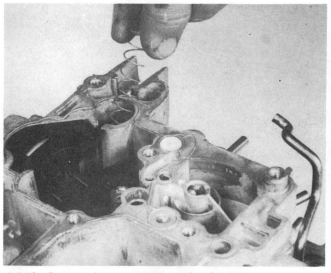

8.3/19   Remove the pump return spring from the pump well

8.3/20   Remove the plastic filler block that covers the float valve

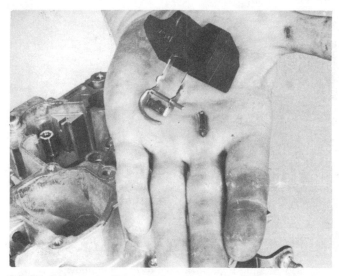

8.3/21   Remove the float and lever assembly, float valve and stabilizing spring (if used) by pulling up on the hinge pin

8.3/22   Remove the float valve seat and gasket (left) and the extended metering jet (right) from the float bowl

8.3/23   Using needle nose pliers, pull out the white plastic retainer and remove the pump discharge spring and check ball (do not pry on the retainer to remove it)

4

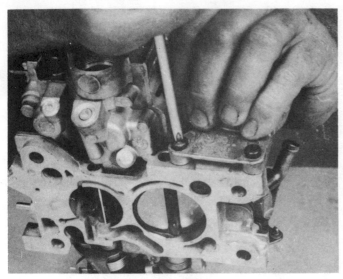

8.3/24   Remove the screws that retain the choke housing to the throttle body

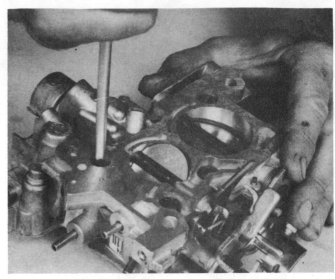

8.3/25   Remove the screws that retain the float bowl to the throttle body

8.3/26   Separate the float bowl from the throttle body

8.3/27   Carefully file the heads off the pop rivets that retain the choke cover to the choke housing, remove the cover and tap out the remainder of the rivets

8.3/28   Remove the choke coil lever screw and lift out the lever

8.3/29   Remove the intermediate shaft and lever assembly by sliding it out the lever side of the float bowl. For further procedures refer to Step 4 in the text.

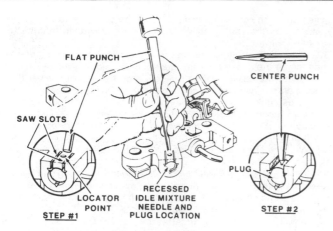

Fig. 4.7 E2SE carburetor idle mixture needle plug removal details (Sec 8)

4   The final step in disassembly involves the idle mixture needle. It is recessed in the throttle body and sealed with a hardened steel plug. The plug should not be removed unless the needle requires replacement or normal cleaning procedures fail to clean the idle mixture passages. If the idle mixture needle must be removed, refer to the accompanying illustration and proceed as follows.

5   Secure the throttle body in a vise so it is inverted with the manifold side up. Use blocks of wood to cushion the throttle body.

6   Locate the idle mixture needle and plug. It should be marked by an indented locator point on the underside of the throttle body. Using a hacksaw, make two parallel cuts in the throttle body on either side of the locator mark. The cuts should be deep enough to touch the steel plug, but should not extend more than 1/8-inch beyond the locator point.

7   Position a flat punch at a point near the ends of the saw marks. Holding it at a 45° angle, drive it into the throttle body until the casting breaks away, exposing the steel plug.

8   Use a center punch to make an indentation in the steel plug. Holding it at a 45° angle, drive the plug from the throttle body casting. **Note:** *If the plug breaks apart, be sure to remove all of the pieces.*

9   Use a 3/16-inch deep socket to remove the idle mixture needle and spring from the throttle body.

Cleaning and inspection

10   Clean the air horn, float bowl, throttle body and related components with clean solvent and blow them out with compressed air. A can of compressed air can be used if an air compressor is not available. *Do not use a piece of wire for cleaning the jets and passages.*

11   The idle speed solenoid, mixture control solenoid, Throttle Position Sensor, electric choke, pump plunger, diaphragm, plastic filler block and other electrical, rubber and plastic parts should *not* be immersed in carburetor cleaner because they will harden, swell or distort.

12   Make sure all fuel passages, jets and other metering components are free of burrs and dirt.

13   Inspect the upper and lower surfaces of the air horn, float bowl and throttle body for damage. Be sure all material has been removed.

14   Inspect all lever holes and plastic bushings for excessive wear and an out-of-round condition and replace them if necessary.

15   Inspect the float valve and seat for dirt, deep wear grooves and scoring and replace it if necessary.

16   Inspect the float valve pull clip for proper installation and adjust it if necessary.

17   Inspect the float, float arms and hinge pin for distortion and binding and correct or replace as necessary.

18   Inspect the rubber cup on the pump plunger for excessive wear and cracks.

19   Check the choke valve and linkage for excessive wear, binding and distortion and correct or replace as necessary.

20   Inspect the choke vacuum diaphragm for leaks and replace if necessary.

21   Check the choke valve for freedom of movement.

22   Check the mixture control solenoid in the following manner.

    a)   Connect one end of a jumper wire to either end of the solenoid connector and the other end to the positive terminal of the battery.

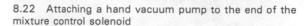

8.22   Attaching a hand vacuum pump to the end of the mixture control solenoid

8.25   Installing the gasket on the bottom of the float bowl

    b)   Connect another jumper wire between the other terminal of the solenoid connector and the negative terminal of the battery.

    c)   Remove the rubber seal and retainer from the end of the solenoid stem and attach a hand vacuum pump to it (photo).

    d)   With the solenoid fully energized (lean position), apply at least 25 in-Hg of vacuum and time the leak-down rate from 20 to 15 in-Hg. The leak-down rate should not exceed 5 in-Hg in five (5) seconds. If leakage exceeds that amount, replace the solenoid.

    e)   To check if the solenoid is sticking in the down position, again apply about 25 in-Hg of vacuum to it, then disconnect the jumper lead to the battery and watch the pump gauge reading. It should fall to zero in less than one (1) second.

Reassembly

23   Before reassembling the carburetor, compare all old and new gaskets back-to-back to make sure they match perfectly. Check especially that all the necessary holes are present and in the proper positions in the new gaskets.

24   If the idle mixture needle and spring have been removed, reinstall them by lightly seating the needle, then back it off three (3) turns. This will provide a preliminary idle mixture adjustment. Final idle mixture adjustment must be made on the vehicle. Proper adjustment must be done using special emission sensing equipment, making it impractical for the home mechanic. To have the mixture settings checked or readjusted, take your vehicle to a GM dealer or other qualified mechanic with the proper equipment.

25   Install a new gasket on the bottom of the float bowl (photo).

26 Mount the throttle body on the float bowl so it is properly in-stalled over the locating dowels on the bowl (photo), reinstall the screws and tighten them evenly and securely (photo). Be sure that the steps on the fast idle cam face toward the fast idle screw on the throttle lever when installed.

27 Inspect the linkage to make sure that the lockout tang properly engages in the slot of the secondary lockout lever and that the linkage moves freely without binding (photo).

28 Attach the choke housing to the throttle body, making sure the locating lug on the rear of the housing sits in the recess in the float bowl (photos).

29 Install the intermediate choke shaft and lever assembly in the float bowl by pushing it through from the throttle lever side.

30 Position the intermediate choke lever in the up position and install the thermostatic coil lever on the end sticking into the choke housing. The coil lever is properly aligned when the coil pick-up tang is in the 12 o'clock position (photo). Install the screw in the end of the in-termediate shaft to secure the coil lever.

31 Three self-tapping screws supplied in the overhaul kit are used in place of the original pop rivets to secure the choke cover and coil

assembly to the choke housing. Thread the screws into the housing, making sure they start easily and are properly aligned (photo), then remove them.

32 Place the fast idle screw on the highest step of the fast idle cam, then install the choke cover on the housing, aligning the notch in the cover with the raised casting projection on the housing cover flange (photo). When installing the cover, be sure the coil pick-up tang engages the inside choke lever. **Note:** *The thermostatic coil tang is formed so that it will completely encircle the coil pick-up lever. Make sure the lever is inside of the tang when installing the cover (refer to the accompa-nying illustration).*

33 With the choke cover in place, install the self-tapping screws and tighten them securely.

34 Install the pump discharge check ball and spring in the passage next to the float chamber, then place a new plastic retainer in the hole so that its end engages the spring and tap it lightly into place until the retainer top is flush with the bowl surface.

35 Install the main metering jet in the bottom of the float chamber (photo).

36 Install the float valve seat assembly and gasket (photo).

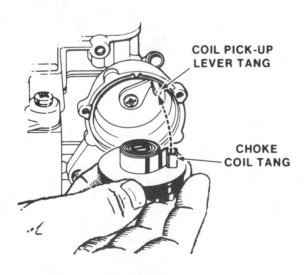

8.26a Mounting the throttle body on the float bowl

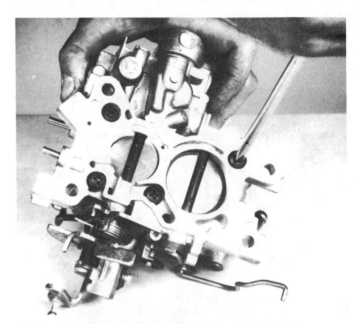

8.26b Installing the throttle body-to-float bowl attaching screws

Fig. 4.8 Details of the E2SE choke housing assembly (Sec 8)

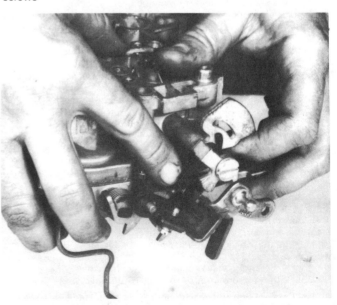

8.27 Checking the engagement of the lockout tang in the secondary lockout lever

8.28a   Attaching the choke housing to the throttle body

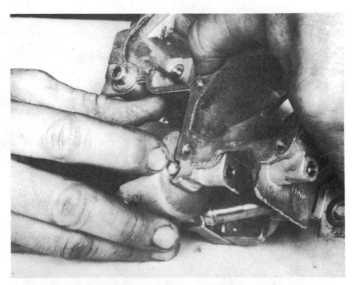

8.28b   The lug at the rear of the choke housing should sit in the bowl recess

8.30   Install the thermostatic coil lever so it is in the 12 o'clock position when the intermediate choke lever is facing up

8.31   The choke cover is reinstalled with the self-tapping screws supplied in the overhaul kit

8.32   Be sure the notch in the choke cover is aligned with the raised casting projection on the housing cover flange

8.35   Installing the main metering jet

8.36   Installing the float valve seat assembly

37 To make float level adjustments easier, bend the float arm up slightly at the notch before installing the float (photo).
38 Install the float valve onto the float arm by sliding the lever under the pull clip. The correct installation of the pull clip is shown in the accompanying illustrations. Install the float pin in the float lever (photo). Install the float assembly by aligning the valve and seat and the float retaining pin and locating channels in the float bowl.
39 To adjust the float level, hold the float pin firmly in place, push down on the float arm at the outer end, against the top of the float valve,

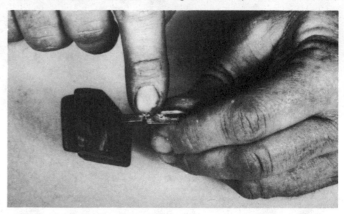

8.37   Prior to installation bend the float arm up slightly at the point shown

8.38   Installing the float retaining pin in the float lever

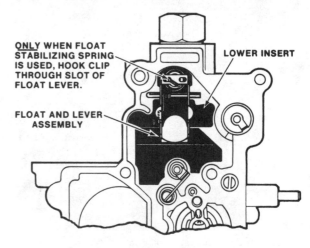

ONLY WHEN FLOAT STABILIZING SPRING IS USED, HOOK CLIP THROUGH SLOT OF FLOAT LEVER.

LOWER INSERT

FLOAT AND LEVER ASSEMBLY

Fig. 4.9 Correct installation of the pull clip on E2SE floats with a stabilizing spring (Sec 8)

8.39   Measuring the float level

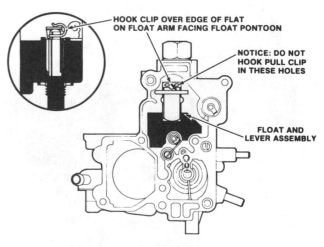

HOOK CLIP OVER EDGE OF FLAT ON FLOAT ARM FACING FLOAT PONTOON

NOTICE: DO NOT HOOK PULL CLIP IN THESE HOLES

FLOAT AND LEVER ASSEMBLY

Fig. 4.10 Correct installation of the pull clip on E2SE floats without a stabilizing spring (Sec 8)

and see if the top of the float is the specified distance from the float bowl surface (photo). Bend the float arm as necessary to achieve the proper measurement by pushing down on the pontoon. See the Specifications for the proper float measurement for your vehicle. Check the float level visually following adjustment.

40 Install the plastic filler block over the float valve so that it is flush with the float bowl surface (photo).

41 If the carburetor is equipped with a Throttle Position Sensor, install the TPS return spring in the bottom of the well in the float bowl. Then install the TPS and connector assembly by aligning the groove in the electrical connector with the slot in the float bowl. When properly installed, the assembly should sit below the float bowl surface.

42 Install a new air horn gasket on the float bowl (photo).

43 Install the pump return spring in the pump well (photo).

44 Reassemble the pump plunger assembly, lubricate the plunger cap with a thin coat of engine oil and install the pump plunger in the pump well (photo).

45 If used, remove the old pump plunger seal and retainer and the old TPS plunger seal and retainer from the air horn. Install new seals and retainers in both locations and lightly stake both seal retainers in three (3) places other than the original staking locations.

46 Install the fast idle cam rod in the lower hole of the choke lever.

47 If so equipped, apply a light coat of silicone grease or engine oil to the TPS plunger and push it through the seal in the air horn so that

8.40 Installing the plastic float block

8.42 Installing a new air horn gasket on the float bowl

8.43 Installing the pump return spring in the pump well

8.44 Installing the pump plunger in the pump well

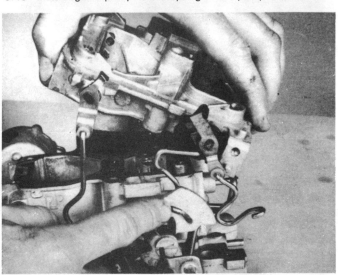

8.49 Engage the fast idle cam link in the fast idle cam prior to installation of the air horn

about one-half of the plunger extends above the seal.

48 Before installing the air horn, apply a light coat of silicone grease or engine oil to the pump plunger stem to aid in slipping it through the seal in the air horn.

49 Rotate the fast idle cam to the Up position so it can be engaged with the lower end of the fast idle cam rod (photo). While holding down on the pump plunger assembly, carefully lower the air horn onto the float bowl and guide the pump plunger stem through the seal.

50 Install the air horn retaining screws and washers, making sure the different length screws are inserted into their respective holes, then tighten them in the sequence illustrated.

51 If so equipped, install a new seal in the recess of the float bowl and attach the hot idle compensator valve.

52 Install a new rubber seal on the end of the mixture control solenoid stem until it is up against the boss on the stem (photo).

53 Using a 3/16-inch socket and a hammer (photo), drive the retainer over the mixture control solenoid stem just far enough to retain the rubber seal, while leaving a slight clearance between them for seal expansion.

54 Apply a light coat of engine oil to the rubber seal and, using a new gasket, install the mixture control solenoid in the air horn. Use a slight twisting motion while installing the solenoid to help the rubber seal slip into the recess.

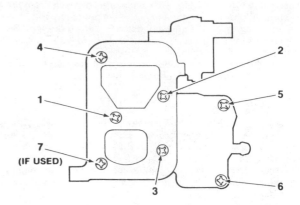

Fig. 4.11 Recommended air horn screw tightening sequence for E2SE carburetor (Sec 8)

8.52 Attaching a new rubber seal to the mixture control solenoid

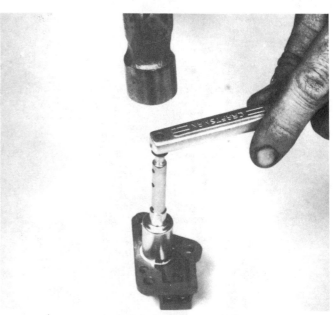

8.53 Using a hammer and a hollow tool to tap the seal retainer onto the mixture control solenoid stem

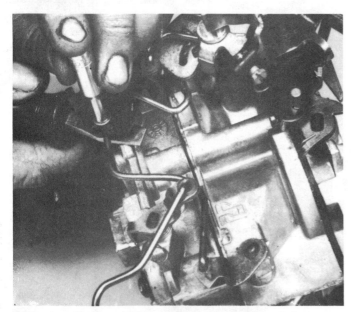

8.56 Attaching a retaining clip to the intermediate choke rod to secure it to the choke lever

8.57 Installing the idle speed solenoid/vacuum break diaphragm assembly

8.58a   Engaging the pump rod with the pump rod lever

55 Install the vent/screen assembly on the air horn.
56 Install a plastic bushing in the hole in the choke lever, with the small end facing out, then, with the intermediate choke lever at the 12 o'clock position, install the intermediate choke rod in the bushing. Install a new retaining clip on the end of the rod. Use a broad flat-blade screwdriver and a 3/16-inch socket as shown in the photo. Make sure the clip is not seated tightly against the bushing and that the linkage moves freely.
57 Reattach the primary and secondary vacuum break links and install the vacuum break and idle speed solenoid assemblies (photo).
58 Engage the pump rod with the pump rod lever (photo), install a new retaining clip on the pump rod and install the pump lever on the air horn with the washer between the lever and the air horn (photo).
59 Reconnect the vacuum break hoses.
60 Install the fuel filter with the hole facing toward the inlet nut.
61 Place a new gasket on the inlet nut and install and tighten it securely. Take care not to over tighten the nut, as it could damage the gasket, leading to a fuel leak.
62 Install a new gasket on the top of the air horn (photo).
63 Check that all linkage hook-ups have been made and that they do not bind.
64 For external linkage adjustment procedures, refer to the accompanying illustrations.

8.58b   Inserting the pump rod mounting screw through the pump rod prior to installation

8.62   Installing a new gasket on top of the air horn

① REMOVE AIR HORN VENT STACK.
② SELECT CORRECT GAGE FROM BT-8104 OR J-9789-135 SERIES FOR CARBURETOR.
③ a USING BT-8104 GAGE SERIES, INSERT BRIDGE
       -OR-
   b USING J-9789-135 GAGE SERIES, REMOVE AIR HORN SCREW NEXT TO OPEN VENT.
④ WITH ENGINE RUNNING AT IDLE, CHOKE WIDE-OPEN, INSERT GAGE IN BRIDGE OR GUIDE HOLE, AND ALLOW IT TO FLOAT FREELY.

NOTICE: DO NOT PRESS DOWN ON GAGE. FLOODING OR FLOAT DAMAGE COULD RESULT.

⑤ OBSERVE AT EYE LEVEL THE MARK ON GAGE THAT LINES UP WITH TOP OF BRIDGE OR AIR HORN CASTING. SETTING SHOULD BE WITHIN ±1.588mm (1/16") OF SPECIFIED FLOAT LEVEL SETTING.
   INCORRECT FUEL PRESSURE WILL ADVERSELY AFFECT FUEL LEVEL.
⑥ IF NECESSARY, REMOVE AIR HORN AND ADJUST FLOAT LEVEL TO SPECIFICATION.

BT-8104

J-9789-135

Fig. 4.12 E2SE carburetor external float check procedure (Sec 8)

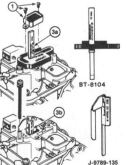
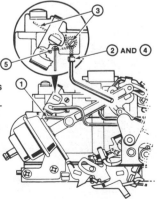

① IF NECESSARY, REMOVE INTERMEDIATE CHOKE ROD, TO GAIN ACCESS TO LOCK SCREW.
② LOOSEN LOCK SCREW USING 3/32" (2.381mm) HEX WRENCH.
③ TURN TENSION-ADJUSTING SCREW CLOCKWISE UNTIL AIR VALVE OPENS SLIGHTLY.
   TURN ADJUSTING SCREW COUNTER-CLOCKWISE UNTIL AIR VALVE JUST CLOSES. CONTINUE COUNTER-CLOCKWISE SPECIFIED NUMBER OF TURNS.
④ TIGHTEN LOCK SCREW.
⑤ APPLY LITHIUM BASE GREASE TO LUBRICATE PIN AND SPRING CONTACT AREA.

Fig. 4.13 E2SE carburetor air valve spring adjustment procedure (Sec 8)

4

① IF RIVETED, DRILL OUT AND REMOVE RIVETS. REMOVE CHOKE COVER AND COIL ASSEMBLY.
② PLACE FAST IDLE SCREW ON HIGH STEP OF FAST IDLE CAM.
③ PUSH ON INTERMEDIATE CHOKE LEVER UNTIL CHOKE VALVE IS CLOSED.
④ INSERT .085" (2.18mm) PLUG GAGE IN HOLE.
⑤ EDGE OF LEVER SHOULD JUST CONTACT SIDE OF GAGE.
⑥ SUPPORT AT "S" AND BEND INTERMEDIATE CHOKE ROD TO ADJUST.

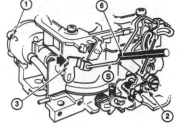
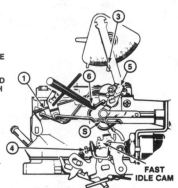

Fig. 4.14 E2SE carburetor choke coil lever adjustment procedures (typical) (Sec 8)

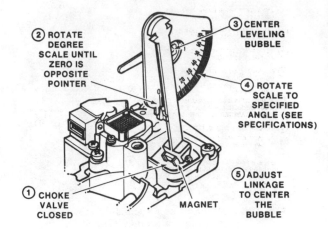

② ROTATE DEGREE SCALE UNTIL ZERO IS OPPOSITE POINTER
③ CENTER LEVELING BUBBLE
④ ROTATE SCALE TO SPECIFIED ANGLE (SEE SPECIFICATIONS)
⑤ ADJUST LINKAGE TO CENTER THE BUBBLE
① CHOKE VALVE CLOSED
MAGNET

Fig. 4.15 Measuring the E2SE carburetor choke valve angle with an angle gauge (Sec 8)

① ATTACH RUBBER BAND TO INTERMEDIATE CHOKE LEVER.
② OPEN THROTTLE TO ALLOW CHOKE VALVE TO CLOSE.
③ SET UP ANGLE GAGE AND SET ANGLE TO SPECIFICATIONS.
④ PLACE FAST IDLE SCREW ON SECOND STEP OF CAM AGAINST RISE OF HIGH STEP.
⑤ PUSH ON CHOKE SHAFT LEVER TO OPEN CHOKE VALVE AND TO MAKE CONTACT WITH BLACK CLOSING TANG.
⑥ SUPPORT AT "S" AND ADJUST BY BENDING FAST IDLE CAM ROD UNTIL BUBBLE IS CENTERED.

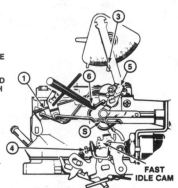

Fig. 4.16 E2SE carburetor choke rod fast idle cam adjustment procedure (Sec 8)

PLUGGING AIR BLEED HOLES

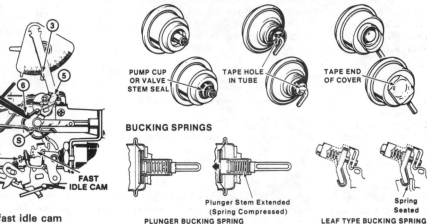

PUMP CUP OR VALVE STEM SEAL
TAPE HOLE IN TUBE
TAPE END OF COVER

BUCKING SPRINGS

Plunger Stem Extended (Spring Compressed)
PLUNGER BUCKING SPRING
Spring Seated
LEAF TYPE BUCKING SPRING

Fig. 4.17 E2SE carburetor vacuum break adjustment details (Sec 8)

⑤ AIR VALVE ROD MUST NOT RESTRICT PLUNGER FROM RETRACTING FULLY. IF NECESSARY, SUPPORT AT "S-S" AND BEND ROD (SEE ARROW) TO PERMIT FULL PLUNGER TRAVEL. FINAL ROD CLEARANCE MUST BE SET AFTER VACUUM BREAK SETTING HAS BEEN MADE. WHERE APPLICABLE, PLUNGER STEM MUST BE EXTENDED FULLY TO COMPRESS BUCKING SPRING.
⑥ TO CENTER BUBBLE, EITHER:
A ADJUST WITH 1/8" (3.175 mm) HEX WRENCH (VACUUM STILL APPLIED).
-OR-
B SUPPORT AT "6-S" AND BEND WIRE-FORM VACUUM BREAK ROD. (VACUUM STILL APPLIED).
① ATTACH RUBBER BAND TO INTERMEDIATE CHOKE LEVER.
② OPEN THROTTLE TO ALLOW CHOKE VALVE TO CLOSE.
③ SET UP ANGLE GAGE AND SET ANGLE TO SPECIFICATION.
④ RETRACT VACUUM BREAK PLUNGER USING VACUUM SOURCE, AT LEAST 18" HG. PLUG AIR BLEED HOLES WHERE APPLICABLE.

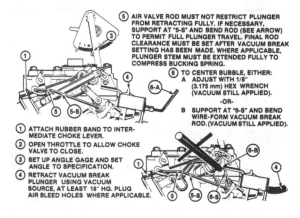

Fig. 4.18 E2SE carburetor primary vacuum break adjustment procedure for models with dual vacuum break units (Sec 8)

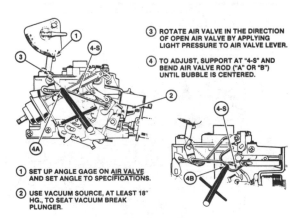

③ ROTATE AIR VALVE IN THE DIRECTION OF OPEN AIR VALVE BY APPLYING LIGHT PRESSURE TO AIR VALVE LEVER.
④ TO ADJUST, SUPPORT AT "4-S" AND BEND AIR VALVE ROD ("A" OR "B") UNTIL BUBBLE IS CENTERED.
① SET UP ANGLE GAGE ON AIR VALVE AND SET ANGLE TO SPECIFICATIONS.
② USE VACUUM SOURCE, AT LEAST 18" HG., TO SEAT VACUUM BREAK PLUNGER.

Fig. 4.19 E2SE carburetor air valve link adjustment procedure (Sec 8)

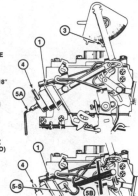

1. ATTACH RUBBER BAND TO INTER-MEDIATE CHOKE LEVER.
2. OPEN THROTTLE TO ALLOW CHOKE VALVE TO CLOSE.
3. SET UP ANGLE GAGE AND SET ANGLE TO SPECIFICATION.
4. RETRACT VACUUM BREAK PLUNGER USING VACUUM SOURCE, AT LEAST 18" HG. PLUG AIR BLEED HOLES WHERE APPLICABLE.
   WHERE APPLICABLE, PLUNGER STEM MUST BE EXTENDED FULLY TO COMPRESS PLUNGER BUCKING SPRING.
5. TO CENTER BUBBLE, EITHER:
   A. ADJUST WITH 1/8" (3.175 mm) HEX WRENCH (VACUUM STILL APPLIED)
      -OR
   B. SUPPORT AT "5-S", BEND WIRE-FORM VACUUM BREAK ROD (VACUUM STILL APPLIED)

Fig. 4.20 E2SE carburetor secondary vacuum break adjustment procedure (Sec 8)

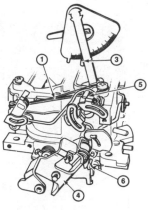

1. ATTACH RUBBER BAND TO INTER-MEDIATE CHOKE LEVER.
2. OPEN THROTTLE TO ALLOW CHOKE VALVE TO CLOSE.
3. SET UP ANGLE GAGE AND SET ANGLE TO SPECIFICATIONS.
4. HOLD THROTTLE LEVER IN WIDE OPEN POSITION.
5. PUSH ON CHOKE SHAFT LEVER TO OPEN CHOKE VALVE AND TO MAKE CONTACT WITH BLACK CLOSING TANG.
6. ADJUST BY BENDING TANG UNTIL BUBBLE IS CENTERED.

Fig. 4.21 E2SE carburetor unloader adjustment procedure (Sec 8)

9 Carburetor (DCH340/DFP340) — overhaul and adjustment

Note: *Carburetor overhaul is an involved procedure that requires some experience. The home mechanic without much experience should have the overhaul done by a dealer service department or repair shop. Because of running production changes, some details of the unit overhauled here may not exactly match those of your carburetor, although the home mechanic with previous experience should be able to detect the differences and modify the procedure.*

Disassembly

1 Remove the two throttle return springs.
2 Disconnect the accelerator pump lever.
3 Remove the choke lead connector mounting bracket from the carburetor.
4 Disconnect the switch vent valve lead wire.
5 Disconnect the choke connecting rod from the counter (fast idle) lever by removing the circlip.
6 Disconnect the vacuum hose from the choke chamber. Remove the four screws from the choke chamber assembly and remove the assembly.
7 Remove the circlip retaining the vacuum break diaphragm plunger to the secondary throttle lever. Remove the diaphragm assembly screws and remove the diaphragm from the carburetor.
8 Remove the float chamber screws and separate the float chamber

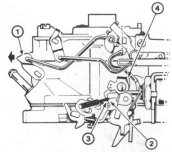

1. HOLD CHOKE VALVE WIDE OPEN BY PUSHING DOWN ON INTERMEDIATE CHOKE LEVER.
2. OPEN THROTTLE LEVER UNTIL END OF SECONDARY ACTUATING LEVER IS OPPOSITE TOE OF LOCKOUT LEVER.
3. GAGE CLEARANCE - DIMENSION SHOULD BE .025".
4. IF NECESSARY TO ADJUST, BEND LOCKOUT LEVER TANG CONTACTING FAST IDLE CAM.

Fig. 4.22 E2SE carburetor secondary lockout adjustment procedure (Sec 8)

from the throttle chamber.
9 Remove the screws from the base of the accelerator pump and remove the accelerator pump assembly.
10 Remove the fuel inlet nipple and strainer. Be careful not to distort the strainer during removal.

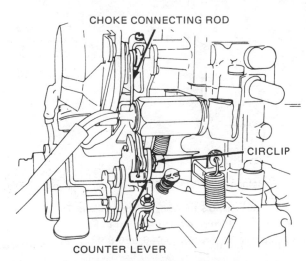

Fig. 4.23 The choke rod is retained on the fast idle lever with a small circlip (Sec 9)

CHOKE CONNECTING ROD
CIRCLIP
COUNTER LEVER

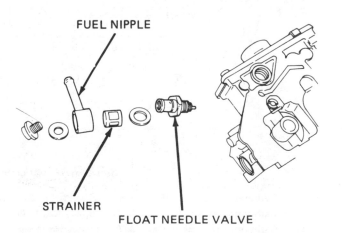

Fig. 4.24 Exploded view of the inlet fuel nipple and float needle valve (Sec 9)

FUEL NIPPLE
STRAINER
FLOAT NEEDLE VALVE

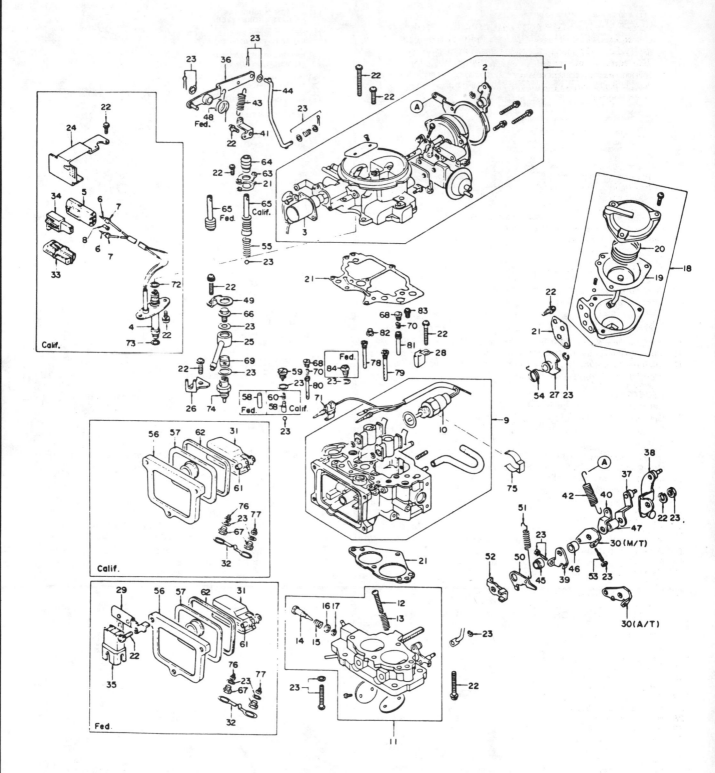

Fig. 4.25 DCH/DFP 340 carburetor — exploded view (Sec 9)

Carburetor assembly, Fed. (Incl. Key No. 1 thru 3, 9 thru 23, 25 thru 32, 35 thru 59, 61 thru 71 and 74 thru 84)
Carburetor assembly, Calif. M/T (Incl. Key No. 1 thru 28, 30 thru 34, 36 thru 47 and 49 thru 83)
Carburetor assembly, Calif. A/T (Incl. Key No. 1 thru 28, 30 thru 34, 36 thru 47 and 49 thru 83)

11 Using a six-point socket, remove the float needle valve.
12 Remove the three screws from the float bowl cover and remove the cover. Carefully remove the float and float collar.
13 Remove the jets from the top of the float chamber (refer to the accompanying illustration).
14 Remove the injector weight plug and the injector weight and check ball. On California models there will also be a spring.

Note: The DCH/DFP 340 series carburetors contain several subassemblies which vary in their component parts depending upon the sales destination of the car (California or other) and whether the car is equipped with a manual or automatic transmission. Therefore, not all parts listed in the carburetor breakdown below are included in all carburetors.

1 Chamber assembly, choke, carb., Fed.(Incl. Key No. 2, 3)
1 Chamber assembly, choke, carb., Calif. (Incl. Key No. 2 thru 8)
2 Lever, counter, choke, carb.
3 Valve, solenoid, sw. vent.
4 Valve, solenoid, duty, Calif.
5 Connector, 3P, Calif.
6 Terminal, duty solenoid, Calif.
7 Seal, duty solenoid, Calif.
8 Plug, duty solenoid, Calif.
9 Chamber assembly, float, Fed. (Incl. Key No. 10)
9 Chamber assembly, float, Calif. (Incl. Key No. 10)
10 Valve, solenoid, slow cut, Fed.
10 Valve, solenoid, slow cut, Calif.
11 Chamber assembly, throttle, Fed. (Incl. Key No. 12 thru 17)
11 Chamber assembly, throttle, Calif. M/T (Incl. Key No. 12 thru 17)
11 Chamber assembly, throttle, Calif. A/T (Incl. Key No. 12 thru 17)
12 Screw, throttle adj., carb.
13 Spring, throttle adj., carb.
14 Screw, idle adj., carb.
15 Spring, idle adj., carb.
16 Washer, idle adj., carb.
17 Seal, rubber, idle adj., carb.
18 Chamber assembly, diaphragm (Incl. key No. 19, 20)
19 Diaphragm, carb.
20 Spring, diaphragm, carb.
21 Gasket kit, carb., overhaul, Fed.
21 Gasket kit, carb., overhaul, Calif.
22 Screw and washer kit (A), carb., Fed.
22 Screw and washer kit (A), carb., Calif.
23 Screw and washer kit (B), carb.
24 Bracket, connector, Calif.
25 Nipple, fuel, carb.
26 Plate, stopping, carb.
27 Cam, fast idle, F42, Fed.
27 Cam, fast idle, F52, Calif. M/T
27 Cam, fast idle, F53, Calif. A/T
28 Holder, lead wire, carb.
29 Hanger, connector, Fed.
30 Lever, fast adj., carb., M/T
30 Lever, fast adj., carb., A/T
31 Float, fuel, carb.
32 Plate, lock, drain plug
33 Connector, 2P, Calif.
34 Connector, 1P, Calif.
35 Connector, 3P, Fed.
36 Lever, pump, carb.

37 Lever, accl., carb.
38 Lever, cruise, carb.
39 Lever, kick, carb.
40 Hanger, spring A, carb.
41 Hanger, spring B, carb.
42 Spring, main, carb.
43 Spring, assist, carb.
44 Rod, pump, carb.
45 Sleeve, carb.
46 Collar, shaft A, carb.
47 Collar, shaft B, carb.
48 Spring, pump lever, Fed.
49 Lever, lock, carb.
50 Plate, return, carb.
51 Spring, throttle, S
52 Lever, adj., carb.
53 Screw, fast idle, carb.
54 Spring, cam, carb.
55 Spring, piston return, carb., Fed.
55 Spring, piston return, carb., Calif.
56 Cover, lever gauge
57 Gauge, level
58 Weight, injector, Fed.
58 Weight, injector, Calif.
59 Screw, pump set, carb.
60 Spring, injector, Calif.
61 Collar, C, carb.
62 Seal, rubber, carb.
63 Plate, cyl., carb.
64 Cover, dust, carb.
65 Piston, carb., Fed.
65 Piston, carb., Calif.
66 Screw, nipple set, carb.
67 Plug, drain fuel, carb.
68 Plug, taper, carb.
69 Filter, carb.
70 Spring, slow jet
71 Connector, lead wire
72 O-ring, carb., S9, Calif.
73 O-ring, carb., S7, Calif.
74 Valve, needle, 1.8, carb., Fed.
74 Valve, needle, 2.0, carb., Calif.
75 Clip, lead wire, carb.
76 Jet, main, P, #114, Fed.
76 Jet, main, P, #93, Calif.
77 Jet, main, S, #170, Fed.
77 Jet, main, S, #180, Calif.
78 Bleed, air main, P, #120, Fed.
78 Bleed, air main, P, #100, Calif.
79 Bleed, air main, S, #70, Fed.
79 Bleed, air main, S, #90, Calif.
80 Jet, slow, P, #50, Fed.
80 Jet, slow, P, #53, Calif.
81 Jet, slow, S, #100, Fed.
81 Jet, slow, S, #125, Calif.
82 Bleed, air, slow, P, #150, Fed.
82 Bleed, air, slow, P, #120, Calif.
83 Bleed, air, slow, S, #110, Fed.
83 Bleed, air, slow, S, #130, Calif.
84 Valve, power, #50, Fed.

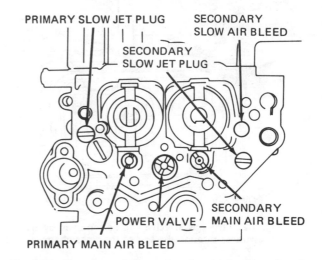

Fig. 4.26 Float assembly components (typical of all models except California) (Sec 9)

Fig. 4.27 Locations of the various jets in the float chamber (Sec 9)

4

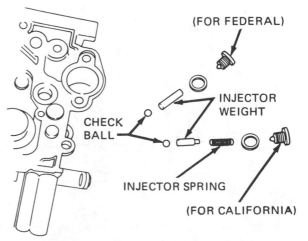

Fig. 4.28 Exploded view of the injector weight and ball (Sec 9)

15 Using a screwdriver, remove the power valve from the base of the float chamber (be sure that the screwdriver blade fits the valve head snugly).
16 Remove the two main jet plugs from the top of the float chamber and remove the primary and secondary main jets.
17 Remove the primary slow air bleed jet from the bottom of the choke chamber (refer to the accompanying illustration).
18 Do not remove the primary throttle valve, secondary throttle valve or choke valve. Also, on California models, do not remove the slow and main actuators.

Cleaning and inspection
19 Clean the choke chamber, float chamber and throttle chamber with clean solvent and blow them out with compressed air. Do not use a piece of wire for cleaning the jets and passages.
20 Do not immerse any rubber or plastic parts in solvent because they will harden, swell or distort.
21 Make sure all fuel passages, jets and other metering components are free of burrs and dirt.
22 Inspect the upper and lower surfaces of the choke chamber, float chamber and throttle chamber for damage. Be sure all gasket material has been removed.
23 Inspect all lever holes for excessive wear and an out-of-round condition.

24 Inspect the fuel inlet strainer for corrosion and damage.
25 Inspect the rubber cup on the pump plunger for excessive wear or cracks.
26 Inspect the float, float arms and float collar for distortion and binding and correct or replace as necesary.
27 Check the choke valve and linkage for excessive wear, binding and distortion and correct or replace as necessary.

Reassembly
28 Reassembly is the reverse of disassembly, but refer to the following steps:
29 On all vehicles except California models, be careful not to bend the valve rod when installing the power valve.
30 Be careful not to bend the piston connecting rod when reassembling the accelerator pump.
31 If the main actuator was removed, be sure to apply grease to the O-ring before installation and tighten it carefully to avoid damaging the O-ring.

Float level adjustment
32 The float level is checked by measuring the stroke of the needle valve.
33 Invert the float chamber and raise the float completely. Measure the clearance between the fully seated valve stem and the

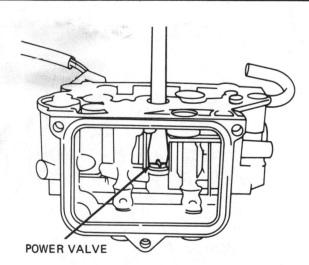

Fig. 4.29 The power valve can be removed by inserting a screwdriver through the top of the float chamber (Sec 9)

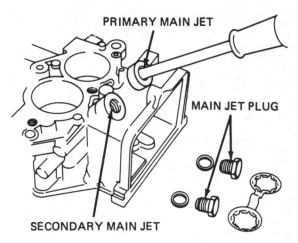

Fig. 4.30 Be sure to use the proper size screwdriver when removing the main jets (Sec 9)

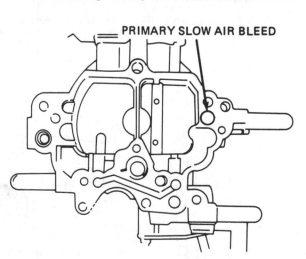

Fig. 4.31 The primary slow air bleed location (Sec 9)

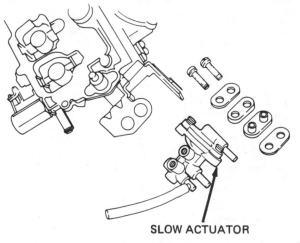

Fig. 4.32 The slow actuator, although detached for illustrative purposes here, must not be removed on California models (Sec 9)

float tang. A number 53 drill bit works well for this procedure (the specified clearance is 1.5 mm). The drill bit should just fit between the tang of the raised float and the valve stem — do not force it!

Primary throttle valve adjustment
34 Close the choke valve completely.
35 Turn the throttle stop screw all the way in.
36 Measure the clearance between the throttle valve and the wall of the throttle valve chamber. Again, a drill bit will work well as a gauge.

Use a number 54 or 55 drill bit for vehicles equipped with a manual transmissions. A number 51, 52 or 53 bit will work for vehicles equipped with an automatic transmissions.
37 If necessary, adjust the throttle valve opening by turning the fast idle screw.

Secondary throttle valve adjustment
38 The secondary throttle valve should begin to open when the primary throttle valve opens to an angle of 47 degrees. Using a drill bit as a

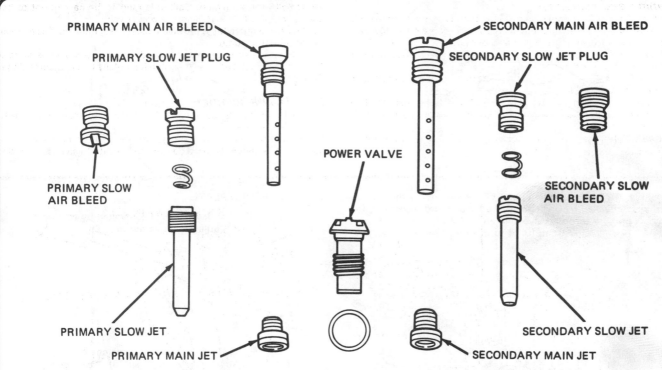

Fig. 4.33 Identification of the various jets used in the DCH/DFP 340 carburetor Sec 9)

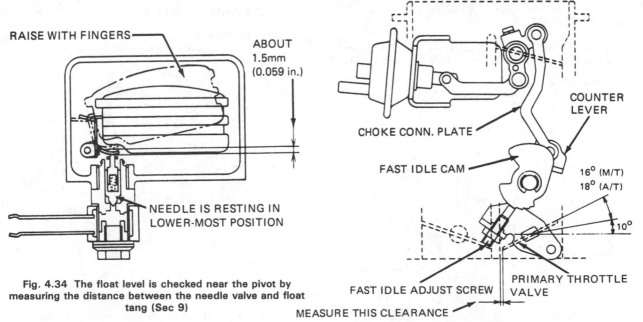

Fig. 4.34 The float level is checked near the pivot by measuring the distance between the needle valve and float tang (Sec 9)

Fig. 4.35 Primary throttle valve clearance is measured with the fast idle screw on the highest step of the fast idle cam (Sec 9)

gauge, measure the clearance between the center of the primary throttle valve and the throttle chamber wall when the return plate is brought into contact with the kick lever. Standard clearance is 0.24 to 0.30 inches (6.1 to 7.6 mm).

39 If necessary, adjust the opening point of the secondary throttle valve

by bending the kick lever where it comes into contact with the return plate.

Kick lever adjustment

40 Close the primary throttle valve by turning the throttle adjustment

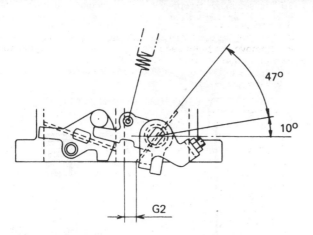

Fig. 4.36 The opening point of the secondary throttle valve is checked by positioning the linkage and measuring the primary throttle valve clearance. G2 clearance is 6.1 to 7.6mm (0.24 to 0.30 in) (Sec 9)

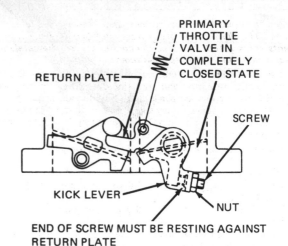

Fig. 4.37 Kick lever lash is eliminated by turning the adjustment screw (Sec 9)

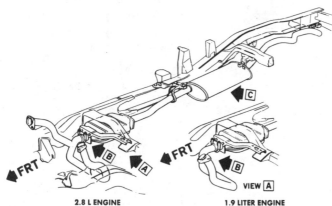

Fig. 4.38 Typical exhaust system component layout (Sec 10)

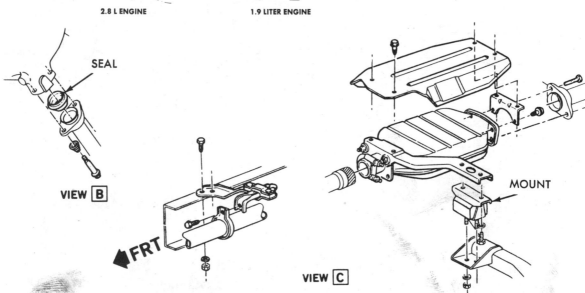

Fig. 4.39 Exploded view of exhaust system fittings (Sec 10)

screw out (count the turns for future reference).

41 Loosen the locknut on the kick lever screw and turn the screw until it comes into contact with the return plate. Tighten the lock screw.

42 Reset the throttle adjustment screw.

---

10   Exhaust system components — removal and installation

Caution: *The vehicle's exhaust system generates very high temperatures and should be allowed to cool down completely before any of the components are touched. Be especially careful around the catalytic converter, where the highest temperatures are generated.*

Due to the high temperatures and exposed locations of the exhaust system components, rust and corrosion can 'freeze' parts together. Liquid penetrating oils are available to help loosen frozen fasteners. However, in some cases it may be necessary to cut the pieces apart with a hacksaw or cutting torch. The latter method should be employed only by persons experienced in this work.

1 Raise the vehicle and support it securely on jackstands.

Front exhaust pipe

2 Remove the bolts securing the exhaust pipe to the exhaust manifold(s).

3 Remove the clamp securing the exhaust pipe to the catalytic converter.

4 Separate the exhaust pipe from the exhaust manifold(s) and the catalytic converter.

5 Installation is the reverse of the removal procedure. Be sure to install new 'doughnut' gaskets in the exhaust manifold(s) and new nuts and bolts.

Catalytic converter

Caution: *Make sure the catalytic converter has been allowed sufficient time to cool before attempting removal.*

6 Remove the converter-to-front exhaust pipe clamp.

7 Remove the coverter-to-crossmember bracket at the crossmember.

8 Remove the bolts securing the rear of the converter to the converter/intermediate pipe and remove the converter.

9 Installation is the reverse of the removal procedure. Be sure to use new nuts and bolts.

Intermediate exhaust pipe, muffler and tailpipe

10 The intermediate pipe, muffler and tailpipe are all one unit.

11 Remove the intermediate pipe-to-frame bracket.

12 Remove the bolts securing the intermediate pipe to the catalytic converter.

13 Remove the muffler/tailpipe assembly rear hanger bolts at the crossmember just behind the muffler and at the frame near the end of the tailpipe. Separate the muffler/tailpipe/intermediate pipe assembly from the vehicle.

17 Installation is the reverse of removal. Be sure to use new nuts and bolts.

4

Chapter 5 Engine electrical systems

Refer to Chapter 13 for information related to 1985 and later models

Contents

Specifications

Ignition pickup coil air gap (1.9L only)	0.12 to 0.20 in (0.3 to 0.5mm)
Starter motor brush length, type two	
Standard	0.62 in (16mm)
Service limit	0.47 in (12mm)

1 Ignition system — general information and precautions

The ignition system is composed of the battery, distributor, coil, ignition switch, spark plugs and the primary (low tension) and secondary (high tension) wiring circuits.

A high energy ignition (HEI) distributor is used on all vehicles, and all models use a separately mounted coil. California vehicles equipped with the V6 engine also incorporate electronic spark timing (EST) and an electronic control module (ECM), which monitors data from various engine sensors, computes the desired spark timing and signals the distributor to change the timing accordingly. Non-California vehicles are equipped with vacuum and centrifugal advance mechanisms. On all models the distributor uses a magnetic pickup assembly which contains a permanent magnet, a pole piece with internal teeth and a pickup coil in place of the traditional ignition point assembly.

The secondary (spark plug) wire used with the HEI system is a carbon-impregnated cord conductor encased in an 8 mm (5/16-inch) diameter rubber jacket with an outer silicone jacket. This type of wire will withstand very high temperatures and still provide insulation for the HEI's high voltage. For more information on spark plug wiring refer to Chapter 1. **Note:** *Because of the very high voltage generated by the HEI system extreme care should be taken whenever an operation involving ignition components is performed. This not only includes the distributor, coil, control module and spark plug wires, but related items that are connected to the system as well (such as the plug connections, tachometer, and testing equipment). Consequently, before any work is performed, the ignition should be turned off and the negative battery cable disconnected.*

2 Battery — removal and installation

1   The battery is located at the front of the engine compartment. It is held in place by a hold-down clamp near the bottom of the battery case.

2   Hydrogen gas is produced by the battery, so keep open flames and lighted cigarettes away from it at all times.

3   Always keep the battery in an upright position. Spilled electrolyte should be rinsed off immediately with large quantities of water. Always wear eye protection when working around a battery.

4   Always disconnect the negative (-) battery cable first, followed by the positive (+) cable.

5   After the cables are disconnected from the battery, remove the hold-down clamp.

6   Carefully lift the battery out of the engine compartment.

7   Installation is the reverse of removal. The cable clamps should be tight, but do not overtighten them as damage to the battery case could occur. The battery posts and cable ends should be cleaned prior to connection (see Chapter 1).

3   Battery — emergency jump starting

Refer to the *Booster battery (jump) starting* procedure at the front of this manual.

4   Battery cables — check and replacement

1   Periodically inspect the entire length of each battery cable for damage, cracked or burned insulation and corrosion. Poor battery cable connections can cause starting problems and decreased engine performance.
2   Check the cable-to-terminal connections at the ends of the cables for cracks, loose wire strands and corrosion. The presence of white, fluffy deposits under the insulation at the cable terminal connection is a sign the cable is corroded and should be replaced. Check the terminals for distortion, missing mounting bolts or nuts and corrosion.
3   If only the positive cable is to be replaced, be sure to disconnect the negative cable from the battery first.
4   Disconnect and remove the cable(s) from the vehicle. Make sure the replacement cable(s) is the same length and diameter.
5   Clean the threads of the starter or ground connection with a wire brush to remove rust and corrosion. Apply a light coat of petroleum jelly to the threads to ease installation and prevent future corrosion. Inspect the connections frequently to make sure they are clean and tight.
6   Attach the cable(s) to the starter or ground connection and tighten the mounting nut(s) securely.
7   Before connecting the new cable(s) to the battery, make sure they reach the terminals without having to be stretched.
8   Connect the positive cable first, followed by the negative cable. Tighten the nuts and apply a thin coat of petroleum jelly to the terminal and cable connection.

5   Ignition system — check

Caution: *Because of the very high voltage generated by the HEI system, extreme care should be taken whenever an operation is performed involving ignition components. This not only includes the distributor, coil, control module and spark plug wires, but related items that are connected to the system as well, such as the plug connections, tachometer and any test equipment. Consequently, before any work is performed, the ignition should be turned off or the battery ground cable disconnected.*

1   If the engine turns over but will not start, remove the spark plug wire from a spark plug and, using an insulated tool, hold the wire about 1/4-inch from a good ground and have an assistant crank the engine. **Note:** *A special tool, ST-125, is available for making the above test. It is available from your dealer and auto parts stores.*
2   If there is no spark, check another wire in the same manner. A few sparks, then no spark, should be considered as no spark.
3   If there is good spark, check the spark plugs (refer to Chapter 1) and/or the fuel system (refer to Chapter 4).
4   If there is a weak spark or no spark, unplug the coil lead from the distributor, hold it about 1/4-inch from a good ground and check for spark as described above.
5   If there is no spark, have the system checked by a dealer or repair shop.
6   If there is a spark, check the distributor cap and/or rotor (refer to Chapter 1).
7   Further checks of the HEI ignition system must be done by a dealer or repair shop.

6   Distributor — removal and installation

Removal
1   Disconnect the ground cable from the battery.

L4 (1.9L and 2.0L engines)
2   Disconnect the plug wires from the spark plugs and remove the

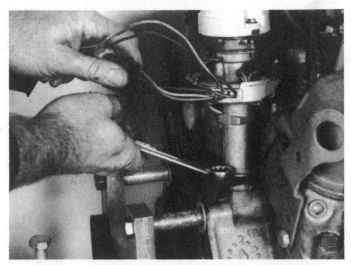

6.14   Removing the distributor hold-down clamp bolt (V6 engine shown out of vehicle)

spark plug wire clips from the cam/rocker arm cover.
3   Disconnect the secondary (large) coil wire at the coil.
4   Unplug the distributor ignition wire where it enters the wiring harness.
5   Mark the position of the rotor on the outside of the distributor body.
6   Remove the bolt attaching the distributor bracket to the engine block.
7   Make matching marks on the base of the distributor and the engine block to insure that you will be able to put the distributor back in the same position.
8   Lift the distributor slowly. As you lift it the rotor will turn slightly. When it stops turning make another mark on the distributor body to show where it is pointing when the gear on the distributor is disengaged. This is the position the rotor should be in when you begin reinstallation.
9   Remove the distributor. Avoid turning the crankshaft with the distributor removed, as this will change the timing position of rotor and require retiming the engine.

LR2 (V6 engine)
10   Disconnect the wiring harness connectors from the side of the distributor cap.
11   With a screwdriver press down on the two cap holddown pins, turn them a half turn and remove the cap.
12   Make matching marks on the base of the distributor and the engine block to insure that you will be able to put the distributor back in the same position.
13   Mark the position of the rotor on the outside of the distributor body.
14   Remove the holddown bolt and clamp.
15   Lift the distributor slowly. As you lift it the rotor will turn slightly. When it stops turning make another mark on the distributor body to show where it is pointing when the gear on the distributor is disengaged. This is the position the rotor should be in when you begin reinstallation.
16   Remove the distributor. Avoid turning the crankshaft with the distributor removed, as this will change the timing position of the rotor and require retiming the engine.

Installation if the crankshaft was not turned after distributor removal
17   Position the rotor in the exact location (second mark on the housing) when the distributor was removed.
18   Lower the distributor into the engine. To mesh the gears at the bottom of the distributor it may be necessary to turn the rotor slightly.
19   With the base of the distributor seated against the engine block turn the distributor housing to align the marks made on the distributor base and the engine block.
20   With the distributor all the way down and the marks aligned the rotor should point to the first mark made on the distributor housing.
21   On V6 engines place the holddown clamp in position and loosely install the holddown bolt. On L4 engines install the holddown bolt through the distributor bracket.

5

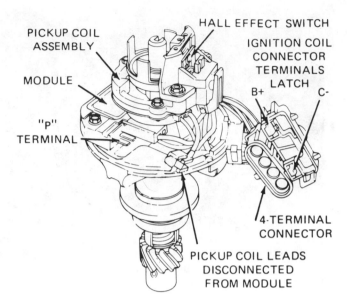

Fig. 5.1 Distributor used with separately mounted coil with Hall effect switch installed (Sec 7)

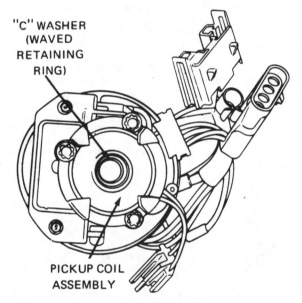

Fig. 5.3 Pickup coil installation details (distributors with separately mounted coil) (Sec 7)

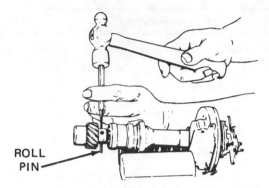

Fig. 5.2 Removing the roll pin from the distributor shaft and gear (Sec 7)

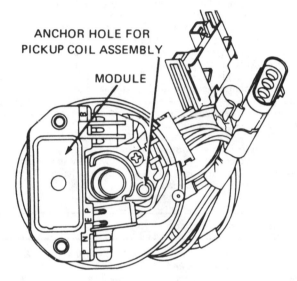

Fig. 5.4 Separately mounted coil distributor with the pickup coil removed (Sec 7)

22 Reconnect the ignition wiring harness.
23 Install the distributor cap. If the secondary wiring harness was removed from the cap, reinstall it.
24 Reconnect the coil wire, and, if removed, the spark plug wires and clips.
25 Check the ignition timing (Chapter 1).

Installation if the crankshaft was turned after distributor removal

26 Remove the number one spark plug.
27 Place your finger over the spark plug hole while turning the crankshaft with a wrench on the pulley bolt at the front of the engine.
28 When you feel compression continue turning the crankshaft slowly until the timing mark on the crankshaft pulley is aligned with the 0 on the engine timing indicator.
29 On V6 engines position the rotor between the number one and six spark plug terminals on the cap. On L4 engines position the rotor between the number one and three terminals.
30 Complete the installation by referring to Steps 21 through 25.

7 Ignition pickup coil — replacement

V6 and 2.0L four-cylinder engines
1 Remove the distributor from the engine as previously described.
2 Remove the two rotor mounting screws and remove the rotor.
3 Disconnect the pickup coil leads from the module.
4 On models with a Hall-effect switch, remove the switch retaining screws and the switch.
5 Mark the distributor gear and shaft so they can be reassembled in the same position.
6 Carefully mount the distributor in a soft-jawed vice and, using a hammer and punch, remove the roll pin from the distributor shaft and gear.
7 Remove the gear and washers from the shaft.
8 Carefully pull the shaft out through the top of the distributor.
9 Remove the 'C' washer retaining ring at the center of the distributor and remove the pickup coil.
10 Installation is the reverse of the removal procedure.

1.9L four-cylinder engine
11 Remove the distributor from the engine as described in Section 6.
12 Remove the rotor.
13 Remove the mounting screws from the vacuum controller and remove the vacuum controller.
14 Disconnect the wiring leads from the pickup coil. Remove the screw retaining the wiring harness and remove the harness from the distributor housing.

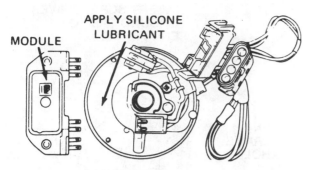

Fig. 5.5 Module installation on a distributor without an internal capacitor (Sec 9)

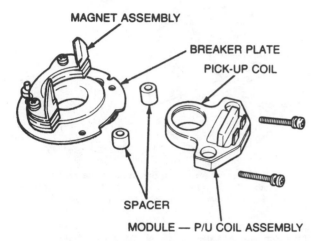

Fig. 5.7 Two spacers are used between the pickup coil and breaker plate on this distributor (1.9 liter engines only) (Sec 7)

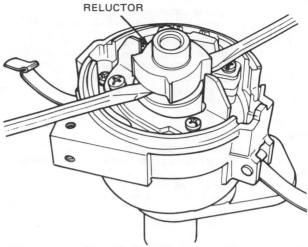

Fig. 5.6 On 1.9 liter engines, the reluctor should be pried up from two sides when removed (Sec 7)

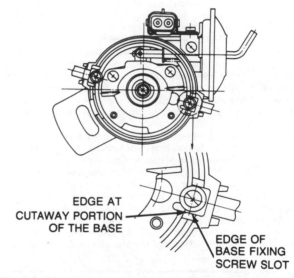

Fig. 5.8 When installing the breaker plate on this distributor, the edge of the screw slot must be flush with the cutaway portion of the base (1.9 liter engines only) (Sec 7)

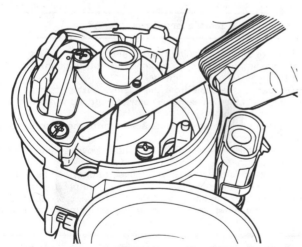

Fig. 5.9 On 1.9 liter engines, be sure to adjust the reluctor air gap after replacing the pickup coil (Sec 8)

15 Using two screwdrivers, carefully pry the reluctor from the rotor shaft as shown in the accompanying illustration.
16 Remove the mounting screws from the breaker plate assembly and remove the assembly from the distributor housing.
17 Remove the pickup coil mounting screws and separate the pickup coil from the breaker plate.
18 Installation is the reverse of the removal procedure.
19 Adjust the air gap after replacing the pickup coil (Sec 8).

8   Air Gap (1.9 liter engine) — adjustment

1 Before measuring the air gap, the engine must be rotated until one of the four reluctor teeth line up with the stator (an assistant or remote starter switch is helpful here). Crank the starter motor intermittently until the reluctor and stator line up.
2 Using a feeler gauge, measure the air gap between the reluctor and the stator and compare it to the Specifications.
3 If necessary, adjust the air gap by loosening the two stainless steel screws and moving the pole piece.
4 Recheck the air gap and tighten the screws.

9   Ignition module — replacement

1 Remove the distributor.
2 Remove the pickup coil assembly.
3 Disconnect the wiring harness from the module, remove the two mounting screws and remove the module.
4 Installation is the reverse of the removal procedure. Before installing the module apply silicone lubricant to the housing on which the module mounts.

10 Ignition coil — removal and installation

V6 and 2.0L four-cylinder engines

1 Disconnect the negative battery cable.
2 Disconnect the ignition switch lead at the coil.
3 Disconnect the coil to distributor wires at the coil.
4 Remove the screws holding the coil to the engine block and remove the coil.
5 Installation is the reverse of the removal procedure.

1.9L four-cylinder engine

6 Disconnect the negative battery cable.
7 Disconnect the primary terminal connector and high tension lead from the coil.
8 Disconnect the resistor lead wire.
9 Remove the bracket attaching bolts and remove the coil and condenser.
10 Installation is the reverse of the removal procedure.

11 Charging system — general information and precautions

The charging system is made up of the alternator, voltage regulator and battery. These components work together to supply electrical power for the engine ignition, lights, radio, etc.

The alternator is turned by a drivebelt at the front of the engine. When the engine is operating, voltage is generated by the internal components of the alternator to be sent to the battery for storage.

The purpose of the voltage regulator is to limit the alternator voltage to a pre-set value. This prevents power surges, circuit overloads, etc., during peak voltage output. On all models with which this manual is concerned, the voltage regulator is contained within the alternator housing.

The charging system does not ordinarily require periodic maintenance. The drivebelts, electrical wiring and connections should, however, be inspected at the intervals suggested in Chapter 1.

Take extreme care when making circuit connections to a vehicle equipped with an alternator and note the following. When making connections to the alternator from a battery, always match correct polarity. Before using electric-arc welding equipment to repair any part of the vehicle, disconnect the wires from the alternator and the battery terminal. Never start the engine with a battery charger connected. Always disconnect both battery leads before using a battery charger.

12 Charging system — check

1 If a malfunction occurs in the charging circuit, do not immediately assume that the alternator is causing the problem. First check the following items:

    The battery cables where they connect to the battery (make sure the connections are clean and tight)
    The battery electrolyte specific gravity (if it is low, charge the battery)
    Check the external alternator wiring and connections (they must be in good condition)
    Check the drivebelt condition and tension (see Chapter 1)
    Check the alternator mount bolts for tightness
    Run the engine and check the alternator for abnormal noise

2 Using a voltmeter, check the battery voltage with the engine off. It should be approximately 12-volts.
3 Start the engine and check the battery voltage again. It should now be approximately 14 to 15-volts. If it does not rise when the engine is started or if it exceeds 15-volts, proceed to Step 4.
4 Locate the test hole in the back of the alternator and ground the tab that is located inside the hole by inserting a screwdriver blade into the hole and touching the tab and the case at the same time. **Note:** *Do not run the engine with the tab grounded any longer than necessary to obtain a voltmeter reading. The alternator, if it is charging, is running unregulated at this point. This condition may overload the electrical system and cause damage to the components.*
5 The reading on the voltmeter should be 15-volts or higher with the

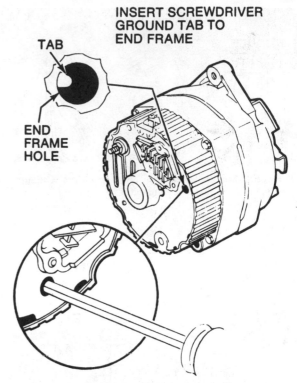

INSERT SCREWDRIVER GROUND TAB TO END FRAME

TAB

END FRAME HOLE

Fig. 5.10 Location of the test hole in the rear of the alternator (2.0 liter four-cylinder and V6 engines only — inset shows grounding procedure) (Sec 12)

tab grounded in the test hole.
6 If the voltmeter indicates low battery voltage, the alternator is faulty and should be replaced with a new one (refer to Section 13).
7 If the voltage reading is 15-volts or higher and a no-charge condition is present, the regulator or field circuit is the problem. Remove the alternator and have it checked further by an auto electric shop.

13 Alternator — removal and installation

1 Remove the bolt retaining the negative battery cable to the alternator adjusting bracket, if so equipped. If not, disconnect the cable from the negative battery terminal.
2 Disconnect the cable from the positive battery terminal.
3 Disconnect the two electrical connectors from the rear of the alternator (photo).
4 Remove the bolt retaining the alternator to the adjusting bracket (photo).
5 Remove the alternator pivot bolt and remove the alternator from the vehicle.
6 Installation is the reverse of removal, noting the following:
7 Reconnect the positive battery cable before reattaching the negative cable at the alternator bracket.
8 Adjust the alternator drivebelt (refer to Chapter 1).

14 Alternator brushes — replacement

1 Remove the alternator from the vehicle (refer to Section 13).
2 Scribe a match mark on the front and rear end frame housings of the alternator to facilitate reassembly.
3 From the rear of the alternator, insert a paper clip through the rear end frame to hold the brushes in place (photo).
4 Remove the four (4) through-bolts holding the front and rear end frames together, then separate the end frames with the paper clip still in place (photos).
5 Remove the bolts holding the stator to the rear end frame and separate the stator from the end frame (photo).

13.3   Disconnect the BAT terminal wire and electrical connector from the alternator

13.4   Remove the bolt retaining the alternator to the adjusting bracket

14.3   Paper clip inserted from rear of the alternator to hold the brushes in place during disassembly and reassembly

14.4a   Separating the alternator front and rear end frames

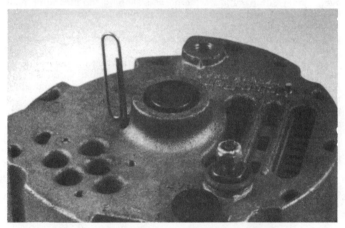

14.4b   Details of the alternator rear end frame

- A   Brush holder
- B   Paper clip retaining brushes
- C   Regulator
- D   Resistor (not all models)
- E   Diode trio
- F   Rectifier bridge

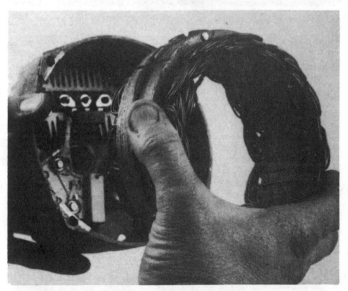

14.5   Separating the stator from the rear end frame

5

6   Remove the nuts attaching the diode trio to the rectifier bridge and remove the trio (photo).

7   Remove the paper clip from the rear of the end frame while holding your hand over the end of the brush holder to catch the brushes as they are released.

8   Remove the screws retaining the regulator and resistor (if equipped) to the end frame and remove the regulator (photo).

9   Remove the brushes from the regulator by slipping the brush retainer off the regulator (photo).

10   Remove the springs from the brush holder.

11   Installation is the reverse of the removal procedure, noting the following.

12   When installing the brushes in the brush holder, install the brush closest to the end frame first. Slip the paper clip through the rear of the end frame to hold the brush, then insert the second brush and push the paper clip in to hold both brushes while reassembly is completed. The paper clip should not be removed until the front and rear end frames have been bolted together.

15   Starting system — general information

The function of the starting system is to crank the engine. This system is composed of a starting motor, solenoid and battery. The battery sup-

plies the electrical energy to the solenoid, which then completes the circuit to the starting motor which does the actual work of cranking the engine.

The solenoid and starting motor are mounted together at the lower right side of the engine. No periodic lubrication or maintenance is required.

The electrical circuits of the vehicle are arranged so the starter motor can only be operated when the clutch pedal is depressed (manual transmission) or the transmission selector lever is in Park or Neutral (automatic transmission).

Never operate the starter motor for more than 30 seconds at a time without pausing to allow it to cool for at least two minutes. Excessive cranking can cause overheating, which can seriously damage the starter.

16   Starter motor — testing in vehicle

1   If the starter motor does not turn at all when the switch is operated, make sure that the shift lever is in Neutral or Park (automatic transmission) or that the clutch pedal is depressed (manual transmission).

2   Make sure that the battery is charged and that all cables, both at the battery and starter solenoid terminals, are secure.

3   If the motor spins but the engine is not being cranked, then the overrunning clutch in the starter motor is slipping and the motor must be removed from the engine and disassembled.

4   If, when the switch is actuated, the starter motor does not operate at all but the solenoid clicks, then the problem is in the main solenoid contacts or the starter motor itself.

5   If the solenoid plunger cannot be heard when the switch is actuated, the solenoid itself if defective or the solenoid circuit is open.

6   To check out the solenoid, connect a jumper lead between the battery (+) and the S terminal on the solenoid. If the starter motor now operates, the solenoid is OK and the problem is in the ignition or neutral start switches or in the wiring.

7   If the starter motor still does not operate, remove the starter/solenoid assembly for disassembly, testing and repair.

8   If the starter motor cranks the engine at an abnormally slow speed, first make sure that the battery is charged and that all terminal connections are tight. If the engine is partially seized, or has the wrong viscosity oil in it, it will crank slowly also.

9   Run the engine until normal operating temperature is reached, then disconnect the coil wire from the distributor cap and ground it on the engine.

10   Connect a voltmeter positive lead to the starter motor terminal of the solenoid and then connect the negative lead to ground.

11   Actuate the ignition switch and take the voltmeter readings as soon as a steady figure is indicated. Do not allow the starter motor to turn for more than 30 seconds at a time. A reading of 9-volts or more, with the starter motor turning at normal cranking speed, is normal. If the reading is 9-volts or more but the cranking speed is slow, the motor is faulty. If the reading is less than 9-volts and the cranking speed is slow, the solenoid contacts are probably burned.

14.6   Removing the diode trio from the rectifier bridge

14.8   Removing the regulator from the rear end frame

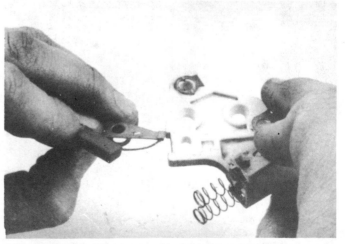

14.9   Removing a brush assembly from the regulator

17 Starter motor — removal and installation

1 Disconnect the cable from the negative battery terminal.
2 Remove the starter brace and shield, if so equipped.
3 From beneath the vehicle, remove the two starter motor-to-engine bolts. On 1.9L four-cylinder engines there is a bolt under the starter and a nut on a stud at the top. Let the starter drop down far enough to allow removal of the nuts attaching the wires to the starter solenoid and battery cable (photo). Support the starter while the wires are removed.
4 Remove the starter.
5 Remove the starter.
6 Installation is the reverse of removal. Make sure that the shims, if so equipped, are properly reinstalled (photo).

18 Starter solenoid — removal and installation

V6 and 2.0L four-cylinder engines

1 After removing the starter as described in Section 17 disconnect the field strap from the solenoid.
2 Remove the two screws which secure the solenoid housing to the starter end frame.
3 Twist the solenoid in a clockwise direction to disengage the flange from the starter body (photo).
4 To install, first make sure the return spring is in position on the plunger, then insert the solenoid body into the starter housing and turn the solenoid counterclockwise to engage the flange.
5 Install the two solenoid screws and connect the field strap.

1.9L four-cylinder engine

6 After removing the starter as described in Section 17 disconnect the strap from the 'M' terminal on the solenoid.
7 Remove the two bolts which secure the solenoid to the starter and remove the solenoid.
8 Installation is the reverse of the removal procedure.

19 Starter motor brushes — replacement

V6 and 2.0L four-cylinder engines

1 Remove the starter and solenoid assembly from the vehicle as described in Section 17.
2 Remove the solenoid from the starter housing (refer to Section 18).
3 Remove the starter motor through bolts after marking the relationship of the commutator end frame to the field frame housing to simplify reassembly.
4 Remove the end frame from the field frame housing (photo).

5 Mark the relationship of the field frame housing to the drive end housing and pull the field frame housing away from the drive end housing and over the armature.
6 Unbolt the brushes and brush supports from the brush holders in the field frame housing (photo).
7 To install new brushes, attach the brushes to the brush supports, making sure they are flush with the bottom of the supports, and bolt the brushes/supports to the brush holders.
8 Install the field frame over the armature, with the brushes resting on the first step of the armature collar at this point (photo).
9 Make sure the field frame is properly aligned with the drive end housing, then push the brushes off the collar and into place on the armature.
10 The remaining installation steps are the reverse of those for removal.

1.9L four-cylinder engine

11 Remove the starter and solenoid assembly from the vehicle (refer to Section 17).
12 Remove the solenoid from the starter housing as described in Section 18.
13 Remove the dust cover, ring and thrust washer.
14 Remove the two screws and the through-bolts.
15 Remove the rear cover from the starter housing.
16 Raise the brush spring and remove the brush. Remove the brush holder assembly.
17 The brush and brush lead can now be removed from the starter housing.
18 Installation is the reverse of removal.

18.3 Withdrawing the solenoid assembly from the starter housing

19.4 Removing the end frame from the field frame housing

19.6 Unbolting a brush and brush support from the brush holder

19.8 Installing the field frame over the armature (note the position of the brushes on the armature collar)

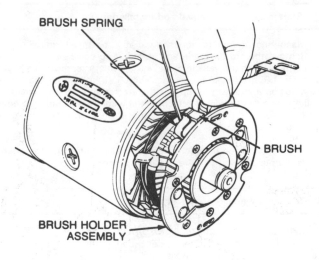

Fig. 5.11 Pulling up on the brush spring allows removal of the brush (1.9 liter engines) (Sec 19)

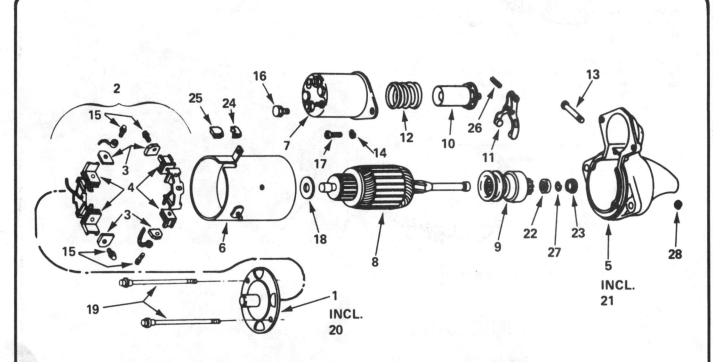

Fig. 5.12 Components used in the Type One starter motor (Sec 19)

1 Frame-commutator end	11 Shift lever	20 Bushing — commutator end
2 Brush and holder pkg.	12 Plunger return spring	21 Bushing — drive end
3 Brush	13 Shift lever shaft	22 Pinion stop collar
4 Brush holder	14 Lockwasher	23 Thrust collar
5 Housing — drive end	15 Screw—brush attaching	24 Grommet
6 Frame and field assm.	16 Screw — field lead to switch	25 Grommet
7 Solenoid switch	17 Screw — switch attaching	26 Plunger pin
8 Armature	18 Leather washer — brake	27 Pinion stop retaining ring
9 Drive assembly	19 Through bolt	28 Lever shaft retaining ring
10 Plunger		

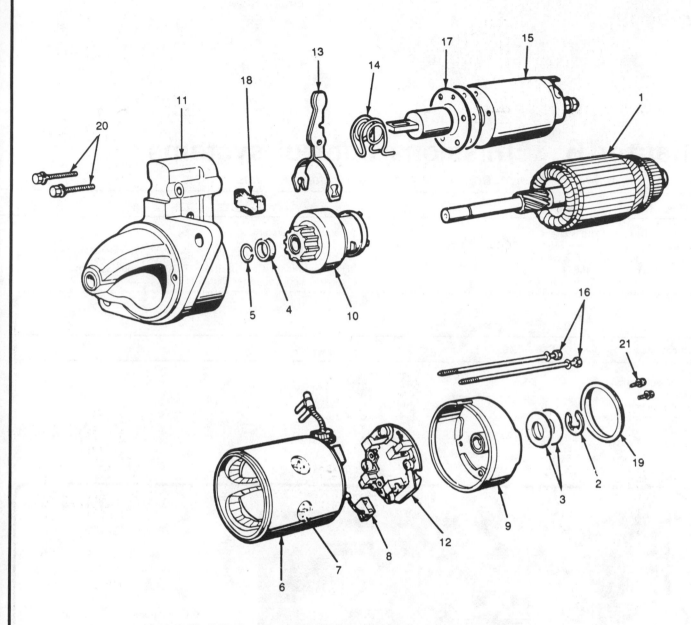

Fig. 5.13 Components used in the Type Two starter motor (Sec 19)

1 Armature assembly	8 Brush	15 Solenoid
2 'E' ring	9 Rear cover assembly	16 Through bolt
3 Thrust waser	10 Pinion assembly	17 Dust cover
4 Pinion stop	11 Gear case assembly	18 Gasket
5 Clip	12 Brush holder assembly	19 Dust cover
6 Frame assembly	13 Shift lever	20 Bolt
7 Screw	14 Torsion spring	21 Screw

Chapter 6 Emissions control systems

Refer to Chapter 13 for information related to 1985 and later models

Contents

Specifications

Torque specifications	Ft-lbs
EGR valve	25
AIR pump pulley	24
Air management valve	20 to 35
Air pump	13
Oxygen sensor	30

Fig. 6.1 Locations of the various emission control system components (V6 engine shown)

A EGR valve
B Air management valve
C Check valve
D Air pump

1 General information

To prevent pollution of the atmosphere from burned and evaporating gases, a number of emissions control systems are incorporated on the vehicles covered by this manual. The combination of systems used depends on the year in which the vehicle was manufactured, the locality to which it was originally delivered and the engine type. The major systems incorporated on the vehicles with which this manual is concerned include the:

Closed Loop Emissions Control System
Air Injection Reactor (AIR)
Fuel Control System
Electronic Spark Timing (EST)
Early Fuel Evaporation (EFE)
Exhaust Gas Recirculation (EGR)
Evaporative Emissions Control (EECS)
Transmission Converter Clutch (TCC)
Positive Crankcase Ventilation (PCV)
Thermostatically Controlled Air Induction (TCA)

On California vehicles all of these systems are linked, directly or indirectly, to the Computer Command Control System (CCCS).

The Sections in this Chapter include general descriptions, checking procedures (where possible) and component replacement procedures (where applicable) for each of the systems listed above.

Before assuming that an emissions control system is malfunctioning, check the fuel and ignition systems carefully. In some cases special tools and equipment, as well as specialized training, are required to accurately diagnose the causes of a rough running or difficult to start engine. If checking and servicing become too difficult or if a procedure is beyond the scope of the home mechanic, consult your dealer service department. This does not necessarily mean, however, that the emissions control systems are particularly difficult to maintain and repair. You can quickly and easily perform many checks and do most (if not all) of the regular maintenance at home with common tune-up and hand tools. **Note:** *The most frequent cause of emissions system problems is simply a loose or broken vacuum hose or wiring connection. Therefore, always check the hose and wiring connections first.*

Pay close attention to any special precautions outlined in this Chapter. It should be noted that the illustrations of the various systems may not exactly match the system installed on your particular vehicle due to changes made by the manufacturer during production or from year to year.

A Vehicle Emissions Control Information label is located in the engine compartment of all vehicles with which this manual is concerned. This label contains important emissions specifications and setting procedures, as well as a vacuum hose schematic with emissions components identified. When servicing the engine or emissions systems, the VECI label in your particular vehicle should always be checked for up-to-date information.

2 Computer Command Control System (CCCS)

General description

This electronically controlled emissions system, which is used only on California models, is linked with as many as nine other related emissions systems. It consists mainly of sensors (as many as 15) and an Electronic Control Module (ECM). Completing the system are various engine components which respond to commands from the ECM.

In many ways, this system can be compared to the central nervous system in the human body. The sensors (nerves) constantly gather information and send this data to the ECM (brain) which processes the data and, if necessary, sends out a command for some type of vehicle (body) change.

Here's a specific example of how one portion of this system operates. An oxygen sensor, mounted in the exhaust manifold and protruding into the exhaust gas stream, constantly monitors the oxygen content of the exhaust gas as it travels through the exhaust pipe. If the percentage of oxygen in the exhaust gas is incorrect, an electrical signal is sent to the ECM. The ECM takes this information, processes it and then

6

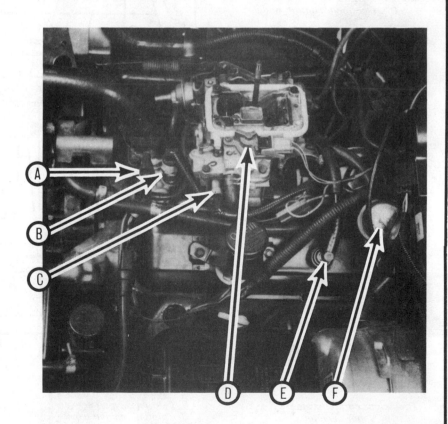

Fig. 6.2 Locations of the various emission control system components (V6 engine shown)

A *Thermal vacuum switch*
B *Coolant sensor/EFE heater switch*
C *Throttle position sensor connector (2.0L and V6 only)*
D *Mixture control solenoid sensor (2.0L and V6 only)*
E *PCV valve*
F *AIR system deceleration valve (V6 engine only)*

sends an electrical command to the carburetor Mixture Control (M/C) solenoid telling it to change the fuel/air mixture. To be effective, all this happens in a fraction of a second, and it goes on continuously while the engine is running. The end result is a fuel/air ratio which is constantly kept at a predetermined 'exact' proportion, regardless of driving conditions.

Testing

One might think that a system which uses exotic electrical sensors and is controlled by an on-board computer would be difficult to diagnose. This is not necessarily the case.

The Computer Command Control System has a built-in diagnostic system which indicates a problem by flashing a 'Check Engine' light on the instrument panel. When this light comes on during normal vehicle operation, a fault has been detected.

Perhaps more importantly, the exact cause of this fault is determined and automatically stored in the ECM memory. Thus, troubleshooting this system is easily accomplished by you or a dealer mechanic.

To extract this information from the ECM memory you must use a short jumper wire to ground a 'Test' terminal. This terminal is part of a wiring connector located just behind the dashboard, to the right of the steering column. A small, rectangular plate is used to cover the connector, which must be pried out of place to provide access to the terminals.

With the connector exposed to view, push one end of the jumper wire into the 'Test' terminal and the other end into the 'Ground' terminal. **Note:** *Do not start the engine with the 'Test' terminal grounded.*

Turn the ignition to the On position — *not* the Start or Run positions. The 'Check Engine' light should flash Trouble Code 12, indicating that the diagnostic system is working. Code 12 will consist of one flash, followed by a short pause, and then two flashes in quick succession.

After a longer pause, the code will repeat itself two more times.

If no other codes have been stored, Code 12 will continue to repeat itself until the jumper wire is disconnected. If additional Trouble Codes have been stored, they will follow Code 12. Again, each Trouble Code will flash three times before moving on.

The ECM can also be checked for stored codes with the engine running. Completely remove the jumper wire from the 'Test' and 'Ground' terminals, start the engine and then plug the jumper wire back in. With the engine running, all stored Trouble Codes will flash. However, Code 12 will flash only if there is a fault in the distributor reference circuit.

Once the code(s) have been noted, use the Trouble Code Identification information which follows to locate the source of the fault. **Note:** *Whenever the positive battery cable is disconnected all stored Trouble Codes in the EMC are erased. Be aware of this before you disconnect the battery for servicing or replacement of electrical components, engine removal, etc.*

It should be noted that the self-diagnosis feature built into this system does not detect all possible faults. If you suspect a problem with the Computer Command Control System, but a 'Check Engine' light has not come on, have your local dealer perform a 'system performance check.'

Furthermore when diagnosing an engine performance, fuel economy or exhaust emissions problem (which is not accompanied by a 'Check Engine' light) do not automatically assume the fault lies in this system. Perform all standard troubleshooting procedures, as indicated elsewhere in this manual, before turning to the Computer Command Control System.

Finally, since this is an electronic system, you should have a basic knowledge of automotive electrics before attempting any diagnosis. Damage to the ECM, PROM or related components can easily occur if care is not exercised.

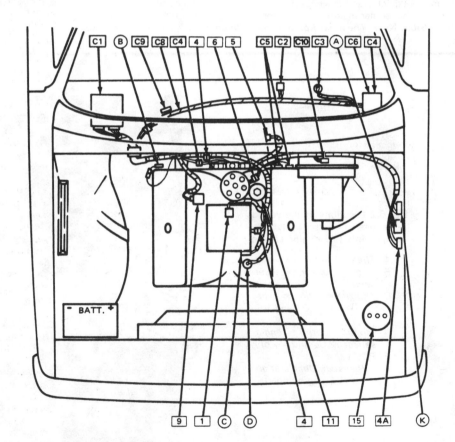

Fig. 6.3 Locations of emission system and related components (California V6 model shown)

Computer system
- C1 Electronic control module (ECM)
- C2 ALCL connector
- C3 'Check engine' light
- C4 System power
- C5 System ground
- C6 Fuse panel
- C8 Computer control harness
- C9 Remote lamp driver
- C10 Dwell connector

Air/Fuel system
- 1   Mixture control
- 4   Heated grid EFE connector
- 4A Heated grid EFE relay

Transmission converter clutch control system
- 5   Transmission converter clutch connector

Ignition system
- 6   Electronic spark timing connector

Air injection system
- 9   Air divert solenoid valve

Exhaust gas recirculation control system
- 11 Exhaust gas recirculation valve

Fuel vapor control system
- 15 Vapor canister

Sensors/Switches
- A Vacuum sensor
- B Exhaust oxygen sensor
- C Throttle position sensor
- D Coolant sensor/EFE heater switch
- K WOT relay

Trouble Code Identification

Following is a list of the Trouble Codes which may be encountered while diagnosing the Computer Command Control System. Also included are simplified troubleshooting procedures. If the problem persists after these checks have been made, the vehicle must be diagnosed by a professional mechanic who can use specialized diagnostic tools and advanced troubleshooting methods to check the system. Procedures marked with an asterisk (*) indicate component replacements which may not cure the problem in all cases. For this reason, you may want to seek professional advice before purchasing replacement parts.

To clear the Trouble Code(s) from the ECM memory, unplug the ECM electrical pigtail at the positive (+) battery cable.

Trouble Code	Circuit or system	Probable cause
12 (one flash, pause, two flashes)	No reference pulses to ECM	This code should flash whenever the 'Test' terminal is grounded with the ignition On and the engine not running. If additional Trouble Codes are stored (indicating a problem), they will appear after this code has flashed three times With the engine running, the appearance of this code indicates that no references from the distributor are reaching the ECM. Carefully check the four-terminal EST connector at the distributor
13 (one flash, pause, three flashes)	Oxygen sensor circuit	Check for a sticking or misadjusted throttle position sensor Check the wiring and connectors from the oxygen sensor Replace oxygen sensor (see Chapter 1)
14 (one flash, pause, four flashes)	Coolant sensor circuit	**Note:** *If the engine is experiencing overheating problems (as indicated by high temperature gauge readings or the 'hot' light coming on), rectify by referring to Chapters 1 and 3 before continuing.* Check all wiring and connectors from the coolant sensor *Replace coolant sensor (located at front of left-hand cylinder head on V6; front of engine block on four-cylinder)
15 (one flash, pause, five flashes)	Coolant sensor circuit	See above, plus: Check the wiring connections at the ECM
21 (two flashes, pause, one flash)	TPS circuit	Check for sticking or misadjusted TPS plunger Check all wiring and connections at the TPS and at the ECM *Adjust or replace TPS (see Chapter 4)
22 (two flashes, pause, two flashes)	TPS circuit	Check TPS adjustment (Chapter 4) Check ECM connector *Replace TPS (Chapter 4)
23 (two flashes, pause, three flashes)	M/C solenoid circuit	Check the electrical connections at the M/C solenoid (see Chapter 4). If OK, clear the ECM memory and recheck for code(s) after driving the vehicle Check wiring connections at the ECM Check wiring from M/C solenoid (Chapter 4)
24 (two flashes, pause, four flashes)	Vehicle speed sensor (VSS) circuit	**Note:** *A fault in this circuit should be indicated only while the vehicle is in motion. Disregard code 24 if set when drive wheels are not turning.* Check connections at the ECM Check the TPS setting (Chapter 4)

6

Trouble code	Circuit or system	Probable cause
32 (three flashes, pause, two flashes)	Baro sensor circuit	Check for a short between sensor terminals B and C or the wires leading to these terminals Check the wire leading to ECM terminal 1 Check the ECM connections Check the wires leading to ECM terminals 21 and 22 *Replace Baro sensor (located in the engine compartment, attached to the firewall)
33 (three flashes, pause, three flashes)	MAP sensor	Check vacuum hose(s) from MAP sensor Check electrical connections at ECM *Replace MAP sensor
34 (three flashes, pause, four flashes)	Vacuum sensor circuit	Check the wiring leading to terminals 20, 21 and 22 of the ECM Check the connections at the ECM Check the vacuum sensor wiring and connections *Replace vacuum sensor (located in the engine compartment)
41 (four flashes, pause, one flash)	No distributor signals	Check all wires and connections at the distributor Check distributor pick-up coil connections (Chapter 5) Check vacuum sensor circuit (see above)
42 (four flashes, pause, two flashes)	Bypass or EST problem	**Note:** *If the vehicle will not start and run, check the wire leading to ECM terminal 12.* **Note:** *An improper HEI module can cause this trouble code.* Check the EST wire leading to the HEI module E terminal Check all distributor wires Check the wire leading from EST terminal A to ECM terminal 12 and the wire from EST terminal C to ECM terminal 11 Check all ECM connections *Replace HEI module
43 (four flashes, pause, three flashes)	Electronic Spark Control (ESC) system	Check wire leading to ECM terminal L Check the wiring connector' at the ESC controller and at the ECM Check wire from knock sensor to ESC controller; if necessary, reroute it away from other wires such as spark plug, etc.
44 (four flashes, pause, four flashes)	Lean exhaust	Check for a sticking M/C solenoid (Chapter 4) Check ECM wiring connections, particularly terminals 14 and 9 Check for vacuum leakage at carburetor base gasket, vacuum hoses or intake manifold gasket Check for air leakage at air management system-to-exhaust ports and at decel valve *Replace oxygen sensor

Trouble code	Circuit or system	Probable cause
45 (four flashes, pause, five flashes)	Rich exhaust	Check for a sticking M/C solenoid (Chapter 4) Check wiring at M/C solenoid connector Check the evaporative charcoal canister and its components for the presence of fuel (Chapters 1, 6) *Replace oxygen sensor
51 (five flashes, pause, one flash)	PROM problem	The PROM is located inside the ECM and is very delicate and easily broken. All diagnostic procedures should be done by a dealer mechanic.
54 (five flashes, pause, four flashes)	M/C solenoid	Check all M/C solenoid and ECM wires and connections *Replace the M/C solenoid (see Chapter 4)
55 (five flashes, pause, five flashes)	Oxygen sensor circuit	Check for corrosion on the ECM connectors and terminals Make sure that the four-terminal EST wiring harness is not too close to electrical signals such as spark plug wires, distributor housing, alternator, etc. Check the wiring of the various sensors *Replace the oxygen sensor

3 Fuel Control System

General description

1 The function of this system is to control the flow of fuel through the carburetor idle main metering circuits. The major components of the system are the mixture control (M/C) solenoid and the oxygen sensor.

2 The M/C solenoid changes the fuel/air mixture by allowing more or less fuel to flow through the carburetor. The M/C solenoid, located in the carburetor air horn, is in turn controlled by the ECM, which provides a ground for the solenoid. When the solenoid is energized the fuel flow through the carburetor is reduced, providing a leaner mixture, and when the ECM removes the ground path the solenoid de-energizes and allows more fuel flow.

3 The ECM determines the proper fuel mixture required by monitoring a signal sent by the oxygen sensor located in the exhaust stream. When the mixture is lean the oxygen sensor voltage is low and the ECM commands a richer mixture. Conversely, when the mixture is rich, the oxygen sensor voltage is higher and the ECM commands a leaner mixture.

Checking

Oxygen sensor

4 If the vehicle is equipped with a 1.9 liter engine, make sure that the oxygen sensor is replaced every 30,000 miles.

5 The proper operation of the sensor depends on the four conditions which follow:

6 *Electrical conditions:* The low voltages and low currents generated by the sensor depend upon good, clean connections which should be checked whenever a malfunction of the sensor is suspected or indicated.

7 *Outside air supply:* The sensor is designed to allow air circulation to the internal portion of the sensor. Whenever the sensor is removed and installed or replaced, make sure the air passages are not restricted.

8 *Proper operating temperature:* The ECM will not react to the sensor signal until the sensor reaches approximately 600°F (360°C). This factor must be taken into consideration when evaluating the performance of the sensor.

9 *Non-leaded fuel:* The use of non-leaded fuel is essential for proper operation of the sensor. Make sure the fuel you are using is of this type.

10 In addition to observing the above conditions, special care must be taken whenever the sensor is handled. Violation of any of these cautionary procedures may lead to sensor failure. **Note:** *Do not attempt to measure the voltage output of the oxygen sensor, because the current drain from a conventional voltmeter would be enough to permanently damage the sensor. For the same reason, never hook up test leads, jumpers or other electrical connections.*

Mixture control solenoid

11 Check the wiring connectors and wires leading to the mixture control solenoid for looseness, fraying and other damage. Repair or replace any damaged wiring as necessary.

12 Check the mixture control solenoid for apparent physical damage. Replace it if damage is found.

6

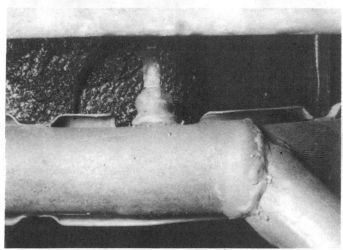

3.13 The oxygen sensor may be located in the exhaust pipe, as shown, or in the exhaust manifold.

Component replacement

Oxygen sensor

13 Disconnect the wire and unscrew the sensor from the manifold. Follow the installation instructions supplied with the new sensor.

Mixture control solenoid

14 For E2SE carburetors, refer to Chapter 4.

4 Electronic Spark Timing (EST)

1 Electronic Spark Timing is used on all California models. The EST distributor contains no vacuum or centrifugal advance, depending on commands from the ECM instead. The ECM receives a reference pulse form the distributor, indicating both engine RPM and crankshaft position, determines the proper spark advance for the engine operating conditions and sends an EST pulse to the distributor.

2 Under normal operating conditions, the ECM will always control the spark advance; however, under certain conditions such as cranking or setting base timing, the distributor can operate independently of ECM control. This condiditon is called 'bypass' and is determined by the bypass lead from the ECM to the distributor. When the bypass lead is over two volts, the ECM will control the spark; however, disconnecting the four-terminal EST connector, or grounding the bypass lead, will cause the engine to operate in the bypass mode.

3 For further information (and checking and component replacement procedures) regarding the EST distributor, refer to Chapter 5.

5 Air Injection Reactor (AIR) system

General description

1 The AIR system helps reduce hydrocarbons and carbon monoxide levels in the exhaust by injecting air into the exhaust ports of each cylinder during cold engine operation or directly into the catalytic converter during normal operation. It also helps the catalytic converter reach proper operating temperature quickly during warm-up.

2 The AIR system uses an air pump to force the air into the exhaust stream. An air management valve, controlled by the vehicle's electronic control module (ECM) directs the air to the correct location depending on engine temperature and driving conditions. During certain situations, such as deceleration, the air is diverted to the air cleaner to prevent backfiring from too much oxygen in the exhaust stream. On V6 engines only a deceleration (gulp) valve is used to help prevent backfiring during high vacuum conditions. The deceleration valve allows air to flow into the intake manifold and enter the air/fuel mixture to lean the rich condition created at high vacuum when the throttle closes upon deceleration. One-way check valves are also used in the AIR system's air lines to prevent exhaust gases from being forced back through the system.

3 The following components are utilized in the AIR system: an engine driven air pump; air control, air switching and divert management valves; a deceleration valve (V6 only); air flow and control hoses; check valves; and a dual bed catalytic converter.

Checking

4 Because of the complexity of this system it is difficult for the home mechanic to make a proper diagnosis. If the system is suspected of not operating properly, individual components can be checked.

5 Begin any inspection by carefully checking all hoses, vacuum lines and wires. Be sure they are in good condition and that all connections are tight and clean. Also make sure that the pump drivebelt is in good condition and properly adjusted.

6 To check the pump allow the engine to reach normal operating temperature and run it at about 1500 rpm. Locate the hose running from the air pump and squeeze it to feel the pulsations (photo). Have an assistant increase the engine speed and check for a parallel increase in air flow. If this is observed as described, the pump is functioning properly. If it is not operating in this manner a faulty pump is indicated.

7 The check valve can be inspected by first removing it from the air line. Attempt to blow through it from both directions. Air should only pass through it in the direction of normal air flow. If it is either stuck open or stuck closed the valve should be replaced.

8 To check the air management valve disconnect the vacuum signal line at the valve (photo). With the engine running see if vacuum is present in the line. If not, the line is clogged. If vacuum is present have the valve checked by a dealer or other qualified mechanic.

9 To check the deceleration valve remove the air cleaner and plug the air cleaner vacuum source. With the engine running at the specified idle speed remove the small deceleration valve signal hose from the manifold vacuum source, then reconnect the signal hose and listen for air flow through the ventilation pipe and into the deceleration valve. There should also be a noticeable engine speed drop when the signal hose is reconnected. If the air flow does not continue for at least one second, or the engine speed does not drop noticeably, check the deceleration valve hoses for restrictions or leaks. If no restrictions or leaks are found replace the deceleration valve.

Component replacement

Drivebelt

10 Loosen the pump mounting bolt and the pump adjustment bracket bolt.

5.6 The air pump hose can be squeezed to check pump output

5.8 The vacuum signal to the air management valve can be checked after removing the vacuum hose

11 Move the pump inboard until the belt can be removed.

12 Install the new belt and adjust it (refer to Chapter 1).

AIR pump pulley and filter

13 Compress the drivebelt to keep the pulley from turning and loosen the pulley bolts.

14 Remove the drivebelt as described above.

15 Remove the mounting bolts and lift off the pulley (photo).

16 If the fan-like filter must be removed, grasp it firmly with needle-nose pliers, as shown in the accompanying illustration, and pull it from the pump. **Note:** *Do not insert a screwdriver between the filter and pump housing as the edge of the housing could be damaged. The filter will usually be distorted when pulled off. Be sure no fragments fall into the air intake hose.*

17 The new filter is installed by placing it in position on the pump, placing the pulley over it and tightening the pulley bolts evenly to draw the filter into the pump. Do not attempt to install a filter by pressing or hammering it into place. **Note:** *It is normal for the new filter to have an interference fit with the pump housing and, upon initial operation, it may squeal until worn in.*

18 Install the drivebelt and, while compressing the belt, tighten the pulley bolts to the specified torque.

19 Adjust the drivebelt tension.

Hoses and tubes

20 To replace any tube or hose always note how it is routed first, either with a sketch or with numbered pieces of tape.

21 Remove the defective hose or tube and replace it with a new one of the same material and size and tighten all connections.

Check valve

22 Disconnect the pump outlet hose at the check valve (photo).

23 Remove the check valve from the pipe assembly, making sure not to bend or twist the assembly.

24 Install a new valve after making sure that it is a duplicate of the part removed, then tighten all connections.

Air management valve

25 Remove the air cleaner.

26 Disconnect the vacuum signal line from the valve. Also disconnect the air hoses and wiring connectors.

27 If the mounting bolts are retained by tabbed lock washers, bend the tabs back, then remove the mounting bolts and lift the valve off the adaptor or bracket.

28 Installation is the reverse of the removal procedure. Be sure to use a new gasket when installing the valve.

Air pump

29 Remove the air pump output hose.

30 If the pulley must be removed from the pump it should be done prior to removing the drivebelt as described elsewhere in this Section.

31 If the pulley is not being removed, remove the drivebelt.

32 Remove the pump mounting bolts and separate the pump from the engine (photo).

33 Installation is the reverse of the removal procedure. **Note:** *Do not tighten the pump mounting bolts until all components are installed.*

34 Following installation adjust the drivebelt tension as described in Chapter 1.

Deceleration valve

35 Disconnect the vacuum hoses from the valve (photo).

5.15 To replace the air pump filter, remove these three pulley mounting bolts and remove the pulley

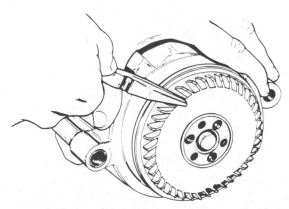

Fig. 6.4 **Removing the air pump filter fan (remove as shown — do not insert any tool behind the fan as damage to the pump may result (Sec 5)**

5.32 Location of the air pump mounting bolts

5.35 AIR system deceleration valve — V6 engine only

6

36 Remove the screws retaining the valve to the engine bracket (if present) and remove the valve.
37 Install a new valve and reconnect all hoses.

6   Early Fuel Evaporation (EFE) system

General description

1   This unit provides rapid heat to the intake air supply on California model engines by means of a ceramic heater grid which is integral with the carburetor base gasket and located under the primary bore.
2   The components involved in the EFE's operation include the heater grid, a relay, electrical wires and connectors and the ECM.
3   The EFE heater unit is controlled by the vehicle's Electronic Control Module (ECM) through a relay. The ECM senses the coolant temperature level and applies voltage to the heater unit only when the engine temperature is below a predetermined level. At normal operating temperatures the heater unit is off.
4   If the EFE heater is not coming on poor cold engine performance will be experienced. If the heater unit is not shutting off when the engine is warmed up the engine will run as if it is out of tune (due to the constant flow of hot air through the carburetor).

Checking

ECM-equipped models (California only)
5   If the EFE system is suspected of malfunctioning while the engine is cold, first check all electrical wires and connectors to be sure they are clean, tight and in good condition.
6   With the ignition switch in the On position use a circuit tester or voltmeter to check that current is reaching the relay. If not, there is a problem in the wiring leading to the relay, in the ECM's thermo switch or the ECM itself.
7   Next, with the engine cold but the ignition switch On, disconnect the heater unit wiring connector and use a circuit tester or voltmeter to see if current is reaching the heater unit. If so, use a continuity tester to check for continuity in the wiring connector attached to the heater unit. If continuity exists, the system is operating correctly in the cold engine mode.
8   If current is not reaching the heater unit, but is reaching the relay, replace the relay.
9   To check that the system turns off at normal engine operating temperature, first allow the engine to warm up thoroughly. With the engine idling, disconnect the heater unit wiring connector and use a circuit tester or voltmeter to check for current at the heater unit.
10 If current is reching the heater unit a faulty ECM is indicated.
11 For confirmation of the ECM's condition, refer to Section 2 or have the system checked by a dealer or automotive repair shop.

Non-ECM equipped models
12 If the EFE system is suspected of malfunctioning while the engine is cold, first check all electrical wires and connectors to be sure they are clean, tight and in good condition.
13 With the ignition On and the engine cold connect a test light lead to a good ground and probe, alternately, the two terminal leads at the coolant sensor/heater switch.
14 If the light glows at both terminals probe the pink wire at the heater unit connector to be sure current is reaching the heater unit. If the light glows again the EFE system should be functioning properly.
15 If the test light only glows at one of the terminals, the heater switch is defective and must be replaced.
16 If the test light does not glow at all and the lead is definitely connected to a good ground, the wiring betweeen the heater switch and ignition switch is faulty. Locate the short circuit and repair as necessary.

7   Exhaust Gas Recirculation (EGR) system

General description

1   An EGR system is used on all engines with which this manual is concerned. The system meters exhaust gases into the engine induc-

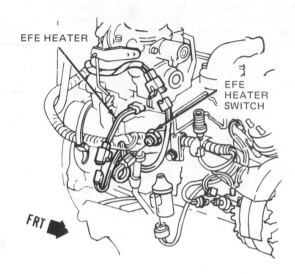

Fig. 6.5 Locations of the EFE heater connector and coolant sensor/heater switch (1.9L engine shown) (Sec 6)

7.15   Typical thermal vacuum switch — V6 engine shown

tion system through passages cast into the intake manifold and into the fuel/air mixture for the purpose of lowering combustion temperatures, thereby reducing the amount of oxides of nitrogen (NOX) formed.
2   The amount of exhaust gas admitted is regulated by a vacuum or backpressure controlled (EGR) valve in response to engine operating conditions. The EGR valve, in turn, is under control of the Thermal Vacuum Switch (TVS).
3   Common engine problems associated with the EGR system are rough idling or stalling when at idle, rough engine performance during light throttle application and stalling during deceleration.

Checking

4   Refer to Chapter 1 for EGR valve checking procedures.
5   If the EGR valve appears to be in proper operating condition,

carefully check all hoses connected to the valve for breaks, leaks or kinks. Replace or repair the valve/hoses as necessary.

6   Due to the interrelationship of the EGR system and the ECM, further checks of the system should be made by referring to Section 2 or having the system checked by a dealer or repair shop.

Component replacement

EGR valve

7   Disconnect the vacuum hose at the EGR valve.

8   Remove the nuts or bolts which secure the valve to the intake manifold or adapter.

9   Lift the EGR valve from the engine.

10   Clean the mounting surfaces of the EGR valve. Remove all traces of gasket material.

11   Place the new EGR valve, with a new gasket, on the intake manifold or adapter and tighten the attaching nuts or bolts.

12   Connect the vacuum signal hose.

TVS

13   Drain sufficient coolant from the radiator to bring the level below the bottom of the TVS (the TVS is located at the front of the intake manifold).

14   Remove the hoses from the valve, labeling them to ensure proper installation.

15   Remove the TVS with a wrench and replace it with a new one (photo).

16   Installation is the reverse of the removal procedure.

---

8   Evaporative Emissions Control system (EEC)

General description

1   This system is designed to trap and store fuel that evaporates from the carburetor and fuel tank which would normally enter the atmosphere and contribute to hydrocarbon (HC) emissions.

2   The system consists of a charcoal-filled canister and lines running to and from the canister. These lines include a vent line from the gas tank, a vent line from the carburetor float bowl or injection unit, an idle purge line into the vehicle's induction system and a vacuum line to the manifold. In addition, there is a purge valve in the canister. The TVS controls the vacuum to the purge valve with an electrically operated solenoid. The fuel tank cap is also an integral part of the system.

3   A tip-off that the system is not operating properly is a strong fuel odor.

Checking

4   Maintenance and replacement of the charcoal canister filter is covered in Chapter 1.

5   Check all lines in and out of the canister for kinks, leaks and breaks along their entire lengths. Repair or replace as necessary.

6   Check the gasket in the gas cap for signs of drying, cracking or breaks. Replace the gas cap with a new one if defects are found.

7   Due to its interrelationship with the TVS, other system checks should be made by referring to Section 2 or having the system checked by a dealer or repair shop.

Component replacement

8   Replacement of the canister filter is covered in Chapter 1.

9   When replacing any line running to or from the canister, make sure the replacement line is a duplicate of the one you are replacing. These lines are often color-coded to denote their particular usage.

---

9   Positive Crankcase Ventilation (PCV) system

General description

1   The positive crankcase ventilation system, or PCV as it is more commonly called, reduces hydrocarbon emissions by circulating fresh air through the crankcase to pick up blow-by gases, which are then rerouted through the carburetor to be burned in the engine.

2   The main components of this simple system are vacuum hoses and a PCV valve, which regulates the flow of gases according to engine speed and manifold vacuum.

Checking

3   The PCV system can be checked quickly and easily for proper operation. This system should be checked regularly as carbon deposited by the blow-by gases will eventually clog the PCV valve and/or system hoses. When the flow of the PCV system is reduced or stopped, common symptoms are rough idling or reduced engine speed at idle.

4   To check for proper vacuum in the system, remove the top plate of the air cleaner and locate the small PCV filter on the inside of the air cleaner housing.

5   Disconnect the hose leading to this filter. Be careful not to break the molded fitting on the filter.

6   With the engine idling, place your thumb lightly over the end of the hose. You should feel a slight pull or vacuum. The suction may be heard as your thumb is released. This will indicate that air is being drawn all the way through the system. If a vacuum is felt, the system is functioning properly. Check that the filter inside the air cleaner housing is not clogged or dirty. If in doubt, replace the filter with a new one, an inexpensive safeguard (refer to Chapter 1).

7   If there is very little vacuum or none at all at the end of the hose, the system is clogged and must be inspected further.

8   Shut off the engine and locate the PCV valve. Carefully pull it from its rubber grommet. Shake it and listen for a clicking sound. That is the rattle of the valve's check needle. If the valve does not click freely, replace it with a new one.

9   Now start the engine and run it at idle speed with the PCV valve removed. Place your thumb over the end of the valve and feel for suction. This should be a relatively strong vacuum which will be felt immediately.

10   If little or no vacuum is felt at the PCV valve, turn off the engine and disconnect the vacuum hose from the other end of the valve. Run the engine at idle speed and check for vacuum at the end of the hose just disconnected. No vacuum at this point indicates that the vacuum hose or inlet fitting at the engine is plugged. If it is the hose which is blocked, replace it with a new one or remove it from the engine and blow it out sufficiently with compressed air. A clogged passage at the carburetor or manifold requires that the component be removed and thoroughly cleaned to remove carbon build-up. A strong vacuum felt going into the PCV valve, but little or no vacuum coming out of the valve, indicates a failure of the PCV valve requiring replacement with a new one.

11   When purchasing a new PCV valve, make sure it is the correct one for your engine. An incorrect PCV valve may pull too little or too much vacuum, possibly leading to engine damage.

Component replacement

12   The replacement procedures for both the PCV valve and filter are covered in Chapter 1.

---

10   Thermostatically-Controlled Air induction system (TCA)

General description

1   The TCA system is provided to improve engine efficiency and reduce hydrocarbon emissions during the initial warm-up period by maintaining a controlled air temperature at the carburetor. This temperature control of the incoming air allows leaner carburetor and choke calibrations.

2   The system uses a damper assembly located in the snorkel of the air cleaner housing to control the ratio of cold and warm air directed into the carburetor. This damper is controlled by a vacuum motor which is, in turn, modulated by a temperature sensor in the air cleaner. On some engines a check valve is used in the sensor, which delays the opening of the damper flap when the engine is cold and the vacuum signal is low.

3   It is during the first few miles of driving (depending on outside temperature) that this system has its greatest effect on engine performance and emissions output. When the engine is cold, the damper flap blocks off the air cleaner inlet snorkel, allowing only warm air from the exhaust manifold to enter the carburetor. Gradually, as the engine warms up, the flap opens the snorkel passage, increasing the amount of cold air allowed in. Once the engine reaches normal operating temperature the flap opens completely, allowing only cold, fresh air to enter.

4   Because of this cold-engine-only function, it is important to periodically check this system to prevent poor engine performance when cold or overheating of the fuel mixture once the engine has reached

6

10.16   The air cleaner temperature sender can be pried off after disconnecting the adjacent vacuum hose from the bottom of the air cleaner

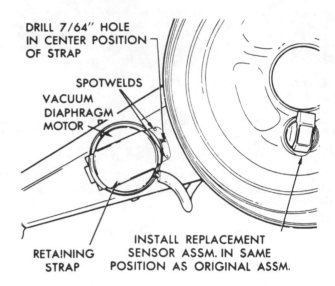

Fig. 6.6 After drilling out the two spot welds, the replacement TCA vacuum motor is installed by drilling a screw mounting hole at the location shown (Sec 10)

operating temperature. If the air cleaner valve sticks in the 'no heat' position, the engine will run poorly, stall and waste gas until it has warmed up on its own. A valve sticking in the 'heat' position causes the engine to run as if it is out of tune (due to the constant flow of hot air to the carburetor).

Checking

5   Refer to Chapter 1 for maintenance and checking procedures for this system. If problems were encountered in the system's performance while performing the routine maintenance checks, refer to the procedures which follow.
6   If the damper door did not close off snorkel air when the cold engine was first started, disconnect the vacuum hose at the snorkel vacuum motor and place your thumb over the hose end, checking for vacuum. If there is vacuum going to the motor, check that the damper door and link are not frozen or binding within the air cleaner snorkel. Replace the vacuum motor if the hose routing is correct and the damper door moves freely.
7   If there was no vacuum going to the motor in the above test, check the hoses for cracks, crimps and proper connection. If the hoses are clear and in good condition, replace the temperature sensor inside the air cleaner housing.

Component replacement

Air cleaner vacuum motor

8   Remove the air cleaner assembly from the engine and disconnect the vacuum hose from the motor.
9   Drill out the two spot welds which secure the vacuum motor retaining strap to the snorkel tube.
10 Remove the motor attaching strap.
11 Lift up the motor, cocking it to one side to unhook the motor linkage at the control damper assembly.
12 To install, drill a 7/64-inch hole in the snorkel tube at the center of the retaining strap.
13 Insert the vacuum motor linkage into the control damper assembly.
14 Using the sheet metal screw supplied with the motor service kit, attach the motor and retaining strap to the snorkel. Make sure the sheet

metal screw does not interfere with the operation of the damper door. Shorten the screw if necessary.
15 Connect the vacuum hose to the motor and install the air cleaner assembly.

Air cleaner temperature sensor

16 Remove the air cleaner from the engine and disconnect the vacuum hoses at the sensor (photo).
17 Carefully note the position of the sensor. The new sensor must be installed in exactly the same position.
18 Pry up the tabs on the sensor retaining clip and remove the sensor and clip from the air cleaner.
19 Install the new sensor with a new gasket in the same position as the old one.
20 Press the retaining clip onto the sensor. Do not damage the control mechanism in the center of the sensor.
21 Connect the vacuum hoses and attach the air cleaner to the engine.

11   Transmission Converter Clutch (TCC)

1   Toward optimizing the efficiency of the emissions control network, the ECM (California models only) controls an electrical solenoid mounted in the automatic transmission of vehicles so equipped. When the vehicle reaches a specified speed, the ECM energizes the solenoid and allows the torque converter to mechanically couple the engine to the transmission, under which conditions emissions are at their minimum. However, because of other operating condition demands (deceleration, passing, idle, etc.), the transmission must also function in its normal, fluid-coupled mode. When such latter conditions exist, the solenoid de-energizes, returning the transmission to fluid coupling. The transmission also returns to fluid-coupling operation whenever the brake pedal is depressed.
2   Due to the requirement of special diagnostic equipment for the testing of this system, and the possible requirement for dismantling of the automatic transmission to replace components of this system, checking and replacing of the components should be handled by a dealer or automotive repair shop.

Chapter 7 Part A   Manual transmission

Contents

Specifications

Torque specifications	Ft-lbs
77mm 4-speed	
Oil filler plug	20
Shift lever cover retaining bolts	10
Transmission-to-engine bolts.......................	55
Crossmember-to-frame bolts........................	25
Mount-to-crossmember bolts	25
Mount-to-transmission bolts	35
77.5mm 4-speed	
Oil filler plug	30
Oil drain plug	30
Shift lever cover retaining bolts	15
Transmission-to-engine bolts	
Six-cylinder	55
Four-cylinder	25
Crossmember-to-frame bolts........................	25
Mount-to-crossmember nuts	25
Mount-to-transmission bolts	35
77mm 5-speed	
Oil filler plug	20
Dust cover bolts	8
Transmission-to-engine bolts.......................	55
Shift lever cover-to-case bolts	10
Crossmember-to-frame bolts........................	35
Mount-to-crossmember bolts	35
Mount-to-transmission bolts	35

7A

1   General information

The 'S' series vehicles covered in this manual are equipped with a standard four-speed or optional five-speed manual transmission. Two different four-speed transmissions are used; a 77mm and a 77.5mm (the figure represents the distance between the mainshaft and countershaft centerlines). All manual transmissions are operated through a floor-mounted gearshift lever assembly attached to the top of the transmission extension housing.

2   Transmission mounts — check and replacement (with transmission in vehicle)

1   Raise the vehicle and support it securely with jackstands. Make sure the vehicle is stable as you may jostle it somewhat in the course of checking the mounts.
2   Push up on the transmission extension housing and note the amount the housing moves (photo).
3   Pull down on the extension housing and note the amount of movement available.

2.2   Location of the extension housing transmission mount (four-wheel drive shown)

3   If the extension housing can be pushed upwards a greater distance than it can be pulled down it is an indication that the rubber is worn and the mount has bottomed out.

4   If the rubber portion of the mount separates from the metal plate when you push upwards the mount should be replaced.

3   Shift lever — removal and installation

1   With the transmission in Neutral, remove the screws from the shift lever boot retainer and slide the boot up the lever.

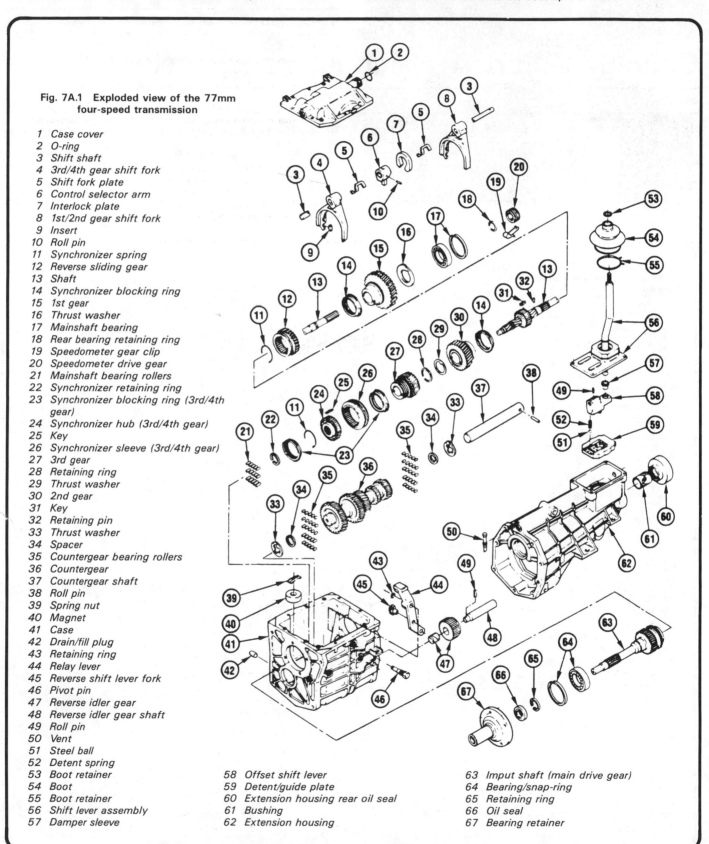

Fig. 7A.1   Exploded view of the 77mm four-speed transmission

1   Case cover
2   O-ring
3   Shift shaft
4   3rd/4th gear shift fork
5   Shift fork plate
6   Control selector arm
7   Interlock plate
8   1st/2nd gear shift fork
9   Insert
10 Roll pin
11 Synchronizer spring
12 Reverse sliding gear
13 Shaft
14 Synchronizer blocking ring
15 1st gear
16 Thrust washer
17 Mainshaft bearing
18 Rear bearing retaining ring
19 Speedometer gear clip
20 Speedometer drive gear
21 Mainshaft bearing rollers
22 Synchronizer retaining ring
23 Synchronizer blocking ring (3rd/4th gear)
24 Synchronizer hub (3rd/4th gear)
25 Key
26 Synchronizer sleeve (3rd/4th gear)
27 3rd gear
28 Retaining ring
29 Thrust washer
30 2nd gear
31 Key
32 Retaining pin
33 Thrust washer
34 Spacer
35 Countergear bearing rollers
36 Countergear
37 Countergear shaft
38 Roll pin
39 Spring nut
40 Magnet
41 Case
42 Drain/fill plug
43 Retaining ring
44 Relay lever
45 Reverse shift lever fork
46 Pivot pin
47 Reverse idler gear
48 Reverse idler gear shaft
49 Roll pin
50 Vent
51 Steel ball
52 Detent spring
53 Boot retainer
54 Boot
55 Boot retainer
56 Shift lever assembly
57 Damper sleeve
58 Offset shift lever
59 Detent/guide plate
60 Extension housing rear oil seal
61 Bushing
62 Extension housing
63 Imput shaft (main drive gear)
64 Bearing/snap-ring
65 Retaining ring
66 Oil seal
67 Bearing retainer

3.2   Location of the shift lever retaining bolts

2   Remove the shift lever retaining bolts at the transmission (photo) and remove the lever assembly by pulling it straight up and out of the extension housing.
3   Installation is the reverse of the removal procedure.

4   Transmission — removal and installation

1   Disconnect the negative battery cable from the battery.
2   On models equipped with a 77.5mm transmission only, remove the starter motor upper mounting bolt.
3   Remove the shift lever assembly from the transmission (refer to Section 3).
4   Raise the vehicle and support it securely on jackstands.
5   Remove the driveshaft, referring to Chapter 8 if necessary.
6   Remove the transfer case on four-wheel drive vehicles (refer to Chapter 7C).
7   Disconnect the speedometer cable from the transmission.
8   Label and detach the wire connectors at the transmission.
9   Disconnect the clutch slave cylinder.
10   On 77.5mm transmissions only, disconnect the exhaust pipe(s) at the manifold. Remove the appropriate body mounting bolts and raise the body as described in Chapter 2D, Section 7. This will provide the

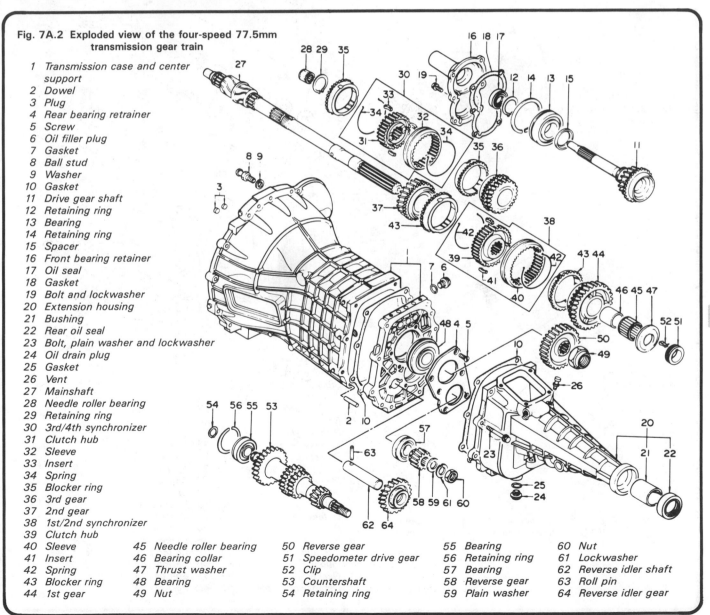

Fig. 7A.2 Exploded view of the four-speed 77.5mm transmission gear train

1   Transmission case and center support
2   Dowel
3   Plug
4   Rear bearing retrainer
5   Screw
6   Oil filler plug
7   Gasket
8   Ball stud
9   Washer
10   Gasket
11   Drive gear shaft
12   Retaining ring
13   Bearing
14   Retaining ring
15   Spacer
16   Front bearing retainer
17   Oil seal
18   Gasket
19   Bolt and lockwasher
20   Extension housing
21   Bushing
22   Rear oil seal
23   Bolt, plain washer and lockwasher
24   Oil drain plug
25   Gasket
26   Vent
27   Mainshaft
28   Needle roller bearing
29   Retaining ring
30   3rd/4th synchronizer
31   Clutch hub
32   Sleeve
33   Insert
34   Spring
35   Blocker ring
36   3rd gear
37   2nd gear
38   1st/2nd synchronizer
39   Clutch hub

40 Sleeve	45 Needle roller bearing
41 Insert	46 Bearing collar
42 Spring	47 Thrust washer
43 Blocker ring	48 Bearing
44 1st gear	49 Nut

50 Reverse gear	55 Bearing
51 Speedometer drive gear	56 Retaining ring
52 Clip	57 Bearing
53 Countershaft	58 Reverse gear
54 Retaining ring	59 Plain washer

60 Nut	
61 Lockwasher	
62 Reverse idler shaft	
63 Roll pin	
64 Reverse idler gear	

7A

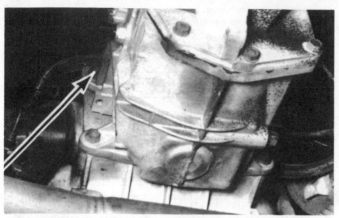

4.16 The upper transmission bolts (arrow indicates upper left bolt) should be removed first, then guide pins should be installed

clearance needed to remove the upper bellhousing bolts.
11 Support the engine/transmission by placing a jack and a block of wood under the engine oil pan.
12 Remove the transmission mount bolts.
13 Remove the hanger supporting the catalytic converter. Take care not to damage the converter.
14 Remove the crossmember bolts, then remove the crossmember and transmission mounts.
15 Remove the dust cover bolts.
16 Remove the transmission-to-clutch housing upper bolts (photo), install guide pins in the holes then remove the lower bolts. The guide pins can be made by cutting the heads off of appropriate size bolts.
17 Lower the jack until the transmission can be withdrawn to the rear and removed.
18 Installation is the reverse of removal. Use the guide pins (photo) as an installation aid. Apply a light coat of high-temperature grease to the imput shaft bearing retainer and to the splined portion of the shaft to ensure free movement of the clutch and transmission components during installation. Be sure to tighten all nuts and bolts to the specified torque.
19 Refill the transmission with the recommended lubricant.

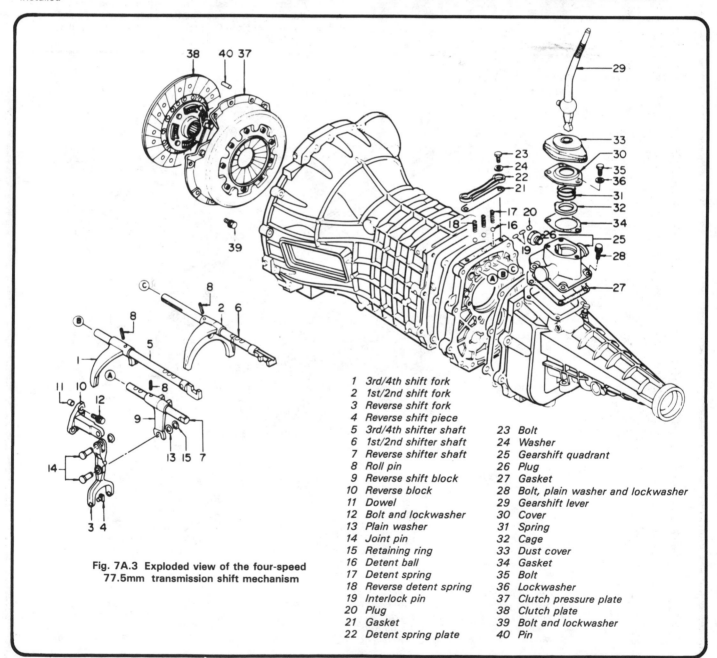

1	3rd/4th shift fork
2	1st/2nd shift fork
3	Reverse shift fork
4	Reverse shift piece
5	3rd/4th shifter shaft
6	1st/2nd shifter shaft
7	Reverse shifter shaft
8	Roll pin
9	Reverse shift block
10	Reverse block
11	Dowel
12	Bolt and lockwasher
13	Plain washer
14	Joint pin
15	Retaining ring
16	Detent ball
17	Detent spring
18	Reverse detent spring
19	Interlock pin
20	Plug
21	Gasket
22	Detent spring plate
23	Bolt
24	Washer
25	Gearshift quadrant
26	Plug
27	Gasket
28	Bolt, plain washer and lockwasher
29	Gearshift lever
30	Cover
31	Spring
32	Cage
33	Dust cover
34	Gasket
35	Bolt
36	Lockwasher
37	Clutch pressure plate
38	Clutch plate
39	Bolt and lockwasher
40	Pin

Fig. 7A.3 Exploded view of the four-speed
77.5mm transmission shift mechanism

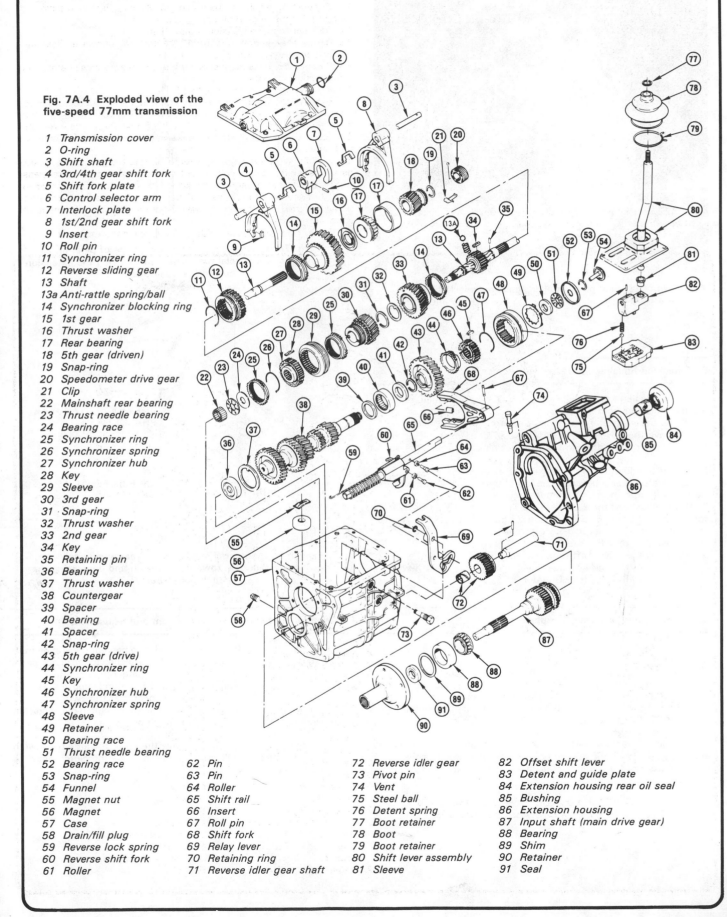

Fig. 7A.4 Exploded view of the five-speed 77mm transmission

1 Transmission cover
2 O-ring
3 Shift shaft
4 3rd/4th gear shift fork
5 Shift fork plate
6 Control selector arm
7 Interlock plate
8 1st/2nd gear shift fork
9 Insert
10 Roll pin
11 Synchronizer ring
12 Reverse sliding gear
13 Shaft
13a Anti-rattle spring/ball
14 Synchronizer blocking ring
15 1st gear
16 Thrust washer
17 Rear bearing
18 5th gear (driven)
19 Snap-ring
20 Speedometer drive gear
21 Clip
22 Mainshaft rear bearing
23 Thrust needle bearing
24 Bearing race
25 Synchronizer ring
26 Synchronizer spring
27 Synchronizer hub
28 Key
29 Sleeve
30 3rd gear
31 Snap-ring
32 Thrust washer
33 2nd gear
34 Key
35 Retaining pin
36 Bearing
37 Thrust washer
38 Countergear
39 Spacer
40 Bearing
41 Spacer
42 Snap-ring
43 5th gear (drive)
44 Synchronizer ring
45 Key
46 Synchronizer hub
47 Synchronizer spring
48 Sleeve
49 Retainer
50 Bearing race
51 Thrust needle bearing
52 Bearing race
53 Snap-ring
54 Funnel
55 Magnet nut
56 Magnet
57 Case
58 Drain/fill plug
59 Reverse lock spring
60 Reverse shift fork
61 Roller

62 Pin
63 Pin
64 Roller
65 Shift rail
66 Insert
67 Roll pin
68 Shift fork
69 Relay lever
70 Retaining ring
71 Reverse idler gear shaft

72 Reverse idler gear
73 Pivot pin
74 Vent
75 Steel ball
76 Detent spring
77 Boot retainer
78 Boot
79 Boot retainer
80 Shift lever assembly
81 Sleeve

82 Offset shift lever
83 Detent and guide plate
84 Extension housing rear oil seal
85 Bushing
86 Extension housing
87 Input shaft (main drive gear)
88 Bearing
89 Shim
90 Retainer
91 Seal

7A

4.18   With the guide pins installed, the transmission and input shaft are easily aligned with the bellhousing and pilot bearing

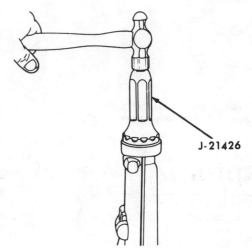

J-21426

Fig. 7A.5   An appropriately-sized piece of pipe, or, as shown here, a special tool is needed to install the extension housing oil seal (Sec 5)

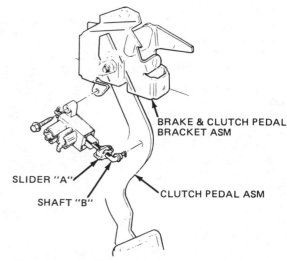

BRAKE & CLUTCH PEDAL BRACKET ASM

SLIDER "A"

SHAFT "B"

CLUTCH PEDAL ASM

Fig. 7A.6   The neutral start switch is easily adjustable by moving the slider (A) toward the switch and depressing the clutch pedal (Sec 7)

5   Extension housing oil seal — replacement

1   The extension housing oil seal can be replaced without removing the transmission from the vehicle.
2   Raise the vehicle and support it securely on jackstands.
3   Remove the driveshaft as described in Chapter 8.
4   Carefully pry out the old seal. Do not nick or scratch the output shaft.
5   Clean the counterbore and examine it for damage.
6   Lubricate the area between the lips of the new seal with transmission oil and coat the outer diameter with sealant.
7   Carefully install the seal, with the lip in, until the flange seats. A special tool, J-214266 (J-33035 on 77.5mm 4-speeds), is available to install the seal. However, a piece of pipe of the proper diameter used with a hammer may be substituted.
8   Reinstall the driveshaft (refer to Chapter 8).
9   Check the transmission fluid level and refill as needed with the recommended lubricant (see Chapter 1).

6   Speedometer gear seal — replacement

1   The speedometer gear seal can be replaced without removing the transmission from the vehicle.
2   Raise the vehicle and support it securely on jackstands.
3   Disconnect the speedometer cable, remove the lock plate to extension bolt and lock washer, then remove the lock plate.
4   Insert a screwdriver in the lock plate fitting and pry the fitting, gear and shaft from the extension housing.
5   Pry out the O-ring.
6   Installation is the reverse of removal, but lubricate the new seal with transmission lubricant and hold the assembly so that the slot in the fitting is toward the lock plate boss on the extension.

7   Neutral start switch — replacement and adjustment

1   This switch is a safety device intended to prevent the engine from being started with the clutch engaged. It is attached to the clutch pedal mounting bracket and is activated by a plunger-type shaft.
2   Remove the screws retaining the hush panel and remove the panel.
3   Disconnect the wiring harness connector at the switch.
4   Remove the switch mounting screw from the clutch pedal bracket and disengage the shaft from the clutch pedal.
5   Installation is the reverse of removal.
6   To adjust the switch simply move the slider towards the switch (see the accompanying illustration) and depress the clutch pedal as far as possible.

Chapter 7 Part B Automatic transmission

Contents

Specifications

Transmission type
1982 . . . . 200C
1983 and 1984 . . . . 200C, 700-R4

Torque Specifications	Ft-lbs
Transmission-to-engine bolts	
four-cylinder	25
V6	55
Driveplate-to-converter bolts	35
Inspection cover bolts	
four-cylinder	7
V6	25
Dipstick tube brace-to-transmission bolt	8
Transmission crossmember-to-frame bolts	25
Transmission mount-to-crossmember bolts	25
Catalytic converter/exhaust pipe bracket bolts	15
TV cable-to-transmission bolts/nuts	31
Torque arm bracket-to-transmission bolts	31
Shift cable pin-to-shift lever nut	8
Torque arm-to-rear axle bracket bolts	100
Driveshaft strap bolts	16

1 General information

Due to the complexity of the clutches and the hydraulic control system, and because of the special tools and expertise required to perform an automatic transmission overhaul, it should not be undertaken by the home mechanic. Therefore, the procedures in this Chapter are limited to general diagnosis, routine maintenance and adjustment and transmission removal and installation.

If the transmission requires major repair work it should be left to a dealer service department or a reputable automotive or transmission repair shop. You can, however, remove and install the transmission yourself and save the expense, even if the repair work is done by a transmission specialist.

Adjustments that the home mechanic may perform include those involving the throttle valve cable, the shift linkage and the neutral safety switch.

Caution: *Never tow a disabled vehicle at speeds greater than 30 mph or distances over 50 miles unless the driveshaft has been removed. Failure to observe this precaution may result in severe transmission damage caused by lack of lubrication.*

2 Diagnosis — general

Automatic transmission malfunctions may be caused by four general conditions: poor engine performance, improper adjustments, hydraulic malfunctions and mechanical malfunctions. Diagnosis of these problems should always begin with a check of the easily repaired items: fluid level and condition, shift linkage adjustment and throttle linkage adjustment. Next, perform a road test to determine if the problem has been corrected or if more diagnosis is necessary. If the problem persists after the preliminary tests and corrections are completed, additional diagnosis should be done by a dealer service department or a reputable automotive or transmission repair shop.

3 Shift linkage — check and adjustment

Note: *Apply the parking brake and block the wheels to prevent the vehicle from rolling.*

1   Position the shift lever in the Neutral position.

2   Working under the vehicle, loosen the clamp screw attaching the shift rod to the transmission control lever (B in the accompanying illustration).
3   Make sure that the transmission lever (A) is in the neutral detent.
4   Hold the clamp flush against the control lever while tightening the clamp screw finger-tight.
5   Tighten the clamp screw while making sure no force is exerted in either direction against the shift rod.

4   Throttle valve (TV) cable assembly — description and adjustment

1   The throttle cable should not be thought of as just an automatic downshift cable, but rather as a cable that controls the line pressure, shift feel and shift timing, as well as part throttle and detent downshifts. The function of the cable combines the functions of the vacuum modulator and downshift (detent) cable found on other model transmissions.
2   The TV cable is attached to the link at the throttle lever and bracket assembly at the transmission and to the throttle lever at the carburetor.
3   Whenever the TV cable has been disconnected from the carburetor it must be adjusted after reconnection.
4   The engine should be off.
5   If not previously done, remove the air cleaner, labeling all hoses as they are removed to simplify installation.
6   Depress and hold down the metal readjust tab at the engine end of the TV cable.
7   While holding the tab down move the slider until it stops against the fitting.
8   Release the readjust tab.
9   Manually open the carburetor lever to the full throttle stop posi-

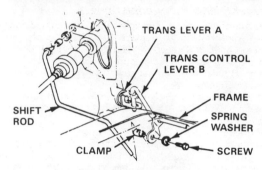

Fig. 7B.1 Details of the components involved in adjusting the shift linkage (Sec 3)

tion. The cable will ratchet through the slider and automatically re-adjust itself.
10 Release the carburetor lever.
11 Road test the vehicle. If delayed or only full-throttle shifts occur have the vehicle checked by a dealer.

5   Neutral safety and back-up light switch — replacement and adjustment

1   When the switch is operating properly, the back-up lights should come on only when the transmission is in Reverse and the engine should start only with the transmission lever in Park or Neutral.

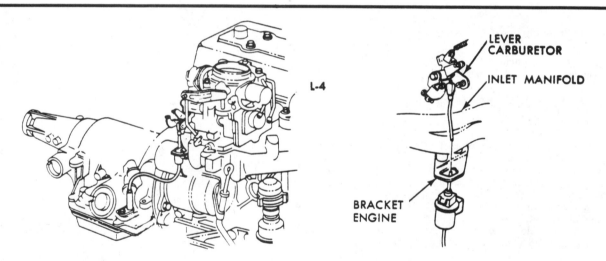

Fig. 7B.2 Details of the TV/detent cable installation (four-cylinder engine shown) (Sec 4)

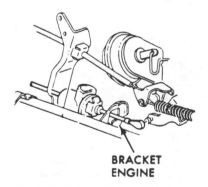

Fig. 7B.3 Typical TV cable adjustment slider and engine bracket for a V6 engine (Sec 4)

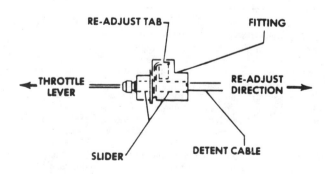

Fig. 7B.4 Details of a typical TV cable adjuster (Sec 4)

Replacement (and initial adjustment)

2   The neutral safety and back-up light switch is mounted on the lower part of the steering column. To replace the switch, simply remove the two mounting bolts and separate the switch from the column.
3   Move the shift lever to the Neutral position.
4   Insert a 0.89-inch diameter gauge pin 3/8-inch into the gauge hole on the new switch.
5   Insert the carrier tang on the switch into the shift tube slot in the steering column and install and tighten the switch mounting bolts.
6   Remove the gauge pin.
7   Move the shift lever into the Park position.
8   Return the shift lever to the Neutral position. The gauge pin should now fit into the switch gauge hole without any binding. If the pin does not fit readjust the switch as described in the following steps:

Adjustment

9   To reset the adjustment on the original switch, move the shift lever to the Neutral position and loosen the switch mounting bolts.
10   Insert the gauge pin as described in Step 4.
11   Tighten the mounting bolts and remove the gauge pin.
12   Check the operation of the switch.

6   Transmission — removal and installation

Note: *Before removing the transmission from four-wheel drive vehicles the transfer case must be removed as described in Chapter 7C.*

1   Disconnect the cable from the negative battery terminal.
2   Remove the air cleaner, labeling all hoses as they are disconnected to simplify installation.
3   Disconnect the TV cable at the carburetor.
4   Remove the transmission fluid dipstick from the tube.
5   Remove the upper bolt retaining the dipstick tube and separate the tube from the transmission.
6   Raise the vehicle and support is securely on jackstands.
7   Remove the driveshaft (refer to Chapter 8).
8   Disconnect the speedometer cable at the transmission.
9   Disconnect the TCC wire connector at the transmission if so equipped.
10   On four-wheel drive vehicles remove the crossmember mounting bolts and detach the crossmember. Be sure to separate the brake line from the crossmember.
11   Remove the mounting bolts from the exhaust crossover pipe and

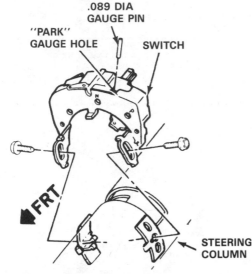

Fig. 7B.5 A gauge pin (or drill bit) is needed to adjust the neutral safety switch (Sec 5)

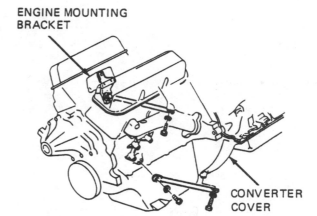

Fig. 7B.6 Location of the transmission support brackets (typical) (Sec 6)

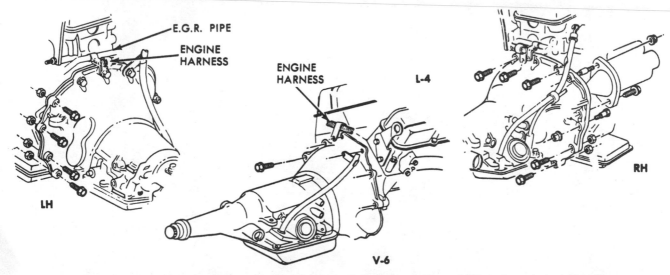

Fig. 7B.7 Transmission-to-engine mounting bolt details (2.0L four-cylinder and V6 engines shown) (Sec 6)

7B

catalytic converter and remove the crosssover pipe and converter as an assembly.

12 Remove the support bracket bolts at the inspection cover, if so equipped.

13 Remove the bolts retaining the inspection cover and detach the cover.

14 Remove the now-exposed converter-to-driveplate bolts. It will be necessary to turn the crankshaft to bring each of the bolts into view (use a wrench on the large bolt at the front of the crankshaft). Mark the relative position of the converter and driveplate with a scribe so they can be reinstalled in the same position. Engage a large screwdriver in the teeth of the driveplate to prevent movement as the bolts are loosened.

15 Disconnect the catalytic converter support bracket, if not done previously.

16 Disconnect the exhaust pipe(s) at the manifold.

17 Remove the appropriate body mounting bolts and raise the body of the vehicle as described in Chapter 2D, Section 7. This will provide the clearance needed to remove the upper bellhousing bolts.

18 Using a floor jack and a piece of wood placed between the jack and the transmission, support the transmission and remove the rear mount bolt.

19 Lower the transmission as far as possible without causing the engine or transmission to contact the firewall, then disconnect the TV cable assembly and the oil cooler lines at the transmission.

20 Support the engine at the oil pan rail with a jack and remove the transmission-to-engine bolts. The upper bolts should be removed first.

21 Move the transmission to the rear and down. If necessary, carefully pry it free from the driveplate. Keep the rear of the transmission down at all times to keep the converter from falling out. The converter can be held in place with a strap.

22 Installation is the reverse of the removal procedure, with the following additional instructions.

23 Before installing the driveplate-to-converter bolts make sure that the weld nuts on the converter are flush with the driveplate and that the converter can be turned freely by hand in this position. Start the mounting bolts and tighten them finger-tight, then tighten them to the specified torque. This will insure proper alignment of the converter.

24 Adjust the shift linkage (refer to Section 3).

25 Adjust the TV cable (refer to Section 4).

Chapter 7 Part C Transfer case

Contents

Specifications

Torque specifications	Ft-lb
Lock plate retaining bolts	25
Front output yoke nut	110
Vacuum switch	20
Shift lever nut	15
Transfer case half attaching bolts	20
Rear retainer bolts	15
Extension housing bolts	20
Drain/fill plug	35
Transfer case adapter bolts (automatic only)	25
Shift bracket bolt	55
Shift pivot bolt	100
Shifter adjusting bolt (A)	30

1 Shifter — removal and installation

1   Disconnect the negative cable from the battery.
2   From inside the vehicle, remove the shifter console mounting screws and lift out the console.
3   Remove the shifter boot.
4   Loosen the jam nut from the bottom of the shifter and unscrew the shifter from its base.

5   Detach the electrical connectors and remove the mounting bolt from the selector switch. Remove the selector switch.
6   Raise the vehicle and support it securely on jackstands.
7   Disconnect the shift rod from the shifter by prying it out with a screwdriver.
8   Remove the pivot and adjusting bolts (photo).
9   Installation is the reverse of removal. Adjust the shifter mechanism as described in Section 2.

7C

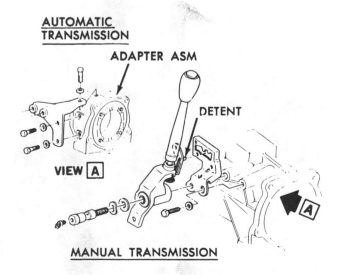

Fig. 7C.1 Details of the shifter components (Sec 1)

1.8 Location of the transfer case shifter pivot bolt (the rubber boot must be pulled back to remove the adjusting bolt, hidden from view)

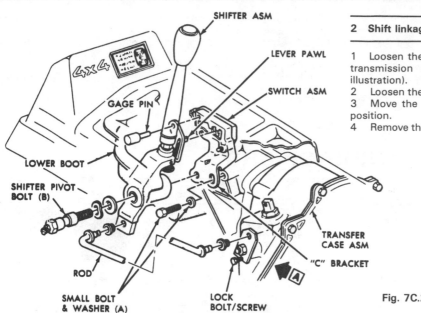

SHIFTER ASM

LEVER PAWL

SWITCH ASM

GAGE PIN

LOWER BOOT

SHIFTER PIVOT
BOLT (B)

ROD

SMALL BOLT
& WASHER (A)

LOCK
BOLT/SCREW

TRANSFER
CASE ASM

"C" BRACKET

2   Shift linkage — adjustment

1   Loosen the small bolt on the shift lever bracket attached to the transmission extension housing (bolt A in the accompanying illustration).
2   Loosen the shifter pivot bolt (B in the accompanying illustration).
3   Move the transfer case shifter (inside the vehicle) to the 4 HI position.
4   Remove the shifter console and boot. Slide the boot up the shifter.

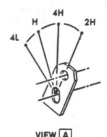

4H

H   2H

4L

VIEW A

Fig. 7C.2 Transfer case shift linkage assembly — exploded
view (Sec 2)

2.5 A 5/16-inch drill bit works fine as a gauge pin when adjusting the shift linkage

3.6 The transfer case front output shaft yoke should be marked so that the front driveshaft can be reinstalled in the same position

3.10 The catalytic converter hanger bolts must be removed before the transmission/transfer case mount can be removed

3.14 A floor jack is used to support the weight of the transfer case during removal procedures and to lower the case out of the vehicle

5   Insert an 8 mm gauge pin (a 5/16-inch drill bit works fine) through the shifter and shifter bracket (photo).
6   Insert a locking bolt or screw through the transfer case shift lever as shown in the accompanying illustration.
7   Tighten the small bolt (A) to the specified torque.
8   Tighten the shifter pivot bolt to the specified torque.
9   Remove the gauge pin and lock bolt or screw.
10 Install the shifter boot and console.

3   Transfer case — removal and installation

1   Move the transfer case shifter to the 4 HI position.
2   Disconnect the negative battery cable.
3   Raise the vehicle and support it securely on jackstands.
4   Remove the skid plate mounting bolts and detach the skid plate, if equipped.
5   Drain the oil from the transfer case.
6   Mark the transfer case front output shaft yoke and driveshaft so they can be reassembled in the same relative position (photo). Disconnect the front driveshaft from the transfer case.
7   Mark the rear axle yoke and driveshaft to simplify reassembly, then remove the rear driveshaft.
8   Disconnect the speedometer cable and vacuum harness at the transfer case.
9   Remove the shifter lever as described in Section 1. Disconnect the shift rod from the transfer case.
10   Remove the catalytic converter hanger bolts at the converter (photo).
11   Place a floor jack under the transmission oil pan and raise the transmission slightly. Position a block of wood between the jack head and the oil pan to prevent damage to the pan.
12   Remove the transmission mount bolts. Remove the mount and catalytic converter hanger.
13   Lower the transmission and transfer case.
14   While supporting the weight of the transfer case with the floor jack (photo), remove the transfer case mounting bolts. On automatic-transmission equipped vehicles the shifter bracket must be removed from the transfer case adapter before the upper mounting bolt can be removed.
15   Separate the transfer case from the extension housing and remove it from the vehicle.
16   Before installation position a new gasket on the transfer case.
17   Install the transfer case, aligning the splines of the input shaft while sliding the transfer case forward until seated against the transmission.
18   Install the transfer case mounting bolts and tighten them to the specified torque. Be sure to install the shift lever bracket on vehicles equipped with an automatic transmission.
19   Raise the transfer case and install the mount and hanger bracket. Install the retaining bolts and tighten them to the specified torque.

20   Install the catalytic converter hanger bolts at the converter and tighten them securely.
21   Attach the shift linkage to the transfer case and install the shift lever.
22   Connect the speedometer cable and vacuum hose.
23   Install the front and rear driveshafts, using the alignment marks for reference.
24   Fill the transfer case with the specified lubricant.
25   Install the skid plate (if equipped) and lower the vehicle.
26   Connect the negative battery cable.

4   Transfer case — disassembly, inspection and reassembly

Disassembly

1   Remove the fill and drain plugs.
2   Remove the front yoke (photo).
3   Remove the yoke seal washer. Discard the seal washer and yoke nut.
4   Set the transfer case on its side, positioning the front case on wood blocks.
5   Shift the transfer case to the 4 LO position (photo). The top of the transfer case lever should be in the far left detent.
6   Remove the extension housing mounting bolts and detach the extension housing. Tap the shoulder of the extension housing with a soft-faced hammer to break the seal.

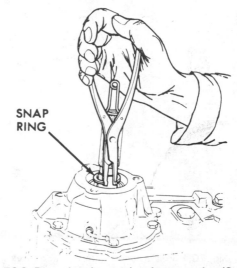

SNAP RING

Fig. 7C.3 Removing the rear bearing snap-ring (Sec 4)

4.2 A breaker bar can be inserted through the front yoke to facilitate removal of the yoke nut

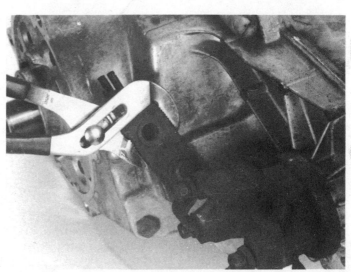

4.5 Before beginning disassembly, the top of the shifter must be in the far left detent position (4 LO)

7C

4.13 The case must be pried apart only at the pry slots cast into the case

4.14 Raising the mainshaft slightly will allow the output shaft and drive chain to be removed as an assembly

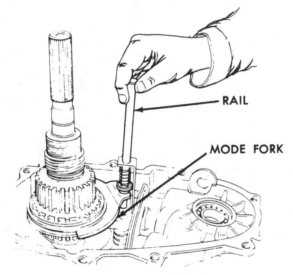

RAIL

MODE FORK

Fig. 7C.4 Pull up and rotate the mode fork rail to remove the fork and rail from the transfer case (Sec 4)

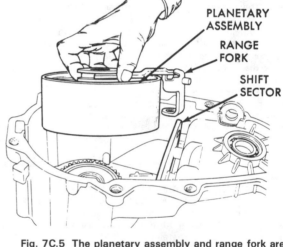

PLANETARY ASSEMBLY

RANGE FORK

SHIFT SECTOR

Fig. 7C.5 The planetary assembly and range fork are removed as an assembly (Sec 4)

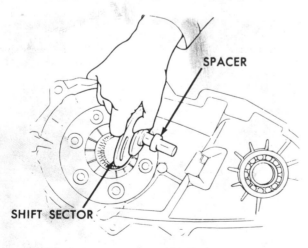

SPACER

SHIFT SECTOR

Fig. 7C.6 Removing the shift sector, shaft and spacer from the transfer case (Sec 4)

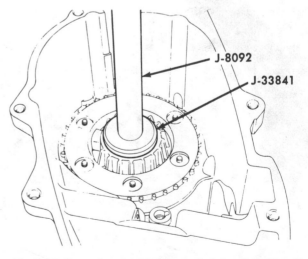

J-8092

J-33841

Fig. 7C.7 Removing the front input shaft bearings (Sec 4)

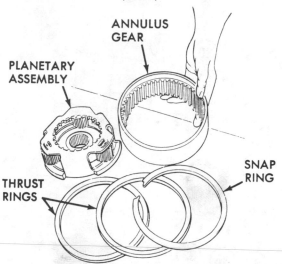

Fig. 7C.8 A special tool (as shown) or a slide hammer can be used to remove the front output shaft rear bearing (Sec 4)

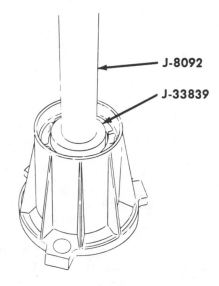

Fig. 7C.9 Press the extension housing bushing from the housing (Sec 4)

ANNULUS GEAR

PLANETARY ASSEMBLY

SNAP RING

THRUST RINGS

Fig. 7C.10 Planetary assembly components (Sec 4)

7   Remove and discard the snap-ring from the mainshaft rear bearing.
8   Remove the rear retainer mounting bolts and tap the shoulder of the retainer to break the seal.
9   Remove the rear retainer and pump housing from the transfer case.
10 Remove the pump seal from the pump housing.
11 Remove the speedometer drive gear from the mainshaft.
12 Remove the pump gear from the mainshaft.
13 Remove the rear case attaching bolts from the front case. Separate the cases by prying only at the slots cast into the ends of the transfer case (photo).
14 Remove the front output shaft and drive chain as an assembly. The mainshaft can be raised slightly to allow the front output shaft to clear the case (photo).
15 Pull up on the mode fork rail until it clears the range fork. Rotate the mode fork and rail and remove them from the transfer case.
16 Pull up on the mainshaft, separating it from the planetary assembly and remove the mainshaft from the transfer case.
17 Remove the planetary assembly and range fork from the transfer case.
18 Remove the planetary thrust washer and input gear from the transfer case.
19 Remove the input gear thrust bearing and front thrust washer from the transfer case.
20 Remove the shift sector detent spring and retaining bolt.
21 Remove the shift sector, shaft and spacer from the transfer case.

22 Remove the retaining bolts from the lock plate and separate the lock plate from the transfer case.
23 Using an expansion tool such as GM No. J-29369-1 and a slide hammer, remove the input gear pilot bearing.
24 Using a screwdriver or a brass drift, remove the front output shaft seal, the input shaft seal and the rear extension seal.
25 Press the two input gear roller bearings from the transfer case, using a tool setup as shown in the accompanying illustration.
26 Using an expansion tool and slide hammer as shown in the accompanying illustration, remove the output shaft rear bearing.
27 Using a hammer and drift, remove the rear mainshaft bearing from the rear retainer.
28 Using a screwdriver, pry out the snap-ring retaining the front output shaft bearing.
29 Remove the front output shaft bearing from the case using a hammer and punch.
30 Press the extension housing bushing from the housing using a tool setup as shown in the accompanying illustration.
31 To disassemble the mainshaft, first remove the synchronizer hub snap-ring.
32 Tap the synchronizer hub from the mainshaft, using a soft-faced hammer.
33 Remove the drive sprocket and thrust washer.
34 Using an appropriately-sized collar (such as GM No. J-33826), press the two roller bearings from the drive sprocket.
35 Remove the synchronizer keys and retaining rings.
36 To disassemble the planetary gear, first remove the snap-ring that retains the planetary gear to the annulus gear.
37 Remove and discard the outer thrust ring.
38 Remove the planetary assembly from the annulus gear.
39 Remove the inner thrust ring from the planetary assembly and discard it.

Inspection
40 Wash all parts thoroughly in solvent. Make sure that all old oil, dirt and metal particles are removed. Clean out each oil feed port and channel in each case half with compressed air. After cleaning the parts should be laid out for inspection.
41 Inspect all gear teeth for evidence of excessive wear or damage. Check all gear splines for burrs, nicks, wear or damage. Minor nicks or scratches can be removed with an oil stone, but replace any part showing significant wear or damage.
42 Inspect all snap-rings and thrust washers and replace any that show signs of wear, distortion or damage.
43 Inspect the two case halves for cracks, damaged mating surfaces, stripped bolt threads or distortion. Replace as necessary.
44 Inspect the low range lockplate in the front case. If the lock plate teeth or the plate hub are cracked, chipped or excessively worn, replace

7C

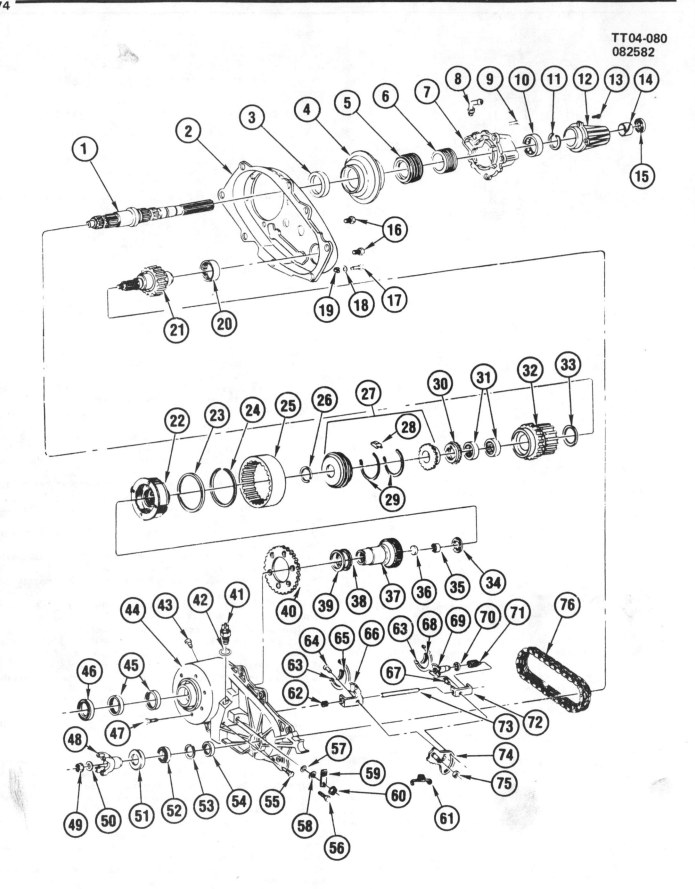

TT04-080
082582

Fig. 7C.11 Exploded view of the NP 207 transfer case components (Sec 4)

1 Main drive shaft
2 Housing
3 Oil pump housing seal
4 Oil pump housing
5 Oil pump
6 Speedometer drive gear
7 Bearing retainer
8 Vent connector
9 Bolt
10 Bearing
11 Snap-ring
12 Extension
13 Bolt
14 Bushing
15 Seal
16 Plug
17 Bolt
18 Washer
19 Dowel
20 Bearing
21 Front output shaft
22 Planetary gear carrier
23 Thrust washer
24 Retainer ring
25 Annulus gear
26 Retaining ring
27 Synchronizer assembly
28 Strut
29 Spring
30 Stop ring
31 Bearing
32 Sprocket
33 Thrust washer
34 Thrust washer
35 Bearing
36 Plug
37 Main drive gear assembly
38 Thrust bearing
39 Thrust washer
40 Lock plate
41 Indicator light switch
42 Seal
43 Plug
44 Housing
45 Bearing
46 Seal
47 Bolt
48 Yoke
49 Nut
50 Rubber washer
51 Deflector
52 Seal
53 Retaining ring
54 Bearing
55 Screw
56 Screw
57 Seal
58 Retainer
59 Lever
60 Nut
61 Spring assembly
62 Bushing
63 Pad
64 Pin
65 Pad
66 Fork assembly
67 Pin
68 Pad
69 Fork assembly
70 Cup
71 Spring
72 Bracket assembly
73 Shaft
74 Sector
75 Spacer
76 Drive chain

the lock plate and the lock plate attaching bolts.

45 Inspect all needle, roller and thrust bearings. Check the condition of the bearing bores in both cases. Also check the bearing bores in the input gear, rear output shaft and rear retainer. Replace any part that shows signs of excessive wear or damage.

Reassembly

46 To assemble the planetary gear, begin by installing the inner thrust ring.

47 Install the planetary assembly in the annulus gear.

48 Install the outer thrust ring. Install the retaining snap-ring.

49 Begin assembling the mainshaft by using an appropriately-sized collar (GM No. J-33832) to press the front drive sprocket bearing into place.

50 Press the rear bearing into the front drive sprocket with an

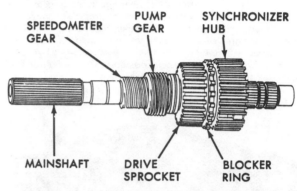

Fig. 7C.12 Mainshaft assembly components (Sec 4)

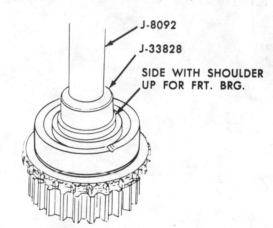

Fig. 7C.13 Installing the front drive sprocket front bearing (Sec 4)

7C

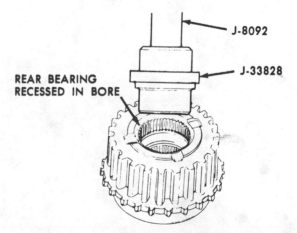

Fig. 7C.14 Installing the front drive sprocket rear bearing (Sec 4)

appropriately-sized collar. The factory GM tool (No. J-33828) should be used here, as the shoulder of the tool is machined to provide the proper bearing recess.

51 Install the drive sprocket thrust washer on the mainshaft.

52 Install the drive sprocket on the mainshaft.

53 Install the blocker ring and synchronizer assembly on the mainshaft. Install a new snap-ring.

54 Install the pump gear on the mainshaft, tapping it with a soft-faced hammer until it is seated.

55 Install the speedometer gear on the mainshaft.

56 Begin transfer case reassembly by installing the lock plate. Coat the case and lock plate surfaces around the bolt holes with Loctite 515 or equivalent.

57 Position the lock plate on the case, aligning the bolt holes. Install the mounting bolts and tighten them to the specified torque.

58 Install the two input shaft roller bearings in the transfer case. GM tool No. J-33830 is machined to provide the proper bearing recess during installation. Using the GM tool, press the bearing in until the tool bottoms in the bore. **Note:** *All of the bearings used in the transfer case must be correctly aligned with the bearing oil feed holes. After installing each bearing, check the bearing position to be sure the oil feed hole is not in any way obstructed by the bearing.*

59 Install the front output shaft rear bearing. Again, GM tool No. J-33832 is machined to provide the proper recess.

60 Install the front output shaft front bearing, using tool No. J-33832.

61 Install the front output shaft bearing snap-ring.

62 Install the front output shaft seal using a length of pipe of the appropriate diameter.

63 Install the spacer on the shift sector shaft and install the sector in the transfer case.

64 Install the shift lever and retaining nut and tighten the nut to the specified torque.

65 Install the shift sector detent spring and retaining bolt.

66 Press the input gear pilot bearing into place, using an installation tool such as GM No. J-33829.

67 Install the input gear front thrust bearing and input gear in the transfer case.

68 Install the planetary gear thrust washer on the input gear. Install the range fork on the planetary assembly and install the planetary assembly in the transfer case (photo).

69 Install the mainshaft in the transfer case, making sure the thrust washer is aligned with the input gear and planetary assembly.

70 Install the mode fork on the synchronizer sleeve and rotate it so that it lines up with the range fork. Slide the mode fork rail down through

4.68 Correct installation of the planetary assembly in the transfer case

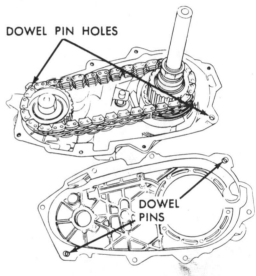

Fig. 7C.15 Align the dowel pin holes when assembling the cases to avoid disturbing the sealant bead (Sec 4)

4.70 Correct installation of the mode fork rail and bracket

4.75 The pump gear and speedometer drive gear are installed on the mainshaft as shown

the range fork until the rail bottoms out in the case bore (photo).

71 Position the drive chain on the front output shaft and on the mainshaft drive sprocket. Install the front output shaft in the transfer case. The mainshaft can be raised slightly to allow the output shaft to seat completely.

72 Install the magnet in the pocket in the transfer case.

73 Apply a 1/8-inch bead of Loctite 515 or the equivalent to the mating surface of the front case half.

74 Install the rear case on the front case, aligning the dowel pins. Install the attaching bolts and tighten them to the specified torque. Install the two bolts and washers used in the dowel pin holes.

75 Install the pump gear and speedometer drive gear on the mainshaft (photo).

76 Install the output bearing in the rear retainer using an installation tool such as GM No. J-33833. Press the bearing in until it is completely seated in the bore.

77 Install the pump seal in the pump housing using GM tool No. J-33835 or a pipe of the appropriate diameter. Apply some petroleum jelly to the pump housing tabs and install the pump housing in the rear retainer.

78 Apply a 1/8-inch bead of Loctite 515 or the equivalent to the mating surface of the rear retainer. Attach the rear retainer to the transfer case. Tighten the bolts to the specified torque.

79 Install a new snap-ring on the mainshaft. Pull up on the mainshaft to seat the snap-ring.

80 Install the extension housing bushing using an installation tool such as GM No. J-338265. Press the bushing in until it bottoms in the bore.

81 Install the new extension housing seal using an installation tool such as GM No. J-33843. Seat the seal completely in the bore.

82 Apply a 1/8-inch bead of Loctite 515 or the equivalent to the mating surface of the extension housing. Install the extension housing. Tighten the attaching bolts to the specified torque.

83 Install the front yoke on the output shaft, using a new seal washer and nut. Tighten the nut to the specified torque.

84 Install the drain and filler plugs and tighten them to the specified torque.

7C

Chapter 8   Driveline

Contents

Specifications

Hydraulic clutch pedal travel (measured at the clutch fork)

1.9 liter engine	0.624 in. minimum
2.0 liter engine	0.832 in. minimum

Torque specifications	Ft-lbs
Clutch pedal-to-mounting bracket	25
Clutch reservoir-to-mounting bracket	2.5
Clutch master cylinder-to-cowl	10
Slave cylinder heat shield-to-bellhousing	15
Slave cylinder-to-bellhousing	15
Universal joint retainer strap bolts	15
Rear axle housing cover-to-carrier	30
Brake assembly-to-rear axle housing	35
Rear gear-to-differential case	80
Rear differential pinion shaft lock screw	20
Rear differential carrier cover bolts	20
Bearing cap-to-carrier	60
Filler plug	20
Shift cable housing attaching bolts	35
Drive axle-to-output shaft flange bolts	60
Output shaft tube bracket-to-frame bolts	55

1   Clutch — general information

All manual transmission-equipped vehicles utilize a single dry plate, diaphragm spring-type clutch. Operation is through a foot pedal and rod linkage. The unit consists of a pressure plate assembly which contains the pressure plate, diaphragm spring and fulcrum rings. The assembly is bolted to the rear face of the flywheel.

The driven plate (friction or clutch plate) is free to slide along the transmission input shaft and is held in place between the flywheel and pressure plate by the pressure exerted by the diaphragm spring. The friction lining material is riveted to the clutch plate, which incorporates a spring-cushioned hub designed to absorb driveline shocks and to assist in ensuring smooth starts.

Depressing the clutch pedal pushes the throwout bearing forward to bear against the fingers of the diaphragm spring. This action causes the diaphragm spring outer edge to deflect and move the pressure plate to the rear to disengage the pressure plate from the clutch plate.

When the clutch pedal is released, the diaphragm spring forces the pressure plate into contact with the friction linings of the clutch plate and at the same time pushes the clutch plate forward on its splines to ensure full engagement with the flywheel. The clutch plate is now firmly sandwiched between the pressure plate and the flywheel and the drive is taken up.

1984 models

A hydraulic clutch assembly is employed on all 1984 models. The assembly consists of a remote reservoir, a clutch master cylinder and a slave cylinder.

The clutch master cylinder is mounted on the cowl panel in the engine compartment and the slave cylinder is mounted on the engine bellhousing. The master cylinder operates directly off the clutch pedal.

When the clutch pedal is pushed in, hyradulic fluid (under pressure from the clutch master cylinder) flows into the slave cylinder. Because the slave cylinder is also connected to the clutch fork, the fork moves the throwout bearing into contact with the pressure plate release fingers, disengaging the clutch plate.

The hydraulic clutch system locates the clutch pedal and provides clutch adjustment automatically, so no adjustment of the clutch linkage or pedal position is required. **Caution:** *Prior to servicing the clutch or vehicle components that require the removal of the slave cylinder (i.e. transmission and clutch housing removal), the master cylinder pushrod must be disconnected from the clutch pedal. If this is not done, permanent damage to the slave cylinder will occur if the clutch pedal is depressed while the slave cylinder is disconnected.*

If a malfunction of the hydraulic clutch assembly is suspected, verify it by removing the clutch housing dust shield and measuring the clutch slave cylinder pushrod travel as follows.

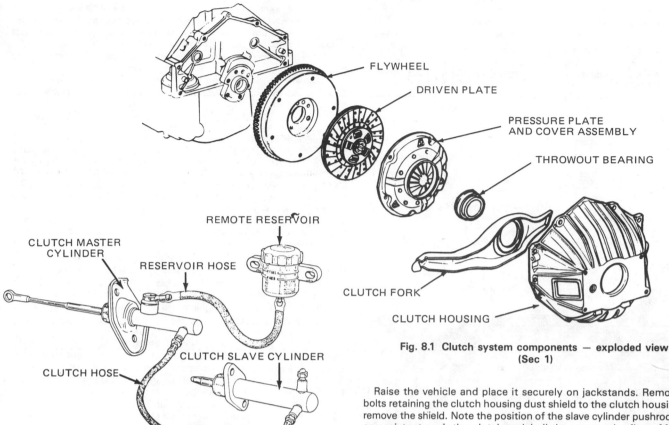

Fig. 8.1 Clutch system components — exploded view
(Sec 1)

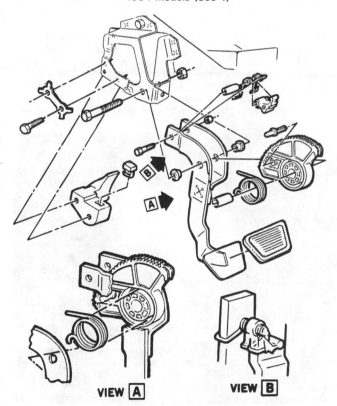

Fig. 8.2 Typical clutch hydraulic components used on
1984 models (Sec 1)

Fig. 8.3 Details of the clutch pedal assembly (Sec 2)

Raise the vehicle and place it securely on jackstands. Remove the bolts retaining the clutch housing dust shield to the clutch housing and remove the shield. Note the position of the slave cylinder pushrod. Have an assistant push the clutch pedal all the way to the floor. Measure the distance the pushrod travels while engaging the clutch fork. If the distance is as specified or more, the clutch hydraulic system is operating correctly. Do not remove it. If the slave cylinder pushrod does not travel at least the specified distance check the reservoir fluid level (the slave cylinder must be in place when the fluid level is checked). **Note:** *Carefully clean the top of the reservoir before removing it to prevent contamination of the system.* Fill the reservoir to the proper level, indicated by a step in the reservoir. Do not overfill the reservoir, as the upper portion must accept fluid that is displaced from the slave cylinder as the clutch wears.

If the reservoir required fluid, examine the hydraulic system components for leakage by removing the rubber boots from the master and slave cylinders and checking for leakage past the pistons. A slight wetting of the surfaces is acceptable, but if excessive leakage is evident, the clutch hydraulic system must be replaced, as a whole, with a new one.

2   Clutch pedal — removal and installation

1   Disconnect the cable from the negative battery terminal.
2   Disconnect the clutch pedal return spring.
3   Remove the screws retaining the underdash hush panel, then remove the hush panel.
4   Disconnect and remove the neutral start switch from the clutch pedal (refer to Chapter 7A).
5   Remove the turn signal and hazard warning flasher mounting bracket screws.
6   Disconnect the clutch actuator rod (clutch master cylinder pushrod on models with hydraulic clutch) from the clutch pedal.
7   Remove the nut from the clutch pedal pivot bolt.
8   Pull the bolt out only far enough to allow removal of the clutch pedal, leaving it engaged through the brake pedal pivot and bracket.
9   Before installing the clutch pedal assembly, inspect and clean all components. Replace all components showing wear with new ones. **Note:** *Do not clean the bushings with solvent; simply wipe them off with a clean rag.*
10   Installation is the reverse of the removal procedure. After installation is complete, adjust the clutch pedal free play (refer to Chapter 1).

8

3   Clutch — removal, inspection and installation

1   Access to the clutch is normally accomplished by removing the transmission, leaving the engine in the vehicle. If, of course, the engine is being removed for major overhaul, then the opportunity should always be taken to check the clutch assembly for wear at the same time.

2   Disconnect the clutch fork pushrod and spring, then remove the clutch housing from the engine block (photo). On models equipped with a hydraulic clutch assembly, remove the slave cylinder heat shield and slave cylinder from the clutch housing before removing the clutch housing.

3   Slide the clutch fork from the ball stud and remove the fork from the dust boot.

4   If necessary, the ball stud can be removed from the clutch housing by unscrewing it.

5   If there are no alignment marks on the clutch cover (an X-mark or white-painted letter) scribe or center-punch marks for indexing purposes during installation.

6   Unscrew the bolts securing the pressure plate and cover assembly one turn at a time in a diagonal sequence to prevent distortion of the clutch cover.

7   With all the bolts and lock washers removed, carefully lift the pressure plate away from the flywheel. Be careful not to drop the clutch plate.

3.2 Locations of the clutch housing mounting bolts (not all are visible)

8   It is not practical to dismantle the pressure plate assembly.

9   If a new clutch plate is being installed, replace the throwout bearing at the same time. This will preclude having to replace it at a later date when wear on the clutch plate is still very little.

10   If the pressure plate assembly must be replaced, a rebuilt unit may be available.

11   Examine the clutch plate friction lining for wear and loose rivets, and the disc for rim distortion, cracks, broken hub springs and worn splines. The surface of the friction linings may be highly glazed, but as long as the clutch material pattern can be seen clearly, this is satisfactory. Compare the amount of lining remaining with a new clutch plate, if possible. If in doubt, replace the clutch plate with a new one.

12   Check the machined faces of the flywheel and the pressure plate. If either are grooved, they should be machined until smooth or replaced.

13   If the pressure plate is cracked or split, replace it with a new one; also, if the condition of the diaphragm spring is suspect, the spring should be checked and replaced if necessary.

14   Check the throwout bearing for smoothness of operation. There should be no harsh or loose spots in it. It should spin reasonably freely, bearing in mind that it has been prepacked with grease. If in doubt, replace the bearing with a new one.

15   It is important that no oil or grease gets on the clutch plate friction linings or the pressure plate and flywheel faces. Always handle the clutch with clean hands and wipe down the pressure plate and flywheel faces with a clean, dry rag before assembly begins.

16   Place the clutch plate against the flywheel, making sure that the longer splined boss faces toward the flywheel (thicker torsional spring assembly projection toward the transmission).

17   Install the pressure plate and clutch cover assembly so that the marks are in alignment. Tighten the bolts only finger tight so that the driven plate is gripped, but can still be moved sideways.

18   The clutch plate must now be aligned so that when the engine and transmission are mated, the input shaft splines will pass through the splines in the center of the clutch hub plate.

19   Alignment can usually be carried out by inserting a round bar or long screwdriver through the hole in the center of the clutch so that the end of the bar rests in the small hole in the end of the crankshaft containing the input shaft pilot bushing (photo). Ideally, an old transmission input shaft or alignment tool should be used. These alignment tools are inexpensive and available at your local auto parts retailer.

20   Using the bearing as a fulcrum, move the bar sideways or up and down to move the clutch plate in whichever direction is necessary to align (center) it.

21   Alignment can be verified by removing the bar and viewing the clutch plate hub in relation to the hole in the center of the clutch cover plate diaphragm spring. When the hub appears exactly in the center of the hole, all is correct. On pressure plate covers which have cutaway edges, the clutch plate can be centered by using the fingers to line up its edges with the edge of the flywheel.

22   Tighten the clutch cover bolts in a diagonal sequence to ensure

3.19   Typical clutch plate alignment tool in use

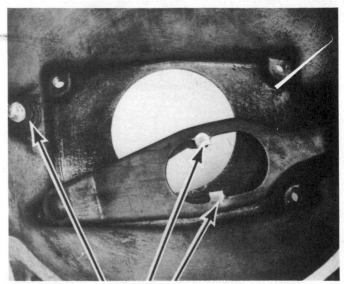

3.23   Clutch fork lubrication points

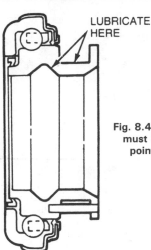

LUBRICATE HERE

Fig. 8.4 The throwout bearing must be lubricated at these points before installation (Sec 3)

that the cover plate is pulled down evenly and without distortion of the flange.

23 Lubricate the clutch fork fingers at the throwout bearing end, and the ball and socket, with a high melting point grease (photo). Also lubricate the throwout bearing collar and groove (see the accompanying illustration).

24 Install the clutch fork and dust boot in the clutch housing and attach the throwout bearing to the fork.
25 Install the clutch housing.
26 Install the transmission (refer to Chapter 7A).
27 Connect the fork pushrod and spring, lubricating the spring and pushrod ends. On models with hydraulic clutch assemblies, attach the slave cylinder and slave cylinder heat shield to the clutch housing.
28 Adjust the clutch linkage (refer to Chapter 1) on models not equipped with a hydraulic clutch assembly.

4 Clutch pilot bearing — removal and installation

Note: *If the engine has been removed from the vehicle, disregard the following steps that do not apply.*
1 Remove the transmission (refer to Chapter 7).
2 Remove the clutch (refer to Section 3).
3 The clutch pilot bearing (bushing), which is pressed into the end of the crankshaft, supports the forward end of the transmission input shaft. It requires attention whenever the clutch is removed from the vehicle.
4 Clean the bearing thoroughly and inspect it for excessive wear or damage. If wear is noted, the bearing must be replaced with a new one.
5 Removal can be accomplished with a special puller, but an alternative method, and one that works very well, is to remove the bearing hydraulically. First, locate a solid steel bar with a diameter that is slightly

4.5A A grease gun works very well for filling the area behind the pilot bearing with heavy grease

4.5B After packing the area behind and in the bearing with grease,...

4.5C ...insert a close fitting steel bar and strike it with a hammer

4.6 A socket or a steel bar can be used to install the new pilot bearing

8

less than the inside diameter of the bearing (19/32-inch should be very close). The bar should just slip into the bearing with very little clearance. Next, pack the bearing and the area behind it (in the crankshaft recess) with heavy grease (photos). Try to eliminate as much air as possible from the recess behind the bearing. Insert the bar into the bearing bore and rap the end of the bar with a hammer (photo). The pressure exerted on the grease will be transferred to the back side of the bearing, forcing it out of the recess. Be sure to clean the grease out of the crankshaft after the bearing has been removed.

6   To install the new bearing, lubricate its outside surface with oil, then drive it into the recess with a socket and a soft-faced hammer (photo). The radius in the bore of the bearing must face *out*. Select a socket that is slightly smaller than the outside diameter of the bearing.

7   Replace the clutch and transmission.

***

5   Clutch slave cylinder — removal, overhaul and installation

1   Raise the vehicle and support it securely on jackstands.
2   Disconnect the hydraulic line at the slave cylinder.
3   Remove the slave cylinder retaining nuts and detach the cylinder.
4   Remove the pushrod and dust cover from the slave cylinder.
5   Using snap-ring pliers, remove the snap-ring from the slave cylinder.
6   Shake out the plunger and spring assembly.
7   Carefully remove the seal from the plunger.
8   Replace the seal and clean all other parts in clean brake fluid. Do not use solvent!
9   Inspect the cylinder bore for scoring and scratches. The bore should be smooth to the touch. Replace the slave cylinder if the cylinder bore is not smooth.
10 Carefully install the seal in the groove on the plunger.
11 Install the spring on the plunger.
12 Lubricate the seal and cylinder bore with clean brake fluid.
13 Install the plunger and spring assembly in the slave cylinder bore.
14 Press in on the plunger and install the snap ring.
15 Apply some grease to the inside of the rubber dust cover (there should be some included with the slave cylinder rebuild kit). Install the dust cover on the slave cylinder.
16 Install the pushrod through the dust cover.
17 Attach the slave cylinder to the vehicle by first installing the hydraulic line.
18 Fill the clutch master cylinder reservoir with clean brake fluid of the specified type and bleed the clutch hydraulic system as described in Section 7.
19 Attach the slave cylinder to the bellhousing and install the retaining nuts. Tighten the nuts to the specified torque.

***

6   Clutch master cylinder — removal, overhaul and installation

1   Remove the insulation panel from behind the clutch pedal.
2   Disconnect the master cylinder pushrod from the clutch pedal.
3   Remove the master cylinder mounting bolts.
4   Disconnect and plug the reservoir hose at the master cylinder.
5   Disconnect and plug the hydraulic line for the slave cylinder at the master cylinder.
6   Remove the master cylinder.
7   Be sure to disassemble the master cylinder on a clean working surface.
8   Slide the dust cover back.
9   Use snap-ring pliers to remove the pushrod circlip and detach the pushrod.
10 Shake out the plunger and spring assembly.
11 Remove the reservoir adapter from the top of the master cylinder by twisting and pulling out.
12 Remove the spring, seal support, recuperation seal and shim from the front of the plunger. Be careful not to damage the plunger surface.
13 Remove the back seal from the rear of the plunger.
14 Replace all seals and clean the remaining parts with clean brake fluid. Inspect the cylinder bore for scoring and scratches. The bore should be smooth to the touch. Replace the master cylinder if any roughness is noted.
15 Reassemble the master cylinder using new seals.
16 Install the back seal in the groove in the plunger.

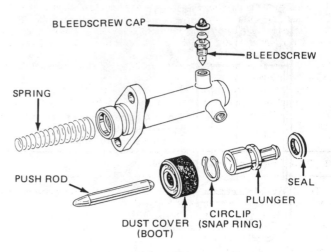

Fig. 8.5   Exploded view of the hydraulic clutch system slave cylinder (Sec 5)

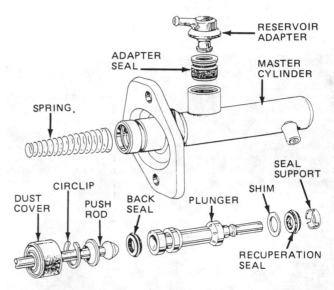

Fig. 8.6   Exploded view of the hydraulic clutch system master cylinder (Sec 6)

17 Install the shim and recuperation seal on the plunger, with the flat of the seal against the shim.
18 Install the seal support in the recuperation seal and snap the ring over the plunger nose.
19 Lubricate the seals and cylinder bore with clean brake fluid.
20 Carefully install the plunger assembly into the master cylinder bore.
21 Install the plunger and circlip in the master cylinder.
22 Install the new reservoir adapter seal and press in the adapter.
23 Attach the master cylinder to the vehicle and tighten the retaining bolts to the specified torque.
24 Connect the pushrod to the clutch pedal and install the retaining clip.
25 Install the hush panel.
26 Connect the reservoir hose and hydraulic line to the master cylinder.
27 Fill the reservoir with the recommended brake fluid and bleed the clutch system as described in Section 7.

***

7   Clutch hydraulic system — bleeding

1   The clutch hydraulic system should be bled whenever any part of the system is disconnected or when a low fluid level has allowed air to be drawn into the master cylinder.

2　Fill the master cylinder with the specified grade of clean brake fluid.
3　Raise the vehicle and support it securely on jackstands.
4　Remove the slave cylinder mounting bolts and hold the slave cylinder at approximately a 45° angle, with the slave cylinder bleed screw at the highest point.
5　Have an assistant depress the clutch pedal all the way while you loosen the bleed screw.
6　Tighten the bleed screw and release the clutch pedal.
7　Repeat Steps 5 and 6 until all air is evacuated from the system.
8　Check the fluid level in the master cylinder reservoir and refill if necessary.

8 Driveshaft — general information

The driveshaft is of tubular construction and may be a one or two-section type depending upon the wheelbase of the vehicle.

On four-wheel drive vehicles the rear wheel driveline is very similar to that described above, but in order to drive the front wheels a driveshaft is incorporated between the transfer case and the front axle. This shaft is basically similar to the shafts used to drive the rear axle.

All driveshafts used to drive the rear wheels have needle bearing type universal joints. Single-section shafts have a splined sliding sleeve at the front end connecting to the output shaft of the transmission, while the two-section shafts have a central slip joint. The purpose of these devices is to accommodate, by retraction or extension, the varying shaft length caused by the movement of the rear axle as the rear suspension deflects. On some four-wheel drive models, due to the extent of the front driveshaft angle, a constant velocity joint is used at the transfer case end of the driveshaft.

The universal joints are lubricated for life and are not serviceable on the vehicle. If a universal joint becomes worn or noisy, a service kit containing cross and bearing assemblies is available. The kit also contains snap-rings which must be installed to substitute for the nylon injection rings installed at the factory during shaft assembly. The entire driveshaft must be removed from the vehicle whenever servicing is necessary and care must be taken when handling it to preserve the balance produced at the factory. Care should also be taken if the vehicle is undercoated. Never allow undercoating or any other foreign material to adhere to the driveshaft as it will disturb the factory balance.

9 Universal joints — wear check

1　Universal joint problems are usually caused by worn or damaged needle bearings. These problems are revealed as vibration in the driveline or clunking noises when the transmission is put in Drive or the clutch is released. In extreme cases they are caused by lack of lubrication. If this happens, you will hear metallic squeaks and ultimately, grinding

and shrieking sounds as the bearings are destroyed.
2　It is easy to check the needle bearings for wear and damage with the driveshaft in place on the vehicle. To check the rear universal joint, turn the driveshaft with one hand and hold the differential yoke with the other. Any movement between the two is an indication of wear. The front universal joint can be checked by holding the driveshaft with one hand and the sleeve yoke in the transmission with the other. Any movement here indicates the need for universal joint repair.
3　If they are worn or damaged, the universal joints will have to be replaced with new ones. Read over the procedure carefully before beginning.

10 Driveshaft out-of-balance correction

1　Vibration of the driveshaft at certain speeds may be caused by any of the following:

Undercoating or mud on the shaft
Loose rear strap mounting bolts
Worn universal joints
Bent or dented driveshaft

2　Vibration which is thought to be coming from the driveshaft is sometimes caused by improper tire balance. This should be one of your first checks.
3　If the shaft is in a good, clean, undamaged condition, it is worth disconnecting the rear end mounting bolts and turning the shaft 180 degrees to see if an improvement is noticed. Be sure to mark the original position of each component before disassembly so the shaft can be returned to the same location.
4　If the vibration persists after checking for obvious causes and changing the position of the shaft, the entire assembly should be checked out by a repair shop or replaced.

11 Driveshaft — removal and installation

One-piece driveshaft
1　Raise the vehicle and place it securely on jackstands.
2　Refer to the accompanying photos for the driveshaft removal procedure.
3　Make sure that the driveshaft is handled carefully during the removal and installation procedures, as it must maintain the factory balance to operate smoothly and quietly.
4　Make sure that the outer diameter of the transmission sleeve yoke is not burred, as it could damage the transmission seal when the driveshaft is installed.
5　Lubricate the sleeve yoke splines with engine oil, then slide the yoke onto the transmission output shaft. Do not force it or use a ham-

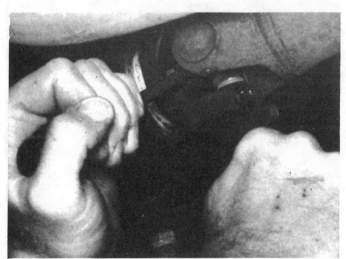

11.2A　Insert a screwdriver through the U-joint to keep the driveshaft from turning and remove the retaining bolts with a wrench

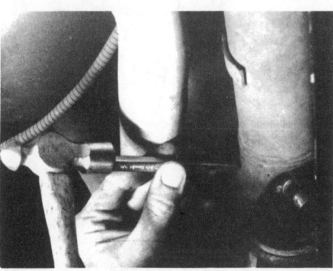

11.2B　Use a punch and hammer to mark the relationship of the driveshaft to the pinion flange

8

mer. If resistance is met, check the splines for burrs.

6　Attach the shaft to the pinion flange. Be sure to align the marks on the shaft and pinion flange that were made before removal.

7　Install the rear bolts and tighten them to the specified torque.

8　Remove the jackstands and lower the vehicle.

Two-piece rear driveshaft

9　The procedure is the same as the one described above with the exception of the need to remove the two bolts which support the center bearing assembly. Be sure to mark the relationship of the front half to rear half of the driveshaft at the center joint.

10　Install the front half first. Attach the center bearing support loosely to the crossmember.

11　Slide the front yoke into the transmission until it bottoms and tighten the center bearing support bolts to the specified torque.

12　Slide the rear half into position and tighten the U-joint retaining bolts to the specified torque.

Front driveshaft (four-wheel drive models only)

13　Raise the vehicle and support it securely on jackstands. Remove the two transmission mount-to-crossmember retaining nuts.

14　Using a hydraulic jack, raise the transfer case about 1/2-inch.

15　Remove the two bolts and nuts from each end of the crossmember (4 total), working through the frame access holes as necessary.

16　Centerpunch or mark the relationship of the driveshaft to the pinion flanges at the transfer case and front differential.

17　Remove the U-joint retaining bolts and detach the driveshaft.

18　Be sure to align the marks upon during installation.

19　Tighten the U-joint retaining bolts to the specified torque.

20　Install the crossmember and tighten the attaching bolts and nuts to the specified torque.

21　Lower the jack supporting the transfer case.

22　Install the transmission mount-to-crossmember retaining nuts and tighten them to the specified torque.

23　Remove the jackstands and lower the vehicle.

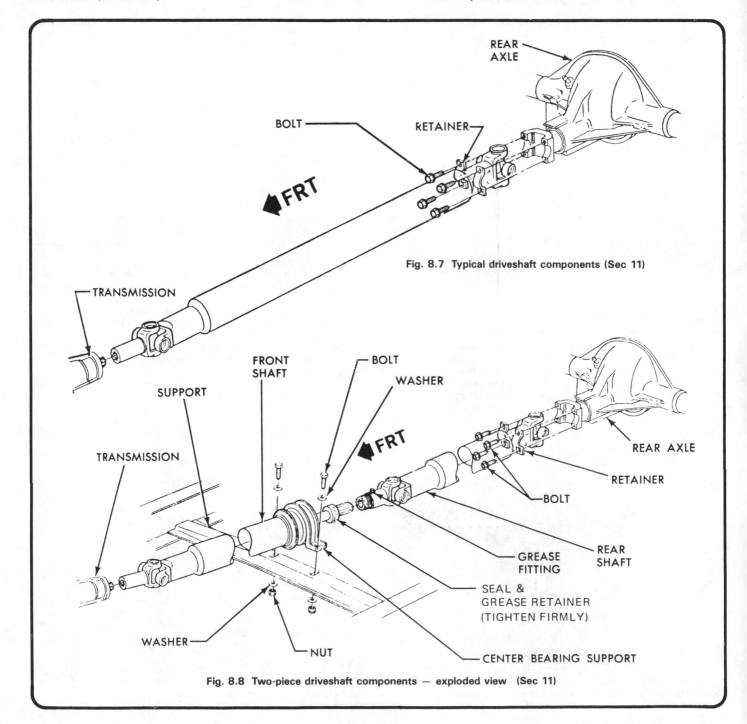

Fig. 8.7 Typical driveshaft components (Sec 11)

Fig. 8.8 Two-piece driveshaft components — exploded view (Sec 11)

12 Universal joints — disassembly, inspection and reassembly

Note: *Always purchase a universal joint service kit(s) for your model vehicle before starting the procedure which follows. Also, read through the entire procedure before beginning work.*

1   Remove the driveshaft (refer to Section 11).
2   Place the shaft on a workbench equipped with a vise.
3   Place the universal joint in the vise with a 1-1/8 inch socket against

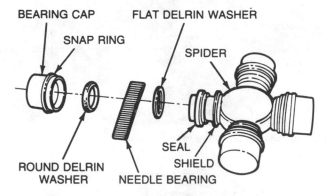

BEARING CAP   FLAT DELRIN WASHER
SNAP RING
SPIDER
ROUND DELRIN WASHER   NEEDLE BEARING   SEAL   SHIELD

Fig. 8.9 Exploded view of a typical universal joint (Sec 12)

one ear of the shaft yoke and a cross press tool placed on the open horizontal bearing cups (photo). A cross press tool, No. J-9522-3, is available from your dealer, or a substitute may be fashioned from 2-1/2 inch by 3/16-inch wall square tube or channel steel (photo). **Note:** *Never clamp the driveshaft tubing itself in a vise, as the tube may be bent.*
4   Press the bearing cup out of the yoke ear, shearing the plastic retaining ring on the bearing. **Note:** *If the cup does not come all the way out of the yoke, it may be pulled free with channel lock pliers, then removed (photo).*
5   Turn the driveshaft 180 degrees and press the opposing bearing cup out of the yoke, again shearing the plastic retainer.
6   Disengage the cross from the yoke and remove the cross. **Note:** *Production universal joints cannot be reassembled because there are no bearing retaining grooves in the production bearing cups. All U-joint service kits contain snap-rings, which will be used when the replacement U-joints are assembled. If your driveshaft has previously had the original U-joints replaced with snap-ring types, remove the snap-rings before pressing the bearing cups out.*
7   If the remaining universal joint is being replaced, press the bearing cups from the slip yoke as detailed above.
8   When reassembling the driveshaft, always install all parts included in the U-joint service kit.
9   Remove all remnants of the plastic bearing retainers from the grooves in the yokes. Failure to do so may keep the bearing cups from being pressed into place and prevent the bearing retainers from seating properly.

12.3A   Pressing a bearing cup out of the front universal joint yoke

12.3B This cross press tool was made from 2-1/2 x 3/16-inch wall thickness square tubing

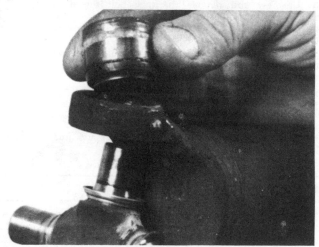

12.4   Removing a bearing cup from the yoke ear after it has been pressed out

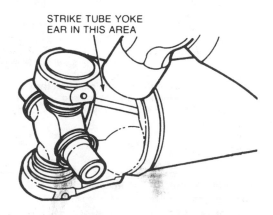

STRIKE TUBE YOKE EAR IN THIS AREA

Fig. 8.10 Seating a U-joint snap-ring (Sec 12)

8

12.11   Assembling a new cross and bearing cup in the driveshaft

12.13   Installing a snap-ring in the groove

12.15   Installing a grease fitting in the U-joint

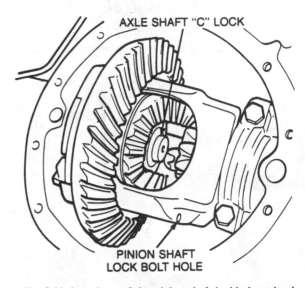

Fig. 8.11 Locations of the pinion shaft lockbolt and axle shaft C-ring lock (Sec 13)

10 Using multi-purpose grease to retain the needle bearings, assemble the bearings, cups and washers. Make sure the bearings do not become dislodged during the assembly and installation procedures.
11 In the vise, assemble the cross and cups in the yoke, installing the cups as far as possible by hand (photo).
12 Move the cross back and forth horizontally to assure alignment, then press the cups into place a little at a time, continuing to center the cross to keep the proper alignment.
13 As soon as one snap-ring groove clears the inside of the yoke, stop pressing and install the snap-ring (photo).
14 Continue to press on the bearing cup until the opposite snap-ring can be installed. If difficulty is encountered, strike the yoke sharply with a hammer. This will spring the yoke ears slightly and allow the snap-ring groove to move into position.
15 Install the grease fitting (photo).
16 Install the driveshaft (refer to Section 11).

13   Axleshaft — removal and installation

1   Raise the rear of the vehicle, support it securely and remove the wheel and brake drum (refer to Chapter 9).
2   Unscrew and remove the pressed steel cover from the differential carrier and allow the oil to drain into a container.
3   Unscrew and remove the lock bolt the differential pinion shaft. Remove the pinion shaft.
4   Push the outer (flanged) end of the axleshaft in and remove the C-ring from the inner end of the shaft.
5   Withdraw the axleshaft, taking care not to damage the oil seal in the end of the axle housing as the splined end of the axleshaft passes through it.
6   Installation is the reverse of removal. Tighten the lock bolt to the specified torque.
7   Always use a new cover gasket and tighten the cover bolts to the specified torque.
8   Refill the axle with the correct quantity and grade of lubricant (Chapter 1).

14   Axleshaft oil seal — replacement

1   Remove the axleshaft as described in the preceding Section.
2   Pry out the old oil seal from the end of the axle housing, using a large screwdriver or the inner end of the axleshaft itself as a lever.
3   Apply high melting point grease to the oil seal recess and tap the seal into position so that the lips are facing in and the metal face is

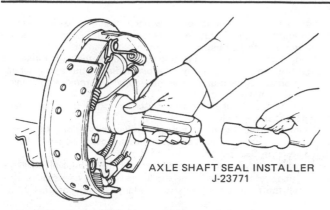

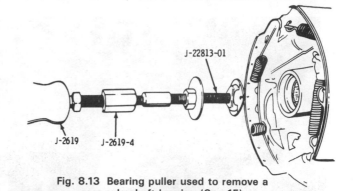

AXLE SHAFT SEAL INSTALLER
J-23771

Fig. 8.12 Installing a rear axle shaft oil seal with the special tool (Sec 14)

Fig. 8.13 Bearing puller used to remove a rear axle shaft bearing (Sec 15)

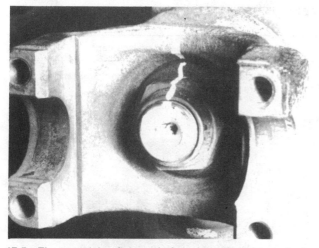

17.5 The rear pinion flange, shaft and nut must be marked before disassembly

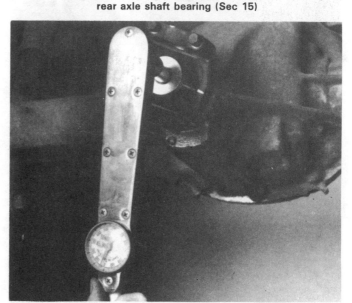

17.7 Checking the pinion bearing preload

visible from the end of the axle housing. When correctly installed, the face of the oil seal should be flush with the end of the axle housing.
4 Installation of the axleshaft is described in the preceding Section.

15 Axleshaft bearing — replacement

1 Remove the axleshaft (refer to Section 13) and the oil seal (refer to Section 14).
2 A bearing puller will be required or a tool which will engage behind the bearing will have to be fabricated.
3 Attach a slide hammer and pull the bearing from the axle housing.
4 Clean out the bearing recess and drive in the new bearing using a piece of pipe *applied against the outer bearing race*. Lubricate the new bearing with gear lubricant. Make sure that the bearing is tapped into the full depth of its recess and that the numbers on the bearing are visible from the outer end of the housing.
5 Discard the old oil seal and install a new one, then install the axleshaft.

16 Rear axle assembly — removal and installation

1 Raise the rear of the vehicle and support it securely on jackstands placed under the frame rails.
2 Position a floor jack under the differential housing. Raise the jack just enough to take up the weight of the rear axle assembly, but not far enough to take the weight of the vehicle off the jackstands.
3 Disconnect the shock absorbers.
4 Remove the brake line junction block bolt at the axle housing, then disconnect the brake lines at the junction block.

5 Lower the jack under the differential housing enough to remove the springs.
6 Remove the rear wheels and brake drums (refer to Chapter 9).
7 Remove the cover from the rear axle assembly and drain the lubricant into a container.
8 Remove the axleshafts (refer to Section 13).
9 Disconnect the brake lines from the axle housing clips.
10 Remove the backing plates.
11 Mark the driveshaft and companion flange, unbolt the driveshaft and support it out of the way on a wire hanger.
12 Remove the rear axle assembly from under the vehicle.
13 Installation is the reverse of the removal procedure. When installation is complete fill the differential with the recommended oil and bleed the brake system.

17 Rear differential pinion seal — replacement

1 Raise the vehicle and support it securely on jackstands.
2 Mark the rear of the driveshaft and the pinion flange so they can be reassembled in the same position.
3 Disconnect the driveshaft from the pinion flange and secure it out of the way by wiring it to the exhaust pipe.
4 If the U-joint bearings are not equipped with a retainer strap, tape the bearings to their journals.
5 Mark the position of the pinion flange, pinion shaft and nut so the proper bearing preload can be set during reassembly (photo).
6 It is a good idea to check the bearing preload before disassembly. This measurement will be needed if a replacement pinion flange has to be installed.
7 To check the pinion bearing preload, remove both rear wheels and

8

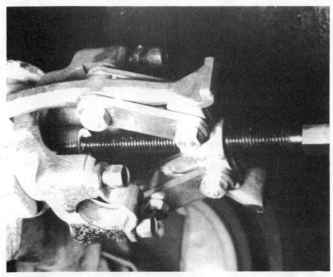

17.9   Using a puller to remove the pinion flange

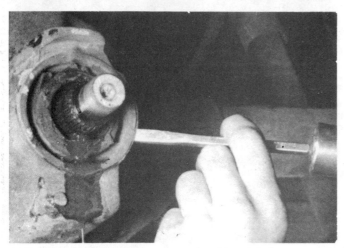

17.10   Use a blunt chisel to remove the old seal, being careful not to damage the differential carrier

17.12   Apply special lubricant to the lip of the new seal

drums. Using an inch-pound torque wrench, check the pinion bearing preload and record it for future reference (photo). The preload is the torque required to just begin turning the pinion shaft.

8   Using a socket and a flange holding tool or a breaker bar inserted through the flange yoke, remove the pinion flange nut and washer.

9   Position a drain pan under the differential and remove the pinion flange with a puller (photo).

10   Drive the oil seal out with a blunt chisel, being careful not to damage the differential carrier (photo).

11   Examine the seal surface of the pinion flange for tool marks, nicks or wear marks (photo). If any damage is found, replace the pinion flange as described in Section 18.

12   Apply special seal lubricant (GM No. 1050169 or equivalent) to the outer diameter of the pinion flange and to the lip of the new seal (photo).

13   Install the replacement seal with a large section of pipe and a hammer.

14   Install the pinion flange and tighten the nut to the position it was marked at before disassembly.

15   Install the flange holder or breaker bar and tighten the flange nut to 1/16-inch (1.59mm) beyond the alignment marks (photo).

18   Rear differential pinion flange — replacement

1   Raise the vehicle and support it securely on jackstands.
2   Remove both rear wheels and drums.

17.11   The sealing surface of the pinion flange should be free of nicks and gouges

17.15   On pinion seal replacement only, tighten the flange nut to 1/16-inch beyond the alignment marks

3 Mark the driveshaft and pinion flange and then disconnect the driveshaft at the rear U-joint. Secure the driveshaft out of the way by wiring it to the exhaust pipe. Tape the joint bearings in place if they are not held by a retainer strap.
4 Check the preload with an inch-pound torque wrench (a dial-type is best) and record it for future use.
5 Remove the pinion flange nut and washer, referring to Section 17 if necessary.
6 Apply special lubricant, GM No. 1050169 or equivalent, to the outside diameter of the replacement pinion flange.
7 Install the pinion flange, washer and pinion flange nut finger tight.
8 While holding the pinion flange as shown in the accompanying illustration, tighten the nut a little at a time, turning the drive pinion several revolutions each time to set the rollers. Check the preload of the bear-

ing each time. Continue until the preload is 3 to 5 inch-pounds more than the measurement obtained before disassembly.
9 Install the brake drums and wheels, then lower the vehicle.

19 Front drive axle — general information

The front drive axle utilizes a right side output shaft tube which can be removed independently to service the tube bearing, seal and output shaft pilot bearing. CV joints are used on the axle, with inner and outer sealing boots. These boots, when replaced by aftermarket 'snap together' boots, can be serviced without disassembling the hub or axle assembly.

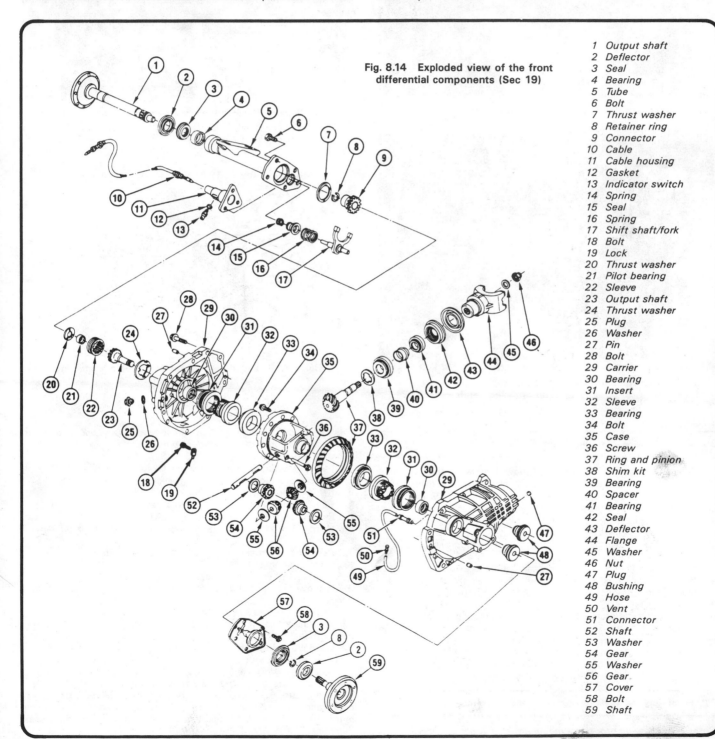

Fig. 8.14 Exploded view of the front differential components (Sec 19)

1	Output shaft
2	Deflector
3	Seal
4	Bearing
5	Tube
6	Bolt
7	Thrust washer
8	Retainer ring
9	Connector
10	Cable
11	Cable housing
12	Gasket
13	Indicator switch
14	Spring
15	Seal
16	Spring
17	Shift shaft/fork
18	Bolt
19	Lock
20	Thrust washer
21	Pilot bearing
22	Sleeve
23	Output shaft
24	Thrust washer
25	Plug
26	Washer
27	Pin
28	Bolt
29	Carrier
30	Bearing
31	Insert
32	Sleeve
33	Bearing
34	Bolt
35	Case
36	Screw
37	Ring and pinion
38	Shim kit
39	Bearing
40	Spacer
41	Bearing
42	Seal
43	Deflector
44	Flange
45	Washer
46	Nut
47	Plug
48	Bushing
49	Hose
50	Vent
51	Connector
52	Shaft
53	Washer
54	Gear
55	Washer
56	Gear
57	Cover
58	Bolt
59	Shaft

8

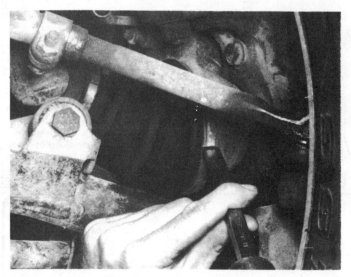

20.2   Removing the boot retaining bands

20.3   After removing the inner and outer retaining bands, the old boot can be cut off and removed

20.5   The replacement CV boot can be slipped into place and secured with the adhesive and retaining bands

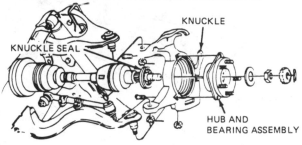

DO NOT BACK OFF NUT TO INSTALL NEW COTTER PIN.

KNUCKLE SEAL   KNUCKLE   HUB AND BEARING ASSEMBLY

Fig. 8.15 Exploded view of the front hub and steering knuckle components (Sec 21)

20 CV joint boot — replacement

1   The inner and outer CV joints (axleshaft U-joints) on the four wheel drive models must be kept dirt free. It is a very good idea to check the CV joint dust boots regularly for splits and tears. The CV joint boots can be replaced by the home mechanic without disassembling the front axle by using one of the 'wraparound' aftermarket boots available from your local auto parts retailer.

2   Using a chisel and hammer, remove the retaining bands from the affected boot (photo).

3   Cut the old boot off and remove it from the axle (photo).

4   If any sign of dirt is evident inside the boot, remove the grease and thoroughly clean the CV joint, then repack it with the grease supplied with the boot kit.

5   Install the replacement boot following the directions included with the kit (photo). Note: *Be sure not to get any grease on the adhesive area at the seams.*

6   Install the replacement retaining bands and let the adhesive set (according to manufacturer's instructions) before driving the vehicle.

21 Front hub and axle bearings — removal, servicing and installation

Note: *The following procedure requires special tools, such as an arbor press, and should be performed by someone with some prior experience. Read through the entire procedure before deciding to carry out the operations described.*

1   Loosen the lug nuts on the wheel(s) to be removed.

2   Raise the vehicle and support it securely on jackstands.

3   Remove the wheel(s).

4   Remove the front brake caliper as described in Chapter 9.

5   Pull the brake rotor off the hub assembly.

6   Using a 1-3/8 inch diameter deep socket and a breaker bar, remove the axle nut.

7   Remove the upper and lower hub retaining bolts from the rear of the steering knuckle.

8   Remove the steering knuckle as described in Chapter 11.

9   Remove the six bolts attaching the tri-pot housing to the drive flange.

10 Remove the axle assembly.

11 To disassemble the outer CV joint, first remove the inner clamp from the boot seal by cutting it off with sidecutters.

12 Tap lightly around the outside of the outer seal retainer until the seal and retainer can be slid back from the outer race (CV housing).

13 Using snap-ring pliers, spread the ears of the race retaining ring apart and separate the axleshaft from the outer race (CV housing).

14 The bearing balls can be removed with a brass drift. Gently tap on the edge of the bearing cage until the cage is tilted enough to allow removal of the first ball. The remaining balls can be removed in the same manner.

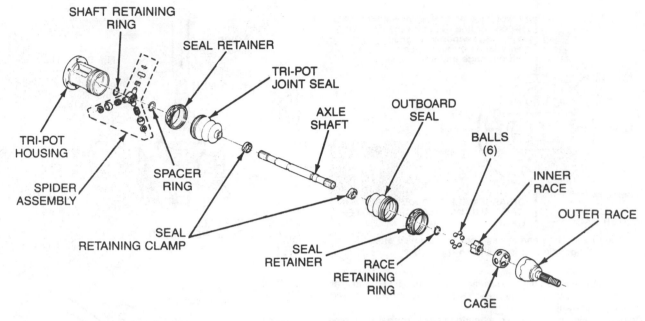

Fig. 8.17 Right side drive axle components — exploded view (Sec 21)

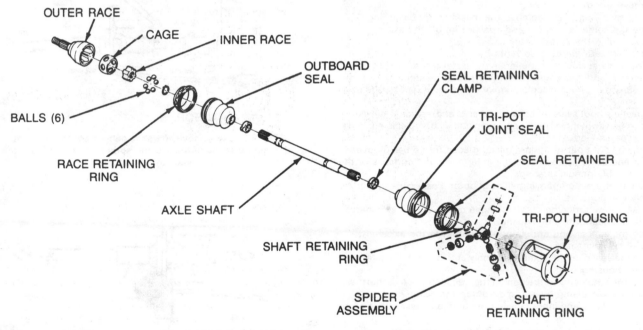

Fig. 8.16 Left side drive axle components — exploded view (Sec 21)

8

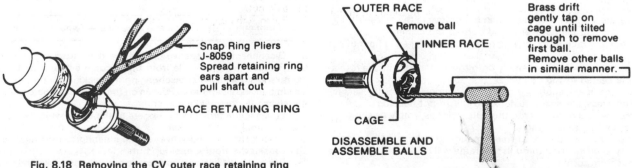

Fig. 8.18 Removing the CV outer race retaining ring
(Sec 21)

Fig. 8.19 Removing the bearing balls (Sec 21)

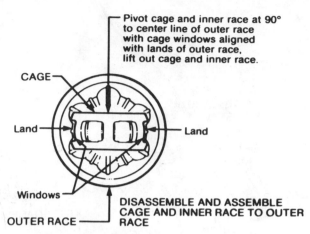

Pivot cage and inner race at 90°
to center line of outer race
with cage windows aligned
with lands of outer race,
lift out cage and inner race.

CAGE

Land   Land

Windows

OUTER RACE

DISASSEMBLE AND ASSEMBLE
CAGE AND INNER RACE TO OUTER
RACE

Fig. 8.20 The bearing cage can be removed after positioning it as shown (Sec 21)

15 The bearing cage can now be removed by pivoting it 90° and aligning the cage windows with the outer race land as shown in the accompanying illustration.
16 Remove the inner race from the bearing cage in the same fashion.
17 To service the spider assembly, first repeat Steps 11 and 12.
18 Remove the tri-pot housing.
19 Using snap-ring pliers, remove the axleshaft retaining ring.
20 Slide the spider assembly and spacer ring off the axle.
21 Disassemble the spider bearing.
22 Clean all metal parts in solvent.
23 Inspect the surfaces of the inner and outer races, the cages and ball bearings, and the spider assembly needle bearings. Check for roughness, scoring, heat discoloration or excessive wear. Replace parts as necessary.
24 Inspect the boot seals for holes and cracks and replace as necessary (it is good preventive maintenance to replace all boot seals while the axle is disassembled).
25 Apply a light coat of lithium-based grease to the ball grooves in the inner and outer races and to the inner and outer surfaces of the spider assembly needle bearings.
26 Refer to the accompanying illustration and assemble the spider assembly components.
27 Install a new retaining clamp or hose clamp on the axleshaft.
28 Slide the seal onto the axleshaft.
29 Slide the spacer ring and spider bearing onto the axleshaft.
30 Install the shaft retaining ring.
31 Slide the seal over the spider assembly and install the seal retainer and tri-pot housing.
32 Place the small end of the seal in its groove in the axleshaft, slip the seal retaining clamp over it and tighten the clamp.
33 Install the cage and inner race in the outer joint assembly's outer race.
34 Install the balls in the same manner as they were removed.
35 Pack the joint with grease.
36 Install a new seal retaining clamp or hose clamp on the axleshaft.
37 Slip the seal retainer over the outer joint seal and install them on the axleshaft.
38 Place the small end of the seal in the groove in the axleshaft, slip the seal retaining clamp over it and tighten the clamp.
39 Position the race retaining ring on the axleshaft just in front of the groove.
40 Press the outer joint assembly onto the axleshaft until the retaining ring is seated in the groove.
41 Support the axleshaft in a press with supports under the seal retainer and press the seal retainer onto the tri-pot housing.
42 Press the seal retainer onto the outer joint assembly as shown in the accompanying illustration.
8 Remove the two carrier-to-frame mounting bolts. An 18mm combination wrench inserted through the frame will be needed to hold the upper nut from turning.
9 Lift up and rotate the carrier until the necessary clearance is gained for removal.
10 Installation is the reverse of removal.

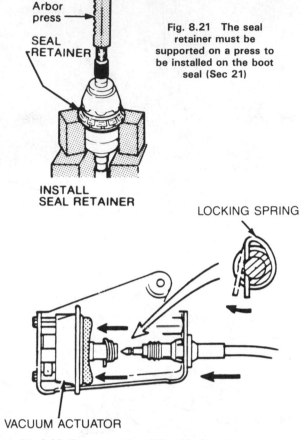

Arbor
press

SEAL
RETAINER

Fig. 8.21 The seal retainer must be supported on a press to be installed on the boot seal (Sec 21)

INSTALL
SEAL RETAINER

LOCKING SPRING

VACUUM ACTUATOR

Fig. 8.22 To remove the shift cable from the vacuum actuator, disengage the locking spring and press in on the vacuum actuator...

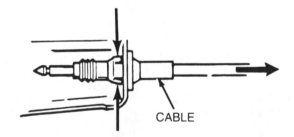

CABLE

Fig. 8.23 ...then squeeze the cable locking fingers and remove the cable from the bracket (Sec 22)

22 Front output shaft, tube and tube seal — removal and installation

1 Disconnect the negative cable from the battery.
2 Remove the shift cable from the vacuum actuator on top of the right fender well by first disengaging the locking spring (refer to the accompanying illustration). Push in on the vacuum actuator diaphragm to release the grooved cable end.
3 Squeeze the two locking fingers of the cable with pliers and pull the cable out of the bracket.
4 Unlock the steering wheel at the steering column.
5 Loosen the front wheel lug nuts.
6 Raise the vehicle and support it securely on jackstands.
7 Remove the front wheels.
8 Remove the engine drivebelt shield.
9 Remove the skid plate (if equipped).

22.13 The shift cable can be removed after pulling the cable housing away from the output shaft tube flange

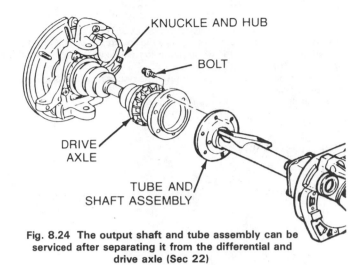

Fig. 8.24 The output shaft and tube assembly can be serviced after separating it from the differential and drive axle (Sec 22)

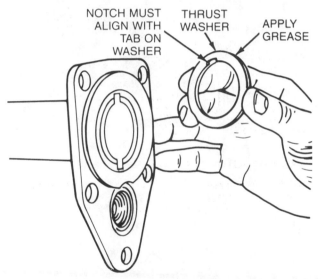

Fig. 8.25 The differential carrier thrust washer must be installed as shown (Sec 22)

10 Disconnect the right side upper balljoint (refer to Chapter 11).
11 Remove the drive axle-to-tube assembly attaching bolts. Insert a drift through the opening in the top of the brake caliper and into a brake rotor vane to keep the axle from turning.
12 Disconnect the four-wheel drive indicator light electrical connection from the switch.
13 Remove the switch/cable housing mounting bolts from the inner flange on the output shaft tube. Pull the housing away enough to gain access to the cable locking spring and disengage the spring (photo). Remove the cable assembly. Do not unscrew the cable coupling nut unless the cable is being replaced.
14 Remove the two tube assembly mounting bolts from the frame.
15 Remove the two remaining tube assembly bolts from the differential housing.
16 Carefully remove the tube assembly from the vehicle.
17 Remove the output shaft from the tube by striking the inside of the flange with a soft-faced hammer while holding the tube.
18 Using a large screwdriver, pry the output shaft tube seal from the tube.
19 Remove the tube bearing using a bearing removal tool such as GM No. J-33893.
20 Drive the shift cable housing seal out of the tube flange with a drift punch or socket.
21 Install the new shift cable housing seal using an appropriate size socket.

22 Install the tube bearing (GM special tool No. J-33844 is machined to provide the proper bearing recess).
23 Install the output shaft tube seal using a socket equivalent to the diameter of the seal outer flange. The flange of the seal must be flush with the tube outer surface when installed.
24 Before installing the tube assembly, make sure that the sleeve, thrust washers and connectors are in place in the differential.
25 Apply Loctite 514 or equivalent to the tube-to-differential carrier mating surface.
26 Apply some grease to the thrust washer and install the washer as shown in the accompanying illustration.
27 Carefully install the tube assembly and install the first mounting bolt at the one o'clock position (do not torque).
28 Pull the assembly down and install the cable and switch housing, and remaining four attaching bolts. Tighten the bolts to the specified torque.
29 Install the two tube assembly mounting bolts in the frame and tighten them to the specified torque.
30 Install the shift cable by pushing it into the shift fork hole (the cable will automatically snap into place).
31 Connect the wire lead for the four-wheel drive indicator light to the indicator switch.
32 Connect the upper balljoint (refer to Chapter 11).
33 Install the drive axle attaching bolts by installing one bolt, then rotating the axle to install the remaining five bolts. Insert a drift punch between the brake caliper and rotor vane and tighten the bolts to the specified torque.
34 Install the skid plate (if equipped) and drivebelt shield.
35 Install the wheel and lower the vehicle.
36 Push the shift cable into place in the vacuum actuator and attach the negative battery cable.

23 Front differential output shaft pilot bearing — replacement

1 Remove the tube and output shaft assembly as described in Section 22.
2 Remove the pilot bearing from the output shaft using GM tool No. J-34011.
3 Install the replacement bearing using GM tool No. J-33842.

24 Front differential carrier — removal and installation

1 Remove the output shaft as described in Section 22. Both sets of front wheel lug nuts should be loosened before raising the vehicle.
2 Remove the bolt securing the steering stabilizer to the frame.
3 Scribe the location of the steering idler arm and remove the idler arm mounting bolts from the frame member.
4 Move the steering linkage towards the front of the vehicle.
5 Remove the axle vent hose from the fitting on the carrier.
6 Remove the left drive axle from the carrier by removing the six bolts.

8

Insert a drift punch through the top of the caliper and into a brake rotor vane to keep the axle from turning.

7   Disconnect the front driveshaft (Section 11).

8   Remove the two carrier-to-frame mounting bolts. An 18mm combination wrench inserted through the frame will be needed to hold the upper nut from turning.

9   Lift up and rotate the carrier until the necessary clearance is gained for removal.

10 Installation is the reverse of removal.

25   Front differential carrier bushing — replacement

1   Remove the tube and shaft assembly as described in Section 22.

2   Remove the differential carrier as described in Section 24.

3   Press the bushing out of the carrier ear.

4   Press the replacement bushing into the carrier ear using a press tool. Use a spacer to prevent the bushing from being installed too deeply.

Chapter 9 Brakes

Contents

Specifications

Disc brakes

Rotor thickness after resurfacing (minimum)	0.980 in
Discard thickness	0.965 in
Disc runout (maximum)	0.005 in
Disc thickness variation (maximum)	0.0005 in

Rear drum brakes

Drum diameter	
Standard	9.50 in
Service limit	9.59 in
Drum taper (maximum)	0.003 in
Out-of-round (maximum)	0.002 in
Wheel cylinder bore diameter	0.748 in

Master cylinder

Piston diameter	0.945 in

Torque specifications	**Ft-lbs**
Brake pedal-to-bracket nut	22
Brake pedal bracket-to-dash screw	18
Parking brake control assembly-to-console screw	9
Combination valve-to-master cylinder screw	15
Brake line-to-master cylinder nut	18
Brake line-to-combination valve nut	17
Brake line-to-brake hose nut	18
Front flexible hose bracket-to-frame	8
Rear flexible hose bracket-to-frame	8
Junction block-to-axle housing screw	20
Lug nuts	
Standard wheel	80
Aluminum wheel	105
Power cylinder housing-to-master cylinder nut	20
Power cylinder studs-to-dash attaching nuts	15
Caliper mount-to-steering knuckle bolt	35
Splash shield-to-steering knuckle bolt	10
Caliper bleeder valve	11
Front brake hose-to-caliper bolt	32
Parking brake lever retaining nut	30 to 40
Parking brake lever mounting bracket bolt	24 to 38
Banjo housing retaining bolt	18 to 30

9

---

1 General information

All vehicles covered by this manual are equipped with hydraulically operated front and rear brake systems. All front brake systems are disc type, while the rear brake systems are drum brakes.

The hydraulic system consists of separate front and rear circuits. The master cylinder has separate reservoirs for the two circuits, and in the event of a leak or failure in one hydraulic circuit, the other circuit will remain operative. A visual warning of circuit failure or air in the system is given by a warning light activated by displacement of the piston in the brake distribution (pressure differential warning) switch from its normal 'in balance' position.

The parking brake mechanically operates the rear brakes only, and is activated by a pull-handle.

A combination valve, located in the engine compartment, consists of three sections providing the following functions:

The metering section limits pressure to the front brakes until a predetermined front imput pressure is reached and until the rear brakes are activated. There is no restriction at inlet pressures below 3 psi, allowing pressure equalization during non-braking periods.

The proportioning section proportions outlet pressure to the rear brakes after a predetermined rear imput pressure has been reached, preventing early rear wheel lock-up under heavy brake loads. The valve is also designed to assure full pressure to the rear brakes should the front brakes fail, and vice versa.

The pressure differential warning switch is designed to continuously compare the front and rear brake pressure from the master cylinder and energize the dash warning light in the event of either front or rear brake system failure. The design of the switch and valve are such that the switch will stay in the warning position once a failure has occured. The only way to turn the light off is to repair the cause of the failure and apply a brake pedal force of 450 psi.

The power brake booster, utilizing engine manifold vacuum and atmospheric pressure to provide assistance to the hydraulically operated brakes, is located in the engine compartment, adjacent to the cowl. All brakes are self-adjusting.

After completing any operation involving the disassembly of any part of the brake system, always test drive the vehicle to check for proper braking performance before resuming normal driving. When testing the brakes, perform the tests on a clean, dry, flat surface. Conditions other than these can lead to inaccurate test results. Test the brakes at various speeds with both light and heavy pedal pressure. The vehicle should stop evenly without pulling to one side or the other. Avoid locking the brakes because this slides the tires and diminishes braking efficiency and control.

Tires, vehicle load and front end alignment are factors which also affect braking performance.

Torque values given in the Specifications are for dry, unlubricated fasteners.

2 Front disc brake pads — replacement

Note: *Disc brake pads should be replaced on both wheels at the same time.*

1   Whenever you are working on the brake system be aware that asbestos dust is present and be careful not to inhale any of it, because it has been proven to be harmful to your health.
2   Remove the cover from the brake fluid reservoir and siphon off about two ounces of the fluid into a container and discard it.
3   Raise the front of the vehicle and place it securely on jackstands.
4   Remove the front wheel, then reinstall two wheel lugs (flat side toward the rotor) to hold the rotor in place. Work on one brake assembly at a time, using the assembled brake for reference if necessary.
5   Push the piston back into its bore. If necessary, a C-clamp can be used, but a flat bar will usually do the job. As the piston is depressed to the bottom of the caliper bore, the fluid in the master cylinder will rise. Make sure that it does not overflow. If necessary, siphon off more of the fluid as directed in Step 2.
6   Now refer to the accompanying photographs and perform the procedure illustrated. Start with photograph 2.6/1.

2.6/1   Use an Allen wrench to remove the two caliper mounting bolts. Check the bolt threads for damage

2.6/2   Remove the brake line retaining clip (mounted to frame rail in upper left of photo) and separate the brake line from the retainer. Remove the inside pad from the caliper

2.6/3   Remove the anti-rattle clip with pliers

2.6/4   Break the outer pad loose with a screwdriver

2.6/5   Separate the outer pad from the caliper

2.6/6   After cleaning the caliper, install the anti-rattle clip to the new pad and install the inner pad

2.6/7   Attach the outer pad to the caliper

2.6/8   Apply multi-purpose grease to the ends of the caliper mounting bracket surfaces

9

2.6/9   Install the caliper over the disc onto the mounting bracket. Do not get any grease on the pad linings

2.6/10   Install the mounting bolts and tighten them securely. Reattach the brake hose to the retaining clip on the frame

2.6/11 After refilling the master cylinder and pumping the brake pedal to seat the pad, use channel-lock pliers to bend the upper ears of the outboard pad until the ears are flush with the caliper housing, with no radial clearance

3 Front disc brake caliper — removal and installation

1   Whenever you are working on the brake system be aware that asbestos dust is present and be careful not to inhale any of it, because it has been proven to be harmful to your health.
2   Remove the cover from the brake fluid reservoir and siphon off about two ounces of the fluid into a container and discard it.
3   Raise the front of the vehicle and place it securely on jackstands.
4   Remove the front wheel. Remove the caliper from one brake assembly at a time, using the assembled brake for reference if necessary.
5   Push the piston back into its bore. If necessary, a C-clamp can be used, but a flat bar will usually do the job. As the piston is depressed to the bottom of the caliper bore, the fluid in the master cylinder will rise. Make sure that it does not overflow. If necessary, siphon off more of the fluid as directed in Step 2.
6   Remove the banjo fitting bolt holding the brake hose (photo), then remove and discard the copper seal rings found on either side of the banjo fitting. **Note:** *Always use new copper seals when reinstalling the brake hose (photo).*
7   Remove the Allen head bolts holding the caliper to the mounting bracket and separate the caliper from the rotor.
8   Installation is the reverse of removal. Lubricate the ends of the caliper mounting bracket surfaces before attaching the caliper to the bracket. Tighten all bolts to the specified torque.

3.6A Remove the banjo fitting nut

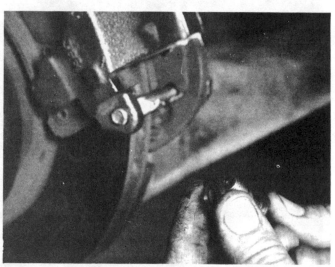

3.6B Be sure to use new copper seal rings when installing the brake hose

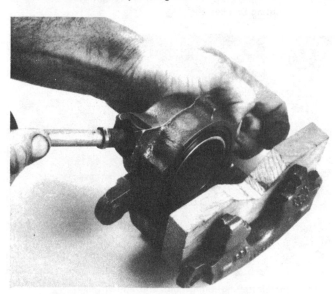

4.4 Compressed air is used to move the piston out of the caliper bore (use a wooden block as a cushion)

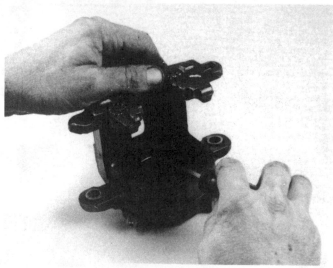

4.5 Pry the dust boot out of the caliper bore

4 Front disc brake caliper — overhaul

Note: *Purchase a brake caliper overhaul kit for your particular vehicle before beginning this procedure.*

1   Refer to Section 3 and remove the caliper.

2   Refer to Section 2 and remove the brake pad assemblies.

3   Clean the exterior of the brake caliper with brake fluid (never use gasoline, kerosene or cleaning solvents), then place the caliper on a clean workbench.

4   Place a wooden block or shop rag in the caliper as a cushion, then use compressed air to remove the piston from the caliper (photo). Use only enough air pressure to ease the piston out of the bore. If the piston is blown out, even with the cushion in place, it may be damaged. **Caution:** *Never place your fingers in front of the piston in an attempt to catch or protect it when applying compressed air — serious injury could occur.*

5   Carefully pry the dust boot out of the caliper bore (photo).

6   Using a wood or plastic tool, remove the piston seal from the groove in the caliper bore. Metal tools may cause bore damage.

7   Remove the caliper bleeder valve, then remove and discard the sleeves and bushings from the caliper ears. Also discard all rubber parts.

8   Clean the remaining parts with brake fluid. Allow them to drain and then shake them vigorously to remove as much fluid as possible.

9   Carefully examine the piston for nicks and burrs and loss of plating. If surface defects are present parts must be replaced. Check the caliper bore in a similar way, but polishing with crocus cloth is permissible to remove light corrosion and stains. Discard the mounting bolts if they are corroded or damaged.

10   When assembling, lubricate the piston bores and seal with clean brake fluid. Position the seal in the caliper bore groove (photo).

11   Lubricate the piston with clean brake fluid, then install a new boot in the piston groove with the fold toward the open end of the piston (photo).

12   Insert the piston squarely into the caliper bore, then apply force to bottom the piston in the bore (photo).

13   Position the dust boot in the caliper counterbore, then use a drift to drive it into position (photo). Make sure that the boot is evenly installed below the caliper face.

14   Install the bleeder valve.

15   The remainder of the installation procedure is the reverse of the removal procedure. Always use new copper gaskets when connecting the brake hose and bleed the system as described in Section 13.

4.6   Remove the piston seal from the caliper groove

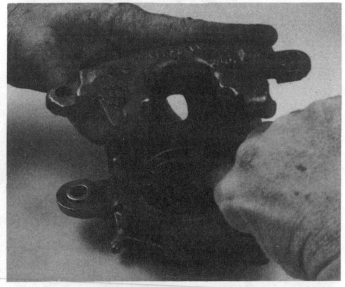

4.10   Position the seal in the caliper bore groove

4.11   Install a new dust boot in the piston groove with the folds toward the open end of the piston

4.12   Square the piston in the bore

9

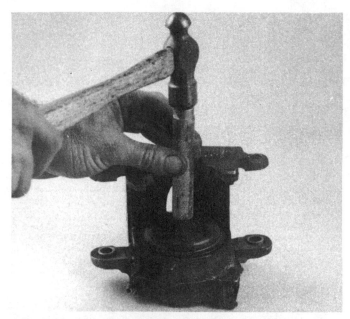

4.13 Use a hammer and driver to seat the boot in the caliper housing counterbore

5.5 Check the brake rotor runout with a dial indicator

5.6 Use a micrometer to check rotor thickness

6.5/1 Remove the wheel mounting stud lockwashers

6.5/2 Mark the relationship of the axle and brake drum

6.5/3 Remove the brake drum (if it cannot be pulled off refer to the text)

5 Disc brake rotor — inspection, removal and installation

1 Raise the vehicle and place it securely on jackstands.
2 Remove the appropriate wheel.
3 Remove the brake caliper assembly (refer to Section 3 or 5).
Note: *It is not necessary to disconnect the brake hose. After removing the caliper mounting bolts, hang the caliper out of the way on a piece of wire. Never hang the caliper by the brake hose because damage to the hose will occur.*
4 Inspect the rotor surfaces. Light scoring or grooving is normal, but deep grooves or severe erosion is not. If pulsating has been noticed during application of the brakes, suspect disc runout.
5 Attach a dial indicator to the caliper mounting bracket, turn the rotor and note the amount of runout. Check both inboard and outboard surfaces (photo). If the runout is more than the maximum allowable, the rotor must be removed from the vehicle and taken to an automotive machine shop for resurfacing.
6 Using a micrometer, measure the thickness of the rotor (photo). If it is less than the minimum specified, replace the rotor with a new one. Also measure the disc thickness at several points to determine variations in the surface. Any variation over 0.0005 inch may cause pedal pulsations during brake application. If this condition exists and

the disc thickness is not below the minimum, the rotor can be removed and taken to an automotive machine shop for resurfacing.
7 To remove and install the rotor refer to Chapter 1, Wheel bearing check and repack.

6 Rear drum brake shoes — replacement

1 Whenever you are working on the brake system, be aware that asbestos dust is present. It has been proven to be harmful to your health, so be careful not to inhale any of it.
2 Raise the vehicle and place it securely on jackstands.
3 Release the parking brake handle.
4 Remove the wheel and tire assembly. **Note:** *All four rear shoes should be replaced at the same time, but to avoid mixing up parts, work on only one brake assembly at a time.*
5 Now refer to the accompanying photographs and perform the brake shoe replacement procedure. Start with Photo 6.5/1. **Note:** *If the brake drum cannot be easily pulled off the axle and shoe assembly, make sure that the parking brake is completely released, then squirt some penetrating oil around the center hub area. Allow the oil to soak in and try to pull the drum off again. If the drum still cannot be pulled off,*

6.5/4 Use a brake spring tool to remove the primary shoe return spring from the anchor pin pivot

6.5/5 Remove the spring after unhooking it from the primary brake shoe

6.5/6 Push on the bottom of the automatic adjuster actuator lever and remove the actuator link from the top of the lever

6.5/7 Remove the actuator link and secondary shoe return spring from the anchor pin pivot with a brake spring tool

9

6.5/8   The actuator link and secondary shoe return spring after removal

6.5/9   Remove the shoe guide from the anchor pin

6.5/10   Remove the primary shoe holddown spring and pin

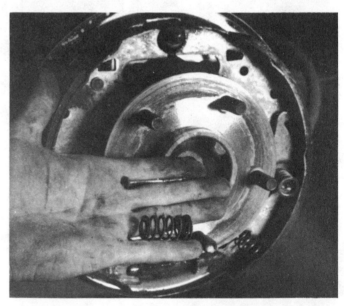

6.5/11   The primary shoe holddown spring and pin after removal

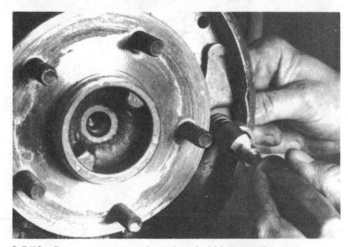

6.5/12   Remove the secondary shoe holddown spring and pin. This pin and spring are shorter than the primary shoe units

6.5/13   Remove the actuator lever, pawl and lever return spring. The L mark on the lever denotes the left side brake assembly

6.5/14 Turn the adjuster wheel all the way in

6.5/15 Pivot the secondary shoe to the rear and down

6.5/16 Remove the secondary shoe from the adjusting screw spring

6.5/17 Remove the adjusting screw and spring

6.5/18 The longer hook on the spring goes toward the rear

6.5/19 Pull the parking brake strut and spring assembly from behind the axle flange

9

6.5/20 Pull out on the primary shoe and pivot it down until it is free of the backing plate

6.5/21 Remove the spring from the parking brake lever

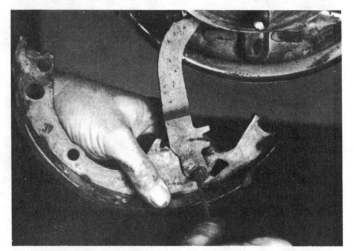

6.5/22 Remove the E-clip retaining the parking brake lever to the primary shoe

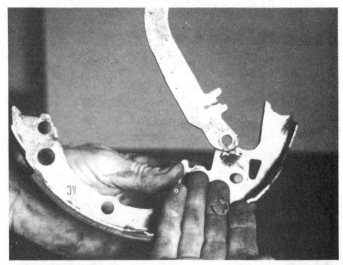

6.5/23 With the E-clip removed the shoe may be separated from the parking brake lever

6.5/24 Check the shoe guide pads for wear, making sure a ridge has not formed which could hang-up the shoe. If a ridge is present it can be removed with 150-grit emery paper. This step completes the removal procedure. Check all springs for tension and replace as necessary, then check the wheel cylinder for leakage. Refer to Section 10 for wheel cylinder rebuilding procedures

6.5/25 Lubricate the shoe guide pads and wheel cylinder ends with multi-purpose grease

6.5/26 Lightly lubricate the pivot pin with multi-purpose grease.

6.5/27 Attach the parking brake lever to the primary shoe and the spring to the lever. The primary shoe has the shorter lining

6.5/28 Install the primary shoe in position on the backing plate and install the holddown spring

6.5/29 Place the parking brake strut into position in the primary shoe slot

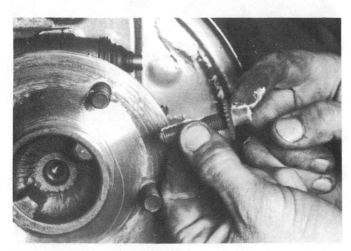

6.5/30 Lubricate both ends of the adjuster

6.5/31 Engage the short hook end of the adjusting spring in the hole in the primary shoe, with the hook inserted from the front

9

6.5/32 Engage the long hook end of the spring in the hole in the secondary shoe, with the hook inserted from the rear

6.5/33 With the adjuster positioned between the shoes, pivot the secondary shoe into place on the backing plate

6.5/34 Attach the pawl to the actuator lever and install the actuator assembly in place inside the secondary shoe

6.5/35 Attach the bushing to the actuator and shoe

6.5/36 Install the shoe holddown spring

6.5/37 Install the shoe guide, with the rounded side in

6.5/38 Install the rear hook of the secondary shoe return spring in the shoe

6.5/39 Assemble the actuating link to the spring

6.5/40 Attach the spring and actuating link to the anchor pin

6.5/41 Attach the actuating link to the parking brake actuating lever

6.5/42 Attach the primary shoe return spring to the shoe...

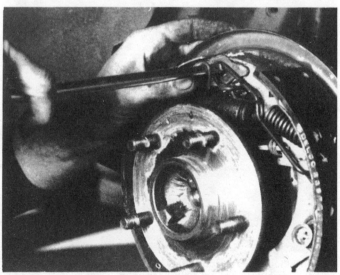

6.5/43 ...and to the anchor pin

9

6.5/44   With all parts installed, rock the assembly back and forth with your hands to insure that all parts are seated

6.6   Location of the maximum diameter mark inside the brake drum

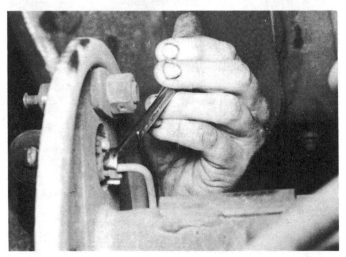

7.2   Remove the brake line fitting from the rear of the wheel cylinder

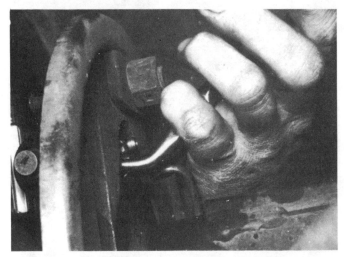

7.3A   Remove the wheel cylinder retaining clip with needle-nose pliers

7.3B   Method of removing the retaining clip using two awls (cylinder has been removed from backing plate for illustration purposes)

7.12   Place a screwdriver handle between the wheel cylinder and axle flange while the retaining clip is installed from the rear

the brake shoes will have to be retracted. This is accomplished by first removing the lanced cutout in the backing plate with a hammer and chisel. With this lanced area punched in, pull the lever off the adjusting screw wheel with one small screwdriver while turning the adjusting wheel with another small screwdriver, moving the shoes away from the drum. The drum may now be pulled off.

6   Before reinstalling the drum, it should be checked for cracks, score marks, deep scratches and 'hard spots,' which will appear as small discolored areas. If the hard spots cannot be removed with fine emery cloth and/or if any of the other conditions listed above exist, the drum must be taken to an automotive machine shop to have it turned. If the drum will not 'clean up' before the maximum drum diameter is reached in the machining operation, the drum will have to be replaced with a new one. **Note:** *The maximum diameter is cast into each brake drum (photo).*

7   Install the brake drum, lining up the marks made before removal if the old brake drum is used, and install the wheel stud lock washers.

8   Mount the wheel and tire, install the wheel lugs and tighten to specification, then lower the vehicle.

9   Make a number of forward and reverse stops to adjust the brakes until a satisfactory pedal action is obtained.

7   Wheel cylinder (drum brakes) — removal, overhaul and installation

Note: *Obtain the wheel cylinder rebuild kits before beginning this procedure.*

1   Remove the brake shoes (refer to Section 6).

2   Remove the brake line fitting from the rear of the wheel cylinder (photo). Cap the brake line to prevent contamination.

3   Using curved needle-nose pliers, remove the wheel cylinder retaining clip (photo), from the rear of the wheel cylinder. Alternatively, insert two awls into the access slots between the cylinder pilot and the retainer locking tabs and bend both tabs away at the same time (photo).

4   Remove the cylinder and place it on a clean workbench.

5   Remove the bleeder valve, seals, pistons, boots and spring assembly from the cylinder body.

6   Clean the wheel cylinder with brake fluid, denatured alcohol or brake system cleaner. *Do not, under any circumstances, use petroleum-based solvents to clean brake parts.*

7   Use compressed air to remove excess fluid from the wheel cylinder and to blow out the passages.

8   Check the cylinder bore for corrosion and scoring. Crocus cloth may be used to remove light corrosion and stains, but the cylinder must be replaced with a new one if the defects cannot be removed easily, or if the bore is scored.

9   Lubricate the new seals with clean brake fluid.

10   Assemble the brake cylinder, making sure the boots are properly seated.

11   Place the wheel cylinder in position in the backing plate.

12   Secure the cylinder in place with a new retaining clip by first starting the brake line fitting into the threads of the wheel cylinder, then placing a screwdriver handle between the wheel cylinder and the axle flange to hold the cylinder in place while the retaining clip is pushed into place with curved needle-nose pliers (photo). Make sure the clip and cylinder are securely in place, then remove the screwdriver and tighten the brake line fitting.

13   Bleed the brake system (refer to Section 13).

8   Master cylinder — removal, overhaul and installation

1   A master cylinder overhaul kit should be purchased before beginning this procedure. The kit will include all the replacement parts necessary for the overhaul procedure. The rubber replacement parts, particularly the seals, are the key to fluid control within the master cylinder. As such, it's very important that they be installed securely and facing in the proper direction. Be careful during the rebuild procedure that no grease or mineral-based solvents come in contact with the rubber parts.

2   Completely cover the front fender and cowling area of the vehicle, as brake fluid can ruin painted surfaces if it is spilled.

3   Disconnect the brake line connections. Rags or newspapers should be placed under the master cylinder to soak up the spilled fluid.

4   Remove the two master cylinder mounting nuts, move the bracket retaining the combination valve forward slightly, taking care not to bend the hydraulic lines running to the combination valve, and remove the master cylinder from the vehicle.

5   Remove the reservoir cover and reservoir diaphragm, then discard any remaining fluid in the reservoir.

6   Remove the primary piston lock ring by depressing the piston and prying the ring out with a screwdriver.

7   Remove the primary piston assembly with a wire hook, being careful not to scratch the bore surface.

8   Remove the secondary piston assembly in the same manner.

9   Place the master cylinder in a vise and pry the reservoir from the cylinder body with a pry bar (photo).

10   Do not attempt to remove the quick take-up valve from the cylinder body, as this valve is not serviceable.

11   Remove the reservoir grommets.

12   Inspect the cylinder bore for corrosion and damage. If any corrosion or damage is found, replace the master cylinder body with a new one, as abrasives cannot be used on the bore.

13   Lubricate the new reservoir grommets with silicone brake lube and press the grommets into the master cylinder body, making sure they are properly **seated**.

14   Lay the reservoir on a hard surface and press the master cylinder body onto the reservoir, using a rocking motion (photo).

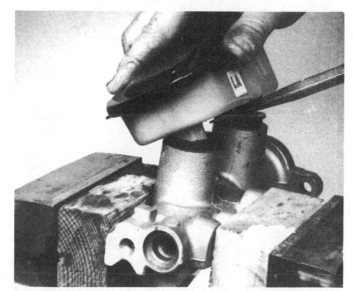

8.9   Pry the plastic reservoir from the master cylinder body

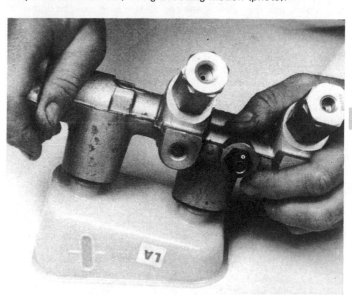

8.14   Press the master cylinder body onto the reservoir

9

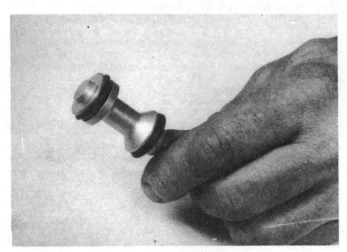

8.15   The secondary seals must be installed with the lips facing out

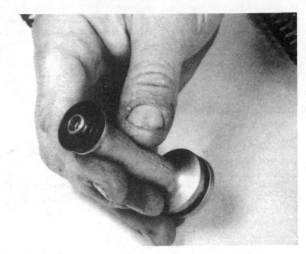

8.18   The primary seal must be installed with the lip facing away from the piston

15   Remove the old seals from the secondary piston assembly and install the new seals so that the cups face *out* (photo).
16   Attach the spring retainer to the secondary piston assembly.
17   Lubricate the cylinder bore with clean brake fluid and install the spring and secondary piston assembly in the cylinder.
18   Disassemble the primary piston assembly, noting the position of the parts, then lubricate the new seals with clean brake fluid and install them on the piston (photo).
19   Install the primary piston assembly in the cylinder bore, depress it and install the lock ring.
20   Inspect the reservoir cover and diaphragm for cracks and deformation. Replace any damaged parts with new ones and attach the diaphragm to the cover.
21   **Note:** *Whenever the master cylinder is removed, the complete hydraulic system must be bled. The time required to bleed the system can be reduced if the master cylinder is filled with fluid and 'bench bled' (refer to Steps 22 through 25) before the master cylinder is installed on the vehicle.*
22   Insert threaded plugs of the correct size into the cylinder outlet holes and fill the reservoirs with brake fluid (the master cylinder should be supported in such a manner that brake fluid will not spill out of it during the bench bleeding procedure).
23   Loosen one plug at a time and push the piston assembly into the bore to force air from the master cylinder. To prevent air from being drawn back into the cylinder, the appropriate plug must be tightened before allowing the piston to return to its original position.
24   Stroke the piston three or four times for each outlet to assure that all air has been expelled.
25   Refill the master cylinder reservoirs and install the diaphragm and cover assembly. **Note:** *The reservoirs should only be filled to the top of the reservoir divider to prevent overflowing when the cover is installed.*
26   Carefully install the master cylinder by reversing the removal steps, then bleed the brakes at the wheel bleed valves (refer to Section 13).

---

9   Hydraulic brake hoses and lines — inspection and replacement

---

1   About every six months, with the vehicle raised and placed securely on jackstands, the flexible hoses which connect the steel brake lines with the front and rear brake assemblies should be inspected for cracks, chafing of the outer cover, leaks, blisters and other damage. These are important and vulnerable parts of the brake system and inspection should be complete. A light and mirror will prove helpful for a thorough check. If a hose exhibits any of the above conditions, replace it with a new one as follows:

Front brake hose
2   Using a back-up wrench, disconnect the brake line from the hose

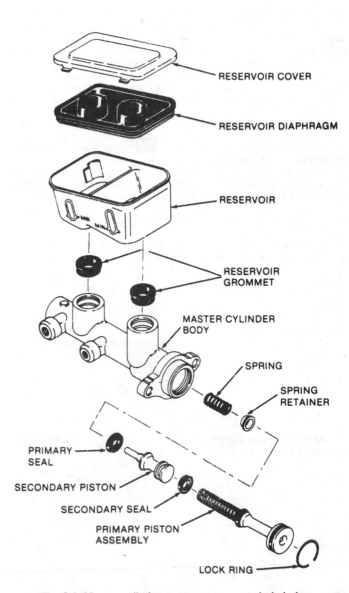

RESERVOIR COVER

RESERVOIR DIAPHRAGM

RESERVOIR

RESERVOIR GROMMET

MASTER CYLINDER BODY

SPRING

SPRING RETAINER

PRIMARY SEAL

SECONDARY PISTON

SECONDARY SEAL

PRIMARY PISTON ASSEMBLY

LOCK RING

Fig. 9.1 Master cylinder components — exploded view (Sec 8)

FRAME
BRACKET   REAR   BRAKE
AXLE   HOSE
FRAME
BRACKET

A

B

REAR
AXLE

HOSE

BRACKET

VIEW A   **VIEW B**

Fig. 9.2 Rear brake hose routing and mounting (Sec 9)

fitting, being careful not to bend the frame bracket or brake line.

3   Use pliers to remove the U-clip from the female fitting at the bracket, then remove the hose from the bracket.

4   At the caliper end of the hose, remove the bolt from the banjo fitting then remove the hose and the copper gaskets on either side of the banjo fitting.

5   When installing the hose, always use new copper gaskets on either side of the banjo fitting and lubricate all bolt threads with clean brake fluid before installing them.

6   With the fitting flange engaged with the caliper locating ledge, attach the hose to the caliper and tighten it to the specified torque.

7   Without twisting the hose, install the female fitting in the hose bracket (it will fit the bracket in only one position).

8   Install the U-clip retaining the female fitting to the frame bracket.

9   Using a back-up wrench, attach the brake line to the hose fitting and tighten it to the specified torque.

10   When the brake hose installation is complete there should be no kinks in the hose. Also, make sure the hose does not contact any part of the suspension. Check this by turning the wheels to the extreme left and right positions. If the hose makes contact, remove the hose and correct the installation as necessary.

Rear brake hose

11   Locate the junction block at the rear axle and disconnect the two steel brake lines from the block.

12   Using a back-up wrench, remove the hose at the female fitting, being careful not to bend the bracket or steel lines.

13   Remove the U-clip with pliers and separate the female fitting from the bracket.

14   Note the position of the junction block carefully so that it may be reinstalled in precisely the same position.

15   Remove the bolt attaching the junction block to the axle and remove the hose from the block.

16   When installing, thread both steel line fittings into the junction block at the rear axle.

17   Bolt the junction block to the axle, then tighten the block bolt and steel lines to the specified torque.

18   Without twisting the hose, install the female end of the hose in the frame bracket (it will fit the bracket in only one position).

19   Install the U-clip retaining the female end to the bracket.

20   Using a back-up wrench, attach the steel line fitting to the female fitting, tightening it to the specified torque. Again, be careful not to bend the bracket or steel line.

21   Check that the hose installation did not loosen the frame bracket. Retorque the bracket if necessary.

22   Fill the master cylinder reservoirs and bleed the system (refer to Section 13).

Steel brake lines

23   When it becomes necessary to replace steel lines, use only double-walled steel tubing. Never substitute copper tubing because copper is subject to fatigue cracking and corrosion. The outside diameter of the tubing is used for sizing.

24   Auto parts stores and brake supply houses carry various lengths of prefabricated brake line. Depending on the type of tubing used, these sections can either be bent by hand into the desired shape or be bent in a tubing bender.

25   If prefabricated lengths are not available obtain the recommended steel tubing and fittings to match the line to be replaced. Determine the correct length by measuring the old brake line, and cut the new tubing to length, leaving about 1/2-inch extra for flaring the ends.

26   Install the fittings onto the cut tubing and flare the ends using an ISO flaring tool.

27   Using a tubing bender, bend the tubing to match the shape of the old brake line.

28   Tube flaring and bending can usually be performed by a local auto parts store if the proper equipment mentioned in Steps 26 and 27 is not available.

29   When installing the brake line, leave at least 3/4-inch clearance between the line and any moving parts.

---

10   Combination valve — check and replacement

Check

1   Disconnect the electrical connector from the pressure differential switch (photo). **Note:** *When disconnecting the connector, squeeze the connector side lock releases, moving the inside tabs away from the switch, then pull up. Pliers may be used as an aid if necessary.*

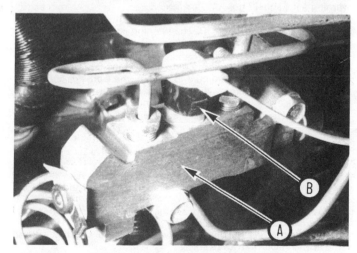

10.1   The combination valve (A) is located just under the master cylinder, with the pressure differential switch (B) located at the center of the valve

9

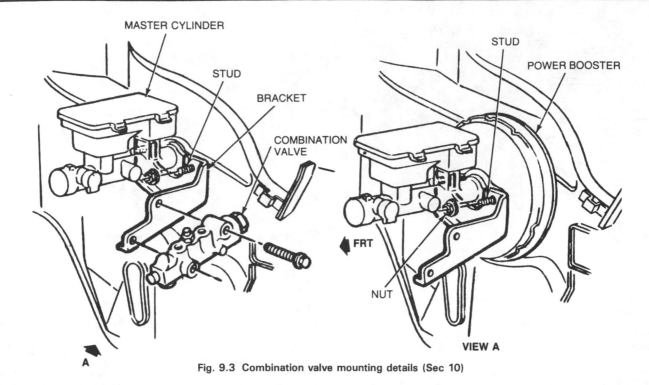

Fig. 9.3 Combination valve mounting details (Sec 10)

2   Using a jumper wire, connect the switch wire to a good ground, such as the engine block.
3   Turn the ignition key to the On position. The warning light in the instrument panel should light up.
4   If the warning light does not light, either the bulb is burned out or the electrical circuit is defective. Replace the bulb (refer to Chapter 10) or repair the electrical circuit as necessary.
5   When the warning light functions correctly, turn the ignition switch off, disconnect the jumper wire and reconnect the wire to the switch terminal.
6   Make sure the master cylinder reservoirs are full, then attach a bleeder hose to one of the rear wheel bleeder valves and immerse the other end of the hose in a container partially filled with clean brake fluid.
7   Turn the ignition switch on.
8   Open the bleeder valve while a helper applies moderate pressure to the brake pedal. The brake warning light on the instrument panel should light.
9   Close the bleeder valve before the helper releases the brake pedal.
10   Reapply the brake pedal with moderate to heavy pressure. The brake warning light should go out.
11   Attach the bleeder hose to one of the front brake bleeder valves and repeat Steps 8 through 10. The warning light should react in the same manner as in Steps 8 and 10.
12   Turn the ignition switch off.
13   If the warning light did not come on in Steps 8 and 11, but does light when a jumper is connected to ground, the warning light switch portion of the combination valve is defective and the combination valve must be replaced with a new one since the components of the combination valve are not individually serviceable.

Replacement
14   Place a container under the combination valve and protect all painted surfaces with newspapers or rags.
15   Disconnect the hydraulic lines at the combination valve, then plug the lines to prevent further loss of fluid and to protect the lines from contamination.
16   Disconnect the electrical connector from the pressure differential switch (refer to Step 1 if necessary).
17   Remove the bolt holding the valve to the mounting bracket and remove the valve from the vehicle.
18   Installation is the reverse of the removal procedure.
19   Bleed the entire brake system (refer to Section 13). *Do not move the vehicle until a firm brake pedal is attained.*

11 Parking brake — adjustment

1   The parking brake cables may stretch over a period of time, necessitating adjustment. Also, the parking brake should be checked for proper adjustment whenever the rear brake cables have been disconnected. If the parking brake handle travel is less than 13 or more than 17 ratchet clicks, the parking brake needs adjustment.
2   Pull the parking brake handle exactly two ratchet clicks.
3   Raise the vehicle and support it securely on jackstands.
4   Locate the adjusting nut on the rear side of the equalizer bracket. To keep the brake cable stud from turning, hold it with one wrench and turn the adjusting nut with another wrench until the left rear wheel can just be turned in reverse (using two hands) but is locked when you attempt to turn it forward (photo).
5   Release the parking brake and make sure that both rear wheels turn freely and that there is no brake drag in either direction, then remove the jackstands and lower the vehicle.

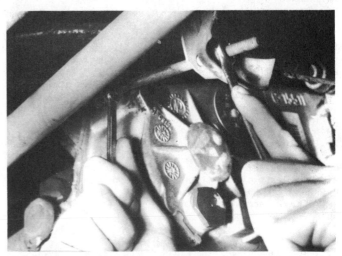

11.4 Hold the brake cable stud with one wrench while turning the adjusting nut with another

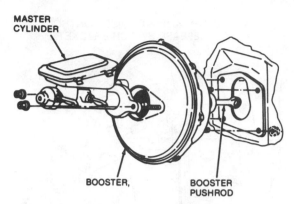

Fig. 9.4 Power brake booster mounting details (Sec 12)

12 Power brake booster — inspection, removal and installation

1   The power brake unit requires no special maintenance apart from periodic inspection of the hoses and inspection of the air filter beneath the boot at the pedal pushrod end.

2   Dismantling of the power brake unit requires special tools. If a problem develops, it is recommended that a new or factory-exchange unit be installed rather than trying to overhaul the original booster.

3   Remove the mounting nuts which hold the master cylinder to the power brake unit. Position the master cylinder out of the way, being careful not to strain the lines leading to the master cylinder. If there is any doubt as to the flexibility of the lines, disconnect them at the cylinder and plug the ends.

4   Disconnect the vacuum hose leading to the front of the power brake booster. Cover the end of the hose.

5   Loosen the four nuts that secure the booster to the firewall. Do not remove these nuts at this time.

6   Inside the vehicle, disconnect the power brake pushrod from the brake pedal. Do not force the pushrod to the side when disconnecting it.

7   Now remove the four booster mounting nuts and carefully lift the unit out of the engine compartment.

8   When installing, loosely install the four mounting nuts and then connect the pushrod to the brake pedal. Tighten the nuts to the specified torque and reconnect the vacuum hose and master cylinder. If the hydraulic brake lines were disconnected, the entire brake system should be bled to eliminate any air which has entered the system (refer to Section 13).

13 Hydraulic system — bleeding

1   Bleeding of the hydraulic system is necessary to remove air whenever it is introduced into the brake system.

2   It may be necessary to bleed the system at all four brakes if air has entered the system due to low fluid level, or if the brake lines have been disconnected at the master cylinder.

3   If a brake line was disconnected only at a wheel, then only that wheel cylinder (or caliper) must be bled.

4   If a brake line is disconnected at a fitting located between the master cylinder and any of the brakes, that part of the system served by the disconnected line must be bled.

5   If the master cylinder has been removed from the vehicle, refer to Section 8, Step 21 before proceeding with the procedure which follows.

6   If the master cylinder is installed on the vehicle but is known to have, or is suspected of having air in the bore, the master cylinder must be bled before any wheel cylinder (or caliper) is bled. Follow Steps 7 through 16 to bleed the master cylinder while it is installed on the vehicle.

7   Remove the vacuum reserve from the brake power booster by applying the brake several times with the engine off.

8   Remove the master cylinder reservoir cover and fill the reservoirs with brake fluid, then keep checking the fluid level often during the bleeding operation, adding fluid as necessary to keep the reservoirs full. Reinstall the cover.

9   Disconnect the forward brake line connection at the master cylinder.

10   Allow brake fluid to fill the master cylinder bore until it begins to flow from the forward line connector port (have a container and shop rags handy to catch and clean up spilled fluid).

11   Reconnect the forward brake line to the master cylinder.

12   Have an assistant depress the brake pedal very slowly (one time only) and hold it down.

13   Loosen the forward brake line at the master cylinder to purge the air from the bore, retighten the connection, then have the brake pedal released slowly.

14   Wait 15 seconds (important).

15   Repeat the sequence, including the 15 second wait, until all air is removed from the bore.

16   After the forward port has been completely purged of air, bleed the rear port in the same manner.

17   To bleed the individual wheel cylinders or calipers, first refer to Steps 7 and 8.

18   Have an assistant on hand, as well as a supply of new brake fluid, an empty clear plastic container, a length of 3/16-inch plastic, rubber or vinyl tubing to fit over the bleeder valve and a wrench to open and close the bleeder valve. The vehicle may have to be raised and placed on jackstands for clearance.

13.23A   Attach a hose to the bleeder valve on the rear drum assembly

13.23B   Bleeding a front disc brake caliper

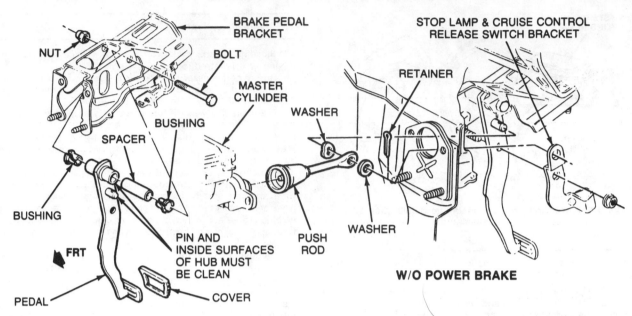

Fig. 9.5 Brake pedal mounting assembly (Sec 14)

19 Beginning at the right rear wheel, loosen the bleeder valve slightly, then tighten it to a point where it is snug but can still be loosened quickly and easily.
20 Place one end of the tubing over the bleeder valve and submerge the other end in brake fluid in the container.
21 Have the assistant pump the brakes a few times to get pressure in the system, then hold the pedal firmly depressed.
22 While the pedal is held depressed, open the bleeder valve just enough to allow a flow of fluid to leave the valve. Watch for air bubbles to exit the submerged end of the tube. When the fluid flow slows after a couple of seconds, close the valve again and have your assistant release the pedal. If the pedal is released before the valve is closed again, air can be drawn back into the system.
23 Repeat Steps 21 and 22 until no more air is seen leaving the tube, then tighten the bleeder valve and proceed to the left rear wheel, the right front wheel and the left front wheel, in that order, and perform the same procedure (photos). Be sure to check the fluid in the master cylinder reservoir frequently.
24 Never use old brake fluid because it attracts moisture which will deteriorate the brake system components.
25 Refill the master cylinder with fluid at the end of the operation.
26 If any difficulty is experienced in bleeding the hydraulic system, or if an assistant is not available, a pressure bleeding kit is a worthwhile investment. If connected in accordance with the instructions, each bleeder valve can be opened in turn to allow the fluid to be pressure ejected until it is clear of air bubbles without the need to replenish the master cylinder reservoir during the process.

14 Brake pedal — removal and installation

1 Disconnect the cable from the negative battery terminal.
2 Disconnect the clutch pedal return spring (if equipped with a manual transmission).
3 Remove the clip retainer from the pushrod pin which travels through the pedal arm.
4 Remove the nut from the pedal shaft bolt. Slide the shaft out far enough to clear the brake pedal arm.
5 The brake pedal can now be removed, along with the spacer and bushing. The clutch pedal (if equipped) will remain in place.
6 When installing, lubricate the spacer and bushings with lightweight grease and tighten the pivot nut to the specified torque.

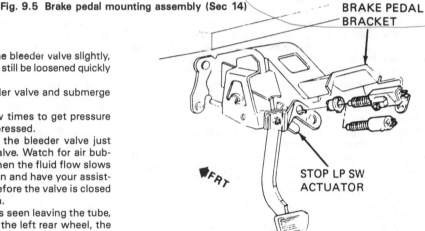

Fig. 9.6 Stop light switch installation details (Sec 15)

15 Stop light switch — removal, installation and adjustment

1 The switch is located on a flange or bracket protruding from the brake pedal support.
2 With the brake pedal in the fully released position, the plunger on the body of the switch should be completely pressed in. When the pedal is pushed in, the plunger releases and sends electrical current to the stop lights at the rear of the vehicle.
3 If the stop lights are inoperative and it has been determined that the bulbs are not burned out, push the stop light switch into the tubular clip, noting that audible clicks can be heard as the threaded portion of the switch is pushed through the clip toward the brake pedal.
4 Pull the brake pedal all the way to the rear against the pedal stop until no further clicks can be heard. This will seat the switch in the tubular clip and provide the correct adjustment.
5 Release the brake pedal and repeat Step 4 to ensure that no further clicks can be heard.
6 Make sure that the stop lights are working.
7 If the lights are not working, disconnect the electrical connectors at the stop light switch and remove the switch from the clip.
8 Install a new switch and adjust it by performing Steps 3 through 6, making sure the electrical connectors are hooked up.

Chapter 10 Chassis electrical system

Contents

1 General information

The electrical system is a 12-volt, negative ground type. Power for the lights and all electrical accessories is supplied by a lead/acid-type battery which is charged by the alternator.

This chapter covers repair and service procedures for the various electrical components not associated with the engine. Information on the battery, alternator, distributor and starter motor can be found in Chapter 5.

It should be noted that whenever portions of the electrical system are worked on, the negative battery cable should be disconnected to prevent electrical shorts and/or fires.

2 Electrical troubleshooting — general information

A typical electrical circuit consists of an electrical component, any switches, relays, motors, etc. related to that component and the wiring and connectors that connect the component to both the battery and the chassis. To aid in locating a problem in any electrical circuit, wiring diagrams for each model are included at the end of this Chapter.

Before tackling any troublesome electrical circuit, first study the appropriate diagrams to get a complete understanding of what makes up that individual circuit. Trouble spots, for instance, can often be narrowed down by noting if other components related to that circuit are operating properly or not. If several components or circuits fail at one

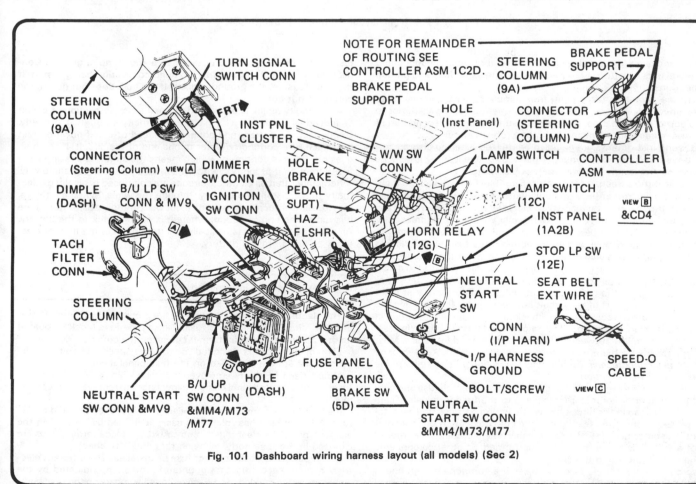

Fig. 10.1 Dashboard wiring harness layout (all models) (Sec 2)

10

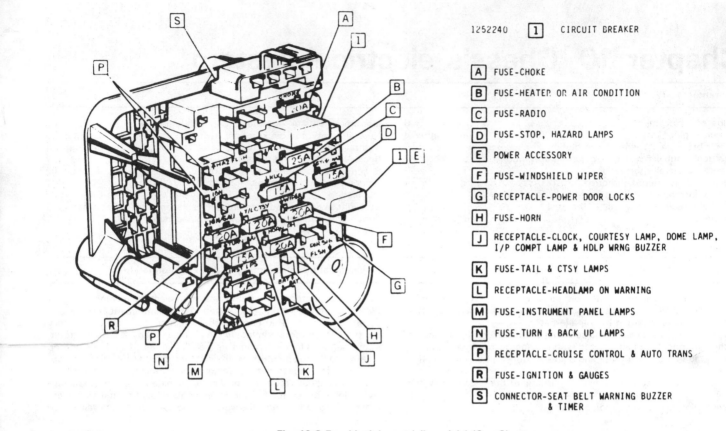

1252240 [1] CIRCUIT BREAKER

[A] FUSE-CHOKE

[B] FUSE-HEATER OR AIR CONDITION

[C] FUSE-RADIO

[D] FUSE-STOP, HAZARD LAMPS

[E] POWER ACCESSORY

[F] FUSE-WINDSHIELD WIPER

[G] RECEPTACLE-POWER DOOR LOCKS

[H] FUSE-HORN

[J] RECEPTACLE-CLOCK, COURTESY LAMP, DOME LAMP,
    I/P COMPT LAMP & HDLP WRNG BUZZER

[K] FUSE-TAIL & CTSY LAMPS

[L] RECEPTACLE-HEADLAMP ON WARNING

[M] FUSE-INSTRUMENT PANEL LAMPS

[N] FUSE-TURN & BACK UP LAMPS

[P] RECEPTACLE-CRUISE CONTROL & AUTO TRANS

[R] FUSE-IGNITION & GAUGES

[S] CONNECTOR-SEAT BELT WARNING BUZZER
    & TIMER

Fig. 10.2 Fuseblock layout (all models) (Sec 3)

time, chances are the problem lies in the fuse or ground connection, as several circuits often are routed through the same fuse and ground connections.

Electrical problems often stem from simple causes, such as loose or corroded connections, a blown fuse or melted fusible link. Prior to any electrical troubleshooting, always visually check the condition of the fuse, wires and connections in the problem circuit.

If testing instruments are going to be utilized, use the diagrams to plan ahead of time where you will make the necessary connections in order to accurately pinpoint the trouble spot.

The basic tools needed for electrical troubleshooting include a circuit tester or voltmeter (a 12-volt bulb with a set of test leads can also be used), a continuity tester (which includes a bulb, battery and set of test leads) and a jumper wire, preferably with a circuit breaker incorporated, which can be used to bypass electrical components.

Voltage checks should be performed if a circuit is not functioning properly. Connect one lead of a circuit tester to either the negative battery terminal or a known good ground. Connect the other lead to a connector in the circuit being tested, preferably nearest the battery or fuse. If the bulb of the tester goes on, voltage is reaching that point (which means the part of the circuit between that connector and the battery is problem free). Continue checking along the entire circuit in the same fashion. When you reach a point where no voltage is present, the problem lies between there and the last good test point. Most of the time the problem is due to a loose connection. *Keep in mind that some circuits receive voltage only when the ignition key is in the Accessory or Run position.*

A method of finding shorts in a circuit is to remove the fuse and connect a test light or voltmeter in its place to the fuse terminals. There should be no load in the circuit. Move the wiring harness from side-to-side while watching the test light. If the bulb goes on, there is a short to ground somewhere in that area, probably where insulation has rubbed off of a wire. The same test can be performed on other components of the circuit, including the switch.

A ground check should be done to see if a component is grounded properly. Disconnect the battery and connect one lead of a self-powered

test light such as a continuity tester to a known good ground. Connect the other lead to the wire or ground connection being tested. If the bulb goes on, the ground is good. If the bulb does not go on, the ground is not good.

A continuity check is performed to see if a circuit, section of circuit or individual component is passing electricity through it properly. Disconnect the battery and connect one lead of a self-powered test light such as a continuity tester to one end of the circuit. If the bulb goes on, there is continuity, which means the circuit is passing electricity through it properly. Switches can be checked in the same way.

Remember that all electrical circuits are composed basically of electricity running from the battery, through the wires, switches, relays, etc. to the electrical component (light bulb, motor, etc.). From there it is run to the body (ground) where it is passed back to the battery. Any electrical problem is basically an interruption in the flow of electricity to and from the battery.

3 Fuses — general information

The electrical circuits of the vehicle are protected by a combination of fuses, circuit breakers and fusible links. The fuse block is located on the underside of the instrument panel on the driver's side (photo).

Each of the fuses is designed to protect a specific circuit and the various circuits are identified on the fuse panel itself.

Miniaturized fuses are employed in the fuse block. These compact fuses, with blade terminal design, allow fingertip removal and replacement.

If an electrical component has failed, your first check should be the fuse. A fuse which has 'blown' is easily identified by inspecting the element inside the clear plastic body. Also, the blade terminal tips are exposed in the fuse body, allowing for continuity checks.

It is important that the correct fuse be installed. The different electrical circuits need varying amounts of protection, indicated by the amperage rating molded in bold, color-coded numbers on the fuse body.

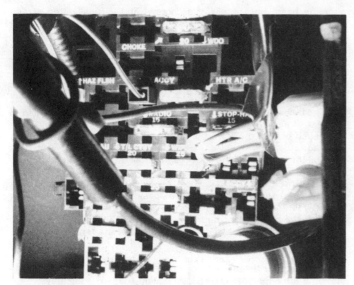

3.1 Location of the fuse block (typical)

7.3 Locations of the mounting screws for the headlight retaining ring

At no time should the fuse be bypassed with pieces of metal or foil. Serious damage to the electrical system could result.

If the replacement fuse immediately fails, do not replace it again until the cause of the problem is isolated and corrected. In most cases, this will be a short circuit in the wiring caused by a broken or deteriorated wire.

4 Fusible links — general information

In addition to fuses, the wiring is protected by fusible links. These links are used in circuits which are not ordinarily fused, such as the ignition circuit.

Although the fusible links appear to be a heavier gauge than the wire they are protecting, the appearance is due to the thick insulation. All fusible links are four wire gauges smaller than the wire they are designed to protect.

The location of the fusible links on your particular vehicle may be determined by referring to the wiring diagram(s) at the end of this Chapter.

The fusible links cannot be repaired, but a new link of the same size wire can be put in its place. The procedure is as follows:

a) Disconnect the battery ground cable.
b) Disconnect the fusible link from the starter solenoid.
c) Cut the damaged fusible link out of the wiring just behind the connector.
d) Strip the insulation back approximately 1/2-inch.
e) Position the connector on the new fusible link and crimp it into place.
f) Use rosin core solder at each end of the new link to obtain a good solder joint.
g) Use plenty of electrical tape around the soldered joint. No wires should be exposed.
h) Connect the fusible link at the starter solenoid. Connect the battery ground cable. Test the circuit for proper operation.

5 Circuit breakers — general information

A circuit breaker is used to protect the headlight wiring and is located in the light switch. An electrical overload in the system will cause the lights to go on and off, or in some cases to remain off. If this happens, check the entire headlight circuit immediately. Once the overload condition is corrected, the circuit breaker will function normally.

Circuit breakers are also used with accessories such as power windows, power door locks and rear window defogger.

The circuit breakers in your particular vehicle may be found by referring to the wiring diagram(s) at the end of this Chapter.

6 Turn signals and hazard flashers — check and replacement

1   Small canister-shaped flasher units are incorporated into the electrical circuits for the directional signals and hazard warning lights.
2   When the units are functioning properly an audible click can be heard when the circuit is in operation. If the turn signals fail on one side only and the flasher unit cannot be heard, a faulty bulb is indicated. If the flasher unit can be heard, a short in the wiring is indicated.
3   If the turn signal fails on both sides, the problem may be due to a blown fuse, faulty flasher unit or switch, or a broken or loose connection. If the fuse has blown check the wiring for a short circuit before installing a new fuse.
4   The hazard warning lights are checked as in Section 3 above.
5   When replacing either of the flasher units be sure to buy a replacement of the same capacity. Compare the new flasher to the old one before installing it.

7 Headlight sealed beam unit — removal and installation

1   When replacing the headlight do not turn the spring-loaded adjusting screws or the headlight aim will be changed.
2   Remove the headlight bezel screws and the decorative bezel.
3   Remove the screws which secure the retaining ring (photo) and withdraw the ring. Support the light as this is done.
4   Pull the sealed beam out slightly and disconnect the wires from the rear of the light.
5   Position the new sealed beam close enough to connect the wires. Make sure that the numbers molded into the lens are at the top.
6   Install the retaining ring with the mounting screws.
7   Install the bezel and check for proper operation. If the adjusting screws were not turned the new headlight should not require adjustment.

10

8 Headlights — adjustment

1   Any adjustments made by the home mechanic that affect the aim of the headlights should be considered temporary only. After adjustment, always have the beams readjusted by a facility with the proper aligning equipment as soon as possible. In some states, these facilities must be state-authorized. Check with your local motor vehicle department concerning the laws in your area.
2   Adjustment screws are provided at the front of each headlight to

8.2A   The side screw adjusts the beam left and right

8.2B   The screw in the top adjusts the headlight beam up and down

9.8   These two mounting screws for the taillight lens assembly are accessible after lowering the tailgate

alter the beam horizontally (side screw) and vertically (top screw) (photos). When making adjustments, be careful not to scratch the paint on the body.

***

9   Bulbs — replacement

Front

1   The bulbs for the parking and turn signal lights are accessible from the rear of each unit.

2   Reach behind the front bumper and twist the socket out of the housing.

3   Pull the bulb out of the socket and install the replacement (photo).

Side marker

4   The front side marker lights are accessible from under the front wheel well.

5   Turn the bulb socket counterclockwise 90° to detach it.

6   Pull the bulb out of the socket and install the replacement.

Rear

7   The bulbs for the taillights, brake lights, turn signal lights and back-up lights are all accessible after removing the lens assembly.

8   Using a Torx bit screwdriver, remove the four lens assembly mounting screws. The inner two screws can be removed after lowering the tailgate (photo).

9   Remove the appropriate bulb socket by squeezing the lock on the assembly and turning it counterclockwise, or by simply turning the socket out of the panel (photo).

10   Pull the bulb out of the socket and install the replacement.

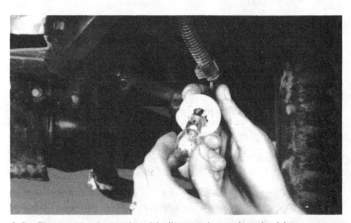

9.3   The parking/turn signal bulbs can be replaced without removing the lens assembly

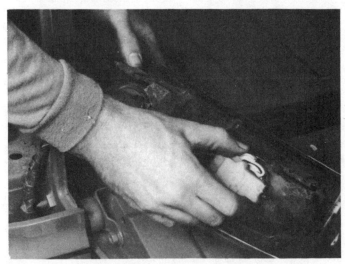

9.9   All rear light bulbs are accessible from the rear of the taillight lens assembly

License plate bulb

11 Remove the screw retaining the lens/socket assembly and pull the assembly out of the bumper.
12 Twist the socket out of the lens and replace the bulb.

10 Radio — removal and installation

1 Disconnect the negative cable from the battery.
2 Remove the center instrument panel bezel (a number 15 Torx bit screwdriver is needed).
3 Remove the four mounting screws from the radio bracket and pull the radio forward (photo).
4 Disconnect the antenna lead from the rear of the radio.
5 Disconnect the speaker and electrical plugs from the rear of the radio (photo).
6 Installation is the reverse of removal.

11 Instrument cluster — removal and installation

1 Disconnect the negative battery cable.
2 Remove the five mounting screws from the instrument cluster trim plate and detach the trim plate (photo).
3 Remove the four mounting screws from the instrument panel face plate and detach the face plate (photo).

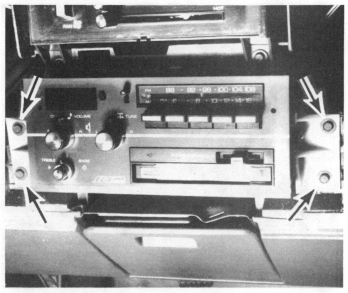

10.3 Locations of the radio mounting screws

10.5 All electrical leads to the radio can be removed by simply unplugging the connectors

11.2 Locations of the mounting screws for the instrument cluster trim plate (two are out of view on the right side)

11.3 Locations of the four instrument cluster faceplate screws.

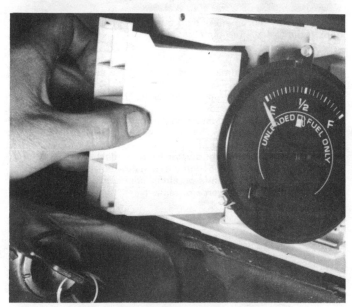

11.4 Removing the instrument light grid

10

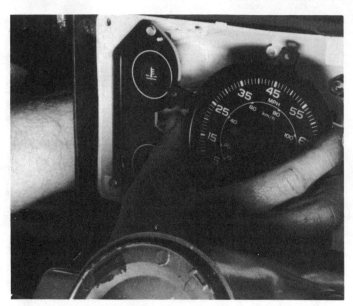

11.5A   After locating the speedometer cable in the rear of the instrument cluster...

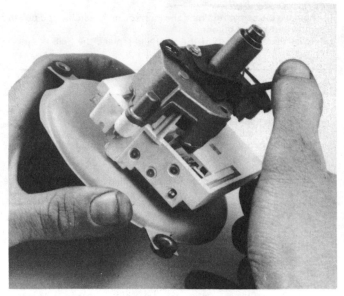

11.5B   ...release the retaining tab as shown and disengage the cable (speedometer shown out of vehicle for illustrative purposes)

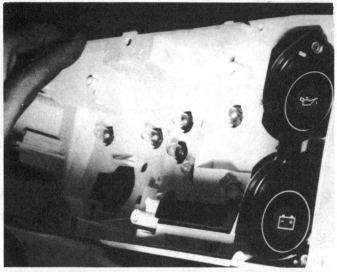

11.6   Pull the instrument cluster away just enough to detach the C-4 system bulb

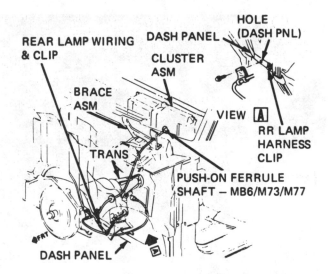

Fig. 10.3 Speedometer cable routing (Sec 12)

4   Remove the instrument light grid from the center of the cluster (photo).
5   From behind the instrument cluster, reach behind the speedometer and disconnect the speedometer cable by releasing the tab (photos).
6   Pull the instrument cluster away from the dashboard just enough to detach the C-4 system bulb from the center of the instrument cluster (photo).
7   Remove the instrument cluster from the dashboard.
8   The fuel gauge and speedometer can now be detached by removing the three mounting bolts on either component.
9   Installation is the reverse of removal.

12   Speedometer cable — replacement

1   Disconnect the cable from the negative battery terminal.
2   Disconnect the speedometer cable from the transmission or transfer case, as applicable.
3   Remove the instrument cluster as described in Section 11.
4   Slide the old cable out of the upper end of the casing, or, if broken,

from both ends of the casing.
5   If speedometer operation has been noisy, but the speedometer cable appears to be in good condition, take a short piece of speedometer cable with a tip that fits the speedometer and insert it in the speedometer socket. Spin the piece of cable between your fingers. If binding is noted, the speedometer is faulty and should be replaced.
6   Inspect the speedometer cable casing for sharp bends and cracks, especially at the transmission end. If cracks are noted replace the casing with a new one.
7   When installing the cable perform the following operations to ensure quiet operation:
8   Wipe the cable clean with a lint-free cloth.
9   Flush the bore of the casing with solvent and blow it dry with compressed air.
10   Place some speedometer cable lubricant in the palm of one hand.
11   Feed the cable through the lubricant and into the casing until the lubricant has been applied to the lower two-thirds of the cable. Do not over-lubricate.
12   Seat the upper cable tip in the speedometer and snap the retainer onto the casing.
13   The remaining installation steps are the reverse of those for removal.

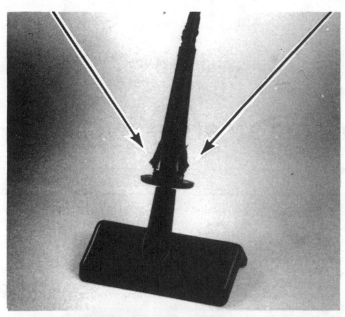

13.3 The parking brake release cable handle can be removed after depressing the retaining fingers

13.5 Location of release button for the headlight switch knob

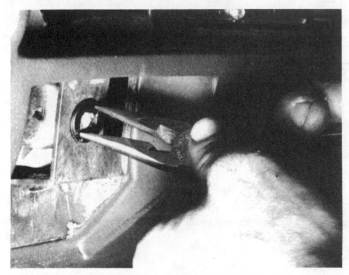

13.6 Removing the headlight switch retaining nut

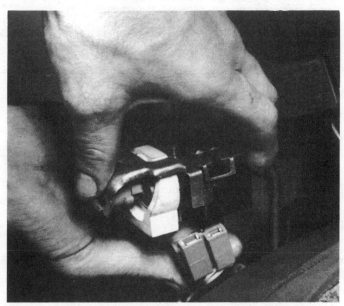

13.7 Disconnecting the headlight switch wiring harness

13 Headlight switch — removal and installation

1 Disconnect the negative cable from the battery.
2 Disconnect the parking brake release cable from the ratchet mechanism.
3 Press in on the retaining fingers of the release cable handle and remove the handle (photo).

4 Pull the dashboard panel insert down to gain access to the switch assembly.
5 Pull the headlight switch knob out and press in on the release button (photo). Remove the switch knob.
6 Using needle-nose pliers, remove the switch retaining nut (photo).
7 Disconnect the headlight switch from the wiring harness and remove the switch (photo).
8 Installation is the reverse of removal.

10

Wiring diagrams — pages 245 - 256

Chapter 11 Suspension and steering systems

Refer to Chapter 13 for specifications related to 1988 and later models

Contents

Specifications

Torque specifications	Ft-lbs
Steering linkage	
Steering knuckle-to-tie-rod end nut	40
Tie-rod clamp nuts	14
Tie-rod-to-relay rod nut	40
Pitman arm-to-relay rod nut	40
Pitman arm-to-steering gear nut	185
Idler arm-to-relay rod nut	40
Idler arm-to-frame nut	50
Power steering pump	
Reservoir bolt	35
Flow control fitting	35
Pressure hose fitting	20
Power steering gear	
Gear-to-frame bolts	80
High pressure line fitting at gear	20
Oil return line fitting at gear	20
Coupling flange bolt	30
Coupling flange nut	20
Steering wheel and column	
Steering wheel-to-shaft nut	30
Turn signal switch attaching screws	35 in-lbs
Ignition switch attaching screws	35 in-lbs
Bracket-to-steering column support nuts	25
Toe-pan-to-dash screws	45 in-lbs
Toe-pan clamp screws	60 in-lbs
Bracket-to-steering column bolt	30
Cover-to-housing screws	100 in-lbs
Clamp-to-steering shaft nut	55
Support-to-lock plate screws	60 in-lbs
Front suspension (two-wheel drive)	
Shock absorber upper nut	8
Shock absorber-to-control arm bolts	20
Upper control arm-to-frame nuts	45
Lower control arm-to-frame nuts,	
weight on wheels	65
Upper control arm pivot shaft nuts	85
Stabilizer bar link nuts	13
Stabilizer bar bracket-to-frame bolts	24
Lower balljoint	90
Upper balljoint	65

Front suspension (four-wheel drive)
Shock absorber nuts 55
Lower control arm-to-frame nuts 92
Upper control arm-to-frame nuts 70
Lower balljoint 83
Upper balljoint 50
Drive axle hub retaining nut 174
Drive axle hub-to-steering knuckle bolts 77
Torsion bar crossmember retainer bolts 25
Rear suspension
Shock absorber upper bolts 15
Shock absorber lower nut 50
Leaf spring U-bolts (final torque) 85
Leaf spring eye bolts 88
Leaf spring rear shackle-to-frame bolt 88

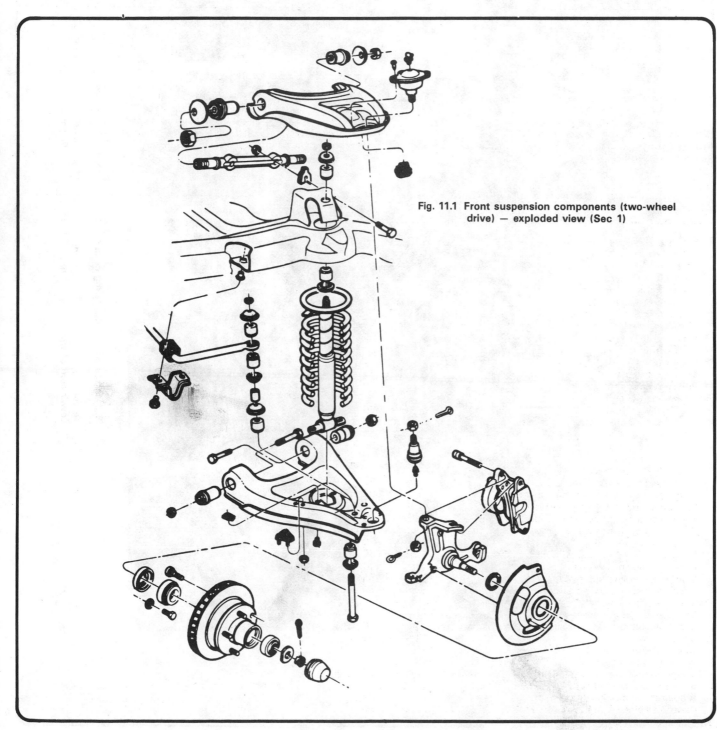

Fig. 11.1 Front suspension components (two-wheel drive) — exploded view (Sec 1)

11

Fig. 11.2 Suspension and steering components (four-wheel drive shown)

1 Tie-rod
2 Lower control arm
3 Relay rod
4 Steering stabilizer
5 Stabilizer bar
6 Torsion bar

224

2.6 Location of the front shock absorber upper mount (four-wheel drive shown)

3.2 Location of the rear shock absorber upper mount

1 Front suspension — general information

The front suspension on both two-wheel drive and four-wheel drive vehicles is fully independent, allowing each wheel to compensate for road surface changes without appreciably affecting the opposite wheel.

Each wheel is connected independently to the frame by a steering knuckle, upper and lower balljoints and upper and lower control arms. The front wheels are held in proper relationship to each other by tie-rods, which are connected to the steering knuckles and to a relay rod assembly.

Two-wheel drive

Chassis suspension is handled by coil springs mounted between the lower control arms and the frame. Shock absorbers are mounted inside each coil spring, bolted to the lower control arm and passing through the upper control arm to bolt to the upper control arm frame bracket.

Side roll is controlled by a stabilizer bar mounted to the frame in rubber bushings. Rubber grommeted link bolts attach the ends of the stabilizer bar to the lower control arms.

Four-wheel drive

The basic layout of the front suspension on the four-wheel drive is the same as that of the two-wheel drive, with the exception of the replacement of the coil springs with torsion bars. These allow the front drive axles access to the drive hubs.

The torsion bars are mounted to the lower control arms and are anchored in a frame crossmember with an adjustable arm to control the trim height of the vehicle.

2 Front shock absorber — removal and installation

Two-wheel drive
1 Raise the vehicle and support it securely on jackstands.
2 Remove the upper shock absorber stem nut. Use an open end wrench to keep the upper stem from turning.
3 Remove the two bolts at the lower shock mount and pull the shock absorber out through the bottom of the lower control arm.
4 Installation is the reverse of removal. Be sure to tighten the nuts/bolts to the specified torque.

Four-wheel drive
5 Raise the vehicle and support it securely on jackstands.
6 Remove the nut and bolt from the upper shock absorber mount (photo).
7 Remove the nut and bolt from the lower mount on the control arm.

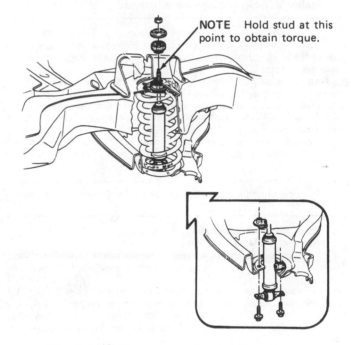

NOTE Hold stud at this point to obtain torque.

Fig. 11.3 Front shock absorber mounting details (two-wheel drive) (Sec 2)

8 Compress the shock absorber enough to slide it off the mounts and remove it from the vehicle.
9 Installation is the reverse of removal. Be sure to tighten the nuts/bolts to the specified torque.

3 Rear shock absorber — removal and installation

1 Raise the vehicle and support it securely on jackstands.
2 Remove the two bolts and nuts at the upper shock absorber mount (photo).
3 Remove the nut and washer at the lower mount.
4 Slide the shock absorber off the lower mount and detach it from the vehicle.
5 Installation is the reverse of removal. Be sure to tighten the nuts/bolts to the specified torque.

11

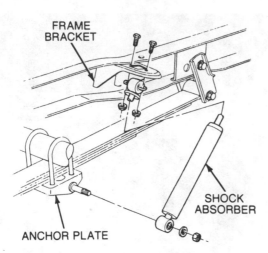

FRAME
BRACKET

SHOCK
ABSORBER

ANCHOR PLATE

**Fig. 11.4 Rear shock absorber mounting details (all models)
(Sec 3)**

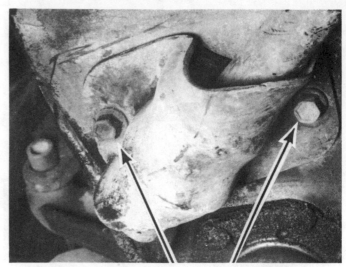

4.2 Location of the stabilizer bar-to-control arm bolts (four-wheel drive shown)

4.3 Location of the stabilizer bar-to-frame bolts (four-wheel drive shown)

4 Stabilizer bar — removal and installation

1   Raise the vehicle and support it securely on jackstands.
2   Two-wheel drive: Remove the bolts from each end of the stabilizer bar at the lower control arms. Note the positions of the grommets and spacers (photo).
   Four-wheel drive: Disconnect the torsion bars (see Section 10) from the crossmember to allow free movement of the lower control arms. Remove the stabilizer bar mounting cups from the lower control arms.
3   Remove the mounting bolts from the frame and detach the stabilizer bar, bushings and brackets (photo)
4   Installation is the reverse of removal. Install the control arm nuts first, then the frame bolts. Tighten all fasteners to the specified torque.

5 Steering knuckle and balljoints, two-wheel drive — removal and installation

1   Raise the vehicle and support it securely on jackstands.
2   Remove the wheel and tire.
3   Place a floor jack or jackstand under the lower control arm spring seat, raising it just enough to take all spring pressure off the upper control arm.
4   Remove the tie-rod from the steering knuckle (see Section 13).
5   Remove the cotter pin and nut from the lower balljoint stud.
6   Use GM tool No. J-23742 or equivalent to remove the lower balljoint stud from the steering knuckle as shown in the accompanying illustration.
7   Remove the cotter pin and nut from the upper balljoint stud.
8   Use GM tool No. J-23742 to remove the stud from the steering knuckle as shown in the accompanying illustration.
9   Remove the lower balljoint from the control arm by pressing it out as shown in the illustration.
10 The upper balljoint is removed by using a 1/8-in diameter bit to drill 1/4-in deep into the four mounting rivets.
11 Drill off the rivet heads using a 1/2-in bit.
12 Remove the rivets with a small punch and slide the balljoint out of the control arm.
13 To install the lower balljoint position the new unit in the lower control arm and press it in until it bottoms. The grease purge opening on the seal must be facing inwards, towards the engine.
14 Place the balljoint stud in the steering knuckle, thread on the nut and tighten it to 90 ft-lb (120 Nm). Tighten additionally as necessary to line up the slot in the nut with the hole in the stud and install the cotter pin.
15 Lubricate the balljoint with chassis grease.
16 Install the new balljoint in the upper control arm, using the four attaching bolts which came with the balljoint, and tighten the nuts to 8 ft-lb (11 Nm).

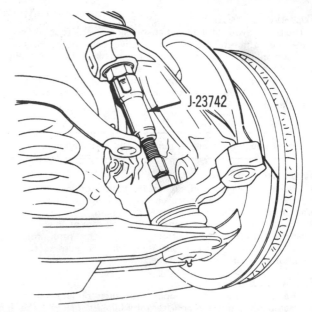

J-23742

**Fig. 11.5 This expansion tool is used to break the balljoint
loose (two-wheel drive) (Sec 5)**

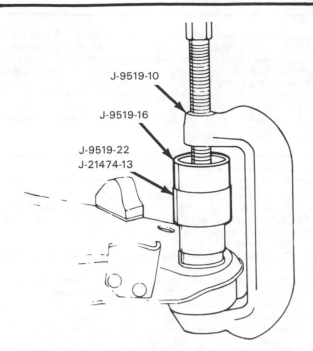

J-9519-10
J-9519-16
J-9519-22
J-21474-13

Fig. 11.6 Removing the lower balljoint from the control arm (Sec 5)

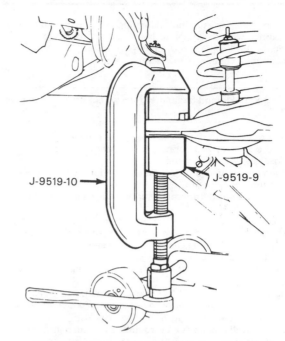

J-9519-10
J-9519-9

Fig. 11.7 Lower balljoint installation (Sec 5)

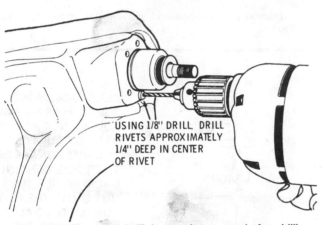

USING 1/8" DRILL, DRILL RIVETS APPROXIMATELY 1/4" DEEP IN CENTER OF RIVET

Fig. 11.8 The upper balljoint can be removed after drilling out the rivets (all models) (Sec 5)

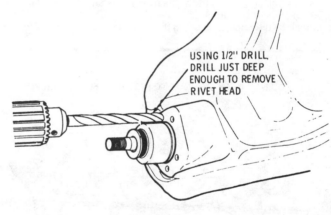

USING 1/2" DRILL, DRILL JUST DEEP ENOUGH TO REMOVE RIVET HEAD

Fig. 11.9 Removing the rivet heads (Sec 5)

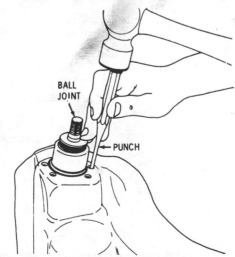

BALL JOINT
PUNCH

Fig. 11.10 The balljoint rivets must be driven out with a punch (Sec 5)

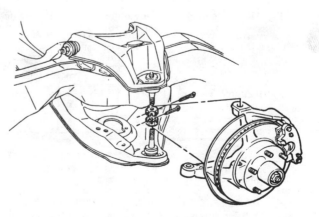

Fig 11.11 Steering knuckle mounting details (two-wheel drive shown) (Sec 5)

11

17 Place the balljoint stud in the steering knuckle, thread on the nut, and tighten to 65 ft-lb (90 Nm). Install the cotter pin.
18 Lubricate the balljoint with chassis grease.
19 Replace the wheel and lower the vehicle.

6 Steering knuckle and balljoints, four-wheel drive — removal and installation

1 Loosen the lug nuts of the wheel to be removed.
2 Raise the vehicle and support it securely on jackstands.
3 Remove the wheel and tire.
4 Position a hydraulic jack or jackstand under the lower control arm to support the control arm.
5 Remove the tie-rod from the steering knuckle as described in Section 13.
6 Remove the spindle cotter key, nut cover, nut and washer.
7 If the steering knuckle seal is to be changed remove the three bolts holding the hub and bearing assembly to the steering knuckle and slide the hub out of the knuckle.
8 Remove the cotter pins and nuts from the upper and lower balljoint studs.
9 Using GM tool No. J-34026 or equivalent remove the balljoint studs from the steering knuckle. **Note:** *Do not use a 'pickle fork' type of balljoint tool, as this can damage the balljoint seals.*
10 Use a 1/8-in diameter drill bit to drill 1/4-in deep into the balljoint mounting rivets (four rivets on the upper control arm and four on the lower).
11 Drill off the rivet heads using a 1/2-in drill bit.
12 Use a small punch to remove the rivet shafts and the balljoints will fall out of the control arms.
13 Install the new balljoints using the attaching nuts and bolts which came with the new balljoints. Tighten the nuts to 8 ft-lb (11 Nm).
14 Place the balljoint studs in the steering knuckle and thread on the nuts. Tighten the upper balljoint nut to 50 ft-lb (68 Nm) and the lower balljoint to 83 ft-lb (113 Nm). Tighten the nuts further as necessary to install the cotter keys.
15 Reinstall the tie-rod and tighten to 35 ft-lb (48 Nm).
16 Grease the new ball joints.
17 The remainder of the installation is the reverse of the removal procedure.

7 Upper control arms — removal and installation

1 Raise the vehicle and support it securely on jackstands.
2 Support the lower control arm with a hydraulic jack or jackstand. The support point must be as close to the balljoint as possible to give the maximum leverage on the coil spring or torsion bar.
3 Remove the wheel.
4 Disconnect the upper balljoint from the steering knuckle (Sections 5 and 6).
5 Two-wheel drive: Remove the upper control arm bolts and detach the upper control arm. Note the position of the alignment shims which are installed between the pivot shaft and frame. They will have to be reinstalled in the same position when replacing the control arm.
   Four-wheel drive: Mark the positions of the camber adjusting cups then remove the pivot bolts.
6 Replace the bushings in the control arm. On two-wheel drive use a C-clamp and receiver cup to remove the bushings. A threaded puller and receiver cup works well to remove the bushings on four-wheel drive vehicles.
7 Installation is the reverse of removal. Tighten all bolts to specified torque.

DO NOT BACK OFF NUT TO INSTALL NEW COTTER PIN.

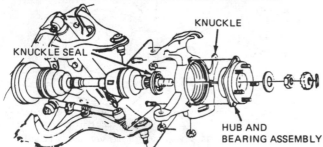
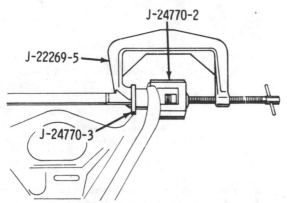

Fig. 11.12 Steering knuckle mounting details (four-wheel drive) (Sec 6)

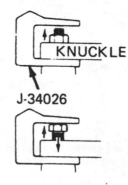

PLACE J-34026 INTO POSITION AS SHOWN. LOOSEN NUT AND BACK OFF UNTIL THE NUT CONTACTS THE TOOL. CONTINUE BACKING OFF THE NUT UNTIL THE NUT FORCES THE BALL STUD OUT OF THE KNUCKLE.

Fig. 11.13 Tool used to break the balljoints loose on four-wheel drive models (Sec 6)

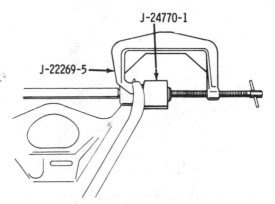

Fig. 11.14 Removing the upper control arm bushing (Sec 7)

Fig. 11.15 Upper control arm bushing installation (Sec 7)

8 Lower control arms — removal and installation

Two-wheel drive

1 Remove the coil spring as described in Section 9.
2 Remove the lower balljoint stud as described in Section 5.
3 Remove the lower control arm, guiding it out through the opening in the splash shield.
4 Using a blunt chisel drive the bushing flare down flush with the rubber bushing.
5 Remove the bushings and install new ones as shown in the accompanying illustrations.
6 Use a flaring tool to flare the replacement bushing as shown in the accompanying illustration.
7 Installation is the reverse of the removal procedure.

Four-wheel drive

8 Raise the vehicle and support it on jackstands.
9 Unload the torsion bar as described in Section 10.
10 Unbolt the stabilizer bar mounting cups on both sides and pivot the stabilizer bar down to clear the control arm.
11 Remove the lower shock absorber mounting bolt.
12 Remove the inner control arm pivot bolts.
13 Remove the lower balljoint stud as described in Section 6.
14 Referring to the accompanying illustrations, remove the old control arm bushings and install new bushings.
15 Installation is the reverse of the removal procedure.

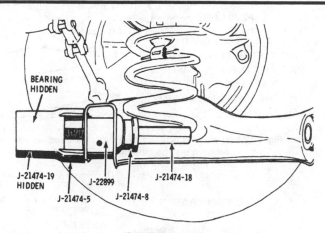

Fig. 11.16 Removing the lower control arm front bushing on two-wheel drive vehicles (Sec 8)

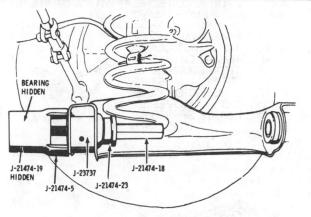

Fig. 11.17 Front bushing installation on two-wheel drive vehicles (Sec 8)

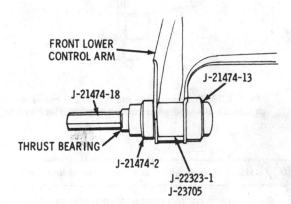

Fig. 11.18 On two-wheel drive models the bushing must be flared after installation (Sec 8)

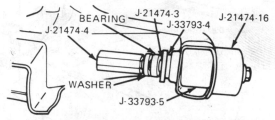

Fig. 11.19 Removal of lower control arm front bushing on four-wheel drive vehicles (Sec 8)

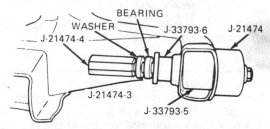

Fig. 11.20 Removal of lower control arm rear bushing on four-wheel drive vehicles (Sec 8)

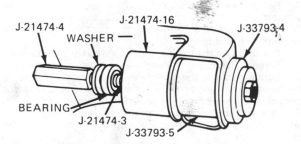

Fig. 11.21 Installation of lower control arm front bushing on four-wheel drive vehicles (Sec 8)

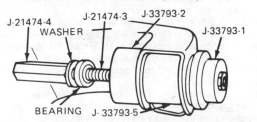

Fig. 11.22 Installation of lower control arm rear bushing on four-wheel drive vehicles (Sec 8)

11

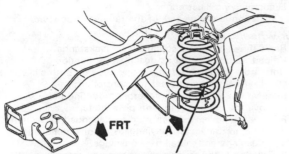

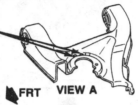

SPRING TO BE INSTALLED WITH TAPE AT LOWEST POSITION. BOTTOM OF SPRING IS COILED HELICAL, AND THE TOP IS COILED FLAT WITH A GRIPPER NOTCH NEAR END OF SPRING COIL.

AFTER ASSEMBLY, END OF SPRING COIL MUST COVER ALL OR PART OF ONE IN-SPECTION DRAIN HOLE. THE OTHER HOLE MUST BE PARTLY EXPOSED OR COM-PLETELY UNCOVERED. ROTATE SPRING AS NECESSARY.

Fig. 11.23 The coil spring must be installed as shown (Sec 9)

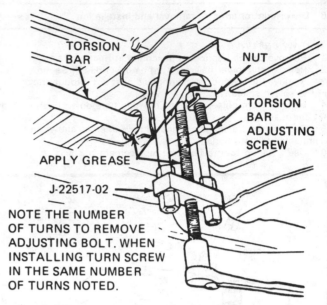

NOTE THE NUMBER OF TURNS TO REMOVE ADJUSTING BOLT. WHEN INSTALLING TURN SCREW IN THE SAME NUMBER OF TURNS NOTED.

Fig 11.24 A special preload tool must be used to relieve tension on the torsion bar (Sec 10)

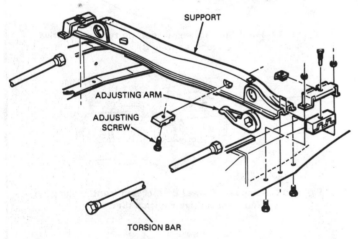

Fig. 11.25 Exploded view of the torsion bar suspension components (four-wheel drive only) (Sec 10)

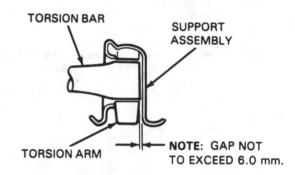

NOTE: GAP NOT TO EXCEED 6.0 mm.

Fig. 11.26 The clearance measurement indicated here should be checked after torsion bar installation (Sec 10)

9 Front coil springs — removal and installation

1   Raise the vehicle and support it on jackstands placed under the outside frame rails. The lower control arms must be free to move.
2   Remove the wheel and tire.
3   Remove the shock absorber-to-lower control arm bolts and push the shock up into the coil spring.
4   Disconnect the stabilizer bar at the lower control arm.
5   Use GM tool No. J-23028 or equivalent, mounted on a jack, to sup-port the inner control arm bushings. Raise the jack just enough to remove the tension from the bushing pivot bolts.
6   Install a chain around the spring and through the control arm as a safety precaution.
7   Remove the rear pivot bolt, then the front bolt.
8   Lower the control arm and spring. When all tension is removed from the spring remove the safety chain and work the spring out of the con-trol arm pocket. Do not apply force to the control arm-to-steering knuckle balljoint to remove the spring. Proper maneuvering will allow the spring to come free.
9   Installation is the reverse of the removal procedure.

10 Torsion bar, four-wheel drive — removal and installation

1   Raise the vehicle and support it securely on jackstands.
2   Install a special preload tool over the torsion bar support as shown in the accompanying illustration.
3   Counting the number of turns, remove the torsion bar adjusting screw.
4   Remove the nuts and bolts from the support retainer. Remove the support retainer.
5   Slide the torsion bar forward in the lower control arm until it clears the torsion bar support.
6   Pull down on the torsion bar and detach it from the control arm.
7   Remove the adjusting arm from the torsion bar support.
8   Before installing the torsion bar apply some grease to the top of the adjusting arm and to the end of the adjusting bolt. Also, apply some grease to the hex-shaped surface of the torsion bar.
9   Finally, check the torsion arm-to-support assembly clearance (refer to the accompanying illustration) after installation.

11 Rear leaf spring — removal and installation

1   Raise the vehicle until the weight is off the rear spring to be work-ed on, but the tire is still touching the ground.

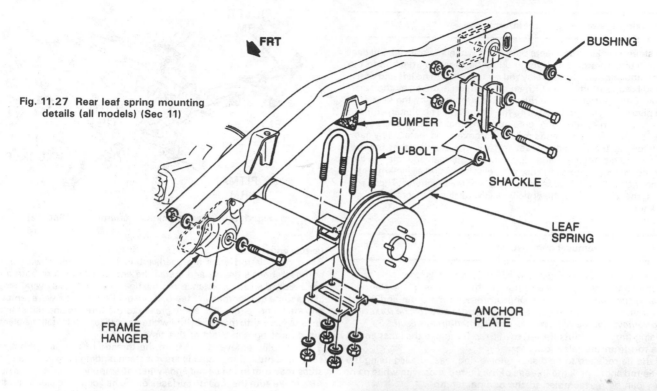

Fig. 11.27 Rear leaf spring mounting details (all models) (Sec 11)

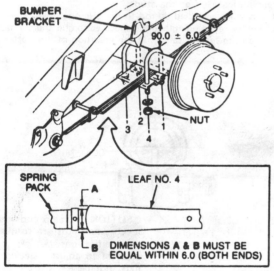

Fig. 11.28 Checking the alignment and arc of the spring leafs (Sec 11)

11.3 The rear leaf spring must be free to pivot down, so loosen the spring-to-shackle nut

2   Support the frame securely on jackstands.
3   Loosen, but do not remove, the spring-to-shackle retaining nut (photo).
4   Remove the U-bolt retaining nuts and detach the U-bolts.
5   Rotate the spring anchor plate on the shock absorber until the plate clears the spring.
6   Remove the nut and bolt securing the spring shackle to the frame.
7   Remove the nut and bolt from the front hanger and detach the spring.
8   If the spring eye bushings are worn or damaged they must be replaced by an automotive repair shop with the necessary hydraulic press and associated tools.
9   Clean the axle spring pad before installing the spring.
10 Attach the spring at the front hanger but do not tighten the bolt to the final torque.
11 Attach the spring shackle to the frame (be sure the open end of

the shackle faces foward), but do not tighten the bolt to the final torque.
12 Make sure that the shackle bolt in the rear spring eye is loose.
13 Position the axle spring pad on the spring so that the center bolt head seats into the hole in the spring pad seat.
14 Rotate the anchor plate into position and install the U-bolts finger-tight.
15 Tighten the U-bolt nuts, in a criss-cross pattern, to 20 ft-lb.
16 Lower the vehicle completely and tighten the U-bolt nuts to the specified torque.
17 Check to be sure that the leaves are properly seated by comparing the side overhang dimension on each side (A and B in the accompanying illustration).
18 Check the height dimension between the bumper bracket and the axle tube as shown in the accompanying illustration.
19 Tighten the front and rear spring eye bolts and the shackle-to-frame bolts to the specified torque.

12 Steering system — general information

The steering linkage connects both front wheels to the steering gear through a pitman arm. The right and left tie-rods are attached to the steering knuckles and to the relay rod by balljoints. The left end of the relay rod is supported by the pitman arm, which is driven by the steering gear. The right end of the relay rod is supported by the idler arm, which pivots on a support bolted to the frame rail. The pitman arm and idler arm move in symmetrical arcs and remain parallel to each other.

The tie-rods and tie-rod ends may be removed and installed by carefully following the procedures set forth in the Section that follows. However, the replacement and alignment of the relay rod, pitman arm and/or the idler arm requres the use of special tools and alignment equipment not normally in the possession of the home mechanic. These procedures, therefore, should be done by a GM dealer or a front-end alignment shop.

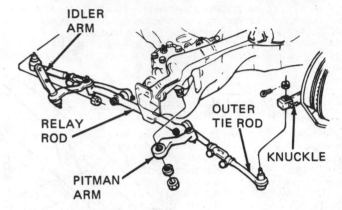

Fig. 11.29 Steering linkage components (Sec 12)

13 Tie-rods — removal and installation

1   Raise the vehicle and place it securely on jackstands.
2   Remove the cotter pins and nuts from the ends of the tie-rod.
3   Using the puller as shown (photo), remove the outer end of the tie-rod from the steering knuckle. **Note:** *Do not use a 'pickle fork' type tool to remove the tie-rod end, as seal damage may result.*
4   Using the same tool referred to in Step 3 remove the inner end of the tie-rod from the relay rod.
5   If the tie-rods are to be disassembled and reassembled using the same tie-rod ends, mark the threads of the tie-rod ends with white paint so they can be reassembled to the original length.
6   If new tie-rod ends are to be installed carefully measure the overall length of the tie-rod assembly before removing the tie-rod ends so the assemblies can be adjusted to the original length.
7   To remove the tie-rod ends loosen the clamp nuts and unscrew the tie-rod ends.

8   If new tie-rod ends are used, lubricate the threads with multi-purpose chassis grease and install the ends, making sure both ends are threaded an equal distance into the tie-rod and that the overall length is the same as recorded in Step 6. If the old tie-rod ends were removed and are being reinstalled, apply grease to the threads and reinstall the ends to the depth marked by the white paint (Step 5). Install the clamps but do not tighten them at this time.
9   Carefully remove all dirt from the threads of the tie-rod balljoint studs and nuts. If the threads are not clean binding may occur and the studs may turn in the tie-rod ends when attempting to tighten the nuts. Also make sure the tapered surfaces of the balljoints are clean and that the seals are installed on the studs.
10 Attach the assembled tie-rod to the steering linkage.
11 Tighten the retaining nuts to the specified torque, then, if necessary, tighten the nuts farther to permit the insertion of the cotter pins.

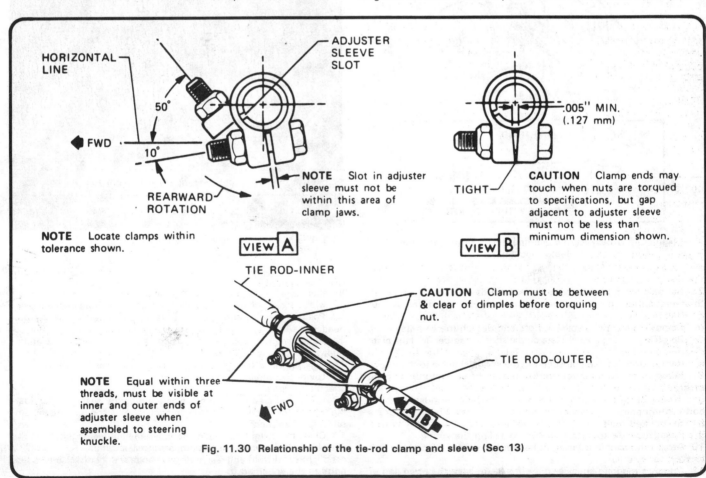

Fig. 11.30 Relationship of the tie-rod clamp and sleeve (Sec 13)

12 Refer to the accompanying illustration and adjust the tie-rod clamps as shown, then tighten the clamps to the specified torque.
13 Lubricate the tie-rod ends with the specified grease.
14 Remove the jackstands and lower the vehicle.
15 A front end alignment must now be performed by a GM dealer or an alignment shop.

14 Power steering system — general information

With the optional power steering gear, hydraulic pressure is generated in an engine-driven pump and supplied through hoses to the steering box spool valve. When the steering wheel is turned and force is applied to the steering shaft, hydraulic pressure is added and power assistance is given to the turning effort.

The sections which follow concern procedures that can be performed by the home mechanic. However, due to the requirements for special tools and diagnostic procedures, major repairs to the power steering system should be performed by a dealer or reputable repair shop.

15 Power steering system — bleeding

1 This is not a routine operation and normally will only be required when the system has been dismantled and reassembled.
2 Fill the reservoir to the correct level with the recommended fluid and allow it to remain undisturbed for at least two minutes.
3 Start the engine and run it for two or three seconds only. Check the reservoir and add more fluid as necessary.
4 Repeat the operations described in the preceding paragraph until the fluid level remains constant.
5 Raise the front of the vehicle until the wheels are clear of the ground.
6 Start the engine and run it at about 1500 rpm. Turn the steering from stop to stop. Check the reservoir fluid level.
7 Lower the vehicle to the ground and, with the engine still running, move the vehicle forward sufficiently to obtain full right lock, followed by full left lock. Recheck the fluid level. If the fluid in the reservoir is getting foamy allow the vehicle to stand for a few minutes with the engine off, then repeat the previous operations. At the same time check the belt tightness. Check to make sure the power steering hoses are not touching any part of the vehicle such as sheet metal or the exhaust manifold.
8 The procedures above will normally remedy an extreme foam condition and/or a noisy pump. If, however, either or both conditions persist after a few trials, the power steering system will have to be checked by a dealer. Do not drive the vehicle until the conditions have been remedied.

16 Power steering gear — removal and installation

1 Disconnect the cable from the negative battery terminal.
2 Remove the coupling shield.
3 Disconnect the pressure and return hoses attached to the power steering gear assembly.
4 Plug or tape the ends of the disconnected hoses and the holes in the power steering housing to prevent contamination.
5 Remove the nuts, lockwashers and bolts at the steering coupling-to-steering shaft flange.
6 Remove the pitman arm locknut and washer. Mark the position of the pitman arm in relation to the shaft and disconnect the pitman arm with a puller.
7 Remove the bolts securing the steering gear to the frame and separate it from the vehicle.
8 When installing the gear place it in position so that the coupling mounts properly to the flanged end of the steering shaft. Secure the gear to the frame, install the washers and bolts, then tighten down the bolts to the specified torque.
9 Secure the steering coupling to the flanged end of the column with the lock washers and nuts. Tighten the nuts.
10 Install the pitman arm, lining up the marks made during disassembly, and tighten the nut.
11 Connect the coupling shield and negative battery cable.

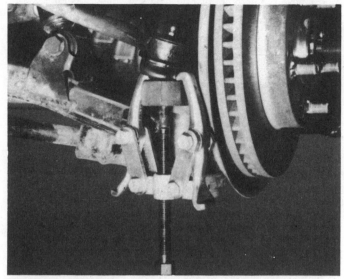

13.3 Using a puller to separate the tie-rod from the steering knuckle

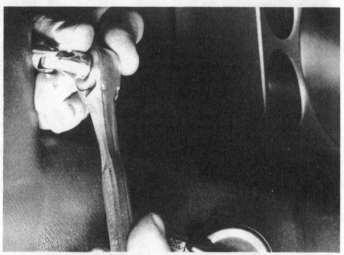

18.2 Removing the steering wheel shroud

17 Power steering pump — removal and installation

1 Disconnect the hydraulic hoses from the pump and keep them in the raised position to prevent the fluid from leaking out until they can be plugged.
2 Remove the pump drivebelt by loosening the pump mounts and pushing it in toward the engine.
3 Unscrew and remove the pump mounting bolts and braces and remove the pump.
5 Installation is the reverse of removal.
6 Prime the pump by turning the pulley in the reverse direction to that of normal rotation (counterclockwise as viewed from the front) until air bubbles cease to emerge from the fluid when observed through the reservoir filler cap.
7 Install the drivebelt and adjust it as described in Chapter 1.
8 Bleed the system as described in Section 15.

18 Steering wheel — removal and installation

1 Disconnect the negative battery cable from the battery.
2 Use a 7mm socket to remove the steering wheel shroud screws on the underside of the steering wheel (photo). Detach the shroud (photo).

11

3   Remove the horn contact bushing and spring (photo).
4   Remove the retainer clip and steering wheel retaining nut. A socket and breaker bar will be needed to remove the retaining nut.
5   Mark the steering wheel and steering shaft so the wheel can be reinstalled in the same position (photo).
6   Use a steering wheel puller to remove the steering wheel from the column (photo).
7   Installation is the reverse of removal.

19   Steering column switches — removal and installation

1   Remove the steering wheel as described in Section 18.
2   Pry the shaft lock cover off the steering column (photo).
3   Use an expansion tool to compress the lockplate and remove the lockplate retaining ring (photo).
4   Remove the expansion tool and detach the lockplate.
5   Remove the cancelling cam.
6   Remove the upper bearing spring and washer.
7   Remove the mounting screw from the base of the turn signal lever

and detach the turn signal lever.
8   Remove the hazard signal knob screw on the outside of the steering column and detach the hazard signal knob (photo).
9   Remove the three mounting screws (photo) from the signal switch assembly and remove the assembly.
10   If the switch assembly is not being replaced, it can be left hanging from the steering column.
11   To remove the ignition switch, first remove the switch retaining screw from inside the column (photo).
12   Turn the ignition switch to the Run position and pull the switch out.
13   To replace the signal switch assembly, first remove the steering column trim cover (photo).
14   Remove the four bolts and two nuts from the steering column-to-dashboard brace to free the wiring harness.
15   Disconnect the switch wiring harness at the bottom of the column (photo) and attach a routing wire to the end of the switch harness.
16   Remove the switch and wiring harness from the steering column.
17   Attach the replacement switch wiring harness to the routing wire and install the harness in the column.
18   Connect the wiring harness. Install the two bracket nuts and the four bolts.
18   The rest of installation is the reverse of removal.

18.3 Removing the horn contact and spring

18.5 The steering wheel and shaft should be marked before removing the steering wheel

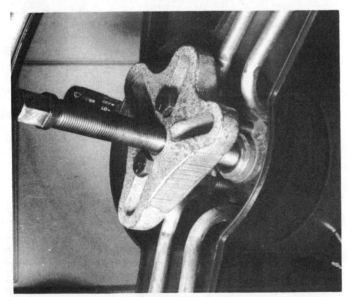

18.6 Using a steering wheel puller to remove the steering wheel

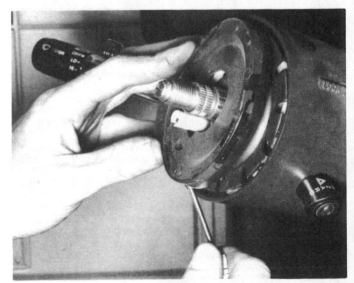

19.2 Removing the steering column shaft lock cover

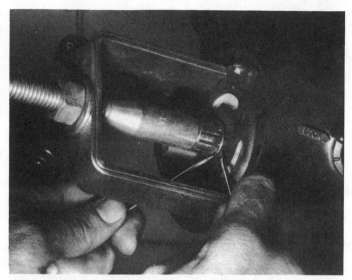

19.3 An expansion tool preloads the lockplate, allowing removal of the retaining ring

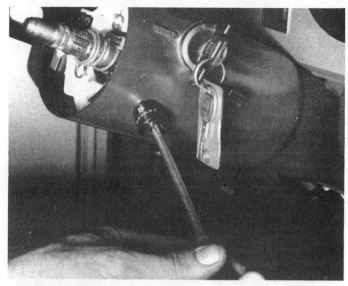

19.8 Removing the hazard signal knob

19.9 Location of the turn signal switch mounting screws

19.11 Location of the ignition switch retaining screw

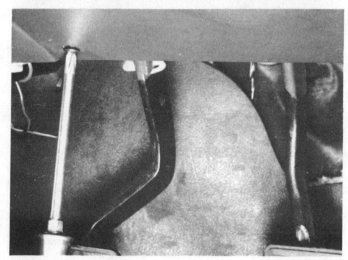

19.13 Removing the steering column trim cover

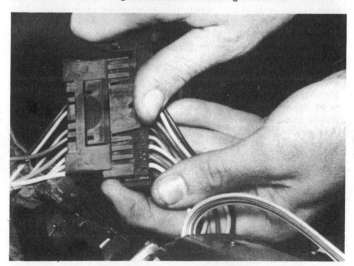

19.15 The turn signal switch wiring harness is disconnected at the bottom of the steering column

11

Chapter 12 Body

Contents

Specifications

Torque specifications	Ft-lb
Hood mounting bolts	20
Hood hinge-to-fender bolts	20
Endgate glass-to-hinge bolts	50 in-lb

1 General information

Chevrolet and GMC utility vehicles are built with body on separate frame construction. The frame is ladder-type, consisting of two C-section steel side rails joined by a variable number of crossmembers. All crossmembers are riveted, with the exception of the one under the transmission, which is bolted in to facilitate transmission removal and installation. The number of crossmembers in the frame depends on the vehicle wheelbase and load rating.

Front fenders, hood, inner fender panels and grilles are bolted to the cab and the radiator support at the front of the vehicle. The radiator support is attached to the front frame rails and insulated with rubber donuts. Bolts retain the support.

Bumpers are bolted to the frame horns at the front and to the frame rails at the rear via mounting brackets.

Doors, seats and dashboard are all bolted to the cab and are individually replaceable.

2 Body — maintenance

1   The condition of your vehicle's body is very important, because it is on this that the second-hand value will mainly depend. It is much more difficult to repair a neglected or damaged body than it is to repair mechanical components. The hidden areas of the body, such as the fender wells, the frame, and the engine compartment, are equally important, although obviously do not require as frequent attention as the rest of the body.
2   Once a year, or every 12 000 miles, it is a good idea to have the underside of the body and the frame steam cleaned. All traces of dirt and oil will be removed and the underside can then be inspected carefully for rust, damaged brake lines, frayed electrical wiring, damaged cables, and other problems. The front suspension components should be greased after completion of this job.
3   At the same time, clean the engine and the engine compartment using either a steam cleaner or a water soluble degreaser.
4   The fender wells should be given particular attention, as undercoating can peel away and stones and dirt thrown up by the tires can cause the paint to chip and flake, allowing rust to set in. If rust is found, clean down to the bare metal and apply an anti-rust paint.
5   The body should be washed once a week (or when dirty). Wet the vehicle thoroughly to soften the dirt, then wash it down with a soft sponge and plenty of clean soapy water. If the surplus dirt is not washed off very carefully, it will in time wear down the paint.
6   Spots of tar or asphalt coating thrown up from the road should be removed with a cloth soaked in solvent.
7   Once every six months, give the body and chrome trim a thorough wax job. If a chrome cleaner is used to remove rust from any of the vehicle's plated parts, remember that the cleaner also removes part of the chrome, so use it sparingly.

3 Upholstery and carpets — maintenance

1   Every three months, remove the carpets or mats and clean the interior of the vehicle (more frequently if necessary). Vacuum the upholstery and carpets to remove loose dirt and dust.
2   If the upholstery is soiled, apply upholstery cleaner with a damp sponge and wipe it off with a clean, dry cloth.

4   Vinyl trim — maintenance

Vinyl trim should not be cleaned with detergents, caustic soaps or petroleum-based cleaners. Plain soap and water or a mild vinyl cleaner is best for stains. Test a small area for color fastness. Bubbles under the vinyl can be corrected by piercing them with a pin and then working the air out.

5   Hinges and locks — maintenance

Every 3000 miles or three months, the door, hood and tailgate hinges and locks should be lubricated with a few drops of oil. The striker plates should also be given a thin coat of grease to reduce wear and ensure free movement.

6   Body repair — minor damage

See color photo sequence

Repair of minor scratches

If the scratch is very superficial and does not penetrate to the metal of the body, repair is very simple. Lightly rub the scratched area with a fine rubbing compound to remove loose paint and built-up wax. Rinse the area with clean water.

Apply touch-up paint to the scratch, using a small brush. Continue to apply thin layers of paint until the surface of the paint in the scratch is level with the surrounding paint. Allow the new paint at least two weeks to harden, then blend it into the surrounding paint by rubbing with a very fine rubbing compound. Finally, apply a coat of wax to the scratch area.

If the scratch has penetrated the paint and exposed the metal of the body, causing the metal to rust, a different repair technique is required. Remove all loose rust from the bottom of the scratch with a pocket knife, then apply rust-inhibiting paint to prevent the formation of rust in the future. Using a rubber or nylon applicator, coat the scratched area with glaze-type filler. If required, the filler can be mixed with thinner to provide a very thin paste, which is ideal for filling narrow scratches. Before the glaze filler in the scratch hardens, wrap a piece of smooth cotton cloth around the tip of a finger. Dip the cloth in thinner and then quickly wipe it along the surface of the scratch. This will ensure that the surface of the filler is slightly hollow. The scratch can now be painted over as described earlier in this section.

Repair of dents

When repairing dents, the first job is to pull the dent out until the affected area is as close as possible to its original shape. There is no point in trying to restore the original shape completely as the metal in the damaged area will have stretched on impact and cannot be restored to its original contours. It is better to bring the level of the dent up to a point which is about 1/8-inch below the level of the surrounding metal. In cases where the dent is very shallow, it is not worth trying to pull it out at all.

If the back side of the dent is accessible, it can be hammered out gently from behind using a soft-faced hammer. While doing this, hold a block of wood firmly against the opposite side of the metal to absorb the hammer blows and prevent the metal from being stretched out.

If the dent is in a section of the body which has double layers, or some other factor that makes it inaccessible from behind, a different technique is required. Drill several small holes through the metal inside the damaged area, particularly in the deeper sections. Screw long, self-tapping screws into the holes just enough for them to get a good grip in the metal. Now the dent can be pulled out by pulling on the protruding heads of the screws with locking pliers.

The next stage of repair is the removal of paint from the damaged area and from an inch or so of the surrounding metal. This is easily done with a wire brush or sanding disk in a drill motor, although it can be done just as effectively by hand with sandpaper. To complete the preparation for filling, score the surface of the bare metal with a screwdriver or the tang of a file (or drill small holes in the affected area). This will provide a very good grip for the filler material. To complete the repair, see the Section on filling and painting.

Repair of rust holes or gashes

Remove all paint from the affected area and from an inch or so of the surrounding metal using a sanding disk or wire brush mounted in a drill motor. If these are not available, a few sheets of sandpaper will do the job just as effectively. With the paint removed, you will be able to determine the severity of the corrosion and decide whether to replace the whole panel, if possible, or repair the affected area. New body panels are not as expensive as most people think and it is often quicker to install a new panel than to repair large areas of rust.

Remove all trim pieces from the affected area (except those which will act as a guide to the original shape of the damaged body, i.e. headlight shells, etc.). Then, using metal snips or a hacksaw blade, remove all loose metal and any other metal that is badly affected by rust. Hammer the edges of the hole in to create a slight depression for the filler material.

Wire brush the affected area to remove the powdery rust from the surface of the metal. If the back of the rusted area is accessible, treat it with rust-inhibiting paint.

Before filling is done, block the hole in some way. This can be done with sheet metal riveted or screwed into place, or by stuffing the hole with wire mesh.

Once the hole is blocked off, the affected area can be filled and painted (see the following sub-section on filling and painting).

Filling and painting

Many types of body fillers are available, but generally speaking, body repair kits which contain filler paste and a tube of resin hardener are best for this type of repair work. A wide, flexible plastic or nylon applicator will be necessary for imparting a smooth and contoured finish to the surface of the filler material.

Mix up a small amount of filler on a clean piece of wood or cardboard (use the hardener sparingly). Follow the manufacturer's instructions on the package, otherwise the filler will set incorrectly.

Using the applicator, apply the filler paste to the prepared area. Draw the applicator across the surface of the filler to achieve the desired contour and to level the filler surface. As soon as a contour that approximates the original one is achieved, stop working the paste. If you continue, the paste will begin to stick to the applicator. Continue to add thin layers of filler paste at 20-minute intervals until the level of the filler is just above the surrounding metal.

Once the filler has hardened, the excess can be removed with a body file. From then on, progressively finer grades of sandpaper should be used, starting with a 180-grit paper and finishing with 600-grit wet-or-dry paper. Always wrap the sandpaper around a flat rubber or wooden block, otherwise the surface of the filler will not be completely flat. During the sanding of the filler surface, the wet-or-dry paper should be periodically rinsed in water. This will ensure that a very smooth finish is produced in the final stage.

At this point, the repair area should be surrounded by a ring of bare metal, which in turn should be encircled by the finely feathered edge of good paint. Rinse the repair area with clean water until all of the dust produced by the sanding operation is gone.

Spray the entire area with a light coat of primer. This will reveal any imperfections in the surface of the filler. Repair the imperfections with fresh filler paste or glaze filler and once more smooth the surface with sandpaper. Repeat this spray-and-repair procedure until you are satisfied that the surface of the filler and the feathered edge of the paint are perfect. Rinse the area with clean water and allow it to dry completely.

The repair area is now ready for painting. Spray painting must be carried out in a warm, dry, windless and dust-free atmosphere. These conditions can be created if you have access to a large indoor work area, but if you are forced to work in the open, you will have to pick the day very carefully. If you are working indoors, dousing the floor in the work area with water will help settle the dust which would otherwise be in the air. If the repair area is confined to one body panel, mask off the surrounding panels. This will help minimize the effects of a slight mismatch in paint color. Trim pieces such as chrome strips, door handles, etc., will also need to be masked off or removed. Use masking tape and several thicknesses of newspaper for the masking operations.

Before spraying, shake the paint can thoroughly, then spray a test area until the spray painting technique is mastered. Cover the repair area with a thick coat of primer. The thickness should be built up using several thin layers of primer rather than one thick one. Using 600-grit wet-or-dry sandpaper, rub down the surface of the primer until it is

12

This photo sequence illustrates the repair of a dent and damaged paintwork. The procedure for the repair of a hole is similar. Refer to the text for more complete instructions

After removing any adjacent body trim, hammer the dent out. The damaged area should then be made slightly concave

Use coarse sandpaper or a sanding disc on a drill motor to remove all paint from the damaged area. Feather the sanded area into the edges of the surrounding paint, using progressively finer grades of sandpaper

The damaged area should be treated with rust remover prior to application of the body filler. In the case of a rust hole, all rusted sheet metal should be cut away

Carefully follow manufacturer's instructions when mixing the body filler so as to have the longest possible working time during application. Rust holes should be covered with fiberglass screen held in place with dabs of body filler prior to repair

Apply the filler with a flexible applicator in thin layers at 20 minute intervals. Use an applicator such as a wood spatula for confined areas. The filler should protrude slightly above the surrounding area

Shape the filler with a surform-type plane. Then, use water and progressively finer grades of sandpaper and a sanding block to wet-sand the area until it is smooth. Feather the edges of the repair area into the surrounding paint.

Use spray or brush applied primer to cover the entire repair area so that slight imperfections in the surface will be filled in. Prime at least one inch into the area surrounding the repair. Be careful of over-spray when using spray-type primer

Wet-sand the primer with fine (approximately 400 grade) sandpaper until the area is smooth to the touch and blended into the surrounding paint. Use filler paste on minor imperfections

After the filler paste has dried, use rubbing compound to ensure that the surface of the primer is smooth. Prior to painting, the surface should be wiped down with a tack rag or lint-free cloth soaked in lacquer thinner

Choose a dry, warm, breeze-free area in which to paint and make sure that adjacent areas are protected from over-spray. Shake the spray paint can thoroughly and apply the top coat to the repair area, building it up by applying several coats, working from the center

After allowing at least two weeks for the paint to harden, use fine rubbing compound to blend the area into the original paint. Wax can now be applied

12

very smooth. While doing this, the work area should be thoroughly rinsed with water and the wet-or-dry sandpaper periodically rinsed as well. Allow the primer to dry before spraying additional coats.

Spray on the top coat, again building up the thickness by using several thin layers of paint. Begin spraying in the center of the repair area and then, using a circular motion, work out until the whole repair area and about two inches of the surrounding original paint is covered. Remove all masking material 10 to 15 minutes after spraying on the final coat of paint. Allow the new paint at least two weeks to harden, then use a very fine rubbing compound to blend the edges of the new paint into the existing paint. Finally, apply a coat of wax.

7   Body repair — major damage

1   Major damage must be repaired by an auto body shop specifically equipped to perform body repairs. These shops have available the specialized equipment required to do the job properly.
2   If the damage is extensive, the frame must be checked for proper alignment or the vehicle's handling characteristics may be adversely affected and other components may wear at an accelerated rate.
3   Due to the fact that all of the major body components (hood, fenders, etc.) are separate and replaceable units, any seriously damaged components should be replaced rather than repaired. Sometimes these components can be found in a wrecking yard that specializes in used vehicle components (often at considerable savings over the cost of new parts).

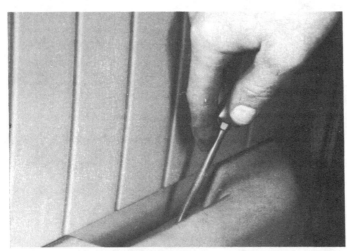

8.2 The armrest can be removed by sliding it to the rear after removing the mounting screws

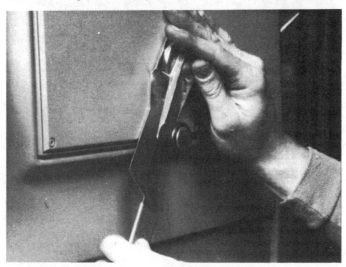

8.3   Although a small screwdriver can be used, the inexpensive tool shown here saves time when removing the window regulator handle retaining spring clip

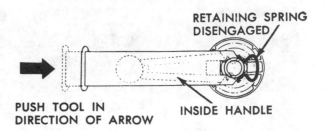

PUSH TOOL IN
DIRECTION OF ARROW

RETAINING SPRING
DISENGAGED

INSIDE HANDLE

Fig. 12.1 The special spring clip tool is shaped to fit the clip without slipping off (Sec 8)

8   Door trim panel — removal and installation

1   Remove the door handle trim frame.
2   Remove the armrest mounting screws and slide the armrest to the rear (photo). Remove the armrest.
3   Using a special tool available at your local auto parts retailer (photo) or a small screwdriver, remove the window handle retaining spring clip.
4   Carefully remove the clips retaining the trim panel to the door, using a screwdriver (photo), or special tool (available at your local auto parts retailer).
5   Release the two latches at the top of the trim panel and detach the panel.
6   Installation is the reverse of removal. If any trim panel retaining clips were broken during removal, they can be inexpensively replaced (available at your local auto parts retailer).

9   Door exterior handle and lock cylinder — removal and installation

1   Raise the window completely.
2   Remove the door trim panel as described in Section 8.
3   Pry back the water deflector enough to gain access to the exterior handle mounting hardware.
4   Pry the linkage rod out of the door handle lever with a screwdriver.
5   Remove the two nuts retaining the handle to the door sheet metal and detach the handle.
6   Installation is the reverse of removal.
7   To remove the lock cylinder detach the linkage rod from the lock lever and slide the retainer forward with pliers to disengage it from the lock unit. The lock can be removed from the outside.
8   Installation is the reverse of removal.

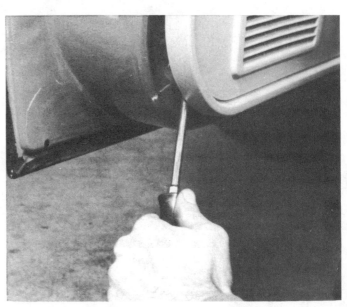

8.4 Removing the door trim panel

10 Door glass and window regulator — removal and installation

1 Remove the trim panel as described in Section 8.
2 On models equipped with power windows, disconnect the negative battery cable from the battery.
3 Use a putty knife to completely remove the water deflector.

4 To replace the window glass lower the glass until the window regulator roller is visible through the door access hole.
5 Remove the window glass retaining bolts and disengage the window regulator roller from the sash channel. Lower the glass into the door and rotate it upward to remove it.
6 To replace the window regulator raise the window completely and tape both sides of the glass to the top of the door with a single piece

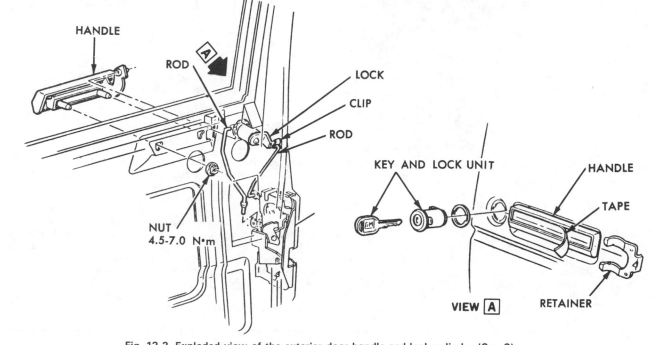

Fig. 12.2 Exploded view of the exterior door handle and lock cylinder (Sec 9)

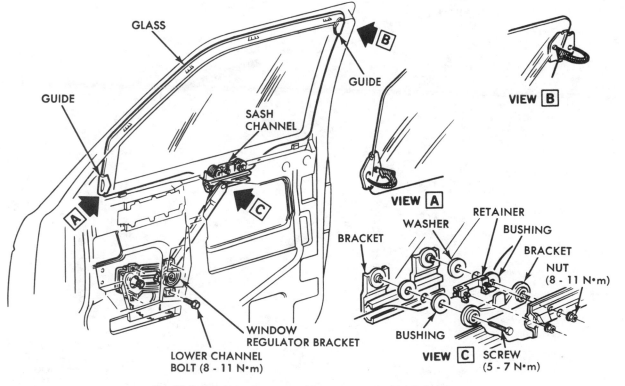

Fig. 12.3 Window glass assembly mounting details (Sec 10)

12

10.7 Location of the window regulator mounting bolts

of cloth-backed tape.

7 Remove the window regulator mounting bolts (photo).

8 On power windows maneuver the regulator as necessary and disconnect the motor wiring harness.

9 Disengage the roller or regulator lift arm from the glass run channel.

10 Remove the regulator through the door panel access hole.

11 Installation is the reverse of removal.

11 Rear cab window — removal and installation

1 Using a screwdriver from the inside of the cab, pry carefully around the weatherstrip lip, forcing the weatherstripping out. Have an assistant pull on the window assembly to remove it with the weatherstripping attached.

2 On sliding type rear windows, using a screwdriver and pliers, remove the sliding glass stopper from the channel.

3 From the channel track, remove the four screws holding the two fixed frames.

4 With the window assembly standing vertically on its lower edge, place a folded rag near the center of the window frame to protect the channel.

5 Stand on the rag with one foot and gently lift the top edge of the frame and remove the sliding windows and fixed frames.

6 Move the rag toward either end of the channel frame and remove the two non-sliding windows in the same manner.

7 To install the rear window, first transfer the weatherstripping from the non-sliding window(s) being replaced to the new window(s).

8 Apply soapy water to the contact face of the weatherstripping surrounding the glass channel and to the glass channel flange.

9 The remaining assembly steps are the reverse of those for disassembly. It is probable that the old weatherstripping has become weather-hardened and may develop water leaks. Replace the weatherstripping with new material if any such deterioration is indicated.

10 Once the rear window is assembled, apply a working cord along the weatherstripping groove, as shown in the accompanying illustration.

11 Begin the installation in the center of the lower part of the glass.

12 Attach the window assembly to the body by pulling on the cord from the inside while an assistant pushes along the weatherstripping from the outside.

13 Seat the window assembly by tapping around the circumference of the glass with your open hand.

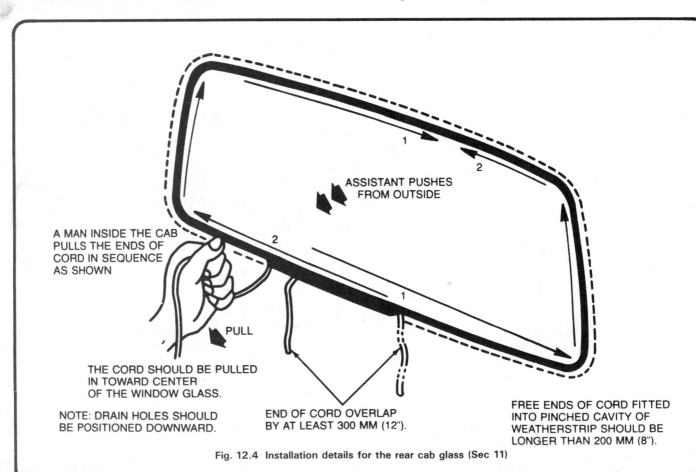

Fig. 12.4 Installation details for the rear cab glass (Sec 11)

12   Hood — removal and installation

1   Raise the hood.
2   Place protective pads along the edges of the engine compartment to prevent damage to the painted surfaces.
3   Disconnect the cable from the negative battery terminal.
4   Disconnect the underhood light electrical connector, if equipped.
5   Scribe lines on the underside of the hood, around the hood mounting bracket, so the hood can be installed in the same position (photo).
6   Apply white paint around the bracket-to-hood bolts so they can be aligned quickly and accurately during installation.
7   Remove the bracket-to-hood bolts and, along with an assistant, separate the hood from the vehicle.
9   Installation is the reverse of the removal procedure.

13   Tailgate/endgate — removal and installation

Endgate

1   Support the endgate in an open position.
2   Remove the support cables from the sides.
3   Remove the hinge pins at the base.
4   Detach the endgate from the vehicle.
5   Installation is the reverse of removal.

Tailgate

6   The tailgate can be removed simply by disconnecting the support arms and removing the hinge pins at the base of the tailgate.

14   Tailgate/endgate latch and handle — removal and installation

1   Remove the handle mounting screws from the inside.
2   Detach the linkages from the retaining clips at the handle.
3   Remove the latch mounting bolts at each side.
4   Remove the latches and linkages through each side of the tailgate/endgate.
5   Installation is the reverse of removal.

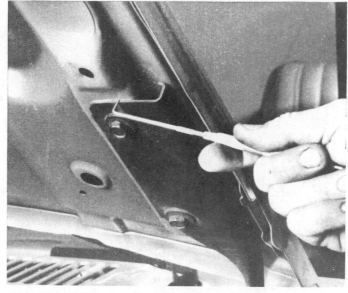

12.5   Scoring a line around the hood mounting bracket

15   Endgate glass assembly — removal and installation

1   Open the endgate. Using a grease pencil, mark the hinge location on the ouside of the glass.
2   While an assistant supports the endgate, remove the retaining clips from the strut assemblies (a scratch awl works well as a removal tool.)
3   With the assistant still supporting the endgate, remove the bolts attaching the endgate to the hinges and detach it.
4   Loosely install the hinge bolts and then align the endgate with the location marks. Tighten the bolts to the specified torque.
5   The rest of installation is the reverse of removal.

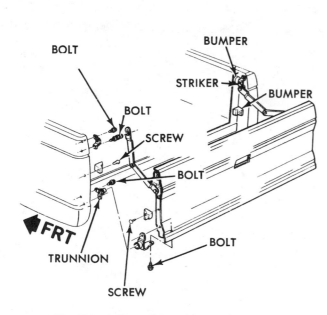

Fig. 12.5 Tailgate installation details (Sec 13)

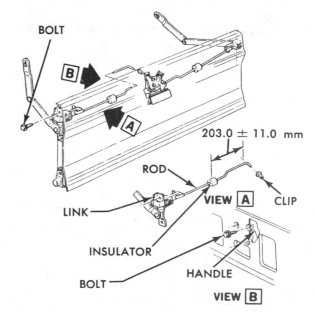

Fig. 12.6 Exploded view of the tailgate latch and linkage (Sec 14)

12

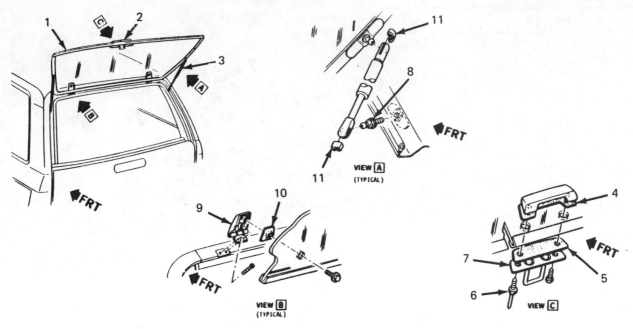

Fig. 12.7 Endgate glass assembly mounting details (Sec 15)

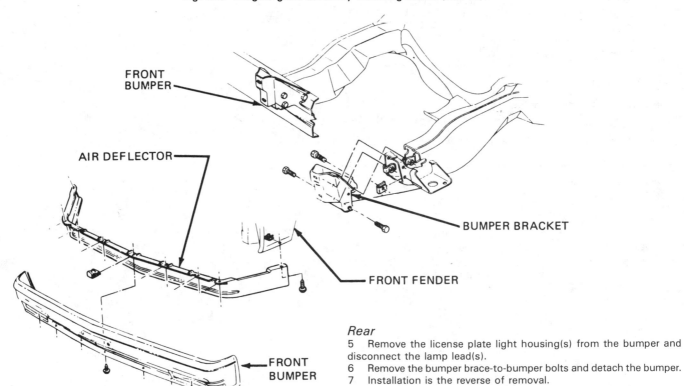

Fig. 12.8 Front bumper and air deflector mounting bolt
locations (Sec 16)

16   Bumpers — removal and installation

Front

1   Remove the right and left side parking lights from the housings
in the bumper.
2   Remove the air dam mounting bolts at the right and left side lower
fender flanges.
3   Remove the bumper brace-to-frame bolts and detach the bumper.
4   Installation is the reverse of removal.

Rear

5   Remove the license plate light housing(s) from the bumper and
disconnect the lamp lead(s).
6   Remove the bumper brace-to-bumper bolts and detach the bumper.
7   Installation is the reverse of removal.

17   Grille — removal and installation

1   Remove the headlight trim frames.
2   Remove the grille mounting screws from the front of the grille.
3   Remove the grille.
4   Installation is the reverse of removal.

18   Windshield replacement

Due to the requirements for special handling techniques, the windshield glass should be replaced by a dealer or auto glass shop.

Wiring Diagrams

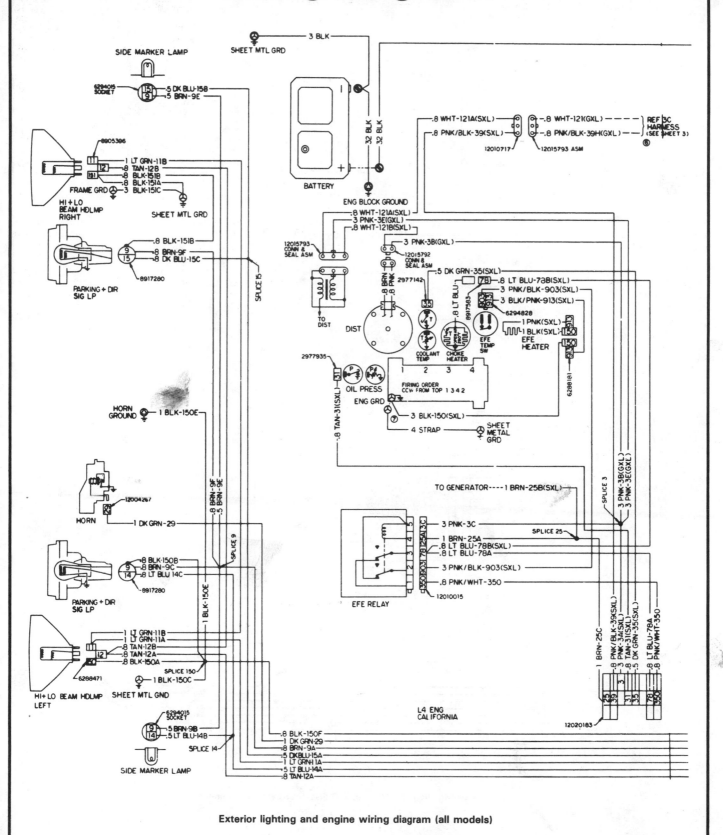

Exterior lighting and engine wiring diagram (all models)

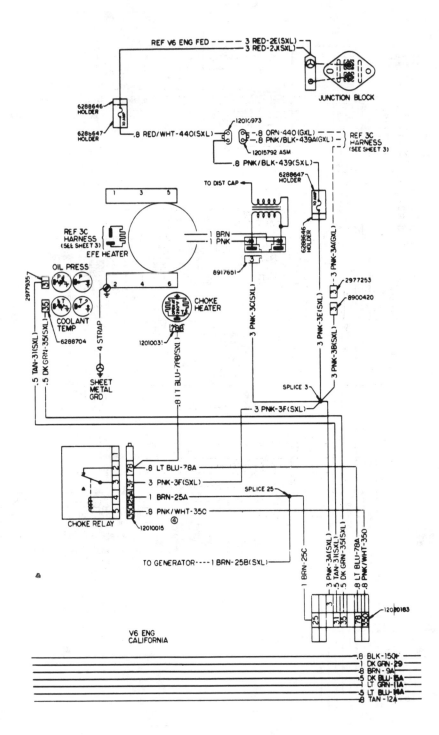

Engine wiring diagram (V6 and 2.0 liter four-cylinder engine)

247

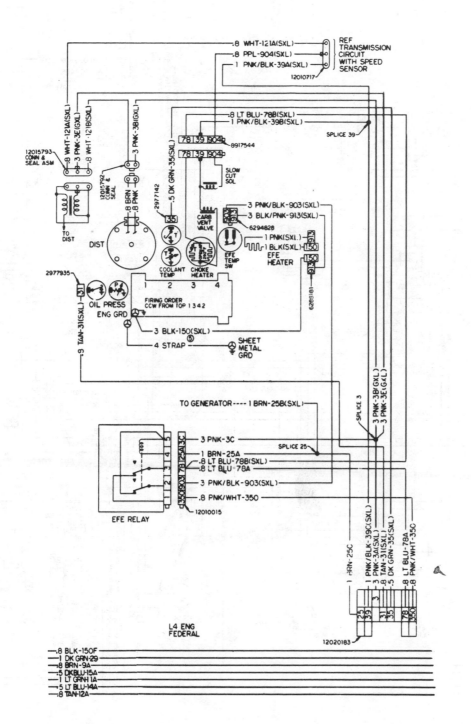

Engine wiring diagram (V6 and 2.0 liter four-cylinder engine) (continued)

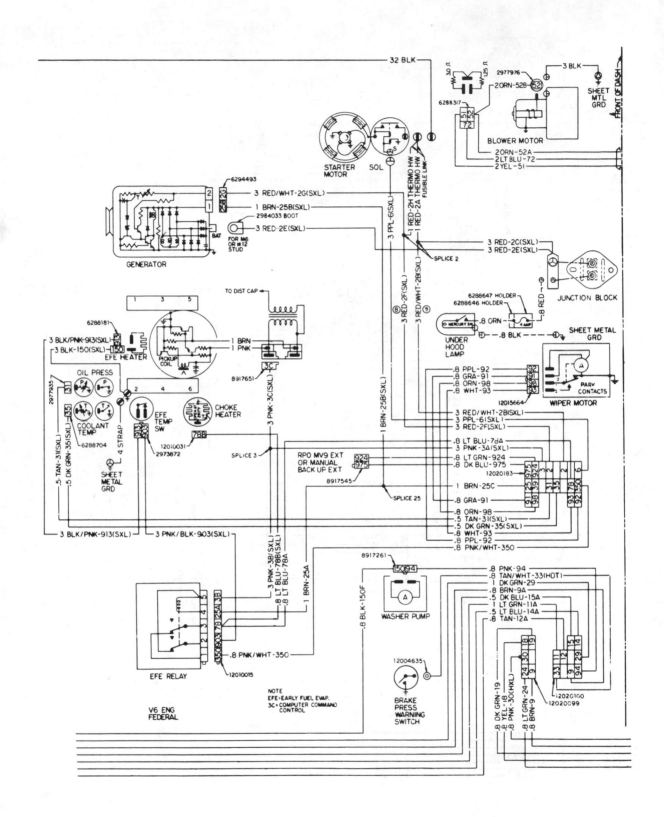

Charge circuit and engine wiring diagrams (V6 model shown — others similar)

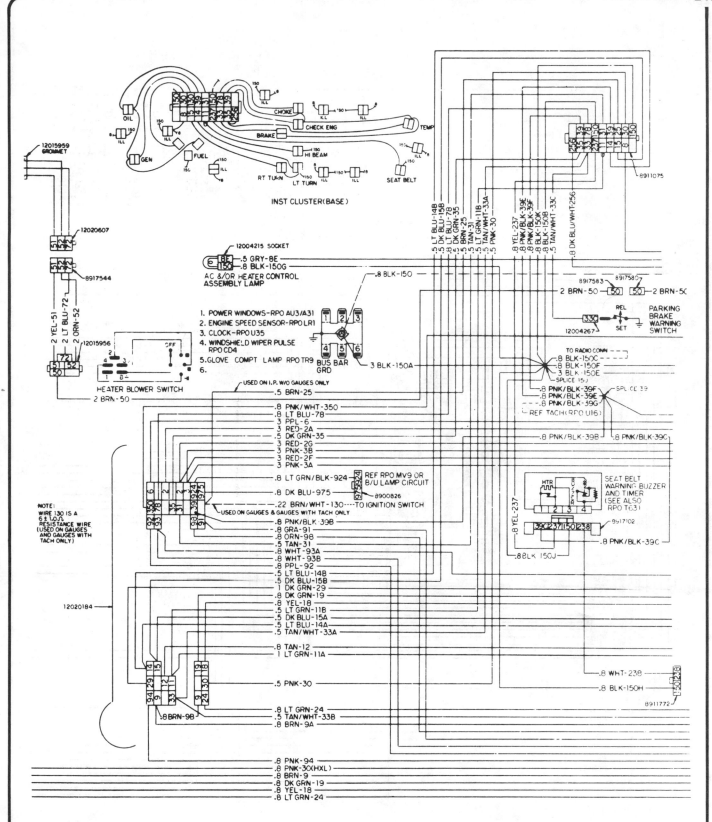

Dashboard harness and instrument cluster wiring diagram (all models)

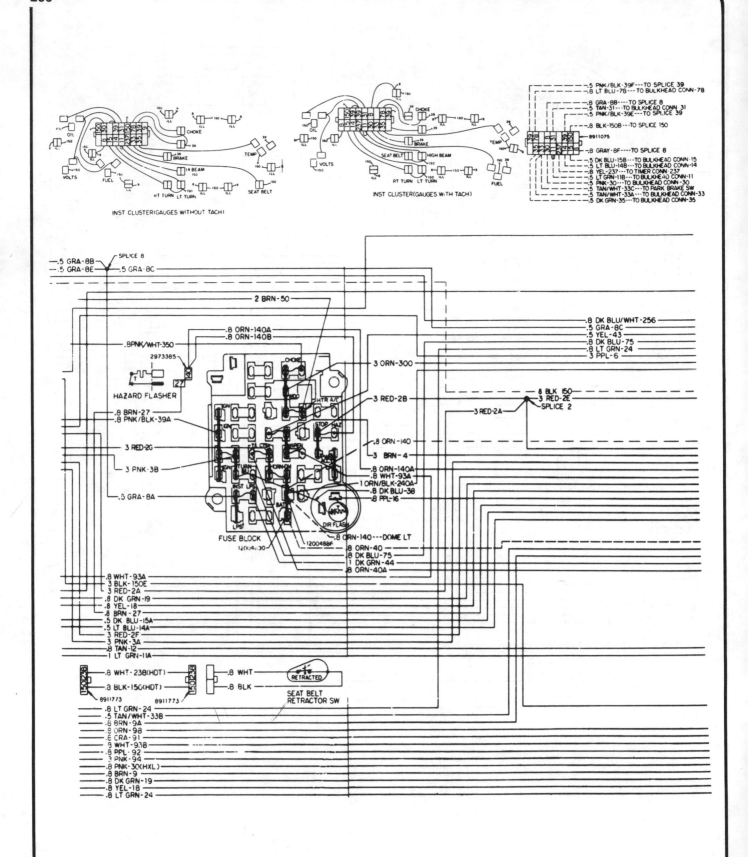

INST CLUSTER(GAUGES WITHOUT TACH)

INST CLUSTER(GAUGES WITH TACH)

Power distribution wiring diagram (all models)

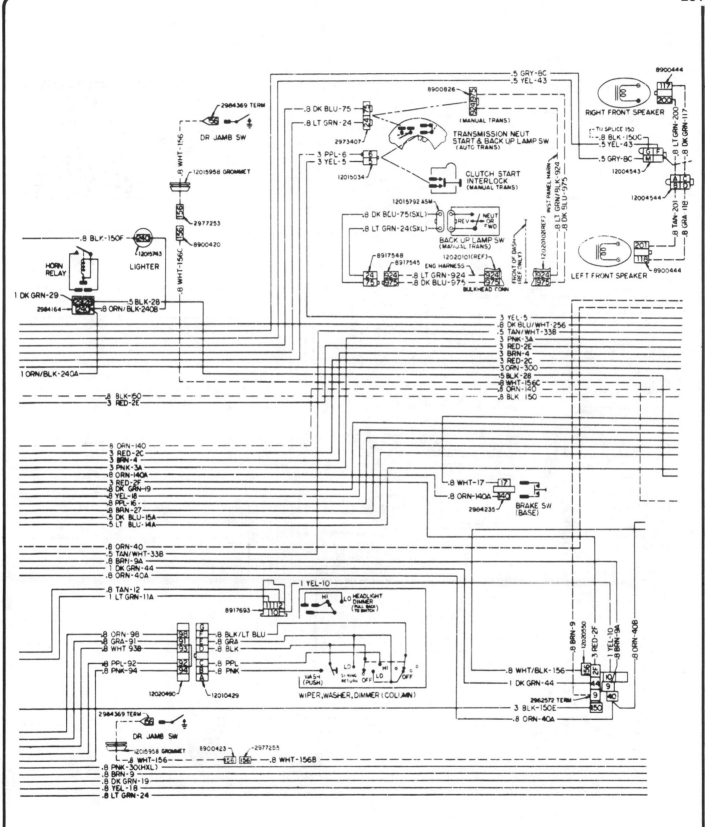

Power distribution wiring diagram — continued (all models)

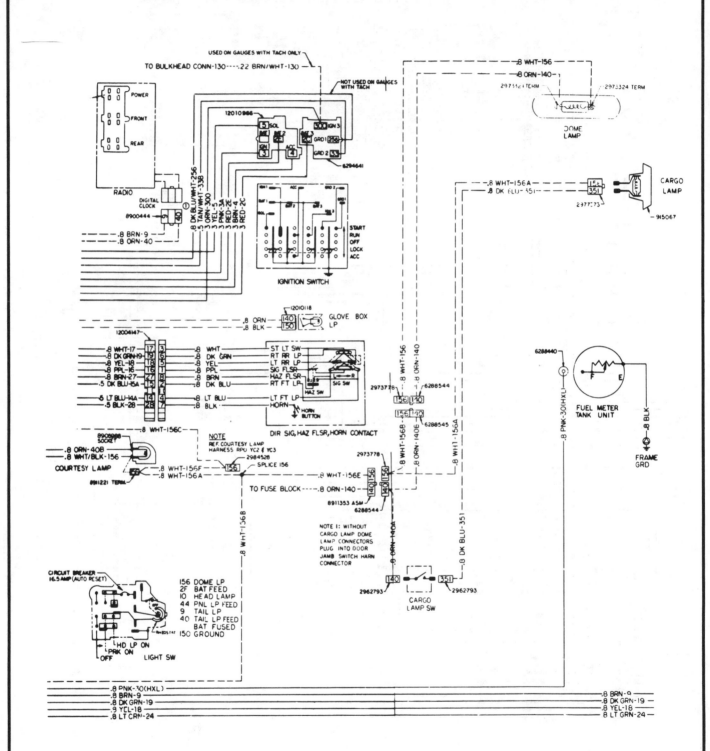

Ignition switch and signal operations wiring diagram (all models)

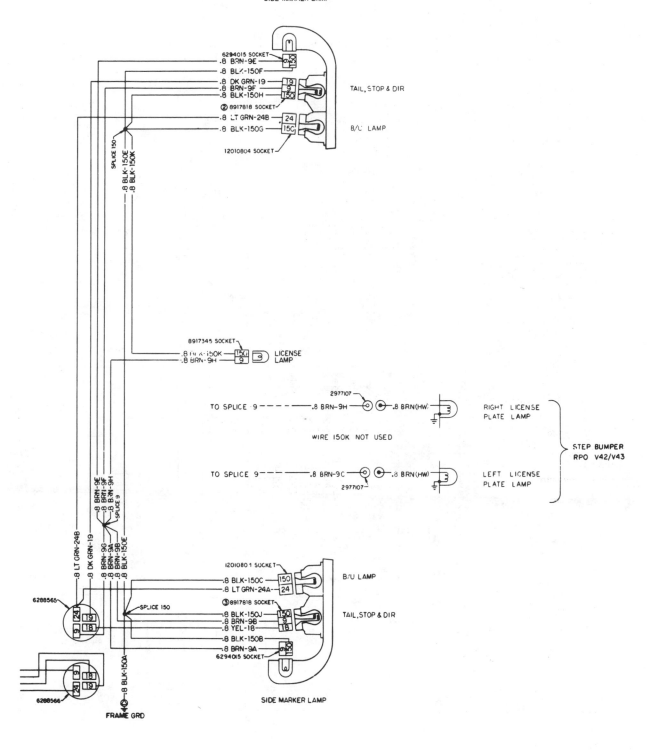

Chassis exterior wiring diagram (all models)

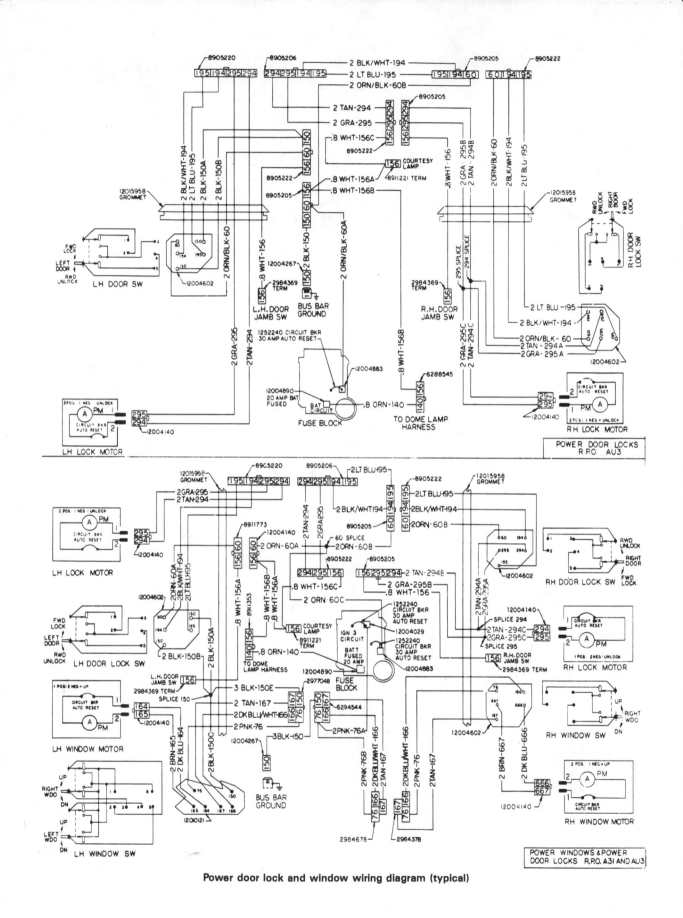

Power door lock and window wiring diagram (typical)

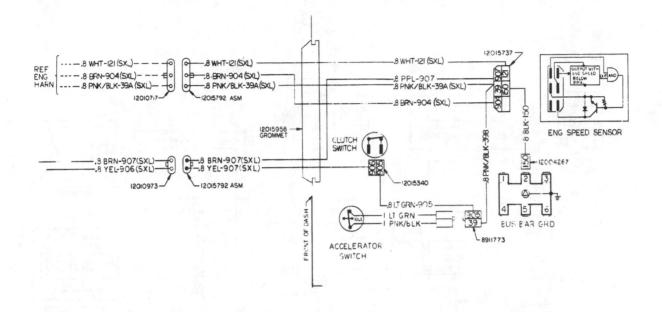

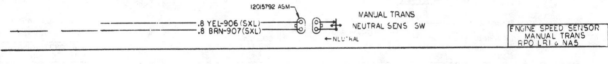

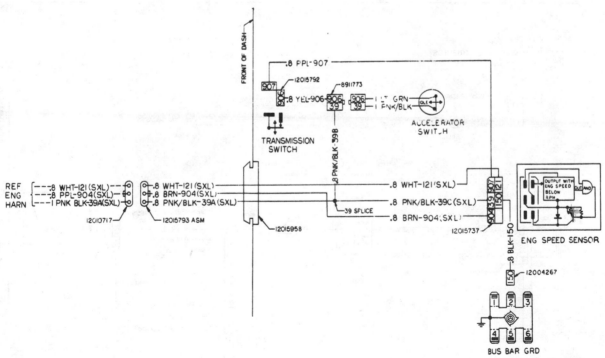

Engine speed sensor wiring diagram (typical)

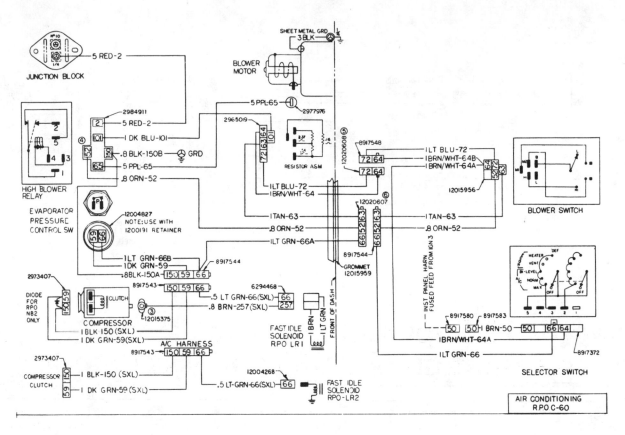

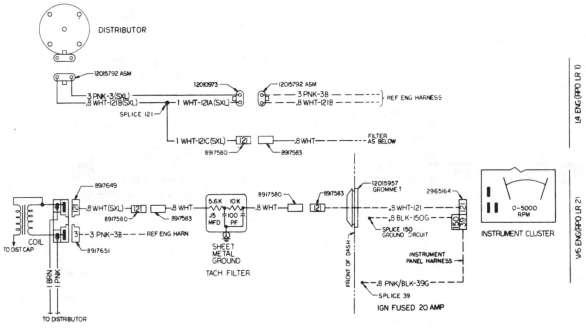

Air conditioning and tachometer wiring diagram (typical)

Chapter 13 Supplement: Revisions and information on 1985 and later models

Contents

13

1   Introduction

This Supplement contains specifications and service procedure changes that apply to Chevrolet and GMC S and T-series trucks manufactured from 1985 on. Also included is information related to previous models that was not available at the time of original publication of this manual.

Where no differences (or very minor differences) exist between 1984 models and later models, no information is given. In those instances, the original material included in Chapters 1 through 12 should be used.

Before beginning a service or repair procedure, check this Supplement for new specifications and procedure changes. Make note of the supplementary informaton and be sure to include it while following the original procedure(s) in Chapters 1 through 12.

2   Specifications

Note: *The following specifications are revisions of or supplementary to those listed at the beginning of each Chapter of this manual. The original specifications apply unless alternative information is included here.*

Tune-up and routine maintenance

Engine oil viscosity	See accompanying chart
Engine oil capacity	
2.5 liter L4 engine	3 qts (without new filter)
4.3 liter V6 engine	4 qts (without new filter)
Cooling system capacity	
2.5 liter L4 engine	11.5 qts
4.3 liter V6 engine	13.5 qts

Torque specifications	**Ft-lbs**	**Nm**
Oil pan drain plug (2.5 liter L4 engine)	25	34
Wheel lug nuts		
Two wheel drive	71	96
Four wheel drive	93	126

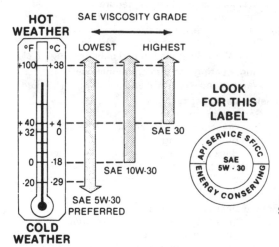

RECOMMENDED SAE VISCOSITY GRADE ENGINE OILS

For best fuel economy and cold starting, select the lowest SAE viscosity grade oil for the expected temperature range

2.5 liter four-cylinder (L4) engine

All models

General

Cylinder numbers (front-to-rear)	1–2–3–4
Firing order	1-3-4-2

Valves and related components
Valve face angle 45-degrees
Valve seat angle 46-degrees

1985 through 1987 models
Stem-to-guide clearance
  Intake .... 0.001 to 0.0027 in (0.0254 to 0.06858 mm)
  Exhaust
    Top .... 0.001 to 0.0027 in (0.0254 to 0.06858 mm)
    Bottom .... 0.002 to 0.0037 in (0.0508 to 0.09398 mm)
Valve seat width
  Intake .... 0.035 to 0.074 in (0.896 to 1.897 mm)
  Exhaust .... 0.058 to 0.097 in (1.468 to 2.468 mm)
Valve installed height (intake and exhaust) .... 1.690 in (42.893 mm)
Valve spring pressure and length (intake and exhaust)
  Valve closed .... 1.660 in (42.132 mm) at 78 to 86 lbs
  Valve open .... 1.254 in (31.827 mm) at 122 to 180 lbs

Crankshaft and connecting rods
Crankshaft endplay .... 0.0035 to 0.0085 in (0.0889 to 0.2159 mm)
Connecting rod endplay (side clearance) .... 0.006 to 0.022 in (0.1524 to 0.5588 mm)
Main bearing journal diameter .... 2.300 in (58.42 mm)
Main bearing oil clearance .... 0.0005 to 0.0022 in (0.0127 to 0.05588 mm)
Connecting rod bearing journal diameter .... 2.000 in (50.8 mm)
Connecting rod bearing oil clearance .... 0.0005 to 0.0026 in (0.0127 to 0.0660 mm)
Crankshaft journal taper/out-of-round limit .... 0.0005 in (0.0127 mm)

Engine block
Cylinder bore diameter .... 4.000 in (101.6 mm)
Out-of-round limit .... 0.0014 in (0.0356 mm)
Taper limit .... 0.0005 in (0.0127 mm)

Pistons and rings
Compression ring side clearance .... 0.0015 to 0.0030 in (0.0381 to 0.0762 mm)
Compression ring end gap
  Upper .... 0.010 to 0.022 in (0.254 to 0.559 mm)
  Lower .... 0.010 to 0.027 in (0.254 to 0.686 mm)
Oil ring end gap .... 0.015 to 0.055 in (0.381 to 1.397 mm)

Camshaft
Lobe lift (intake and exhaust) .... 0.398 in (10.109 mm)
Bearing journal diameter .... 1.869 in (47.4726 mm)
Bearing oil clearance .... 0.0007 to 0.0027 in (0.01778 to 0.069 mm)

Torque specifications	Ft-lbs	Nm
Main bearing cap bolts	70	95
Connecting rod cap nuts	32	44
Oil pan bolts	6	8
Oil pump-to-block bolts	22	30
Oil pump cover bolts	10	14
Crankshaft pulley hub bolt	160	220
Flywheel-to-crankshaft bolts	44	60
Intake manifold-to-cylinder head bolts		
1985 and 1986 (Fig. 13.10)		
Bolt B	25	34
Bolt C	37	50
Bolt D	28	38
1987 (all)	25	34
Exhaust manifold-to-cylinder head bolts		
1985	37	50
1986 and 1987 (Fig. 13.14)		
Bolt A	36	50
Bolt B	32	43
Fuel pump-to-block bolts	18	25
Timing cover-to-block bolts	7	10
Timing cover-to-oil pan bolts	7	10
Rocker arm bolts	20	27
Cylinder head bolts		
1985 and 1986	92	125
1987		
Bolt 9	30*	41*
All others	22**	30**

13

1985 through 1987 models (continued)

Rocker arm cover bolts	6	8
Camshaft thrust plate-to-block bolts	7	10

** *Plus an additional 90-degrees rotation*
** *Plus an additional 120-degrees rotation*

1988 and later models

Valves and related components

Stem-to-guide clearance	
Intake	0.0010 to 0.0025 in
Exhaust	0.0013 to 0.0030 in
Valve seat width	
Intake	0.035 to 0.075 in
Exhaust	0.058 to 0.097 in
Valve spring installed height	1.440 in
Valve spring pressure and length (intake and exhaust)	
Valve closed	1.440 in at 71 to 78 lbs
Valve open	1.440 in at 158 to 170 lbs

Crankshaft and connecting rods

Crankshaft endplay	0.0035 to 0.0085 in
Connecting rod endplay (side clearance)	0.006 to 0.002 in
Main bearing journal diameter	2.300 in
Main bearing oil clearance	0.0005 in
Connecting rod bearing oil clearance	0.0005 to 0.0026 in
Crankshaft journal taper/out-of-round limit	0.0005 in

Engine block

Cylinder bore diameter	4.000 in
Out-of-round limit	0.001 in
Taper limit	0.005 in

Pistons and rings

Compression ring side clearance	0.002 in
Compression ring end gap	
Upper	0.010 to 0.020 in
Lower	0.010 to 0.020 in
Oil ring end gap	0.020 to 0.060 in

Camshaft

Lobe lift (intake and exhaust)	0.232 in
Bearing journal diameter	1.869 in
Bearing oil clearance	0.0007 to 0.0027 in

Torque specifications	Ft-lbs	Nm
Main bearing cap bolts	65	88
Connecting rod cap nuts	30	40
Oil pan bolts	8	10
Oil pump-to-block bolts	18	25
Oil pump cover bolts	11	14
Crankshaft pulley hub bolt	25	34
Flywheel-to-crankshaft bolts		
Automatic	55	75
Manual	65	90
Intake manifold bolts	25	34
Exhaust manifold bolts		
Front and rear exhaust tubes	32	43
Center exhaust tube	36	50
Timing cover-to-block bolts	9	10
Timing cover-to-oil pan bolts	22	
Rocker arm bolts	22	30
Cylinder head bolts		
Bolt 9	18*	25*
All others	26*	35*
Rocker arm cover bolts	6	8
Camshaft thrust plate-to-block bolts	9	10

* *Plus an additional 90-degree rotation*

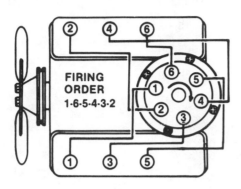

**4.3L V6 ENGINE CYLINDER NUMBERS AND
DISTRIBUTOR SPARK PLUG WIRE
TERMINAL LOCATIONS**

4.3 liter V6 engine

General

Cylinder numbers (front-to-rear)	
Left (driver's) side	1–3–5
Right side	2–4–6
Firing order	1-6-5-4-3-2
Bore and stroke	4.000 x 3.480 in
Oil pressure	10 psi at 500 rpm; 30 to 55 psi at 2000 rpm
Compression pressure	150 psi
Maximum variation between cylinders	20 psi

Engine block

Cylinder bore diameter	3.9995 to 4.0025 in
Taper limit	0.001 in
Out-of-round limit	0.002 in

Pistons and rings

Piston-to-cylinder bore clearance	
Standard	0.0007 to 0.0017 in
Service limit	0.0027 in
Piston ring-to-groove side clearance	
Standard	
Compression rings	0.0012 to 0.0032 in
Oil control ring	0.002 to 0.007 in
Service limit	
Compression rings	0.0033 in
Oil control ring	0.008 in
Piston ring end gap	
Standard	
Top compression ring	0.010 to 0.020 in
Second compression ring	0.010 to 0.025 in
Oil control ring	0.015 to 0.055 in
Service limit	
Top compression ring	0.030 in
Second compression ring	0.035 in
Oil control ring	0.065 in
Piston pin	
Diameter	0.9270 to 0.9273 in
Pin-to-piston clearance limit	0.001 in
Pin-to-rod interference fit	0.0008 to 0.0016 in

Crankshaft

Main journal	
Diameter	
No. 1 journal	2.4484 to 2.4493 in
No. 2 and 3 journals	2.4481 to 2.4490 in
No. 4 journal	2.4479 to 2.4488 in
Taper limit	0.001 in
Out-of-round limit	0.001 in

13

Main bearing oil clearance
  Standard
    No. 1 journal .... 0.0008 to 0.0020 in
    No. 2 and 3 journals .... 0.0011 to 0.0023 in
    No. 4 journal .... 0.0017 to 0.0032 in
  Service limit
    No. 1 journal .... 0.001 to 0.0015 in
    No. 2 and 3 journals .... 0.001 to 0.0025 in
    No. 4 journal .... 0.0025 to 0.0035 in
Connecting rod journal
  Diameter .... 2.2487 to 2.2497 in
  Taper limit .... 0.001 in
  Out-of-round limit .... 0.001 in
Connecting rod bearing oil clearance
  Standard .... 0.0013 to 0.0035 in
  Service limit .... 0.0035 in
Connecting rod end play (side clearance) .... 0.006 to 0.014 in
Crankshaft end play .... 0.002 to 0.006 in

Cylinder heads and valve train
Head warpage limit .... 0.003 in per 6 in span/0.006 in overall
Valve seat angle..................................... 46°
Valve seat width
  .... 1/32 to 1/16 (0.0313 to 0.0625) in
  Exhaust .... 1/16 to 3/32 (0.0625 to 0.0938) in
Valve seat runout limit .... 0.002 in
Valve face angle..................................... 45°
Minimum valve margin width .... 1/32 in
Valve stem-to-guide clearance
  Standard .... 0.0010 to 0.0027 in
  Service limit
    Intake .... 0.0037 in
    Exhaust .... 0.0047 in
Valve spring free length .... 2.030 in
Valve spring damper (inner spring) free length .... 1.860 in
Valve spring installed height
  Intake .... 1-23/32 (1.7188) in
  Exhaust .... 1-19/32 (1.5938) in
Valve spring pressure and length (intake and exhaust)
  Closed .... 76 to 84 lbs. at 1.70 in
  Open .... 194 to 206 lbs. at 1.25 in

Camshaft
Bearing journal
  Diameter....................................... 1.8682 to 1.8692 in
  Out-of-round limit .... 0.001 in
Lobe lift
  Intake .... 0.357 in
  Exhaust .... 0.390 in
End play .... 0.004 to 0.012 in

Torque specifications   Ft-lbs (unless otherwise indicated)
Rocker arm cover bolts................................ 90 in-lbs
Intake manifold bolts 36
Exhaust manifold bolts
  Center bolts 26
  All others 20
Cylinder head bolts*................................. 65
Timing chain cover bolts.............................. 120 in-lbs
Camshaft sprocket bolts.............................. 21
Vibration damper bolt 70
Oil pan
  Bolts/studs .... 100 in-lbs
  Nuts .... 200 in-lbs
Rear main oil seal housing bolts .... 135 in-lbs
Flywheel bolts 65
Driveplate bolts 55
Main bearing cap bolts 80
Connecting rod cap nuts............................. 45
Oil pump bolts .... 100 in-lbs

Use Permatex number 2 on the bolt threads

Cooling, heating and air conditioning systems

Torque specifications	Ft-lbs	Nm
Water pump mounting bolts	22	30

Fuel and exhaust systems

Rochester 2SE and E2SE carburetors (1985 models)

Float adjustment
  Carburetor numbers . . . . 1/8-inch (3.3 mm)
    17085356
    17085358
    17085368
  Carburetor numbers . . . . 5/32-inch (3.6 mm)
    17085348
    17085350
    17085352
    17085354
    17085360
    17085362
    17085364
    17085366
    17085372
    17085374
    17085452
    17085453
    17085458
  Carburetor numbers . . . . 9/32-inch (7.0 mm)
    17085357
    17085359
    17085369
    17085371
  Carburetor numbers . . . . 11/32-inch (8.4 mm)
    17085351
    17085355
    17085363
    17085367
Air valve spring adjustment
  Carburetor numbers 1/2-turn
    17085452
    17085453
    17085458
  Carburetor numbers 3/4-turn
    17085372
    17085374
  All others . . . . 1 turn
Fast idle cam (choke rod) adjustment
  Carburetor numbers . . . . 28°
    17085452
    17085453
    17085458
  All others . . . . 22°
Primary vacuum break adjustment
  Carburetor numbers . . . . 30°
    17085352
    17085354
    17085355
    17085364
    17085366
    17085367
  Carburetor numbers . . . . 32°
    17085348
    17085350
    17085357
    17085360
    17085362
    17085363
    17085372
    17085374
  All others . . . . 25°
Secondary vacuum break adjustment
  Carburetor numbers . . . . 34°
    17085352
    17085354
    17085355
    17085364
    17085366
    17085367
  Carburetor numbers . . . . 35°
    17085452
    17085453
    17085458

13

Secondary vacuum brake adjustment (continued)

Carburetor numbers	36°
17085348	
17085350	
17085351	
17085360	
17085362	
17085363	
17085372	
17085374	
All others	30°

Unloader adjustment

Carburetor numbers	45°
17085452	
17085453	
17085458	
Carburetor numbers	30°
17085356	
17085357	
17085358	
17085359	
17085368	
17085369	
17085370	
17085371	
All others	40°

Torque specifications	Ft-lbs *(unless otherwise indicated)*	Nm
TBI fuel meter cover screws	28 in-lbs	3.16
TBI IAC valve	13	18
TBI mounting bolts	10 to 15	14 to 20
TBI mounting stud	3 to 6	4 to 8
TBI mounting nut	10 to 15	14 to 20
TBI fuel line fittings	17	23

Suspension and steering systems

Torque specifications	Ft-lbs	Nm
Tie-rod stud nuts	35	47
Adjuster tube clamp bolts/nuts	14	19
Relay rod ball stud-to-idler arm nut		
2WD	35	47
4WD	60	82
Relay rod ball stud-to-Pitman arm nut		
2WD	35	47
4WD	60	82
Inner tie-rod ball stud-to-relay rod nut		
2WD	35	47
4WD	60	82
Steering shock absorber ball stud nut	45	62
Power steering pump mounting bolts		
Four-cylinder engine	20	27
V6 engines	36	50
Power steering pump rear brace nut		
Four-cylinder engine	18.5	25
V6 engines	33	45

3   Special maintenance techniques

Some parts on later model vehicles have an electrostatic discharge sensitive sticker applied to them (Fig. 13.1). When installing or servicing any parts with this sticker, the following guidelines should be followed:

Avoid touching the electrical terminals of the part
Always ground the package to a known good ground on the vehicle before removing the part from the package
Always touch a known good ground before handling the part

4   Tune-up and routine maintenance

Drivebelt check and adjustment

1   As of the 1987 model year, a single serpentine drivebelt is used in place of multiple V-belts. These belts require no adjustment, as it

NOTICE

CONTENTS SENSITIVE
TO
STATIC ELECTRICITY

HANDLE IN ACCORDANCE WITH STATIC CONTROL
PROCEDURES GM9107P AND GM9108P,
OR GM DIVISIONAL SERVICE MANUALS.

Fig. 13.1   Some late model electrical components have this label on the package or part, indicating that both you and the part should be grounded before handling (Sec 3)

is taken care of by a spring-loaded tensioner pulley. The belt should be replaced when the wear indicator on the tensioner reaches its maximum travel. Inspect the belt for missing ribs, fraying and other signs of abnormal wear.

2   To replace the belt, insert a 1/2-inch breaker bar into the tensioner pulley, then rotate the tensioner counterclockwise to release belt tension.

3   Remove the drivebelt from the pulleys, noting how it is routed in the accompanying illustrations.

4   Install the belt starting with the bottom pulleys, then release the tension on the tensioner pulley to allow final installation.

Fuel filter replacement

5   The fuel filter on four-cylinder models is located at the left rear corner of the cylinder head. On V6 engine equipped vehicles it is located on the front of the engine, to the left of the water pump.

6   Relieve the fuel system pressure (refer to Section 9 in this Supplement).

7   Using a backup wrench on the fuel filter canister, disconnect the fuel lines from each side of the filter. Inspect the 0-rings on each fuel line and replace them if necessary.

8   Loosen the fuel filter clamp bolt and remove the filter.

9   Position the new filter in the clamp, tighten the clamp bolt and connect the fuel lines.

10 Pressurize the fuel system by turning the ignition key on for at least two seconds, then check the fittings for leaks.

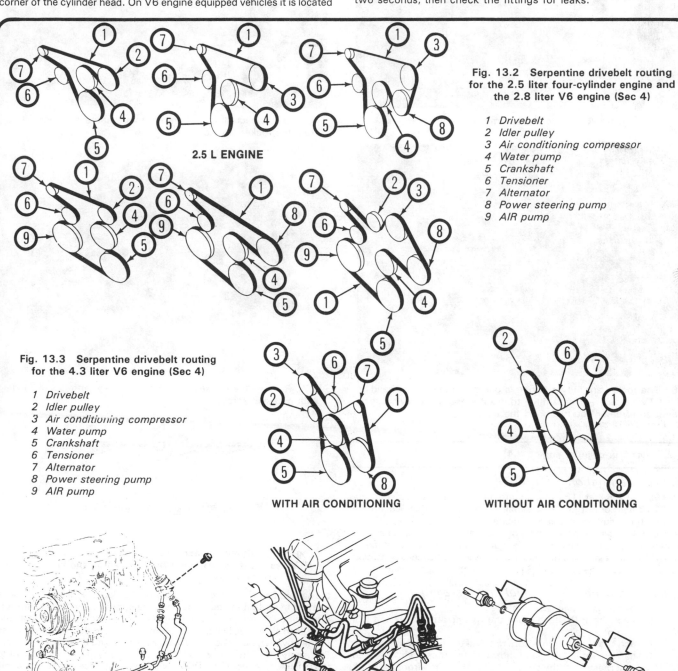

2.5 L ENGINE

Fig. 13.2   Serpentine drivebelt routing for the 2.5 liter four-cylinder engine and the 2.8 liter V6 engine (Sec 4)

1 Drivebelt
2 Idler pulley
3 Air conditioning compressor
4 Water pump
5 Crankshaft
6 Tensioner
7 Alternator
8 Power steering pump
9 AIR pump

Fig. 13.3   Serpentine drivebelt routing for the 4.3 liter V6 engine (Sec 4)

1 Drivebelt
2 Idler pulley
3 Air conditioning compressor
4 Water pump
5 Crankshaft
6 Tensioner
7 Alternator
8 Power steering pump
9 AIR pump

WITH AIR CONDITIONING

WITHOUT AIR CONDITIONING

Fig. 13.4   Fuel filter location — 2.5 liter four-cylinder engine (Sec 4)

Fig. 13.5   Fuel filter location — V6 engine (Sec 4)

Fig. 13.6   The 0-rings (arrows) must be in good condition or fuel leaks will result when the line fittings are retightened (Sec 4)

13

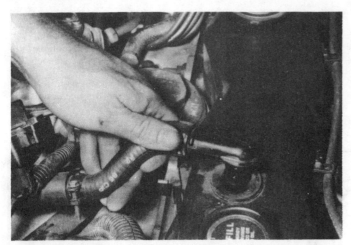

5.2   Pull the PCV valve hose from the rocker arm cover

5.3   Disconnect all four spark plug wire harness retainer clips from the rocker arm cover

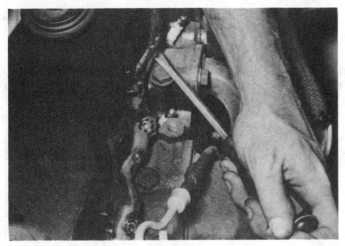

5.6   The rocker arm cover flange is glued to the cylinder head with RTV sealant — if you have to pry it loose, try to avoid using too much force or you will bend the flange

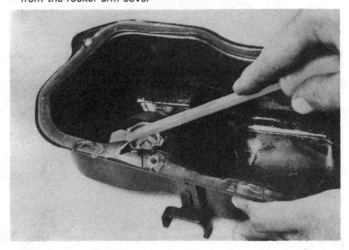

5.7   Remove the old sealant from the rocker arm cover flange with a gasket scraper

5   2.5 liter four-cylinder engine (L4)

General information

In 1985, a 2.5 liter (151 cubic inch) engine was introduced in the S-10/S-15 light duty truck. The repair procedures in this Section are based on the assumption that the engine is still installed in the vehicle. Therefore, if this information is being used during a complete engine overhaul — with the engine already out of the vehicle and on a stand — many of the steps included here will not apply. Specifications pertaining to this engine can be found in Section 2 of this Supplement.

Rocker arm cover — removal and installation

1   Remove the air cleaner assembly.
2   Disconnect the PCV hose from the rocker arm cover and TBI assembly (photo).
3   Label each spark plug wire before removal to ensure correct installation. Unsnap the retaining clips (photo) on the rocker arm cover to free the wire harness from the cover. Unplug the wires from the spark plugs and from the distributor terminals and set the wire harness aside.
4   Loosen the throttle body mounting nut and bolts to provide clearance for removal of the EGR valve, then remove the EGR valve (refer to Section 9 of this Supplement).
5   Remove the rocker arm cover bolts.
6   Remove the rocker arm cover. If the cover is stuck to the cylinder head, use a soft-face hammer or a block of wood and a hammer to dislodge it. If the cover still won't come loose, pry on it carefully at several points until the sealant is broken loose (photo), but do not distort

Fig. 13.7   Apply a continuous 3/16-inch diameter bead of RTV sealant (arrow) to the cylinder head as shown (Sec 5)

the sealing flange surface. Gently pry on the flange at several locations to avoid bending it. **Note:** *If you bend the flange, set it on a flat surface after removal and tap it with a soft-face hammer until it's flat again.*
7   Clean all dirt, oil and old sealant material from the sealing surfaces of the cover and cylinder head with a scraper and degreaser (photo).
8   Apply a continuous 3/16-inch wide bead of RTV-type sealant to the cylinder head-to-rocker arm cover mating surface. Be sure to apply the sealant inboard of the bolt holes.
9   Place the rocker arm cover on the cylinder head while the sealant is still wet and install the mounting bolts. Tighten the bolts a little at a time to the specified torque.
10   Install the EGR valve and tighten the bolts to the specified torque.
11   Tighten the throttle body mounting nut and bolts to the specified torque.
12   Attach the spark plug wire boots to the spark plugs and the distributor terminals in the same order in which they were removed. Snap

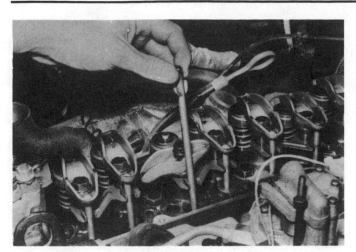

5.16   Loosen the rocker arm bolt, rotate the rocker arm, then lift out the pushrod

5.18   Make sure the pushrod guides are kept in order too, if they are removed

the wire harness retaining clips back onto the rocker arm cover.
13 Install the PCV hose between the rocker arm cover and the throttle body assembly.
14 Install the air cleaner assembly. **Note:** *Make sure that the manifold absolute pressure (MAP) sensor vacuum line and the Thermac motor temperature sensor line are properly installed.*

Valve train components — replacement (cylinder head in place)

15 Remove the rocker arm cover (refer to Steps 1 – 7 in this Section).
16 If only a pushrod is to be replaced, loosen the rocker arm bolt enough to allow the rocker arm to be rotated to the side so that it will clear the pushrod. Pull the pushrod out of the hole in the cylinder head (photo).
17 If a valve spring or valve guide oil seal is to be replaced, remove the rocker bolt and pivot and lift off the rocker arm. Then remove the spark plug from the affected cylinder.
18 If all the pushrods and rocker arms are removed , they must be kept in the proper order for reinstallation. The best way to organize them is to store them in clearly labelled boxes. **Note:** *Do not mix up the pushrod guides (photo). They must be kept in order for proper re-installation.*
19 There are two ways to hold the valve in place while the valve spring is removed. If you have access to compressed air, install an air hose adapter in the spark plug hole. These adapters are sold by most auto parts stores. Most quality compression gauges have a lower extension hose that will serve the same purpose. One end of the extension screws into the spark plug hole and the other end has a quick-connect air fitting that attaches to the compression gauge. This quick-connect fitting can be attached to a compressor air hose. Bring the piston to top dead center on the compression stroke to ensure that both valves are closed before applying air pressure. Once the cylinder is pressurized, the valves will remain closed while the spring is removed.
20 If you don't have access to compressed air, bring the piston of the appropriate cylinder to slightly before top dead center on the compression stroke. Feed a long piece of 1/4-inch rope or cord into the cylinder through the spark plug hole until it fills the combustion chamber. Be sure to leave the end of the rope hanging out of the spark plug hole so that it can be removed when the procedure is completed.
21 Turn the crankshaft with a wrench in the normal direction of rotation until a slight resistance is felt. This will be the rope compressing between the piston top and the valves, effectively holding the valves closed while the valve spring is removed. **Caution:** *Make sure before inserting the rope that the piston is coming up on the compression stroke with both valves closed. If the rope is inserted on the exhaust stroke when the exhaust valve is open to expel the burned gas and the intake valve is starting to open to allow a fresh charge into the engine, the valves can easily be bent when the piston is brought up to compress the rope.*
22 Install a valve spring compressor over the valve spring.
23 Remove the keeper halves, then release pressure on the tool. If, after the spring is compressed, the valve spring retainer will not release

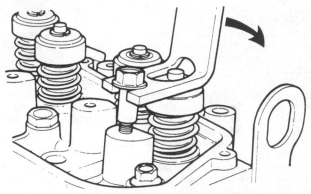

Fig. 13.8   A lever-type valve spring compressor is used to compress the spring and remove the keepers to replace seals or springs while the head is installed (Sec 5)

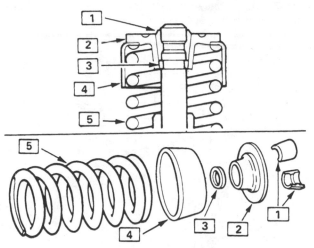

Fig. 13.9   Typical valve components — exploded view (Sec 5)

1 Keepers	4 Shield
2 Retainer	5 Spring
3 O-ring	

from the keepers, squirt the retainer with penetrating oil and tap the top of the spring compressor lightly with a hammer.
24 Remove the valve spring compressor, retainer, spring, damper (inner spring) and valve stem O-ring seal. Note the relationship between the components before removing them.

13

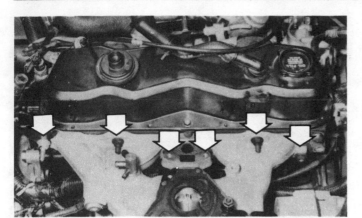

5.44   Location of the intake manifold mounting bolts

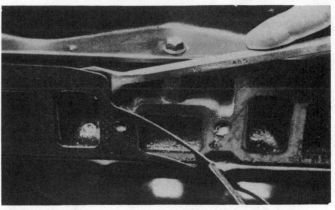

5.45   Remove the old intake manifold gasket with a scraper —
don't leave any material on the mating surface

25 Install a new seal on the valve guide (not all engines are equipped
with valve guide seals). Using a hammer and a deep socket, gently
tap the seal into place until it is completely seated on the guide. Do
not twist or cock the seal during installation or it will not seal properly
on the valve stem.

26 Set the valve springs, shield and retainer in place. Compress the
springs and carefully install the O-ring oil seal in the lower groove of
the valve stem. Make sure the seal is not twisted — it must lie perfectly
flat in the groove.

27 Position the keepers in the upper groove, then slowly release the
compressor and make sure the keepers seat properly. Apply a small
dab of grease to each keeper to hold it in place if necessary.

28 Once the springs, retainer and keepers are installed, the valve stem
O-ring seal must be checked to make sure it does not leak. This procedure requires a vacuum pump and special adapter (GM tool no.
J-23994), so it may be a good idea to have it done by a dealer service
department, repair shop or automotive machine shop. The adapter is
positioned on the valve retainer and vacuum is applied with the hand
pump. If the vacuum cannot be maintained, the seal is leaking and must
be checked/replaced before the engine is run.

29 Coat the bearing surfaces of the rocker arm and pivot with a moly-
base grease or engine assembly lube.

30 Install the rocker arm. The engine valve mechanism requires no
special valve lash adjustment. Simply tighten the rocker arm bolt to
the specified torque.

Intake manifold — removal and installation

31 Disconnect the cable from the negative battery terminal.

32 Remove the air cleaner assembly. Tag each hose with a piece of
numbered or colored tape as it is disconnected to simplify installation.

33 Relieve the fuel pressure (refer to Section 9 of this Supplement).

34 Drain the cooling system (Chapter 1).

35 Remove the PCV valve and hose at the throttle body housing.

36 Label and disconnect the fuel line fittings at the throttle body.

37 Label and disconnect the vacuum lines and electrical leads from
the fuel injection assembly and intake manifold.

38 Disconnect the throttle cable from the throttle linkage by prying
the C-clip off with a screwdriver. Remove the linkage rod by popping
it off with a screwdriver. Carefully note how the linkage rod is installed
before removing it.

39 If your vehicle is equipped with an automatic transmission, disconnect and remove the downshift linkage. Note how the components
are installed.

40 If your vehicle is equipped with a cruise control, disconnect the
linkage.

41 Disconnect the heater hose and water pump bypass hose from the
intake manifold.

42 Disconnect the alternator by removing the belt tensioning nut and
bolt. Remove the alternator bracket.

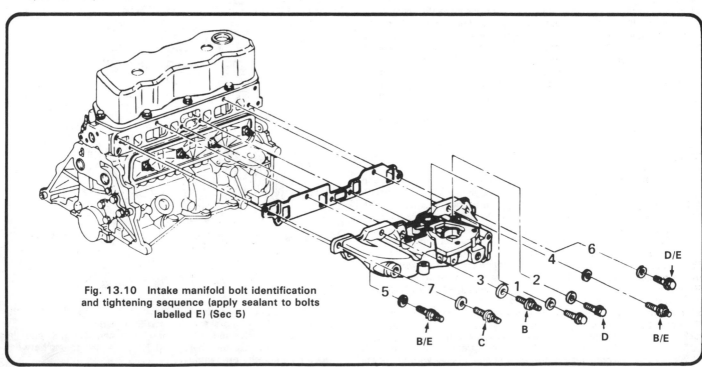

Fig. 13.10 Intake manifold bolt identification
and tightening sequence (apply sealant to bolts
labelled E) (Sec 5)

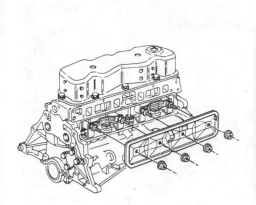

Fig. 13.11 Remove the four pushrod cover nuts, then carefully pry off the cover (Sec 5)

5.67 Don't forget to install new rubber sealing washers around the pushrod cover mounting studs or oil will leak past the studs

5.68 Install the pushrod cover while the sealant is still wet — be sure that the semi-circular cutout (arrow) is facing down

43 Disconnect the coil mounting nuts, coil lead and coil wire, then remove the coil.

44 Remove the intake manifold mounting bolts and separate the manifold from the cylinder head (photo). Do not pry between the manifold and the head as damage to the gasket sealing surfaces may result.

45 Remove the intake manifold gasket with a gasket scraper (photo).

46 If the intake manifold itself is being replaced, transfer all components still attached to the old manifold to the new one.

47 Clean the cylinder head and manifold gasket surfaces. All gasket material and sealing compound must be removed prior to installation.

48 Place a new intake manifold gasket on the manifold, hold the manifold in position against the cylinder head and install the mounting bolts finger tight.

49 Tighten the mounting bolts a little at a time in the proper sequence to the specified torque.

50 Install the alternator bracket. Install the alternator belt tension adjustment nut and bolt and adjust the belt (see Section 4 of this Supplement).

51 Reposition the TBI linkage rod and reattach the throttle cable.

52 Reattach the heater hose fitting to the underside of the intake manifold.

53 Reconnect the fuel feed and return lines.

54 Reattach the PCV valve, elbow and hose between the rocker arm cover and the TBI housing.

55 Reattach the remaining vacuum lines and electrical connectors.

56 Install the coil assembly. Reconnect the coil lead and coil wire.

57 Install the air cleaner.

58 Fill the radiator with coolant, start the engine and check for leaks.

Pushrod cover — removal and installation

59 Remove the air cleaner assembly. Tag each hose with a piece of numbered or colored tape as it is disconnected to ensure correct installation.

60 Remove the intake manifold (as previously described in this Section).

61 Remove the wire harness from the pushrod cover.

62 Disconnect the fuel lines and clips at the pushrod cover.

63 Loosen the four pushrod cover nuts.

64 Remove the pushrod cover by carefully prying it off with a screwdriver. **Caution:** *Careless prying may damage the sealing surface of the cover. If you bend the cover during removal, place it on a flat surface and straighten it with a soft-face hammer.*

65 Clean the sealing surfaces on the pushrod cover and cylinder block with a gasket scraper and solvent.

66 Apply a continuous 3/16-inch diameter bead of RTV-type sealant to the sealing surface of the pushrod cover.

67 Install new rubber pushrod cover mounting stud washers (photo).

68 Install the cover while the sealant is still wet. Make sure that the semi-circular cutout in the edge of the pushrod cover is facing down (photo).

69 Tighten the retaining nuts gradually until they're snug, then tighten

them to the specified torque.

70 Secure the fuel lines and clips to the pushrod cover.

71 Reattach the wire harness to the pushrod cover.

72 Install the intake manifold.

73 Install the air cleaner.

Hydraulic lifters — removal, inspection and installation

74 A noisy valve lifter can be isolated when the engine is idling. Place a length of hose or tubing near the position of each valve while listening at the other end of the tube. Or remove the rocker arm cover and, with the engine idling, place a finger on each of the valve spring retainers, one at a time. If a valve lifter is defective, it will be evident from the shock felt at the retainer as the valve seats.

75 The most likely cause of a noisy valve lifter is a piece of dirt trapped between the plunger and the lifter body.

76 Remove the rocker arm cover (as previously outlined in this Section).

77 Loosen both rocker arm bolts at the cylinder with the noisy lifter and rotate the rocker arms away from the pushrods. Remove the pushrod guide plates and pushrods.

78 Remove the intake manifold (following steps 31 through 45 in this Section).

79 Remove the pushrod cover.

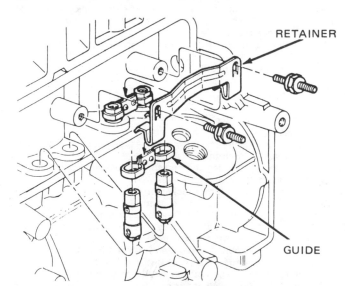

RETAINER

GUIDE

Fig. 13.12 The lifter guides are held in place by the retainer (Sec 5)

13

5.80   Remove the lifter guide — if you are removing more than one guide, keep them in order to ensure that they are installed in their original locations

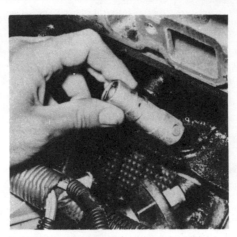

5.81   On newer engines which haven't become sticky with sludge and varnish, the lifters can usually be removed without any special tools

5.82   If you are removing more than one lifter, keep them in order with a clearly labelled box

80 Remove the lifter guide retainer by unscrewing the pushrod cover studs. Remove the lifter guide (photo).
81 There are several ways to extract a lifter from its bore. A special hydraulic lifter removal tool is available, but isn't absolutely necessary. On newer engines without a lot of varnish buildup, lifters can often be removed with a small magnet or even with your fingers (photo). A small scribe can also be used to pull the lifter out of the bore. **Caution:** *Do not use pliers of any type to remove a lifter unless you intend to replace it with a new one because they will damage the precision machined and hardened surface finish of the lifter, rendering it useless.*
82 Store the lifters in a clearly labelled box to insure their reinstallation in the same lifter bores (photo).
83 It is easier to simply replace a worn lifter with a new one than to repair a defective lifter. The internal components are not available separately — you must buy a lifter as a complete assembly. But sometimes, disassembling and cleaning the internal components of a dirty lifter will restore normal operation. For complete disassembly, inspection and reassembly procedures, refer to Chapter 2B.
84 The lifters must be installed in their original bores. Coat each lifter roller with moly-base grease or engine assembly lube.
85 Lubricate the bearing surfaces of the lifter bores with engine oil.
86 Install the lifter(s) in the lifter bore(s). **Note:** *Make sure that the oil orifice is facing toward the front of the engine.*
87 Install the lifter guide(s) and retainer(s).
88 Install the pushrods, pushrod guide plates, rocker arms and rocker arm retaining bolts. **Caution:** *Make sure that each pair of lifters is on the base circle of the camshaft; that is, with both valves closed, before tightening the rocker arm bolts.*
89 Tighten the rocker arm bolts to the specified torque.
90 Install the pushrod cover.
91 Install the intake manifold.
92 Install the rocker arm cover.
93 Install the air cleaner.

Exhaust manifold — removal and installation

94 Disconnect the negative battery cable.
95 Remove the air cleaner assembly and the pre-heat ducting between the exhaust manifold and the air cleaner.
96 Unbolt the air conditioning compressor (if equipped) and lay it aside. *Do not disconnect the refrigerant lines. Personal injury may result.*
97 Remove the dipstick tube bracket bolt.
98 Raise the vehicle and support it securely on jackstands.
99 Disconnect the exhaust pipe-to-exhaust manifold flange bolts. **Note:** *These bolts are often corroded, so you may have to apply penetrating oil to break them loose.*
100 If necessary, support the exhaust system with a piece of wire. If all the mounting springs are in place and in good shape, the exhaust system will remain in place without additional support.
101 Remove the oxygen sensor connector wire from its retaining clip and disconnect the electrical connector from the wire harness. **Note:** *It is not necessary to remove the oxygen sensor from the manifold*

unless you are replacing the manifold. If you do remove the sensor from the old manifold, be sure to install it with an anti-seize compound in the new one.
102 Lower the vehicle.
103 Loosen and remove the exhaust manifold retaining bolts and washers. Loosen the end ones first and then the middle ones. You may have to apply penetrating oil to the fastener threads, because they're often corroded.
104 Remove the exhaust manifold and gasket from the engine. **Note:** *The oil dipstick tube may be knocked loose during removal of the exhaust manifold. Be sure to push it back into the block before reinstallation of the exhaust manifold.*
105 Clean the gasket mating surfaces on the cylinder head and the exhaust manifold with a wire brush. All leftover gasket material and carbon deposits must be removed.
106 Place a new exhaust manifold gasket on the cylinder head, then place the manifold in position and install the mounting bolts finger tight. **Note:** *You can drop the factory gasket into position with the exhaust manifold already in place and the bottom retaining bolts loosely installed.*
107 The exhaust bolts are numbered from 1 to 7. Tighten them a little at a time in the proper sequence to the specified torque.
108 Raise the vehicle and support it securely on jackstands.

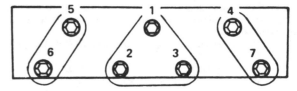

Fig 13.13   1985 model exhaust manifold installation — tighten all bolts in the order shown to the specified torque (Sec 5)

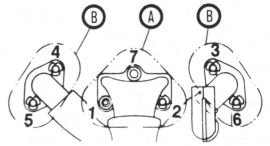

Fig 13.14   1986 and later model exhaust manifold installation — tighten group A bolts to 36 ft-lbs (50 Nm) and group B bolts to 32 ft-lbs (43 Nm) in the sequence shown (Sec 5)

5.129 Push the head bolts through the "bolt holes" of your cardboard tracing in the exact locations they occupy in the head

5.130 If you can't jar the head loose, pry it up with a large screwdriver at the overhang just behind and below the thermostat housing

5.134 Before cleaning the cylinder block-to-head mating surface, stuff clean rags into the cylinder bores to prevent debris from falling into them

109 Reconnect the oxygen sensor lead wire to the wire harness.
110 Install a new exhaust manifold flange gasket between the exhaust manifold and the exhaust pipe.
111 Tighten the exhaust manifold-to-exhaust pipe flange bolts.
112 Install the EFI throttle cable bracket and tighten it securely.
113 Install the pre-heat ducting between the exhaust manifold and the air cleaner.
114 Install the air cleaner assembly.
115 Start the engine and check for exhaust leaks between the exhaust manifold and cylinder head and between the exhaust manifold and the exhaust pipe.

Cylinder head — removal and installation

116 Relieve the fuel system pressure (Section 9 of this Supplement).
117 Remove the cable from the negative terminal of the battery.
118 Drain the cooling system (Chapter 1).
119 Remove the air cleaner assembly. Tag each hose with numbered or colored tape as it is disconnected to facilitate reassembly.
120 Detach the exhaust manifold from the cylinder head.
121 Remove the intake manifold (as described in this Section).
122 Remove the air conditioning compressor and bracket (if equipped) and lay it aside. *Do not disconnect the refrigerant lines.*
123 Remove the rocker arm cover (as previously described).
124 Remove the rocker arms and pushrods (as previously outlined).
125 Remove the generator and brackets and lay them aside.
126 Remove the fuel filter and fuel line brackets from the rear of the cylinder head.
127 Disconnect the wiring harness bracket and ground strap from the rear of the cylinder head.
128 Unplug and label the wiring connectors from the sensors on the rear of the cylinder head and the thermostat housing.
129 Using the new head gasket, trace an outline of the cylinders and the bolt pattern onto a piece of cardboard. Loosen the head bolts 1/4-turn at a time each until they can be removed by hand. Remove the cylinder head bolts. Insert the bolts into the cardboard outline in the same order in which they are installed in the head (photo).
130 Using a hammer and a block of wood, tap the cylinder head free and remove it. If the cylinder head is stuck to the engine block, pry it free only at the overhang on the thermostat end of the head (photo). **Caution:** *If you pry on the cylinder head anywhere else, you may damage the sealing surfaces.*
131 Place the head on a block of wood to prevent damage to the gasket surface and/or valves.
132 Remove the cylinder head gasket and discard it.
133 If a new cylinder head is being installed, transfer all of the external components from the old cylinder head to the new one.
134 Stuff clean rags into the cylinders to prevent debris from falling into them. Remove all dirt, oil and old gasket material from the gasket surfaces of the cylinder head and block (photo). The surfaces must also be free of nicks and scratches. Clean up all retaining bolt threads and cylinder block threaded holes with a tap and die set. Dirt will affect

bolt torque.
135 Lay a new gasket on the cylinder block, making sure that the gasket is positioned correctly.
136 Carefully lower the cylinder head into place, making sure that it is positioned over the dowel pins.
137 Coat the threads of the cylinder head retaining bolts and the under sides of the bolt heads with sealing compound. Install them in the cylinder head finger tight. Do not tighten any of the bolts at this time.
1985 and 1986 engines
138 Tighten the cylinder head bolts in at least three steps, following the sequence shown in the acompanying illustration until the specified torque is reached.
1987 and later engines
139 Gradually tighten the cylinder head bolts in the sequence shown in the accompanying illustration to the Step 1 torque figure shown in the Specifications.

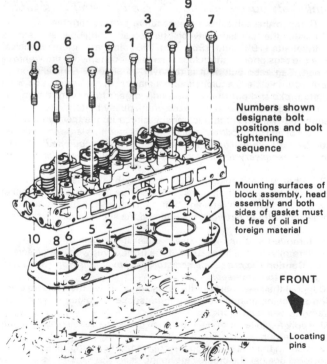

Numbers shown designate bolt positions and bolt tightening sequence

Mounting surfaces of block assembly, head assembly and both sides of gasket must be free of oil and foreign material

FRONT

Locating pins

Fig. 13.15 The cylinder head bolts must be tightened in three stages to the specified torque in the numerical sequence shown above; apply sealant to the threads and undersides of the bolt heads (Sec 5)

13

5.175   Using a large screwdriver, carefully pry the seal out of the timing gear cover

5.176   Installing the timing gear cover oil seal

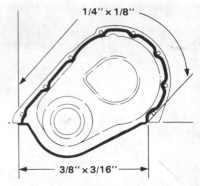

Fig. 13.16   Lay a 1/4-inch wide by 1/8-inch high bead of RTV sealant along the sealing flange of the timing cover above the oil pan (where it contacts the block) and a 3/8-inch wide by 3/16-inch high bead along the sealing surface between the cover and the oil pan (Sec 5)

140 Repeat the sequence, bringing them to the second specified torque on all bolts except number 9. Tighten number 9 to its specified torque.
141 Repeat the sequence. Turn all bolts, except number 9, 120 degrees (1/3-turn). Turn number 9 an additional 90 degrees (1/4-turn).
142 Install the pushrods and the rocker arms.
143 Install the rocker arm cover.
144 Reconnect the radiator hose to the thermostat housing.
145 Install the intake manifold.
146 Install the exhaust manifold.
147 Install the air conditioning compressor and belt (if equipped).
148 Install the alternator bracket and belt.
149 Reconnect all the fuel lines, electrical connectors and vacuum hoses that were disconnected.
150 Install the air cleaner assembly.
151 Refill the cooling system with fresh coolant.
152 Connect the cable to the negative terminal of the battery.
153 Start the engine and check for oil, compression and coolant leaks.

Crankshaft pulley and hub — removal and installation

154 Remove the cable from the negative battery terminal.
155 Loosen the accessory drivebelt tension adjusting bolts and remove the drivebelts (1985 and 1986). On 1987 and later model vehicles, rotate the tensioner counterclockwise to relieve tension, then remove the belt. Tag each belt as it is removed to simplify reinstallation.
156 If your vehicle is equipped with a manual transmission, apply the parking brake and put the transmission in gear to prevent the engine from turning over, then remove the crank pulley bolts. If your vehicle is equipped with an automatic transmission, remove the starter motor (Chapter 5) and immobilize the starter ring gear with a large screwdriver. **Note:** *On both manual and automatic transmission equipped vehicles, it may be necessary to use a breaker bar because the bolts are very tight.*
157 To break the crankshaft hub retaining bolt loose, thread a bolt into one of the pulley bolt holes. Place a large breaker bar and socket on the crankshaft hub retaining bolt. Immobilize the hub by wedging a large screwdriver between the bolt and the socket, then remove the bolt.
158 Remove the crank hub. Use a puller if necessary.
159 Carefully pry the oil seal out of the front cover with a large screwdriver. **Caution:** *Do not gouge or distort the cover or it won't seal properly around the new seal.*
160 Install the new seal with the lip facing in. Drive the seal into place using a seal installation tool or a large socket. A block of wood and a hammer will also work.
161 Apply a thin layer of multi-purpose grease to the seal contact surface of the hub.
162 Position the pulley hub on the crankshaft nose and slide it on until it bottoms against the crankshaft timing gear. Note that the slot in the hub must be aligned with the Woodruff key in the end of the crankshaft. The crankshaft hub bolt can also be used to press the hub into position.
163 Tighten the hub-to-crankshaft bolt to the specified torque.
164 Install the crank pulley on the hub. Coat the pulley-to-hub bolts

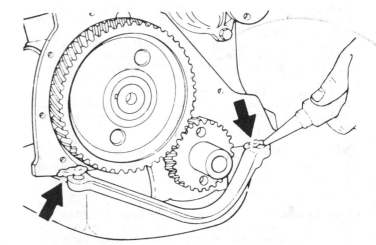

Fig. 13.17   Also apply a dab of sealant at the joints between the oil pan and the engine block (Sec 5)

with thread locking compound before installation.
165 Install the drivebelts.

Timing gear cover and front oil seal — removal and installation

166 Remove the cable from the negative terminal of the battery.
167 Detach the power steering fluid reservoir from the radiator shroud (if equipped).
168 Remove the upper fan shroud.
169 remove the drivebelt(s).
170 Unbolt the alternator and bracket and lay it aside.
171 Remove the crankshaft pulley and hub (as previously outlined).
172 Remove the timing cover-to-block bolts.
173 Remove the timing cover by carefully prying it loose. **Note:** *The timing cover is installed with RTV sealant so it isn't easy to pry it off. The sealing flange between the timing cover and the oil pan will probably be bent during removal. Try to minimize the damage to the sealing flange during removal or it may be too damaged to be straightened.*
174 Using a scraper and degreaser, remove all the old sealant from the mating surfaces of the timing gear cover, engine block and oil pan.
175 Remove the front oil seal by carefully prying it out of the timing gear cover with a large screwdriver (photo). Do not distort the cover.
176 Install the new seal with the lip facing toward the inside of the cover. Drive the seal into place using a seal installation tool or a large socket and hammer (photo). A block of wood will also work.
177 Apply a 3/8-inch wide by 3/16-inch thick bead of RTV-type gasket sealant to the timing gear cover flange at the sealing surface between

5.187   The oil pump driveshaft retainer plate is on the rear of the cylinder block, just below the pushrod cover and just above the oil filter

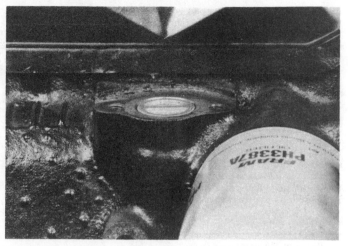

5.191   If the slotted oil pump driveshaft is properly mated with the oil pump gear tang, the top of the bushing will be flush with the retainer plate mounting surface

the timing cover and the oil pan, a 1/4-inch wide by 1/8-inch thick bead of RTV-type gasket sealant between the cover and the block and a dab of sealant at the joints between the oil pan and the engine block.
178 Place the timing gear cover in position and loosely install a couple of bolts to support it.
179 Lubricate the cover seal and insert the hub through the seal. As the hub slides onto the end of the crankshaft, it will center the timing gear cover.
180 Install the remaining timing gear cover mounting bolts and tighten them to the specified torque.
181 Install the crankshaft hub and pulley.
182 Install the alternator, bracket and drivebelt(s).
183 Reinstall the upper fan shroud.
184 Mount the power steering fluid reservoir to the radiator shroud (if removed).
185 Reattach the cable to the negative terminal of the battery.

Oil pump driveshaft — removal and installation

186 Disconnect the cable from the negative terminal of the battery.
187 Remove the oil pump driveshaft retainer plate bolts (photo).
188 Remove the oil pump driveshaft and bushing with a magnet.
189 Clean the sealing surfaces on the cylinder block and the retainer plate.
190 Inspect the bushing and driveshaft for wear.
191 Install the bushing and oil pump driveshaft in the block. The shaft driven gear must mesh with the camshaft drive gear and the slot in the lower end of the shaft must mate with the oil pump gear tang. When installed correctly, the top of the shaft bushing will be flush with the retainer plate mounting surface (photo).
192 Apply a 1/16-inch bead of RTV-type sealant to the retainer plate so that it completely seals around the oil pump driveshaft hole in the block.
193 Lay the retainer plate in position on the block and tighten the mounting bolts securely.

Oil pan — removal and installation

Note: *The engine must be removed from the vehicle before the oil pan can be removed.*
194 Remove the engine as described in Chapter 2 part D.
195 Remove the oil pan retaining bolts. Remove the oil pan.
196 Clean the mating surfaces of the oil pan and cylinder block.
197 Apply RTV sealant to the oil pan flange (Fig. 13.18).
198 Install the oil pan and tighten the retaining bolts to the specified torque.
199 Install the engine (see Chapter 2 Part D).

Oil pump — removal and installation

200 Remove the oil pan (as previously described).
201 Remove the two oil pump flange mounting bolts and the screen bracket nut from the main bearing cap bolt.

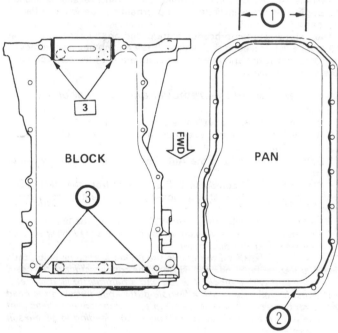

Fig. 13.18   Oil pan sealant application details (Sec 5)

1 3/8 inch wide by   2 3/16 inch wide by   3 1/8 inch bead at
   3/16 inch thick   1/8 inch thick   points indicated

202 Remove the oil pump and screen assembly.
203 For inspection procedures, refer to Chapter 2 Part B.
204 To install the pump, align the shaft so that the gear tang mates with the slot on the lower end of the oil pump driveshaft. The oil pump should slide easily into place over the oil pump driveshaft lower bushing. If it doesn't, pull it off and turn the tang until it is aligned with the pump driveshaft slot.
205 Install the pump mounting bolts and the screen bracket nut. Tighten them to the specified torque.
206 Reinstall the oil pump.

Flywheel/driveplate and rear main bearing oil seal — removal and installation

Note: *The rear main bearing oil seal is a one-piece unit and can be replaced without removal of the oil pan or crankshaft.*

207 Remove the tranmission (Chapter 7). Follow all precautionary notes.

13

208 If your vehicle is equipped with a manual transmission, remove the pressure plate and clutch disc (Chapter 8).

209 Remove the flywheel (manual transmission) or driveplate (automatic transmission) retaining bolts and separate it from the crankshaft.

210 Using a screwdriver or pry bar, carefully remove the rear main oil seal from the block.

211 Using solvent, thoroughly clean the crankshaft-to-seal and block mating surfaces.

212 Apply a light coat of engine oil to the outside surface of the new seal.

213 Using your fingertips, press the new seal evenly into position in the block.

214 Install the flywheel or driveplate and tighten the bolts to the specified torque.

215 If your vehicle is equipped with a manual transmission, reinstall the clutch disc and pressure plate (Chapter 8).

216 Reinstall the transmission (Chapter 7).

---

6   4.3 liter V6 engine

General information

This Section is devoted to in-vehicle repair procedures for the 4.3L V6 engine. All information concerning engine removal and installation and engine block and cylinder head overhaul can be found in Part D of Chapter 2.

The following repair procedures are based on the assumption that the engine is installed in the vehicle. If the engine has been removed from the vehicle and mounted on a stand, many of the steps outlined here will not apply.

Rocker arm covers — removal and installation

Removal — general
1   Disconnect the negative cable from the battery.
2   Remove the air cleaner assembly and heat stove tube.

Removal — right side
3   Detach the hose from the AIR system exhaust check valve or diverter valve.
4   Remove the A/C compressor (if equipped) from the bracket and position it out of the way. Do not loosen or disconnect the compressor lines.
5   Remove the oil filler tube, the PCV valve and the choke wires.
6   Detach the spark plug wires from the plugs, then lay the spark plug wire harness over the distributor.
7   Use a T-30 TORX bit to remove the rocker arm cover bolts, then detach the cover from the head. **Note:** *If the cover is stuck to the head, bump one end with a block of wood and a hammer to jar it loose. If that doesn't work, try to slip a flexible putty knife between the head and cover to break the gasket seal. Don't pry at the cover-to-head joint or damage to the sealing surfaces may occur (leading to oil leaks in the future).*

Removal — left side
8   Detach the vacuum brake line from the intake manifold fitting.
9   Detach the alternator. Lay it aside, out of the way, without disconnecting the wires.
10   Remove the accelerator and TVS cable bracket from the intake manifold.
11   Refer to Paragraphs 5 and 6 above for the next steps.
12   Use a T-30 TORX bit to remove the rocker arm cover bolts, then detach the cover from the head. **Note:** *If the cover is stuck to the head, bump one end with a block of wood and a hammer to jar it loose. If that doesn't work, try to slip a flexible putty knife between the head and cover to break the gasket seal. Don't pry at the cover-to-head joint or damage to the sealing surfaces may occur (leading to oil leaks in the future).*

Installation
13   The mating surfaces of each cylinder head and rocker arm cover must be perfectly clean when the covers are installed. Use a gasket scraper to remove all traces of sealant and old gasket material, then clean the mating surfaces with lacquer thinner or acetone. If there's sealant or oil on the mating surfaces when the cover is installed, oil leaks may develop.
14   Clean the mounting bolt threads with a die to remove any corrosion

and restore damaged threads. Make sure the threaded holes in the head are clean — run a tap into them to remove corrosion and restore damaged threads.

15   The gaskets should be mated to the covers before the covers are installed. Apply a thin coat of RTV sealant to the cover flange, then position the gasket inside the cover lip and allow the sealant to set up so the gasket adheres to the cover. If the sealant isn't allowed to set, the gasket may fall out of the cover as it's installed on the engine.
16   Carefully position the cover on the head and install the bolts.
17   Tighten the bolts in three or four steps to the specified torque.
18   The remaining installation steps are the reverse of removal.
19   Start the engine and check carefully for oil leaks as the engine warms up.

Rocker arms and pushrods — removal, inspection, installation and adjustment

Removal
20   Detach the rocker arm cover(s) from the cylinder head(s).
21   Beginning at the front of one cylinder head, loosen and remove the rocker arm stud nuts. Store them separately in marked containers to ensure that they will be reinstalled in their original locations. **Note:** *If the pushrods are the only items being removed, loosen each nut just enough to allow the rocker arms to be rotated to the side so the pushrods can be lifted out.*
22   Lift off the rocker arms and pivot balls and store them in the marked containers with the nuts (they must be reinstalled in their original locations).
23   Remove the pushrods and store them separately to make sure they don't get mixed up during installation (photo).

6.23   A perforated cardboard box can be used to store the pushrods to ensure that they are reinstalled in their original locations — note the label indicating the front of the engine

Inspection
24   Check each rocker arm for wear, cracks and other damage, especially where the pushrods and valve stems contact the rocker arm faces.
25   Make sure the hole at the pushrod end of each rocker arm is open.
26   Check each rocker arm pivot area for wear, cracks and galling. If the rocker arms are worn or damaged, replace them with new ones and use new pivot balls as well. Check the rocker arm studs for wear. The studs must be replaced by an automotive machine shop, since they must be pressed into place and protrude a precise amount.
27   Inspect the pushrods for cracks and excessive wear at the ends. Roll each pushrod across a piece of plate glass to see if it's bent (if it wobbles, it's bent).

Installation
28   Lubricate the lower end of each pushrod with clean engine oil or moly-base grease and install them in their original locations. Make sure each pushrod seats completely in the lifter.

6.29 The ends of the pushrods and the valve stems should be lubricated with moly-base grease prior to installation of the rocker arms

6.30 Moly-base grease applied to the privot balls will ensure adequate lubrication until oil pressure builds up when the engine is started

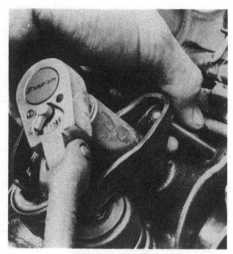

6.32 Rotate each pushrod as the rocker arm nut is tightened to determine the point at which all play is removed, then tighten each nut an additional one full turn

29 Apply moly-base grease to the ends of the valve stems and the upper ends of the pushrods before positioning the rocker arms over the studs (photo).

30 Set the rocker arms in place, then install the pivot balls and nuts. Apply moly-base grease to the pivot balls to prevent damage to the mating surfaces before engine oil pressure builds up (photo). Be sure to install each nut with the **flat** side against the pivot ball.

Valve adjustment

31 Bring the number one piston to top dead center on the compression stroke.

32 Tighten the rocker arm nuts (number one cylinder only) until all play is removed at the pushrods. This can be determined by rotating each pushrod between your thumb and index finger as the nut is tightened (photo). You'll be able to feel the point at which all play is eliminated because the pushrod will no longer turn.

33 Tighten each nut an additional one full turn (360°) to center the lifters. Valve adjustment for cylinder number one is now complete.

34 Turn the crankshaft 120° in the normal direction of rotation until the next piston in the firing order (number six) is at TDC on the compression stroke. The distributor rotor should be pointing in the direction of terminal number six on the cap.

35 Repeat the procedure described in Paragraphs 32 and 33 for the number six cylinder valves.

36 Turn the crankshaft another 120° and adjust the number five cylinder valves. Continue turning the crankshaft 120° at a time and adjust both valves for each cylinder before proceeding. Follow the firing order sequence — a cylinder number illustration is also included — in the Specifications.

37 Install the rocker arm covers. Start the engine, listen for unusual valvetrain noises and check for oil leaks at the rocker arm cover joints.

Valve springs, retainer and seals — replacement in vehicle

Note: Broken valve springs and defective valve stem seals can be replaced without removing the cylinder heads. Two special tools and a compressed air source are normally required to perform this operation, so read through this section carefully and rent or buy the tools before beginning the job. If compressed air isn't available, a length of nylon rope can be used to keep the valves from falling into the cylinder during this procedure.

38 Remove the rocker arm cover from the affected cylinder head. If all of the valve stem seals are being replaced, remove both rocker arm covers.

39 Remove the spark plug from the cylinder which has the defective component. If all of the valve stem seals are being replaced, all of the spark plugs should be removed.

40 Turn the crankshaft until the piston in the affected cylinder is at top dead center on the compression stroke. If you are replacing all of the valve stem seals, begin with cylinder number one and work on the valves for one cylinder at a time. Move from cylinder-to-cylinder following the firing order sequence (1-6-5-4-3-2).

41 Thread an adapter into the spark plug hole (photo) and connect an air hose from a compressed air source to it. Most auto parts stores can supply the air hose adapter. **Note:** *Many cylinder compression gauges utilize a screw-in fitting that may work with your air hose quick-disconnect fitting.*

42 Remove the nut, pivot ball and rocker arm for the valve with the defective part and pull out the pushrod. If all of the valve stem seals are being replaced, all of the rocker arms and pushrods should be removed.

43 Apply compressed air to the cylinder. The valves should be held in place by the air pressure. If the valve faces or seats are in poor condition, leaks may prevent air pressure from retaining the valves — refer to the alternative procedure below.

44 If you don't have access to compressed air, an alternative method can be used. Position the piston at a point just before TDC on the compression stroke, then feed a long piece of nylon rope through the spark plug hole until it fills the combustion chamber. Be sure to leave the end of the rope hanging out of the engine so it can be removed easily. Use a large breaker bar and socket to rotate the crankshaft in the normal direction of rotation until **slight** resistance is felt.

6.41 Use compressed air, if available, to hold the valves closed when the springs are removed — the air hose adapter (arrow) threads into the spark plug hole and accepts the hose from the compressor

13

6.45a Once the spring is depressed the keepers can be removed with a magnet or needle-nose pliers (a magnet is preferred to prevent dropping the keepers)

6.45b The stamped steel lever-type valve spring compressor is usually less expensive than the type that grips the spring coils

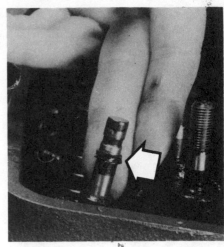

6.46 The O-ring seal (arrow) should be replaced with a new one each time the keepers and retainer are removed

45 Stuff shop rags into the cylinder head holes above and below the valves to prevent parts and tools from falling into the engine, then use a valve spring compressor to compress the spring/damper assembly. Remove the keepers with small needle-nose pliers or a magnet (photo). **Note:** *A couple of different types of tools are available for compressing the valve springs with the head in place. One type, shown here, grips the lower spring coils and presses on the retainer as the knob is turned, while the other type utilizes the rocker arm stud and nut for leverage (photo). Both types work very well, although the lever type is usually less expensive.*

46 Remove the spring retainer or rotator, oil shield and valve spring assembly, then remove the valve stem O-ring seal and the umbrella-type guide seal (the O-ring seal will most likely be hardened and will probably break when removed, so plan on installing a new one each time the original is removed) (photo). **Note:** *If air pressure fails to hold the valve in the closed position during this operation, the valve face and/or seat is probably damaged. If so, the cylinder head will have to be removed for additional repair operations.*

47 Wrap a rubber band or tape around the top of the valve stem so the valve won't fall into the combustion chamber, then release the air pressure. **Note:** *If a rope was used instead of air pressure, turn the crankshaft slightly in the direction opposite normal rotation.*

48 Inspect the valve stem for damage. Rotate the valve in the guide and check the end for eccentric movement, which would indicate that the valve is bent.

49 Move the valve up-and-down in the guide and make sure it doesn't

bind. If the valve stem binds, either the valve is bent or the guide is damaged. In either case, the head will have to be removed for repair.

50 Reapply air pressure to the cylinder to retain the valve in the closed position, then remove the tape or rubber band from the valve stem. If a rope was used instead of air pressure, rotate the crankshaft in the normal direction of rotation until **slight** resistance is felt.

51 Lubricate the valve stem with engine oil and install a new umbrella-type guide seal.

52 Install the spring/damper assembly and shield in position over the valve.

53 Install the valve spring retainer or rotator. Compress the valve spring assembly and carefully install the new O-ring seal in the lower groove of the valve stem. Make sure the seal isn't twisted — it must lie perfectly flat in the groove (photo).

54 Position the keepers in the upper groove. Apply a small dab of grease to the inside of each keeper to hold it in place if necessary (photo). Remove the pressure from the spring tool and make sure the keepers are seated. Check the seals with a vacuum pump.

55 Disconnect the air hose and remove the adapter from the spark plug hole. If a rope was used in place of air pressure, pull it out of the cylinder.

56 Install the rocker arm(s) and pushrod(s).

57 Install the spark plug(s) and hook up the wire(s).

58 Install the rocker arm cover(s).

59 Start and run the engine, then check for oil leaks and unusual sounds coming from the rocker arm cover area.

6.53 Make sure the O-ring seal under the retainer is seated in the groove and not twisted before installing the keepers

6.54 Apply a small dab of grease to each keeper as shown here before installation — it will hold them in place on the valve stem as the spring is released

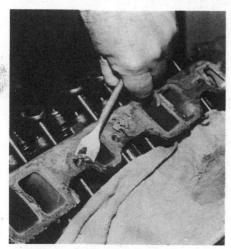

6.68 After covering the lifter valley, use a gasket scraper to remove all traces of sealant and old gasket material from the head and manifold mating surfaces

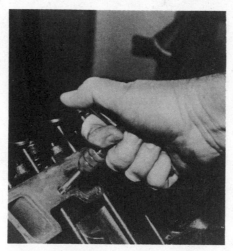

6.69a The bolt hole threads must be clean and dry to ensure accurate torque readings when the manifold mounting bolts are installed

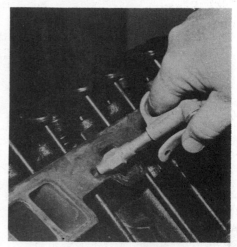

6.69b Clean the bolt holes with compressed air, but be careful — wear safety goggles!

Intake manifold — removal and installation

60 Disconnect the negative cable from the battery, then refer to Chapter 1 and drain the cooling system.
61 Remove the air cleaner assembly.
62 Remove the carburetor and choke components or the fuel injection unit, as necessary, to expose the intake manifold mounting bolts.
63 Detach the upper radiator hose from the thermostat housing and remove the alternator brace (if not already done). The thermostat housing may have to be detached to provide room for removal of the left front manifold bolt.
64 Remove the rocker arm covers.
65 Remove the distributor.
66 If there is a heater hose fitting on the intake manifold, remove the hose.
67 Loosen the manifold mounting bolts in 1/4-turn increments until they can be removed by hand. The manifold will probably be stuck to the cylinder heads and force may be required to break the gasket seal. A large pry bar can be positioned under the cast-in lug near the thermostat housing to pry up the front of the manifold, but make sure all bolts have been removed first! **Caution:** *Do not pry between the block and manifold or the heads and manifold or damage to the gasket sealing surfaces may occur, leading to vacuum leaks.*

Installation

Note: *The mating surfaces of the cylinder heads, block and manifold must be perfectly clean when the manifold is installed. Gasket removal solvents in aerosol cans are available at most auto parts stores and may be helpful when removing old gasket material that's stuck to the heads and manifold (since the manifold is made of aluminum, aggressive scraping can cause damage). Be sure to follow the directions printed on the container.*

68 Use a gasket scraper to remove all traces of sealant and old gasket material, then clean the mating surfaces with lacquer thinner or acetone. If there's old sealant or oil on the mating surfaces when the manifold is installed, oil or vacuum leaks may develop. When working on the heads and block, cover the lifter valley with shop rags to keep debris out of the engine (photo). Use a vacuum cleaner to remove any gasket material that falls into the intake ports in the heads.
69 Use a tap of the correct size to chase the threads in the bolt holes, then use compressed air (if available) to remove the debris from the holes (photos). **Warning:** *Wear safety glasses or a face shield to protect your eyes when using compressed air!* Remove excessive carbon deposits and corrosion from the exhaust, EGR and coolant passages in the heads and manifold.
70 Apply a 3/16-inch wide bead of RTV sealant to the front and rear manifold mating surfaces of the block (Fig. 13.19). Make sure the beads extend up the heads 1/2-inch on each side.
71 Apply a thin coat of RTV sealant around the coolant passage holes on the cylinder head side of the new intake manifold gaskets (there

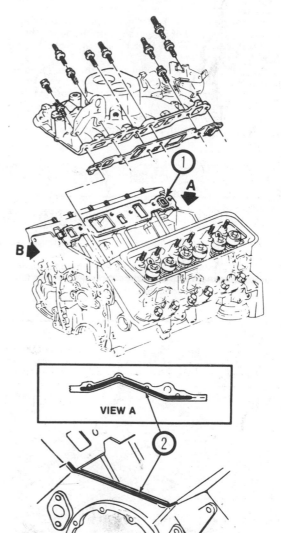

Fig. 13.19 Intake manifold sealant application details (Sec 6)

1 Port blocking plate   2 RTV sealant

13

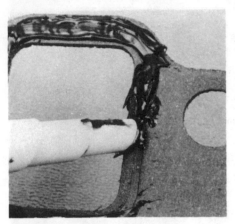

6.71   RTV sealant should be used around the coolant passage holes in the new intake manifold gaskets

6.72   Be sure to install the gaskets with the marks UP!

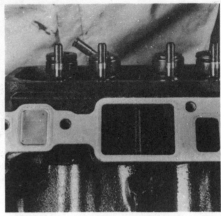

6.73   The rear coolant passages on some models are blocked off — make sure the gasket is installed with the blocked off hole at the rear!

is normally one hole at each end) (photo).

72   Position the gaskets on the cylinder heads, with the ears at each end overlapping the bead of RTV sealant on the head. The upper side of each gasket will have a THIS SIDE UP label stamped into it to ensure correct installation (photo).

73   Make sure all intake port openings, coolant passage holes and bolt holes are aligned correctly. **Note:** *The gaskets used on some later models have the rear coolant passages blocked off (photo). Be sure the gaskets are installed with the blocked off passages at the rear of the engine.* Some gaskets may have small tabs which must be bent over until they're flush with the rear surface of each head.

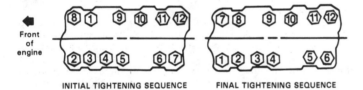

Fig. 13.20   Intake manifold bolt tightening sequence — note that the initial sequence differs from the final sequence (Sec 6)

74   Carefully set the manifold in place while the sealant is still wet. **Caution:** *Don't disturb the gaskets and don't move the manifold fore-and-aft after it contacts the sealant on the block.*

75   Apply non-hardening sealant (such as Permatex Number 2) to the manifold bolt threads. Install the bolts and tighten them to the specified torque following the recommended sequence (Fig. 13.20). Work up to the final torque in two stages and note that two different tightening sequences must be followed, one for each stage.

76   The remaining installation steps are the reverse of removal. Start the engine and check carefully for oil and coolant leaks at the intake manifold joints.

Exhaust manifolds — removal and installation

Removal

77   Disconnect the negative cable from the battery.

78   Remove the carburetor heat stove pipe between the exhaust manifold and air cleaner snorkel (if equipped).

79   Disconnect the oxygen sensor wire.

80   Remove the AIR hose at the check valve and the AIR pipe bracket from the manifold stud (if equipped).

81   Disconnect the spark plug wires from the spark plugs (refer to Chapter 1 if necessary). If there is any danger of mixing the plug wires up, label them with small pieces of tape.

82   Remove the spark plugs (Chapter 1).

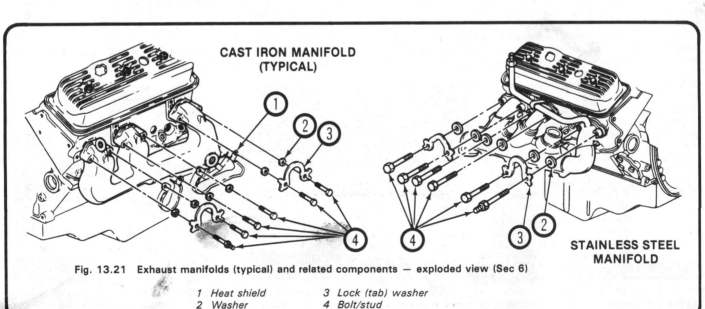

Fig. 13.21   Exhaust manifolds (typical) and related components — exploded view (Sec 6)

1   Heat shield
2   Washer
3   Lock (tab) washer
4   Bolt/stud

6.95   To avoid mixing up the head bolts, use a new gasket to transfer the bolt hole pattern to a piece of cardboard, then punch holes to accept the bolts

83   Remove the nuts and detach the exhaust pipe from the manifold. Penetrating oil may be required to loosen the nuts — they are usually frozen on the studs. Do not use excessive force if the nuts are frozen — the studs could be sheared off quite easily.

84   Remove all accessories, such as the alternator or air conditioning compressor, bolted to the exhaust manifold, along with any mounting brackets.

85   Remove the two front and two rear manifold mounting bolts first, then the two center bolts. Separate the manifold from the head. Some models use tabbed washers under the manifold bolts to keep the bolts from vibrating loose. The tabs will have to be flattened before the bolts can be removed.

Installation

86   Check the manifold for cracks and make sure the bolt threads are clean and undamaged. The manifold and cylinder head mating surfaces must be clean before the manifolds are reinstalled — use a gasket scraper to remove all carbon deposits. Transfer the heat stove assembly (if used) to the new manifold.

87   Apply anti-seize compound to the bolt threads and exhaust pipe-to-manifold nut studs. Position the manifold, tab washers and heat shields (if equipped) on the head and install the mounting bolts (Fig. 13.21).

88   When tightening the mounting bolts, work from the center to the ends and be sure to use a torque wrench. Tighten the bolts in three equal steps until the specified torque is reached.

89   The remaining installation steps are the reverse of removal. Use a new ''doughnut'' gasket between the pipe and manifold.

90   Start the engine and check for exhaust leaks.

Cylinder heads — removal and installation

Note: *The engine must be completely cool when the heads are removed. Failure to allow the engine to cool off could result in head warpage.*

Removal

91   Remove the rocker arm covers.

92   Remove the intake manifold. Note that the cooling system must be drained to prevent coolant from getting into internal areas of the engine when the manifold and heads are removed. The alternator, power steering pump, air pump and air conditioner compressor brackets (if equipped) must be removed as well.

93   Detach both exhaust manifolds.

94   Remove the pushrods.

95   Using a new head gasket, outline the cylinders and bolt pattern on a piece of cardboard (photo). Be sure to indicate the front of the engine for reference. Punch holes at the bolt locations.

96   Loosen the head bolts in 1/4-turn increments until they can be removed by hand. Work from bolt-to-bolt in a pattern that's the reverse of the tightening sequence (Fig. 13.23). **Note:** *Don't overlook the row of bolts on the lower edge of each head, near the spark plug holes.* Store the bolts in the cardboard holder as they're removed; this will ensure that the bolts are reinstalled in their original holes.

97   Lift the heads off the engine. If resistance is felt, DO NOT pry between the head and block as damage to the mating surfaces will result. To dislodge the head, place a block of wood against the end of it and strike the wood block with a hammer. Store the heads on blocks of wood to prevent damage to the gasket sealing surfaces.

98   Cylinder head disassembly and inspection procedures are covered in detail in Chapter 2, Part D.

Installation

99   The mating surfaces of the cylinder heads and block must be perfectly clean when the heads are installed.

100 Use a gasket scraper to remove all traces of carbon and old gasket material, then clean the mating surfaces with lacquer thinner or acetone. If there's oil on the mating surfaces when the heads are installed, the gaskets may not seal correctly and leaks may develop. When working on the block, cover the lifter valley with shop rags to keep debris out of the engine. Use a vacuum cleaner to remove any debris that falls into the cylinders.

101 Check the block and head mating surfaces for nicks, deep scratches and other damage. If damage is slight, it can be removed with a file — if it's excessive, machining may be the only alternative.

102 Use a tap of the correct size to chase the threads in the head bolt holes. Mount each bolt in a vise and run a die down the threads to remove corrosion and restore the threads (photo). Dirt, corrosion, sealant and damaged threads will affect torque readings.

103 Position the new gaskets over the dowel pins in the block (photo). **Note:** *If a steel gasket is used, apply a thin, even coat of sealant such as K&W Copper Coat to both sides prior to installation (photo). Steel gaskets must be installed with the raised bead UP. The composition gasket must be installed dry — don't use sealant.*

104 Carefully position the heads on the block without disturbing the gaskets.

105 Before installing the head bolts, coat the threads with a *non-hardening sealant* such as Permatex Number 2.

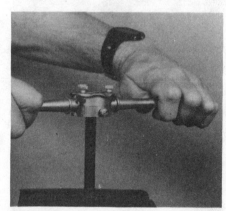

6.102   A die should be used to remove sealant and corrosion from the head bolt threads prior to installation

6.103a   Locating dowels (arrows) are used to position the gaskets and heads on the block

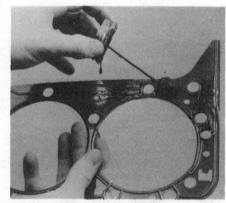

6.103b   Steel gaskets should be coated with a sealant such as K&W Copper Coat before installation

13

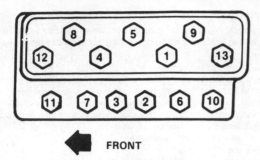

Fig. 13.22   Cylinder head bolt tightening sequence (Sec 6)

106 Install the bolts in their original locations and tighten them finger tight. Follow the recommended sequence and tighten the bolts in several steps to the specified torque (Fig. 13.22).
107 The remaining installation steps are the reverse of removal.
108 Change the engine oil and filter (Chapter 1), then start the engine and check carefully for oil and coolant leaks.

Top Dead Center (TDC) for number one piston — locating

109 Top Dead Center (TDC) is the highest point in the cylinder that each piston reaches as it travels up-and-down when the crankshaft turns. Each piston reaches TDC on the compression stroke and again on the exhaust stroke, but TDC generally refers to piston position on the compression stroke. The timing marks on the vibration damper installed on the front of the crankshaft are referenced to the number one piston at TDC on the compression stroke.
110 Positioning the piston(s) at TDC is an essential part of many procedures such as rocker arm removal, valve adjustment, timing chain and sprocket replacement and distributor removal.
111 In order to bring any piston to TDC, the crankshaft must be turned using one of the methods outlined below. When looking at the front of the engine, normal crankshaft rotation is *clockwise.* **Warning:** *Before beginning this procedure, be sure to place the transmission in Neutral and unplug the wire connector at the distributor to disable the ignition system.*

  a)   The preferred method is to turn the crankshaft with a large socket and breaker bar attached to the vibration damper bolt threaded into the front of the crankshaft.
  b)   A remote starter switch, which may save some time, can also be used. Attach the switch leads to the S (switch) and B (battery) terminals on the starter motor. Once the piston is close to TDC, use a socket and breaker bar as described in the previous paragraph.
  c)   If an assistant is available to turn the ignition switch to the Start position in short bursts, you can get the piston close to TDC without a remote starter switch. Use a socket and breaker bar as described in Paragraph a) to complete the procedure.

112 Make a mark on the distributor housing directly below the number one spark plug wire terminal on the distributor cap. **Note:** *The terminal numbers are marked on the spark plug wires near the distributor (photo).*
113 Remove the distributor cap.
114 Turn the crankshaft (see Paragraph 3 above) until the line on the vibration damper is aligned with the zero mark on the timing plate (photo). The timing plate and vibration damper are located low on the front of the engine, near the pulley that turns the drivebelt.
115 The rotor should now be pointing directly at the mark on the distributor housing (photo). If it isn't, the piston is at TDC on the exhaust stroke.
116 To get the piston to TDC on the compression stroke, turn the crankshaft one complete turn (360°) clockwise. The rotor should now be pointing at the mark. When the rotor is pointing at the number one spark plug wire terminal in the distributor cap (which is indicated by the mark on the housing) and the ignition timing marks are aligned, the number one piston is at TDC on the compression stroke.
117 After the number one piston has been positioned at TDC on the compression stroke, TDC for any of the remaining cylinders can be located by turning the crankshaft 120° at a time and following the firing order.

Timing cover, chain and sprockets — removal and installation

Removal

118 Remove the water pump.
119 Remove the bolts and separate the crankshaft drivebelt pulley from the vibration damper (photo).
120 Position the *number four* piston at TDC on the compression stroke. **Caution:** *Once this has been done, DO NOT turn the crankshaft until the timing chain and sprockets have been reinstalled!*
121 Remove the bolt from the front of the crankshaft, then use a puller to detach the vibration damper (photo). **Caution:** *Don't use a puller with jaws that grip the outer edge of the damper. The puller must be the type shown in the illustration that utilizes bolts to apply force to the damper hub only.*
122 Remove the bolts and separate the timing chain cover from the block. It may be stuck — if so, use a putty knife or screwdriver to break the gasket seal (photo). The cover is easily distorted, so be very careful when prying it off.
123 Remove the three bolts from the end of the camshaft (photo), then detach the camshaft sprocket and chain as an assembly. The sprocket on the crankshaft can be removed with a two or three jaw puller, but be careful not to damage the threads in the end of the crankshaft. **Note:** *If the timing chain cover oil seal has been leaking, install a new one.*

Installation

124 Use a gasket scraper to remove all traces of old gasket material and sealant from the cover and engine block. Stuff a shop rag into the opening at the front of the oil pan to keep debris out of the engine. Clean the cover and block sealing surfaces with lacquer thinner or acetone.

6.112   The spark plug wires are numbered to correspond to their respective cylinders (arrow)

6.114   Turn the crankshaft until the line on the vibration damper is directly opposite the zero mark on the timing plate

6.115   If the rotor is pointing directly at the mark on the distributor housing, as shown here, the number one piston is at TDC on the compression stroke

6.119   The vibration damper bolt (arrow) is usually very tight, so use a six-point socket and a breaker bar to loosen it (the three other bolts hold the pulley to the vibration damper)

6.121   Use the recommended puller to remove the vibration damper — if a puller that applies force to the outer edge is used, the damper will be damaged!

6.122   A putty knife or screwdriver can be used to break the timing chain cover-to-block seal, but be careful when prying it off as damage to the cover may result

125 Check the cover flange for distortion, particularly around the bolt holes. If necessary, place the cover on a block of wood and use a hammer to flatten and restore the gasket surface.

126 If new parts are being installed, be sure to align the keyway in the crankshaft sprocket with the Woodruff key in the end of the crankshaft. Press the sprocket onto the crankshaft with the vibration damper bolt, a large socket and some washers or tap it gently into place until it's completely seated. **Caution:** *If resistance is encountered, DO NOT hammer the sprocket onto the crankshaft. It may eventually move onto the shaft, but it may be cracked in the process and fail later, causing extensive engine damage.*

127 Loop the new chain over the camshaft sprocket, then turn the sprocket until the timing mark is in the 6 o'clock position. Mesh the chain with the crankshaft sprocket and position the camshaft sprocket

on the end of the cam. If necessary, turn the camshaft so the dowel pin fits into the sprocket hole with the timing mark in the 6 o'clock position. When correctly installed, the marks on the sprockets will be aligned as shown in Fig. 13.23. **Note:** *The number four piston must be at TDC on the compression stroke as the chain and sprockets are installed (see Paragraph 120 above).*

128 Apply Locktite to the camshaft sprocket bolt threads, then install and tighten them to the specified torque. Lubricate the chain with clean engine oil.

129 Check the oil pan-to-block joints to make sure that all excess sealant is removed.

130 Apply RTV sealant to the U-shaped channel on the bottom of the cover.

131 Apply a thin layer of RTV sealant to both sides of the new gasket, then position it on the engine block (the dowel pins and sealant will hold it in place).

132 Since the oil pan seal in the bottom of the cover must be compressed in order to position the cover over the dowel pins and thread the bolts into the block, the cover is nearly impossible to install unless the oil pan is removed first. It can be done, but it's very difficult, time consuming and frustrating.

6.123   Remove the three small bolts from the end of the camshaft (arrows)

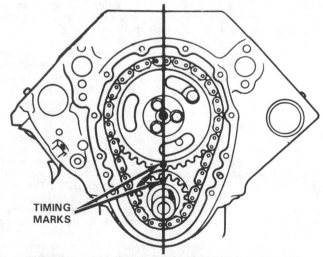

TIMING MARKS

Fig. 13.23   With the number four piston at TDC on the compression stroke and the timing marks on the cam and crankshaft sprockets in the 6 and 12 o'clock positions, a straight line should pass through the camshaft timing mark, the center of the camshaft, the crankshaft timing mark and the center of the crankshaft (Sec 6)

13

6.140   The lifters on an engine that has accumulated many miles may have to be removed with a special tool — be sure to store the lifters in an organized manner to make sure they are reinstalled in their original locations

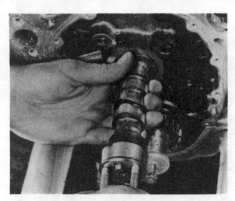

6.141   Long bolts can be threaded into the camshaft bolt holes to provide a handle for removal and installation of the camshaft — support the cam near the block as it's withdrawn

6.147   After the camshaft is in place, turn it until the dowel pin (arrow) is in the 3 o'clock position as shown here

133 Remove the oil pan, then install the timing chain cover. After the cover bolts have been tightened securely, reinstall the oil pan.
134 Lubricate the oil seal contact surface of the vibration damper hub with moly-base grease or clean engine oil, then install the damper on the end of the crankshaft. The keyway in the damper must be aligned with the Woodruff key in the crankshaft nose. If the damper cannot be seated by hand, slip a large washer over the bolt, install the bolt and tighten it to push the damper into place. Remove the large washer and tighten the bolt to the specified torque.
135 The remaining installation steps are the reverse of removal.

Camshaft, bearings and lifters — removal, inspection and installation
Camshaft lobe lift check
136 In order to determine the extent of cam lobe wear, the lobe lift should be checked before camshaft removal. Refer to Section 16 in Chapter 2, Part D for the procedure.
137 After the check is complete, compare the results to the Specifications. If camshaft lobe lift is less than specified, cam lobe wear has occurred and a new camshaft should be installed.

Removal
138 Refer to the appropriate steps and remove the intake manifold, the rocker arms, the pushrods and the timing chain and camshaft sprocket. The radiator should be removed as well (Chapter 3).
139 There are several ways to extract the lifters from the bores. A special tool designed to grip and remove lifters is manufactured by many tool companies and is widely available, but it may not be required in every case. On newer engines without a lot of varnish buildup, the lifters can often be removed with a small magnet or even with your fingers. A machinist's scribe with a bent end can be used to pull the lifters out by positioning the point under the retainer ring in the top of each lifter. **Caution:** *Don't use pliers to remove the lifters unless you intend to replace them with new ones (along with the camshaft). The pliers will damage the precision machined and hardened lifters, rendering them useless.*
140 Before removing the lifters, arrange to store them in a clearly labelled box to ensure that they're reinstalled in their original locations. **Note:** *On engines equipped with roller lifters, the retainer and restrictors must be removed before the lifters are withdrawn. Remove the lifters and store them where they won't get dirty (photo). DO NOT attempt to withdraw the camshaft with the lifters in place.*
141 Thread two 6-inch long 5/16–18 bolts into two of the camshaft sprocket bolt holes to use as a handle when removing the camshaft from the block (photo).
142 Carefully pull the camshaft out. Support the cam near the block so the lobes don't nick or gouge the bearings as it's withdrawn.

Inspection
143 Refer to Section 16 in Part D of Chapter 2 for the camshaft, lifter and bearing inspection procedure.

Bearing replacement
144 Camshaft bearing replacement requires special tools and expertise

that place it outside the scope of the home mechanic. Take the block to an automotive machine shop to ensure that the job is done correctly.
Installation
145 Lubricate the camshaft bearing journals and cam lobes with moly-base grease or engine assembly lube.
146 Slide the camshaft into the engine. Support the cam near the block and be careful not to scrape or nick the bearings.
147 Turn the camshaft until the dowel pin is in the 3 o'clock position (photo).
148 Refer to Paragraphs 124 through 135 and install the timing chain and sprockets.
149 Lubricate the lifters with clean engine oil and install them in the block. If the original lifters are being reinstalled, be sure to return them to their original locations. If a new camshaft was installed, be sure to install new lifters as well (except for engines with roller lifters).
150 The remaining installation steps are the reverse of removal.
151 Before starting and running the engine, change the oil and install a new oil filter (see Chapter 1).

Oil pan — removal and installation
Note: *The following procedure is based on the assumption that the engine is in place in the vehicle. If it's been removed, merely unbolt the oil pan and detach it from the block.*
Removal
152 Disconnect the negative cable from the battery.
153 Remove the distributor cap to keep it from being crushed as the engine is lifted.
154 Unbolt the radiator shroud and move it back over the fan.
155 Raise the vehicle and support it securely on jackstands.
156 Drain the engine oil (Chapter 1).
157 If the vehicle is equipped with a single exhaust, unbolt the crossover pipe at the exhaust manifolds.
158 If the vehicle is equipped with an automatic transmission, remove the converter inspection cover. If the vehicle is equipped with a manual transmission, remove the flywheel inspection cover.
159 Remove the starter.
160 Turn the crankshaft until the timing mark on the vibration damper is pointed straight down.
161 Remove the motor mount through bolts.
162 Use an engine hoist or a floor jack and block of wood under the oil pan to lift the engine approximately three inches. **Caution:** *The oil pump pick-up is very close to the bottom of the oil pan and it can be damaged easily if concentrated pressure from a jack is applied to the pan. Use the block of wood to spread the load over a wide area.* When lifting the engine, check to make sure the distributor isn't hitting the firewall and the fan isn't hitting the radiator.
163 Place blocks of wood between the crossmember and the engine block in the area of the motor mounts to hold the engine in the raised position, then remove the floor jack or engine hoist.
164 Remove the oil pan mounting bolts/nuts. Most models are equipped with a reinforcement strip on each side of the oil pan which

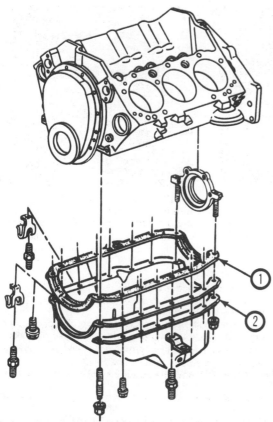

Fig. 13.24   The gasket (1) is a one-piece molded rubber part and reinforcement strips (2) are used on each side of the oil pan (Sec 6)

may come loose after the bolts/nuts are removed (Fig. 13.24).

165 Carefully separate the pan from the block. Don't pry between the block and pan or damage to the sealing surfaces may result and oil leaks could develop. You may have to turn the crankshaft slightly to maneuver the front of the pan past the crank counterweights.

Installation

166 Clean the gasket sealing surfaces with lacquer thinner or acetone. Make sure the bolt holes in the block are clean.

167 Check the oil pan flange for distortion, particularly around the bolt holes. If necessary, place the pan on a block of wood and use a hammer to flatten and restore the gasket surface.

168 The rubber gasket should be checked carefully and replaced with a new one if damage is noted. Apply a small amount of RTV sealant to the corners of the semi-circular cutouts at both ends of the pan,

then attach the rubber gasket to the pan.

169 Carefully position the pan against the block and install the bolts/nuts finger tight (don't forget the reinforcement strips, if used). Tighten the bolts/nuts in three steps to the specified torque. Start at the center of the pan and work out toward the ends in a spiral pattern.

170 The remaining steps are the reverse of removal. **Caution:** *Don't forget to refill the engine with oil before starting it (see Chapter 1).*

171 Start the engine and check carefully for oil leaks at the oil pan.

Oil pump — removal and installation

172 Remove the oil pan.

173 While supporting the oil pump, remove the pump-to-rear main bearing cap bolt. On some models, the oil pan baffle may have to be removed first.

174 Lower the pump and remove it along with the pump driveshaft. Note that on most models a hard nylon sleeve is used to align the pump shaft and driveshaft. Make sure the sleeve is in place on the pump driveshaft. If it isn't, check the oil pan for pieces of the sleeve, clean them out of the pan and obtain a new sleeve for the pump driveshaft.

175 If a new oil pump is installed, make sure the pump driveshaft is mated with the shaft inside the pump.

176 Position the pump on the engine and make sure the slot in the upper end of the driveshaft is aligned with the tang on the lower end of the distributor shaft. The distributor drives the oil pump, so it is absolutely essential that the components mate properly.

177 Install the mounting bolt and tighten it to the specified torque.

178 Install the oil pan.

Crankshaft oil seals — replacement

Front seal — timing cover in place

179 Remove the water pump and separate the drivebelt pulley from the vibration damper, then refer to Paragraphs 120 and 121 and detach the vibration damper from the crankshaft.

180 Carefully pry the seal out of the cover with a seal removal tool or a large screwdriver (photo). Be careful not to distort the cover or scratch the wall of the seal bore. If the engine has accumulated a lot of miles, apply penetrating oil to the seal-to-cover joint and allow it to soak in before attempting to pull the seal out.

181 Clean the bore to remove any old seal material and corrosion. Position the new seal in the bore with the open end of the seal facing IN. A small amount of oil applied to the outer edge of the new seal will make installation easier — don't overdo it!

182 Drive the seal into the bore with GM tool no. J-23042A or a large socket and hammer until it's completely seated (Fig. 13.25). Select a socket that's the same outside diameter as the seal (a section of pipe can be used if a socket isn't available).

183 Reinstall the vibration damper and all other components removed to gain access to the seal.

Front seal — timing cover removed

184 Use a punch or screwdriver and hammer to drive the seal out of the cover from the back side. Support the cover as close to the seal bore as possible (photo). Be careful not to distort the cover or scratch the wall of the seal bore. If the engine has accumulated a lot of miles,

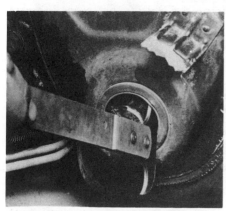

6.180   The front crankshaft oil seal can be removed with a seal removal tool (shown here) or a large screwdriver

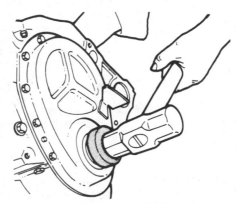

Fig. 13.25   Installing the front crankshaft oil seal with GM tool no. J-23042A (Sec 6)

6.184   While supporting the cover near the seal bore, drive the old seal out from the inside with a hammer and punch or screwdriver

13

6.186   Clean the bore, then apply a small amount of oil to the outer edge of the seal and drive it squarely into the opening with a large socket and a hammmer — DO NOT damage the seal in the process!

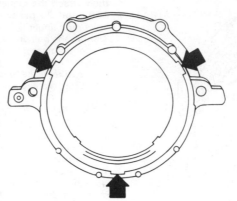

Fig. 13.26   To remove the seal from the housing, insert the tip of the screwdriver into each notch (arrows) and lever the seal out (Sec 6)

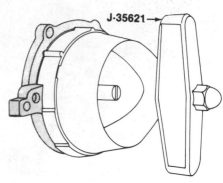

Fig. 13.27   GM tool no. J-35621 is recommended for seal installation with the housing attached to the engine (Sec 6)

apply penetrating oil to the seal-to-cover joint on each side and allow it to soak in before attempting to drive the seal out.

185 Clean the bore to remove any old seal material and corrosion. Support the cover on blocks of wood and position the new seal in the bore with the open end of the seal facing IN. A small amount of oil applied to the outer edge of the new seal will make installation easier — don't overdo it!

186 Drive the seal into the bore with a large socket and hammer until it's completely seated (photo). Select a socket that's the same outside diameter as the seal (a section of pipe can be used if a socket isn't available).

Rear seal

187 Rear seal replacement requires removal of the transmission, clutch assembly and flywheel (manual transmission equipped vehicles) or torque converter and driveplate (automatic transmission equipped vehicles).

188 The old seal can be removed from the housing by inserting a large screwdriver into the notches provided and prying it out (Fig. 13.26). Be sure to note how far it's recessed into the housing bore before removing it; the new seal will have to be recessed an equal amount. Be very careful not to scratch or otherwise damage the bore in the

housing or oil leaks could develop.

189 Check the seal lip contact surface very carefully for scratches and nicks that could damage the new seal lip and cause oil leaks. If the crankshaft is damaged, the only alternative is a new or different crankshaft.

190 Make sure the housing is clean, then apply a thin coat of engine oil to the outer edge of the new seal. Apply moly-based grease to the seal lips. The seal must be pressed squarely into the housing bore, so hammering it into place is not recommended. If you don't have access to GM tool no. J-35621 (Fig. 13.27) remove the oil pan and unbolt the seal housing from the block. Sandwich the housing and seal between two smooth pieces of wood and press the seal into place with the jaws of a large vise. The pieces of wood must be thick enough to distribute the force evenly around the entire circumference of the seal. Work slowly and make sure the seal enters the bore squarely.

191 The seal lips must be lubricated with clean engine oil or moly-based grease before the seal/housing is slipped over the crankshaft and bolted to the block. Use a new gasket — no sealant is required — and make sure the dowel pins are in place before installing the housing (Fig. 13.28).

192 Tighten the nuts/screws a little at a time until they're all snug.

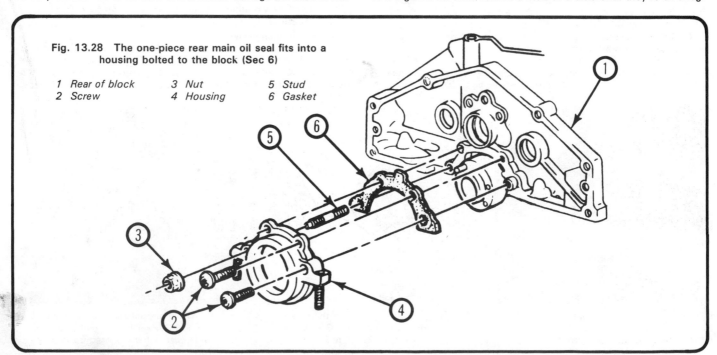

Fig. 13.28   The one-piece rear main oil seal fits into a housing bolted to the block (Sec 6)

1   Rear of block
2   Screw
3   Nut
4   Housing
5   Stud
6   Gasket

7.1   Removing the camshaft thrust plate bolts

---

7   General engine overhaul procedures

Camshaft — removal and installation (2.5 liter four-cylinder engine)

Note: *It is assumed that the engine is already out of the vehicle and the rocker arm cover has been removed. This procedure is not possible with the engine installed. Once lobe lift has been determined (Chapter 2 Part D), the pushrods, the pushrod cover, the valve lifters, the distributor, the oil pump driveshaft, the front pulley and hub and the timing gear cover must be removed (Section 5 of this supplement) before the camshaft can be extracted.*

1   Remove the camshaft thrust plate bolts by rotating the camshaft until the access holes in the timing gear are aligned with them (photo).
2   Remove the camshaft and timing gear through the front of the block. **Caution:** *To avoid damage to the camshaft bearings as the lobes pass over the bearing surfaces, extract the camshaft carefully. Support it with one hand near the engine block.*
3   Refer to Chapter 2 Part D for camshaft inspection procedures.
4   If the timing gear must be removed from the camshaft, it must be pressed off. If you don't have access to a press, take it to an automotive machine shop. The thrust plate must be positioned so that the Woodruff key in the shaft does not damage it when the shaft is pressed off.
5   If the gear has been removed, it must be pressed back on prior to installation of the camshaft.

   a)   Support the camshaft in an arbor press by placing press plate adapters behind the front journal.

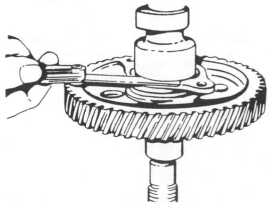

Fig 13.29   Checking camshaft thrust plate end clearance with a feeler gauge (Sec 7)

   b)   Place the gear spacer ring and the thrust plate over the end of the shaft.
   c)   Install the Woodruff key in the shaft keyway.
   d)   Position the camshaft gear and press it onto the shaft until it bottoms against the gear spacer ring.
   e)   Use a feeler gauge to check the end clearance. It should be 0.0015 to 0.005-inch. If the clearance is less than 0.0015-inch, the spacer ring should be replaced. If the clearance is more than 0.005-inch, the thrust plate should be replaced.

6   Before installing the camshaft, coat each of the lobes and journals with engine assembly lube or moly-base grease.
7   Slide the camshaft into the engine block, again taking care not to damage the bearings (photo). Align the marks on the gears.
8   With the timing marks aligned (photo), push the camshaft in to seat it. The access holes should be aligned with the thrust plate bolt holes. Apply Locktite to the threads, then install the bolts and tighten them to the specified torque.

Crankshaft — removal (4.3 liter V6 engine)

9   Follow the procedure in Chapter 2, Part D, but note that the rear seal housing must be unbolted from the block before the crankshaft can be removed. Refer to Section 6 in this Chapter for information and illustrations related to the rear seal and housing.

Crankshaft — installation and main bearing oil clearance check

2.5 liter four-cylinder engine
10   The flanged thrust bearing must be installed in the number five

7.7   The camshaft lobes and journals should be lubricated prior to installation of the camshaft in the block

7.8   The camshaft and crankshaft gears must be positioned so that the timing marks (arrows) line up

13

cap and saddle. Aside from this difference, the procedure described in Chapter 2 Part D, Section 22, can be followed.

4.3 liter V6 engine

11 Follow the procedure in Part D of Chapter 2, but note that the rear seal and housing must be bolted to the block after the cranksahft has been installed. Refer to Section 6 in this Chapter for information and illustrations related to the rear seal and housing.

8 Cooling, heating and air conditioning systems

Water pump — removal and installation (4.3 liter V6 engine)

Warning: *The engine must be completely cool before beginning this procedure.*

1 Detach the negative battery cable from the battery, then drain the coolant from the radiator (Chapter 1).
2 Remove the drivebelts (see Chapter 1).
3 Remove the upper fan shroud.
4 Remove the fan and fan clutch assembly.
5 Remove the water pump pulley.
6 Loosen the hose clamps and detach the lower radiator hose and heater hose from the water pump fittings. If they're hard to remove, grasp each hose, at the fitting, with a large pair of Channel-lock pliers and twist it to break the seal, then pull it off.
7 If necessary to gain access to the water pump fasteners, remove the alternator, air pump, power steering pump or A/C compressor brackets as necessary.
8 Remove the bolts and detach the pump from the engine (Fig. 13.30).

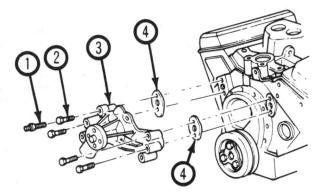

Fig. 13.30 4.3 liter V6 engine water pump mounting details (Sec 8)

1	Stud	3 Water pump
2	Bolt	4 Gaskets

9 Using a gasket scraper, remove all traces of old gasket material and sealant from the engine block. Clean the mating surfaces on the block and the new pump with lacquer thinner or acetone.
10 When installing the new pump, use new gaskets. Coat both sides of the new gaskets with a thin layer of RTV sealant.
11 Apply GM sealant no. 1052080 or equivalent to the mounting bolt threads.
12 Hold the pump in position and install the bolts. Tighten them to the specified torque in a criss-cross pattern. Don't overtighten them or the pump may be distorted.
13 Reinstall all parts removed for access to the pump.
14 Refill the cooling system, run the engine and check for leaks.

9 Fuel and exhaust systems

General Information

On 1985 and later models, Throttle Body Injection was used in place of a carburetor (2.5 liter engine only). From 1986 on, TBI was also standard equipment on V6 engines.

Fuel pressure relief procedure (TBI only)

1 **Warning:** *Before servicing any fuel system component on a fuel injected vehicle, relieve the fuel pressure to minimize the risk of fire and personal injury. Gasoline is extremely flammable, so extra precautions must be taken when working on any part of the fuel system. Do not smoke or allow open flames or bare light bulbs near the work area. Also, do not work in a garage if a natural gas-type appliance with a pilot light is present.*
2 Remove the fuse marked *Fuel Pump* from the fuse block in the passenger compartment.
3 Crank the engine over. It will start and run until the fuel supply remaining in the fuel lines is depleted. When the engine stops, engage the starter again for another three seconds to ensure that any remaining pressure is dissipated.
4 With the ignition turned to Off, replace the fuel pump fuse. Unless this procedure is followed before servicing fuel lines or connections, fuel spray (and possible injury) may occur.

Fuel pump — testing (TBI only)

Warning: *Gasoline is extremely flammable, so extra precautions must be taken when working on any part of the fuel system. Do not smoke or allow open flames or bare light bulbs near the work area. Also, do not work in a garage if a natural gas-type appliance with a pilot light is present.*

5 The fuel pump for both four-cylinder and V6 powered models is located in the fuel tank, is sealed and is not repairable.
6 When the key is first turned on without the engine running, the ECM will turn the fuel pump relay on for two seconds. This builds up the fuel pressure quickly. If the engine is not started within two seconds, the ECM will shut the fuel pump off and wait until the engine starts. As soon as the engine is cranked, the ECM will turn the relay on and run the fuel pump.
7 As a backup system to the fuel pump relay, the fuel pump can also be turned on by the oil pressure switch. The oil pressure switch is a normally open switch which closes when the oil pressure reaches about 4 psi. If the fuel pump relay fails, the oil pressure switch will run the fuel pump.
8 An inoperative fuel pump relay can result in long cranking times, particularly if the engine is cold. The oil pressure switch acts as a backup to the relay and will turn on the fuel pump as soon as the oil pressure reaches about 4 psi.
9 When the ignition is turned to On, the Electronic Control Module (ECM) will turn on the in-tank fuel pump. It will remain on as long as the engine is cranking or running and the ECM is receiving High Energy Ignition (HEI) distributor reference pulses.
10 The fuel pump test terminal is terminal G of the assembly line communication link (ALCL) located in the passenger compartment under the dashboard, to the right of the steering column. When the engine is stopped, the pump can be activated by applying battery voltage to the test terminal.
11 Before beginning the following sequence of tests, make sure that the fuel tank has fuel in it.
12 Relieve fuel system pressure (refer to steps 2 and 3). Install a pressure gauge in the line between the fuel filter and the inlet fitting of the TBI (photo).
13 Turn the ignition switch to the On position. The fuel pump should run for two seconds. The pump should pressurize the system at 9 to 13 psi. Pressure may drop slightly when the pump stops.
14 If there is no fuel pressure, check the fuel pump fuse. If the fuse is blown, check the wiring associated with the fuel pump (see the wiring diagrams at the end of this Supplement).
15 If the fuse is good and there is no fuel pressure, listen for the fuel pump running while applying battery voltage to the fuel pump test connector. If it runs, check for a restriction in the fuel delivery line or a restricted fuel filter.
16 If there is fuel pressure but it is less than specified, pinch the fuel return line. Apply voltage to the fuel pump test terminal. If the pressure is still low, either the fuel pump, the fuel pump-to-fuel line coupling hose or the pulsator on the pump inlet is faulty.
17 If there is fuel pressure but it is above the specified pressure, disconnect the injector connector, disconnect the primary coil connectors, then disconnect the fuel return line flexible hose and attach a 5/16-inch diameter flex hose to the throttle body side of the return line. Insert the other end into an approved fuel container. Note the fuel pressure within two seconds after the ignition is turned on. This test will deter-

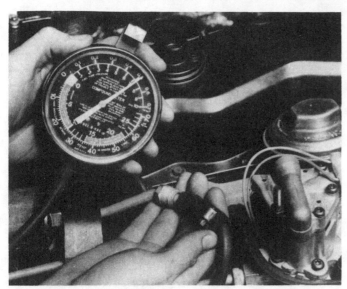

9.12   To test fuel pump operation, install a pressure gauge in the line between the fuel filter and the inlet fitting of the TBI, then turn the ignition switch to On

Fig. 13.31   Throttle Body Injection (TBI) has very few components (Sec 9)

1 Fuel injector	4 Throttle Position
2 Fuel pressure regulator	Sensor (TPS)
3 Idle Air Control (IAC)	5 Fuel meter cover

mine if the high fuel pressure is due to a restricted fuel return line or a faulty fuel pressure regulator.
18   If the fuel pressure is now within the specified limits, locate and repair the restriction in the fuel return line.
19   If fuel pressure is still high, replace the fuel meter cover.
20   If the specified fuel pressure is attained but bleeds down, pinch the return line and recheck the pressure gauge. If the pressure holds, replace the fuel meter cover.
21   If the fuel pressure does not hold, check the pressure again, this time pinching the pressure hose after the specified pressure is obtained. If the pressure holds, check for a leaking pump coupling hose, a leaking pulsator or a faulty in-tank pump.
22   If the pressure does not hold with the pressure line pinched after pressure buildup, check for a leaking throttle body injector.
23   A leaking injector can be diagnosed by disconnecting the injector connector, turning on the ignition to allow fuel pressure to build up and looking into the throttle body to see if the injector drips. Inspect the injector and seals. If the seals do not appear to be damaged or leaking, replace the injector.
24   If there is no fuel pressure and the fuel pump fuse is good, check the fuel pump relay and connector for burned or loose wires.

Fuel lines and fittings — repair and replacement (TBI only)

Warning: *Gasoline is extremely flammable, so extra precautions must be taken when working on any part of the fuel system. Do not smoke or allow open flames or bare light bulbs near the work area. Also, do not work in a garage if a natural gas-type appliance with a pilot light is present.*

25   Always relieve the fuel pressure before servicing fuel lines or fittings as described at the beginning of this Section.
26   The fuel feed and return lines extend from the fuel gauge sending unit to the engine compartment. The lines are secured to the underbody with clip and screw assemblies. Both fuel feed lines must be properly routed and maintained and should be occasionally inspected for leaks, kinks or dents.
27   If evidence of dirt is found in the system or fuel filter during disassembly, the line should be disconnected and blown out. Check the fuel strainer on the fuel gauge sending unit for damage or deterioration.
28   If replacement of a fuel feed, fuel return or emission line is called for, use welded steel tubing meeting GM Specification 124-M or its equivalent.
29   Do not use copper or aluminum tubing to replace steel tubing. These materials do not have satisfactory durability to withstand normal vehicle vibrations.
30 **Warning:** *If a section of fuel line is damaged, the entire line must be replaced. Do not attempt to repair fuel lines with fuel hose. Fuel*

injection systems operate under high pressure and replacing fuel lines with anything other than original equipment-quality materials may create a hazardous condition.

Fuel injection system (TBI) — general information

Electronic fuel injection (EFI) provides optimum mixture ratios at all engine speeds and loads and offers immediate throttle response characteristics. It also enables the engine to run at the leanest possible air/fuel mixture ratio, greatly reducing exhaust gas emissions.
Both the four-cylinder and V6 engines are equipped with a throttle body injection (TBI) unit, which replaces a conventional carburetor atop the intake manifold. The system is controlled by an Electronic Control Module (ECM), which monitors engine performance and adjusts the air/fuel mixture accordingly.
The TBI unit is computer controlled by the Electronic Control Module (ECM) and supplies the correct amount of fuel during all engine operating conditions.
An electric fuel pump located in the fuel tank with the fuel gauge sending unit pumps fuel to the TBI through the fuel feed line and an inline fuel filter. The pump is designed to provide pressurized fuel at about 18 psi. A pressure regulator in the TBI keeps fuel available to the injector at a constant pressure between 9 and 13 psi. Fuel in excess of injector needs is returned to the fuel tank by a separate line. The injector, located in the TBI, is controlled by the ECM.
The basic TBI unit is made up of two major casting assemblies: A throttle body with an Idle Air Control (IAC) valve controls air flow and a throttle position sensor monitors throttle angle. A fuel body consists of a fuel meter cover with a built-in pressure regulator and a fuel injector to supply fuel to the engine (photo).
The throttle body portion of the TBI unit contains ports located at, above and below the throttle valve. These ports generate the vacuum signals for the exhaust gas recirculation (EGR) valve, manifold absolute pressure (MAP) sensor and the canister purge system.
The fuel injector is a solenoid operated device controlled by the ECM. The ECM turns on the solenoid, which lifts a normally closed ball valve off its seat. The fuel, which is under pressure, is injected in a conical spray pattern at the walls of the throttle body bore above the throttle valve. The fuel which is not used by the injector passes through the pressure regulator before being returned to the fuel tank.
The pressure regulator is a diaphragm-operated relief valve with injector pressure on one side and air cleaner pressure on the other. The function of the regulator is to maintain a constant pressure at the injector at all times by controlling the flow in the return line.

13

9.37 The fuel pressure regulator is installed in the fuel meter cover and pre-adjusted by the factory — do not remove the four retaining screws (arrows) or you may damage the regulator!

The purpose of the idle air control valve is to control engine idle speed while preventing stalls due to changes in engine load. The IAC valve, mounted on the throttle body, controls bypass air around the throttle valve. By moving a conical valve in, to decrease air flow, or out, to increase air flow, a controlled amount of air can move around the throttle valve. If rpm is too low, more air is bypassed around the throttle valve to increase rpm. If rpm is too high, less air is bypassed around the throttle valve to decrease rpm.

During idle, the proper position of the IAC valve is calculated by the ECM based upon battery voltage, coolant temperature, engine load and engine rpm. If the rpm drops below a specified rpm, and the throttle valve is closed, the ECM senses a near stall condition. The ECM will then calculate a new valve position to prevent stalls based on barometric pressure.

Throttle Body Injection (TBI) — component removal and installation

Note: *Because of its relative simplicity, a throttle body assembly does not have to be removed from the intake manifold or completely disassembled during component replacement. However, for the sake of clar-*
ity, *the following procedures are depicted in the accompanying photos on a TBI assembly removed from the vehicle.*

31 Relieve the fuel pressure.
32 Disconnect the cable from the negative terminal of the battery.
33 Remove the air cleaner.

Fuel meter cover and fuel injector
34 Remove the injector electrical connector by squeezing the two tabs together and pulling straight up.
35 Unscrew the five fuel meter cover retaining screws and lockwashers securing the fuel meter cover to the fuel meter body. Note the location of the two short screws.
36 Remove the fuel meter cover. **Caution:** *Do not immerse the fuel meter cover in solvent. It might damage the pressure regulator diaphragm and gasket.*
37 The fuel meter cover contains the fuel pressure regulator. The regulator is pre-set and plugged at the factory. If a malfunction occurs, it cannot be serviced. It must be replaced as a complete assembly. **Warning:** *Do not remove the screws securing the pressure regulator to the fuel meter cover (photo). It has a large spring inside which is tightly compressed. If accidentally released, it could cause injury. Disassembly might also cause a fuel leak between the diaphragm and the regulator container.*
38 With the old fuel meter cover gasket in place to prevent damage to the casting, carefully pry the injector from the fuel meter body with a screwdriver until it can be lifted free (photos). **Caution:** *Use care in removing the injector to prevent damage to the electrical connector terminals, the injector fuel filter, the O-ring and the nozzle (photo).*
39 The fuel meter body should be removed from the throttle body if it needs to be cleaned. To remove it, remove the fuel feed and return line fittings (photo) and the Torx screws that attach the fuel meter body to the throttle body.
40 Remove the old gasket from the fuel meter cover and discard it. Remove the large O-ring and steel back-up washer from the upper counterbore of the fuel meter body injector cavity. Clean the fuel meter body thoroughly in solvent and blow dry.
41 Remove the small O-ring from the nozzle end of the injector. Carefully rotate the injector fuel filter back-and-forth and remove the filter from the base of the injector (photo). Gently clean the filter in solvent and allow it to drip dry. It is too small and delicate to dry with compressed air. **Caution:** *The fuel injector itself is an electrical component. Do not immerse it in any type of cleaning solvent.*
42 The fuel injector is not serviceable. If it is malfunctioning, replace it as an assembly.
43 Install the clean fuel injector nozzle filter on the end of the fuel injector with the larger end of the filter facing the injector so that the filter covers the raised rib at the base of the injector. Use a twisting motion to position the filter against the base of the injector.
44 Lubricate a new small O-ring with automatic transmission fluid.

9.38a Carefully pry the injector from the fuel meter body

9.38b Note the position of the terminals on top and the dowel pin on the bottom of the injector (in relation to the fuel meter cover) when you lift the injector out of the cover

9.38c A typical TBI injector

1 *Electrical terminals*   3 *O-ring*
2 *Injector fuel filter*   4 *Nozzle*

Push the O-ring onto the nozzle end of the injector until it presses against the injector fuel filter.

45 Insert the steel back-up washer in the top counterbore of the fuel meter body injector cavity.

46 Lubricate a new large O-ring with automatic transmission fluid and install it directly over the back-up washer. Be sure that the O-ring is seated properly in the cavity and is flush with the top of the fuel meter body casting surface. **Caution:** *The back-up washer and large O-ring must be installed before the injector or improper seating of the large O-ring could cause fuel to leak.*

47 Install the injector in the cavity in the fuel meter body, aligning the raised lug on the injector base with the cast-in notch in the fuel meter body cavity. Push straight down on the injector with both thumbs until it is fully seated in the cavity. **Note:** *The electrical terminals of the injector should be approximately parallel to the throttle shaft.*

48 Install a new fuel outlet passage gasket on the fuel meter cover and a new fuel meter cover gasket on the fuel meter body (photo).

9.39   The fuel inlet and outlet fittings must be removed before the fuel meter body can be detached from the throttle body

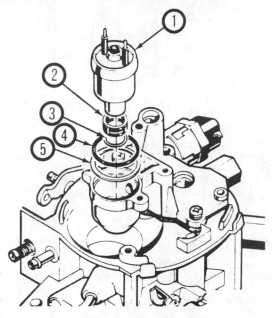

Fig. 13.32   Remove the large O-ring and steel backup washer from the injector cavity of the fuel meter body (Sec 9)

1 Fuel injector	4 Large O-ring
2 Filter	5 Steel backup washer
3 Small O-ring	

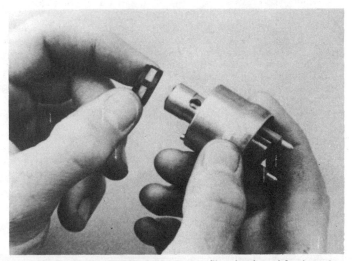

9.41   Gently rotate the fuel injector filter back-and-forth and carefully pull it off the nozzle

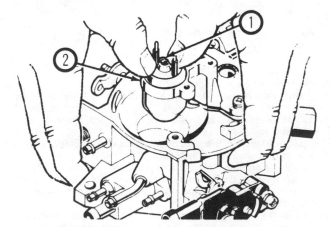

Fig. 13.33   Push straight down with both thumbs to install the injector in the fuel meter body cavity (Sec 9)

1 Fuel injector   2 Fuel meter body

9.48   Position the fuel outlet passage gasket and the fuel meter cover gasket properly

13

9.49   Install a new dust seal in the recess of the fuel meter body

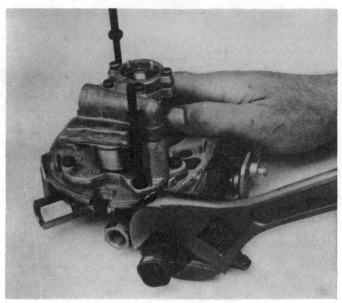

9.55   Remove the IAC valve with a large wrench, but be careful, it's a delicate device

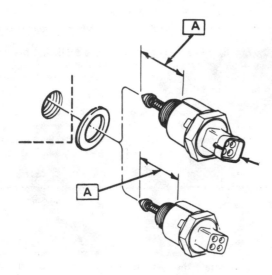

Fig. 13.34   Distance A should be less than 1-1/8 inch for either style Idle Air Control Valve — if it isn't, determine what style valve you have and adjust it accordingly (Sec 9)

9.65   The Throttle Position Switch is mounted on the side of the TBI unit

49   Install a new dust seal into the recess on the fuel meter body (photo).

50   Attach the fuel meter cover to the fuel meter body, making sure that the pressure regulator dust seal and cover gaskets are in place.

51   Apply a thread locking compound to the threads of the fuel meter cover screws. Install the screws (the two short screws go next to the injector) and tighten them to the specified torque. **Note:** *Service repair kits include a small vial of thread compound with directions for use. If material is not available, use Loctite 262, GM part number 1052624, or equivalent. Do not use a higher strength locking compound than recommended, as this may prevent subsequent removal of the screws or cause breakage of the screwhead if removal becomes necessary.*

52   Plug in the electrical connector to the injector.

53   Install the air cleaner.

Idle Air Control (IAC) valve

54   Unplug the electrical connector at the Idle Air Control valve.

55   Remove the Idle Air Control valve with a wrench on the hex surface only (photo).

56   Before installing a new Idle Air Control valve, measure the distance the valve is extended. The measurement should be made from the motor housing to the end of the cone. The distance should be no greater than 1-1/8 inch. If the cone is extended too far, damage may occur

to the valve when it is installed.

57   Identify the replacement IAC valve as either a Type I (with a collar at the electric terminal end) or a Type II (without a collar). If the measured dimension A is greater than 1-1/8 inch, the distance must be reduced as follows:

   Type I — Exert firm pressure on the valve to retract it (a slight side-to-side movement may be helpful).

   Type II — Compress the retaining spring of the valve while turning the valve in with a clockwise motion. Return the spring to its original position with the straight portion of the spring aligned with the flat surface of the valve.

58   Install the new Idle Air Control valve on the throttle body. Use the new gasket supplied with the assembly. Tighten the IAC valve to the specified torque.

59   Plug in the electrical connector.

60   Install the air cleaner.

61   Start the engine and allow it to reach operating temperature. The

Electronic Control Module (ECM) will reset the idle speed when the vehicle is driven above 35 mph.

Throttle Position Sensor (TPS)

62 The Throttle Position Sensor (TPS) is connected to the throttle shaft on the TBI unit. As the throttle valve angle is changed (as the accelerator pedal is moved), the output of the TPS also changes. At a closed throttle position, the output of the TPS is below 1.25-volts. As the throttle valve opens, the output increases so that, at wide-open throttle, the output voltage should be approximately 5-volts.

63 A broken or loose TPS can cause intermittent bursts of fuel from the injector and an unstable idle, because the ECM thinks the throttle is moving. A problem in any of the TPS circuits will set either a Code 21 or 22 (see *Trouble Codes*, Chapter 6).

64 The TPS is not adjustable. The ECM uses the reading at idle for the zero reading. If the TPS malfunctions, it is replaced as a unit.

65 Unscrew the two Torx screws (photo) and remove the TPS.

66 Install the new TPS. **Note:** *Make sure that the tang on the lever is properly engaged with the stop on the TBI.*

---

10   Engine electrical systems

Charging system — general information

All 1986 and later V6 powered vehicles and all 1987 and later models utilize a new style alternator, designated the CS-130. This alternator has no test hole in the end frame and it is not serviceable.

Charging system — check

1 Check to make sure the drivebelt is tensioned properly and not slipping (see Chapter 1).

2 Verify that the battery and alternator connections are clean and tight.

3 With the ignition switch turned to the On position and the engine stopped, the charge indicator light on the instrument panel should be glowing brightly.

4 If your vehicle does not have a charge indicator light, proceed to Step 9.

5 If the light is not on, disconnect the wiring harness at the rear of the alternator and ground the L terminal wire. If the light now glows, replace the alternator.

6 If the light does not glow, check the bulb. If the bulb is not burned out, locate the open circuit between the grounded terminal and the engine control switch.

7 With the engine running, the light should be off. If it is on, detach the wiring harness at the alternator. If the light goes out, replace the alternator.

8 If the light is still on, trace the L terminal wire, looking for a short to ground.

9 On vehicles without a charge indicator light, detach the connector from the alternator and probe terminal L and terminal I (if used) on the wiring harness side with a voltmeter connected to ground.

10 With the ignition switch On and the engine not running, a reading of 12 to 14-volts should be attained.

11 If the voltmeter reads zero, an open circuit exists between the battery and the terminal being tested.

12 Reattach the harness connector and run the engine at moderate speed with all accessories turned off.

13 Using a voltmeter, measure the voltage across the battery terminals. If the voltage indicated is above 16-volts, replace the alternator.

14 Additional checks should be performed by a dealer service department or a repair shop.

Alternator — removal and installation (4.3 liter V6 engine)

15 Disconnect the negative cable from the battery, then remove the drivebelt(s).

16 Disconnect the wires from the back of the alternator. Mark them with pieces of tape to ensure correct reinstallation.

17 Remove the brace bolt from the back of the alternator and the two mounting bolts (Fig. 13.35).

18 Installation is the reverse of the removal procedure.

Ignition system — general information

19 Beginning in 1988, an EST distributor with a sealed module connector and separate coil is used on all models.

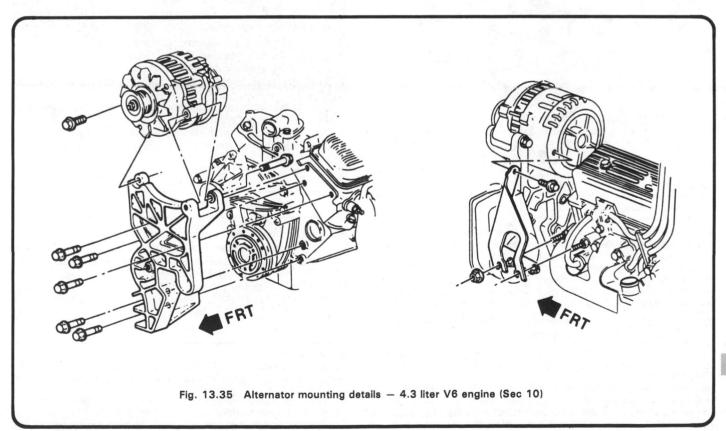

Fig. 13.35   Alternator mounting details — 4.3 liter V6 engine (Sec 10)

13

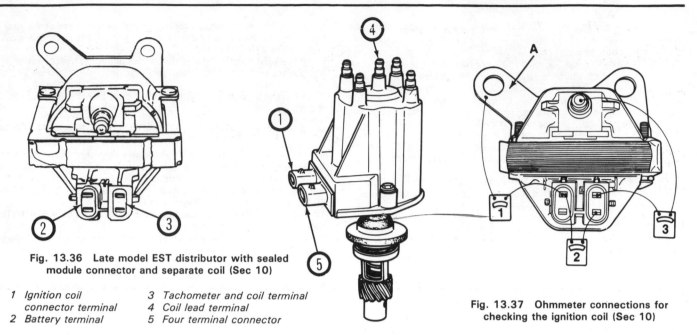

Fig. 13.36   Late model EST distributor with sealed module connector and separate coil (Sec 10)

1   Ignition coil
    connector terminal
2   Battery terminal
3   Tachometer and coil terminal
4   Coil lead terminal
5   Four terminal connector

Fig. 13.37   Ohmmeter connections for checking the ignition coil (Sec 10)

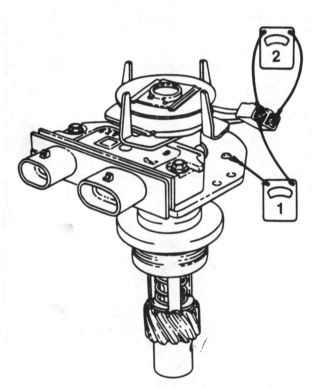

Fig. 13.38   Ohmmeter connections for checking the pick-up coil (Sec 10)

Ignition coil – check

20   Disconnect the coil wire from the center terminal of the distributor and detach the ignition switch wire from the coil (Fig. 13.36).
21   Connect an ohmmeter as shown in Fig. 13.37 for test number 1. Using the high scale, the reading should be infinite. If it isn't, replace the coil.
22   Connect the ohmmeter as shown in test 2. On the low scale, the reading should be very low or zero. If not, replace the coil.
23   Connect the ohmmeter as shown in test 3. On the high scale, the reading should not be infinite. If it is, replace the coil.

Pick-up coil – check

24   Disconnect the negative cable from the battery.
25   Remove the distributor cap.
26   Disconnect the pick-up coil connector from the module.
27   Connect an ohmmeter as shown in Fig. 13.38 for test 1. The reading should be infinite. If not, replace the pick-up coil.
28   Reconnect the ohmmeter as shown in test 2 and flex the pick-up coil leads by hand. The ohmmeter should show a constant reading of between 500 and 1500 ohms. If not, or if the reading varies as the leads are flexed, replace the pick-up coil.

Ignition coil – removal and installation

29   Disconnect the negative cable from the battery.
30   Disconnect the wires from the coil terminals.
31   Remove the secondary lead from the coil.
32   Remove the nuts holding the coil bracket to the engine bracket or manifold.
33   Drill out the two rivets holding the coil to the coil bracket and separate the coil from the bracket.
34   Attach the new coil to the bracket with bolts and nuts.
35   The remainder of installation is the reverse of the removal procedure.

---

11   Emissions control systems

Trouble codes

The following trouble codes, along with the trouble codes listed in Chapter 6, may be encountered when diagnosing problems related to the throttle body injection system and/or the emissions control systems. Aside from these differences, the emissions control systems on newer vehicles are very similar in design and operation to the systems described in Chapter 6.

---

12   Brakes

Rear wheel anti-lock brakes – general information

Beginning in 1990, all models are equipped with a Rear Wheel Anti-Lock brake system (RWAL). This system monitors the rear wheel speed and when it senses a wheel speed decrease, modulates the hy-

Trouble Code	Circuit or system	Probable cause
Code 32 . . . . (3 flashes, pause, 2 flashes)	EGR system	The EGR solenoid should not be energized and vacuum should not pass to the EGR valve. The diagnostic switch should close at about 2-inches of vacuum. With vacuum applied, the switch should close. Replace the EGR valve.*
Code 33 . . . . (3 flashes, pause, 3 flashes)	MAP sensor	Check the vacuum hoses from the MAP sensor. Check the electrical connections at the ECM. Replace the MAP sensor.*
Code 34 . . . . (3 flashes, pause, 4 flashes)	MAP sensor	Code 34 will set when the signal voltage from the MAP sensor is too low. Instead, the ECM will substitute a fixed MAP value and use the TPS to control fuel delivery. Replace the MAP sensor.*
Code 35 . . . . (3 flashes, pause, 5 flashes)	Idle Air Control	Code 35 will set when the closed throttle speed is 50 rpm above or below the correct idle speed for 30 seconds. Replace the IAC.*
Code 43 . . . . (4 flashes, pause, 3 flashes)	Electronic Spark Control	Check the voltage at the ECM A-B connector terminal B7; it should be over 6-volts unless the system is sensing detonation. Check for a loose connection. Replace the ESC sensor and/or module.*
Code 55 . . . . (5 flashes, pause, 5 flashes)	ECM	Be sure that the ECM ground connections are tight. If they are, replace the ECM.*

* Component replacement may not cure the problem in all cases. For this reason, you may want to seek professional advice before purchasing replacement parts.

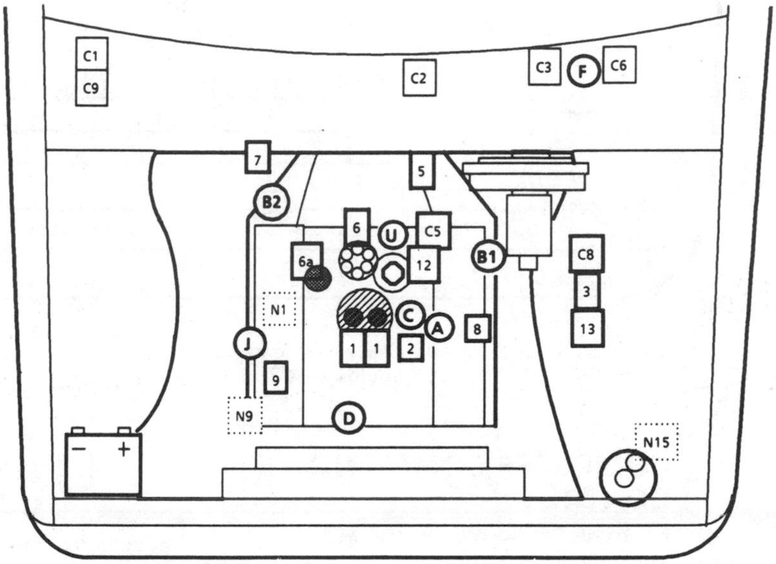

Fig. 13.39 Emissions control system and related component locations – 2.5 liter four-cylinder engine (1987 model shown, others similar) (Sec 11)

☐ **COMPUTER COMMAND CONTROL**

C1 Electronic Control Module (E.C.M.)
C2 ALDL diagnostic connector
C3 "SERVICE ENGINE SOON" light
C5 ECM harness ground
C6 Fuse panel
C8 Fuel pump test connector

☐ **ECM CONTROLLED COMPONENTS**

1 Fuel injector
2 Idle air control
3 Fuel Pump relay
5 Transmission Converter Clutch Connector
6 Electronic Spark Timing Distributor (E.S.T.)
13 A/C relay

○ **ECM INFORMATION SENSORS**

A Manifold pressure (M.A.P.)
B Exhaust oxygen
C Throttle position (T.P.S.)
D Coolant temperature
F Vehicle speed (V.S.S.)
G Power Steering Pressure
T Manifold Air Temperature (M.A.T.)

⬚ **EMISSION COMPONENTS (NOT ECM CONTROLLED)**

N1 Crankcase vent valve (PCV)
N17 Fuel Vapor Canister

draulic pressure to the rear brakes, inhibiting their tendency to lock up. The system consists of a control unit, located under the driver's seat, the hydraulic unit, which contains solenoids to pulse the brake line pressure, the speed sensor, mounted in the axle housing, a system electrical check connector, a pressure differential switch, located near the master cylinder, and a system fuse.

Each time the engine is started, the amber ABS warning light on the dashboard comes on for a brief time and then goes out, indicating the system is operating properly. If the dashboard light comes on and stays on while the vehicle is in operation, the ABS system should be checked. About the only check the home mechanic can make is to inspect the ABS fuse to determine if it's burned out. Due to the

complicated nature of this system, further diagnosis should be done by a dealer service department.

13   Chassis electrical system

Wiring diagrams

Wiring diagrams for later model vehicles are included at the end of this Supplement. Due to space limitations we are not able to provide every diagram for all years. However, the diagrams included are typical for later models.

13

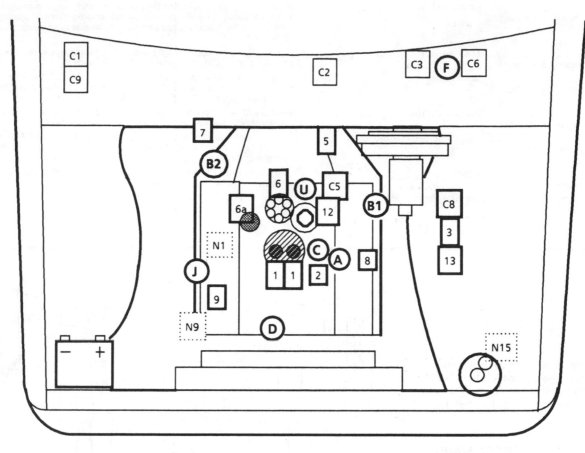

Fig. 13.40   Emissions control system and related component locations —
V6 engine (1987 model shown, others similar) (Sec 11)

☐ COMPUTER COMMAND CONTROL

C1   Electronic Control Module (E.C.M.)
C2   ALDL diagnostic connector
C3   "SERVICE ENGINE SOON" light
C5   ECM harness ground
C6   Fuse panel
C8   Fuel pump test connector
C9   Elapsed Timer Module

○ ECM INFORMATION SENSORS

A   Manifold Absolute Pressure (M.A.P.)
B1   Exhaust oxygen (Federal)
B2   Exhaust Oxygen (California)
C   Throttle position (T.P.S.)
D   Coolant temperature
F   Vehicle speed (V.S.S.)
J   Electronic Spark Control Knock (E.S.C.)
U   EGR vacuum diagnostic switch

☐ ECM CONTROLLED COMPONENTS

1   Fuel injector
2   Idle air control
3   Fuel pump relay
5   Transmission Converter Clutch Connector
6   Electronic Spark Timing Distributor (E.S.T.)
6a   Remote ignition coil
7   Electronic Spark Control module (E.S.C.)
8   Oil pressure switch
9   Electric Air Control solenoid (E.A.C.)
12   Exhaust Gas Recirculation Vacuum Solenoid
13   A/C Relay

⠿ EMISSION COMPONENTS (NOT ECM CONTROLLED)

N1   Crankcase vent valve (PCV)
N9   Air Pump
N15 Fuel Vapor Canister

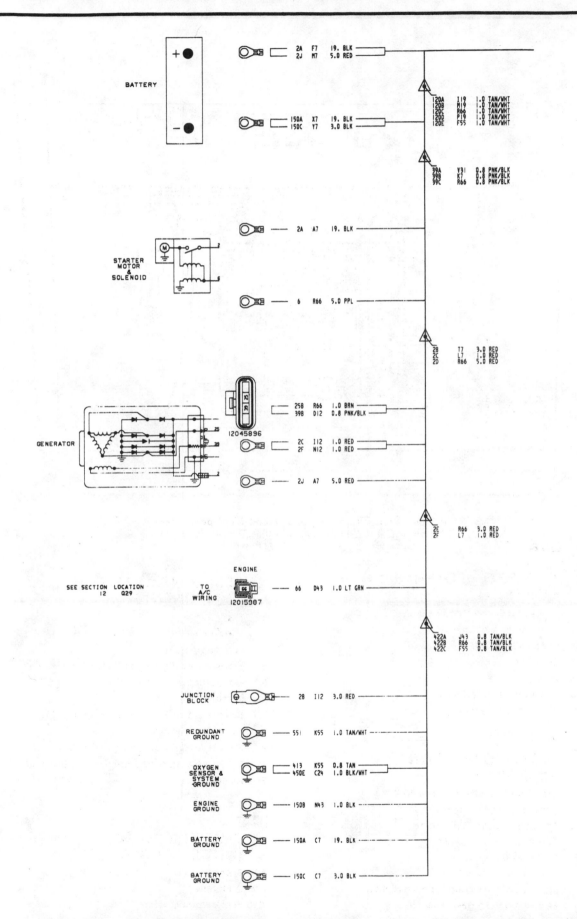

Engine wiring harness — four-cylinder engine with Throttle Body Injection (TBI) (1987 shown) (1 of 6)

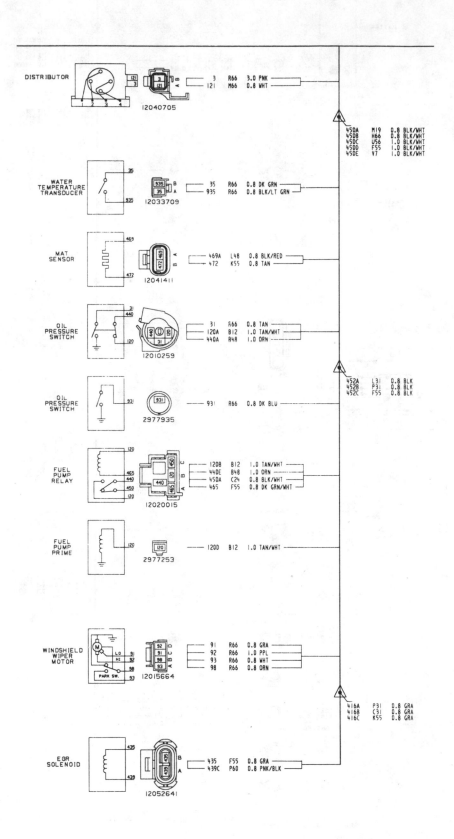

Engine wiring harness — four-cylinder engine with Throttle Body Injection (TBI) (1987 shown) (2 of 6)

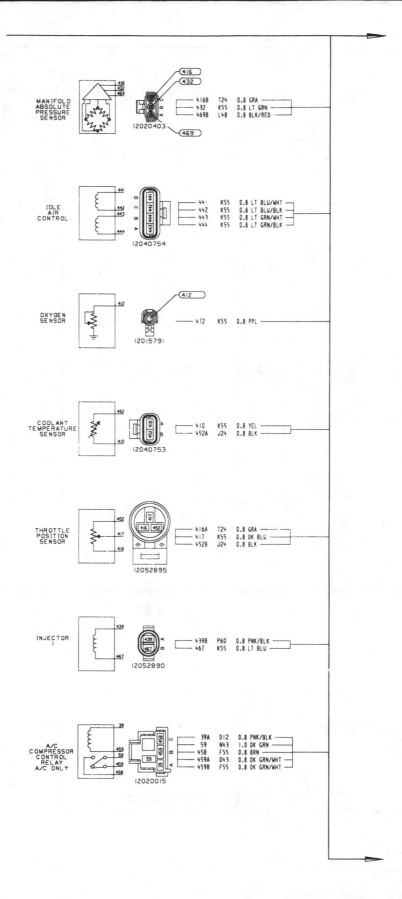

Engine wiring harness — four-cylinder engine with Throttle Body Injection (TBI) (1987 shown) (3 of 6)

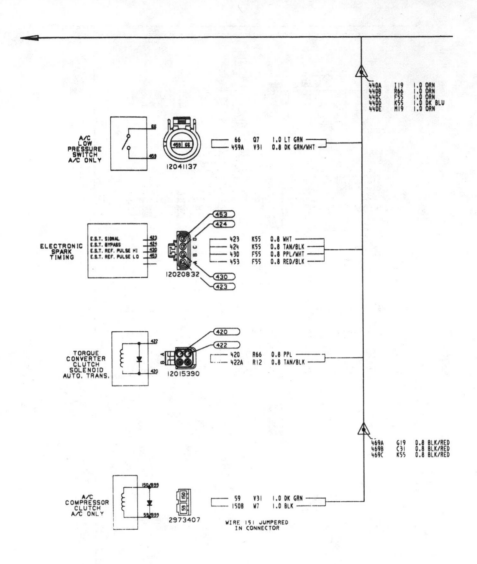

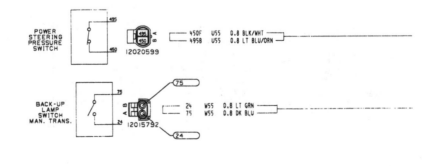

Engine wiring harness — four-cylinder engine with Throttle Body Injection (TBI) (1987 shown) (4 of 6)

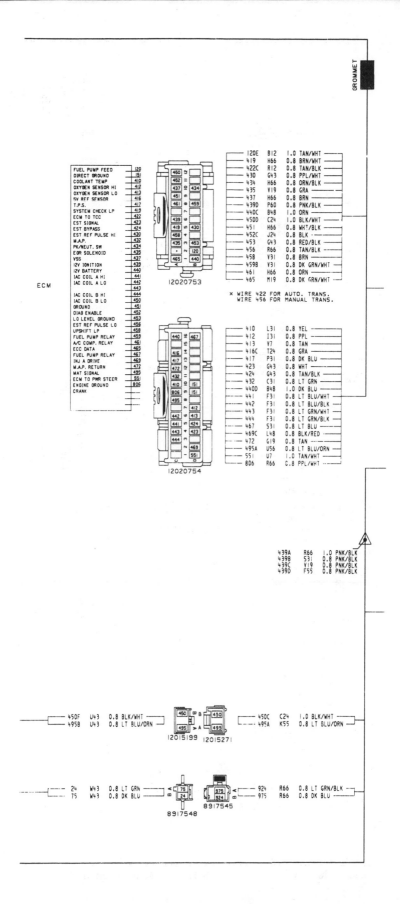

ECM

FUEL PUMP FEED	120		
DIRECT GROUND	151		
COOLANT TEMP	410		
OXYGEN SENSOR HI	412		
OXYGEN SENSOR LO	413		
5V REF SENSOR	416		
T.P.S.	417		
SYSTEM CHECK LP	419		
ECM TO TCC	422		
EST SIGNAL	423		
EST BYPASS	424		
EST REF PULSE HI	430		
M.A.P.	432		
PK/NEUT. SW	434		
EGR SOLENOID	435		
VSS	437		
12V IGNITION	439		
12V BATTERY	440		
IAC COIL A HI	441		
IAC COIL A LO	442		
	443		
IAC COIL B HI	444		
IAC COIL B LO	450		
GROUND	451		
DIAG ENABLE	452		
LO LEVEL GROUND	453		
EST REF PULSE LO	456		
UPSHIFT LP	458		
FUEL PUMP RELAY	459		
A/C COMP. RELAY	461		
ECC DATA	465		
FUEL PUMP RELAY	467		
INJ A DRIVE	469		
M.A.P. RETURN	472		
MAT SIGNAL	495		
ECM TO PWR STEER	551		
ENGINE GROUND	806		
CRANK			

12020753

120E	B12	1.0	TAN/WHT
419	H66	0.8	BRN/WHT
422C	R12	0.8	TAN/BLK
430	G43	0.8	PPL/WHT
434	H66	0.8	ORN/BLK
435	V19	0.8	GRA
437	H66	0.8	BRN
439D	P60	0.8	PNK/BLK
440C	B48	1.0	ORN
450D	C24	1.0	BLK/WHT
451	H66	0.8	WHT/BLK
452C	J24	0.8	BLK
453	G43	0.8	RED/BLK
456	R66	0.8	TAN/BLK
458	V31	0.8	BRN
459B	V31	0.8	DK GRN/WHT
461	H66	0.8	ORN
465	M19	0.8	DK GRN/WHT

× WIRE 422 FOR AUTO. TRANS.
WIRE 456 FOR MANUAL TRANS.

12020754

410	L31	0.8	YEL
412	I31	0.8	PPL
413	Y7	0.8	TAN
416C	T24	0.8	GRA
417	P31	0.8	DK BLU
423	G43	0.8	WHT
424	G43	0.8	TAN/BLK
432	C31	0.8	LT GRN
440D	B48	1.0	DK BLU
441	F31	0.8	LT BLU/WHT
442	F31	0.8	LT BLU/BLK
443	F31	0.8	LT GRN/WHT
444	F31	0.8	LT GRN/BLK
467	S31	0.8	LT BLU
469C	L48	0.8	BLK/RED
472	G19	0.8	TAN
495A	U56	0.8	LT BLU/ORN
551	U7	1.0	TAN/WHT
806	R66	0.8	PPL/WHT

439A	R66	1.0	PNK/BLK
439B	S31	0.8	PNK/BLK
439C	V19	0.8	PNK/BLK
439D	F55	0.8	PNK/BLK

450F	U43	0.8	BLK/WHT
495B	U43	0.8	LT BLU/ORN

12015199   12015271

450C	C24	1.0	BLK/WHT
495A	K55	0.8	LT BLU/ORN

24	W43	0.8	LT GRN
75	W43	0.8	DK BLU

8917548   8917545

924	R66	0.8	LT GRN/BLK
975	R66	0.8	DK BLU

Engine wiring harness — four-cylinder engine with Throttle Body Injection (TBI) (1987 shown) (5 of 6)

13

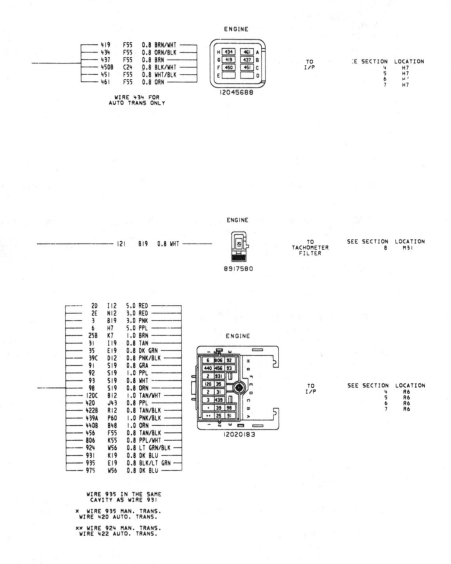

Conversion factors

Length (distance)

Inches (in)	X 25.4	= Millimetres (mm)	X 0.0394	= Inches (in)	
Feet (ft)	X 0.305	= Metres (m)	X 3.281	= Feet (ft)	
Miles	X 1.609	= Kilometres (km)	X 0.621	= Miles	

Volume (capacity)

Cubic inches (cu in; in³)	X 16.387	= Cubic centimetres (cc; cm³)	X 0.061	= Cubic inches (cu in; in³)
Imperial pints (Imp pt)	X 0.568	= Litres (l)	X 1.76	= Imperial pints (Imp pt)
Imperial quarts (Imp qt)	X 1.137	= Litres (l)	X 0.88	= Imperial quarts (Imp qt)
Imperial quarts (Imp qt)	X 1.201	= US quarts (US qt)	X 0.833	= Imperial quarts (Imp qt)
US quarts (US qt)	X 0.946	= Litres (l)	X 1.057	= US quarts (US qt)
Imperial gallons (Imp gal)	X 4.546	= Litres (l)	X 0.22	= Imperial gallons (Imp gal)
Imperial gallons (Imp gal)	X 1.201	= US gallons (US gal)	X 0.833	= Imperial gallons (Imp gal)
US gallons (US gal)	X 3.785	= Litres (l)	X 0.264	= US gallons (US gal)

Mass (weight)

Ounces (oz)	X 28.35	= Grams (g)	X 0.035	= Ounces (oz)
Pounds (lb)	X 0.454	= Kilograms (kg)	X 2.205	= Pounds (lb)

Force

Ounces-force (ozf; oz)	X 0.278	= Newtons (N)	X 3.6	= Ounces-force (ozf; oz)
Pounds-force (lbf; lb)	X 4.448	= Newtons (N)	X 0.225	= Pounds-force (lbf; lb)
Newtons (N)	X 0.1	= Kilograms-force (kgf; kg)	X 9.81	= Newtons (N)

Pressure

Pounds-force per square inch (psi; lbf/in²; lb/in²)	X 0.070	= Kilograms-force per square centimetre (kgf/cm²; kg/cm²)	X 14.223	= Pounds-force per square inch (psi; lbf/in²; lb/in²)
Pounds-force per square inch (psi; lbf/in²; lb/in²)	X 0.068	= Atmospheres (atm)	X 14.696	= Pounds-force per square inch (psi; lbf/in²; lb/in²)
Pounds-force per square inch (psi; lbf/in²; lb/in²)	X 0.069	= Bars	X 14.5	= Pounds-force per square inch (psi; lbf/in²; lb/in²)
Pounds-force per square inch (psi; lbf/in²; lb/in²)	X 6.895	= Kilopascals (kPa)	X 0.145	= Pounds-force per square inch (psi; lbf/in²; lb/in²)
Kilopascals (kPa)	X 0.01	= Kilograms-force per square centimetre (kgf/cm²; kg/cm²)	X 98.1	= Kilopascals (kPa)
Millibar (mbar)	X 100	= Pascals (Pa)	X 0.01	= Millibar (mbar)
Millibar (mbar)	X 0.0145	= Pounds-force per square inch (psi; lbf/in²; lb/in²)	X 68.947	= Millibar (mbar)
Millibar (mbar)	X 0.75	= Millimetres of mercury (mmHg)	X 1.333	= Millibar (mbar)
Millibar (mbar)	X 0.401	= Inches of water (inH₂O)	X 2.491	= Millibar (mbar)
Millimetres of mercury (mmHg)	X 0.535	= Inches of water (inH₂O)	X 1.868	= Millimetres of mercury (mmHg)
Inches of water (inH₂O)	X 0.036	= Pounds-force per square inch (psi; lbf/in²; lb/in²)	X 27.68	= Inches of water (inH₂O)

Torque (moment of force)

Pounds-force inches (lbf in; lb in)	X 1.152	= Kilograms-force centimetre (kgf cm; kg cm)	X 0.868	= Pounds-force inches (lbf in; lb in)
Pounds-force inches (lbf in; lb in)	X 0.113	= Newton metres (Nm)	X 8.85	= Pounds-force inches (lbf in; lb in)
Pounds-force inches (lbf in; lb in)	X 0.083	= Pounds-force feet (lbf ft; lb ft)	X 12	= Pounds-force inches (lbf in; lb in)
Pounds-force feet (lbf ft; lb ft)	X 0.138	= Kilograms-force metres (kgf m; kg m)	X 7.233	= Pounds-force feet (lbf ft; lb ft)
Pounds-force feet (lbf ft; lb ft)	X 1.356	= Newton metres (Nm)	X 0.738	= Pounds-force feet (lbf ft; lb ft)
Newton metres (Nm)	X 0.102	= Kilograms-force metres (kgf m; kg m)	X 9.804	= Newton metres (Nm)

Power

Horsepower (hp)	X 745.7	= Watts (W)	X 0.0013	= Horsepower (hp)

Velocity (speed)

Miles per hour (miles/hr; mph)	X 1.609	= Kilometres per hour (km/hr; kph)	X 0.621	= Miles per hour (miles/hr; mph)

Fuel consumption*

Miles per gallon, Imperial (mpg)	X 0.354	= Kilometres per litre (km/l)	X 2.825	= Miles per gallon, Imperial (mpg)
Miles per gallon, US (mpg)	X 0.425	= Kilometres per litre (km/l)	X 2.352	= Miles per gallon, US (mpg)

Temperature

Degrees Fahrenheit = (°C x 1.8) + 32   Degrees Celsius (Degrees Centigrade; °C) = (°F - 32) x 0.56

*It is common practice to convert from miles per gallon (mpg) to litres/100 kilometres (l/100km), where mpg (Imperial) x l/100 km = 282 and mpg (US) x l/100 km = 235

Index

HAYNES AUTOMOTIVE MANUALS

NOTE: New manuals are added to this list on a periodic basis. If you do not see a listing for your vehicle, consult your local Haynes dealer for the latest product information.

ALFA-ROMEO
531 Alfa Romeo Sedan & Coupe '73 thru '80

AMC
Jeep CJ – see JEEP (412)
694 Mid-size models, Concord, Hornet, Gremlin & Spirit '70 thru '83
934 (Renault) Alliance & Encore all models '83 thru '87

AUDI
615 4000 all models '80 thru '87
428 5000 all models '77 thru '83
1117 5000 all models '84 thru '88
207 Fox all models '73 thru '79

AUSTIN
049 Healey 100/6 & 3000 Roadster '56 thru '68
Healey Sprite – see MG Midget Roadster (265)

BLMC
260 1100, 1300 & Austin America '62 thru '74
527 Mini all models '59 thru '69
***646** Mini all models '69 thru '88

BMW
276 320i all 4 cyl models '75 thru '83
632 528i & 530i all models '75 thru '80
240 1500 thru 2002 all models except Turbo '59 thru '77
348 2500, 2800, 3.0 & Bavaria '69 thru '76

BUICK
Century (front wheel drive) – see GENERAL MOTORS A-Cars (829)
***1627** Buick, Oldsmobile & Pontiac Full-size (Front wheel drive) all models '85 thru '90
Buick Electra, LeSabre and Park Avenue; Oldsmobile Delta 88 Royale, Ninety Eight and Regency; Pontiac Bonneville
***1551** Buick Oldsmobile & Pontiac Full-size (Rear wheel drive)
Buick Electra '70 thru '84, Estate '70 thru '90, LeSabre '70 thru '79
Oldsmobile Custom Cruiser '70 thru '90, Delta 88 '70 thru '85, Ninety-eight '70 thru '84
Pontiac Bonneville '70 thru '86, Catalina '70 thru '81, Grandville '70 thru '75, Parisienne '84 thu '86
627 Mid-size all rear-drive Regal & Century models with V6, V8 and Turbo '74 thru '87
Regal – see GENERAL MOTORS (1671)
Skyhawk – see GENERAL MOTORS J-Cars (766)
552 Skylark all X-car models '80 thru '85

CADILLAC
***751** Cadillac Rear Wheel Drive all gasoline models '70 thru '90
Cimarron – see GENERAL MOTORS J-Cars (766)

CAPRI
296 2000 MK I Coupe all models '71 thru '75
283 2300 MK II Coupe all models '74 thru '78
205 2600 & 2800 V6 Coupe '71 thru '75
375 2800 Mk II V6 Coupe '75 thru '78
Mercury Capri – see FORD Mustang (654)

CHEVROLET
***1477** Astro & GMC Safari Mini-vans all models '85 thru '90
554 Camaro V8 all models '70 thru '81
***866** Camaro all models '82 thru '90
Cavalier – see GENERAL MOTORS J-Cars (766)
Celebrity – see GENERAL MOTORS A-Cars (829)
625 Chevelle, Malibu & El Camino all V6 & V8 models '69 thru '87

449 Chevette & Pontiac T1000 all models '76 thru '87
550 Citation all models '80 thru '85
***1628** Corsica/Beretta all models '87 thru '90
274 Corvette all V8 models '68 thru '82
***1336** Corvette all models '84 thru '89
704 Full-size Sedans Caprice, Impala, Biscayne, Bel Air & Wagons, all V6 & V8 models '69 thru '90
Lumina – see GENERAL MOTORS (1671)
319 Luv Pick-up all 2WD & 4WD models '72 thru '82
626 Monte Carlo all V6, V8 & Turbo models '70 thru '88
241 Nova all V8 models '69 thru '79
***1642** Nova and Geo Prizm all front wheel drive models, '85 thru '90
***420** Pick-ups '67 thru '87 – Chevrolet & GMC, all V8 & in-line 6 cyl 2WD & 4WD models '67 thru '87
***1664** Pick-ups '88 thru '90 – Chevrolet & GMC all full-size (C and K) models, '88 thru '90
***1727** Sprint & Geo Metro '85 thru '91
***831** S-10 & GMC S-15 Pick-ups all models '82 thru '90
***345** Vans – Chevrolet & GMC, V8 & in-line 6 cyl models '68 thru '89
208 Vega all models except Cosworth '70 thru '77

CHRYSLER
***1337** Chrysler & Plymouth Mid-size front wheel drive '82 thru '89
K-Cars – see DODGE Aries (723)
Laser – see DODGE Daytona (1140)

DATSUN
402 200SX all models '77 thru '79
647 200SX all models '80 thru '83
228 B-210 all models '73 thru '78
525 210 all models '78 thru '82
206 240Z, 260Z & 280Z Coupe & 2+2 '70 thru '78
563 280ZX Coupe & 2+2 '79 thru '83
300ZX – see NISSAN (1137)
679 310 all models '78 thru '82
123 510 & PL521 Pick-up '68 thru '73
430 510 all models '78 thru '81
372 610 all models '72 thru '76
277 620 Series Pick-up all models '73 thru '79
720 Series Pick-up – see NISSAN Pick-ups (771)
376 810/Maxima all gasoline models '77 thru '84
124 1200 all models '70 thru '73
368 F10 all models '76 thru '79
Pulsar – see NISSAN (876)
Sentra – see NISSAN (982)
Stanza – see NISSAN (981)

DODGE
***723** Aries & Plymouth Reliant all models '81 thru '89
***1231** Caravan & Plymouth Voyager Mini-Vans all models '84 thru '89
699 Challenger & Plymouth Saporro all models '78 thru '83
236 Colt all models '71 thru '77
419 Colt (rear wheel drive) all models '77 thru '80
610 Colt & Plymouth Champ (front wheel drive) all models '78 thru '87
***556** D50 & Plymouth Arrow Pick-ups '79 thru '88
***1668** Dakota Pick-up all models '87 thru '90
234 Dart & Plymouth Valiant all 6 cyl models '67 thru '76
***1140** Daytona & Chrysler Laser all models '84 thru '89
***545** Omni & Plymouth Horizon all models '78 thru '90
***912** Pick-ups all full-size models '74 thru '90
***349** Vans – Dodge & Plymouth V8 & 6 cyl models '71 thru '89

FIAT
080 124 Sedan & Wagon all ohv & dohc models '66 thru '75
094 124 Sport Coupe & Spider '68 thru '78
310 131 & Brava all models '75 thru '81
479 Strada all models '79 thru '82
273 X1/9 all models '74 thru '80

FORD
***1476** Aerostar Mini-vans all models '86 thru '90
788 Bronco and Pick-ups '73 thru '79
***880** Bronco and Pick-ups '80 thru '90
014 Cortina MK II all models except Lotus '66 thru '70
295 Cortina MK III 1600 & 2000 ohc '70 thru '76
268 Courier Pick-up all models '72 thru '82
789 Escort & Mercury Lynx all models '81 thru '90
560 Fairmont & Mercury Zephyr all in-line & V8 models '78 thru '83
334 Fiesta all models '77 thru '80
754 Ford & Mercury Full-size, Ford LTD & Mercury Marquis ('75 thru '82); Ford Custom 500, Country Squire, Crown Victoria & Mercury Colony Park ('75 thru '87); Ford LTD Crown Victoria & Mercury Gran Marquis ('83 thru '87)
359 Granada & Mercury Monarch all in-line, 6 cyl & V8 models '75 thru '80
773 Ford & Mercury Mid-size, Ford Thunderbird & Mercury Cougar ('75 thru '82); Ford LTD & Mercury Marquis ('83 thru '86); Ford Torino, Gran Torino, Elite, Ranchero pick-up, LTD II, Mercury Montego, Comet, XR-7 & Lincoln Versailles ('75 thru '86)
***654** Mustang & Mercury Capri all models including Turbo '79 thru '90
357 Mustang V8 all models '64-1/2 thru '73
231 Mustang II all 4 cyl, V6 & V8 models '74 thru '78
204 Pinto all models '70 thru '74
649 Pinto & Mercury Bobcat all models '75 thru '80
***1026** Ranger & Bronco II all gasoline models '83 thru '89
***1421** Taurus & Mercury Sable '86 thru '90
***1418** Tempo & Mercury Topaz all gasoline models '84 thru '89
1338 Thunderbird & Mercury Cougar/XR7 '83 thru '88
***1725** Thunderbird & Mercury Cougar '89 and '90
***344** Vans all V8 Econoline models '69 thru '90

GENERAL MOTORS
***829** A-Cars – Chevrolet Celebrity, Buick Century, Pontiac 6000 & Oldsmobile Cutlass Ciera all models '82 thru '89
***766** J-Cars – Chevrolet Cavalier, Pontiac J-2000, Oldsmobile Firenza, Buick Skyhawk & Cadillac Cimarron all models '82 thru '90
***1420** N-Cars – Buick Somerset '85 thru '87; Pontiac Grand Am and Oldsmobile Calais '85 thru '90; Buick Skylark '86 thru '90
***1671** GM: Buick Regal, Chevrolet Lumina, Oldsmobile Cutlass Supreme, Pontiac Grand Prix, all front wheel drive models '88 thru '90

GEO
Metro – see CHEVROLET Sprint (1727)
Tracker – see SUZUKI Samurai (1626)
Prizm – see CHEVROLET Nova (1642)

GMC
Safari – see CHEVROLET ASTRO (1477)
Vans & Pick-ups – see CHEVROLET (420, 831, 345, 1664)

(continued on next page)

Listings shown with an asterisk (*) indicate model coverage as of this printing. These titles will be periodically updated to include later model years — consult your Haynes dealer for more information.

Haynes North America, Inc., P.O. Box 978, Newbury Park, CA 91320 • (818) 889-5400 • (805) 498-6703

HAYNES AUTOMOTIVE MANUALS (continued from previous page)

NOTE: New manuals are added to this list on a periodic basis. If you do not see a listing for your vehicle, consult your local Haynes dealer for the latest product information.

HONDA
- **138**   360, 600 & Z Coupe all models '67 thru '75
- **351**   Accord CVCC all models '76 thru '83
- ***1221**   Accord all models '84 thru '89
- **160**   Civic 1200 all models '73 thru '79
- **633**   Civic 1300 & 1500 CVCC all models '80 thru '83
- **297**   Civic 1500 CVCC all models '75 thru '79
- ***1227**   Civic all models '84 thru '90
- ***601**   Prelude CVCC all models '79 thru '89

HYUNDAI
- ***1552**   Excel all models '86 thru '89

ISUZU
- ***1641**   Trooper & Pick-up, all gasoline models '81 thru '90

JAGUAR
- **098**   MK I & II, 240 & 340 Sedans '55 thru '69
- ***242**   XJ6 all 6 cyl models '68 thru '86
- ***478**   XJ12 & XJS all 12 cyl models '72 thru '85
- **140**   XK-E 3.8 & 4.2 all 6 cyl models '61 thru '72

JEEP
- ***1553**   Cherokee, Comanche & Wagoneer Limited all models '84 thru '89
- **412**   CJ all models '49 thru '86

LADA
- ***413**   1200, 1300, 1500 & 1600 all models including Riva '74 thru '86

LAND ROVER
- **314**   Series II, IIA, & III all 4 cyl gasoline models '58 thru '86
- **529**   Diesel all models '58 thru '80

MAZDA
- **648**   626 Sedan & Coupe (rear wheel drive) all models '79 thru '82
- ***1082**   626 & MX-6 (front wheel drive) all models '83 thru '90
- ***267**   B1600, B1800 & B2000 Pick-ups '72 thru '90
- **370**   GLC Hatchback (rear wheel drive) all models '77 thru '83
- **757**   GLC (front wheel drive) all models '81 thru '86
- **109**   RX2 all models '71 thru '75
- **096**   RX3 all models '72 thru '76
- **460**   RX-7 all models '79 thru '85
- ***1419**   RX-7 all models '86 thru '89

MERCEDES-BENZ
- ***1643**   190 Series all four-cylinder gasoline models, '84 thru '88
- **346**   230, 250 & 280 Sedan, Coupe & Roadster all 6 cyl sohc models '68 thru '72
- **983**   280 123 Series all gasoline models '77 thru '81
- **698**   350 & 450 Sedan, Coupe & Roadster all models '71 thru '80
- **697**   Diesel 123 Series 200D, 220D, 240D, 240TD, 300D, 300CD, 300TD, 4- & 5-cyl incl. Turbo '76 thru '85

MERCURY
See FORD Listing

MG
- **475**   MGA all models '56 thru '62
- **111**   MGB Roadster & GT Coupe all models '62 thru '80
- **265**   MG Midget & Austin Healey Sprite Roadster '58 thru '80

MITSUBISHI
- ***1669**   Cordia, Tredia, Galant, Precis & Mirage '83 thru '90
-       Pick-up – *see Dodge D-50 (556)*

MORRIS
- **074**   (Austin) Marina 1.8 all models '71 thru '80
- **024**   Minor 1000 sedan & wagon '56 thru '71

NISSAN
- **1137**   300ZX all Turbo & non-Turbo models '84 thru '89
- ***1341**   Maxima all models '85 thru '89
- ***771**   Pick-ups/Pathfinder gas models '80 thru '88
- ***876**   Pulsar all models '83 thru '86
- ***982**   Sentra all models '82 thru '90
- ***981**   Stanza all models '82 thru '90

OLDSMOBILE
-       Custom Cruiser – *see BUICK Full-size (1551)*
- **658**   Cutlass all standard gasoline V6 & V8 models '74 thru '88
-       Cutlass Ciera – *see GENERAL MOTORS A-Cars (829)*
-       Cutlass Supreme – *see GENERAL MOTORS (1671)*
-       Firenza – *see GENERAL MOTORS J-Cars (766)*
-       Ninety-eight – *see BUICK Full-size (1551)*
-       Omega – *see PONTIAC Phoenix & Omega (551)*

PEUGEOT
- **161**   504 all gasoline models '68 thru '79
- **663**   504 all diesel models '74 thru '83

PLYMOUTH
- **425**   Arrow all models '76 thru '80
-       *For all other PLYMOUTH titles, see DODGE listing.*

PONTIAC
-       T1000 – *see CHEVROLET Chevette (449)*
-       J-2000 – *see GENERAL MOTORS J-Cars (766)*
-       6000 – *see GENERAL MOTORS A-Cars (829)*
- **1232**   Fiero all models '84 thru '88
- **555**   Firebird all V8 models except Turbo '70 thru '81
- ***867**   Firebird all models '82 thru '89
-       Full-size Rear Wheel Drive – *see Buick, Oldsmobile, Pontiac Full-size (1551)*
-       Grand Prix – *see GENERAL MOTORS (1671)*
- **551**   Phoenix & Oldsmobile Omega all X-car models '80 thru '84

PORSCHE
- ***264**   911 all Coupe & Targa models except Turbo & Carrera 4 '65 thru '89
- **239**   914 all 4 cyl models '69 thru '76
- **397**   924 all models including Turbo '76 thru '82
- ***1027**   944 all models including Turbo '83 thru '89

RENAULT
- **141**   5 Le Car all models '76 thru '83
- **079**   8 & 10 all models with 58.4 cu in engines '62 thru '72
- **097**   12 Saloon & Estate all models 1289 cc engines '70 thru '80
- **768**   15 & 17 all models '73 thru '79
- **081**   16 all models 89.7 cu in & 95.5 cu in engines '65 thru '72
- **598**   18i & Sportwagon all models '81 thru '86
-       Alliance & Encore – *see AMC (934)*
- **984**   Fuego all models '82 thru '85

ROVER
- **085**   3500 & 3500S Sedan 215 cu in engines '68 thru '76
- ***365**   3500 SDI V8 all models '76 thru '85

SAAB
- **198**   95 & 96 V4 all models '66 thru '75
- **247**   99 all models including Turbo '69 thru '80
- ***980**   900 all models including Turbo '79 thru '88

SUBARU
- **237**   1100, 1300, 1400 & 1600 all models '71 thru '79
- ***681**   1600 & 1800 2WD & 4WD all models '80 thru '89

SUZUKI
- ***1626**   Samurai/Sidekick and Geo Tracker all models '86 thru '89

TOYOTA
- ***1023**   Camry all models '83 thru '90
- **150**   Carina Sedan all models '71 thru '74
- **229**   Celica ST, GT & liftback all models '71 thru '77
- **437**   Celica all models '78 thru '81
- ***935**   Celica all models except front-wheel drive and Supra '82 thru '85
- **680**   Celica Supra all models '79 thru '81
- **1139**   Celica Supra all in-line 6-cylinder models '82 thru '86
- **361**   Corolla all models '75 thru '79
- **961**   Corolla all models (rear wheel drive) '80 thru '87
- ***1025**   Corolla all models (front wheel drive) '84 thru '91
- ***636**   Corolla Tercel all models '80 thru '82
- **230**   Corona & MK II all 4 cyl sohc models '69 thru '74
- **360**   Corona all models '74 thru '82
- ***532**   Cressida all models '78 thru '82
- **313**   Land Cruiser all models '68 thru '82
- **200**   MK II all 6 cyl models '72 thru '76
- ***1339**   MR2 all models '85 thru '87
- **304**   Pick-up all models '69 thru '78
- ***656**   Pick-up all models '79 thru '90

TRIUMPH
- **112**   GT6 & Vitesse all models '62 thru '74
- **113**   Spitfire all models '62 thru '81
- **028**   TR2, 3, 3A, & 4A Roadsters '52 thru '67
- **031**   TR250 & 6 Roadsters '67 thru '76
- **322**   TR7 all models '75 thru '81

VW
- **091**   411 & 412 all 103 cu in models '68 thru '73
- **159**   Beetle & Karmann Ghia all models '54 thru '79
- **238**   Dasher all gasoline models '74 thru '81
- ***884**   Rabbit, Jetta, Scirocco, & Pick-up all gasoline models '74 thru '89 & Convertible '80 thru '89
- **451**   Rabbit, Jetta & Pick-up all diesel models '77 thru '84
- **082**   Transporter 1600 all models '68 thru '79
- **226**   Transporter 1700, 1800 & 2000 all models '72 thru '79
- **084**   Type 3 1500 & 1600 all models '63 thru '73
- **1029**   Vanagon all air-cooled models '80 thru '83

VOLVO
- **203**   120, 130 Series & 1800 Sports '61 thru '73
- **129**   140 Series all models '66 thru '74
- **244**   164 all models '68 thru '75
- ***270**   240 Series all models '74 thru '90
- **400**   260 Series all models '75 thru '82
- ***1550**   740 & 760 Series all models '82 thru '88

SPECIAL MANUALS
- **1479**   Automotive Body Repair & Painting Manual
- **1654**   Automotive Electrical Manual
- **1480**   Automotive Heating & Air Conditioning Manual
- **1763**   Ford Engine Overhaul Manual
- **482**   Fuel Injection Manual
- **1666**   Small Engine Repair Manual
- **299**   SU Carburetors thru '88
- **393**   Weber Carburetors thru '79
- **300**   Zenith/Stromberg CD Carburetors thru '76

See your dealer for other available titles

4-1-91

---

* Listings shown with an asterisk (*) indicate model coverage as of this printing. These titles will be periodically updated to include later model years — consult your Haynes dealer for more information.

Over 100 Haynes motorcycle manuals also available

Haynes North America, Inc., P.O. Box 978, Newbury Park, CA 91320 • (818) 889-5400 • (805) 498-6703